American Literary Scholarship

1986

American Literary Scholarship

An Annual / 1986

Edited by David J. Nordloh

Essays by Philip F. Gura, Claudia D. Johnson, Kent P. Ljungquist, Brian Higgins, Vivian R. Pollak, Hamlin Hill, Richard A. Hocks, Reed Way Dasenbrock, M. Thomas Inge, Gerry Brenner, William J. Scheick, James Woodress, John J. Murphy and Stephen L. Tanner, Virginia Spencer Carr, Jerome Klinkowitz, Linda Wagner-Martin, Richard J. Calhoun, Walter J. Meserve, Michael J. Hoffman, F. Lyra, Marc Chénetier, Rolf Meyn, Laura Coltelli, Massimo Bacigalupo, Hiroko Sato

Duke University Press Durham North Carolina 1988

 Library of Congress Catalog Card number 65–19450. ISBN 0–8223–0802–9. Printed in the United States of America by Heritage Printers, Inc.

Foreword

The difficulties of identifying scholars willing to devote a significant amount of time and effort to an enterprise like *ALS* and of meeting ever-tightening publishing deadlines occasionally affect the table of contents. This year, for example, there is no chapter on Black Literature; it will be restored next year, however, under the authorship of R. Baxter Miller (Univ. of Tennessee). There is no section on Scandinavian contributions in the Foreign Contributions chapter; it will also return next year, prepared by Jan Nordby Gretlund (Odense Universitet, Denmark). On the other hand, there are two sections on Italian contributions—for 1985 by Laura Coltelli (Univ. of Pisa), received too late for *ALS 1985*, and for 1986 by Massimo Bacigalupo (Univ. of Genoa).

Besides the two new contributors already identified, there will be only a few changes in chapter authors between this volume and *ALS 1987*. The place of Kent J. Ljungquist (Worcester Polytechnic Institute), who has done the chapter on Poe since 1983, will be taken by Benjamin Franklin Fisher IV (Univ. of Tennessee). Richard A. Hocks (Univ. of Missouri) is overseas this year, and Susan Griffin (Univ. of Louisville) has agreed to take over the Henry James chapter in his absence. And Linda Wagner-Martin (Michigan State Univ.), who agreed to do the chapter on Poetry: 1900 to the 1940s for this volume (and who in the past has also contributed the chapters on Poetry: 1930s to the Present and on Faulkner), is yielding to Melody Zajdel (Montana State Univ.). My gratitude to these parting authors for their help, and a warm welcome to the new contributors.

The arrangements for the chapter on 19th-Century Literature and for the editorship of *ALS 1987* are a bit more complicated—and interrelated. James Woodress, the founding editor of this series, supplies the chapter this year, and has also generously agreed to step back in "just this once" as editor of *ALS 1987*. I will move from the editor's position to preparation of the 19th-century chapter, where I got my start with the company. And J. Albert Robbins, who has coedited *ALS* with Jim Woodress for so many years, will prepare the chapter on General Reference Works.

As someone who had prepared individual chapters for these volumes, I already knew the kind of hard work and dedication required to make *ALS* a success. Having lived through my first experience as editor, I can appreciate even more fully what the many scholars who collaborate in its creation give of themselves in making it the continuously effective retrospect of scholarship that it is. I want to express my appreciation for the patience, the enthusiasm, and the goodwill of the more than two dozen participants whose essays appear here.

I also want to thank the various persons and institutions whose assistance has been so essential to this volume. I am grateful to the staff of the Indiana University Library for help in identifying and locating materials, particularly Ann Bristow and Patricia Riesenman of the Reference Department and Anthony Shipps, the English Subject Librarian; to Professor James L. Harner (Bowling Green State Univ., Ohio), chairman of the *Festschriften* and Other Collections Section of the *MLA International Bibliography*, who supplies us with relevant titles; and to Eileen M. Mackesy, Director of the MLA Center for Bibliographical Services, who provides a preprint of the American literature portions of the *International Bibliography* and thus supports chapter authors in their efforts to be both comprehensive and timely. I am grateful too for the able professional assistance and the equanimity of the editorial staff at Duke University Press in supervising all aspects of the production of this volume.

Authors and presses are reminded to send review copies of relevant 1987 publications to the 1987 editor, Professor James Woodress, Department of English, University of California–Davis, Davis, California 95616.

David J. Nordloh

Indiana University

Table of Contents

Key to Abbreviations

Festschriften, Essay Collections, and Books Discussed in More Than One Chapter

American Incarnation / Myra Jehlen, *American Incarnation: The Individual, the Nation, and the Continent* (Harvard)

American Literary Magazines / Edward E. Chielens, ed., *American Literary Magazines: The Eighteenth and Nineteenth Centuries* (Greenwood)

The American Newness / Irving Howe, *The American Newness: Culture and Politics in the Age of Emerson* (Harvard)

The American Sublime, Mary Arensberg, ed. (SUNY)

Amid Visions and Revisions / Barney J. Hollis, ed., *Amid Visions and Revisions: Poetry and Criticism in Literature and the Arts* (Morgan State)

Atlantic Double-Cross / Robert Weisbuch, *Atlantic Double-Cross: American Literature and British Influence in the Age of Emerson* (Chicago)

Auctor Ludens / Gerald Guinness and Andrew Hurley, eds., *Auctor Ludens: Essays on Play in Literature* (Benjamins)

Bergson, Eliot, and American Literature / Paul Douglass, *Bergson, Eliot, and American Literature* (Kentucky)

A Companion to Melville Studies / John Bryant, ed., *A Companion to Melville Studies* (Greenwood)

Continuities / Marvin Fisher, *Continuities and Ideas in American Literature* (Univ. Press)

Critical Angles / Marc Chénetier, ed., *Critical Angles: European Views of Contemporary American Literature* (So. Ill.)

Doing Tropology / James M. Mellard, *Doing Tropology: Analyses of Literary Desire* (Illinois)

Emerson and His Legacy / Stephen Donadio et al., eds., *Emerson and His Legacy: Essays in Honor of Quentin Anderson* (So. Ill.)

Essaying Biography / Gloria G. Fromm, ed., *Essaying Biography: A Celebration for Leon Edel* (Hawaii)

Ezra Pound Among Poets / George Bornstein, ed., *Ezra Pound Among Poets* (Chicago)

The Failure of Modernism / Andrew Ross, *The Failure of Modernism* (Columbia)

The Fall into Eden / David Wyatt, *The Fall into Eden: Landscape and Imagination in California* (Cambridge)

Faulkner and Humor / Doreen Fowler and Ann J. Abadie, eds., *Faulkner and Humor* (Miss.)

Faulkner and Women / Doreen Fowler and Ann J. Abadie, eds., *Faulkner and Women* (Miss.)

The Flying Machine / Laurence Goldstein, *The Flying Machine and Modern Literature* (Indiana)

The Frenzy of Renown / Leo Braudy, *The Frenzy of Renown: Fame and Its History* (Oxford)

The Futurist Moment / Marjorie Perloff, *The Futurist Moment: Avant-garde, Avant Guerre, and the Language of Rupture* (Chicago)

Gender and Reading / Elizabeth A. Flynn and Patrocinio P. Schweickart, eds., *Gender and Reading: Essays on Readers, Texts, and Contexts* (Hopkins)

Herman Melville / Harold Bloom, ed., *Herman Melville* (Chelsea House)

Ideology and Classic American Literature / Sacvan Bercovitch and Myra Jehlen, eds., *Ideology and Classic American Literature* (Harvard)

Intellectual Life in Ante-Bellum Charleston / Michael O'Brien and David Moltke-Hansen, eds., *Intellectual Life in Ante-Bellum Charleston* (Tenn.)

Interface / Daniel Royot, ed., *Interface: Essays on History, Myth and Art in American Literature* (Valéry, 1985)

L'Amerique et l'Europe: Realités et représentations (GRENA)

Literature and Lore of the Sea / Patricia Ann Carlson, ed., *Literature and Lore of the Sea* (*Costerus* 52)

Literature and the Visual Arts / Suzanne Ferguson and Barbara Groseclose, eds., *Literature and the Visual Arts in Contemporary Society* (Ohio State, 1985)

Melville's Later Novels / William B. Dillingham, *Melville's Later Novels* (Georgia)

My Life a Loaded Gun / Paula Bennett, *My Life a Loaded Gun: Female Creativity and Feminist Poetics* (Beacon)

New England Literary Culture / Lawrence Buell, *New England Literary Culture: From Revolution Through Renaissance* (Cambridge)

The Nineteenth-Century American Short Story / A. Robert Lee, ed., *The Nineteenth-Century American Short Story* (Barnes and Noble)

No Fairer Land / J. Lasley Dameron and James W. Mathews, eds., *No Fairer Land: Studies in Southern Literature Before 1900* (Whitson)

On the Modernist Long Poem / Margaret Dickie, *On the Modernist Long Poem* (Iowa)

The Play & Its Critics / Michael Bertin, ed., *The Play & Its Critics: Essays for Eric Bentley* (Univ. Press)

Poe and Our Times / Benjamin Franklin Fisher IV, ed., *Poe and Our Times: Influences and Affinities* (Balt. Poe Soc.)

The Poem as Utterance / R. A. York, *The Poem as Utterance* (Methuen)

The Poetics of Gender / Nancy K. Miller, ed., *The Poetics of Gender* (Columbia)

The Politics of American English / David Simpson, *The Politics of American English* (Oxford)

Pound, Yeats, Eliot and the Modernist Movement / C. K. Stead, *Pound, Yeats, Eliot and the Modernist Movement* (Rutgers)

Reconstructing American Literary History / Sacvan Bercovitch, ed., *Reconstructing American Literary History* (Harvard)

Reinventing the Americas / Bell Gale Chevigny and Gari Laguardia, eds., *Reinventing the Americas: Comparative Studies of the Literature of the United States and Spanish America* (Cambridge)

Revival / Ted R. Spivey, *Revival: Southern Writers in the Modern City* (Florida)

Revolution and the Word / Cathy N. Davison, *Revolution and the Word: The Rise of the Novel in America* (Oxford)

The School of Hawthorne / Richard Brodhead, *The School of Hawthorne* (Oxford)

The Scope of the Fantastic / Robert A. Collins and Howard D. Pearce, eds., *The Scope of the Fantastic—Theory, Technique, Major Authors* (Greenwood, 1985)

Sex, Politics and Science / Ruth B. Yeazell, ed., *Sex, Politics and Science in the Nineteenth-Century Novel* (Hopkins)

Studien zur englischen und amerikanischen Prosa / Maria Diedrich and Christoph Schoneich, eds., *Studien zur englischen und amerikanischen Prosa nach dem ersten Weltkrieg: Festschrift für Kurt*

Otten zum 60. Geburtstag (Darmstadt: Wissenschaftliche Buchgesellschaft)

Theodicies in Conflict / Richard Forrer, *Theodicies in Conflict: A Dilemma in Puritan Ethics and Nineteenth-Century American Literature* (Greenwood)

Theorie und Praxis / Winfried Herget et al., eds., *Theorie und Praxis im Erzählen des 19. und 20. Jahrhunderts: Studien zur englischen und amerikanischen Literatur zu Ehren von Willi Erzgräber* (Narr)

Third Force Psychology / Bernard Paris, ed., *Third Force Psychology and the Study of Literature* (Fairleigh Dickinson)

Twentieth Century Literatures / Bela Kopeczi and Georgy M. Vajda, eds., *Proceedings of the 8th Congress of the International Comparative Literature Association, II: Twentieth Century Literatures Originating in Different Cultures* (Stuttgart: Bieber, 1980)

Virgil in a Cultural Tradition / Richard A. Cardwell and Janet Hamilton, eds., *Virgil in a Cultural Tradition: Essays to Celebrate the Bimillenium* (Nottingham)

Washington and Washington Writing / David McAleavey, ed., *Washington and Washington Writing* (GW 12)

When People Publish / Frederick Busch, *When People Publish: Essays on Writers and Writing* (Iowa)

Words and Deeds / Taylor Stoehr, *Words and Deeds: Essays on the Realistic Imagination* (AMS Press)

Writing the South / Richard Gray, *Writing the South: Ideas of an American Region* (Cambridge)

Periodicals, Annuals, Series

ABBW / *AB Bookman's Weekly*
ABC / *American Book Collector*
ABR / *American Benedictine Review*
Aevum
Agenda
AI / *America Imago*
AL / *American Literature*
ALR / *American Literary Realism, 1870–1910*
ALS / *American Literary Scholarship*
American Neptune
AmerP / *American Poetry*
AmerS / *American Studies*
Amst / *Amerikastudien*
AN&Q / *American Notes and Queries*
Angelicum
Anglo-American Studies
Annales du GERB / *Annales du Groupe d'Etudes et de Recherches Britanniques* (Bordeaux)
AppalJ / *Appalachian Journal*
APR / *American Poetry Review*
AQ / *American Quarterly*
AR / *The Antioch Review*
ArAA / *Arbeiten aus Anglistik und Amerikanistik*
Archiv / *Archiv für das Studium der Neueren Sprachen und Literaturen*
ArQ / *Arizona Quarterly*
ASInt / *American Studies International*
Atlantic
ATQ / *American Transcendental Quarterly*
BALF / *Black American Literature Forum*
Boundary / *Boundary 2*
BSJ / *The Baker Street Journal*
BSUF / *Ball State Univ. Forum*
BuR / *Bucknell Review*
Caliban (Toulouse, France)
California (formerly *New West*)
Callaloo: A Black South Journal of Arts and Letters
C&L / *Christianity and Literature*
CanL / *Canadian Literature*
CASS / *Canadian-American Slavic Studies*
CEA / *CEA Critic*
CentR / *The Centennial Review*
ChiR / *Chicago Review*
CimR / *Cimarron Review*
CL / *Comparative Literature*

CLAJ / College Language Assn. Journal
CLC / Columbia Library Columns
CLQ / Colby Library Quarterly
CLS / Comparative Literature Studies
CML / Classical and Modern Literature
Coda: Poets and Writers Newsletter
CollL / College Literature
CompD / Comparative Drama
Concord Saunterer
ConL / Contemporary Literature
Costerus: Essays in English and American Language and Literature
CP / Concerning Poetry
CQ / The Cambridge Quarterly
CRAA / Centre de Recherche sur l'Amérique Anglophone (Université de Grenoble III)
Crazyhorse
CRevAS / Canadian Review of American Studies
Crit / Critique: Studies in Modern Fiction
CritI / Critical Inquiry
Criticism: A Quarterly for Literature and the Arts
CritQ / Critical Quarterly
CRUX: A Journal on the Teaching of English
CSE / Center for Scholarly Editions
DeltaES / Delta: Revue de Centre d'Etudes et de Recherche sur les Ecrivains du Sud aux Etats-Unis (Montpellier, France)
DGQ / Dramatist Guild Quarterly
DicS / Dickinson Studies
DLB / Dictionary of Literary Biography (Gale)
DQR / Dutch Quarterly Review of Anglo-American Letters
DrN / Dreiser Newsletter
DSA / Dickens Studies Annual: Essays on Victorian Fiction
EA / Etudes Anglaises
EAA / Estudos Anglo-Americanos (São Paulo, Brazil)
EAL / Early American Literature
EAS / Essays in Arts and Sciences
ECr / L'Esprit Créateur
EdWN / Edith Wharton Newsletter
EIC / Essays in Criticism
EigoS / Eigo Seinen (Tokyo)
EIHC / Essex Institute Historial Collections
ELH [formerly *Journal of English Literary History*]
ELN / English Language Notes
ELWIU / Essays in Literature (Western Ill. Univ.)
EON / The Eugene O'Neill Newsletter
ES / English Studies
ESJ / European Studies Journal
ESQ: A Journal of the American Renaissance
Expl / Explicator
Extrapolation: A Journal of Science Fiction and Fantasy
Fabula (Univ. de Lille, France)
Field: Contemporary Poetry and Poetics
FJ / Faulkner Journal (Ohio Northern Univ.)
Flannery O'Connor Bulletin
ForLing / Forum Linguisticum (Lake Bluff, Ill.)
GaR / Georgia Review
Genre
Gothic
GRENA / Groups d'Etudes et de Recherches Nord-Américaines (Aix: Université de Provence)
Hayden's Ferry Review
HC / Hollins Critic
HemR / Hemingway Review
HJR / Henry James Review
HLQ / Huntington Library Quarterly
HTR / Harvard Theological Review
HudR / The Hudson Review
HumanS / Human Studies: A Journal for Philosophy and the Social Sciences
IJAS / Indian Journal of American Studies
IUR / Irish University Review
James Dickey Newsletter
JAmS / Journal of American Studies
JASAT /Journal of the American Studies Association of Texas
JEP / Journal of Evolutionary Psychology
JHI / Journal of the History of Ideas
JJQ / James Joyce Quarterly
JLN / Jack London Newsletter
JML / Journal of Modern Literature

JNT / Journal of Narrative Technique
JPC / Journal of Popular Culture
JPRS / The Journal of Pre-Raphaelite Studies
Kalki: Studies in James Branch Cabell
LAmer / Letterature d'America: Rivista Trimestrale
L&H / Literature and History
L&S / Language and Speech
Lang&S / Language and Style
LanM / Les Langues Modernes
LBR / Luso-Brazilian Review
LCrit / Literary Criterion (Mysore, India)
Legacy: A Journal of Nineteenth-Century American Women Writers
Ling&L / Lingua e Literatura (São Paulo, Brazil)
LitR / Literary Review: An International Journal of Contemporary Writing (Madison, N.J.)
LJHum / Lamar Journal of the Humanities
LRN / Literary Research Newsletter
MarkhamR / Markham Review
MD / Modern Drama
MFS / Modern Fiction Studies
MHLS / Mid-Hudson Language Studies
Midamerica: The Yearbook of the Society for the Study of Midwestern Literature
Midstream: A Quarterly Jewish Review
MissQ / Mississippi Quarterly
MissR / Missouri Review
MLN [formerly *Modern Language Notes*]
MLQ / Modern Language Quarterly
MLS / Modern Language Studies
MMisc / Midwestern Miscellany
Mosaic: A Journal for the Interdisciplinary Study of Literature
Mother Jones
MQ / Midwest Quarterly (Pittsburg, Kan.)
MQR / Michigan Quarterly Review
MR / Massachusetts Review
MTJ / Mark Twain Journal
Names: Journal of the American Name Society
N&Q / Notes and Queries
NAS / Norwegian-American Studies (Northfield, Minn.)
National Review
NCF / Nineteenth-Century Fiction
NCL / Nineteenth-Century Literature
NConL / Notes on Contemporary Literature
NDQ / North Dakota Quarterly
Neohelicon: Acta Comparationis Universarum
Neophil / Neophilologus (Groningen, Netherlands)
NEQ / New England Quarterly
NER / New England Review & Bread Loaf Quarterly
NewC / The New Criterion
New Republic
New York Quarterly
NHR / Nathaniel Hawthorne Review
NMAL: Notes on Modern American Literature
NMW / Notes on Mississippi Writers
NOR / New Orleans Review
Novel: A Forum on Fiction
NYRB / New York Review of Books
NYTBR / New York Times Book Review
OhR / Ohio Review
OL / Orbis Litterarum: International Review of Literary Studies
ON / The Old Northwest
OntarioR / Ontario Review
PAAS / Proceedings of the American Antiquarian Society
Pacific Studies
Paideuma: A Journal Devoted to Ezra Pound Scholarship
P&L / Philosophy and Literature
PAPA / Papers of the Arkansas Philological Assn.
PBSA / Papers of the Bibliographical Society of America
PCL / Perspectives on Contemporary Literature
PCP / Pacific Coast Philology
PCSM / Publications of the Colonial Society of Massachusetts
PLL / Papers on Language and Literature
PMHB / Pennsylvania Magazine of History and Biography
PMHS / Proceedings of the Massachusetts Historical Society

PMLA: Publications of the Modern Language Assn.
PNotes / Pynchon Notes
PoeS / Poe Studies
POMPA / Publications of the Mississippi Philological Assn.
PoT / Poetics Today (Jerusalem)
PQ / Philological Quarterly
Prospects: An Annual Journal of American Cultural Studies
PVR / Platte Valley Review
QJS / The Quarterly Journal of Speech
RALS / Resources for American Literary Study
RANAM / Recherches Anglaises et Américaines
R&L / Religion and Literature
Raritan, A Quarterly Review
ReAL / RE: Artes Liberales
REALB / REAL: The Yearbook of Research in English and American Literature (Berlin)
RecL / Recovering Literature: A Journal of Contextualist Criticism
Renascence: Essays on Value in Literature
Representations
RFEA / Revue Française d'Etudes Américaines (Paris)
RLet / Revista Letras (Paraná, Brazil)
RLMC / Rivista di Letterature Moderne e Comparate (Pisa, Italy)
RP&P / Romanticism Past and Present
RSA / Rivista di Studi Anglo-americani (Abano terme, Italy)
SAF / Studies in American Fiction
Sagetrieb: A Journal Devoted to Poets in the Pound-H.D.-Williams Tradition
SALit / Chu-Shikoku Studies in American Literature
SAQ / South Atlantic Quarterly
SAR / Studies in the American Renaissance
SatR / Saturday Review
SB / Studies in Bibliography
SCRev / South Central Review
SDR / South Dakota Review
SECC / Studies in Eighteenth-Century Culture
SELit / Studies in English Literature (Tokyo)
SFS / Science-Fiction Studies
Shenandoah
SHR / Southern Humanities Review
SJS / San Jose Studies
SLitI / Studies in the Literary Imagination
SLJ / Southern Literary Journal
SMy / Studia Mystica
SNNTS / Studies in the Novel (North Texas State Univ.)
SoAR / South Atlantic Review
SoQ / Southern Quarterly
SoR / Southern Review
SoSt / Southern Studies
Southern Magazine (Little Rock, Ark.)
SR / Sewanee Review
SSF / Studies in Short Fiction
StQ / Steinbeck Quarterly
Style
TA / Theatre Annual
TCBS / Transactions of the Cambridge Bibliographical Society
TCL / Twentieth-Century Literature
TCW / Turn-of-the-Century Women
Theoria: A Journal of Studies in the Arts, Humanities and Social Sciences (Natal, S. Africa)
ThoreauQ / Thoreau Quarterly
ThS / Theatre Survey
TJ / Theatre Journal
TLS / Times Literary Supplement (London)
TriQ / TriQuarterly
TSLL / Texas Studies in Literature and Language
TSWL / Tulsa Studies in Women's Literature
TUSAS / Twayne's United States Authors Series
TWN / The Thomas Wolfe Review
UTQ / University of Toronto Quarterly
VC / Virginia Cavalcade
Verri / Il Verri: Rivista di Letterature
Vinduet (Oslo, Norway)
VQR / Virginia Quarterly Review
VS / Victorian Studies
WAL / Western American Literature
WCPMNewsl / Willa Cather Pioneer Memorial Newsletter

WCWR / William Carlos Williams Review
WE / Winesburg Eagle: The Official Publication of the Sherwood Anderson Society
West Hills Review
WF / Western Folklore
WHR / Western Humanities Review
WMQ / William and Mary Quarterly
WS / Women's Studies
WSJour / Wallace Stevens Journal
WWR / Walt Whitman Quarterly Review
YER / Yeats Eliot Review
YES / Yearbook of English Studies
YR / Yale Review
YULG / Yale University Library Gazette

Publishers

ABC-Clio / Santa Barbara, Calif.: ABC-Clio Information Services
Abrams / New York: Harry N. Abrams
Alabama / University: Univ. of Alabama Press
Allen & Unwin (London)
American Library Association (Chicago)
Amherst / Amherst, Mass.: Amherst College Press
AMS Press (New York)
Archon / Hamden, Conn.: Archon Books
Arkansas / Fayetteville: Univ. of Arkansas Press
Atheneum / New York: Atheneum Publishers
Balt. Poe Soc. / Baltimore: Baltimore Poe Society
Barnes and Noble (Totowa, N.J.)
Beacon / Boston: Beacon Press
Benjamins / Philadelphia: J. Benjamins Publishing Co.
Berg / Shakopee, Minn.: Berg Publishing Co.
Black Sparrow / Santa Rosa, Calif.: Black Sparrow Press
Black Swan Press (Redding Ridge, Conn.)
Blackwell / New York: Basil Blackwell
Bowling Green : Bowling Green, Ohio: Bowling Green State Univ. Popular Press
Braziller / New York: George Braziller
Calif. / Berkeley: Univ. of California Press
Cambridge / Cambridge and New York: Cambridge Univ. Press
Camden House (Columbia, S.C.)
Carl Winter (Heidelberg)
Catholic Univ. / Washington, D.C.: Catholic Univ. of America Press
Central Arkansas / Conway: Univ. of Central Arkansas Press
Chelsea House (New York)
Chicago / Chicago: Univ. of Chicago Press
City Lights (San Francisco)
Clarendon / Oxford: Clarendon Press
Columbia / New York: Columbia Univ. Press
Cordelia / Santa Barbara, Calif.: Cordelia Editions
Cornell / Ithaca, N.Y.: Cornell Univ. Press
Creative Arts / Berkeley, Calif.: Creative Arts Book Co.
Crown / New York: Crown Publishers
Dalkey Archive / Elmwood Park, Ill.: Dalkey Archive Press
Delacorte / New York: Delacorte Press
Delaware / Newark: Univ. of Delaware Press
Doubleday / New York: Doubleday and Co.
Duke / Durham, N.C.: Duke Univ. Press
Ecco / New York: Ecco Press
Faber / Winchester, Mass.: Faber & Faber
Fairleigh Dickinson / Madison, N.J.: Farleigh Dickinson Univ. Press
Farrar, Straus & Giroux (New York)
Florida / Gainesville: Univ. Presses of Florida
Florida State / Tallahassee: Florida State Univ. Press
Gale / Detroit: Gale Research Co.

Garland / New York: Garland Publishing Co.
Georgia / Athens: Univ. of Georgia Press
Gordian / New York: Gordian Press
Göteborg Sweden: Acta Universitatis Gothoburgensis
Greenwood / Westport, Conn.: Greenwood Press
Hall / Boston: G. K. Hall & Co.
Harper / New York: Harper and Row
Harvard / Cambridge, Mass.: Harvard Univ. Press
Hawaii / Honolulu: Univ. of Hawaii Press
Heinemann / New York: James H. Heinemann
Hopkins / Baltimore: Johns Hopkins Univ. Press
Houghton Mifflin / Boston: Houghton Mifflin Co.
Humanities / Atlantic Highlands, N.J.: Humanities Press International
Illinois / Urbana: Univ. of Illinois Press
Indiana / Bloomington: Indiana Univ. Press
International / New York: International Universities Press
Iowa / Iowa City: Univ. of Iowa Press
Kansas / Lawrence: Univ. Press of Kansas
Kent State / Kent, Ohio: Kent State Univ. Press
Kentucky / Lexington: Univ. Press of Kentucky
Knopf / New York: Alfred A. Knopf
Lefkowicz / Fairhaven, Mass.: Edward J. Lefkowicz
Limberlost Press (Boise, Idaho)
Little, Brown / Boston: Little, Brown & Co.
Longman / White Plains, N.Y.: Longman
LSU / Baton Rouge: Louisiana State Univ. Press
McGraw-Hill (New York)
Maclay / Baltimore, Md.: Maclay & Associates
Macmillan (New York)
Mass. / Amherst: Univ. of Massachusetts Press
Mellen / Lewiston, N.Y.: Edwin Mellen Press
Mercer / Macon, Ga.: Mercer Univ. Press
Methuen (London)
Michigan / Ann Arbor: Univ. of Michigan Press
Minnesota / Minneapolis: Univ. of Minnesota Press
Miss. / Jackson: Univ. Press of Mississippi
Missouri / Columbia: Univ. of Missouri Press
MLA / New York: Modern Language Assn.
Morgan State / Baltimore: Morgan State Univ. Press
Morrow / New York: William Morrow
Narr / Tübingen: G. Narr
Natl. Poetry Found. / Orono, Me.: National Poetry Foundation
Nebraska / Lincoln: Univ. of Nebraska Press
New Directions / New York: New Directions Publishing Corp.
N. Mex. / Albuquerque: Univ. of New Mexico Press
No. Car. / Chapel Hill: Univ. of North Carolina Press
Norton / New York: W. W. Norton & Co.
Nottingham / Nottingham: Univ. of Nottingham
NYU / New York: New York Univ. Press
Ohio State / Columbus: Ohio State Univ. Press
Oklahoma / Norman: Univ. of Oklahoma Press
Oxford / New York: Oxford Univ. Press
Pantheon / New York: Pantheon Books
Penguin / New York: Penguin Books
Penn. / Philadelphia: Univ. of Pennsylvania Press
Penn. State / University Park: Pennsylvania State Univ. Press
Peregrine Smith Books (Layton, Utah)
Peter Lang / New York: Peter Lang Publishing Co.

Princeton / Princeton, N.J.: Princeton Univ. Press
Prometheus / Buffalo, N.Y.: Prometheus Press
Putnam's / New York: G. P. Putnam's Sons
Research Publishing (Washington, D.C.)
RK Editions (New York)
Rodopi / Netherlands: Editions Rodopi
Routledge / London: Routledge and Kegan Paul
Rutgers / New Brunswick, N.J.: Rutgers Univ. Press
St. Martin's / New York: St. Martin's Press
Scarecrow / Metuchen, N.J.: Scarecrow Press
Schocken / New York: Schocken Books
Scholars' Facsimiles / Delmar, N.J.: Scholars' Facsimiles and Reprints
Scholars Press (Decatur, Ga.)
Scribner's / New York: Charles Scribner's Sons
Sheep Meadow Press (Riverdale-on-Hudson, N.Y.)
Simon & Schuster (New York)
So. Car. / Columbia: Univ. of South Carolina Press
So. Ill. / Carbondale: Southern Illinois Univ. Press
SUNY / Albany: State Univ. of New York Press
Susquehanna / Susquehanna Univ. Press (Penn.)
TCG / New York: Theatre Communications Group
Tenn. / Knoxville: Univ. of Tennessee Press
Texas / Austin: Univ. of Texas Press
Times Books (New York)
Toronto / Univ. of Toronto Press
Turkey Press (Santa Barbara, Calif.)
Twayne / Boston: Twayne Publishers
UMI / Ann Arbor, Mich.: University Microfilms International
UMI Research Press (Ann Arbor, Mich.)
Ungar / New York: Frederick Ungar Publishing Co.
Univ. Press / Lanham, Md.: Univ. Press of America
Valéry / Montpelier, France: Université Paul Valéry
Viking / New York: Viking Press
Virginia / Charlottesville: Univ. Press of Virginia
Washington / Seattle: Univ. of Washington Press
Wayne State / Detroit, Mich.: Wayne State Univ. Press
Whitston / Troy, N.Y.: Whitston Publishing Co.
Wisconsin / Madison: Univ. of Wisconsin Press
Yale / New Haven, Conn.: Yale Univ. Press

Part I

1. Emerson, Thoreau, and Transcendentalism

Philip F. Gura

This year saw a substantial harvest of scholarship and criticism for those interested in Emerson, Thoreau, and Transcendentalism. Among book-length studies, for example, there was an outstanding intellectual biography of Thoreau, a reconstruction of the first draft of his *Week on the Concord and Merrimack Rivers*, another volume in the Princeton edition of his works, an edition of Emerson's poetry notebooks, and, outweighing any other work published in 1986 on *any* aspect of antebellum literature, a magisterial study of New England literary culture that should prove as much a benchmark as F. O. Matthiessen's *American Renaissance* (1941) and Perry Miller's *The Transcendentalists: An Anthology* (1950). In addition, there were many fine essays, particularly on some of Emerson's less frequently discussed works and the relationship of Thoreau to the concerns of contemporary critical theorists. Indeed, now critics of many persuasions begin to travel a good deal in the Concord and Boston of the 1830s, '40s, and '50s to verify their notions of the relation of language to meaning. Some of what the theoreticians say will not surprise intellectual historians who long have appreciated the Transcendentalists' linguistic sophistication. On the other hand, it is clear that in some cases these same theoreticians have revivified texts that hitherto have seemed virtually exhausted; under exotic modes of cultivation some old rootstocks yield as much food for thought in 1986 as they did in 1836 or 1854.

i. Edited Texts, Calendars, General Studies

The monumental edition of Emerson's *Journals and Miscellaneous Notebooks* now completed, scholars are turning their attention to other manuscripts left by the Concord sage. One of the first fruits of these new editorial labors is *The Poetry Notebooks of Ralph Waldo*

Emerson (Missouri), ed. Ralph H. Orth, Albert J. von Frank, Linda Allardt, and David W. Hill. This hefty volume consists of the nine notebooks Emerson devoted solely to poetry, additional relevant manuscripts, analyses of the poems, and Emerson's own indexes to his volumes. Textual scholars will welcome the way the editors have sifted through the various layers of Emerson's pencil drafts to show his often elaborate process of revision, and the editors' detailed analyses of the poems do indeed provide "all of the information necessary for an understanding of the genesis, growth, transformation, significance, [and] ultimate fate . . . of each distinct poetic entity" included in the volume. I also duly note that the editors have chosen *not* to print texts already published in the *JMN*, those to appear in the forthcoming *Topical Notebooks of Ralph Waldo Emerson*, and those in separate manuscripts that do not differ appreciably from the poems included here. As meticulously and judiciously prepared as the *JMN*, this is an indispensable volume for Emerson scholars.

Linck C. Johnson has performed an equally important task in *Thoreau's Complex Weave: The Writing of* A Week on the Concord and Merrimack Rivers (Virginia). The author of the historical introduction to the Princeton edition of *A Week*, Johnson now has provided an even more detailed study of the genesis of Thoreau's first book and as well as an "edited text of the reconstructed first draft." In his commentary he offers "an analysis of the method" by which Thoreau constructed it, assesses "the impact of events on its emerging form and underlying structure," and speculates on "the relationship between its design and the overall pattern of [Thoreau's] early literary career." Also valuable is Johnson's appendix of some of the passages omitted in the second draft of *A Week* that Thoreau prepared between 1846 and 1849, in particular those that most illuminate his immediate thematic concerns. Even without the reconstructed text, this is one of the best recent studies of *A Week*. Any graduate student who doubts the worth—and the potential excitement—of preparing textual studies should turn to this volume, a model of conservative but very fine scholarship.

K. P. Van Anglen has edited Thoreau's *Translations* (Princeton) in the ongoing edition of this author's works, and, as with the other volumes in this series, the lengthy introduction alone is almost worth the price of admission. This book contains all of Thoreau's "literary translations," defined as "substantial, independent works conceived for an audience, even if not published." Here, then, we have four pieces that first were published in the *Dial* (*The Prometheus Bound* of Aeschylus, selections from the *Anacreontea*, selections from the odes of Pindar, and "Fragments from Pindar") as well as another group of Pindaric odes, *The Seven Against Thebes* of Aeschylus, and "The Transmigrations of the Seven Brahmans." In addition to providing a detailed history of Thoreau's interest in these texts and classical literatures generally, Van Anglen also offers an important statement on the significance of the translations in the context of Thoreau's intellectual development and literary career. In particular, he makes a strong case for the importance of such translations to Thoreau's long-standing interest in primitive religions and literature—and, by implication, the contemporary poet's relation to such a past—as well as to his virtual obsession with the nature and origin of language, particularly his attempt, as he put it in "Walking," "to [nail] words to their primitive senses." Although many readers may puzzle over why so ostensibly "minor" a volume has appeared in this edition before, say, a work like *Cape Cod*, Van Anglen's intelligent framing of Thoreau's translations by his larger concerns as a writer and thinker takes a bit of the edge off the question.

A real treat this year was Irving Sablosky's *What They Heard: Music in America, 1852–1881, From the Pages of "Dwight's Journal of Music"* (LSU), a generous selection from John Sullivan Dwight's pathbreaking efforts in musical journalism and criticism. All Transcendentalist scholars know that Dwight edited this journal—for 1,051 issues!—but few read in it because of its relative scarcity; now they have no excuse to neglect this fascinating side of the Brook Farmer's career. Herein we find, among other things, Dwight's reports on Boston's famed Handel and Haydn Society and New York's Philharmonic Society, and his reaction to the visits to America of such European luminaries as Jenny Lind and Anton Rubinstein. We also learn that, Dwight's consuming passion for Beethoven, Bach, and Mozart notwithstanding, he was willing to report not only on Verdi's and Wagner's operas but also on Stephen Foster's folk melodies and the music of Afro-Americans and the Moravians. Sablosky's volume is a veritable treasure trove of information about music in 19th-century America, as important to the serious student of classical music as to the Transcendentalist scholar.

In "Turning from the Orthodox: Emerson's Gospel Lectures" (*SAR*, pp. 69–112), Karen Kalinevitch prints six gospel lectures (begun on 8 March 1831) that Emerson delivered to the youth of his Boston congregation. These important documents show Emerson building arguments toward his "Lord's Supper" sermon (1832), for in these discussions he seriously questions the divine authority of Scripture and frequently cites the German "Higher Critics" to buttress his case. He emerges as a more sophisticated exegetical scholar than we hitherto have considered him. Elizabeth Maxfield-Miller performs an equally valuable editorial labor in the final part of "Elizabeth of Concord: Selected Letters of Elizabeth Sherman Hoar (1814–1878) to the Emersons, Family, and the Emerson Circle (Part Three)" (*SAR*, pp. 113–98). Maxfield-Miller includes 74 letters written by this Concord woman between 1840 and 1878. Added to her previous work on Hoar (see *ALS 1984* and *1985*), her efforts with this correspondence have made generally available a truly important source for study of the entire Concord circle of writers and thinkers.

Of interest to scholars concerned with Hawthorne's relation to the same Concordians is Edwin Haviland Miller's "Calendar of the Letters of Sophia Peabody Hawthorne" (*SAR*, pp. 199–281), for among her many correspondents were such important figures as Elizabeth Palmer Peabody and James and Annie T. Fields. Helen R. Deese has compiled "A Calendar of the Poems of Jones Very" (*SAR*, p. 305–72), tallying 850 different poems. Because Very often gave the same works different titles, and wrote different poems that included the same first lines, she has provided as well both first-line and title indexes and has cross-referenced them, enabling scholars for the first time to use with relative ease the various editions of Very's poetry. With Guy R. Woodall, Deese has also compiled another valuable reference work, "A Calendar of Lectures Presented by the Boston Society for the Diffusion of Useful Knowledge (1829–1847)" (*SAR*, pp. 17–67). This society was one of the most patrician of such early groups, and, to make its activities more known to scholars, Deese and Woodall give a brief history of the society as well as a detailed calendar of its 15 annual lecture series. Their editorial notes identify lecturers and their subjects, and the times and places of the 266 lectures delivered under the group's auspices. Finally, Joel Myerson and Daniel Shealy provide "Three Contemporary Accounts of Louisa May Alcott, with Glimpses of Other Concord Notables" (*NEQ* 59:109–22), from letters by Elizabeth Susan Greene, Bessie Holyoke, and Anne B. Adams.

Three general studies, which touch on many figures besides Emerson, Thoreau, and the Transcendentalists, deserve special mention. In his chapter on "The Soul of Language: The Transcendentalist Alternative," in *The Politics of American English*, David Simpson compares the Transcendentalists' attempts to recover a primitive, universal language to Cooper's "emphatic and unambiguous challenge to the whole tendency to impose upon nature through the exercise of the figuring imagination." Unlike Cooper, then, whose language raised questions "about the differences and tensions between the various elements in the social contract," the Transcendentalists, in Simpson's view, understood language as "a medium that can embrace in harmonious synthesis every human being and every natural object." This particular chapter is solid but breaks no new ground vis-à-vis the Transcendentalists and language. The earlier chapters, however—especially that on Cooper—are insightful.

So too is all of Robert Weisbuch's *Atlantic Double-Cross*, which contains many pages of interest to students of Transcendentalism. Weisbuch's is a major study of Anglo-American literary relations, following the work of Walter Jackson Bate and Harold Bloom on the subject of influence but breaking new ground through imaginative juxtaposition of works that display how "the American [romantic] undertakes a complex, subtle argument similar in its revisionary rites to the argument [the] English romantics take up in relation to Milton." The most important chapters for our purposes are "Thoreau's Dawn and the Lake School's Night," in which Weisbuch reads *Walden* against both Coleridge's "Dejection: An Ode" and Wordsworth's work generally; and "History, Time, and Spirit: Whitman against Wordsworth, Carlyle and Emerson against Themselves," in which *On Heroes and Hero Worship* is compared to *Representative Men.* In the former section Weisbuch argues for Thoreau's struggle to establish the possibility of an "earliness," an awakening of life and an open-endedness of opportunity in America through his Walden Pond experiment, as opposed to the "lateness" of those English writers who, as Emerson noted in *English Traits*, already had come to represent the constrictions of "linear and historical time." In his section on Emerson and Carlyle, Weisbuch expands this argument, for he views the latter as maintaining "an historical sense of decline against a wavering belief in a permanent value, still historically visible if infinite at its edges." On the contrary, Emerson blatantly employed "history unto its dissolution into invisible qualities." A brief summary does not do justice to the subtlety and complexity of Weisbuch's book, which should be required reading in its entirety for all Transcendentalist scholars because Emerson, who had been concerned with influence at least since *Nature*, is its touchstone.

Without doubt the most significant book of the year was Lawrence Buell's *New England Literary Culture*, a comprehensive literary history informed not only by the most current trends in critical theory (while remaining blessedly free of the jargon that dulls the effect of so many of its applications) but also by the most recent historical and bibliographical scholarship. I have already assessed elsewhere (*ESQ* 32:68–78) what I consider the great achievement of this work, so I will keep my comments here to a minimum. The sections of direct relevance to readers of this *ALS* chapter are "New England Poetics: Emerson, Dickinson, and Others"; "New England Oratory from Everett to Emerson"; "Literary Scripturism"; and "Lococentrism from Dwight to Thoreau." But because Buell provides, as no one ever has, an engaging description and acute assessment of hundreds of the literary works against which the canonized masterpieces of the antebellum period later emerged, this profound and wide-ranging study bears reading in its entirety by all students of American literature and culture. Like Matthiessen's *American Renaissance*, it is pathbreaking in a way that should spawn scores, if not more, of dissertations; like Miller's *The Transcendentalists*, it details a story that few of us have known in its full complexity and as such provides a new starting point for our understanding of the entire period from 1780 to 1860. Buell's scholarship is extraordinarily humbling, and his writing always is lucid. *New England Literary Culture* quite simply is one of *the* books of this generation of scholars.

Finally, in *The American Newness*, first delivered as the Charles E. Massey, Sr., Lectures in the History of American Civilization at Harvard, Irving Howe offers an overview of the American Renaissance that focuses particularly on Emerson in the 1830s and '40s, when he first recognized the opportunity for men to disentangle themselves from historical conditions and to elevate the self to the center of authority. Elegantly composed, as befits a series of lectures by so distinguished a critic, this slim volume objectively adds little to our understanding of the period. It does, however, remind us that Emerson can indeed be viewed as "one of the most political of Americans" because he understood the potentiality of the American Revolution in the realm of mind and spirit.

ii. Emerson

The major study of Emerson this year was David Van Leer's *Emerson's Epistemology: The Argument of the Essays* (Cambridge). In this dense but rewarding work Van Leer is particularly interested in the early 19th-century's "commitment to philosophical idealism," and so, taking his cue from Matthiessen, who reminded us that we still had to write a book called "The Age of Swedenborg," he zeroes in on "the way idealism promised potential divinity to man through its recognition that the soul makes its own world." Practically speaking, he has tried to "translate Emerson's private vocabulary into the more public one of traditional philosophy," and thus treats the major essays of the 1830s and '40s as though they were organized philosophical statements. The topic of the book thus becomes "Emerson's philosophy narrowly defined—his confrontation with certain traditional nineteenth-century questions about ethics and especially epistemology." It is worth mentioning that Van Leer is not so much interested in sources or influences—herein the *JMN* do not figure largely—but in the fact that he regards Emerson as a great 19th-century epistemologist like Kant. "Finally," then, Van Leer rather humbly tells us, his "hypothetical account [of Emerson as systematic thinker] means only to disprove the claim that Emerson cannot be read seriously as a philosopher." Although this book reads as slowly as molasses pours, as a tour de force in philosophical thinking it is well worth the Emersonian's while, even if some wits will no doubt quip that, as with people who begin to look like their dogs, the author's style has absorbed some of the opaqueness of Emerson's and Kant's.

There were several essays, a few of them quite significant, that dealt with general issues in Emerson's work. One of the weaker efforts was Ormond Seavey's "Emerson as Itinerant" (*Emerson and His Legacy*, pp. 1–22), in which we learn the not overly startling fact that as Emerson went through his vocational crisis in the 1830s he was "basically revising his notion of what an audience was, and ultimately what society was." Seavey tries to link Emerson's "itinerancy" to very different controversies over that issue in the Great Awakening; instead of spending so much time reviewing what we all know about that earlier period, he would have done much better to examine in more depth contemporary religious politics in Emerson's Boston, in which, as Joseph Conforti and others recently have shown, the Awakening was an issue in very different ways. More substantial is Peter Carafiol's "Reading Emerson: Writing History" (*CentR* 30: 431–51), in which he discusses the fact that Emerson's own notions of Transcendentalism, as best expressed in "The Transcendentalist," have too often been the starting point for later thinking about the movement; that is, that we have accepted his polarities of "thought" and "feeling" as a key to the group's concerns without carefully analyzing *how* he expresses his thoughts on these issues. Carafiol demonstrates that if one looks carefully at how Emerson speaks about Transcendentalism, he is in fact uncertain of precisely how to define the New Thought and so produced "a new sort of prose, one that calls in turn for a new way of reading that does *not* seek to resolve his various statements into one clearer meaning." Carafiol thus sees Emerson as trying to compose "an alternative *to* metaphysical philosophy, one with important implications for literary theory," for the key to his thought is not unity but variety or multiplicity. For Carafiol, then, Emerson understands Transcendentalism as a method of examining the world and our relation to it, not as a logical, coherent system. Elegantly argued, this piece is well worth anyone's time, even if he is not particularly interested in the way Carafiol transforms Emerson into a herald of the theoreticians. Stephen Donadio, in "Emerson, Poe, and the Ruins of Convention" (*Emerson and His Legacy*, pp. 67–92), comes to similar conclusions by a different route. Comparing Emerson in certain ways to Poe, usually taken as his opposite, Donadio shows how disorientation, a pervasive disorder, and a disregard for institutional authority characterize both men's work. This leads him to note that the striking thing about Emerson and Poe is the way in which they regularly represent themselves as "conforming to established and familiar models which they proceed systematically to reduce to ruins." As in Carafiol's reading, Emerson produces "fragmentary structures" which paradoxically have come to be "apprehended as aesthetic wholes."

The most powerful essay on Emerson this year was, hands down, David Leverenz's "The Politics of Emerson's Man-Making Words" (*PMLA* 101:38–56). Leverenz begins with the simple-enough observation that, despite Emerson's vagueness, he has two distinct interpretive communities—intellectuals and businessmen. Contemplating this, Leverenz suggests that "Emerson's prose begins to make sense not in and of itself or in relation to intellectual or literary traditions but as an implicitly political response to contemporary

American expectations of becoming a man." If, for example, both Harold Bloom and Woody Hayes still find Emerson "strong," as they indeed do, it is because "Emerson's various paradoxes reflect contradictions in the energizing ideology of individualism, which erected an ideal of free, forceful, and resourceful white men on the presumption of depersonalized servitude from several subordinated groups." Centering on a lovely and powerful reading of "Experience," Leverenz argues that Emerson dreamed of "an intelligentsia that could preserve the patrician values of culture over business and politics," while also wishing to empower culture "with the capital of American manhood." This is one of the best attempts to understand Emerson's continuing fascination for Americans that I have come across.

Less original but still worthwhile for what she has found in manuscript sources is Barbara Packer's "Origin and Authority: Emerson and the Higher Criticism" (*Reconstructing American Literary History*, pp. 67–92). Packer discusses how Emerson's early interest in scriptural exegesis, particularly as it was nurtured by his brother William's trip to Göttingen in 1824, carried over to his poetic theory. Her conclusion that over time the "names and technical vocabulary of higher critics" disappeared from his writing but "their sophisticated models for imagining the relationship between inspiration and text continued to fascinate him" will not surprise readers of, say, Julie Ellison's *Emerson's Romantic Style* (1984). Stephen Railton's "Seeing and Saying: The Dialectic of Emerson's 'Eloquence'" (*Emerson and His Legacy*, pp. 48–66) similarly fails to deliver significant news. As befits someone contributing an essay to a collection honoring Quentin Anderson, Railton argues that in *Nature* Emerson's method is not dialectical but imperial; that is, in this seminal piece Emerson makes no attempt at synthetic statement but rather simply dismisses any potential opposition to his thought. Even as he sought to be appreciated by his audience, then, he demanded acceptance on his own terms, something apparent to any careful reader of his works.

John Michael, in "Emerson's Chagrin: Benediction and Exhortation in 'Nature' and 'Tintern Abbey'" (*MLN* 101:1067–85), is similarly concerned with Emerson's view of himself vis-à-vis his audience, but in this well-balanced appraisal he sees him as much more tentative than Railton allows. Michael claims that "we have too long remained deaf to Emerson's persistent anxieties that everywhere modify the optimistic upsurges and affirmations" of his individualism. With this in mind, he finds most instructive Emerson's ambivalent relation to Wordsworth, in whose statements about the poet, particularly in "Tintern Abbey" and the prefaces to *Lyrical Ballads*, he saw reflected his own "self doubt" and "longing for confirmation." In "The Private Voice behind the Public Text: Two Emerson Sermons" (*ESQ* 32:173–82), Susan L. Roberson explores the question of Emerson's public role from a different direction, closely reading two of his sermons (of 20 September 1829 and 21 October 1832) to demonstrate how, throughout the six years of his ministry, he struggled to "empower the self against fears of failure." She convincingly demonstrates the close linkage between Emerson's thoughts in his journals and those he presented to his congregation: starting from a belief that the individual was indeed formed and controlled by society, over the course of his ministerial career he "willed into being a new religion whose flag bearer was nurtured by the private voice of God." This is a nice essay to understand just what can be done by a textual scholar who opens her materials to the realms of biography and intellectual history.

Others essays also focused on *Nature*. Jerry A. Herndon, for example, in "Emerson's *Nature* and Whitman's 'Song of Myself' " (*REAL* 4:195–232), argues that scholars have not focused enough on the influence of Emerson's first book on the good gray poet, choosing instead to emphasize the importance of works like "The Poet." In this elaborate, convincing essay Herndon demonstrates "the seminal importance of this Transcendentalist document in the 'long foreground' . . . of Whitman's poetic development"; he indicates as well how Whitman managed to go his own way as the poet of American democracy. Less rewarding is Dennis Donoghue's "Emerson at First: A Commentary on *Nature*" (*Emerson and His Legacy*, pp. 23–47), little more than an explication of each selection of *Nature* that displays this critic's characteristic intelligence but fails to bring anything new to the scholarship.

In "The Journey and the Mirror: Emerson and the American Arts" (*Prospects* 10 [1985]:353–408), Betty E. Chmaj assesses the impact of "The American Scholar" on four art forms—architecture, literature, painting, and music—among Emerson's contemporaries as well as subsequent American artists. She does well to remind us of his influence on architects like Sullivan and Wright, and on composers like Ives, but what she has to say about the Luminist painters, or about Thoreau and Whitman, only recapitulates what we have learned earlier elsewhere. In contrast, Robert E. Burkholder contributes a fine piece of contextual scholarship in his "Emerson, Kneeland, and the Divinity School Address" (*AL* 58:1–14), in which he reminds us that the infamous Abner Kneeland sat in a Boston jail, convicted of blasphemy, at the same time that Emerson addressed the graduates at the Divinity School. The implication is that in the Jacksonian period charges of infidelity such as Emerson incurred implied anti-establishment social and political views as well, something to which Emerson was very sensitive as he tailored his address. The furor that followed his performance surprised and troubled him because by some he was viewed as an ally of infidel Democrats like Kneeland, an impression augmented by Kneeland and his associates, who applauded Emerson's effort to beard the Unitarians in their own den. Emerson's journal entries in the days and weeks following his address, Burkholder notes, show him trying to reestablish his social and political credentials.

If Burkholder's is a model of careful historical scholarship, Michael Strelow's "Emerson Abroad and at Home: The Making of the Paradigm in *Essays,* [sic] *First Series*" (*ATQ* 59:43–51) stands as a cautionary example of how one's imagination can run away with ideas. Strelow begins by suggesting that Emerson's famous epiphany in the Jardin des Plantes about the universal laws of nature is akin to what historian of science Robert Kuhn has called a "paradigm shift"; thence, somehow, he moves on to a discussion of railroads and the Age of Jackson. I will let him state his own case. "From Cuvier and company Emerson learned to distrust the myriad possible surfaces life perpetrated like a magician. From Jackson and the Jacksonians the young Emerson saw instuitive [sic] flashes—the light within—at work in American politics. The *Essays,* [sic] *First Series* are in some important ways a record of this fashion." Hmmm. Leonard R. Neufeldt and Christopher Barr, in "'I Shall Write Like a Latin Father': Emerson's 'Circles'" (*NEQ* 59:92–108), do better at explaining what Emerson was up to in the 1840s, though they take us there via the minefields of critical theory. In Emerson's famous essay of 1841 they locate one of his chief concerns in that period of his life, "that of finding a stable center and authoritative moment, expression, or mode of action in a centrifugal field." They also have performed the, to me, astonishing feat of introducing readers of *NEQ* to Derrida! A lighter effort in this same direction is

David Shimkin's "Emerson's Playful Habit of Mind" (*ATQ* 62:3–16), which argues that "playfulness" best characterizes Emerson's philosophical position. Put another way, the unity of Emerson's works is achieved by "touting rather than reconciling contradictions of statement and image."

Three essays deal with *English Traits*, perhaps a sign that this book finally is becoming more appreciated. In "The Edge of Urbanity: Emerson's *English Traits*" (*ESQ* 32:96–109), Julie Ellison continues her provocative work on Emerson by noting that part of his strategy in this book is to depict the British as primitives, as he adopts the role of a representative of high culture visiting them. She regards Emerson's as an "ironic urbanity," which she identifies as "one of the later modalities" of his "aggressiveness." She also notes his observation that England, in her words, has become a "social machine signifying the triumph of culture over nature," a fact epitomized by the country's closed class structure that excluded Jews, blacks, and others. Finally, Ellison is intent on demonstrating that certain themes persist in Emerson's writings from the 1830s through the 1850s, particularly his aversion to metaphysical reductionism. Richard Bridgman, in "From Greenough to Nowhere: Emerson's *English Traits*" (*NEQ* 59:469–85), sees an Emerson more ambivalent about his nation's superiority. Emerson was willing to maintain—through his invocation in the first chapter of the book of the American sculptor Horatio Greenough—that with its commitment to a functional and organic aesthetic America represented a new wave that would wash over Britain's crumbling civilization. Concomitantly, though, he lamented the fact that by the 1850s America still had not achieved its destined greatness. "He saw English insufficiency as clearly as he felt the need for American succession," Bridgman notes; but Emerson also was haunted by the possibility that "England's limitations might finally prove to be the world's." Carl F. Hovde's "English and American Traits" (*Emerson and His Legacy*, pp. 66–83) offers, though less powerfully, the same argument, for he views the book as "admonitory about American characteristics" and a witness to, among other things, the possibility that man is limited in what he can achieve.

Finally, there were some brief discussions of Emerson's poetry and poetic theory. In "A Perverted Poetics: Bryant's and Emerson's Concern for a Developing American Literature" (*ATQ* 61:15–22), Steve Olson notes that in his fourth lecture on poetry (1825) Bryant acknowledges both the need for originality as well as the importance of tradition in a genuinely American poetry, a theme Emerson announced in "The American Scholar." In "Emerson and Byron" (*ATQ* 62:59–62) Larry Bielawski reads "Self-Reliance" as "antithetical" to the ideas found in *Childe Harold*, claiming that Emerson rejects Byron's celebration of a pathetic, misanthropic wanderer who seeks things that do not already reside in his soul. In "The Meeting of the Twain: Emerson's 'Hamatreya' " (*ELN* 23:47–51), Alice Hall Petry plays with the title of this poem and suggests that it is a pun on *hamartia*, from Aristotle's discussion of the *tragic hero*. It also means *earth-mother*, and Petry shows how each half of the poem focuses on one of these meanings. And J. Lasley Dameron, in "Emerson's 'Each and All' and Goethe's 'Eins und Alles' " (*ES* 67:327–30), notes that an 1839 issue of the *North American Review* carried a translation of Goethe's poem as "One and All," suggesting that this might be the reason Emerson changed the title of *his* poem from "Each in All," as it appeared in 1839 in the *Western Messenger*, to "Each and All" in the 1847 edition of his poetry.

iii. Thoreau

The outstanding work on Thoreau was Robert D. Richardson, Jr.'s *Henry David Thoreau: A Life of the Mind* (Calif.), an intellectual biography to stand aside, if not quite surpass, Sherman Paul's *The Shores of America* (1958). Unlike Paul, of course, Richardson has had the benefit of Walter Harding's lifetime investigation of Thoreau's life as well as of the textual scholarship made available by the Princeton edition of Thoreau's works. In one hundred brief but compelling chapters, covering the period from Thoreau's commencement at Harvard in 1837 to his death in 1862, Richardson brilliantly traces the growth of Thoreau "as a writer, as a naturalist, and as a reader," a task in part so successful because he has located and consulted quite literally *all* the books his subject is known to have read. Indeed, it is finally the breadth and depth of Richardson's attempt to know what Thoreau was reading, thinking, and saying at any given point in his career, and his ability to link such information to the development of Thoreau as an artist, that is most remarkable. Add to this the lucidity of his prose, and, as the University of California Press rightly gambled, you have an indispensable scholarly work that will sell as a trade edition. Richardson's book is required reading for everyone who reads this chapter of *ALS*. And do not overlook the beautiful wood engravings designed especially for this work by Barry Moser, one of America's foremost artists in the genre.

The only other book on Thoreau was David A. Dombrowski's *Thoreau the Platonist* (Peter Lang), as restricted and unattractive a book (mine had its covers bound upside down) as Richardson's is catholic and handsome. Dombrowski treats the sources that led Thoreau to become a Platonist, outlines the conceptual structure of his universe (Platonic, of course), discusses his theism and vegetarianism, which derived from his understanding of the world, and investigates the Platonic basis of language in his works. All this is fine, but the book would be much stronger had the author understood, as Richardson does, the breadth and complexity of the sources of Thoreau's ideas. A glance at the bibliography, for example, shows Dombrowski seemingly unaware of the many recent essays that treat Thoreau's philological interests and which thus bear on his arguments concerning language. Dombrowski recapitulates some of his ideas in "Thoreau, Sainthood, and Vegetarianism" (*ATQ* 60:25–36), in which he also argues that "Thoreau's vegetarian position makes sense and can be given a rational defense today" if one understands that it was based in a model of sainthood that "forces all moral agents at least to consider the possibility that meat-eating is morally reprehensible." Anyone who occasionally is tempted to seize a woodchuck and devour it raw might find some food for thought herein.

There were several essays that treated Thoreau from the perspectives of contemporary critical theory. In "Thoreau's Composition of the Narrator: From Sexuality to Language" (*BuR* 30[1985]:121–42), Ross J. Pudaloff attempts to "trace Thoreau's stance toward those aspects of his self and life which were sometimes obscure to him, which were sometimes deeply troubling, and, most important, which constitute the raw material out of which he constructed the narrators of his texts." For Pudaloff the touchstone here is Michel Foucault, for Pudaloff understands Thoreau "as a literary figure that identifies a certain discursive practice arising in response to the nineteenth century's invention of psychological man." To read him thus is to see, for example, that "the chaos of 'Ktaadn' and the order of *Walden* do not negate each other" but rather mark "the boundaries of the transformations possible within the discursive practice of idealism in nineteenth-century America." This is a thorny article but an interesting discussion of how the language of Thoreau's texts allows him to subjugate his body to Reason.

Henry Golemba, in "Thoreau's Working Audience: The Reader as Other and Character" (*ELWIU* 13:89–102), shifts the spotlight from Thoreau the "author" to his presumed "reader," whom Golemba sees not as "a passive consumer of the text nor a mere 'Dear Reader' convention" but as a presence that plays "an active aesthetic role in Thoreau's narrative construction and creation of personae." Thoreau, Golemba believes, creates an imagined reader who is inside the text, "actively engaged in shaping its significance whether in his/her role of audience as character or as participant in the creative process of reading." This, too, is a provocative piece, more so, say, than Timothy Gould's "Reading On: *Walden*'s Labors of Succession" (*ThoreauQ* 16[1984]:119–36), which concludes, unremarkably, that "to learn reading from Emerson and Thoreau is to learn how to keep reading exactly in the prospect of becoming unsettled."

I turn now to essays that deal primarily with specific texts. In "'Further Down the Stream of Time': Memory and Perspective in Thoreau's *A Week on the Concord and Merrimack Rivers*" (*ThoreauQ* 16[1984]:93–118), H. Daniel Peck studies what he considers Thoreau's "most insistently and explicitly temporal work," particularly his "attempt to immerse himself in the river of time in order to recover from time one of his most deeply felt losses," that of his brother John. This is a lovely close reading of certain key passages in *A Week*, rewarding for its judiciousness and intelligence if not for pyrotechnic theoretical premises. All readers who love Thoreau's first book, for example, will appreciate how "right" Peck is when he concludes that the book "implicitly argues that memory does not order the past sequentially but layers it into levels of value and meaning whose relation to one another is more poetic than historical." A more challenging, if finally less satisfying, essay is Malini Schueller's "Carnival Rhetoric and Extra-Vagance in Thoreau's *Walden*" (*AL* 58:33–45), in which M. M. Bakhtin is the critic of the day. Schueller is interested in the fact that in *Walden* Thoreau champions "a metaphysics of difference, challenging the sameness of socially instituted rhetoric and urging nonconformity"; but, and for Schueller here is the rub, "as a poet-priest he finally attempts to authorize only his unique rhetoric, to privilege the ideology of a single, authoritative 'I.'" Thus his "carnivalization" of rhetoric—his laughter that destroys forms of authority—ironically "metamorposes into a hierarchical counter-ideology." It struck me, finally, that this is simply a highfalutin way of discussing Thoreau's admitted self-righteousness.

Meg McGavran Murray offers an ingenious reading of one of Thoreau's parables in "Thoreau's Moon Mythology: Lunar Clues to the Hieroglyphics of *Walden*" (*AL* 58:15–32). She is interested in the different mythological heroes whom Thoreau associates with the moon, particularly Cynthia, Endymion's young lover, and Isis. In Murray's view Thoreau is the votary of Isis/Diana/Cynthia, seeking their wisdom. Murray notes, for example, that a hound is the dog associated with all these three, and that in Plutarch's account of Isis and Osiris a dove represents wisdom and a horse, mankind. If the reader hasn't yet seen the point, Murray thus deciphers Thoreau's famous story about having lost a hound, a bay horse, and a turtledove! More important, she believes that many of the central images in *Walden* come from the Osiris myth. Much more lightweight is Ian Marshall's "Thoreau's Walden Odyssey" (*ATQ* 59: 53–62), which speculates that, contrary to popular scholarly opinion, the *Odyssey*, with its story of a mythic wanderer, was more important to Thoreau during his Walden Pond years than was the *Iliad*. After we learn this, we still are left with—ho-hum—*Walden* as a modern epic.

Bruce Greenfield provides a top-notch reading of *The Maine Woods* in "Thoreau's Discovery of America: A First Contact" (*ESQ* 32:80–95). Greenfield notes that in Thoreau's description of Maine's wild landscape he neglects to mention anything about the initial Native American/White contacts, primarily because he wishes to interpret it as "empty," awaiting *his* discovery. "Ktaadn," then, is an account of a journey through which Thoreau "tries to disencumber both the traveler and the land from their visible relations with Indian and Euro-American society." Because it occurs in the realm of the imagination and is re-created by each reader, this recovery is a "personal event which can be repeated in successive generations." This essay contributes significantly to Thoreau's complicated response to wilderness and the people who passed through it. Less interesting is "The Journal, Self-Culture, and the Genesis of 'Walking' " (*ThoreauQ* 16[1984]:137–55), in which William Rossi tries to explain, through recourse to the phrase "self-culture" that David Robinson has made so central to Transcendentalist studies, the links between Thoreau's composition in his journals, his practice of walking, and the essay by that title. There is nothing startling in Rossi's account.

In "The Language of Prophecy: Thoreau's 'Wild Apples'" (*NEQ* 59:212–30), Steven Fink, working the same vein as Schueller (see above), discusses the contradiction between Thoreau's desire for independence and his wish to engage and convince an audience, to find a discourse faithful to his personal vision that yet was intelligible to the wider community. Fink, too, sees such contradictions in *Walden* and locates them as well in Thoreau's late essay "Wild Apples," which he, obviously under Sacvan Bercovitch's influence, regards as "a highly crafted personal autobiography, a national biography, and an American jeremiad." This is a good close reading of an essay which demonstrates how even in his last years Thoreau "had never given up his desire for acclaim in the literary marketplace" nor "ever lost the conviction of his calling to be a prophet to America." In "A 'Life without Principle' Manuscript Fragment: What to Make of a Diminished Thing?" (*ELWIU* 12[1985]: 139–44), Ronald Wesley Hoag makes more than one might think possible. He performs a bit of literary sleuthing with regard to a few words of Thoreau manuscript he came across and argues for their importance in understanding Thoreau's process of revision. Finally, I note one essay that I was not able to see before copy deadline, Kevin Radaker's "Luminism in Thoreau's *A Week on the Concord and Merrimack Rivers*" (*MHLS* 9:31–37).

iv. Other Transcendentalists

In "To the Edges of Ideology: Margaret Fuller's Centrifugal Evolution" (*AQ* 38:173–201), Bell Gale Chevigny offers a powerful statement about how the life of this extraordinary woman and her critique of American ideology were sanitized and distorted after her tragic death. Pointing to the editors of her *Memoirs* (Emerson, Clarke, and W. H. Channing) as well as to Hawthorne and James, Chevigny demonstrates how much of what Fuller had learned from her experience in Europe—that, for example, the American Revolution had not gone far enough in eliminating social injustice—was dropped from their "re-representation" of her life and writings. From their statements about her, that is, one would not guess that by 1850 the former editor of the *Dial* sought to revitalize the American revolutionary ideal to support the sovereignty of the working classes and to effect a Fourierist liberation from institutionalized gender constraints. By the end of the 19th century, then, a certain "ideological closure" had been attained with regard to the meaning of Fuller's life and a myth of a "domestic" Fuller "established for the sentimentalist." Chevigny's essay is an example of the best work being done in the "new historicism." Tepid by contrast is Sharon George's "Margaret Fuller's *Dial* Criticism: The Merging of the Scottish Common Sense and Romantic Traditions" (*ATQ* 62:17–28), in which she displays how from the Common Sense school Fuller absorbed the notion that the critic should educate the public yet did not believe that as such she was obligated to teach only the ideas and values that already had gained critical acceptance. This is solid work but hardly astonishing. The same can be said of Elizabeth Hardwick's "The Genius of Margaret Fuller" (*NYRB* 33,vi:14–22), more interesting about Hardwick than about Fuller.

In "Conservative Voices in the *Western Messenger*: William Greenleaf Eliot and Harm Jan Huidekoper" (*HTR* 77[1984]:331–52), Judith Green argues that it is important to remember that the *Western Messenger* was not so much a Transcendentalist periodical as one which emphasized the "scriptural basis for a Unitarian interpretation of Christianity." To illustrate this, she focuses on the contributions of two men who frequently wrote for its pages and who—unlike some others, admittedly better known, whose essays and verse appeared therein—continued to live in the West. Green's reminder that the *Western Messenger* was a moderating force in the Transcendentalist controversy is welcome, as is David R. Williams's essay on a figure who, if despising Transcendentalism, still greatly influenced its foremost exponent. In "The Wilderness Rapture of Mary Moody Emerson: One Calvinist Link to Transcendentalism" (*SAR*, pp. 1–16), Williams discusses Miss Emerson's probable influence on her nephew, particularly her encouragement of him to "enter into the wilderness of his soul and there experience the terror and the ecstasy of conversion." This is a good study of early 19th-century Calvinism, particularly as to how it emphasized the "dualistic desire for self-denial and the substitution of God in the place of self," notions which, after being filtered through Emerson's reading, were restated in his version of the philosophy of the New School. To accompany this essay we also have Phyllis Cole's "The Divinity School Address of Mary Moody Emerson: Women's Silence and Women's Speech in the American Puritan Tradition" (*Harvard Divinity Bul-*

letin 16,ii:4–6). Cole provides an overview of Miss Emerson's life and writings and speaks particularly to the importance of her "Almanacks" or diaries to the recovery of American women's literature. Finally, I note that Kenneth Walter Cameron published *Transcendental Curriculum or Bronson Alcott's Library* (Transcendental, 1984).

University of North Carolina, Chapel Hill

2. Hawthorne

Claudia D. Johnson

Scholars writing on Hawthorne in 1986 depart from tradition in being significantly more self-conscious about the critical methods they apply to his work. Lawrence Buell, Jonathan Arac, and E. Miller Budick, among others, take up the issue, Arac pointing out the general reluctance of Americanists to come to terms with new critical methods, Budick explaining her preference for historicity over psychology as a critical approach, and Buell locating his work in a historicism between New Criticism and deconstruction. In 1986 the new historicists encroached even further on literary ground once held by the old literary historians and the once New Critics. Unlike feminist critics who have in recent years, and continue in 1986, to write on Hawthorne, deconstructionists in general have failed to stake out significant claims in Hawthorne country as the new historicists have, though the debt the new historicism owes to the deconstruction of literary and historical scholarship is not to be ignored.

As a result of this development, even more attention than usual has been given to the conflicting forces within the cultural context of Hawthorne's fiction. As always, a number of critics in 1986 consider the effect of Calvinism on Hawthorne, the balance of interpretation now swinging in the direction of Calvinism's negative rather than positive influence, to demonstrate Hawthorne's fictional rejection of the Puritans' destructive absolutism as they upheld the rigid letter of the law to the detriment of spirit. There are also significant investigations of the ideological constraints placed upon art and sexuality not just by Puritanism, but by the Protestantism and materialism of Hawthorne's own day. The effect that rationalism and Transcendentalism had on Hawthorne's fiction also forms part of the emphasis on intellectual history. The more sophisticated work on Hawthorne for the year includes provocative arguments for an already familiar thesis, that Hawthorne's artistic dilemma was inextricably bound up with the ideologies that defined America: since art was obviously in a state of becoming and the nation was regarded as complete, the two were largely antithetical.

Theoretical conviction and interpretation intersect as the critic who has decided to "remain in history" finds Hawthorne himself and Hawthorne's characters struggling with the identical imperative to remain in history. From such a perspective scholars in 1986 speculated about the effect that Hawthorne's early uneasiness with his vocation and his country may have on his eventual artistic decline.

Two other characteristics of the scholarship for 1986 may well follow from the move away from the old New Criticism: an interpretive propensity for national and aesthetic allegory and a continuing, somewhat iconoclastic, examination of literary history. Increasingly, Hawthorne scholars are moving outside the confines of the traditional canon to look at the literary forms and writers popular at the time Hawthorne was learning his craft. In some of the finest work on Hawthorne this year, Richard H. Brodhead explores the reasons why the canon develops as it does, the effect Hawthorne's place in the canon had on the work of other writers, and especially the effect of that place on Hawthorne's own career.

i. Primary Materials

After several years of significant additions to the store of primary texts, particularly the Ohio State Centenary Edition letters, little in 1986 falls under the category of newly available primary material. However, an eighth number of *The Spectator*, the family newspaper edited by Hawthorne in his teens, having in 1982 been deposited in the Essex Institute of Salem along with other papers belonging to his sister Elizabeth, was published in facsimile on the cover of *NHR* and accompanied by a report on its substance (Thomas Woodson, "A New Installment of Hawthorne's *Spectator*," *NHR* 12,ii:1–3). This issue shows his reaction to clerical politics in Salem, revealing him to be as skeptical of the clergy at 16 as he was throughout his adult life.

ii. General Studies

Substantial sections of four 1986 book-length studies of 19th-century literary culture in America take into account more than one work by Hawthorne. The fresh readings within new, provocative, but convincingly argued historical frames make three of these studies important contributions to scholarship. The object of Lawrence Buell's *New England Literary Culture* is to redefine literary history through a historiographical middle ground, specifically an "ideology of provincialism" which he locates between New Criticism and deconstruction. Several works by Hawthorne, some of them compared with popular works by noncanonical writers like Harriet Beecher Stowe and Elizabeth Barstow Stoddard, lend themselves to Buell's purpose. For example, by using historical frames of reference in "Young Goodman Grown" to illustrate the narrator's undercutting of what the protagonist perceives as truth, Buell finds a kinship between Emerson and Hawthorne, both of whom question the provincial New England orthodox view of reality which tends to divide the self. Hawthorne used history to explore the social realities of his own day in *The House of the Seven Gables*, a romance in the Walter Scott tradition and one in which he linked the changelessness of Puritan-dominated New England with gothicism. While recognizing the importance of Puritanism to the culture in which Hawthorne shared, Buell is also attentive to the impact made by the rationalism that intervened between the American Renaissance and Puritanism. Although Hawthorne privately railed against the liberal church and publicly satirized Transcendentalism, the decline in theological rigor gave him the distance he needed to examine Puritanism's constraints on the self and its skewed view of reality. Finally, by transcending the provincial limits of place and time in *The Scarlet Letter*, he could turn to the realities of the heart.

Myra Jehlen's "Transgression and Transformation" (*American Incarnation*, pp. 153–84) uses *The Scarlet Letter* and *The Marble Faun* to explore America as a symbol of the country's material landscape with its spirit of liberalism, idealism, and individualism. Her interpretation of *The Scarlet Letter* turns on the novel's conclusion. Hester, who has entered the novel in rebellion against the social conventions which represent America, returns in acquiescence, advising the women, whose very unhappiness damns them and taints their protests, to submit to a condition that, by implication, they deserve and that is never likely to improve. The spirit of the letter Hester wears dies with her, losing its original symbolic evocativeness, the gloom and hopelessness of both character and letter betraying Hawthorne's guilt for his own radicalism in adulterously conceiving a fictional "other" America. Because America was regarded as complete, Jehlen posits, the novelist, who denies America's completion by reinventing it, becomes blasphemer. The ending of the novel, by affirming the values of America initially challenged by Hester and the author, necessarily denies the usefulness of their travail. In "Prophetic Pictures" Hawthorne also graphically illustrates the dangerous blasphemies and double binds of the fiction-making he commits and then persistently scrutinizes. Like the painter in "Prophetic Pictures" who enlarges our understanding of history in taking upon himself the role of prophet, the writer is damned for using his powers because it is an assumption of divinity. But failure to use his gifts is equally damning. The romance, which separated reality and fiction, allowed Hawthorne "to exercise more freely the very power he feared." *The Marble Faun* finds Hawthorne's artists escaping from America into European artistic culture, then redeeming themselves by leaving art behind to return to the New World. The fiction itself leaves behind the complications of *The Scarlet Letter* to escape largely into allegory. The art, passion, and rejuvenation of the Old World are left without a future, and Hawthorne like Kenyon is shamed into silence. Jehlen's reading of Hawthorne against Transcendentalism is especially valuable. Hawthorne, she argues, brings greater complexity to the concept of transcendental perception because he recognizes the "natural fact" as a puzzle with multiple dimensions, the author as separated from rather than united with transcendental truth.

Hawthorne's literary decline is addressed by Richard Brodhead in *The School of Hawthorne* (Oxford). Brodhead's title means those writers—Melville, Howells, James, and Faulkner chief among them—whose vision and education as writers derive from Hawthorne or at least a tradition commonly associated with Hawthorne. That the history of a literary brotherhood, to which Hawthorne was the key, is canonical is scarcely surprising; that Brodhead acknowledges and explains his book's canonical character in the preface and first and third chapters is an interesting further indication of the current impulse to reexamine the canon in light of a more complete literary history in which noncanonical works play a revealing part. Brodhead continually asks why the canon developed as it did. Hawthorne seems unlikely as the key formulator of an American canon, the founder of a literary tradition: he is neither authoritarian nor a prosyletizer. Yet Brodhead supposes that it is Hawthorne's very openness, his refusal to authorize literary absolutes, that has made his tradition accessible to such diverse writers. Like Jehlen, Brodhead brings originality and richness of insight to his thesis, exploring the importance of prophecy to Hawthorne's work, to his conception of authorship, and to his impact on Melville, who imperfectly understood that Hawthorne's prophecy eluded "the conceptual commitments such energies bring along" (p. 44). Brodhead opens up a new level of understanding by reasoning that Hawthorne's literary disablement after 1852 was ironically and adversely affected by his finding himself at the center of a solidifying American literary tradition. His brief rendering of *The Marble Faun* as a sign of Hawthorne's literary collapse is exceptionally well done.

By contrast to the Buell, Jehlen, and Brodhead books, most of the newness in Irving Howe's *The American Newness* is in the title. The scholarship in the Hawthorne section is noticeably unsophisticated, even given the trend to diminish footnotes. One has to wonder why Howe belabors what has now become the obvious: "My Kinsman, Major Molineux" is ironic; Hawthorne is devoted to inwardness; he and Emerson have different attitudes toward the past.

Three major articles dealing with more than one work of Hawthorne's appeared in 1986. E. Miller Budick, "The World as Spectator: Hawthorne's Historical Art" (*PMLA* 101:218–32), contends that Hawthorne used history in what were basically psychological and moral fictions in order to prevent romance from becoming totally engulfed in dreams. From such a point of view, which necessitates granting "Young Goodman Brown" literal plausibility, for example, history, seen as a mediator between determinism and free will, is faith in Scripture and Christian renewal. Brown's own ahistorical moralism damns him as the "ahistorical moral absolutism" of his ancestors had damned them. Similarly, Robin Molineux is mistakenly led to believe that he can gain his independence at the expense of history.

William M. Ferraro, in "An Interpretation of Hawthorne and the American Character" (*SAQ* 85:165–75), finds that Hawthorne's fiction illustrates the necessity in American culture to cope with two dilemmas: the social one wherein society and the self are at cross-purposes, and the aesthetic one wherein practicality is in conflict with beauty, inquisitiveness with sensibility, insecurity with stability. Attempts to deal with the social dilemma by moving to an unreal world (*The Blithedale Romance*) or escaping worldly anxiety ("The Maypole of Merrymount") are doomed. Characters also seek personal escapes, as do Hester and Owen Warland, or, like Hawthorne's scientists, attempt to take hold of and alter the dilemma through the power of knowledge.

Like Ferraro's essay, Sargent Bush, Jr.'s "Hawthorne's Domestic Narratives of the 1830s" (*BI* 45:38–49) has a dualistic structure: the quest in Hawthorne's fiction is opposed to, and the initial step in, the affirmation of home. His work before 1830 is characterized by his characters' initial need to break with home in pursuit of adventure only to circle back home in acceptance of domestic values. The main characters of the period are "dislocated questers." This early pattern, apparent in "Young Goodman Brown," "The Ambitious Guest," and "Wakefield," persists in some form even in the later novels and helps to explain Hawthorne's popularity with an audience that liked domestic narratives.

A note and the abstract of an address, both on Hawthorne's work in general, appeared in *NHR* in 1986: J. Lasley Dameron's "Hawthorne and the Popular Concept of the Prose Romance" (12,i:21) and Richard D. Rust's " 'I Seek For Truth': Hawthorne's Use of the Talisman" (12,i:5–7). Dameron writes that in the 1850s Hawthorne popularized the prose romance, his prefaces setting forth the theoretical basis of a genre that was already widely accepted. Rust argues for the importance in Hawthorne's work of the concept of the talisman, defined as a representation of intuitively perceived truth, most often available to youths and artists. In *The Scarlet Letter* the A, and its embodiment in Pearl, are talismans which eventually give Hester a new understanding of herself and others. In *The Blithedale Romance* Zenobia's flower is a talisman which conveys something of her hidden history to Coverdale.

Several essays on other figures contain observations about Hawthorne's influence. As always, studies of Henry James include his criticism of or debt to Hawthorne. Evan Carton's review-essay "Henry James the Critic" (*Raritan* 5,iii:118–36) contends that James's use of the word "charming" to describe Hawthorne is not only a clue that he failed to read Hawthorne seriously, but also betrays James's need to protect himself from the value he placed on what he saw as Hawthorne's kind of charm. William Harmon has a note on T. S. Eliot's reading of James on Hawthorne: "Hawthorne and Thackeray: Two Notes on Eliot's Reading and Borrowing" (*YER* 8:123–24).

While Carton examines Hawthorne's effect on James, Bell Gale

Chevigny, in "To the Edges of Ideology: Margaret Fuller's Centrifugal Evolution" (*AQ* 38:175–99), explores Hawthorne's contribution to the legend of Fuller in *The Blithedale Romance* and *The Marble Faun.* Even though one might at first argue Hawthorne's sympathy for Fuller in matching Zenobia's fanaticism with Hollingsworth's, her last appearances in the novel show her wish to submit to Hollingsworth, her incompleteness, and her moral fall, a portrait that was formed out of the gossip about Fuller and Ossoli that came Hawthorne's way. In *The Marble Faun* he "repeats his earlier assault on her for impurity" in his characterization of Miriam, by removing the fictionalized Fuller from the social action that explained her real-life existence in Italy.

Harold Bloom's *Nathaniel Hawthorne: Modern Critical Views* (Chelsea House) collects in 1986 previously published essays.

iii. Novels

The Scarlet Letter continues to generate far more attention than Hawthorne's other work, three studies of that novel appearing in what is undoubtedly one of the year's most important and controversial collections of literary essays in any field. Edited by Sacvan Bercovitch and Myra Jehlen, who also contributed the volume's key essays, *Ideology and Classic American Literature* (Harvard) establishes a theoretical foundation for the new historicism, bringing it to the forefront of American studies with considerable impact.

Readers may find Myra Jehlen's use of *The Scarlet Letter* in "The Novel and the American Middle Class" (pp. 125–44) less rewarding than her chapter on Hawthorne's novel in her own book (see above), in part because the psychological complexity of the characters gets lost in her reading of the novel as an allegory of art and America. Again, her interests include the differences between the realistic novel, which ends in "painful retreat," and the romance, which ends in transcendence and escape. She interprets *The Scarlet Letter* as an affirmation of the family in Protestant society, and opposes family to the passion and individualism of Hester. She concludes that "it was Hawthorne too who saw most clearly that sex is the wilderness within while American literature is a saga of civilization."

Jonathan Arac's "The Politics of *The Scarlet Letter*" in the same volume (pp. 247–66) is an attempt to raise theoretical issues that he notes have rarely been considered by Americanists. Because Arac believes that authors cannot escape political engagement, his stated intention is to avoid the indeterminacy of Geoffrey Hartman who contends that fiction is protected from specific political statement, its authors without complete authority. Thus Arac sees Hawthorne, steering a middle way between indeterminacy and authorial control, as making a political statement about the 19th-century in his novel of the 17th-century. *The Scarlet Letter* becomes the unfolding allegory of Hawthorne's 1850 situation; Hester's life is an echo of Hawthorne's literary life. Politics boiled down to the issue of slavery and abolitionism, and, even in New England, morality was sacrificed for expediency. Action, while it might be necessary to maintain economic momentum, was also potentially dangerous in that it could easily disrupt the fragile, uneasy peace of a slave society. Therefore, the successful candidate, like Franklin Pierce, had to run on his personality and promise not to take any hasty action. The tension between motion and regulation in shaping 19th-century American politics and law was the fabric from which Hawthorne fashioned not only the campaign biography but *The Scarlet Letter* as well. The possibilities that 19th-century political tensions hold for literary interpretation are especially well argued by Arac. Sometimes the move to interpretation of specific characters in *The Scarlet Letter* proceeds with less ease, and readers may well ask to be more persuasively convinced of some of the more precise points of interpretation—for example, that the "ideological possibility" represented by Dimmesdale is passion.

A third essay in *Ideology and Classic American Literature*, Emory Elliott's "The Problem of Authority in *Pierre*" (pp. 337–51), presents *The Scarlet Letter* as an introduction to Melville, a writer who also tried to work through the problem confronted by the artist in a nation where the predominant ideology was antagonistic to artistic and sexual identity. Hester, the outcast artist, bears some resemblance to the hermit philosophers of an earlier period in American literature; Dimmesdale is the Man of God whose effectiveness depends on sexual self-repression. Sublimation of artistic impulses in the 17th century, which took the form in *The Scarlet Letter* of Dimmesdale's sermons and Hester's embroidery, was a means not available to artists like the narrator of "The Custom-House." Elliott's essay raises other interesting questions outside the scope of his essay: the 19th-century ideology that repressed the sexuality of males was doubly applied to women like the character who dominates Hawthorne's masterwork and like the scribbling women, disparaged by Hawthorne, who may well have found in art, as Hester did, a way to sublimate their sexuality.

Two other books appearing in 1986 contain studies of *The Scarlet Letter*. Richard Forrer's "Nathaniel Hawthorne's *The Scarlet Letter*: Another Hybrid Theodicy" (*Theodocies in Conflict*, pp. 137–61) is a study of the opposing rationalistic and Calvinistic worldviews balanced through the imagination and awakened moral consciousness of the narrator. The validity of Forrer's contention is considerably damaged by his curious omission of "The Custom-House." Russell J. Reising's *The Usable Past: Theory and the Study of American Literature* (Methuen), in making the point that a new vision of minor authors can throw light on major ones, presents *The Scarlet Letter* in a literary context that includes the popular genre of the sentimental historical novel which also pits independent characters against repressive Puritan communities.

James Walter, in "The Letter and the Spirit in Hawthorne's Allegory of American Experience" (*ESQ* 32:36–51), offers an interesting parallel to Myra Jehlen's work on *The Scarlet Letter*. Both use closure as a focal point of discussion but arrive at rather different conclusions. At the same time that Hester's tombstone would seem to represent a grimness borne of finality and certitude, writes Walter, the novel itself leads the reader in another direction, to experience verities discernible with the imagination or the "eye of faith" even though ambiguities remain. This "natural visionary experience" is the promise seen in the light shining on Hester's A, even on the tombstone which becomes a "figure" of the novel. By contrast, the letter of Puritan law reduces complexities to selective, simple typologies. In *The Scarlet Letter* 17th-century literalism in history and 19th-century materialism meet as a contrast to vision, imagination, intuition. "The letter" is again the center of discussion in Pamela Bunting's "Miss A and Mrs. B: The Letter of Pleasure in *The Scarlet Letter* and *As for Me and My House*" (*NDQ* 54,ii:30–40). In comparing the fiction of Sinclair Ross with Hawthorne's, Bunting makes some useful observations about both works. How workable the actual comparsion is is dubious.

Very few studies of Hawthorne in 1986 take a psychological approach. In one of them, "Mother-Daughter Identification in *The Scarlet Letter*" (*Mosaic* 19:101–15), Lois A. Cuddy examines Pearl's bonding with Hester from a perspective of feminism and modern concepts of child development, which, she contends, places in a new light Hawthorne's other portraits of children. In a second psychological study, "*The Scarlet Letter*: Hawthorne, Freud, and the Transcendentalists" (*ATQ* 61:23–36), Daniel Clay argues that *The Scarlet Letter* is Hawthorne's rejection of Concord Transcendentalism, an attempt to "resolve his Oedipal complex" which he associated with Transcendentalism, particularly during his stay at Brook Farm. The three main adult characters act out an Oedipal triangle, Hester as mother, Chillingworth as father, and Dimmesdale as son/lover.

One book-length study of *The Scarlet Letter* was published in 1986. Nina Baym's *The Scarlet Letter: A Reading* (Twayne), though not addressed to scholars, is not only a sound, accessible introduction to one novel for beginning students, but also a valuable introduction to a way of reading literature, with ample explanations of literary conventions.

Three articles on *The Scarlet Letter*—John C. Gerber's "Form and Content in *The Scarlet Letter*" (1944); Frederick Crews's "The Ruined Wall," from *The Sins of the Fathers* (1966); and James M. Cox's "*The Scarlet Letter*: Through the Old Manse and the Custom House" (1975)—are reprinted in *Romanticism: Critical Essays in American Literature* ed. James Barbour and Thomas Quirk (Garland). Seven articles on *The Scarlet Letter*, only one of them new, appeared in Chelsea House's Modern Critical Interpretations series under Hawthorne's title, introduced and edited by Harold Bloom. The new essay, Scott Derrick's "*The Scarlet Letter* and the Masculinity of Art" (pp. 121–27), is a rereading of the novel in light of Hawthorne's biographical sketch of Ann Hutchinson, disclosing his view of women as inferior creatures who needed to stay in their places. There is a vast difference between the strong, intelligent, witty Hutchinson revealed in actual historical records and Hawthorne's account of her and his portrait of the finally acquiescent Hester Prynne who admires her but whose vocation as mother has saved her. Hawthorne's dilemma day in his conviction that writing should be masculine and his suspicion of writing that arose from the female principle.

Other scholarship on *The Scarlet Letter* includes source studies, Salem Custom House findings, and an investigation of a famous 19th-century painting of Hester and Pearl. Frederick Newberry, in "A Red Hot A and a Lustful Divine: Sources for *The Scarlet Letter*" (*NHR* 12,ii:21–22), finds possible prototypes of Dimmesdale and

Hester in Charles Edward Banks's 1885 *History of York, Maine* and Winthrop's *History of New England.* The historical counterparts are the Reverend Stephen Batchiller, defrocked for " 'soliciting the chastity of another man's wife'," and Batchiller's own wife, who in 1651 was branded with an A for her adultery.

Another source study for *The Scarlet Letter* has received coverage on National Public Radio, Laurie N. Rozakis's "Another Possible Source of Hawthorne's Hester Prynne" (*ATQ* 59:63–71). In Boston's King's Chapel Burial Grounds, on a path that Hawthorne undoubtedly frequented in walking from the Custom House to the Athenaeum, Rozakis found the grave of Elizabeth Payne, whose tomb is marked by a large "A," along with a very old plaque identifying the woman buried there as the model for Hester Prynne. Payne is described in court records as having been tried and acquitted for the murder of her child. Today the case is complicated by the misuse and now archaic use by archivists and historians of the words "spinster," "illegitimate," and "fornication," as well as by the presence of the "A" on Payne's tomb, for the letter there seems to have had nothing to do with adultery. Thomas Pribek's "Hawthorne's Blackstone" (*AN&Q* 24,ix–x:142–44), a third source study, enlarges on Hawthorne's reference in *The Scarlet Letter* to "the Reverend Mr. Blackstone . . . who rides through our early annals, seated on the back of a bull." The early source, Pribek has found, is Francis Baylies's *An Historical Memoir of the Colony of New Plymouth,* which describes Blackstone as having planted the first orchard in New England and tamed a bull on which he occasionally rode. Pribek contends that the reference reinforces Pearl's childlike association with nature.

The first of two notes on the Salem Custom House is Hugh J. Dawson's "*The Scarlet Letter*'s Angry Eagle and the Salem Custom House" (*Essex Institute Historical Collections* 122:30–34). By examining the eagle first carved by Joseph True in 1826, Dawson sees Hawthorne as having deliberately or through faulty memory misrepresented the eagle as it appeared on the Custom House roof and as having overlooked True's meaningful departures from the usual representation of the national emblem. A second note, Edwin Haviland Miller's "Hawthorne at the Salem Custom House" (*NHR* 12,i:15–16), is an account of a prose portrait of Hawthorne from a memoir called "Jottings from Memory from 1823 to 1901" by Henry B. Hill, who found Hawthorne to be a "hard-looking customer" when he worked in the Salem Custom House. "No man displayed more meanness of character than Hawthorne did in his criticisms" of the old employees who, Hill claimed, "served the Custom House honestly and conscientiously."

The subject of another article by Hugh J. Dawson is the 19th-century painting of Hester and Pearl. In "Huges Merle's *Hester et Perle* and Nathaniel Hawthorne's *The Scarlet Letter*" (*The Journal of the Walters Art Gallery* 44:123–27), Dawson investigates how Hawthorne could have been reported as admiring the painting when it seems unlikely to have made its way to the United States until after Hawthorne's death. The answer lies in Dawson's discovery of photographs taken of the original and undoubtedly shown to Hawthorne.

Fanshawe receives attention in a note and in the abstract of a paper. In "A Harleian Miscellany: *Fanshawe*," (*NHR* 12,ii:19), Carol Bensick argues that the narrator endorses the ideas of the disinherited angler who influences Fanshawe in his refusal of Ellen. Hawthorne's suppressed selves are represented by his characters in *Fanshawe*, according to Barbara Snow Hartman, whose "*Fanshawe* and Hawthorne's Strategy to 'Open an Intercourse with the World' " is abstracted in *NHR* (12,ii:19). Hawthorne was able to draw upon these selves for *The Scarlet Letter*, creating from the failed first novel, the successful later fiction.

Apart from brief comments in general studies, *The House of the Seven Gables* was not the subject of discussion in 1986. A number of articles were written on *The Blithedale Romance*, however. Not surprisingly, in three of these the writers seek to unravel the mysterious narration of Miles Coverdale. Beverly Hume, in "Restructuring the Case Against Hawthorne's Coverdale" (*NCF* 40: 387–99), contends that key narrative contradictions reveal Coverdale to be, if not the literal murderer of Zenobia, as John Harmon McElroy and Edward L. McDonald propose, at least murderous in intent. Coverdale's madness, which closely corresponds to 19th-century studies of insanity, can be traced in his obsession, his use of his friends, and his identification with Fourier. Also interested in the effect of Coverdale's madness on his narration, Thomas F. Strychacz in "Coverdale and Women: Feverish Fantasies in *The Blithedale Romance*" (*ATQ* 62:29–46) takes issue with Nina Baym's thesis that Hawthorne shares his age's condescension toward women. Rather, Strychacz contends, Coverdale is an ironic narrator through whom

Hawthorne criticizes the view of women at the time. George Monteiro's "Hawthorne's Summer Romance" (*DQR* 16:97–108) goes against two decades of scholarship which would seem to have thoroughly discredited his contention that Coverdale is the voice of Hawthorne: "there is no profit, and little point, in casting him as a character." A fourth article on the novel, Byron L. Stay's "Hawthorne's Fallen Puritans: Eliot's Pulpit in the *Blithedale Romance*" (*SNNTS* 18:283–90), centers on the scenes set against Eliot's Pulpit to show that the Blithedalers, who shared with the Puritans their Utopian fervor, have retained the rigidity of their forebears but lost their spirit and their grasp of morality. Finally, Hubert Zapf's "The Poetological Theme in Hawthorne's *The Blithedale Romance*" (*ATQ* 6:73–80) proposes that in the romance both plot and metaplot are inquiries into the relationship between fiction and reality. The interplay between the plot, external reality, and the metaplot, comprising Coverdale's filtered and unreliable view of reality, leads the reader not to an absolute truth but to a shifting one, a "continual process of interpretation and self-interpretation." Only an abstract of Patricia Marks's paper, "Hawthorne and the Aesthetic Fallacy: The Transformation of Hilda" (*NHR* 12,ii:21), deals with *The Marble Faun*. *The Marble Faun*'s unwieldiness results from its mix of fictional genres, particularly the gothic novel and bildungsroman. What Marks calls the "aesthetic fallacy," the myth of womanhood in the 19th century, leads Hawthorne to idolize the static, noncreative Hilda and reprove the creative, independent Miriam.

Two studies of *Septimius Felton* explore the relationship between Hawthorne's concept of immortality and his artistic decline. James D. Wallace, in "Immortality in Hawthorne's *Septimius Felton*" (*SAF* 14,i:19–33), contends that the novel is more like a metaphysical exploration than a 19th-century novel because it is an inquiry into the tension between two ideas of immortality, posterity on the one hand and literal physical immortality on the other. Like the failed artist Septimius, Hawthorne wanted immortality and strived to reach it in this last novel where, ironically, the hero is not Septimius but Hagburn, who finds immortality in the world as husband and soldier. So, in effect, the novel "damned the very detachment, isolation and emotional distance that had created it; the novel imploded on its author." Terence Martin develops a similar thesis in "Septimius Felton and Septimius Norton: Matters of History and Immortality" (*NHR* 12,i:1–4) by tracing the evolution of Hawthorne's many drafts of the novel. Hawthorne's theme is brought "to a point of existential frustration" as Septimius is reduced to an incomplete weakling hiding from history, while his foil is the war hero implicated in history. Thus Hawthorne is shown sustaining his conviction in the necessity of remaining engaged in history at the same time that he reveals an abiding fascination with escaping it.

iv. Short Works

Hawthorne's tales received attention both in scholarly journals and on the modern stage, where his work has often been dramatized. A montage of his tales, written for the Williamston (Massachusetts) Theatre Festival by Lou Berger and Kenneth Cavander, was presented as *Hawthorne Country*. The authors, using as a base "The Minister's Black Veil," try to capture some of Hawthorne's simpler themes by placing many of his characters in the same community at the same time. Thus, a young Reverend Hooper is introduced to town by a cynical Goodman Brown and later unites Georgiana and Aylmer (changed to Walter) in matrimony. This melding of plots and characters who speak in modern dialogue is initially off-putting, but the actual production was given a very positive review by Lea Newman in *NHR* (2,ii:14–15).

As always, the most frequently written-about tales are "Young Goodman Brown" and "Rappaccini's Daughter." One section on Hawthorne's work in general, but using "Young Goodman Brown" as its prime illustration, is Taylor Stoehr's "Hawthorne's Faith in Words" (*Words and Deeds*, pp. 23–41). Stoehr sees Hawthorne, the first author he examines, as unsure of the truths taught by experience and the imagination. In "Young Goodman Brown" the problem of discovering reality is presented through the use of dream, where the imaginary and the real merge. The destructive force of Brown's life derives from his having lived it as if the spiritual truth he experienced was a natural truth.

In addition to the section in Stoehr's book, three notes were published on the tale. Patricia W. Shaw, in "Checking Out Faith and Lust: Hawthorne's 'Young Goodman Brown' and Updike's 'A and P'" (*SSF* 86:321–23), argues, as the title suggests, that Goodman Brown is a source for one of John Updike's characters because of the tale's New England setting, the main character's naïveté in dealing with sexually and intellectually sophisticated females, the emblematic use of the color pink, and the theme of sexual guilt. Michael Tritt's "'Young Goodman Brown' and the Psychology of Projection" (*SSF* 86:113–17), using Freud and textbook psychology, explores Brown's projection of his own unacknowledged, unconscious guilt onto others in the community. Bill Christophersen's "'Young Goodman Brown' as Historical Allegory: A Lexical Link" (*SSF* 86:202–04) persuasively establishes further connections between Hawthorne's story and Puritanism with repeated use of the word "errand," an echo of Danforth's "Errand into the Wilderness." Christophersen uses as his support Hawthorne's fondness for the idea of the covenant and city upon a hill during the devil's baptism, his references to Moses, so central to Puritan typology, and his inversions of other images in Exodus.

Helmbrecht Breinig's "Crushed Butterflies and Broken Fountains: Hawthorne between Christian Idealism, Romanticism, and Modernism" (*Theorie und Praxis*, pp. 233–48) takes up two of Hawthorne's tales. Breinig submits that "The Artist of the Beautiful" and "Rappaccini's Daughter" demonstrate a very modern distrust of language and reality and show Hawthorne even leaning in the direction of textual autonomy, though his moral and religious beliefs prevented him from allowing himself to assume that he could lose control. Three articles on "Rappaccini's Daughter" take up the matter of how allusions can unravel this complex tale. Mary Cappello, in "'Rappaccini's Daughter' as Translation" (*PQ* 65:263–76), contends that Hawthorne's translation of events, relationships, and signifiances results in a tale about how characters, especially Giovanni, translate the world in light of past experience and present fears and desires, thus challenging the reader's powers of translation as well. As Giovanni translates what he sees simplistically in light of his past experience, so does the reader who uses only those allusions which are most familiar. Cappello concludes that to read the tale using only one allusion as its key is to fall into the trap which the story warns us against. One might suspect from David L. Cowles's title, "A Profane Tragedy: Dante in Hawthorne's 'Rappaccini's Daughter'" (*ATQ* 60:5–24), that he is in danger of committing Cappello's error of allusive translation. His point is to show biographical evidence for Hawthorne's familiarity with Dante, to whom the American author went for his characters and their situations, including Giovanni's damning lack of faith in Beatrice. Robert Schwartz, in "'Rappaccini's Daughter' and 'Sir Hugh, or, The Jew's Daughter'" (*WF* 45:

21–33), suggests that folklore study can assist the reader of the tale when the limitations of allegory and psychology have been reached. He illustrates his point by using the ballad, "Sir Hugh, or, The Jew's Daughter," which parallels Hawthorne's tale in a number of ways: both have a walled garden, lush vegetation including a particularly striking flower, and a passive seductress. Parallel study of the ballad adds a racial dimension to the story and confirms Hawthorne's fascination with forbidden unions.

"The Minister's Black Veil" is the subject of a note by William V. Davis, "Hawthorne's 'The Minister's Black Veil': A Note on the Significance of the Subtitle" (*SSF* 23:453–54). In what is more a statement of belief than a persuasive argument, Davis takes issue with the view that Hooper is a villain. Rather he has sacrificed himself in order to symbolize the darkness in human nature.

Two of Hawthorne's more frequently anthologized tales are the subjects of an article and a note. Stephen Youra, in " 'The Fatal Hand': A Sign of Confusion in Hawthorne's 'The Birth Mark' " (*ATQ* 60: 43–51), contends that the fatal hand belongs not to Georgiana but to Alymer, whose hand fashions the mark he learns to destroy, and the ultimate shaping hand of the author. The fatal disease suffered by Aylmer, the narrator, the author, and readers is overreading and, thus, remaining closed to possibilities of meaning. James McIntosh's "Nature and Frontier in 'Roger Malvin's Burial' " (*NHR* 12,ii:20) draws attention to the mixed language used to describe the frontier and to Reuben Bourne's mixed reactions to the frontier, both of which reflect the inability of the characters to know the wilderness or what their relationship to it should be.

A number of articles and notes were written about tales that are less frequently studied, two on "Sights From a Steeple." Dana Brand's "The Panoramic Spectator in America: A Re-reading of Some of Hawthorne's Sketches" (*ATQ* 62:5–16) also includes "The Old Apple Dealer" and "Main Street." In these three sketches the author comments on the unreliability of the narrator he presents, parodying the spectator-narrator of popular European fiction who is capable of seeing to the heart of characters whom he observes from an isolated post. Such work reveals the uncertainty that Hawthorne felt about his identity as an artist and about the capacity of his audience to comprehend realistic portraits of America. Brand's conclusion is that the complexity and irony of Hawthorne's "minor works" should not be disregarded. On a similar note, Jeffrey H. Richards, in " 'Sights

From a Steeple" (*ATQ* 62:35–41), contends that the narrator of the sketch, rather than being a sensitive observer, is one whose obvious histrionics show him to be a parody and whose effect is to distance the reader from the story and storyteller. In "'Alice Doane's Appeal': A Literary Double of Hoffman's *Die Elixiere des Teufels*" (*CL* 23:1–11), Allienne R. Becker makes a claim for Hawthorne's indebtedness to Hoffman on the basis of his similar use of a multiple fragmented perspective, a mixed narrative voice, doubling, use of the grotesque, incest, and similar actual relationships, events, and names. A number of interesting notes and abstracts of papers on some aspect of less frequently studied sketches and tales appeared in *NHR*: Alfred H. Marks, "Hawthorne's Rill Occupation" (12,i:20); Alfred Weber, "Hawthorne, the Tourist, and His 1832 Journey Through New England and Upstate New York" (12,ii:19–20); Beth L. Lueck, "Hawthorne's 'Sketches from Memory' and the Picturesque Tour" (12,ii:20); Dennis Berthold, "Hawthorne at Fort Ticonderoga: Pictorializing the American Past" (12,ii:20); and William Randel, "Hawthorne and Sir William Pepperrell" (12,ii:19).

v. Biographical Materials

Edwin Haviland Miller's "A Calendar of the Letters of Sophia Peabody Hawthorne" (*SAR*, 1986:199–281) is a revealing portrait of a woman who developed intense crushes on several male and female friends at a time when her literary husband may have been extremely difficult to live with.

NHR also carried several biographical notes and articles whose titles describe them: James O'Donald Mays, "Hawthorne and the Roebuck Hotel" (12,i:15); Melinda Ponder, "Hawthorne and Raymond, Maine" (12,ii:4–9); Daniel Shealy, "'Poor Jimmy's Knock': A Letter on the Death of James T. Fields" (12,i:15–17); and Sister M. Joseph, "Rose of All the Hawthornes" (12,i:12–13). The last is followed by a reprint of a 1922 *New York Times Book Review and Magazine* article, Rose Hawthorne Lathrop's "On Founding a Home for Destitute Victims of Cancer" (12,i:13–15). Finally, William Jenkins's "Nathaniel Hawthorne, Politician" (*CimR* 74:37–43) is a cursory review of Hawthorne's political activity.

University of Alabama

3. Poe

Kent P. Ljungquist

After several years in which interest in Poe had undergone a modest decline, we confronted in 1986 what one scholar has called a Poe "boom." More studies appeared than in any year since 1975, and over a half-dozen books on Poe are promised for 1987. Contributions in 1986 show, however, that increased volume does not necessarily carry comparable substance, nor does it serve to mediate or focus debate. The battle between the "scholars" and the "critics," redefined in the past decade as a conflict between historicists and theorists, continued unabated. Poe specialists of long standing, well acquainted with his biography, the letters, and an attendant body of secondary material, continue to complain about overly speculative theoretical readings. On the other hand, some theorists, unconcerned about the claims of traditional scholarship, decry even the notion that new work on Poe must build on previous evidence. Representing the latter perspective, Douglas Robinson, in a review-essay on four theoretical studies ("Dogmatizing Discourse," *PoeS* 19:35–43), reserves special praise for a book that says almost nothing about Poe as a writer of his own time. Robinson eschews an historical approach because it smacks of "the old, boring, predeconstructive approaches to literature." If this indifference toward Poe as a figure in his social milieu grows, Poe scholarship will probably lose even the uncertain focus and definition it currently has.

i. Hardcore Scholarship: Texts, Bibliography, Biography

The third and fourth volumes in Burton R. Pollin's edition of the *Collected Writings of Edgar Allan Poe* (Gordian), containing contributions to *The Broadway Journal*, follow a unique format. The first of the two volumes presents the text of Poe's "nonfictional prose," and the second Pollin's informative annotations and explanatory material. Although the entire *Broadway Journal* is available in reprint as well as on microfilm, Pollin presents the text in "a composite facsimile edition," that is, with Poe's original items and those Pollin ascribes to him as they appeared in the weekly's pages. Poe's markings in Sarah Helen Whitman's copy constitute much of the evidence used to establish his contributions. Pollin uses internal evidence as well as ancillary knowledge of Poe to make other attributions. Since no comprehensive table of additions to the Poe canon is provided, the scholar will want to use these volumes with some caution. Whatever the quality of educated guesswork, the ascription of brief filler items, often in the absence of Poe's markings, is a chancy process. Scholars will want to gauge the cogency of Pollin's arguments in this regard against William Doyle Hull's unpublished dissertation, "A Canon of the Critical Works of Edgar Allan Poe" (Virginia, 1941).

In reviews of previous volumes in Pollin's edition (*ALS 1983*, pp. 50–51, and *ALS 1985*, pp. 43–44), I have called attention to typographical errors and other problems in documentation, results either of haphazard proofreading or of imperfect synthesis of the textual apparatus. A few problems of this kind recur in *The Broadway Journal* volumes, as evidenced by inconsistent dates for poems by Thomas Hood and James Aldrich (IV, p. 28 and p. 44) and an incorrect reference to Cooper scholar Thomas R. Lounsbury (not F. R. Lounsberry, IV, p. 256). Such small errors are less serious than those in Pollin's discussion of the Longfellow plagiarism controversy, where zeal to prove a thesis leads to several mistakes. Pollin is convinced that the letter of "Outis," the pseudonymous defender of Longfellow, is totally manufactured. Contrary to Pollin's claims, the poem, which Outis attributes to Whittier, is authentic, appearing in the *Yankee and Boston Literary Gazette* (1829). Furthermore, John Neal, as Outis notes, did accuse N. P. Willis and R. H. Dana of plagiarism (also in the *Yankee*). The Dana cited is Richard Henry Dana, Sr., not the author of *Two Years Before the Mast* as Pollin suggests (IV, p. 31).

J. Albert Robbins makes a contribution to primary bibliography by presenting "A New Manuscript of Poe's 'For Annie'" (*SB*, pp. 261–65). Located in the Lilly Library Poe collection, this second complete manuscript version adds an eighth variant text to those previously known. Robbins helpfully provides a full textual collation, and notes that all versions retain the original sequence, with the exception of the newly found text in which two stanzas are reversed.

Three 1986 publications offer information of biographical significance. A pamphlet from the Baltimore Poe Society prepared by

Alexander G. Rose III and Jeffrey A. Savoye, *Such Friends as These: Edgar Allan Poe's List of Subscribers to His Dream Magazine*, lists potential subscribers and contributors to Poe's projected periodicals. This compilation, drawn from a memorandum book in the Enoch Pratt Library, is accompanied by a series of Maria Clemm's riddles. Elena Zimmerman's "Tragic Ingenue: Memories of Elizabeth Arnold Poe," in *No Fairer Land* (pp. 124–43), details the diversity of roles and frequency of appearance of Poe's actress mother. David Poe's theatrical deficiencies also receive comment. The Poe chapter in Frank Shivers, Jr.'s *Maryland Wits and Baltimore Bards* (Maclay, pp. 71–98) presents little new material on the Baltimore years, though it reprints primary documents not readily available elsewhere.

With the publication of I. M. Walker's long-awaited *Edgar Allan Poe: The Critical Heritage* (Routledge), scholars have ready access to a representative sampling of reviews and critiques published before 1850. While the reprinted reviews and notices were previously recorded in Burton R. Pollin's "Poe 'Viewed and Reviewed': An Annotated Checklist of Contemporaneous Notices" (see *ALS 1980*, pp. 43–44), a cursory comparison indicates that Walker's and Pollin's dates and attributions vary in several cases. In addition to an authoritative introduction that charts Poe's difficulties in an antagonistic literary marketplace, Walker includes such items as letters, publicity devices, and obituaries. The appearance of Walker's volume offers the opportunity to point out that no new contemporaneous reviews have been discovered since Pollin's 1980 checklist.

The annual bibliography of secondary criticism regularly appearing in *Poe Studies* has been expanded into "International Poe Bibliography" (*PoeS* 19:11–23) under the direction of Richard Kopley. In addition to studies appearing in American publications, scholars now have a convenient record of items from several foreign countries.

ii. Sources and Influences

With the implacable persistence of a refrain, scholars return to the possible sources of "The Raven." Arnd Bohm, in "A German Source for Edgar Allan Poe's 'The Raven'" (*CLS* 23:310–23), notes thematic parallels in Ludwig Tieck's "Phantasus," which presents a world-weary narrator visited by dreams of an absent love. Bohm's argument is ultimately unconvincing, since he fails to demonstrate why we should take this source more seriously than others previously advanced. Offering more substance despite its brevity, Gerald E. Gerber's note on "Epes Sargent and 'The Raven'" (*PoeS* 19:24) finds suggestive conjunctions of setting, situation, and language in Sargent's "When the Night Wind Bewaileth," a poem published separately in 1843 and in a volume that Poe consulted. George Monteiro's "The Poem as Felony" (*AntR* 44:209–19) touches only briefly on the genesis of "The Raven," but I recommend his essay as an ingenious, entertaining reminiscence of professional and pedagogical adventures with Poe.

Of the other studies that touch on sources, K. E. Bachinger's "How Sherwood Forest Became the Valley of Many-Colored Grass: Peacock's *Maid Marian* as Source for Poe's 'Eleonora'" (*AN&Q* 24:72–75) has a lengthy and self-explanatory title. Jules Zanger's "Poe's 'Berenice': Philosophical Fantasy and Its Pitfalls," in *The Scope of the Fantastic* (pp. 135–42), addresses indebtedness to Platonic doctrines.

If Poe's sources received scant attention in 1986, it was a banner year for analyses of his influence, largely because of an informative, varied collection of essays on *Poe and Our Times*. Before turning to the contents of that volume, I should note two miscellaneous studies relevant to Poe's influence. Burton R. Pollin, in "Stoddard's Elegiac Sonnet on Poe" (*PoeS* 19:32–34), shows that R. H. Stoddard's vilification of Poe temporarily abated with an anonymously published sonnet in the *Southern Literary Messenger* (1850). In "Poe's Endless Voyage: *The Narrative of Arthur Gordon Pym*" (*PLL* 22:276–83), Jules Zanger explains the less than satisfactory uses of Poe's sea narrative by Jules Verne, Charles Dake, and H. P. Lovecraft.

The misuse or abuse of Poe raises the inevitable subject of his reception in France, the subject of the opening essays in *Poe and Our Times*. Roger Forclaz's essay (pp. 9–17), as translated by James Kelly Morris, makes a general statement about the evolution of Poe's French image since the time of Baudelaire. Of all the French artists and intellectuals interested in Poe, Paul Valéry may have been the most insightful and knowledgable, as Lois Vines convincingly argues in her companion essay (pp. 1–8). Drawing material from Valéry's voluminous notebooks, she demonstrates his penetrating comprehension of the significance of *Eureka* as well as of the unique French adaptations of Poe's poetics. (See *ALS 1977*, p. 36, for mention of Vines's previous work on Poe and Valéry.)

For students of Poe's impact on American poetry, Laura Jehn Menides's contribution to *Poe and Our Times* (pp. 78–89) would provide a convenient point of entry. Her thesis that Eliot and Williams both reflected personal obsessions and concerns in their comments on Poe finds confirmation in Jorge Luis Borges's dictum that each writer "creates his own precursors." Maurice Bennett uses this cryptic statement as a point of departure in his superb comparison of "William Wilson" and Borges's "Deutsches Requieum" (pp. 107–23). Bringing a philosophic perspective to bear without sacrificing Poe's uniqueness as a writer of his own time, Bennett monitors Borges's brilliant transformation of narrative into metaphysics. (See the discussion of John Irwin's essay in section iii.b, below.)

The tension between Poe's popular image and his more serious impact occupies several contributors to *Poe and Our Times.* In a witty survey of plays based on Poe's life (pp. 18–31), John E. Reilly points out that Poe has been the subject of more dramatizations than any other American historical figure, with the exception of Washington or Lincoln (and possibly Pocahontas!). Although Sophie Treadwell's *Plumes in the Dust* (1936) approaches a successful melding of drama and biography, Reilly concurs with N. Bryllion Fagin that Poe's toilings in the magazine marketplace do not immediately offer promising materials for vital drama. Volume editor Benjamin Franklin Fisher IV, using the popular Stephen King as a convenient foil, shows how mystery writer John Dickson Carr artfully adapts motifs from Poe's "The Masque of the Red Death" (pp. 99–106). Fans of King may want to compare Fisher's somewhat judgmental conclusions with those of Kenneth Gibbs, who argues, in an essay not in the Fisher collection, that Melville may have influenced *The Shining* more significantly than Poe ("Stephen King and the Tradition of American Gothic," *Gothic* n.s. 1:6–14). Previous students of Poe and our times have noted the paradox that the conservative southerner asserted significant influence on several modern Afro-American authors, notably Ralph Ellison and Richard Wright (*ALS 1975*, pp. 57, 73). Craig Werner, in a full-scale treatment of this subject (pp. 144–56), shows how Ishmael Reed's parodies of Poe subvert dominant social hierarchies. Reed's parodic adaptation of Poe-esque images (asylum, plague, and tomb) may deny the reader certainty, but his freewheeling use of popular material contributes to a kinetic process that prevents social and personal stagnation. In view of William Styron's allusions to "The Pit and the Pendulum" in the best-selling *Sophie's Choice*, it is hardly surprising that Poe would also figure in an earlier Styron novel, *Set This House on Fire*. Linda E. McDaniel finds substantial Poe-esque material in that work to show how Styron develops his main character Mason Flagg into a "Roderick Usher in Our Time" (pp. 137–43).

The remaining essays in Fisher's collection deal with authors not often associated with Poe. Eleanor Dwight records Edith Wharton's mixed comments on Poe's importance, then focuses on one of her supernatural stories, "The Duchess at Prayer" (pp. 49–57). Carol Marshall Peirce contributes a detailed study of affinities between Poe and Tolkien, and attributes most of them to a common "archetypal heritage" (pp. 49–57). Finally, my essay amplifies a suggestion first advanced by James W. Tuttleton that F. Scott Fitzgerald's terrifyingly beautiful heroines owe much to Poe's characterizations (pp. 90–98). From Anne Edwards's *Child of Night* (1975) to Fitzgerald's *Tender Is the Night*, Poe's image is recast in trivial and imposing contexts in the pages of *Poe and Our Times*.

iii. Poe's Works

***a.* Poetry.** The title of Glen Allan Omans's monograph, *Passion in Poe* (Balt. Poe Soc.), may lead some readers to infer that it deals with Poe's amorous adventures. Rather Omans shows, through a painstaking survey of Poe's seven statements highlighting this critical term, that a ban on passion gradually became a staple of his poetic theory. Omans's systematic overview of aesthetic philosophy in America, Britain, and Germany challenges Robert D. Jacobs's alliance of Poe with a Common Sense tradition, as outlined in *Poe: Journalist and Critic* (1969). As Omans brings wide learning to bear on a complicated subject, he reserves his most telling comments for the possible influence of Schiller's *Aesthetic Letters*.

No less learned, the late Helen Ensley's "Metrical Ambiguity in the Poetry of Edgar Allan Poe" (*No Fairer Land*, pp. 144–58) builds on her previous study of Poe's rhymes (*ALS 1981*, p. 50). She argues that "Spirits of the Dead" and "The Valley of Unrest," in particular, are metrically more complex and more varied than tours de force like "The Raven" and "The Bells." Since these less notorious poems are more characteristic of Poe's prosodic techniques, Ensley rightly concludes that Poe's "rythmical bells did not always ring with a clamor and a clang."

***b.* Tales of Ratiocination.** After a spate of studies that have exalted the importance of the detective stories (*ALS 1984*, pp. 60–62), one of the most impressive analyses of 1986 brings to the subject a welcome sense of proportion. In " 'That Metaphysical Art': Mystery and Detection in Poe's Tales" (*Poe and Our Times*, pp. 32–48), Bruce I. Weiner begins by presenting a possible source in *Blackwood's* for "The Man of the Crowd." (See the discussion of "The Man of the Crowd" in section iii.d, below.) He then contrasts Poe's unsolved mysteries, dramatizing an indeterminate struggle for transcendent vision, with the more modest aims of the Dupin stories, which displace the struggle for transcendence with an "air of success." In Weiner's view, Dupin masters lesser mysteries than those presented in the horror tales. After a brief detour in which he questions the ahistorical nature of semiotic approaches, Weiner provides an interesting reading of Poe's comments on Dickens's *Barnaby Rudge*.

If Weiner downplays the importance of French theoretical approaches, John T. Irwin gives added momentum to what promises to be a continuing seminar on "The Purloined Letter." (See *ALS 1977*, pp. 42–43, and *ALS 1979*, p. 44.) His lengthy "Mysteries We Reread, Mysteries of Reading: Poe, Borges, and the Analytic Detective Story" (*MLN* 101:1168–1215) joins the Lacan-Derrida-Johnson debate in examining Poe's tale as a "parable of the act of analysis." Following this intellectual game of one-upmanship among theorists does not make for easy reading—Irwin acknowledges his own "intellectual vertigo" attending a series of self-conscious interpretations. Nevertheless, his scrutiny of the tale's numerical-geometrical structure leads him to an investigation of Borges's literary reading of Poe in "Death and the Compass." The appearance of a translation of that story several years before Lacan's discussion of "The Purloined Letter," Irwin intriguingly speculates, suggests that Borges may be the éminence grise who initiated the entire controversy. (See the discussion of Maurice J. Bennett's essay in section ii, above.)

William Goldhurst approaches self-reflexivity without even a hint of abstruseness in "Self-Reflective Fiction by Poe: Three Tales" (*MLS* 16:4–14), an essay that deals neatly with "The Gold Bug." His discussion of Legrand's disposition and the symbolic scarabaeus lead him to conclude that Poe's tale is an allegory of death and rebirth. Self-referential elements in other neglected tales, Goldhurst adds, help to establish a kinship between the reader's perspective and the distorted vision of Poe's protagonists. In a related study dealing with characterization in "The Gold Bug" ("'His Right of Attendance': The Image of the Black Man in the Works of Poe and Two of His Contemporaries," *No Fairer Land*, pp. 172–84), Elizabeth C. Phillips makes the unexceptionable point that Jupiter conforms to 19th-century racial stereotypes.

Two discussions of Dupin's role in the detective fiction could not be more strikingly at odds. "Poe's Auguste Dupin" by J. Lasley Dameron (*No Fairer Land*, pp. 159–71), a revision of a previously published essay (*ALS 1983*, p. 55), glorifies the heroic qualities of Poe's detective. Judith Fetterley draws on teaching Poe from a feminist perspective to claim that Dupin collaborates in a "masculinist reading" of violent acts against women ("Reading About Reading: 'A Jury of Her Peers,' 'The Murders in the Rue Morgue,' and 'The Yellow Wallpaper'" (*Gender and Reading*, pp. 147–64). Her commentary on reader response and on gender fails to acknowledge either Dennis Eddings's essay on "Poe, Dupin, and the Reader" (*ALS 1984*, pp. 60–61) or J. A. Leo Lemay's psychosexual reading of "The Murders in the Rue Morgue" (*ALS 1982*, p. 51).

***c.* "Ligeia," "The Assignation," "Usher."** In his collaboration with George Woodberry on the 1895 edition of Poe's works, E. C. Stedman made the following statement: "nor is there any such trilogy, in our own literature, of prose romances taking wings of poetry at their will as 'Ligeia,' 'The Assignation,' and 'The Fall of the House of Usher.'" Attention directed at the first and third titles will come as no surprise; scholarship on the second has been sparse, but three studies in 1986 aimed to alleviate this neglect.

Often grouped with the satires in the abortive *Tales of the Folio Club*, "The Assignation" has been regarded either as a hoax or as a lampoon of the tale of passion. Each of the year's three commentaries, however, investigates the tale's more serious themes. In "The Sexual Abyss: Consummation in 'The Assignation'" (*PoeS* 19:7–10), David Ketterer begins by noting the role of Poe's scenic decor. He then examines sexual punning and other comic bawdry that seem to undermine his general thesis that the tale points to an "arabesque" reality beyond death. In "The Flights of a Good Man's Mind: Gothic Fantasy in 'The Assignation'" (*MLS* 16:27–34), Benjamin Franklin Fisher IV also notes sexual overtones, but attributes them to the lubricious propensities of the muddleheaded narrator. A "good man" of decidedly limited imagination, Poe's storyteller fails to comprehend the parable of thwarted artistic creativity enacted by the Countess and the stranger. Fisher's discussion is well attuned to the multiple, subtle functions of Poe's allusiveness, the subject of Edward W. R. Pitcher's " 'To Die Laughing': Poe's Allusion to Sir Thomas More in 'The Assignation' " (*SSF* 23:197–200). The puns on More (and on Tom Moore, as Fisher notes), purported evidence of Poe's satirical purpose, actually underscore the theme of equanimity in the face of death. Pitcher, extending a previous study of "The Assignation" (*ALS 1980*, pp. 49–50), draws evidence from 18th- and 19th-century jest books to prove his point.

The degree to which we can explain what happens in "Usher" became the subject of several commentaries. Beverly Voloshin's "Explanation in 'The Fall of the House of Usher' " (*SSF* 23:419–28) begins promisingly by noting how Lockean epistemology offered a stable relationship between words and things, a conformity between the order of mind and the order of nature. Gothic fictions like "Usher," however, challenged this view with their subtle, ambiguous shadings among natural, supernatural, and psychological phenomena. Voloshin's Lockean framework becomes obscured as her essay progresses, and she fails to cite both Robert Jacobs on Poe's alliance with a Common Sense tradition (section iii.a, above) and Barton Levi St. Armand's essay on Poe and association theory in "Usher" (*ALS 1977*, p. 42). Much of what happens in "Usher" is explicable via medical theories of Poe's time, according to George R. Uba in "Malady and Motive: Medical History and 'The Fall of the House of Usher' " (*SAQ* 85:10–22). Despite his failure to acknowledge Elizabeth Phillips's previous research on the same subject (*ALS 1979*, pp. 36–37), Uba's well-argued study of contemporaneous theories of hypochondriasis, hysteria, and melancholia provides a circumstantial basis for the imaginative substance of the tale. Less consequential is Lynne P. Shackleford's note on the role of the incubus in "Usher" (*Expl* 45:18–19), which posits the influence of Henry Fuseli's painting "The Nightmare." A study that applies a 20th-century mode of explanation, Craig Howes's " 'The Fall of the House of Usher' and Elegiac Romance" (*SLJ* 19:68–78) uses the generic definition of modern romance developed by Kenneth Bruffee to account for the close relationship between the narrator and Usher.

The single study devoted exclusively to "Ligeia," Joseph Andriano's "Archetypal Projection in 'Ligeia': A Post-Jungian Reading" (*PoeS* 19:27–31), displays wide knowledge of Poe scholarship and of relevant psychocriticism. Attending to the ambiguities surrounding the title character's name, Andriano suggests that the range of signifiers associated with Ligeia find reconciliation in one sign: the anima (the feminine unconscious soul of man). Andriano's discussion of the ways in which consciousness conforms to linguistic structures merits comparison with Taylor Stoehr's "Unspeakable Horror in Poe" (*Words and Deeds*, pp. 43–58), a reprint of a previously published essay (*ALS 1979*, pp. 35, 40–41) that deals with "Ligeia."

d. General Studies, "Minor" Tales, Miscellaneous Topics. Making the recent deprecations of Poe by Harold Bloom (*ALS 1985*, p. 50) look tame, Michael Wood's discussion of "Poe's Tales: The Art of the Impossible" (*The Nineteenth-Century American Short Story*, pp. 13–39) begins by claiming that most of his poetry is terrible and that his themes are neither deep nor academically serious. With his threshold of objectivity thus established, Wood debunks Poe's ideas on transcendence, perversity, and the "legibility" of the world. After this series of undocumented assertions, Wood concludes that Poe's shallowness accounts for his impact.

Criticism that sampled Poe's satires turned up more appreciative readings than those provided by Wood. In "Poe's 'The Man That Was Used Up': Another Bugaboo Campaign" (*SSF* 23:281–86), Joan Tyler Mead, after explaining several literary allusions and buried references to Poe's own writings, builds a case that the narrator is the tale's principal figure of deception. Another of Poe's self-dramatizing, self-aggrandizing storytellers, the narrator, according to Mead, conducts his own "bugaboo" campaign. Also exploring self-referential elements, Stuart and Susan Levine, in "'How-to' Satire: Cervantes, Marryatt, Poe" (*MLS* 16:15–26), suggest that "How to Write a Blackwood Article" looks back to the prologue of *Don Quixote* as well as forward to metafictional experiments by Borges and Beckett. In "Poe and the Perfectibility of Man" (*PoeS* 19:1–6), Richard Fusco takes the list of philosophers satirized in "Lionizing" as his point of departure. He then surveys 18th- and 19th-century attitudes toward perfectionism to provide a context for Poe's skepticism on the subject. This well-researched essay finally compares Poe's attitudes with those of George Tucker, author of a discourse on perfectibilian reform published one month before "Lionizing" appeared.

Poe's response to a more specific 19th-century reform movement—the campaign for temperance—is the subject of T. J. Matheson's

"Poe's 'The Black Cat' as a Critique of Temperance Literature" (*Mosaic* 19:69–81). By the time of the tale's publication a more lenient attitude toward alcoholism had captured the popular mind via T. S. Arthur's formulaic stories portraying drunkenness as a physical evil treated by expeditious moral means. Drawing on this social and literary context, Matheson notes how "The Black Cat" both exploits and extends the conventions of temperance literature. Poe's narrator, as other critics have suggested, uses deceptive rhetoric to excuse deeds driven by darker impulses than those that are alcoholically induced. The sound insights of this essay might have been strengthened by showing how its general thesis built on Benjamin Franklin Fisher IV's research on Poe's literary uses of alcohol (*ALS 1978*, pp. 35–56).

The object of increasing attention in recent years, "The Man of the Crowd" may no longer qualify as "minor" fiction. Clearly impressed by the story's significance, Robert H. Byer imposes some hefty ideological baggage in "Mysteries of the City: A Reading of Poe's 'The Man of the Crowd'" (*Ideology and Classic American Literature*, pp. 221–46). Byer sees in the tale a reflection of increasing mechanization brought about by the forces of industrial capitalism. The crowd, he contends, has a restless, unhealthy vitality that masks the process of commodification that engenders its feverish movement. How this Marxist perspective becomes reconciled with Poe's unique political vision Byer never fully explains, nor does he cite previous scholarship on the tale by J. Gerald Kennedy and Dana Brand (*ALS 1985*, pp. 43 and 52). Fisher includes "The Man of the Crowd" in his general discussion of "The Urban Scene of Edgar Allan Poe" (*POMPA*, pp. 39–50). Tracing depictions of cities from the early verse to the detective stories, he finds little optimism in Poe's perspective on urban life, an attitude analogous to that of Carlyle and Ruskin who bewailed the growth of industrial cities.

Another of Poe's physical settings—the sea—is the subject of Emilio De Grazia's "Poe's Other Beautiful Woman" (*Literature and Lore of the Sea*, pp. 176–84). His comments on the sea fiction, however, are less convincing than those he offers on other Poe texts. Reading sexual implications into Arthur Gordon Pym's "incipient passion for the sea," De Grazia sees the fall into Dirk Peters's arms as a homosexual embrace, and he glosses *biche de mer* as a pun on "bitches." When he discusses the sea as a poetic construct or mythic archetype, however, he makes insightful comments on oceanic imagery in the tales about women.

In a wide-ranging essay that touches on a number of stories, Judith P. Saunders's "'If This I Saw': Optic Dilemmas in Poe's Writings" (*ATQ* 62:63–80) outlines the contributions to plot, theme, and imagery made by visual operations. Saunders sees Dupin as a model of perception by which other characters are judged, since he keeps spiritual impulse and sensory impression in harmonious balance. Other tales trace either the excesses of subjective vision or of distorted perspective. Saunders has isolated a significant theme in the fiction, but I wonder whether her essay really advances James W. Gargano's thesis in "The Distorted Perception of Poe's Comic Narrators" (*ALS 1976*, p. 36).

Finally, Michael Clifton identifies the jeweled chain decorating the devil's apartment in "The Duc de L'Omelette" as that of Hecate ("Down Hecate's Chain: Infernal Inspiration in Three of Poe's Tales," *NCL* 41:217–27). In the recurrence of the moon, the vortex, and the prison in Poe's fiction, Clifton discerns mythic and infernal dimensions. He concludes by claiming that these image clusters suggest latent fears in the creative unconscious.

Worcester Polytechnic Institute

4. Melville

Brian Higgins

Nineteen eighty-six was a year of major productivity in Melville studies. Eight books, a special issue of *Essays in Arts and Sciences* devoted to Melville's later life and works, and several lengthy chapters in books were published, in addition to essays and notes in the journals. Some of the work was of exceptionally high caliber. *Moby-Dick* received far more attention this year than any of the other works; otherwise, as in 1985, no dominant trend in scholarship and criticism was evident. Long neglected, Melville's knowledge and use of the pictorial arts steadily continues to attract scholarly interest.

i. General Studies

Undoubtedly the year's most important achievement is *A Companion to Melville Studies*, ed. John Bryant (Greenwood). This stout, 900-page volume, comprising 25 chapters by 26 contributors, is divided into five parts. Part 1 consists of three biographical chapters (discussed in section ii, below). In Part 2 11 chapters treat Melville's works individually or in pairs or groups. The four chapters of Part 3 examine aspects of his thought—his concepts of society, language, religion, and the mind, and his logic in *Moby-Dick*. The three chapters of Part 4 examine Melville's art—its philosophical elements, its blending of comedy and tragedy, and Melville's aesthetics. In Part 5 two chapters explore Melville's influence on "elite" and "popular" culture, while a third examines foreign studies of Melville. The fourth, G. Thomas Tanselle's remarkably comprehensive "Melville and the World of Books," treats several "interlocking matters," including Melville's own reading and book-buying, the collecting of both his own books and commentary on the books, and efforts to establish reliable texts of his works. The *Companion*, as Bryant stresses, is intended not merely as a "fact book" but as an "intellectual guide." Thus, rather than attempting an exhaustive survey of secondary material, the "textual" chapters in Part 2 discuss the value of particular approaches, the nature of the critical debates the works have generated, and opportunities for future study. Less uniformly organized, the topical chapters of Parts 3–5 also identify important issues and relevant scholarship. Not all of the contributors maintain the generally high standard of writing in the collection, but Bryant has brought together an extraordinary amount of good scholarship in one volume. For both teachers and students, the *Companion* will serve as an invaluable resource for years to come.

Robert K. Martin, in *Hero, Captain, and Stranger: Male Friendship, Social Critique, and Literary Form in the Sea Novels of Herman Melville* (No. Car.), examines "a controlling structural pattern" wherein the Hero or "experiencing self" in several of Melville's works is caught between two opposing forces—one embodied in the Dark Stranger, or later the Handsome Sailor, who represents a kind of innocence or state of nature; the other in the Captain, formally and symbolically the representative of legal authority "and hence the force of restraint upon the individual." Martin's subject is the way in which, within this pattern, "sexually charged relationships between men are employed as part of a critique of power in the society that Melville depicted." In his erotic appeal the Dark Stranger "offers the possibility of an alternate sexuality," a nonaggressive homosexuality. Like Whitman, according to Martin, Melville "seriously believed in the radical social potential of male homosexuality" and "used the male couple as a figure of an inherently democratic union of equals which could serve as the basis for a new social organization": through "the affirmation of the values of nonaggressive male-bonded couples," the "power of the patriarchy" could be contested and even defeated. Martin's analyses of the works he treats—*Typee*, *Redburn*, *White-Jacket*, *Moby-Dick*, and *Billy Budd*—are provocative and often perceptive. As the book progresses, however, his insistence on the liberating and transformative potential of nonaggressive homosexuality and on Melville's "masturbatory poetics" is increasingly heavy-handed. Many of his interpretations seem eccentric or extreme. Most readers will probably agree that the works do indeed contain the figures of Hero, Captain, and Stranger; probably very few will wholly accede to the sexual significance Martin finds in their encounter.

William B. Dillingham's long and laborious *Melville's Later Novels* (Georgia) is the third volume of his critical trilogy on Melville (see *ALS 1972*, pp. 42–43, and *ALS 1977*, pp. 59–60). In the late novels, according to Dillingham, Melville is occupied with the idea of survival, writing indirectly about himself, his own "motivations and strong proclivities," and frequently projecting "what could happen to him if certain inner forces gain sway." Melville wrote out of his need to confront and understand warring forces within himself and out of his will to survive his own self-destructive tendencies. Survival in his books (and in his own case) is the result of "genuine inner probing and hard-won self-knowledge" (like Ishmael's); ignorance of self and of warring impulses within the self leads to self-destruction (as in the case of Ahab, Pierre, and other characters). Dillingham is frequently at odds with established critical positions and at times is valuably perceptive, as in his discussion of "The Whiteness of the Whale" and in his chapter "Surviving the Wreck." More often, his new interpretations seem less the result of genuine insight than of his own preoccupations.

William Hamilton's *Melville and the Gods* (Scholars Press, 1985) offers not so much an argument as passages of summary and commentary loosely held together by a concern with Melville's "religious anguish and search." A major failing of the book, besides its many dubious readings, is Hamilton's apparent unawareness of just about all previous treatments of his topic. According to Hamilton, the creation of Ahab was the act that broke the grip of Protestant Christianity on Melville, "the major act by which he affirmed the death of God." Subsequently, Meville came to affirm "the sea as a god that theodicy [did] not compel him to deny."

Herman Melville, ed. Harold Bloom (Chelsea House), brings together, in Bloom's view, "a representative selection of the best criticism" devoted to Melville's works during the last 40 years, arranged in the chronological order of its publication. If the essays and chapters are not always the best of their kind, they do at least represent a number of different approaches to Melville, and it is nice to see Robert Penn Warren's fine essay on "Melville the Poet" reprinted here. But the collection seems mainly a gratuitous piece of bookmaking, designed more to make up the series it belongs to (*Modern Critical Views*) than to meet any genuine need.

Robert K. Wallace's "Melville's Prints and Engravings at the Berkshire Athenaeum" (*EAS* 15:59–90) provides a useful annotated catalog of the three portfolios of Melville's unframed prints and engravings that Eleanor Metcalf donated in 1952, prefaced by a commentary on their relation to stages in Melville's lifelong interest in art and to his own works. Fourteen of the prints and engravings are attractively reproduced.

James Duban's " 'This "All" Feeling': Melville, Norton, and Schleiermacher" (*ELN* 23,iv:38–42) draws attention to a passage in Andrews Norton's *A Discourse on the Latest Form of Infidelity* translating and commenting on lines from Friedrich Schleiermacher's *On Religion* that possibly helped Melville formulate his sentiments about the " 'all' feeling.' "

ii. Biography

Donald Yannella's valuable "Writing the '*Other* Way': Melville, the Duyckinck Crowd, and Literature for the Masses" (*A Companion to Melville Studies*, pp. 63–81) provides new information about the journalistic and financial enterprises of the Duyckinck brothers and Cornelius Mathews in the early 1850s and their willingness to write "altogether" the "*other* way" (for popular success, that is) in contrast to Melville. Yannella also discusses Melville's relations with the Duyckincks and offers an attractive interpretation of "The Fiddler": he suggests that Melville was caricaturing Mathews in his portrait of Hautboy and possibly parodying Evert Duyckinck in his character Standard, while "expressing his own trepidation and ambivalence about the compromise necessity was forcing on him to write that '*other* way' " as a magazine writer. Thomas Farel Heffernan's "Melville the Traveler" (*A Companion to Melville Studies*, pp. 35–61) recounts Melville's travels in the United States and overseas, stressing their importance in the formation of Melville's imagination and in keeping that imagination alive. James Barbour's "Melville Biography: A Life and the Lives" (*A Companion to Melville Studies*, pp. 3–34) gives an "overview" of Melville's life that does not always avoid the temptation to state speculation as fact, then sensibly evaluates the dozen book-length biographical studies that have appeared since the beginning of the 1920s, concluding with a list of some of the biographical gaps that still need to be filled.

Sanford E. Marovitz's "More Chartless Voyaging: Melville and Adler at Sea" (*SAR*, pp. 373–84) hypothesizes that part of the reason for Melville's being "so immediately and profoundly attracted" to George J. Adler on his voyage to England in the fall of 1849 was that "the German philologist simultaneously reflected an image of

Melville's present psychological state and represented to him as well a portentous confrontation with his own fears and intellectual aspirations." Marovitz suggests plausibly that ideas incorporated in the preface to Adler's *A Dictionary of the German and English Languages* were part of their conversations. The ideas "clearly relate to concepts that Melville himself used in the composition of his fiction from *Moby-Dick* on, though he often employed them for ironic purposes." Stanton Garner's "Surviving the Gilded Age: Herman Melville in the Customs Service" (*EAS* 15:1–13) describes the organization of the corruption-ridden New York Custom House and the work Melville did during his service there.

iii. Typee to *White-Jacket*

Melville's early works attracted relatively little attention in 1986. Stephen de Paul in "The Documentary Fiction of Melville's *Omoo*: The Crossed Grammars of Acculturation" (*Criticism* 28:51–72) argues that the loose format of *Omoo* was largely determined by Tahiti, "a site of two disrupted cultures": "patchwork figures," individuals with identities pieced together from fragments of two altered cultures, required a "patchwork text" (composed of personal anecdotes, speculation, historical facts, and fictitious events) in which to become "visible." De Paul handles the complexities of his argument skillfully, but the essay lacks a sense of Melville as a working author, one whose habits of composition led to the production of more than one "patchwork" text.

In "Melville's 'Synthesizing' Narrator, *Mardi*, Fichte, and the *Frühromantiker*," (*RP&P* 10:45–60), Christopher S. Durer examines *Mardi*'s narrative techniques of "fusion" (by means of which the narrator merges the self with his surroundings) and of "synthesis" (by means of which he unifies what he sees into a coherent whole) and finds "striking analogies" between *Mardi* and the ontological views of Fichte and the German Frühromantiker. The influence of *The Faerie Queene* on *Mardi* has long been recognized; in "Spenser and the Structure of *Mardi*" (*SNNTS* 18:258–69), Carole Moses cites further indications of that influence but tells us little about the book's structure. Neal Tolchin, in "The Social Construct of *Redburn*'s 'Mourning Pilgrimage'" (*SNNTS* 18:157–76), reads *Redburn* as an expression of Melville's "conflicted grief" for his father, wherein Melville's anger at Allan "gets displaced and distanced via Jackson and

Bolton" and then "transmuted into incisive social critique." According to Susan Vanzanten Gallagher, "Jack Blunt and His Dream Book" (*AL* 58:614–19), Melville's description in *Redburn* of the *Bonaparte Dream Book* and his account of Jack Blunt's attempts to remember his dreams and of his markings in chalk are very similar to the "contents and procedures" of *Napoleon's Book of Fate*, one of the most popular contemporary dream books.

iv. Moby-Dick and *Pierre*

Stuart M. Frank's *Herman Melville's Picture Gallery: Sources and Types of the "Pictorial" Chapters of* Moby-Dick (Lefkowicz) meets a genuine need. An invaluable supplement to Howard P. Vincent's *The Trying-Out of* Moby-Dick, it reproduces paintings, prints, and other images of whales and whaling that Melville refers to in chapters 55–57 side by side with Melville's text and Frank's detailed notes. The three chapters, as Frank observes, have previously attracted "minimal pictorial attention" even in Vincent.

Kerry McSweeney's Moby-Dick: *Ishmael's Mighty Book* (Twayne) is for the most part a quite able, lucidly written, unspecialized commentary, apparently intended for undergraduate or first-time readers of *Moby-Dick.* It includes no new scholarship and brings nothing new of significance to interpretation of the book. McSweeney would have done well to have consulted Harrison Hayford's "Unnecessary Duplicates: A Key to the Writing of *Moby-Dick*" (see *ALS 1978*, pp. 49–50) before giving his overconfident account of the book's composition.

Dillingham's discussion of "metaphoric whaling" in *Melville's Later Novels* (deep diving into the self "with the goal of discovering at the center a hidden but powerful and sublime identity") and his analyses of the divided natures of Ishmael (torn between his "pale usher" and "sub-sub-librarian" selves) and Ahab (a "self-conceived god" and God-seeker) are often unconvincing. (Dillingham is also immune to Melville's humor—witness his discussion of "The Advocate" and "The Honor and Glory of Whaling," pp. 37–40.) More valuable, though pressed too hard, is his attempt to show the influence of Melville's knowledge of Gnostic thought in his portrayal of Ahab, a topic Harold Bloom addresses briefly in his introduction to *Herman Melville.*

New Essays on Moby-Dick (Cambridge) strive, in the words of their editor, Richard H. Brodhead, "to determine what is central to *Moby-Dick* and to identify what makes Melville's work impressive now." Brodhead himself in his introduction emphasizes the uniqueness of the stand *Moby-Dick* takes toward literature itself—"its quite peculiar attitude, registered on every page, toward what literature is and can be, and toward what it can attempt as a work of literary making." James McIntosh ("The Mariner's Multiple Quest," pp. 23–53) stresses Melville's "fluidity" of mind, particularly as it expresses itself in the book's multiple quests. Carolyn Porter ("Call Me Ishmael, or How to Make Double-Talk Speak," pp. 73–108) examines the rhetorical strategies that enable Melville "to authorize the discourse of a socially marginalized and culturally alienated narrator." Invoking Mikhail Bakhtin, as in her 1985 essay on *Moby-Dick* (see *ALS 1985*, p. 64), Porter argues that Ishmael's narrative authority derives largely from a "double-voiced discourse," in which he both undermines and exploits "the authority inscribed in the landsman's culturally bound and legitimized discourses." T. Walter Herbert, Jr. ("Calvinist Earthquake: *Moby-Dick* and Religious Tradition," pp. 109–40) attempts to show that the 19th-century conflict between Calvinist orthodoxy and liberal Christianity lies at the heart of the book. Bryan Wolf ("When Is a Painting Most Like a Whale?: Ishmael, *Moby-Dick*, and the Sublime," pp. 141–79) attempts to define Melville's version of the sublime in *Moby-Dick* with the aid of Emerson and landscapes (reproduced in the text) by Thomas Cole, Asher B. Durand, and Frederick E. Church. The most valuable essay in the collection is Lawrence Buell's sophisticated analysis of the ways in which *Moby-Dick* can be read as Scripture ("*Moby-Dick* as Sacred Text," pp. 53–72). Buell's analysis of chapter 86, "The Tail" ("an almost paradigmatic illustration of how the cetology chapters in general work"), and the book's use of revelation at its prophetic level and at the level of plot are particularly acute. Criticism in the last 10 or 15 years, Brodhead maintains, has shown signs of steering clear of *Moby-Dick*, with the result that it has failed to benefit from the innovations in critical study in the last decades. How far the book benefits in that way through these essays is open to question. I will probably not be alone in thinking that where they draw most on recent critical innovations they shed least light on the text—with the exception of Buell's essay, which makes adroit use of Paul Ricoeur's "Toward a Hermeneutic of the Idea of Revelation."

A Companion to Melville Studies contains two fine chapters on

Moby-Dick. In Part 2 Walter E. Bezanson's discussion of Ishmael and his treatment of the book as document, drama, and dream are in some respects an extension of his classic essay "*Moby-Dick*: Work of Art." The chapter also contains valuable sections on the book's "germination" and composition. In Part 3 Edwin S. Shneidman breaks new ground in treating the book from a logician's point of view, examining the ways in which Melville is traditionally Aristotelian and the ways in which he is "idiosyncratically, uniquely Melvillean in his thinking."

Donald E. Pease, in his intricate discussion of "the scene of cultural persuasion" at the time of the publication of *Moby-Dick*, is largely concerned with the rhetoric of orators and politicians and its putative effect on listeners, rhetoric he links to Ahab's ("Melville and Cultural Persuasion," *Ideology and Classic American Literature*, pp. 384–417). Pease also claims that ever since Matthiessen's reading of *Moby-Dick* in *American Renaissance*, the book "has been a Cold War text, one that secures in Ishmael's survival a sign of the free world's triumph over a totalitarian power." Pease argues instead that Ishmael's form of freedom does not oppose Ahab as freedom would totalitarianism—rather it compels him to need Ahab. Pease's analysis of the contradictions in Matthiessen's reading of *Moby-Dick* is forceful; his analysis of Ishmael is less convincing, as is his view that Matthiessen's and similar cold war interpretations constitute *the* canonical reading of *Moby-Dick.*

Adopting the premise that self-consciously "American" modern literature "is marked in the United States by the assumption of achieved independence, and in Spanish America by the ongoing pursuit of independence in the context of dependence," Bell Gale Chevigny examines *Moby-Dick* and Alejo Carpentier's *El siglo de las luces* (*Explosion in a Cathedral*) as works that "sustain and problematize" the projects of Emerson and José Marti ("Insatiable unease': Melville and Carpentier and the Search for an American Hermeneutic," *Reinventing the Americas*, pp. 34–59). Chevigny argues that both Melville and Carpentier used the novel to pursue an American hermeneutic, "both a means of interpreting America and an American way of interpreting."

Three essays focus on individual chapters. Harold Hellenbrand's "Behind Closed Doors: Ishmael's Dreams and Hypnagogic Trances in *Moby-Dick*" (*ATQ* 61:47–71), a Freudian reading of "The Counterpane," suggests the ways in which the chapter "revises traces of

Melville's psychobiography" (involving scenes of "primal material, either real or extrapolated" and of "paternal debilitation and madness") and foreshadows parts of Ishmael's reconstruction of Ahab's past and events abroad the *Pequod.* Marilyn Patton's "The Hidden Artist and the Art of Hiding in *Moby-Dick*" (*ATQ* 59:19–34) is a labored exercise in the exegesis of doubleness, in which references to whaling in "Moby Dick" and "The Chart" are construed as references to writing. According to Patton, the image of the artist that emerges "is a contradictory blend of narcissism and monomania, of both Ishmael and Ahab." In the one new essay in *Herman Melville*, "The Symphony" receives what Harold Bloom describes as a "radically advanced reading" from P. Adams Sitney ("Ahab's Name: A Reading of 'The Symphony,'" pp. 223–37).

Two essays deal with influences, though from different perspectives. James S. Leonard rightly points to elements of *Tamburlaine* and *Dr. Faustus* in the portrayal of Ahab ("Melville's Ahab as Marlovian Hero," *ATQ* 62:47–58), though some of the parallels are not as close as he claims; and Frederick Busch, in "The Whale as Shaggy Dog" (*When People Publish*, pp. 65–82), finds "parallel elements" in *Moby-Dick* and Norman Mailer's "The Man Who Studied Yoga." In "Ideational, Interpersonal and Textual Meaning in Melville's *Moby Dick*" (*ForLing* 8[1984]:157–67), James D. Benson and William S. Greaves adopt a linguistic approach, exploring ways in which systemic theory throws light on Melville's "foregrounding."

A more important essay, Paul Royster's "Melville's Economy of Language" (*Ideology and Classic American Literature*, pp. 313–36), argues that the interaction of two processes in *Moby-Dick*—industrial production and literary construction—produced "a work rich in the metaphorical interplay of language and labor," whereas in *Pierre* Melville "abandoned this sense of language's connection to the world." In the two works he "traveled from one extreme to the other: from endorsing language as the world's perfect counterpart to exposing it as a shadow without corresponding substance." In the same process, Royster argues, Melville also moved from a deep commitment to the capitalist economy to an outright condemnation of it, "both as a means of life and as a mode of representation." Royster develops his argument persuasively, though surely he exaggerates when he claims that *Moby-Dick* "grounds its entire system of metaphor in economy" and that writing is "the industry that provides metaphors in *Pierre*." Emory Elliott's "Art, Religion, and the Problem of Authority in *Pierre*" (*Ideology and Classic American Literature*, pp. 337–51) emphasizes the legacy of New England Calvinism and the American Revolution as "cultural facts" that help to shape Pierre's identity and to foster the "ideological inflexibility" that diminishes his ability to become a successful artist.

The most original part of Dillingham's chapters on *Pierre* in *Melville's Later Novels* is his discussion of what he considers to be pervasive "echoes" of John Paul Lavater. The correspondences he cites do not seem sufficiently close to warrant his claim that from his reading of Lavater's *Essays in Physiognomy* and Goethe's autobiography Melville conceived "the notion of making Pierre akin to the physiognomists" and that in physiognomy Melville "discovered a metaphor for his protagonist's blindness." Dillingham's attempts to link *Pierre*, a number of the stories, *The Confidence-Man*, and *Billy Budd* to Melville's interest in Gnosticism are less convincing than his discussion of Gnosticism and *Moby-Dick*.

Paul A. Smith's "Melville's Vision of Flux and Fixity in *Pierre*" (*ESQ* 32:110–21) relies largely on imagery patterns to support its dubious claim that the book's "principal tension" arises from Pierre's "inability to recognize his essentially static nature"; according to Smith, Pierre's failure to understand that life is "a product of flux and an endless cycle of death, decay, and rebirth" brings about the book's "tragicomic denouement." Nicholas Canaday's "Pierre in the Domestic Circle" (*SNNTS* 18:395–402) stresses Pierre's "psychosexual immaturity," the result of "the stultifying, exclusively female" domestic circles that surround him at Saddle Meadows and in the city. Canaday's account of Pierre and his relationships with his mother, Lucy, and Isabel is sketchy at best.

v. Stories

Lea Bertani Vozar Newman's invaluable *A Reader's Guide to the Short Stories of Herman Melville* (Hall) is organized along the same lines as her guide to Hawthorne's stories (see *ALS 1979*, p. 28), with a chapter devoted to each story. The chapters are arranged alphabetically by title; each contains sections on the story's publication history; composition, sources, and influences; relationship to other works by Melville; and interpretations and criticism. Thoroughly researched and offering a convenient access to the large body of scholarship and criticism devoted to the stories, the *Guide* will be a boon to teachers and students alike. It does not, however, make redundant the chapter on the tales by Johannes D. Bergmann in *A Companion to Melville Studies* (pp. 241–78), which discusses the magazines in which Melville published his short fiction (*Harper's* and *Putnam's*) and usefully treats the stories in chronological groupings.

Far less rewarding is Mary-Madeleine Gina Riddle's *Herman Melville's* Piazza Tales: *A Prophetic Vision* (Göteborg, 1985), which attempts to show that through his addition of "The Piazza" and his arrangement of the tales Melville produced "a highly structured and coherent new tale," which considers slavery in its various forms. The order of *The Piazza Tales*, according to Riddle, is consistent with "socio-political events" of the 1850s and "correlates with the progressive complexity of the historical, political, and social development of slavery." The allusions Riddle finds in the tales to sociopolitical events seem more often the product of her own imagination than of Melville's.

The year's most ambitious essay on a single tale is Barton Levi St. Armand's "Melville, Malaise, and Mannerism: The Originality of 'The Piazza'" (*BuR* 30:72–101). In attempting to define Melville's artistry and vision in "The Piazza," St. Armand draws on definitions of Mannerism by students of late 16th-century European art, then draws parallels and distinguishes between Melville's treatment of the picturesque and the aesthetics of Hawthorne, Asher B. Durand, and John Ruskin. In "The Piazza," St. Armand contends, Melville deliberately undermined the style of symbolic romance he had exploited to the full in *Moby-Dick* and created "a new and bold art of calculated irony, paradox, and formal disintegration" (a literary Mannerism).

The only comparable essay, in terms of the range of reference it brings to a tale, is Eric J. Sundquist's "*Benito Cereno* and New World Slavery" (*Reconstructing American Literary History*, pp. 93–122), which relates the story, somewhat obliquely, to American aspirations in the Caribbean during the first half of the 19th century, as well as to the San Domingan slave revolt of 1791 and its impact in the United States. Gloria Horsley-Meacham, on slender evidence, posits Melville's use of the more remote past ("Melville's Dark Satyr Unmasked," *ELN* 23,iii:43–47). In her view the central device of "the shield-like stern-piece" of the *San Dominick* seems to be "a pointed reference to the African conquest of Spanish lands during the eleventh century." Drawing upon this history, she argues, Melville "interprets the slaves' ascendancy to power over Cereno as a resumption of African sovereignty." A revised version of James Kavenagh's essay (*ALS 1984*, p. 77) appears in *Ideology and Classic American Literature* (pp. 352–83) under the title "That Hive of Subtlety: 'Benito Cereno' and the Liberal Hero."

In "Melville's Copyists: The 'Bar-tenders' of Wall Street" (*PLL* 22:176–86), Thomas Pribek focuses mainly on the copyists in "Bartleby" as victims of "a kind of class system of commercial success and subjugation" perpetuated by the lawyer. Pribek's "The 'Safe' Man of Wall Street: Characterizing Melville's Lawyer" (*SSF* 23:191–95) draws attention to a number of slang connotations of the word "safe" which may apply ironically to "the narrator's position as a successful man of law and a political appointee who represents an impersonal—and perhaps immoral—social system." Allan H. MacLaine ("Melville's 'Sequel' to 'Bartleby the Scrivener' and Dickens' 'Story of the Bagman's Uncle' in *Pickwick Papers*: An Unnoticed Link," *ATQ* 60:37–39) was apparently unaware of Michael H. Friedman's earlier attempt to establish the influence of Dickens's tale on the ending of "Bartleby" (*ALS 1984*, p. 76). A. Robert Lee's "Voices Off and On: Melville's Piazza and Other Stories" (*The Nineteenth-Century American Short Story*, pp. 76–102), a companion piece to Lee's essay on *The Confidence-Man* (*ALS 1984*, pp. 78–79), illustrates Melville's "tactics of voicing"—his "manner of making us 'hear' his stories, his styles of narrative disclosure"—particularly in "Bartleby," "The Encantadas," and "Benito Cereno."

Joseph Rosenblum's "A Cock Fight Between Melville and Thoreau" (*SSF* 23:159–67) lends some support to earlier claims that in "Cock A Doodle Doo!" Melville was alluding satirically to Thoreau's *A Week on the Concord and Merrimack Rivers*, but Rosenblum has little to support his contention that "Thoreau was not oblivious or indifferent to these satiric thrusts and, in his final revisions of *Walden*, pointedly replied to them."

vi. Israel Potter and *The Confidence-Man*

In his chapters on *Israel Potter* and *The Confidence-Man*, Dillingham in *Melville's Later Novels* rides his thesis into the ground. In Potter, according to Dillingham, Melville depicts "a man who in search of liberty moves away from the liberating power of self-knowledge," a man whose patriotism makes him "miss opportunities to know himself better" and "to search out honestly his own wondrous and complex facets of being." In Dillingham's reading of *The Confidence-Man*, the center is again the theme of self-knowledge. Not Satan, nor Christ, nor a trickster God, nor Vishnu, nor some mythic folk figure, the Confidence Man is Melville's rendition of "a man with the highest possible degree of self-understanding"—Melville "as he conceives that he could be if he could master the art of self-development." Most of the other characters in the book "permit their enslavement because of self-ignorance"; the Confidence Man "escapes it through self-awareness." Alchemy, "fundamentally the science of self-knowledge," is one of the keys to understanding his character.

John Bryant's analysis of the book's mixture of genres in "Allegory and Breakdown in *The Confidence-Man*: Melville's Comedy of Doubt" (*PQ* 65:113–30) has implications for more familiar, and more plausible, interpretations. According to Bryant, the "ritualistic patterns" of allegory in the first part of the book are "sedulously thwarted" in the second, so that it begins as "a didactic comedy of thought" and ends as "a mimetic comedy of action." Because of the broken patterns and Goodman's ambiguous behavior, it "seems past knowing" whether the Cosmopolitan is a knave, a fool, or "quite an original." Not everyone will agree that the Cosmopolitan is quite as inscrutable as Bryant maintains. Robert Paul Lamb's "The Place of *The Confidence-Man* in Melville's Career" (*SoR* 22:489–505) links the book, not very compellingly, to the heightened value Melville attached to "geniality" and "mutual human sympathy" in his work after *Pierre*.

vii. Poetry

Hershel Parker's "The Character of Vine in Melville's *Clarel* (*EAS* 15:91–113) qualifies Walter Bezanson's description of Vine (generally accepted as Melville's portrait of Hawthorne) in his Hendricks House edition of *Clarel* by analyzing in detail the character's gestures and speeches and the narrator's comments on him. The impression that emerges from Parker's analysis is considerably less favorable than the one from Bezanson's account. Parker finds a self-absorbed, easily distracted Vine, a man lacking in moral and intellectual profundity and declining in aesthetic capacities. Melville had come to understand, Parker concludes—perhaps during the years he worked on *Clarel*—that Hawthorne "had gotten credit for a lot more philosophical and aesthetic profundity than he was capable of." Hawthorne, he had decided, "was not merely burnt-out as an artist at an early age" but in later life "was coasting on an unmerited reputation for mental force, not to say profound intelligence." Wyn Kelley's "Haunted Stone: Nature and City in *Clarel*" (*EAS* 15:15–29) is less convincingly argued. According to Kelley, Jerusalem reenacts in its historical and social cycles "a seemingly natural cycle of growth," whereas the wilderness, lacking vegetative cycles, gives witness only to the "less human geological progress of time." In the city Clarel finds "intimations of spiritualized nature" and senses there "the power of nature to influence man's actions and thoughts." The lines Kelley quotes from the poem are often at odds with her argument. In the one other essay on Melville's poetry, Bryan C. Short interprets *John Marr* as Melville's "inward look at his own creative processes which makes possible the outward-looking, projective stance" of *Billy Budd* ("Memory's Mint: Melville's Parable of the Imagination in *John Marr and Other Sailors*," (*EAS* 15:31–42).

viii. *Billy Budd, Sailor*

The year's most substantial essay on *Billy Budd* is Julian Markels's "The Liberal Bombast of *Billy Budd*" (*EAS* 15:43–58). Markels cogently analyzes the ways in which "psychologically, stylistically, and, therefore, philosophically and politically, the story is at odds with itself." More specifically, Markels calls attention to "the story's internal pressure to puff itself," its intellectual hesitancy before the politics it dramatizes, and its resulting "thirst for complexity" and "obsessive dialectical perspectivism" in the characterization of Vere. Dennis Grunes in "Preinterpretation and *Billy Budd*" (*ELWIU* 13:103–13) begins with the statement that *Billy Budd* was first published 23 years after Melville's death, then misrepresents Guert Gansevoort's role in the *Somers* case. The essay does not improve when Grunes attempts to show that the narrator is unreliable, particularly on the subject of Claggart's evil, in his "preinterpretation" of the story. Robert K. Martin's "Saving Captain Vere: *Billy Budd* from Melville's Novella to Britten's Opera" (*SSF* 23:49–56) argues that the important changes from the story to the opera, notably in the characterization of Vere and the nature of the ending, are in part due to misinterpretation of Melville by E. M. Forster (librettist with Eric Crozier) "but even more to what seems to have been a difference of conception between Forster and Britten." Lastly, John Limon's "The American Stutter" (*Genre* 18[1985]:215–33) makes an elaborate case for *Billy Budd* as the precursor of Robert Coover's *The Universal Baseball Association* and other metafiction of the 1960s.

University of Illinois at Chicago

5. Whitman and Dickinson

Vivian R. Pollak

There was so much material published on Whitman and Dickinson this year that I have undoubtedly missed some work I should like to have read, though too much of what I read was banal and poorly written. Recurrent themes in the Whitman and Dickinson scholarship that I reviewed: (1) gender identity; (2) religious beliefs; (3) the distinction between written and spoken language—this latter category a distant third.

i. Whitman and Dickinson

Was Walt Whitman parodically male, Emily Dickinson parodically female? This almost inevitable question is considered by Sandra M. Gilbert in "The American Sexual Poetics of Walt Whitman and Emily Dickinson" (*Reconstructing American Literary History*, pp. 123–54). Because of the originality of both poets, the answer turns out to be not really, though Gilbert does a nice job of setting up the starker possibility. The essay, in which Gilbert argues that Dickinson was the more radically experimental writer, is richly documented and subtly conceived. The close readings of poems are consistently illuminating, though Gilbert's larger argument (that both poets were writing "not poetry") ignores the strong generic presence of Dickinson's hymn meters. In *The Frenzy of Renown* Leo Braudy brings the two poets together in a section provocatively entitled "Dickinson and Whitman: The Audience of Solitude" (pp. 462–75). Braudy treats both writers against the background of a mass society which attempted to distinguish between popularity (a specious value) and fame (an authentic one). Despite several minor factual errors, his discussion of Dickinson as the show-off of eternity is more probing than his discussion of Whitman, which treats the "Calamus" persona as normative.

I am indebted to Cynthia L. Ragland for able research assistance in the preparation of this chapter.

ii. Whitman

***a.* Bibliography, Editing.** Gay Wilson Allen's *The New Walt Whitman Handbook* has now been reissued in paperback (NYU), with an updated bibliography for 1975–85 and a new "Introduction." In the revised introduction Allen focuses primarily on Whitman's verse technique, new editions of the manuscripts, biography, and on Whitman's reception in China. Xilao Li's "A Selected Bibliography of Walt Whitman in Chinese (1914–1984)" (*WWR* 3:43–47) contains 74 entries, many of them translations of Whitman poems, but only four after 1959. It appears that none of the standard critical works, not excepting Allen's *The Solitary Singer*, are yet available to Whitman's Chinese audience. Many of the entries are difficult to classify. Is "Selected Poems of Whitman" a translation of selected poems or an essay about them? Were the bibliography annotated, its usefulness would be greatly enhanced. In "Walt Whitman, 1838–1939: A Reference Guide: Additional Annotations" (*WWR* 4:24–40), Scott Giantvalley updates his 1981 G. K. Hall bibliography by more than a hundred new entries. He includes books, articles, poems, parodies, translations, reviews of critical works, and a review of a bibliography. So far as I can tell there are no major discoveries, but the commentary is helpful and succinct. In three issues of the *Walt Whitman Quarterly Review*, William White continues to provide thorough bibliographies of more or less recent reviews, books, articles, dissertations, poems, and miscellanea (*WWR* 3:39–43, 48–50, 4:41–43). Having culled through the first one hundred volumes of *Harper's New Monthly Magazine*, Daniel A. Wells presents 39 citations of Whitman (*WWR* 4:16–23). Wells explains that "the number of citations for Whitman approximates those of Holmes and Lowell, about half as many as Longfellow and Hawthorne, the American writers most frequently cited by *Harper's* columnists." Though several of the notices are distinctly hostile and others are mixed, these findings reinforce Robert Scholnick's argument in "Whitman and the Magazines: Some Documentary Evidence" (*AL* 44[1972]:222–46) that Whitman was not as neglected by the American magazines as he claimed to be. The *Harper's* entries range from 1860 through 1896 and are skillfully annotated.

***b.* Biography.** From a biographical perspective Arthur Golden's presentation of "Nine Early Whitman Letters, 1840–1841" (*AL* 58: 342–60) was the most exciting article of the year. Most of the letters were written during Whitman's schoolteaching days on Long Island when he was in his early twenties. All are addressed to his hitherto unknown friend Abraham Paul Leech, a bookkeeper, and were recently acquired by the Library of Congress. In the newly discovered letters Whitman's vehement dislike of his occupation and surroundings is brilliantly expressed. Sarcastic, abusive, and not infrequently depressed, the future poet reveals a bitter and low-spirited side of his nature that he subsequently disguised and transcended. As Joann P. Krieg points out in "The Long Island Letters of Schoolmaster Whitman" (*West Hills Review* 6:41–48): "This is not the mature Whitman who through the hazy memory of old age could look back on the 'dear old fashion'd farmers' of Long Island." There is a deliberate attempt at humor, some of it successful and some of it heavy-handed. And there are complaints that, from a post-*Leaves of Grass* perspective, are unintentionally comical. By way of contrast, these letters highlight the later Whitman's empathetic self-control.

Whitman's more altruistic Civil War persona is represented in Francis B. Dedmond's "'Here Among Soldiers in Hospital': An Unpublished Letter from Walt Whitman to Lucia Jane Russell Briggs" (*NEQ* 59:544–48). Writing from Washington on 26 April 1864, Whitman thanks Mrs. Briggs for her contribution but somewhat immodestly draws attention to his own "inspiration" and "tact" and "genius" in dispensing comfort to the sick and dying. Addressing himself to Whitman's situation toward the end of his life in "Whitman, Charles Aldrich and W. M. Rossetti in 1885: Background to the Whitman Subscription" (*AL* 58:413–21), Roger W. Peattie publishes two letters written by Aldrich to Rossetti that describe the poet's physical circumstances in his Camden row house at 328 Mickle Street. The letters prompted Rossetti to organize the 1885 Whitman subscription. Aldrich, a former newspaper editor, was an Iowa legislator and collector of "autographs, portraits, and memorabilia of numerous American and British public figures." The partially paralyzed Whitman is described as living like a hermit amid poverty and disorder. He impressed Aldrich with his serenity in the midst of distressing physical circumstances, but the collector also caught a glimpse of the angry and embittered Whitman of the earlier years. Aldrich thought Whitman would be better off in a hospital, a proposal that was roundly rejected by another of Whitman's English admirers, Anne Gilchrist. The poet, she explained, was a man to whom "perfect freedom is indispensable."

***c.* Criticism: General.** The most substantial piece of general criticism is also the only book-length study of Whitman published this year. In *The Ecstatic Whitman: Literary Shamanism and the Crisis of the Union* (Ohio State), George B. Hutchinson argues that the shamanistic model of prophetic role-playing "reconciles various interpretations of the poet's religious orientation, his visionary ecstasies, and his psychological make-up." As a public poet, Whitman was certainly engaged in a form of cultural revitalization, but whether or not the shamanistic model is useful for understanding the revivalist aspect of Whitman's sensibility is another matter, and the results here are mixed. "Song of Myself," for example, is treated as a completely successful and unified effort to create a revitalized community, as exemplified by the poet and his audience. As a member of that audience, I find myself responding much more fully to some parts of the poem than to others. Hutchinson's analysis does not account for the resisting or skeptical or unentranced reader. The most valuable parts of the book describe the relationship between Whitman's psychological and political concerns. An impoverished personal life impelled Whitman to take up the prophet's role, Hutchinson argues persuasively; less persuasively he argues that Whitman's concern with shamanic practice enabled him to salvage his own psychic health. *The Ecstatic Whitman* succeeds when it grounds Whitman's political rhetoric in a recognizable historical and biographical context. It is less successful in its insistence that the shaman-poet is always in control of his "inspired" role-playing.

According to M. Jimmie Killingsworth, in "Whitman's Sexual Themes During a Decade of Revision: 1866–1876" (*WWR* 4:7–15), the post-Civil War Whitman was engaged in a massive project of sexual self-censorship which his comparatively belated references to the soul tended to further. Eventually sexuality became a theme among other themes in *Leaves of Grass*, but originally the sex themes were more urgent. Though Killingsworth perhaps overstates the case for the castrating effect of Whitman's revisions especially in the "Calamus" cluster and perhaps understates the case for the soul themes in the pre-Civil War editions, his basic argument is well documented and intuitively appealing.

The argument of Joseph Kronick's "On the Border of History: Whitman and the American Sublime" (*The American Sublime*, pp. 51–82) is more difficult to grasp. The concluding sentence reads: "And the scene of writing is 'strew'd with the wrecks of skeletons,' the texts of poets who violated the margins demarcating the I and the abyss in order to dis-cover language once again in the traces of a sublime always already inscribed in/as the figure of an 'originary' deviation Whitman variously identifies as death, the sea, and writing." Drawing on Edmund Burke, Kant, Emerson, and Bloom, Kronick suggests that Whitman equated death and insight, an assertion which oversimplifies the complexity of Whitman's imagination of death. Similarly, Kronick's assertion that Whitman never denied the existence of an afterlife is injudicious. Readings of such poems as "Out of the Cradle Endlessly Rocking," "Song of Myself," "As I Ebb'd with the Ocean of Life," and "Passage to India" are considerably more intelligible and better balanced than the abstruse commentary that attempts to link them together.

In a spirited reply to Mark Bauerlein's critique of his work, discussed below (see section ii.d.), C. Carroll Hollis eschews the reverential stance that Bauerlein mistakenly attributes to him and once again roundly rejects the notion that Whitman was a prophet ("Is There a Text in This Grass?" *WWR* 3:15–22). Bauerlein suggests that written language does not carry the illocutionary force of an oral utterance; Hollis rejoins that there are degrees of illocutionary force, that Whitman's poetry has some of that force, and that Bauerlein eventually opts for an all-or-nothing position.

***d.* Criticism: Individual Works.** In "The Written Orator of 'Song of Myself': A Recent Trend in Whitman Criticism" (*WWR* 3:1–14), Mark Bauerlein identifies the belief in "an oracular presence" as an important trend in recent Whitman criticism. He discusses John R. Irwin's *American Hieroglyphics* (1980), Calvin Bedient's "Orality and Power (Whitman's 'Song of Myself')" (*Delta*, May 1983), and C. Carroll Hollis's *Language and Style in "Leaves of Grass"* (1983). Bauerlein argues that "Whitman himself initiated the emphasis on speech in 'Song of Myself' both inside and outside the poem." He concludes that unmediated personal presence cannot be achieved through written language and that "what Whitman wanted most he could not have." Some of Bauerlein's assumptions about the authenticity of spoken as opposed to written language strike me as whimsical, but then so too were Whitman's.

This year there were six other essays that focused on "Song of Myself," but only one of them represents a significant contribution to our understanding of this complex text: Robert Weisbuch's "History, Time, and Spirit: Whitman Against Wordsworth, Carlyle and Emerson Against Themselves" (*Atlantic Double-Cross*, pp. 177–92). Weisbuch reads "Song of Myself" as a response to Wordsworth's 1850 *Prelude*. Both poets find their "good in an active passivity," internalize traditional epic conventions, and seek to relax "cultural constraints and the self-consciousness that accompanies them." Weisbuch is particularly astute on the multiple occasions that challenge the very notion of occasionality in the poem.

Further developing the poem's transatlantic connection, Leonard Douglas, in "Walt Whitman's French in 'Song of Myself' " (*WWR* 3:24–27), suggests that several French words in "Song of Myself" are used with sophistication. For Leonard, at least in this instance, Whitman's French is neither boorish nor pedantic but messianic. The article is too recherché to dispel the doubts of the unconverted. One of the more jargon-ridden articles of the year is by Chanita Goodblatt and Joseph Glicksohn. They describe Whitman's "experience of defamiliarization, whereby the dehabituation entailed in the poet's experience is conveyed to the reader," in "Cognitive Psychology and Whitman's 'Song of Myself' " (*Mosaic* 19:83–90). What a pleasure, then, to turn to Arthur Golden's crisply written "The Ending of the 1855 Version of 'Song of Myself' " (*WWR* 3:27–30). Based on an examination of the subsequent editions, Golden refutes the theory that the absence of punctuation at the end of the poem's last line in 1855 was intentional. Examining a part of "Song of Myself," Section 11, Pamela Postma sees the smaller poem as blending Whitman's conception of male and female identity, in "Self-Marriage, Dream Children, and the Poetic Imagination: A New Reading of Whitman's 'Twenty-eight Young Men' " (*ATQ* 61:37–45). Lovemaking in the poem is treated as analogous to poem-making, but Postma's construction of this analogy is imperfectly worked out.

In addition to "Song of Myself" the only other Whitman poem that dominated an individual essay is "When Lilacs Last in the Dooryard Bloom'd." In "Whitman, Washington, and the War: 'Lilacs' Revisited," in *Washington and Washington Writing*, ed. David McAleavey (George Washington University Center for Washington Area Studies No. 12, pp. 30–36), Jerome Loving argues that the war "brought out Whitman's great altruism." Though Loving veers too close to a reading of the poem as Christian allegory, his distinction between the privatized exclusivity of the "Calamus" themes and the more public style of "Lilacs" is well taken. Whitman, he shows, treats "Lincoln's death in a personal way that is also public."

***e.* Affinities and Influences.** Traditional epics subvert the generic conventions of earlier epics, argues Mark Cumming in "Carlyle, Whitman and the Disprisonment of Epic" (*VS* 29:207–26). In comparing *The French Revolution* and *Leaves of Grass,* Cumming argues persuasively that Carlyle and Whitman shared "the nineteenth-century sense of generic disintegration." Refreshingly, Cumming does not highlight the singular importance of "Song of Myself" for his purposes, suggesting instead that all of *Leaves of Grass* can usefully be approached as a modern epic with an authorial hero. Yet most of Cumming's examples are taken from poems written during the last 20 years of Whitman's life when his inspiration had flagged, though there is some discussion of the 1855 "Preface." Carlyle figures again in "Whitman's Personalism, Arnold's Culture" (*Atlantic Double-Cross*), but Robert Weisbuch contends that Arnold's influence on Whitman was significantly greater than Carlyle's. Arnold, he believes, "is the rejected muse of Whitman's finest prose essay, *Democratic Vistas,*" not the "always credited Thomas Carlyle." Both Arnold and Whitman are treated as representatives of their culture, though it was precisely the Arnoldian idea of culture that Whitman rejected. Whitman began the essay with Carlyle in mind, but "Arnold replaced Carlyle as the enemy, once Whitman found himself drawn to his subject."

Another representative Englishman is thought to have influenced Whitman's approach to evolution in 1855. In "A Note on Walt Whitman's Probable Reading of Robert Chambers" (*WWR* 3:23–28), Judith Kent Green argues that *Vestiges of the Natural History of Creation* is worth examining as "representative of the kind of material available to Whitman" before the publication of Darwin's *Origin of Species* in 1859. Her point is well taken. In addition to juxtaposing passages from Chambers and Whitman, if Green had undertaken to summarize Chambers's evolutionary theory further the article would have been even more useful. Robert J. Scholnick provides such a summary in " 'The Password Primeval': Whitman's Use of Science in 'Song of Myself' " (*SAR*, pp. 385–425). Chambers influenced Edward Livingston Youmans, whom Scholnick cogently describes as an important source "for Whitman's understanding of his most important scientific idea, evolution."

Whitman has influenced "modern Chinese literature, which looks to the May Fourth Student Movement in 1919 as its starting point," explains Xilao Li in "Walt Whitman in China" (*WWR* 3:1–8). The article provides a chronology of Whitman's fortunes in China, which have been consistently linked with the tumultuous political history of that country. The Cultural Revolution (1966–69) was a disaster period, but more recently Whitman has been translated, absorbed, studied, and warmly welcomed by the Chinese people. In Germany, despite his self-revisions, Whitman helped Thomas Mann toward a more democratic and fluid sexual politics. Such is the view of Robert K. Martin in the sensitively written "Walt Whitman and Thomas Mann" (*WWR* 4:1–6). Whitman also influenced Bram Stoker, who first wrote the poet in glowing terms in 1872, visited Camden three times between 1884 and 1887, and called Whitman "Master." Whitman was a good father figure to the novelist, speculates Dennis Perry, but one who also reinforced his obsession with the deliciousness of death, as Perry explains in "Whitman's Influence on Stoker's *Dracula*" (*WWR* 3:29–35). Still another author influenced by Whitman is the American Communist Michael Gold, explains Richard Tuerk in "Michael Gold on Walt Whitman" (*WWR* 3:16–23). "For Gold, Whitman represented the Masses," but he ignored "Whitman's emphasis on individualism as well as the more conservative aspects of his political theorizing." An influence study of more general interest is Hugh Witemeyer's "Clothing the American Adam: Pound's Tailoring of Walt Whitman" (*Ezra Pound Among Poets*, pp. 81–105). The early Pound identified with Whitman's nativism, though he objected to Whitman's provincialism and formal laziness. Then for nearly three decades Pound ignored the poet he had earlier considered his only spiritual father among preceding American poets. With the *Pisan Cantos*, begun in 1945 during his imprisonment, Pound strongly identified with "the good grey poet of the Camden years, an American voice unheeded by America, an aging voice whose utterance must come to terms with infirmity and death." The later Pound no longer needed "to stress the superiority of his cultural tailoring." He needed, rather, "to assert his essential American identity with Whitman." Witemeyer's engaging essay contains generous citations of other approaches to the Whitman-Pound relationship.

iii. Dickinson

***a.* Bibliography, Editing.** Dickinson bibliography is currently in good shape, which probably accounts for the paucity of news here. William White, however, provides two useful bibliographies of books and pamphlets, articles and parts of books, reviews, theses, and creative tributes (*DicS* 57:41–45, 59:1–13). There were two new editions of a minute portion of the canon. In a visually elegant coffee-table book, *Emily Dickinson: Lives of a Poet* (Braziller), Christopher Benfey reprints 35 poems, introduced by a longish essay in which he minimizes our knowledge of the poet's biography and implies that Dickinson criticism is still in its infancy. Also visually elegant but more scholarly is R. W. Franklin's edition of *The Master Letters of Emily Dickinson* (Amherst), which includes facsimiles of these problematic texts. Franklin revises the dates of the second and third letters in the three-part sequence and, even more to the point, reverses their order. This new order violates the psychological logic of the narrative, and I am not persuaded that Franklin's argument is definitive.

b. **Biography.** This year there were many readings of Dickinson's poems within the context of her life, though there was no work of purely biographical interest. Two critical biographies deserve special notice here, one of them a book whose biographical focus is strongest in its opening chapters and the other a series of chapters in a book on Dickinson, Plath, and Rich. Both are discussed in the next section.

c. **Criticism: General.** Cynthia Griffin Wolff provides a stimulating and controversial reading of Dickinson's life that is especially good on the background of her parents' lives and on their influence on her self-conception (*Emily Dickinson*, Knopf). There is a fascinating reading of their courtship letters, coupled with a brilliant interpretation of Edward's negative response to his father's religious mania. Less persuasive is Wolff's emphasis on Dickinson's supposed lack of eye contact with her mother as an infant. Even less persuasive from my point of view is Wolff's nomination of Judge Otis Lord as Dickinson's Master. Dickinson is somewhat de-eroticized in Wolff's presentation of her (evidently I am comparing her conception of Dickinson to my own), but the treatment of Dickinson's separation anxieties is strongly motivated and generally compelling. All in all, Wolff's opening biographical chapters (pp. 3–136) provide a rich account of some of the relationships that mattered most to the poet.

The critical power of *Emily Dickinson* derives less from Wolff's use of a biographical frame to interpret the poems than from her steady, almost obsessional attention to Dickinson's religious anxieties. Wolff locates Dickinson's poetic identity in her struggle with God, conceived as a brutally fierce adversary intent on ravishing the human spirit. Extending Allen Tate's important 1932 essay, Wolff argues that Dickinson's poetic mission was to represent the Puritan tradition in its dying hours and to construct a formidable critique of its central myths. Within this framework there are many readings that I find eccentric; yet Wolff captures the ferocity and some of the peacefulness of Dickinson's religious life—there is an autumnal conversion. She conveys the epic power of Dickinson's experience and discovers in her "wrestle with God" a poet more broadly representative of American religious heroism than we had supposed.

In *My Life a Loaded Gun* (pp. 15–94), Paula Bennett takes on the formidable task of linking Dickinson's artistic development to a dynamic model of her emotional life. Bennett's analysis depends on a harsh assessment of the poems Dickinson wrote before September 1861 (her "terror—since September") and on the accuracy of Johnson's dating of the poems, to which he himself assigned only provisional status. Perhaps because of the amount of material Bennett is compressing into a relatively short space—Dickinson's rebellion against her culture's definition of female usefulness during her adolescence; repeated rejections in love; repeated bouts of severe depression; a fantasy marriage—there are links in this argument that do not stand up under close scrutiny. For example, because Bennett's Dickinson is staunchly female-identified, her notion that Dickinson saved herself through a fantasy marriage with the Master is imperfectly motivated. Nevertheless, there is a shrewd discussion of Dickinson's relationship to her mother, a superb reading of the Master letters, and discussion of the Kate Scott Turner Anthon relationship that is infinitely superior to Rebecca Patterson's treatment of this theme in *The Riddle of Emily Dickinson* (1951). Whatever my specific reservations about the particulars of the argument, I found these chapters deeply engaging and consistently stimulating.

Also concerned with the relationship between Dickinson's life and work is Jerome Loving in the somewhat elliptical *Emily Dickinson: The Poet on the Second Story* (Cambridge). The second story to which the title alludes is both the poet's second-story bedroom in "Her Master's House" and the story of her art, in which she mastered her world of experience by distancing herself from it. The second story is organized, Loving contends, by Dickinson's fidelity to "the mind alone." "No American voice," he insists, "is more disembodied than Dickinson's." Dickinson's distrust of nature and of the body is viewed as motivating her passionate engagement with the erotic experience of her brother and sister-in-law. More generally, Dickinson is described as living through "surrogates," though Loving also places some qualified credence in the "flesh-and-blood" crisis of the Master letters. The biographical analysis is less impressive than Loving's ability to place Dickinson squarely at the center of our culture's definitions of failure and success. Effectively challenging the belief that Dickinson's poetry is culturally marginal, Loving's analysis is consistently enlivened by and indeed depends crucially on references to other American writers, especially the high canonical male authors of the 19th century.

A less complicated Dickinson is present in *Emily Dickinson: Looking to Canaan* by John Robinson (Faber). One of several books I reviewed this year designed to make Dickinson more accessible to undergraduates, this volume is part of the Faber Student Guides series, which also includes books on Beckett, Pound, T. S. Eliot, Seamus Heaney, and Edward Thomas. As the subtitle indicates, Robinson tends to view Dickinson as escaping from history and seeking to rid herself of time. Yet he reveals a satiric, breezy Dickinson, defined by her Protestant "aloofness to worldly things." Robinson has an exceptionally attractive prose style, his facts are accurate, and many of the readings are deftly insightful. Much less skillful is Donna Dickenson's *Emily Dickinson* (Berg), which is designed to bridge the gap between scholarly and popular discussions of the poet. The book is based on the mistaken assumption that little is known about Dickinson's life. The author claims to treat Dickinson as a professional poet who failed only to publish her poems rather than as a lovelorn recluse. Predictably, much of the book rehashes biographical clichés. A much better book that is also intended to appeal "to the general reader as well as to the student or academic specialist" is Helen McNeil's *Emily Dickinson* (Pantheon). Her most original insights depend on the Derridean distinction between writing and speech, as described in her fourth and fifth chapters ("The Spoken and the Written," "A Woman Writing Herself"). McNeil discriminates nicely between Dickinson's heuristic written language and the socially gendered conventions of 19th-century feminine discourse. Rather consistently, she argues for "Dickinson's deep acceptance of her sex." The love poems are slighted in her analysis.

As if to refute McNeil's argument that Dickinson distinguished sharply between oral and written self-expression, Cristanne Miller suggests that "Dickinson sees her poetry as a form of speech, as articulate expression meant for others as well as for herself," in "A Letter Is a Joy of Earth: Dickinson's Communication with the World" (*Legacy* n.s. 1:29–39). Thus it is puzzling to read several paragraphs later that "from her early youth, Dickinson thought of language's power in connection primarily with its written form. . . . What is written . . . has a fuller potential of meaning than what is said." Or this: "The distance between pen and voice also makes the language itself seem more powerful because it becomes more absolute." More consistently, Miller suggests that "writing presumes communication" and that "the metaphor of poet as letter writer aptly characterizes Dickinson's art," in that Dickinson's poems effect "controlled intimacy," as do her letters. The article strikes a fine balance between leaning on the obscurity of Dickinson's style and leaning on its clarity. In a telling phrase, Miller calls her "oracularly chatty." There is a fascinating discussion of the formal poetic features of Dickinson's letters and of her use of poems in letters. Miller also addresses Dickinson's habit of writing letters to people with whom she might otherwise have spoken. All in all, this is a piece that opens up important questions about the comparatively neglected relationship between Dickinson's poems and letters.

Suzanne Juhasz's "Writing Doubly: Emily Dickinson and Female Experience" is another article from the *Legacy* special issue on Dickinson (1:5–15), whose editors are to be commended for its exceptional merit. For Juhasz, as for other feminist critics, writing doubly represents "the ontological situation of women in patriarchal culture." Dickinson's speaker, Juhasz shows, "experiences conflicting definitions of appropriate behavior": that of "the dominant culture" and that of "the muted female world." The latter is "grander and more imaginative." In Dickinson's poetry these two worlds "overlap and are experienced simultaneously." The ambiguity of Dickinson's poetry, Juhasz believes, depends on this conjunction of different systems of value. Joanne Dobson, in " 'The Invisible Lady': Dickinson and Conventions of the Female Self" (*Legacy* 1:41–55), is also concerned with Dickinson's ambivalent response to conservative 19th-century values. She examines Dickinson's little girl and wife personae within the context of gendered stereotypes in popular poetry and novels. The argument is well documented for the poems discussed but leaves somewhat less clear how thoroughgoing the influence of conservative cultural values on Dickinson is perceived to be. Gertrude Reif Hughes, however, contends that "female submissiveness was spectacularly uncongenial to Dickinson's absolutist temper." In "Subverting the Cult of Domesticity: Emily Dickinson's Critique of Women's Work" (*Legacy* 1:17–28), Dickinson is described as obeying the letter of the cult in her outer life but defying its spirit in her poetry. This split between Dickinson's biographical and textual selves is too easy and is not justified by an unpersuasive reading of the Master letters as "strikingly . . . unsubmissive." Hughes is on surer ground when she describes Dickinson's re-empowerment of traditionally female activities such as sewing and horticulture in her art.

Joan Burbick focuses on Dickinson's social class as well as on her gender in "Emily Dickinson and the Economics of Desire" (*AL* 58: 361–78). Initially, Burbick seeks to show that Dickinson's poems "both mimic and deprecate the mercantilist vision of her social class." Subsequently, however, Burbick argues that Dickinson's poems accurately describe the effects "of a system of restraint endemic to female sexuality in the nineteenth century," which effectively eliminates the category of social class from her analysis. Nevertheless, Burbick establishes a powerful model for categorizing Dickinson's attitudes toward pleasure, toward deprivation, and toward the "spectres of regulation [that] stalk the poetry." Especially compelling is her description of the Dickinson who was a consummate consumer of sexual pleasure.

Romantic theories of the sublime provide a more abstract context for two essays from *The American Sublime*. The more accessible essay is by Gary Lee Stonum. In "Emily Dickinson's Calculated Sublime" (pp. 101–29), he writes that "unlike Whitman or Melville, who are fascinated by the indefinite, Dickinson usually prefers an accurate count to a wild surmise." "Dickinson and the Haunting of the Self" by Helen Regeiro Elam (pp. 83–99) employs a more specialized vocabulary to show that the sublime for Dickinson "is always a negative moment." In "'An Exchange of Territory': Dickinson's Fascicle 27" (*ESQ* 32:55–67), William Doreski argues that the arrangement of Dickinson's fascicles is linguistic as well as topical. The approach is promising and the subject an important one, but I have yet to see a close study of a Dickinson fascicle that seemed to me to illuminate the sequence as sequence. Despite the originality of its methodology, this article is no exception. An essay by me that would have been more useful had it appeared earlier is "The Second Act: Emily Dickinson's Orphaned Persona," pp. 159–69, in *Nineteenth-*

Century Women Writers of the English-Speaking World, ed. Rhoda B. Nathan (Greenwood). A conference volume published under the auspices of Hofstra University, this collection draws on work originally presented in late 1980. I examine the relationship between childhood bereavement and gender anxiety in Dickinson's life and work, with passing glances at Dickinsonian nostalgia for an undivided self.

***d.* Criticism: Individual Works.** An article that would be strengthened by references to the appropriate criticism, to say nothing of better proofreading in the case of the title, is Phillip Stambovsky's "Emily Dickson's 'The Last Night That She Lived': Explorations of a Witnessing Spirit" (*CP* 19:87–93). The poem is praised as "a study of the psychology of witnessing death." Katherine A. Monteiro effectively places her analysis of "Dickinson's 'Victory Comes Late' " (*Expl* 44:30–32) in a religious rather than a sexual context. She links "Victory" to religious conversion and to the tragedy of the Civil War. There is a nice juxtaposition of one of Dickinson's letters on the battlefield death of the local hero Frazer Stearns with the poem's image of a belated and therefore futile gift to the dying spirit. Addressing "No other can reduce / Our mortal consequence," which David Porter has called "the most impacted of all Dickinson poems," Douglas Novich Leonard offers an alternative reading in "Pictureless Trope: A Dickinson Experiment" (*DicS* 57:28–34). The poem's most cryptic lines have to do with God's estimate of human worth. Leonard's belief that the poem is a "bold experiment . . . without image" is buttressed by his analysis of two clearer previous drafts of the poem which support a more optimistic reading. Leonard calls the final version "succinct," but whatever the poet's intended meaning Porter's "impacted" still holds. Unfortunately, this interesting article is marred by recurring irregularities in the house style of *Dickinson Studies* that are distracting to readers and unfair to authors.

***e.* Affinities and Influences.** In "Reaching Lonely Heights: Sarah Orne Jewett, Emily Dickinson, and Female Initiation" (*CLQ* 22: 75–82), Carol J. Singley suggests that both Jewett and Dickinson describe initiation experiences that are socially alienating. In this they reject the conventions of woman's fiction as reconstructed by Nina Baym. Both Jewett and Dickinson favor nature over capitalism and patriarchy, internalize male power, and derive spiritual insights from their social isolation. This skillful comparison illuminates the social values of both writers. Size is associated with patriarchal abstractions by Fred Miller Robinson in "Strategies of Smallness: Wallace Stevens and Emily Dickinson" (*WSJour* 10:27–35). Smallness signifies an appropriate finitude. Both poets are viewed as disciplining an Emersonian theme, in their emphasis on "the large strength of the small particular." While still in high school Robert Frost was drawn to Emily Dickinson and sustained his interest in her poetry throughout his career. But it was Dickinson's way of "chuckling at trouble, or seeming to" that captured Frost's deepest attention, according to Scott Donaldson in "Frost, Dickinson, and the Strategy of Evasion" (*CP* 19:107–16). Ultimately the essay is less concerned with the Frost-Dickinson relationship than with Frost's uncanny ability to project his loaded gun onto others, seemingly unawares. Dickinson's supposed concern with "the superiority of intuition over rationality for comprehending the mystical experience figures prominently in Roethke's later poems," according to Robert D. Newman in "Emily Dickinson's Influence on Roethke" (*DicS* 57:38–40). The exposition is restricted to "A Light Exists in Spring" and "In Evening Air." In "The Possible Background of 3 Dickinson Poems" (*DicS* 57: 35–38), John R. Byers argues for the influence of *Hamlet* on "The Soul selects her own Society," of a hymn by James Montgomery on "Prayer is the little implement," and of *The House of the Seven Gables* on "I Heard a Fly buzz—when I died." The parallel between the latter poem and the deathbed scene of Judge Pyncheon is compelling. In "'Engine Against th' Almightie': Emily Dickinson and Prayer" (*ESQ* 32:153–72), Dorothy Huff Oberhaus seeks to show that Dickinson's prayer poems can be illuminated by the context of 17th-century devotional poetry. As might be expected, this context tends to make Dickinson sound more humble than she was, but the essay is well researched and on the whole well balanced. Most of the examples are drawn from Herbert.

"A woman's decision to become a writer has historically involved some form of renunciation," argues Suzanne Juhasz in "Renunciation Transformed, the Dickinson Heritage: Emily Dickinson and Margaret Atwood" (*WS* 12:251–70). Juhasz cogently points to Dickinson's need for boundaries that she herself establishes. Contemporary women poets such as Atwood are described as less willing to sacrifice their need for dynamic social relationships. Paul Scott Derrick links Dickinson's poetry to Heidegger's philosophy of language in "Emily

Dickinson, Martin Heidegger and the Poetry of Dread" (*WHR* 40: 27–38). The exposition is lucid and sensitive to the distinction between fear (which is focused) and dread (which is unfocused). But the analysis is marred by an incomplete reading of his central text ("There came a Wind like a Bugle") and by the absence of references to any critics other than Tate and John Crowe Ransom. Another sensitively written piece is by Marianne Boruch, but the focus of "Dickinson Descending" is not particularly clear (*GaR* 41:863–77). In a general sense Boruch is concerned with the response of others to Dickinson. In passing, she mentions Dickinson's importance to such writers as Rich, Ginsberg, Moore, Frost, Berryman, Sexton, and Roethke. Boruch also discusses some of the books and generic conventions to which the poet herself responded, such as Hugh Conway's best-selling novel, *Called Back.*

A good place to end is with Lawrence Buell's highly original and formidably well-documented study of Dickinson in *New England Literary Culture* (pp. 105–36). Buell uses Dickinson as a kind of touchstone for the New England poets such as Longfellow and Emerson who were her precursors and contemporaries. He shows with beautiful clarity that "writing doubly" was also the project of the Fireside Poets and others now forgotten, some of whom deserve to be remembered. Dickinson's brand of "mingled deviance and deference" is described as more "spectacular and conflicted" than that of let us say James Russell Lowell. But for both conventional and unconventional male and female poets writing before the American Civil War, there was a crucial tension "between the bent of private passion and the norms that one was expected to accept and to use one's art to uphold." In its focus on the conflict between private passion and social convention, *New England Literary Culture* is thus empowered by a mighty theme. This theme links Whitman and Dickinson, and for both poets organizes much of the best criticism I encountered this year.

University of Washington

6. Mark Twain

Hamlin Hill

In 1986 most of the celebrating of Mark Twain's 150th and Huck Finn's hundredth birthdays was over, although a substantial number of items on *Huck* appeared. Louis J. Budd surveys the carnage of these birthday parties in detail in "Huck at 100, How Old Is Huckleberry Finn?" (DLB *Yearbook 1985*, pp. 12–19). But the parties were successful enough that there are already plans, in both Hartford and Elmira, for baking a cake for Hank Morgan and *A Connecticut Yankee in King Arthur's Court* in 1989.

i. Biography

The year was one with no major, book-length biographical studies. Resa A. Willis, "'Quietly and Steadily': Olivia Langdon Clemens' Commonplace Book" (*MTJ* 24:17–20), describes the volume which Olivia kept from 1863 until 1870 to preserve quotations she thought significant. Willis switches from a scrutiny of the 108-page commonplace book to Olivia's mother's diary, which recounts Livy's recovery from her teenage neurasthenia. William Baker surveyed Ohio newspapers from 1865 to 1885 for references to Mark Twain. In "Mark Twain and the Shrewd Ohio Audiences" (*ALR* 18[1985]:14–30) he describes over 30 reviews of lectures and hundreds of brief notes, quotations, and allusions. The lecture reviews—in 1869, 1871–72, and 1884–85 (with George Washington Cable)—were almost always favorable. Earl F. Briden undertook a similar survey of Twain's lectures in Rhode Island in "Mark Twain's Rhode Island Lectures" (*MTJ* 24:35–40)—five in all, in 1869 (two), 1875, 1876, and 1884.

The most tantalizing article of the year was Carl Dolmetsch's "Twain and Freud: Vienna's Odd Couple?" (*William & Mary Alumni Gazette Magazine* 54:8–12). Dolmetsch fills in the background of the late '90s in Vienna, when Twain and Freud were both residents, and pinpoints Freud's attendance at a Mark Twain lecture on 1 February 1898. He conjectures, further, that the two might have met a month earlier, on 5 January, at the premier of "The New Ghetto," a play by Theodore Herzel, who knew and sent complimentary tickets to both men. Robert D. Warth, "Mark Twain and the Gorky Affair" (*SAQ* 85:32–39), also fleshes out facts in the 1906 confrontation between radicalism and gentility and includes extracts from Twain's unpublished "A Cloud-Burst of Calamities," a feeble defense of his actions.

Finally, Doris Lanier, "Mark Twain's Georgia Angel Fish" (*MTJ* 24:5–16), fills in the portrait of Frances Nunnally, who met Mark Twain on board ship to England for the honorary degree in 1907. She became one of the senior Angel Fish in the Aquarium Club. Lanier provides details of Frances's biography, quotes extensively from the 41 letters Twain wrote her, and includes new photographs of Frances. Curiously, Lanier insists that the Angel Fish relationship was completely innocent, though she speculates that Frances's father once received an invitation to visit Stormfield in order "to assure this Southern gentleman that there was nothing improper about his [Twain's] relationship with his wife and daughter"!

ii. Editions

Sean Peter Kirst reprints "A Wonderful Potato" in "By Mark Twain?" (*ALR* 18[1985]:69–72), a paragraph about a crossbreed between a yam and a Canada thistle, attributed to Twain in the Fredonia *Censor* on 14 June 1871. (The same paragraph was printed in the Ohio papers surveyed by Baker, above.) John Seelye's introduction to the Penguin Classics *Adventures of Tom Sawyer* focuses on the intricate weaving of melodrama, fantasy, and burlesque Sunday school literature throughout the novel.

With an amazing amount of popular press coverage Robert Sattelmeyer presents "How Nancy Jackson Married Kate Wilson" (*MissR* 10:97–112), the complete text of a fragment from the early 1900s in which a girl, compelled to masquerade as a man, is forced into a marriage with a pregnant girl. The fragment ends abruptly—but not soon enough—with the birth of a boy.

Vic Doyno has edited the 1907 text of *Christian Science* (Prometheus), making one of the most provocative and neglected of the later works readily accessible to readers.

In the strictest sense *A Union Catalog of Clemens Letters*, ed. Paul Machlis (Calif.), is not an edition. But it is a major research tool which deserves to stand with Gale's *Plots and Characters*, Gribben's *Mark Twain's Library*, and Tenney's *Mark Twain: A Reference Guide* as an indispensable reference volume. It is a complete listing of over 10,000 letters by Clemens, arranged alphabetically by addressee in the printed volume and by date and location of writing in microfiche supplements. The microfiche are of course awkward to use, and additional letters will swell the listing (a hundred letters came to light in 1987, as described by Diane Swanbrow in "The Lost Legacy of Mark Twain," *Los Angeles Times Magazine*, 10 May 1987, pp. 16–19, 32). But to know where Clemens was on practically every day of his adult life and to whom he wrote provides Twain students with a scholarly reference work of incalculable value.

iii. General Interpretations

In "Reporting Reality: Mark Twain's Short Stories" (*The Nineteenth-Century American Short Story*, pp. 103–20), Andrew Hook argues that the vitality, innovation, and formal looseness of the short story make it the typical American art form. But Hook finds in Mark Twain's short fiction "a measure of disappointment"; his focus is, improbably, on *The Mysterious Stranger* and "A True Story," which might explain his problem. Marvin Fisher's "'Do Not Bring Your Dog': Mark Twain on the Manners of Mourning" (in his *Continuities*, pp. 106–25) argues that, from the Tomb of Adam sketch in *Innocents Abroad*, Twain attacked "the false piety, the social pretense, and the blatant hypocrisy that typified every subsequent funeral in his work." In Huck's voice Twain finally found "the means of exposing excessive gentility and hypocritical piety without exposing himself."

Tjebbe A. Westendorp focuses on the hoax and tall tale in "'He Backed Me into a Corner and Blockaded Me with a Chair': Strategies of Mark Twain's Literary Campaigns" (*DQR* 16:22–36). Mark Twain's strength purportedly "lies in the intelligent manipulation of his audience by the use of a rich variety of narrative modes, at the center of which lies his obsessive love of impersonation." Harold H. Kolb, Jr., refines the distinction between "mere" humor and the "moral" humor which William Dean Howells kept attributing to Mark Twain. Kolb proposes in "Mere Humor and Moral Humor: The Example of Mark Twain" (*ALR* 19:52–64) that low comedy dominated the early works and a heavy-handed morality dominated the later ones. Only in the middle '70s to late '80s did Mark Twain achieve the necessary harmonious balance between the two extremes.

Four influence studies linked Mark Twain with other writers. Alan Gribben, in " 'That Pair of Spiritual Derelicts': The Poe-Twain Relationship" (*PoeS* 18[1985]:17–21), charts a broad spectrum of parallels, from specific indebtnesses of Twain's to mutually congenial themes and motifs—doubles, ratiocination, and dark irony, for example. Hana Wirth-Nesher outlines convincingly both the parallels in *Huck Finn* and *Great Expectations* and also the American and English cultural differences which make the two protagonists and the two novels strikingly different ("The Literary Orphan as National Hero: Huck and Pip," *DSA* 15:259–73).

William Bedford Clark's essay "Twain and Faulkner: Miscegenation and the Comic Muse" (*Faulkner and Humor*, pp. 97–109) argues that Mark Twain was unable to make "good-natured" humor of the subject of miscegenation in *Pudd'nhead Wilson*, as Faulkner could in *Go Down, Moses*. Faulkner possessed "an acceptance of the absurdities and contradictions of the human experience and an urge to revel in them for their own sake"; on the other hand, the "laughter of *Pudd'nhead Wilson* did not signal a valid exorcism; it provided only a temporary evasion." Joe Sanders compares *Tom Sawyer*, *Huck Finn*, and *Psion* in "Huck, Cat, and/or Civilization: Joan D. Vinge's *Psion* as 'Juvenile' Fiction" (*Extrapolation* 27:76–83), but the article is devoted almost exclusively to the 1982 novel.

Beverly David's *Mark Twain and His Illustrators* (Whitston) carries us through the novice author's first encounters with book publication and ignorance of the importance of illustrations to the strategist who likened the marketing of his works to the military campaign and chose and approved or vetoed the pictures that accompanied his texts.

iv. Individual Works Through 1885

Forrest G. Robinson explores "the fundamental instability of the consciousness" of the narrator in "Patterns of Consciousness in *The Innocents Abroad*" (*AL* 58:46–63), arguing that it is a complex narrative strategy rather than a flaw in technique. The narrator clings "to the illusion of innocence in order that it may be periodically, almost ritually, lost and then retrieved again." Herbert A. Wisbey, Jr., describes "Mark Twain on Petrarch: More Quarry Farm Marginalia" (*MTJ* 24:21–23) from Anna Brownell Jameson's *Memoirs of the Loves of the Poets* (1866). Mark Twain's outrage at both Petrarch and Laura probably provided the inspiration for the late addition of an attack on Petrarch to chapter 19 of *Innocents.*

Laurence McClain has written a masterful textual history and bibliographical description of the unpublished manuscript " 'A Murder, a Mystery, and a Marriage': Mark Twain's Hannibal in Transition" (*LCUT* 37:55–75). The manuscript, from 1876, has echoes of basic motifs and provides, McClain argues, the fulcrum in the evolution of depictions of Hannibal from "romanticized characterizations" to a "place of stasis, sloth, and mindless conformity."

Thomas A. Maik argues in "The Village in *Tom Sawyer*: Myth and Reality" (*ArQ* 42:157–64) along the familiar lines of Fetterley and Towers that the citizens of St. Petersburg are filled with "lies, smugness, hypocrisy, human cruelty, murder, and greed" (though not, I assume, necessarily in that order). In "American Myth in Disguise: Fathers and Sons in *The Prince and the Pauper*" (*AL* 58:203–16), John Daniel Stahl delineates complex parallels in father-son relationships in *Tom* and *Huck* as well as *The Prince and the Pauper.* Stahl suggests that the focus on natural character, the "rags to riches" motif, orphanhood, and the need to define identity in terms of indebtness to and independence from fathers and father figures makes the middle work characteristically American. In "Tom, Huck, and the Young Pilot: Twain's Quest for Authority" (*MissQ* 39:3–19), John E. Bassett treats *Tom, Huck* (in the first sixteen chapters), and "Old Times on the Mississippi" as a "single text" in which youthful protagonists seek strategies for moving into the adult world. Their paths and solutions vary, but their quests are similar.

It appears to be fashionable to examine the duplicity and dissimulation in *Tom Sawyer* and *Huckleberry Finn* in plot, narrative strategy, and reader response. The most thought-provoking and complex of the arguments is Forrest G. Robinson's *In Bad Faith: The Dynamics of Deception in Mark Twain's America* (Harvard). A sophisticated analysis of both *Tom Sawyer* and *Huck* (with generous reference to later works), it builds upon James M. Cox and George Carrington. Robinson argues that "Tom has collaborated with his neighbors in 'bad faith,' the reciprocal deception of self and other, generally in the denial of departures from public codes of correct behavior.... This delicate equipoise of threats to the collective peace of mind would collapse were it not for the fact that bad faith is the ruling characteristic in the social dynamics of the village." Huck, on the other hand, "retreats to bad faith out of the fear of fully expressing, even to himself, what it is that he has seen. As the result, he is as helpless to acquiesce in the culture's bad faith as he is to draw himself out of it; thus he wavers between contrary, incompatible states of mind." Robinson's subtle and sophisticated argument is too complex to summarize adequately here; but special mention should be made of his extensive analyses of Sid Sawyer and Colonel Sherburn.

John E. Bassett is also interested in the strategies of disguise, duplicity, and deception in "*Life on the Mississippi*: Being Shifty in a New Country" (*WAL* 21:39–45). Ranging broadly though briefly through other works, Bassett then focuses on the travel book in his title, to argue that "if sham and falsehood are the villains of the piece, disguise and performance remain the heroes."

James L. Kastely limits himself to *Huck* in "The Ethics of Self-Interest: Narrative Logic in *Huckleberry Finn*" (*NCF* 40:412–37). The middle section of the novel, between chapters 15 and 31, explores "seriously an ethics of self-interest." Huck's and Jim's attempts to establish a community of equals is constantly undermined by the shadow of slavery, which compels Huck to use duplicity and disguise in his own self-interest. He breaks this mold when he helps Mary Jane Wilks, but he is doomed to fail in his attempt when Tom returns to reduce the heroism to farce. All of the essays in Harold Bloom's collection *Mark Twain* (Chelsea House) are reprints except for Cleo McNelly Kearns's "The Limits of Semiotics in *Huckleberry Finn*" (pp. 207–22). Jim attempts to transcend semiotic constraints "on behalf of a social and fraternal concept of liberation: Huck seeks to escape them on behalf of an individual and self-authorizing freedom." Kearns's analysis of signs in their relation to "money, prediction and textual interpretation" provides the central thesis of this challenging analysis.

Tim William Machan argues, in "The Symbolic Narrative of *Huckleberry Finn*" (*ArQ* 12:131–40), that the polar opposites of River (freedom) and shore (convention) break down after the Duke and Dolphin board the raft. Prior to this point in the novel, "the narrative reflects an unequivocal world in which the dangers of convention can be avoided and the rewards of freedom obtained." Afterward, moral relativism takes over and "Huck's goal of freedom . . . gradually disappears."

Henry B. Rule provides a short survey of recent bannings of *Huck* in "A Brief History of the Censorship of *The Adventures of Huckleberry Finn*" (*LJHum* 12:9–18), concentrating on the 1957

New York City and the 1982 Fairfax County, Virginia, furors.

Two studies focused on the physical aspects of *Huck*. Douglas Anderson takes a sophisticated critical look at a handful of E. W. Kemble's illustrations for the first edition in "Reading the Pictures in *Huckleberry Finn*" (*ArQ* 42:101–20). He notes adroitly ways that the drawings underscore, complement, and add symbolic levels to the text itself. While we wait (and wait and wait) for the Iowa/California textual apparatus to appear, Victor Fischer provides some insights in "A New Edition of *Huck Finn*" (DLB *Yearbook 1985*, pp. 23–27). Fischer summarizes the editorial process involved in establishing the text of the Iowa/California edition and provides examples of two brief restorations from the manuscript. This is a tantalizing glimpse, but we must take the complete text on faith until the entire editorial package is in print.

v. Individual Works After 1885

Possibly the fireworks for the centennial of *A Connecticut Yankee* are already beginning; three of the four post-1885 items published in 1986 deal with this novel. Lesley C. Kordecki analyzes narrative voices which alternate between 19th-century slang, formal modern language, and Malorian prose. In "Twain's Critique of Malory's Romance: *Forma tractandi* and *A Connecticut Yankee*" (*NCL* 41:329–48), Kordecki traces "Mark Twain's admiration of, inquiry into, and even competition with some of the tenets of medieval narrative," but concludes that his attempts to parody this mode ultimately fail because "his sensibilities were antithetical to Romance." William J. Collins, "Hank Morgan in the Garden of Forking Paths: *A Connecticut Yankee in King Arthur's Court* as Alternative History" (*MFS* 32:109–14), says that the novel was the first major work of science fiction to travel backward in time rather than into the future, and that Mark Twain encountered most of the dilemmas and explored one of the solutions: alternative history. On the other hand, David Ketterer argues in "'Professor Baffin's Adventures' by Max Adeler: The Inspiration for *A Connecticut Yankee in King Arthur's Court*?" (*MTJ* 24:24–34) that the plot and phrasing in the novel strongly suggest Mark Twain's indebtness to Adler, as does the evasiveness of his denial of the charge of plagiarism in the New York *World* of 12 January 1890 (reprinted in the essay).

William Coyle looks at some of the later fantasies in "Mark

Twain as Fantasist" in his collection of essays *Aspects of Fantasy* (Greenwood), pp. 175–80. Coyle believes that the later fables fail—particularly *Three Thousand Years Among the Microbes*—because Twain could not successfully focus on one concept. Satire intruded, he delighted too much in "plot machinery" rather than character, and memories of Hannibal undercut the fantastic impulse.

Possibly 1986 was the eye of the storm between the activities of 1984 and 1985, which Louis J. Budd authoritatively covered in these pages, and the impending celebrations scheduled for 1988 and 1989. Problems involving many kinds of narrative unreliability dominated the criticism, but in general it was a placid spell in Mark Twain studies.

Texas A&M University

7. Henry James

Richard A. Hocks

Like a huge magnet James continues to attract massive scholarship of every stripe and hue, from Adeline Tintner's "old-fashioned" source/analogue studies (a banner year, even for her) to the most theoretical day-after-tomorrow analysis. I detect a new thematic interest in James's "aestheticizing of capitalism," as James Cox puts it, and more new psychoanalytic readings abound. *The Henry James Review* with its many articles and admirable collection of new *Portrait of a Lady* essays is now so central to James studies I can hardly believe it began only in 1979. Parallel studies probably exceed any other type of work on James, regardless of formal category. Together with all who read this chapter, I too greatly miss and commend Robert Gale's high intelligence and efficiency with this material.

i. Editions, Collections, Biographical Studies

Leon Edel and Lyall H. Powers's *The Complete Notebooks of Henry James* (Oxford) dramatically supplants the classic 1947 Oxford edition by Matthiessen and Murdock. The expanded volume includes all extant notebooks, sketches, scenarios, dictations, and diaries that "escaped accidental loss or intentional destruction." The editorial apparatus, in sharp contrast to Matthiessen/Murdock, stresses not the creative process by which notes evolved into finished novels and tales, but the assumption that the notebooks are "primarily historical, biographical, geographical, and psychological." The editors also identify many persons hidden behind James's initials. The guiding principle, articulated in Edel's introduction, is that James's inveterate note-taking is both a form of art "endowed with the dignity of James's language" and "the reachings-out of a lonely bachelor for companionship." Edel's "Good Angel" motif (James's genius) is exquisite, and given that very emphasis I am not quite as excited by the new "Pocket Diaries," mostly reminders of James's appointments, as are the editors. But for a scholar "on whom nothing is lost" they are, like everything else, wonderfully at hand in a volume that no longer forces you to go elsewhere either for central items now out of print or else, like the "Hugh Merrow" draft, "Deathbed Dictation," or *Finer Grain* description, available only in specialized places; all is now between the covers of one elegant, copiously edited volume.

The Art of Criticism (Chicago) by William Veeder and Susan M. Griffin is the latest, and to my mind the best, available edition of representative James criticism and theory. Although a number of collections have appeared since Blackmur's venerable *Art of the Novel* (1934), this is the one of choice. The selections, nicely divided into "Practicing Novelist as Practical Critic," "Theorist on Fiction and Culture," "The Master and His Prefaces," and "Genius in Old Age," omit the *Poynton* Preface but are otherwise superior in every respect. Most important, the editors' work following each text is a true model of annotation, a mine of information, and a whole course on James's criticism quietly embedded in Veeder/Griffin's superb critical commentary. Also, I wish to pay special notice to W. R. Martin and Warren U. Ober's reprint of *The Finer Grain* (Scholars' Facsimiles). Not only is this volume newly edited and introduced, but it makes available a group of James's very finest tales—of social criticism and modern sensibility—that need to be studied and taught as a volume, like *Dubliners.* The next step is somehow to get this book into the classroom. (The two authors also collaborated this year on "Refurbishing James's 'A Light Man'" [*ArQ* 42:305–14], an Adeline Tintner-like rereading of James's early tale which argues that narrator Maximus Austin's revelatory diary parallels the other Austin's—St. Augustine's—*Confessions*, and thus, pace Leon Edel et al., he is "Light" in the good sense, not bad.)

Examining the letters and extensive unpublished diaries of Violet Hunt, Robert Secor, in "Henry James and Violet Hunt, the 'Improper Person of Babylon'" (*JML* 13:3–36), believes these documents reveal the importance of each to the other during the last decade of James's life, showing "Hunt and James settling into the roles they played for each other, roles that can also be recognized in James's fiction." The flirtatious woman writer in "The Velvet Glove" (usually thought to be Edith Wharton) may have been suggested by Hunt, who "specialized in sexual conquests of literary men," including Maugham, Wells, and Ford. James called her the "Improper Person of Babylon" because he casts her as active and involved with the battles of life while portraying himself as a "'country cousin' tending his flowers" or a "contemplative spider hanging onto the world from the thinnest of threads." Although they were good friends, James, given his own preoccupations (like his character Monteith), withheld the human sympathy she counted on when her relationship with Ford ended in disaster, and for this withdrawal she could "never quite forgive him." Secor's allusions to *The Finer Grain* tales are of interest. Finally, Adeline Tintner's "Biography and the Scholar: *The Life of Henry James*" (*Essaying Biography*, pp. 21–35), lauds Leon Edel as "Boswell" to James's "Johnson" and tells of a whole "new audience" which reads Edel "in lieu of James himself." Tintner explains lucidly the imaginative and dramatic power of Edel's *Life* as well as its "encyclopedic tissue of evidence" indespensable to any scholar. I much recommended her astute comparison of the respective pros and cons of the five-volume "quintet" and newer "definitive" Penguin versions of Edel's *Life*, and of the parallels therein to James himself.

ii. Interpretive Books

The two leading critical books of the year bespeak opposing epistemological and aesthetic assumptions. First, a real sleeper is Richard Freadman's *Eliot, James and the Fictional Self* (St. Martin's), which, unlike so many studies of familiar subjects, truly extends and transforms our understanding of the George Eliot/James issue. Freadman delves deeply into both authors' concepts of narration and character, subtly playing off their kinship and difference. He detects "tension" in Eliot's theory, greater "organicism" in James, and a certain Jamesian "anxiety of influence." But Freadman's book is likewise a profound defense of "liberal-humanism" from the attack of contemporary language theory, and much of his Eliot/James explication doubles as philosophical foundation for the validity of "individual self" and the "referential view of language." He includes global and probing analyses of *Portrait*, *Golden Bowl*, and *Wings of the Dove* matched against comparable Eliot novels. Ultimately, James, unlike Eliot, exhibits a "drift towards phenomenology . . . a less intrusive narrative persona . . . a greater dependence on metaphor and symbolism as modes of characterisation, a more unified aesthetic structure for novels, and a more reticent moral emphasis." What is quietly fine about Freadman is that, despite his allegiance to the "liberal-humanist" tradition, he himself exhibits a deep grasp of contemporary critical theory, which his mind wears lightly but thoroughly, a grasp duplicated as well by his thorough knowledge of recent James scholarship. The ideological antithesis to Freadman is Donna Przybylowicz's powerful *Desire and Repression: The Dialectic of Self and Other in the Late Works of Henry James* (Alabama), a Marxist-psychoanalytic-Lacanian analysis of a disparate group of late writings, including *The Sacred Fount*, *The Sense of the Past*, all various "*Autobiographical*" *Works*, and a number of late tales. A complex "synthesis" of contemporary theory, Przybylowicz's approach reveals James projecting his "divided self" into his work, most often denying "other" or "alterity," which is usually a name for James's own unconscious and a "discourse written without the subject's knowledge." She exhibits James's increasing "intrasubjectivity" and "dissolution of the natural-fact world" after *Maisie*, his "spatialization of time," tendency toward "decenteredness," and movement toward "expressionism" in the late writings. Even so, his "repressions," "retreats," and disguises create a "reactionary" conflict with his technical, formal radicalism. The author is to my mind best on the late nonfiction, especially *The American Scene* and the *Autobiography*, but the entire argument, despite unremitting jargon and a casserole of theorists "synthesized," does hang together. A fuller summary of this intellectually ambitious book is my review of it (*NCL* 42:116–20).

Two other worthy books illustrate from different angles the prevailing view that theme and technique interweave in James. William R. Goetz's *Henry James and the Darkest Abyss of Romance* (LSU) probes subtly the "presence of the author in his work," both fiction and nonfiction, and closely examines his maneuvers in the *Autobiography* and the *Prefaces*—which lie "on the borderline between two genres . . . and thus call for a unique employment of first-person narration." Alternatively, to avoid "fluidity of self-revelation" precludes his use of first person in ghost story or novel; yet just such "outlawed forms" are employed in *Sacred Fount* and *Turn of the Screw*, resulting in irreducible ambiguity. Despite autobiographical resonances, James's distance from Strether in *The Ambassadors* redeems him from *Sacred Fount* and the "abyss of romance," though it also leads Goetz to posit that Strether, unlike James, does not attain much or know "where he is" at the end. Goetz's study reconfirms our view that James's narrative "point of view" is elusive and complex. *Silence in Henry James* by John Auchard (Penn. State) charts James's ties to the "heritage" of "symbolism and decadence." His uses of thematic "silence"—from Newman's refusal to expose the Bellegardes to Fleda Vetch's memorable and Maggie Verver's critical silences—reveal a powerful "dialectic" between "plenum and void," "*vis negativa*" and "*vis positiva,*" all tied to the century-end mind-set of symbolism/decadence, which Auchard interprets broadly. James here, as in many books nowadays, emerges as modern and antimaterialist; silence "plays out its subtle dialectic on the edge of nothingness and sometimes on the brink of collapse." I find interesting the symbiosis drawn between Isabel Archer's "spirituality" and Osmond's decadent "decay." Like Goetz, Auchard is conceptually oriented, though also historically conscious.

Finally, S. Gorley Putt has authored *A Preface to Henry James* (Longman), one of a series designed to guide us through "characteristic difficulties" and reach "intelligent understanding and enjoyment" of the author. Its odd organization comprises "Early James," "Later James," and "Reference Section," which frame twelve chapters of ill-assorted titles and topics. Yet the text itself is an unformulaic and effective hybrid of backgrounds, commentary, and extracts; Putt is particularly keen on the extracts. No attempt is made, as with Edward Wagenknecht's recent handbook/surveys, to deal systematically with the fiction: many major works are confined to "illustrative passages," and the book itself is heavy on middle and very thin on late James. Another contrast to Wagenknecht is the virtual absence of scholarship mentioned other than Leon Edel, after whom, we hear, one "need[s] no further help in finding your way among all the other interpreters and expositors." This paperback is unusually well illustrated, however, and the generally good extracts include fine examples of James's "extravagances [of] verbal affection," such as his letter of condolence to Fanny Stevenson.

iii. Sources, Influences, Background Studies, Parallels

Few books have been more warmly awaited than Adeline R. Tintner's iconographic magnum opus, *The Museum World of Henry James* (UMI Research Press), which culminates this gifted scholar's 40 years of identifying and interpreting the use of real works of art in James's writings. The organization simulates the "departments and galeries" encountered in a museum, but the extended metaphor encompasses James's "appropriation of the accumulated art of the Western world . . . by human consciousness rather than by dollars."

Jamesians know the mosaics of this imposing study, for Tintner's articles have oft been reviewed in *ALS*, and she is now the most prolific scholar in James history with over 200 pieces. *The Museum World* allows us to stop and gaze with admiration at Tintner's special field-within-the-field of James studies, one which offers the special synergism of the art historian and literary scholar. Each reader has his favorite Tintner source or analogue, whether a Memling Flemish Madonna for "Madame de Mauves," a Velasques "Innocent X" for innocent Daisy Miller, various portraits for the spectral "Jolly Corner" alter ego, or, my personal favorites, the Poussin "Arcadian" strain in *The Ambassadors*, specific cases of the "Oriental craze that swept England" for Maggie Verver's memorable "pagoda" (an incredible fusion of symbolic imagery with real architecture) and the haunting Moreau *Oedipus and the Sphinx*, which for me stamps indelibly the John Marcher of "The Beast in the Jungle" forever. Tintner's coverage is from classical to early modern art, but her vast museum world also includes country homes and the Piazza San Marco, "outdoor museums" which analogize rooms or theaters. In a time when critical theory has moved into deconstruction, Tintner has kept the faith in source studies. However, it is important to stress her *critical* use of her subject, as in the following typical observation: "The appropriation of art changes from submission to the visual stimulation of great art in James's early fiction to the art metaphor that stems from a character's consciousness. This becomes especially true in the last four novels." Similarly, Tintner's own iconographic method gains power and depth when applied to late James, for she directs our attention to his visual surfaces in a way reminiscent of what modern art began doing at the beginning of this century, at the same time as James's late fiction.

Even her book slows not Tintner down, however, as she adds five additional items. "Hogarth's *Marriage à la Mode* and Henry James's 'A London Life'" (*JPRS* 7:69–89) probes James's concealed use of Hogarth in an emblematic way by paralleling the "progress" of the "rakish" Berringtons and rendering the tale itself in a sequence of scenes suggesting Hogarth's serial progressions. "Fiction Is the Best Revenge" (*TCW* 2[1985]:42–49) interweaves James's life and art by enumerating how four fellow women writers, Vernon Lee, Mrs. Ward, Edith Wharton, and Olive Garnett, all "took revenge," with varying degrees of affection, by portraying him in their fiction. "James's Legendary Letter to Stark Young Surfaces" (*SoQ* 24:8–16) amplifies last year's "correct version of the letter" (see *ALS 1985*, p. 104), stressing Young's actual disinterest in James's fiction. In "The Private Life of Peter Quin[t]," (*HJR* 7:2–4) Tintner teams with Leon Edel to unearth an "UR-source" for *Turn of the Screw*, Tom Taylor's *Temptation*, which James read when 11!—complete with villain "Peter Quin," a "Miles," even a "Harley Street," thereby supporting James's description of his tale as "potboiler," yet also hinting that James "rewrote" it into a classic. Finally, "The Charles Dickens Imprint on Henry James" (*ABBW* 11[August]:453–54, 486) is Tintner at her best, showing how much *Oliver Twist* "permeates" "Julia Bride" on a "metaphoric level" with Julia as a symbolic Nancy Sikes and Murray Brush as both Sikes and Fagin, thus augmenting James's own two allusions to Dickens's novel in that late tale; she even shows how a Cruikshank illustration supports her thesis.

Calling his study neither "literary criticism [n]or literary history," Michael Anesko's *"Friction with the Market": Henry James and the Profession of Authorship* (Oxford) fills the gap left by James critics who regard the relationship of text to sensitive reader as primary, without interest in the consumer, the public market, or the profession of authorship. Anesko's "sociology of literature" stakes out this neglected territory and recounts thoroughly James's complex relations with mass audience and publisher alike. His book draws heavily on publisher's records, correspondence between James and his editors, and copious documentation pertaining to literary income; and he stresses the middle period, when James himself addresses such issues fictively. What emerges is a Henry James very desirous of yet "suspicious" of a mass audience, a literary professional constantly negotiating with publishers, together with Anesko's own thesis that such "friction" could spur him to greater achievement. Especially interesting is the full discussion of the various battles and complications attending the New York Edition, which Anesko shows, surprisingly, is as "eclectic as . . . the city in which it was published." The assumptions in this study complement Edel and Powers in their new edition of *The Notebooks*, that we see James as a person with daily tasks, problems, appointments, income.

"Henry James on Eliot and Sand" (*SoAR* 51:57–68) by Sandra Corse argues well that early James felt the "appropriating power of imagination" to be a masculine trait and "acute . . . powers of observation" the more passive female quality. Yet he was fascinated by George Eliot and George Sand, who embodied both. Ironically,

James in later criticism of Eliot reverses his original aesthetic stand by suggesting she sometimes lacks "powers of observation," but praises her for subjecting her ideas to the "transforming power of imagination." George Sand, however, receives high praise "not so much in her works as in her life." A "feminine" observer of human nature, Sand nevertheless was "liberated," because she "simply assumed the rights and privileges of the male." For James, then, Eliot and especially Sand repudiate the notion "that women have distinctive mental traits that are inherent." Barbara DeMille's "Lambert Strether and the Tiger: Categories, Surfaces, and Forms in Nietzsche and Henry James" (*SoAR* 51:69–82) intelligently reexamines the intriguing parallels between Nietzsche and James. Although no evidence exists that either read the other, both used the terminology of painting to convey the inseparable link between truth and point of view, "that all perception is colored by the particular light and stance, of a particular time, and of a particular space." To DeMille, Neitzsche's intuitive man, disregarding "rhetorically intensified categories," parallels James's Strether, who "discards categories and prior conceptions." Both authors admit a "totality of vision" which includes "the violent, the sexual, and the uncontrollable passions, even the cruel." "Artistic activity," she concludes, "for both James and Nietzsche inevitably involves conversions of experience into form, but the best artist and the highest art consist in the continual formation and renewal of both the artistic perception *and* the form."

Perceptively addressing the necessity of audience to the creation and definition of self, Lynda S. Boren in "The Performing Self: Psychodrama in Austen, James and Woolf" (*CentR* 30:1–24) affirms that the three give us "novels in which drama offers analogies for life." Although most critics note James's love of theater and use of dramatic technique, "little attention has been given to how that employment of dramatic form also carries a message . . . about the fragile nature of self and the thin line separating a fulfilled existence from its opposite." Boren thinks that perhaps James invests the Governess in *Turn of the Screw* with his own recollected anxiety about his failure as playwright when she proclaims: " 'I now see how, with the word he spoke, the curtain rose on the last act of my dreadful drama and the catastrophe was precipitated.' " Since nowhere is the Governess "reflected but in a drama of her own creation," it is fitting that her "finest performance is the act of writing itself." Boren also discusses the dramatization of self in Austen's *Persuasion* and in Woolf's *To the Lighthouse*.

iv. Criticism: General Essays

James joins hands with Bellow, O'Connor, Percy, and Waugh in Joseph Hynes's "The Fading Figure in the Worn Carpet" (*ArQ* 42: 321–30), a kind of prolegomenon to the critic's need to reemphasize moral values in fiction. All five authors exhibit authentic evil and imply good as its "absence," and all are "conservative humanists, religious or not, who persist in seeking to specify a core of value." Although some Jamesians will not recognize their man (no "phenomenological acrobatics or metafictional mirror-tricks"), it is of real interest to read of James in this particular company, indeed as its progenitor. Also, "The Critical James" by Millicent Bell (*SR* 94:148–59) is a fine overview of his "poetics of fiction"; her thesis is that "we have never really caught him" because this "supposed Aristotle" of New Criticism and "organic unity" is even more pertinent to a postmodernist era. Bell's real theme, in effect, is that James's criticism constantly flies in the face of presumption, which she shows by indicating his malleability in questions of technique and his elastic evaluations of Hawthorne, George Eliot, Balzac, and Flaubert. Especially right is her observation that James "often . . . alter[s] the meaning of the traditional particulates of literary analysis to the point of reversal, rendering a hard-and-fast definition impossible."

"The Semiotics of Economic Language in James's Fiction" (*AL* 58:540–56) by Peggy McCormack treats the "complex use" and "privileged status" of economic language in James. The essay, too, is a complex linguistic/cultural/feminist analysis ("several critical taps at once"). McCormack probes fictive interactions in terms of the "linguistic market place," "exchange system," and "advertising" with its resulting fragmentation of language and human needs; analyzes irony, metaphor, synecdoche, and metonymy as elements converging in James's exposure of a "reified society"; argues that the early fiction leaves characters "victimized," the middle fiction "marginalized," the late fiction "resistant," or, like Maggie Verver, reformulistic. Her multiple approaches and some jargon make tough going, yet this essay is very persuasive that James's "imagination for disaster was attuned to the ways in which both sexes are betrayed" and "must run the gauntlet of this economic exchange system," yet remaining at their best " 'cultural outlaws,' " like James himself, even when using " 'in-law' codes of exchange."

Eric Mottram's " 'The Infected Air' and 'The Guilt of Interference' " (*The Nineteenth-Century American Short Story*, pp. 164–90) ranges back and forth over James's tales detecting Sartre-based ideas of "prison," "enclosure," and "sterility." Although his final claim is that James challenges "that set of beliefs which preach[es] eternal individual freedom while disregarding actual social controls against life," the essay, despite sporadic insights, is not very focused and contains a few factual errors. Likewise, Renford Bambrough's diffuse "Ounces of Example: Henry James, Philosopher," in *Realism in European Literature*, ed. Nicholas Boyle and Martin Swales (Cambridge), pp. 169–82, lauds James's "primacy of the concrete" and rendering of "cognitive states," yet mostly goes hither and yon in short paragraphs in lieu of an integrated thesis. Strangest of all is *Act of Portrayal* by David M. Lubin (Yale, 1985), pp. 123–49, which ostensibly views James's *Portrait* in relation to specific paintings by Eakins and Sargent, yet whose discussion of the novel is tangential except for claiming that most of its characters exhibit "sex-role reversals" and that Isabel is a contradiction of "realism" and "formalism." His general theme—"viewing ourselves in the act of viewing the artist's act of viewing the individual who is himself or herself engaged in viewing"—is never clarified in the James chapter. Daniel R. Schwarz's *The Humanistic Heritage* (Penn.) opens with "James and Lubbock: The Emergence of an Aesthetic of the Novel," pp. 16–40, which argues that James originated "the dilemma of Anglo-American novel criticism: how to focus on technique without sacrificing subject matter." Relying on the work of Sarah Daugherty and James E. Miller, Schwarz's recapitulation of James's critical ideas is very familiar territory for Jamesians, except for this observation: "James believed in the metaphysics of presence [and] while . . . adopted by rhetorical critics and New Criticism, his aesthetic principles are often surprisingly expressionistic." The analysis of Lubbock is good, yet Schwarz's main point—that Lubbock's picture/panoramic/scenic "Talmud" "codified" James's "parables" and "Bible"—is again familiar to us, though well stated. Most valid are his ideas that Lubbock "anticipat[ed] reader-response criticism" and that Lubbock's *own* style, unlike James's, bespeaks reductionism of James's tenets.

"Intention and Readers' Responses," by Kent Bales (*Neohelicon* 13:177–94) is a lively "response" to Wolfgang Iser's influential analysis of "The Figure in the Carpet" as a centerpiece for *Rezeptionsasthetik.* Bales chides Iser for exhibiting the very "repertoire of norms" and "schemata" he would shun, and for numerous "faulty inferences." Ultimately, Bales shows with wit and persuasion the ubiquitous reappearance of "baseline intention"—in James, critics, and readers alike. He also provides useful distinctions between "response" and "reception" theories, hints offhandedly his own promising reading of James's "Carpet," and, while clearly conversant with contemporary theory, provides my favorite phrase of the year, "ideology at the salt factory." My one complaint: the repeated printing of "Corrick" for the character George Corvick. Taylor Stoehr's "Propaganda by the Deed in James" (*Words and Deeds*, pp. 59–95) examines James's realism by analyzing his response to the political and linguistic milieu he inherited from Turgenev and others in the tradition. Stoehr believes that James recounts political truth in *The Princess Casamassima*, yet borrowed details from *Virgin Soil* and *The Times*, mostly the former. In fact, Stoehr alludes profusely to all the writers and texts surrounding James while writing *Princess*, but "the price James and his characters pay for the freedom to create their own linguistic reality is the nagging suspicion that if reality can be created, it perhaps has no substance independent of the creating consciousness." For the author of *The Question of Our Speech*, "the deed of speech—his fiction—was the most serious business of life."

v. Criticism: Individual Novels

Robert K. Martin ably discusses "The Sorrows of Young Roderick: Wertherism in *Roderick Hudson*" (*ESC* 12:387–95) by showing that James drew upon a romantic pattern established by Goethe in *Sorrows of Young Werther*, yet both indulges in and casts off this romantic tradition in his own novel. James goes further than Goethe by enlarging the role of the perceiver through use of his perspective technique, thus moving "away from action toward consciousness." Martin believes that "*Werther*, a work that is at once romantic dream and ironic commentary, helped James find his way to his major fictions and their triumph over romantic fiction." In "The Love Rectangle in *Roderick Hudson*: Another Look at Christina Light" (*SNNTS* 18:353–66), Ronald Emerick discloses the possibility of a "love rectangle" rather than triangle: to " 'Rowland loves Mary Garland loves Roderick loves Christina' " we add " 'loves Rowland' " to complete the romantic picture. Yet Emerick admits it is difficult to analyze Christina's character, owing to James's method of portraying her: he "seldom enters her mind or makes authorial comments about her; therefore, the reader's knowledge . . . is based entirely upon her own words and actions and upon other characters' interpretations of her." Emerick does examine very closely the scenes in which Christina appears with Rowland to prove there is at least "strong evidence of her affection for him as well as an explanation of his failure to perceive that affection."

One of the most important publishing events of this year is a special double issue of *The Henry James Review* devoted to *Portrait of a Lady* (*HJR* 7:1–195), containing 14 new studies on James's perennial masterpiece plus a poem by Martha Collins and editor Daniel M. Fogel's fine introduction. The essays are by the cream of Jamesian scholars and critics: Leon Edel (who discusses the Emersonian/frontier myth of self-reliance), Joseph Wiesenfarth (who addresses perceptively the final six chapters often neglected as a group), Elizabeth Sabistan (who nicely places Isabel in the tradition of "Emma's Daughters"), Sandra K. Fischer (who assesses the novel's circular "womb-like enclosures"), Robert White (who relates the novel to Victorian views toward sexuality, including those of Henry, Sr.), Sandra Djwa (who exhibits the novel's critique of Pateresque aestheticism/decadence), Cheryl B. Torsney (who reveals the "expanionist/imperialist" political background), Lyall H. Powers (who relates the revisions from early to late text to James's personal, erotic inner life), William T. Stafford (who provides fresh insight on James's enigmatic Serena Merle), Peter Buitenhuis (who dissects the novel's transpositions from Hawthorne), Dorothea Krook (who pinpoints various prefigurings of Isabel in James' early tales), Adeline Tintner (who shows—both in prose and pictures—the various icons informing the work), and Marion Richmond (who traces the early reception of the novel *and* offers a separate new comprehensive bibliography on the novel). Unfortunately, *ALS* is just not scaled for adequately reviewing such collections, especially one this important. I find Stafford's subject the most interesting, the quality of the essays extraordinarily high (far better than most book collections), and am only a mite wishful that, apart from Fischer, there were more theory.

Dorothy Berkson, in "Why Does She Marry Osmond? The Education of Isabel Archer" (*ATQ* 60:53–71), emphasizes Isabel's story as an American bildungsroman in which, unlike male protagonists such as Huck, Ishmael, et al., women "find their freedom is limited precisely because they are female," and can "renounce the values of [an oppressive] world but cannot leave it." Berkson examines Isabel's "characteristic" rejection of Warburton and Goodwood (anti-"proprietorship"), acceptance of Osmond (his "self-deprecation" feeds her illusion of giving rather than "dependency"), as well as her final return to Rome (choosing the "role of protector and guide [to Pansy] over the role of dependent"). The reading itself is familiar, but extremely well presented, and certain points are new or newly put: e.g., the Henrietta/Bantling marriage is "unconventional and new"; for Isabel to accept Goodwood would be an "escape from a malignant to a benevolent paternalism." Berkson concludes rightly that James has "remarkable affinity for the lives of women"; still, her explication does suit better the unrevised text she cites.

Iconoclastic is "The Commodity World of *The Portrait of a Lady*" by Michael T. Gilmore (*NEQ* 59:51–74), which argues that James himself joins in the same "commodification," even "ownership of human beings," that functions thematically in the novel. His wish for the book's financial success, his "mixture of aesthetic and pecuniary motives," his "proprietorship" of Isabel voiced in the later Preface, all reveal "late nineteenth-century commodity capitalism." Gilmore provides historical sources to prove the "homology between the refined and elegant world of James's novel and the actual relations of labor and capital at the time he was writing"—a good point; Michael Anesko, Peggy McCormack, and James Cox write of James's financial/aesthetic sensibility. Yet Gilmore's thesis, unlike theirs, simply misses James: confuses the vividness of his moral critique with his own values, forgets that any novelist feels proprietor to his created characters (James less than most), fails to realize that James, no less than Thoreau or Marx, writes social criticism. Gilbert Osmond does not have "the most James-like imagination of the book's characters"—there are several such misreadings. Even Gilmore's best literary point, the presence of two narrators, one "omniscient" and "proprietary," the other an "observer" who "restor[es] to the characters their freedom," is seen by him as "inconsistent," whereas in fact they befit ideally a novel that probes dialectically its theme of an autonomous self and determining forces.

Rewarding and thorough is John Kimmey's "James's London in

The Princess Casamassima" (*NCL* 41:9–31), which notes that in discussing James's use of London in the novel critics have overlooked two important points: the London described comes not from his adult prowlings of the streets the first year he was there but is rather "the culmination of an association" that began with boyhood readings of *Punch*, Dickens, and Thackeray, coupled with visits in the 1850s with his family. When he arrived there alone in 1869 his first impression was of being both "enthralled and terrified like so many foreign visitors." Kimmey sees this dividedness in Millicent Henning and Hyacinth Robinson—"Like the city the two characters and their world form a maze of contradictions." Further, "James presents the metropolis in a multifaceted manner," "conveying its vastness and variety" yet individualizing "its districts and the people inhabiting them"; "dramatizing its immensity," but also showing its "essential rootlessness" through his "mingling of nationalities and classes." Kimmey thinks few Victorian novels give such a rich and varied picture of London, and "not one presents the metropolis so effectively as both a stubborn fact and a projection of the protagonist's complex self." "Hyacinth Robinson or the Princess Casamassima?" (*TSLL* 28: 296–323) by Warren Johnson asserts that, contrary to many readers' views, the novel does have a heroine, Christina Light, whom James admired because he saw himself in her. The only major character ever revived, "her appearances in *Roderick Hudson* and *The Princess* [reveal] the most complete, considered, and confident portrait of the development of the mind and experience of the novelist in a character in James's fictions." Christina's ability to get outside herself, a feat impossible for both Roderick and Hyacinth, parallels the artist's self-distancing in the making of fiction. Unlike the male protagonists in both novels, Christina shows that "one can choose art and get life in an imagining of experience—the dream of possibilities, the discovery of limitations—and the memory of an illusion of freedom."

Keenly argued is Christopher Brown's "The Rhetoric of Closure in *What Maisie Knew*" (*Style* 20:58–65), which demonstrates that the concluding "euphonious language," "repetition," and "rhythmic iteration" in Mrs. Beale's salon is all "penetrating satire," showing "the falseness and puerility of grand resolutions." Brown augments his thesis with earlier "parallelism" in the novel and then cites Maisie's final maturing "closural simplicity" as a striking contrast to the mellifluous "horrors" of the other characters. Ian Milligan's "Some Misprints in *The Awkward Age*" (*N&Q* 33:177–78) notes three misprints in the first book publications of the novel in 1899 and still current in reprints of that text. James corrected them in the New York Edition. David Seed's "Completing the Picture: Deduction and Creation in Henry James's *The Sacred Fount* (*EA* 39:268–80) adds to numerous metafictional readings of James's enigmatic novel by proposing that the man/mask painting at Newmarch "crystalliz[es]" thematic "contrasts" and "focuses many later metaphors of disguise and artifice." Seed emphasizes the narrator's slide "from deduction into creation," seeing him ultimately as emblematic of "the expenditure and waste of imagination," unusual in James only in "how small a stake [he] has in what he is observing." Seed does a good job of indicating the novel's "diverse aspects," including its similarities to *Aspern Papers* and *Turn of the Screw*. Ultimately, the narrator so identifies with his "imaginative structure" that "when the novel ends he quite literally ceases to exist."

Julie Rivkin's sinuous argument, "The Logic of Displacement in *The Ambassadors*" (*PMLA* 101:819–31), uses Derrida's "logic of supplementarity" as its conceptual framework to prove that "Strether's final decision should be seen not as an act of personal preference but as part of a larger textual logic," which is Strether's (and the entire novel's) participation at all points in "mediations," "substitution," "deviation," and "revision," as opposed to a "fixed ground of reference" directly "represented" by Mrs. Newsome and Woollett—who yet are really an "abyss." Rivkin spends much time showing James's later Preface as an extension and epitome of the same "circular deviation." Although her analysis of the Preface and of Maria Gostrey is particularly strong, Rivkin's Derridian approach finally amounts to an examination of Jamesian "operative irony" in a new key—no minor feat. Her reading also illuminates the plurality of the book's title. Michael Seidel's brilliant chapter, in his *Exile and the Narrative Imagination* (Yale), "The Lone Exile: James's *The Ambassadors* and *The American Scene*," pp. 131–63, places the two works against each other in terms of the "exilic" experience of both Strether and James. He then concentrates on the novel and provides some of the best insights I have read recently, insights related to its internationalism but from a fresh perspective: acute verbal/national analogues explicated ("the other side," "coming out," et al.), a fine demonstration of James's "intricate[ly]" combining "comic and epic plots" (with much allusion to Homer), and a stunning discussion of the novel's international "chiasmus" as Strether, a "permanent exile . . . has crossed over to the land of 'difference' and . . . 'come out on the other side.' " For Seidel, the "narrative both imitates the action and allegorizes it"—and every Jamesian should read just how.

Elissa Greenwald gives a new complex analysis to James's known reformulation of *The Marble Faun* in " 'I and the Abyss': Transcendental Romance in *The Wings of the Dove* (*SNNTS* 18:177–92), showing that James "transforms" Hawthorne's "images" (dove, pearls, et al.) into "symbols." At stake is his reconciling the "gap" or "abyss" between flesh and spirit, the real and the romantic, from Hawthorne's legacy; yet the issue is further complicated by James's own "abyss" in his indirect presentation of Milly Theale/Minny Temple. His solution, in art as in life, is to show her spiritual reality strongest by her "absence" in the "power of [Densher's] memory." Greenwald's is a layered analysis, with fine explication of the symbolism of Veronese's *Marriage at Cana*, and of James's searching dialectic of art and human life, of Venice and London. Although James goes beyond Hawthorne to integrate the "worldly and spiritual," Kate and Densher cannot embody such integration in marriage, thus reenacting the "gap" and ironically proving again James's view that "reality is known only along the margin of its disappearance." Michael Moon's "Sexuality and Visual Terrorism in *The Wings of the Dove*" (*Criticism* 28: 427–43) means to link James's moral vision and homoeroticism, principally in the "relation of vision to sexuality and the relation of sexual domination to other forms of domination." The sexual politics of the novel exhibit "visual terrorism," the asserting "powerful gaze" which Moon derives from the passage in which Kate Croy says Aunt Maud " 'terrorizes with her view any other view.' " Yet Moon also says *Wings* is "without genuine female characters—despite the fame of its two heroines," for it presents them only in "their putative relation to the phallic," whereas Densher's important sexual maneuvering is womanly. Moon even cites male servant Eugenio's "erotic[ally] charged" gaze at Densher in this offbeat reading.

James is quietly subversive in Joseph A. Boone's "Modernist Maneuverings in the Marriage Plot: Breaking Ideologies of Gender and Genre in *The Golden Bowl*" (*PMLA* 101:374–88). Boone's postmodernist inquiry reveals James's ambiguity/irresolution to be a "radical response to and reworking of the nineteenth-century marriage plot" and a challenge to the "foundations underlying the marriage institution"—cherished patriarchal assumptions, including female stereotyping. Accompanying the challenge, indeed the very expression of it, is his great narrative experimentation. Boone provides extensive background discussion of 19th-century marriage plotting in fiction, then focuses on *The Golden Bowl* as the epitome of Jamesian subversion, interpreting the problematic "happy ending" of Maggie's reestablishment with Amerigo as anything but the "connubial ideal"; in fact, James provides a "counterplot" to Maggie's winning-back-her-man "fiction," and renders "strange" the "new basis" of their final relationship. Boone is by no means the first to challenge Maggie's heroism or successful resolution, but his philosophical foundation—that the novel is a "double-barreled critique" of the "social institution of marriage" and the fiction reared on it—is new and powerfully argued. Conversely, Patricia McKee's "The Gift of Acceptance," pp. 270–346, in *Heroic Commitment in Richardson, Eliot, and James* (Princeton), argues that *The Golden Bowl* is "a trial" of "faith," a novel about "the fusion of differences" and the "acceptance of differences on their own terms." Critics (like Boone, above) find "indeterminacy" in this novel, but McKee claims we are given *both* indeterminacy and absolutes: "Belief, trust, good faith, and confidence are the conditions that enable meaning to be secured in *The Golden Bowl.*" Addressing many thematic dualities, McKee's main point is that the novel's "generative element" is "acceptance," especially by Maggie and her father, which "replaces need," for such belief breeds confidence even when there are no grounds for either acceptance or belief—an "essential redundancy of James's vision."

vi. Criticism: Individual Tales and Nonfictional Works

Two items elucidate textual nuances in *Daisy Miller*. Ron Childress's "James's *Daisy Miller*" (*Expl* 44,ii:24–25) focuses on the word "afraid" to "clarify the actions and changing attitudes" of the central characters. More substantial and very illuminating is "The Clue from *Manfred* in *Daisy Miller*" by Susan Koprince (*ArQ* 42:293–304), which supersedes prior discussions of Winterbourne's quotation from Byron in the Colosseum just before discovering and rejecting Daisy. Koprince argues deftly that Manfred and Winterbourne are similarly "ambivalent," with capacities for life and destruction (Manfred destroys innocent Astarte), and that Winterbourne is "a pale imitation," a " 'Manfred manque.' " Neither critic, however, uses James's revised text. In " 'Beltraffio': Henry James' Secrecy" (*AI* 43: 211–27), Melissa Knox thinks that James reveals homoeroticism by seeking to conceal it. She asks why he is obsessed with self-worship in this story, and what "narcissism and exhibitionism have to do with his mysteriously alluding to facts which always prolong but inevitably frustrate reader excitement?" The answer, we learn, is that James's elliptical prose "seems to be using words and phrases the way a woman uses cosmetics and jewelry—to decorate, conceal, and ultimately call attention to herself." The cause (as always) is the "obscure hurt," a "real or imagined castration." Better psychoanalysis is Leland S. Person's "Eroticism and Creativity in *The Aspern Papers*" (*L&P* 32:20–31), which analyzes the narrator who "cannot dissociate Aspern-the-poet from Aspern-the-lover," and whose project is a distorted "internalized quest romance." His psychic split, like that of compulsive Poe characters, can have no "love object" save an "idealized" Aspern (made in his own fantasy image), whereas he recoils from the two women, Juliana and Tina, who embody the "real" Aspern, since the letters themselves fuse "eroticism and creativity." He thus "wants to *misread* the letters," even while pursuing them. Person's deft Freudian study handles well the major episodes in the tale and clarifies anew James's unreliable narrator.

"Freud's *Dora* and James's *Turn of the Screw*: Two Treatments of the Female 'Case'" (*Criticism* 28:73–87) by Paula Marantz Cohen uses well the deconstructive method to uncover the "repression" in these two narratives written "within three years" of each other. When discussing Dora's case, "Freud cannot avoid imposing the male point of view—his own and that of his culture—upon Dora's experiences; thus he operates out of [Derridian] 'blindness'—the blindness which comes of repressing something in order to bring coherence to subject-matter that Freud so much wants to be considered a science." Cohen argues acutely that James, who has been labeled "stuffily Victorian in his failure to deal explicitly with sexuality in his fiction," ironically seems more capable than Freud of "counteracting and exposing the limited truths which are based on repression"—in other words, offering a counterpoint and "corrective" to Freud's patriarchy by his ability to identify with the Governess. On the other hand, the Governess mirrors Freud's viewpoint by "pursuing truth from the other side (a '180 degree turn of the screw' of perception)." Stanley Renner's " 'Why Can't They Tell You Why?': A Clarifying Echo of *The Turn of the Screw*" (*SAF* 14:205–13) thinks that James Purdy's tale, published in the late 1950s, "exposes the true story" of James's work: "the dramatization of the terrible developmental damage done to children by the Victorian sexual squeamishness in which they are brought up by the angel in the house, the great governess of the era, guardian of its moral and spiritual purity." In telling the same tale without explanatory cultural context, Purdy suggests "not only the persistence of the phenomenon but also its generalizability" so long as male children, Renner insists, are under care of "maternal figures fearful of sexuality, ambivalent about their own sexual roles, and hostile to the male in his sexual role."

"Illumination and Affection in the Parallel Plots of 'The Rich Boy' and 'The Beast in the Jungle'" (*PLL* 22:406–16) by Patrick D. Murphy argues that Fitzgerald's story can survive "comparative criticism with the best of early twentieth-century short fiction," James's "Beast in the Jungle." Murphy's comparison includes similar "subversion of the moment-of-crisis" themes depicting the protagonists' narcissism and use of "initial and second moments of crisis," creating in both tales antiheroes, anticlimactic endings, and "intensif[ied] foiling of expectations." Murphy overclaims that Fitzgerald's Hunter is more fully developed than Marcher. In "The Beast in the Closet: James and the Writing of Homosexual Panic" (*Sex, Politics and Science*, pp. 148–86), Eve Kosofsky Sedgwick attempts to see Marcher and May in the broader context of late-19th century "homophobia," and James as analogous to James M. Barrie. In her reading, Marcher's "secret" includes the "monstrous" possibility of his homosexuality, which he keeps in "the closet" by psychically denying it. May tries unsuccessfully to uncloset him, to release him, presumably, for sexual expression. At moments this long chapter newly addresses issues pertinent to James's "bachelor fictions," but too much of the discussion is so crabbed and jargon-ridden as at times to resemble, in the author's own phrase, a "hammeringly tendentious blur." Nothing could be more different than veteran critic James W. Gargano's "Imagery as Action in 'The Beast in the Jungle'" (*ArQ* 42:351–67), a brilliant section-by-section analysis of the "imagistic language" of the tale. Gargano explicates James's use of light, torch, seasonal, sibyl-sphinx, burial, time, and beast imagery to bring out the tale's "engrossing tapestry and mosaic." Jamesians know the ingredients of Gargano's analysis, but nobody has put them together so exquisitely; his reading should be saved by all of us who teach the tale, for it exhibits James's poetic density much the same as that, say, of Joyce or Mann. Gargano's additional theme is that Marcher is a "man of divided sensibility who knows that he does not know what his subconscious is trying to reveal to him"—and finally does at the end.

James M. Cox's "The Memoirs of Henry James: Self-Interest as Autobiography" (*SoR* 22:231–51) is the richest analysis of James's autobiographical sensibility since Paul John Eakin (see *ALS 1984*, pp. 130–31). Cox inverts Edel's premise about the revelation of James's life through his art by addressing the ways James's autobiographical art makes, or remakes, his life. Cox elaborates greatly James's "aestheticizing of capitalism," his preoccupation with "appreciation" and "interest" through style and art, and then thoughtfully yet firmly critiques both *The American Scene* and the *Autobiography*, showing how evasions predominate, "how the late style effaces nature almost as much as it displaces history . . . [so that] the fierce process by which land becomes scene, nature becomes culture, and money becomes beauty is what is largely left out of James's encounter with and rejection of the American Scene." Cox's critique also features a more negative reading of the famous Galerie d'Apollon nightmare, a "space of discontinuity" between the first and second volumes of the *Autobiography*, and an image of James "caressing the past" by feeding off the "ghostly presences" of such wounded or killed in the Civil War as brother Wilky or Cabot Russell. Very complex, Cox's essay is more sympathetic than this synopsis suggests. An uneasy deconstructionist without the terminology, he can be a Twainian "squatter" in the midst of "dandy" analysis: i.e., James's "private life of a campaign that failed" was "converted into the public art of a newborn life in literature that succeeded."

Not unrelated is Alfred Habegger's "Henry James's Rewriting of Minny Temple's Letters" (*AL* 58:159–80), which discloses that Alice H. James and her daughter made complete literal transcriptions of the letters which James used for his crowning re-creation of Minny in *Notes of a Son and Brother*, and prints the first four in parallel columns with James's shortened version together with his deletions, substitutions, and omissions. Habegger's claim, meticulously substantiated, is that the "*thoroughness*" of James's editorial revisions was "far more extensive than anyone could have dreamed" and that they "raise some disturbing questions about his use of historical documentation and his general accuracy and truthfulness." Many may agree, although I find the "silvered over" image of Minny almost inevitable given the lifelong morphology of her portrait in James's mind. In particular, the rendering of her as "more isolated and victimized than she probably was" is precisely James's reformulation of her as the character of Milly Theale in *Wings of the Dove*. Habegger urges "long-overdue skepticism" touching James's "transcriptions of the 'American Girl,'" but his own evidence seems to me to confirm our latest view of James's "appropriating" imagination—especially these days in regard to his memoirs. Finally, Annette Larson Benert in "Monsters, Bagmen, and Little Old Ladies: Henry James and the Unmaking of America" (*ArQ* 42:331–43) asserts that in *The American Scene* James's "scourge sweeps broadly over turn-of-the-century America, despite his deep allegiance to the Eastern Establishment, the Tory Tradition that Marxist critics with some justice decry." To Benert, James shows on every page the "hermeneutical eye of the new sociology, seeing beneath the surfaces of places and people their diminution, their difficulty, disaffection, disorder," and she parallels the book with Max Weber's *Protestant Ethic and the Spirit of Capitalism*, because both mourn over the same world—"the West they both inhabited, the America they both saw as the quintessential expression of western civilization." Both share a vision of "the danger of a public ethos that narrows all human motivation, all cultural achievement, all social engagement to the rigors of the marketplace."

vii. Two Prior *Henry James Review* Volumes

Two 1985 issues of *The Henry James Review*, with 10 studies too important to neglect, were not yet available to Robert Gale last year. Volume six offers one of the year's best essays, William Veeder's "Image as Argument: Henry James and the Style of Criticism" (pp. 172–81), a deeply persuasive thesis that as James's critical sensibility evolved away from a priori "moralistic stiffness" he learned "to express his perceptions in a style adequate to their intricacy." Veeder shows with great thoroughness that James gradually embodied a complex "in between" sensibility (between historian/philosopher, scholar/man of the world, even masculine/feminine) comparable to, then surpassing Sainte-Beuve and Arnold, and that he did this with a critical style "that multiplies terms and that particularly elaborates *images*." Veeder's stunning exhibition of James's transforming use of the word "vessel" in response to Zola and elsewhere is a fine (Arnoldian) touchstone for his theme that James developed as a critic just as he did as a novelist, and that his "imagistic mode of figuration" is the key. Second, Darshan Singh Maini's "The Politics of Henry

James" (pp. 158–71) confirms prevailing opinion that he was a "comely conservative," "innocent of politics *qua* politics," and replete with the prejudices of his class, yet he understood the "psychology" and "typology" of politics (which Marxist critics are explicating these days). The essay, lyrical with much literary allusion, includes commentary on *Bostonians*, *The Princess*, *Tragic Muse*, and *Covering End*. Next, Charles Caramello's "Reading Gertrude Stein Reading Henry James" (pp. 182–203) is a long analysis far more on Stein's "cubistic" imagination than on "forerunner" James; yet the two unite in providing similar difficulties for readers and, especially, in their art of "reflexivity."

In addition to Edel/Tintner's "Peter Quin" earlier cited, volume seven offers "In Defense of James's *The Tragic Muse*" by W. R. Macnaughton (pp. 5–12), who admits that the 1890 novel lacks the experimentalism of the fiction surrounding it, yet proposes it as a "loose baggy monster," successful for its four "fully realized" characters, each of whom the critic analyzes and none of whom is "violated" by James's ideas. Laurens M. Dorsey's " 'Somthing Like the Old Dream of the Secret of Life' " (pp. 13–20) focuses closely on the opening of the "germ" Preface of *The Spoils* to explore James's surprising continuity with the aesthetics of Shelley, and to pose important questions regarding the elusive "link between imagination and extramental life" in James's poetics. Her discussion of metaphor evokes Veeder's argument, above. "Henry and Edith: 'The Velvet Glove' as an 'In' Joke" by Jean Frantz Blackall (pp. 21–25) astutely refines the Wharton-related biographical readings of Tintner and Edel by arguing that the "joke is on both Berridge and Amy Evans [the 'Wharton' figure]. If she is unworthy as a writer, he is unkind as a man, and capable through masculine vanity of misreading her motives." Blackall's pinpointing James's use of Wharton-like "hand movements" as part of their "collaborative" joking is very sharp. Next, Marcia Ian's "Consecrated Diplomacy and the Concretion of Self" (pp. 27–33) is a conceptual analysis of Maggie Verver's James-like "labour of detachment" and "*artful* passion" in *The Golden Bowl*, symbolized by the famous pagoda image which for Ian represents in architectural roundness "an impregnable solipsism" already registered in Adam Verver's "happy spells" and gradually acquired by Maggie's "birthing inward" in the course of the book. Ian's view that the novel's two-part structure stands for Maggie's "divided [and "detaching"] mind" is a remarkable idea. "Thorton Wilder as Literary Cubist: An Acknowledged Debt to Henry James" (pp. 34–44) by Lyall H. Powers is a fine blend of source study and literary criticism with extensive analysis of Wilder's *Theophilus North*, a novel set in "James family" Newport and constructed with "cubist simultaneity," a principle Wilder probably learned from *The Awkward Age*, which he owned, annotated, and would have liked to dramatize. Finally, John Halperin's efficient "Elizabeth Bowen and Henry James" (pp. 45–47) points to "temperamental affinity" between the two, including stylistic elements, "magical moments of psychological insight," interest both in "things" and in "ghost" tales, the critique of society, and the "cruelty of innocence."

University of Missouri

8. Pound and Eliot

Reed Way Dasenbrock

This year's article could be subtitled "Between Two Centenaries." The spillover of activity from the 1985 Pound centenary included special issues of *The Yale Review* and *San Jose Studies*, *"What Thou Lovest Well Remains": 100 Years of Ezra Pound*, ed. Richard Ardinger (Limberlost), and a few journalistic denunciations of all this activity. Accounts of the Yale, Kansai, and Hailey centennial conferences by Hugh Witemeyer, Sanehide Kodama, and Robert G. Waite appeared in *Paideuma* (15,i:123–34). The Eliot centenary is in 1988, and celebrations are already being organized on at least three continents. There continues to be more work (and, in my judgment, more interesting work) done on Pound than on Eliot, but if I discern an overall tendency in the year's work on both men, it is to reestablish the centrality of Eliot's position in literary history by showing his widespread influence on many writers, including Ezra Pound. His centenary will doubtless accentuate this trend.

i. Pound

a. Text, Biography, and Bibliography. Nineteen eighty-six offered nothing as important as in recent years, as New Directions published no new volume of correspondence and we are still waiting for several volumes of biography that are under way. But a steady flow of smaller items continued to help fill out Pound's canon and our knowledge of him. The most important of these items is New Directions' tenth printing of *The Cantos*, which adds the hitherto uncollected and virtually unavailable Cantos 72 and 73 as well as a fragment from 1966. But these haphazard additions indicate how urgently the text of *The Cantos* needs work of the caliber of Hans Walter Gabler's work on *Ulysses*, not the kind of impressionistic tinkering with the text represented by these latest changes. I am not at all convinced that either addition should have been included in the poem. The next most important addition to the canon this year is *Ezra Pound, Forked Branches: Translations of Medieval Poems* (Windhover), ed. Charlotte Ward. This edition of 26 previously unpublished Pound translations of work in four languages (Anglo-Saxon, Provençal, Italian, and German) is unfortunately an expensive and rare small press book without a scholarly introduction or notes. Though this will limit the scholarly importance of the book, those who admire Pound's translations of the Provençal and early Italian poets will welcome these additional versions. I personally find Pound inferior to—but overly influenced by—Rossetti as a translator of this material; and these new materials have not changed my mind. Additional evidence of Pound's translating comes to us from two sources: in "Ezra Pound's 'An Opening for *Agamemnon*'" (*Paideuma* 15,ii–iii:117–20), Donald Gallup prints and introduces Pound's 1919 translation of a fragment of the *Agamemnon*; and Raffaella Baccolini, in "Pound's Tribute to H.D." (*CL* 27:435–39), transcribes Pound's 1961 Italian translation of H.D.'s "Regents of the Night."

Breon Mitchell prints and introduces an exchange of eight letters on *Ulysses* between "Ezra Pound and G. B. Shaw: A Long Windy War" (*JJQ* 23:127–36). Paul Hoover prints seven, not just two, letters from Pound in "Two Pound Letters" (*Paideuma* 15,i:95–104); these letters are to Wayne Andrews and James Douglas Peck, two American high school students who between 1930 and 1932 published a literary magazine in French. These are followed by three "Letters to Woodward" (*Paideuma* 15,i:105–20), 1933–34 letters to the American popular historian W. E. Woodward, who curiously and irritatingly is never identified or even given a full name in the *Paideuma* piece. Brita Lindberg-Seyersted continues to update her *Pound/Ford* of 1982 with one more letter from Pound to Ford in "Cher F.: Another Item in the Correspondence Between Ezra Pound and Ford Madox Ford" (*Paideuma* 15,i:71–73). In the same vein Omar Pound provides "Addenda for *Ezra Pound and Dorothy Shakespear: Their Letters, 1909–1914*" (*Paideuma* 15,ii–iii:239–40), further annotations to the letters he and A. Walton Litz edited in 1984. What could have been the most substantial addition in this category this year, Mary de Rachewiltz's "Pound as Son: Letters Home" (*YR* 75:321–30), is disappointingly mostly commentary on Pound's relationship with his mother, though snippets of his letters home are quoted.

John Leigh contributes to our knowledge of Pound's education in "'An Odd Sort of Post-Graduate Course': Ezra Pound's First Course in Modern Poetry Discovered" (*Paideuma* 15,ii–iii:143–45), a description of a fairly good course in modern poetry Pound took with Cornelius Weygandt in 1906–07. Sheri Martinelli's "A Memoir" (*Paideuma* 15,ii–iii:151–62) does not contribute much to our knowledge of anything. G. Schmidt's "The Ezra Pound Stone at Medinaceli" (*Paideuma* 15,ii–iii:125–27) discusses both the raising of a monument to Pound in Spain and Pound's visits to the town that has so honored him. The photographs in Emily Mitchell Wallace's "Some Friends of Ezra Pound: A Photographic Essay" (*YR* 75:331–56) are more interesting than the text, which is a rehash of Pound's relations with Ford, Lewis, and other figures in literary London. James Laughlin's *The Master of Those Who Know: Ezra Pound* (City Lights) contains two talks, "Pound the Teacher," covering mostly familiar ground about the "Ezuversity," and "Pound and the Primitive," largely a cento of the recent Pound criticism Laughlin finds important. His "Ez As Wuz" (*SJS* 12,iii:6–28) is more substantial than either and should have been included in the City Lights book. And William C. Pratt's "The Greatest Poet in Captivity: Ezra Pound at St. Elizabeths" (*SR* 94:619–29) offers no particular revelations in a memoir of a half-dozen visits to Pound in St. Elizabeth's in 1955.

Tim Redman's "Pound's Library: A Preliminary Catalog" (*Paideuma* 15,ii–iii:213–37), a listing of the books in Pound's library (now divided between Brunnenburg and the Humanities Research Center in Austin) annotated by Pound, is perhaps the most useful contribution to Pound studies this year, though a fuller catalog done by a trained bibliographer is urgently needed. An unannotated bibliography of work *on* Pound has been compiled by Beatrice Ricks in *Ezra Pound: A Bibliography of Secondary Works* (Scarecrow). This is simply not very accurate. Typographical and indexing errors abound, and the entries are not organized along subject lines as rigorously as they might be: the majority of entries are placed in the catchall category of general studies even when the title alone (Hugh Kenner's "A Note on CX/778," to cite one obvious example) should have sufficed to ensure its inclusion in a specific section. This means that anyone using the bibliography had best supplement it with articles such as this one which offer at least some clues to the content and scope of secondary sources. Finally, Donald Gallup's "The Ezra Pound Archive at Yale" (*YULG* 60:161–77) is a fascinating account of how Pound's manuscripts came to Yale.

***b.* General Studies.** The most interesting book on Pound this year is Kevin Oderman's *Ezra Pound and the Erotic Medium* (Duke), which is a discussion of Pound's interest in visionary and mediumistic sexuality. Though narrowly defined and likely to cause fits in those who attack Pound for his "phallocentrism," Oderman's study offers an important new perspective on Pound's work. If the book has a fault, it is that Oderman does not push his thesis far enough, perhaps not seeing the relevance of his ideas to works he does not discuss such as *Homage to Sextus Propertius*; but so rarely do we encounter an academic book that does not push its thesis far enough that this fault is almost a virtue.

Martin A. Kayman's *The Modernism of Ezra Pound: The Science of Poetry* (St. Martin's) is a little harder to summarize, as four or five different foci jostle for control. Kayman is interesting on how Pound's poetics respond to a Symbolism/Naturalism divide Pound wants to bridge, and he also gives a useful account of the relation between the "School of images" of 1909 and Pound's Imagism of 1912. The best part of the book continues Ian Bell's work on relating Pound's work to the scientific discourse of the time. But I am not sure that all of this adds up to a book, and Kayman does not really deliver on the political thread that he seems to think ties the various essays together. Kayman raises an important question in asking why "Some of Our Best Poets Are Fascists," but in and around the intermittent barrages of contemporary Marxist terminology he does not really answer it.

To anticipate a point made below, this has been a good year for theoretical work on Pound, even though Alan Durant's defense of such work against Donald Davie in "Pound, Modernism and Literary Criticism: A Reply to Donald Davie" (*CritQ* 28,i–ii:154–66) tends to make one sympathize with Davie. Marianne Korn's "E.P.: The Dance of Words" (*Paideuma* 15,ii–iii:243–51) relates Pound's concept of logopoeia to intertextuality in a way that illuminates *Homage to Sextus Propertius* and is potentially illuminating about other Pound works. Martin A. Kayman connects Pound's theory of the image to his theory of money in "Ezra Pound: The Color of His Money" (*Paideuma* 15,ii–iii:39–52). I find Kayman's argument here interesting but problematic in his unexamined assumption that Pound never changed, that the aesthetics of 1912–14 are the same as the politics of the 1930s. That is explicitly the argument of an unintelligent essay by Robert Lumsden, "Ezra Pound's Imagism" (*Paideuma* 15,ii–iii: 253–64), who argues that Pound remained an Imagist and that there is no significant distinction between image, vortex, ideoplasty, and ideogram; if this were true, why would Pound have used different words?

Pound's politics attracted more attention than his aesthetics this year. Alfred Kazin in "The Fascination and the Terror of Ezra Pound" (*NYRB*, 13 March: 16–24) and Peter Viereck in "Pound at 100: Weighing the Art and the Evil" (*NYTBR*, 29 December 1985) denounce anyone who reads Pound as complicit with Fascism. Less hysterical (and therefore more persuasive) but as hard on Pound is Barry Goldensohn's "Pound and Antisemitism" (*YR* 75:399–421), one of the first detailed discussions of the Rome Radio broadcasts. In the same journal (75:385–98) Lloyd G. Reynolds offers an interesting treatment of Pound's economics by an economist, more sympathetic than one might expect. His central thesis is the seemingly attractive one that what Pound liked about Mussolini could also have been found a little later in the New Deal, and that the tragedy of Pound's politics is that he could not shift his perspective when the realities of American politics changed. But this does not explain why Pound could not change, why he remained fixated on Italian Fascism.

The Pound issue of *San Jose Studies*, the most substantial of the centennial celebrations, finds its central focus in Pound's politics, with four essays on the subject. James E. B. Breslin's "Ezra Pound and the Jews" (12,iii:37–45) combines some interesting speculations on the origins of Pound's anti-Semitism with a vague thesis about his "phallocentrism." William McCraw's central point in his "Fascist of the Last Hour" (pp. 46–57) is the important one that Pound did not recant his politics after World War II, and both he and Fred Moramarco, in "Italy and Ezra Pound's Politics" (pp. 29–36), have some unsettling things to say about the cult of Pound prevalent among the neo-fascists of the Italian MSI even today. Leon Surette's "Economics and Eleusis" (pp. 58–67) is the most substantial of these essays, arguing that Pound's politics and his interest in the occult are related and find their common origin in the *New Age* circle in London.

Another good essay in the same issue is Robert Casillo's "Ezra Pound and Hermes" (pp. 83–104), which discusses the ambivalence toward the figure of Hermes that runs through Pound's works. Casillo elsewhere surveys "The Meaning of Venetian History in Ruskin and Pound" (*UTQ* 55:235–60), a solid contribution to our growing awareness of Ruskin's influence on Pound. I have learned a lot from Casillo's wide-ranging investigations in some of the less explored areas of

Pound studies over the past several years, but there is a relentless and reductive side to his uncovering of negative aspects of Pound's works, a side on display in "Nature, History and Anti-Nature in Ezra Pound's Fascism" (*PLL* 22:284–311), which slides from a balanced treatment of some contradictions in Pound's attitude toward nature to a condemnation of Pound for his hostility to nature that, it seems to me, misses a lot of evidence the other way.

There are only two separate studies of the prose works this year, one a brief note by Eliot Weinberger, "A Note on the Cathay Ideogram" (*Paideuma* 15,ii–iii:141), discussing the ideogram that appears on the cover of *Cathay*. Lionel Kelly, in "*Guide to Kulchur*: The Book as Ball of Light" (*Paideuma* 15,ii–iii:279–90), attempts a reading of this important work, but he never quite comes to grips with his subject. John J. Nolde gives us a good survey of the place of the *Ta Hio* in the Confucian canon and of Pound's interest in and successive translations of that work in "Ezra Pound and the Ta Hio: The Making of a Confucian" (*Paideuma* 15,ii–iii:73–91). Ron Thomas's "E.P.: Hellenic Punster" (*SCRev* 3:57–67) discusses the (serious) puns that run throughout Pound's work. M. L. Rosenthal talks about his "Discovering E.P." (*Paideuma* 15,ii–iii:107–13) in an article that breaks no new ground. But a lot of new ground has been broken this year in Pound studies, less in one magnum opus than in a number of interesting and intelligent contributions.

***c.* Relation to Other Writers.** The most substantial attempt to place Pound in the context of his contemporaries this year is C. K. Stead's *Pound, Yeats, Eliot and the Modernist Movement*. Stead's overall theses are either noncontroversial (Pound and Eliot are central modernists; Yeats is not) or utterly unacceptable (Pound's politics are less distasteful than Eliot's because Pound at least had the courage of his convictions). The value of the book lies in Stead's close readings of many poems by Pound, Eliot, and Yeats. His general thrust is to show Eliot's deep influence on Pound in matters of form and technique, in particular in the development of a central modernist technique Stead calls "aggregation." Margaret Dickie's *On the Modernist Long Poem* has an important theme, the American aspiration toward the long poem. But her curious choice of poets and order of discussion (Eliot, Crane, Williams, Pound: where are H.D., Stevens, Zukovsky, Olson?) prevent her from getting a very good handle on Pound's place in this tradition.

Pound's continuing influence on American poets ignored in Dickie's study is the subject of a number of pieces. Allen Ginsberg's "Pound's Influence" (*APR* 15,iv:7–8) is valuable when it talks about Pound's metrics and prosody, repetitious when it goes over Ginsberg's meetings with Pound once again. Cid Corman's "Working the Desert" (*Sagetrieb* 5:53–56) briefly treats Zukovsky's debt to Pound. Hugh Witemeyer contributes a fascinating article on "The Strange Progress of David Hsin-Fu Wand" (*Paideuma* 15,ii–iii:191–210), one of Pound's disciples from the St. Elizabeths period. But probably the best testimony to the continued influence of Pound comes from *"What Thou Lovest Well Remains": 100 Years of Ezra Pound*, ed. Richard Ardinger (Limberlost). Largely the talks given at the Hailey Centennial Conference, this book does not have a good deal of scholarly value, but pieces by Charles Bukowski, Jim Harrison, and other writers testify to the impact of Pound on their work.

Marjorie Perloff, in her chapter on Pound in *The Futurist Moment*, argues that Pound needs to be considered in a broader context, one that is more international and more concerned with the other arts. Her specific focus is the debt Pound's versification owes to Futurist (and other) manifestos, and this makes good sense even if one has doubts about Perloff's larger argument about the centrality and greatness of Futurism. Perloff's general approach is seconded by JoAnna Isaak's *The Ruin of Representation* (UMI Research Press), which focuses, more problematically, on links between the Russian avant-garde and the English Vorticists, including Pound.

The most important article this year on Pound's relation to his contemporaries is Kathryne V. Lindberg's "Tradition and Heresy: Pound's Dissociation from Eliot" (*Paideuma* 15,ii–iii:9–37), an illuminating essay on Pound's consciously heterodox dissent from Eliot's emerging critical and intellectual orthodoxy in the 1930s that makes excellent use of their correspondence. Shedding further light on this crucial relationship is Eliot's own fine 1950 essay, "Ezra Pound," reprinted in *Agenda* (23,iii–iv:153–63). Pound and *Hugh Selwyn Mauberley* are Ian F. A. Bell's "Oblique Contexts in Yeats: The Homer of 'The Nineteenth Century and After'" (*PQ* 65:335–44). And though Bell takes a lot of space to delineate just one aspect of a four-line poem, he makes the important point that the poem expresses not "regret about the passing of earlier values but affirming of present possibilities"; Yeats, in short, was more sympathetic to Pound's later work (and modernism in general) than has been appreciated. Two good articles in the *Yeats Annual* treat—in contrast—Pound's equally important debt to Yeats. There seems more than a bit of overstatement in the title of James Longenbach's "The Secret Society of Modernism: Pound, Yeats, Olivia Shakespear, and the Abbe de Montfaucon de Villars" (4:103–20), but he makes some interesting connections between Yeats's occult interests and the aesthetics of modernism. Less speculative is Yoko Chiba's "Ezra Pound's Versions of Fenollosa's Noh Manuscripts and Yeats's Unpublished 'Suggestions and Corrections'" (4:121–44); after going over some familiar ground, it shows in detail how Yeats influenced Pound's Noh translations that had in turn such an influence on Yeats. Also focusing on Pound's orientalism is Anthony Tatlow's "The Image of Process: Pound's and Brecht's Response to Chinese Philosophy" (*Twentieth Century Literatures*, pp. 371–79) and Richard Sieburth's "Ideograms: Pound/Michaux" (*ECr* 26,iii:15–27), two straightforward comparisons that help place Pound's Orientalism in a larger context. Finally, Donald Davie discusses some Virgilian echoes in Pound's work despite his anti-Virgilianism in "Virgil's Presence in Ezra Pound and Others" (*Virgil in a Cultural Tradition*, pp. 134–46).

Less substantial studies on Pound's relation to other writers include Celeste Goodridge's "Firm Piloting of Rebellious Fluency: Marianne Moore's Reviews of *The Cantos* of Ezra Pound" (*Paideuma* 15,ii–iii:175–90), which does not make Moore out to be a very important critic of Pound. Kathleen Flanagan's "Ezra Pound and Amy Lowell: English Poetics in Renditions of Chinese Poetry" (*Paideuma* 15,ii–iii:163–73) goes over the contrast between Pound's expert and Lowell's inept translations one more time. John Leigh persuasively argues, in "Arthur Symons and the Evolution of Pound's Concepts of Absolute Rhythm and Precision" (*Paideuma* 15,i:55–59), that Symons was an important influence on Pound's concept of an absolute rhythm without ever quite making it clear what Pound means by "absolute rhythm." John Lash discusses the erotic components of Guido Cavalcanti's art in "Making Sense of 'Donna Mi Priegha'" (*Paideuma* 15,i:83–93) in a study that should be read in the context of Kevin Oderman's work. Carl Grundberg's "Ezra Pound and *Trobar Clus*" (*SJS* 12,iii:119–24) defines the Provençal terms *trobar* and *clus* without saying much about Pound. And finally Mohammed Shaheen in "Pound and Arabic" (*Paideuma* 15,ii–iii:93–106) studies the interest of the Arab world in Pound and Pound's equally slight interest in the Arab world. If I sound a little impatient in this section, that is because too many Pound critics (and the editors of *Paideuma*, unfortunately) feel that it is worthwhile to connect Pound to everyone he can be connected to; my sense, in contrast, is that such efforts are worthwhile only if there is a critical payoff, something that seems lacking in many of these studies.

***d.* The Shorter Poems and Translations.** *The Cantos* continue to win much more attention than the other poetic works this year. John Espey, in "Some Notes on 'The Return'" (*Paideuma* 15,i:33–39), follows up on Pound's reference to the Henri de Regnier prosodic model for "The Return." In "Metre and Translation in Pound's *Women of Trachis*" (*SJS* 12,iii:111–18), Marianina Olcott argues for the interest and fidelity of this neglected translation by Pound, focusing on his rendering of the meters of the original. Otherwise, only *Hugh Selwyn Mauberley* received individual attention, in three studies. Ian F. A. Bell intelligently relates *Mauberley* to Wyndham Lewis's Vorticist concern with surfaces as well as, more traditionally, to Henry James in "A Mere Surface: Wyndham Lewis, Henry James and the 'Latitude' of *Hugh Selwyn Mauberley*" (*Paideuma* 15,ii–iii: 53–71). Traci Gardner's "Pound's *Hugh Selwyn Mauberley*" (*Expl* 44,iii:46–48) relates the phrase "wringing lilies from the acorns" to the Circe episode of the *Odyssey*. In " 'Of King's Treasuries': Pound's Allusion to Ruskin in *Hugh Selwyn Mauberley*" (*Paideuma* 15,i:23–31), Hugh Witemeyer argues persuasively that the reference to Ruskin in *Mauberley* is positive, not negative as has often been assumed.

***e.* The Cantos.** This year provides a torrent of studies of Pound's major work, and for me the most significant aspect of that torrent is that a number of genuinely illuminating studies of *The Cantos* using contemporary theory are beginning to emerge. Until now, most post-structuralist work on Pound has either chastized him for not being a post-structuralist or rewritten him until he resembled one; but both John Steven Childs in *Modernist Form: Pound's Style in the Early Cantos* (Susquehanna) and Jean-Michel Rabaté in *Language, Sexuality, and Ideology in Ezra Pound's Cantos* (SUNY) are actually interested in reading Pound. Childs has an irritating habit of criticizing virtually all previous Pound criticism for its adherence to outmoded critical approaches while at the same time producing readings that rely upon and do not look all that different from the criticism he attacks. His "matrices" and "intertexts" seem much like the old themes and allusions he is so confident he has moved beyond. But when he is not being irrelevantly polemical, Childs has some very interesting things to say. The syntax of *The Cantos* has never been looked at so closely, and he has a valuable discussion of Pound's prosody. There is, in short, some good close reading of the Early Cantos here.

If Childs is primarily a disciple of Riffaterre, Rabaté is one of Lacan, and though I personally find Lacan utterly unintelligible, Rabaté is fortunately not. His central focus is on the interplay of voice and writing in *The Cantos*, and he makes some of the dullest stretches of *The Cantos*—such as the Chinese History Cantos and *Thrones*—seem interesting, not through critical pyrotechnics but simply through his insight and intelligence. This makes the utterly miserable job SUNY Press did in producing the book that much more regrettable.

A number of articles on *The Cantos* are well worth reading this year. My favorite is Michael North's outstanding "Towers and the Visual Map of Pound's *Cantos*" (*CL* 27:17–31), which interprets the significance of the various towers that punctuate *The Cantos* and makes a larger argument about the historicity of the visual in the poem. Analogously, in "Image, Word, and Sign: The Visual Arts as Evidence in Ezra Pound's *Cantos*" (*CritI* 12:347–64), Michael André Bernstein relates Pound's ideas on art to his ideas on usury and—though this is less original than he seems to think—relates both to Ruskin. Walter Sutton's "Coherence in Pound's *Cantos* and William James' Pluralistic Universe" (*Paideuma* 15,i:7–21) relates Pound's attempt at a coherent but polyvalent work to James's philosophy. It is a little unclear whether Sutton's argument is that James is an influence on or an interesting parallel to Pound, but clearly he is arguing for lower or looser standards of coherence to be applied to *The Cantos*. Kay Davis argues just the opposite in "Three Techniques Made New" (*Paideuma* 15,i:46–53), a close reading of the opening of Canto 68 as organized around fugues and choriambic rhythm. This does not persuade me that the Adams Cantos are as carefully organized as she insists, but she nonetheless offers a useful challenge to those like Sutton (or myself) who would argue that we are never going to achieve a totally organized sense of the work. In an article that does not carry much conviction, "Pound: The Prophetic Voice" (*YR* 75:373–84), Louis L. Martz argues for a reading of *The Cantos* as prophetic rather than epic in genre. I would like to request a moratorium on all such either-or attempts to define the genre of

The Cantos as prophecy, epic, Menippean satire, or whatever; it seems fairly obvious by now that *The Cantos* stand in a significant relation to a number of genres but is not a perfect example of any of them. Largely in agreement with me is Victor P. H. Li, who in a suggestive general essay, "The Vanity of Length: The Long Poem as Problem in Pound's *Cantos* and Williams' *Paterson*" (*Genre* 19:3–20), relates the modernist impulse toward length in poetry to a reaction against the lyric poem.

Alan Williamson briefly relates Pound to Jung in "Mythic and Archetypal Methods: A Reading of Canto IV" (*SJS* 12,iii:105–10). A. Walton Litz's "'Remember that I have Remembered': Traces of the Past in *The Pisan Cantos*" (*YR* 75:357–67) adds little that is new on a part of *The Cantos* that has already received much attention. And Peter Dale Scott's "Anger and Poetic Politics in *Rock-Drill*" (*SJS* 12,iii:68–82) unpersuasively argues that Pound put the unsavory aspects of his politics behind him in *Rock-Drill.* In contrast, Francis McKee's "Commentary on the *Drafts and Fragments*" (*Paideuma* 15,ii–iii:265–77) pays needed and useful attention to the most underrated section of the whole poem. And R. Peter Stoicheff's "The Composing and Publication History of Ezra Pound's *Drafts and Fragments*" (*TCL* 32:78–94) provides an extremely interesting treatment of the far from straightforward textual history of the end of Pound's poem. Though Stoicheff does not provide firm editorial recommendations, this is precisely the kind of work a proper edition of *The Cantos* is going to need to draw on.

Paideuma this year offers the usual number of explications of short passages or individual references in individual Cantos. Stephen J. Adams claims that "Apovitch in Canto XII" (15,ii–iii:31–33) is a reference to Carl Sandburg. In "Blum's Bidet Revisited (80/794) or, The Final Solution" (15,ii–iii:147), David Gordon explains the point of Pound's reference in Canto 80 to Blum as "defending a bidet." Jeff Twitchell's "A Church Note" (15,ii–iii:135–40) argues that the St. Etienne of Canto 83 is not St. Etienne of Perigueux but of Toulouse. After 10 years of searching, Walter Baumann has found the source in W. H. Hudson of "Birds, Said Hudson, Are Not Automata (97/678)" (15,ii–iii:121–24). David Gordon again, in "Notes on 'Katze' and 'Wand'" (15,i:75–76), explicates the reference to "Katze" in Canto 102. In "Sir Edward Coke and the Banishment of Usury" (15,i:61–70), Richard Sawyer provides an informative discussion of Coke's commentary on the statute *de Judaismo* alluded to in Canto 108.

C. F. Terrell's *Commentary* is already being supplemented and corrected by all these individual studies, yet we still lack a good working theory of annotating *The Cantos*: is the "fit reader" of *The Cantos* expected to know all these things or look them up? Or did Pound expect us to read *The Cantos* differently?

ii. Eliot

The *Yeats Eliot Review*, buried in *ALS 1984*, is enjoying a second life. A double issue published in 1986 is the final issue published from the University of Alberta, but the journal has found a new home at the University of Arkansas at Little Rock and a new editor in Russell Murphy, whose first issue should appear in late 1987.

***a.* Text and Biography.** In an intemperate but provocative review-essay of recent work on Eliot ("Eliot and His Problems," *SR* 94:510–17), William Harmon argues that the most urgent needs of readers of Eliot right now are, first, "a good collected edition of his prose" and, second, "the selected correspondence." And while I do not agree with his denunciation of much recent critical work on Eliot, his point is surely well taken. Nothing significant has happened to Eliot's texts since the publication of the facsimile of *The Waste Land* in 1971, and biographical work has been hampered by the attitude of the Eliot Estate and by the unavailability of key documents such as the correspondence with Emily Hale. Pound studies offer one immediate contrast, despite the deplorable state of the text of *The Cantos*; even the long unavailable works of Wyndham Lewis are now, thanks to Black Sparrow, widely available and better edited than Eliot's. If textual studies are the foundation of criticism, Eliot criticism is an imposing edifice without a sufficient foundation.

The attitude of the Eliot Estate is, of course, central to all this, and though its concern may have been to thwart "irresponsible" biographical approaches, its refusal to let biographers like Peter Ackroyd quote anything (see *ALS 1984*) has led, paradoxically, to the situation where *only* "irresponsible" biographers can flourish. And this is the context in which the only significant explorations of Eliot's biography this year are plays: Michael Hasting's *Tom and Viv*, the 1984 West End play that provoked an extensive correspondence in *TLS*, has been published (Penguin, 1985); produced but not yet published was Caroline Behr's *Possum in the Bughouse* (reviewed in

TLS, 16 May), a play in which Eliot visits Pound at St. Elizabeths. I have seen neither play performed, but *Tom and Viv* in print seems far from the libelous scandal it has been called. It is a probing but sensitive exploration of a tragic situation that everyone interested in Eliot ought to read, and Hastings's introduction to the Penguin edition both defends the play well and tells amusingly of the opposition the project encountered during Hastings's research and during the play's West End run.

***b.* General Studies.** Quantitatively, a good deal of work fits into this category this year, but little of it merits sustained attention. Marianne Thormahlen had an intriguing concept in *Eliot's Animals* (Lund, Sweden: C. W. K. Gleerup, 1984), but the working out of it is much less satisfying than her earlier *The Waste Land: A Fragmentary Wholeness* (1978). Part of the problem is her humorlessness: she does not find it necessary to discuss *Old 'Possum's Book of Practical Cats* since it is only "a more or less appealing bagatelle." Instead, she tracks every animal image in the rest of the oeuvre, organizing her study according to animal; this acontextual approach simply is not very illuminating.

Even less satisfactory is William Skaff's *The Philosophy of T. S. Eliot: From Skepticism to a Surrealist Poetic, 1909–1927* (Penn.). Though Skaff is well read in the philosophy, anthropology, and comparative religion Eliot studied, he goes over ground already covered by earlier critics such as Howarth and Margolis as if no one had ever written on these topics. Particularly troubling is his failure to remark an excellent essay on "Eliot and Logical Atomism" by Richard Shusterman which advanced virtually the same thesis about Eliot's debt to Bertrand Russell some years earlier. Another problem with Skaff's book is that he means the definite article in his title: Eliot had *one* philosophy, and Skaff can tell us what it is. Moreover, he has an unpersuasive thesis that he rides too hard about the essentially surrealist nature of Eliot's poetry. Despite some useful material on Eliot's intellectual background, this book is (or should be) an embarrassment to the University of Pennsylvania Press.

Agha Shahid Ali's *T. S. Eliot as Editor* (UMI) focuses on Eliot's editing of *The Criterion* and is full of useful information; the author's reverential tone, however, prevents him from analyzing why—in the phrase of Pound he quotes—"the odour of the undertaker's establishment" hung over *The Criterion*. Another published dissertation,

Jeanne Gunner's *T. S. Eliot's Romantic Dilemma: Tradition's Anti-Traditional Elements* (Garland, 1985), is unfortunately a book in search of a subject. Gunner wants to answer the recent Romantic critics' criticism of Eliot's anti-Romanticism, but she accepts too much of their case to be able to answer them. I personally cannot imagine finding both their case against Eliot *and* Eliot's own work compelling, but that is the dilemma out of which this unsuccessful and badly organized book is written. Harold Bloom is perhaps the most important of these critics, so his editing a collection of essays on Eliot might seem a grotesque mismatch. And, indeed, his introduction to *T. S. Eliot: Modern Critical Views* (Chelsea House, 1985) shows Bloom still obsessed with putting modernism in a double bind: Eliot is castigated for not fitting into Bloom's reductive and monolingual vision of poetic tradition as the English Romantic tradition, yet Bloom also argues that Eliot is really a Romantic poet. But after the introduction, Bloom's is a reasonably useful book, reprinting nine good essays on different aspects of Eliot's work by critics from Hugh Kenner to Gregory Jay. R. A. York's *The Poem as Utterance* has an interesting general project, which is to use speech-act theory and pragmatics to explore the relation between poems and utterances in speech, but the chapter on Eliot does not offer much that would help a reader of Eliot.

If most of these books are not very impressive, only some of the articles are better. Two studies of Eliot in *The Literary Criterion* have little to offer: C. T. Thomas's "T. S. Eliot through Western and Eastern Eyes" (21,iv:80–86) has no discernible thesis at all; Ujjal Dutta's point in "Ideology into Criticism: The Case of T. S. Eliot" (21,iii:91–99) is that Eliot's praise of objectivity, being ideologically determined, is itself not objective. In "T. S. Eliot's Symbolical Woman: From Temptress to Priestess" (*MQ* 27:476–86), Susan L. Roberson offers a fairly formulaic interpretation that finds Monica in *The Elder Statesman* to be Eliot's most satisfactory female character because she avoids the either/or dichotomy Roberson finds in the earlier work. However, two good articles explore Eliot's intellectual background. Mark Manganaro's "Dissociation in 'Dead Land': The Primitive Mind in the Early Poetry of T. S. Eliot" (*JML* 13:97–110) focuses on the influence of the anthropologist Lucien Lévy-Bruhl on Eliot's presentation of the isolation of modern man and, more suggestively, of the poet as a kind of contemporary shaman. J. M. Kertzer's concern, in "T. S. Eliot and the Problem of Will" (*MLQ* 45[1984]:373–94), is to relate the "willessness" of many figures in Eliot's early poetry to the philosophies of Bradley and Schopenhauer; Kertzer sees Eliot's desire to get out of the impasse of will as a crucial element in Eliot's conversion. Finally, Aidan Nichols's "T. S. Eliot and Yves Congar on the Nature of Tradition" (*Angelicum* 81[1984]:473–85), while a piece of theology I find opaque, usefully reminds us that Eliot has readers other than students of literature, readers who take Eliot's Christianity and Christian writings as the center of his importance and the major reason to read him. There are a number of T. S. Eliots.

***c.* Relation to Other Writers.** This seems to have been the most lively arena for Eliot studies this year. C. K. Stead's *Pound, Yeats, Eliot and the Modernist Movement* both places Eliot at the very center of modernism and blames him for the movement's failure to sustain itself. He stands at the center of modernism for showing how to construct poems by means of "aggregation," influencing Pound and virtually everyone else in the process. But he caused its demise, according to Stead, by embracing political concerns and by failing to articulate a modernist aesthetic in his criticism; and Eliot's failures are represented in *Four Quartets*, which Stead loathes and denounces. Stead is better where he praises than where he denounces, and his discussion of the failure of the criticism (which contains a perceptive treatment of the relation of Eliot and Auden) is better than his discussion of politics. But everyone interested in Eliot will need to come to terms with his arguments and will be pleased by the centrality he ascribes to Eliot whether he is praising or denouncing him.

Four other books that also make Eliot central are less challenging. Margaret Dickie's *The Modernist Long Poem*, by treating *The Waste Land* first, obscures Eliot's place in the tradition she treats as much as she obscures Pound by placing him last; *The Cantos* were, after all, begun before *The Waste Land*, and it is not at all clear to me that *The Waste Land* is a long poem in the sense that poems by Pound, Williams, Zukovsky, Olson, and others are. In the three chapters devoted to Eliot in *The Failure of Modernism*, Andrew Ross gives Eliot almost as hard a time as Stead does. The failure of modernism for Ross is a confusion between "subjectivity" and "subjectivism," and Eliot's emphasis in his criticism on impersonality is one cause of this confusion. Ross traces back Eliot's interest in objectivity only to his dissertation on Bradley, ignoring the equally important influences on Eliot's doctrine of impersonality of Oriental philosophy,

Irving Babbitt, Bertrand Russell, and Ezra Pound. I am also not sure why Eliot is Ross's scapegoat here, nor why he needs a scapegoat. How modernism is supposed to have failed is never made clear in this book that, trying to be polemical to avoid being conventionally academic, is simply badly argued and poorly focused. Paul Douglass, in *Bergson, Eliot, and American Literature*, defines a line of influence that runs from Bergson through Eliot to Faulkner and other American writers; he does not persuade me that this line of influence was as important as he thinks it is nor that Eliot was ever as Bergsonian as he thinks he was. As opposed to finding Bergson everywhere in modernism, F. C. McGrath finds Pater everywhere in *The Sensible Spirit: Walter Pater and the Modernist Paradigm* (So. Florida), but the two projects are fairly similar and locate Eliot as central to the line of influence they seek to trace. Both books (but particularly McGrath's) demonstrate one unfortunate byproduct of contemporary critical theory, the license it seems to give to more casual influence studies. McGrath claims to be following a "paradigmatic approach" instead of writing a conventional source study, but he never makes it clear how this "paradigmatic approach" is different or superior. Both books, however, are informative about Bergson and Pater, respectively.

The articles on Eliot's relation to other writers are generally more successful than the books this year, at least partially because the article length helps to restrain the tendency to extend a thesis beyond its useful limits. Eliot's relation to Virgil and Dante is examined in a number of studies. E. Porges Watson's "Virgil and T. S. Eliot" (*Virgil in a Cultural Tradition*, pp. 115–33) hunts rather unsuccessfully through Eliot's poetry looking for Virgilian echoes. Neither Eugenio Frongia, in "'A Heap of Broken Images': T. S. Eliot, Dante, and Fellini's 'La Dolce Vita'" (*ESJ* 2,ii[1985]:52–57), nor, surprisingly, Seamus Heaney, in "Envies and Identifications: Dante and the Modern Poet" (*IUR* 15[1985]:5–19), has anything very new to say about Eliot's relationship to Dante. Frongia compares the pessimism and alienation found in Dante, Eliot, and Fellini; Heaney offers some general reflections on his subject.

An even less successful study is Peter M. Brogno's "T. S. Eliot and Blaise Pascal on the Other Side of Despair" (*PAPA* 11,i[Spring 1985]: 13–25), which argues that the two figures had a "shared itinerary to God." As with a number of other weak studies of this kind, it is impossible to figure out whether Brogno is arguing for an influence or a parallel; either he does not see the difference or he thinks the pointing out of parallels is inherently more interesting than I think it is. William Harmon argues for some very specific borrowings in "Hawthorne and Thackeray: Two Notes on Eliot's Reading and Borrowing" (*YER* 8:123–24), listing among other things individual words Eliot might have taken from *Vanity Fair*.

In work on Eliot's intellectual background T. John Jamieson dissociates two influences in "Babbitt and Maurras as Competing Influences on T. S. Eliot" (in *Irving Babbitt in Our Time*, ed. George A. Panichas and Claes G. Ryn [Catholic Univ.]). His essay and—once one allows for the hagiographic tone—the collection of essays of which it is a part are informative on Babbitt, a major and still insufficiently appreciated influence on Eliot. But Thomas R. Nevin strains credulity when he argues, in "Eliot, Babbitt and the 'Dead Master' of 'Little Gidding'" (*YER* 8:90–95), that Babbitt is the "ghost" of "Little Gidding." Louis Menand's "T. S. Eliot and F. H. Bradley" (*Raritan* 5:61–75) also explores an important intellectual influence on Eliot, but his is less an attempt to use Eliot's dissertation on Bradley as a key to his other works than a useful warning about the impossibility of doing that. His caution might have benefited Michael D. Riley, who, in "Eliot, Bradley, and J. Hillis Miller: The Metaphysical Context" (*YER* 8:76–89), criticizes Hillis Miller's early study *Poets of Reality* for underestimating the influence of Bradley's metaphysics on Eliot.

More important work on Eliot's relations to other writers is done by Kathryne V. Lindberg in "Tradition and Heresy: Pound's Dissociation from Eliot" (*Paideuma* 15,ii–iii:9–37), which traces Pound's critique of Eliot in the 1930s. This study shows how valuable it would be to have a *Pound/Eliot* to accompany the already published *Pound/Joyce*, *Pound/Ford*, and *Pound/Lewis*. Ignoring Pound as a mediating figure, Sigrid Renaux makes an unconvincing claim of direct influence in "Ford Madox Ford's Essay on Poetry and T. S. Eliot's *The Waste Land*" (*RLet* 34[1985]:145–54). Randell Helms, in "T. S. Eliot on Gilbert Murray" (*ELN* 23,iv:50–56), criticizes Eliot for his unfair and inaccurate attack on Murray. Michael Long's chapter on Eliot, Pound, and Joyce in *Unreal City: Urban Experience in Modern European Literature and Art*, ed. Edward Timms and David Kelvey (St. Martin's, 1985), contrasts Joyce's emerging affirmation of the city to Eliot's (and Pound's) more pessimistic view. Also in the contrastive vein is Kathleen Henderson Staudt's "The Language of T. S. Eliot's *Four Quartets* and David Jones's *The Anathemata*" (*Renascence* 38:118–40), which contrasts Eliot's private and "negative" spiritual journey with Jones's public and semiotic form of spirituality. James Tetreault explores some less friendly differences in "Parallel Lines: C. S. Lewis and T. S. Eliot" (*Renascence* 38:256–69), focusing primarily on why—despite similarities in their religious positions—Lewis objected so strongly to Eliot's work. Less noteworthy studies on Eliot's relation to later writers are those of Randy W. Oakes and John Desmond. Oakes's "Myth and Method: Eliot, Joyce, and Wolfe in *The Web and the Rock*" (*TWN* 10:23–26) discusses how Wolfe in that book inclines to Joyce's optimism over Eliot's pessimism. Desmond's "Walker Percy and T. S. Eliot: The Lancelot Andrewes Connection" (*SoR* 22:465–77) discusses parallels between Percy and Eliot in their interest in Lancelot Andrewes and between "Gerontion" and *Lancelot*, though again it is unclear whether a line of influence is being argued for.

***d.* The Poems and Plays.** There was almost no separate discussion of the plays this year, and some unusual emphases in the studies of the poems (such as the *Ariel* poems and "Mr. Apollinax"), though as usual *The Waste Land* has garnered the most substantial and the largest number of studies. Of the three studies of "Prufrock," Robert F. Fleissner's "*Quo Vadis Pedes*: Notes on the Liveryman in *Prufrock*" (*ABR* 36[1985]:394–401) offers some unpersuasive speculations on the religious implications of the figure of the Footman in the poem. Robert McNamara's " 'Prufrock' and the Problem of Literary Narcissism" (*CL* 27:356–77) is considerably more substantial, though more tangled than it need be. McNamara sees "Prufrock" as a critique of the introspective poetry of moods it resembles. Mihai Spariosu has much the same point to make in "The Games of Consciousness in 'The Love Song of J. Alfred Prufrock' " (in *Auctor Ludens*), though his discussion is more general and less incisive than McNamara's. John Coakley's "T. S. Eliot's 'Mr. Apollinax' and Frost's 'The Demiurge's Laugh' " (*Expl* 45,i:42–45) sees a parallel between the two poems; Donald J. Childs proposes Professor W. H. Schofield of Harvard as the Professor Channing-Cheetah of the poem in " 'Mr. Apollinax,' Professor Channing-Cheetah, and T. S. Eliot" (*JML* 13:172–

77). A more ambitious study is Clifford J. Ronan's "Eliot's Polypheman Pastorals" (YER 8:109–18), in which Ronan argues that the Sweeney poems and "Prufrock" are indebted to Theocritus's and other versions of the Polyphemus story. But Ronan seems to me to be reaching.

The most substantial work on *The Waste Land* this year is Calvin Bedient's *He Do the Police in Different Voices*: The Waste Land *and Its Protagonist* (Chicago). Bedient has two central theses: that the poem is unified because its diversity of voices is really the performance of a single protagonist, whom Bedient is careful not to identify with the author; and that the poem turns fairly comfortably to religious affirmation in an anticipation of Eliot's "conversion" of the later 1920s. The first thesis is both more controversial and—to this reader—less persuasive: Occam's razor seems to me enough of an argument against the introduction of a "protagonist," while the major reason for wanting to introduce the notion of the protagonist seems to be that it makes the poem personal in theme without being at all autobiographical. This is probably what led the Estate to permit Bedient to quote the *entire poem* across the book, but Bedient does not convince me that he is correct in seeking to reverse the tide of Eliot criticism toward reading the poem in more personal *and* autobiographical terms. But Bedient's study is a must for everyone, and I cannot do justice to the interest of his fine line-by-line commentary here.

Of the twelve essays on *The Waste Land*, the interesting ones are those by David Trotter, Gerald Doherty, and Wendy Steiner. Trotter's "Modernism and Empire: Reading *The Waste Land*" (*CritQ* 28,i–ii:143–53) is a generally persuasive—if in places, tendentious—attempt to relate *The Waste Land* to contemporary anxieties about the state of the British Empire. In "*The Waste Land* as Modernist Discourse" (*OL* 40[1985]:244–57), Doherty argues persuasively that *The Waste Land* successively and systematically invites and then dismantles models of coherence, ways to make the poem fit together; he is less persuasive in arguing that the end product of all this in the poem's close is a Barthesian exhaustion of signifying activity. A less successful theoretical consideration of the poem is Peter Middleton's "The Academic Development of *The Waste Land*" (in *Demarcating the Disciplines*, ed. Samuel Weber [Glyph Textual Studies 1; Minnesota], pp. 153–80). Middleton's central perception seems close to

Doherty's—that the poem openly invites interpretations yet ultimately sanctions none of them—but he takes this perception as the basis of an attack on *The Waste Land* as the ultimate academic poem that represents (and even seems responsible for) the debility of academic criticism. There seems an awful lot of confusion here, as Middleton's cast of mind and prose style alike seem far more academic than Eliot's. Wendy Steiner offers a good rebuttal of Middleton in her excellent comparison of *The Waste Land* to Thomas Pynchon's *The Crying of Lot 49*, "Collage or Miracle: Historicism in a Deconstructed World" (in *Reconstructing American Literary History*). Steiner's central point in the best essay on *The Waste Land* this year is that the poem undercuts ahistorical close readings, that it is unified not in thematic terms but by the activity of the reader reinscribing the poem into cultural history and thereby escaping "the wasteland solipsism that the poem deplores." This smart use of contemporary theory makes the limitations of an essay like Michael P. Dean's "T. S. Eliot's Tiresias: A Unifying Force in *The Waste Land*" (*POMPA* [1984]: 125–33) all the more painfully obvious. Dean goes over the familiar passages about Tiresias and argues that he holds the poem together by giving it a thematic and narrative closure of a kind it simply does not possess. Jewel Spears Brooker's interests in " 'The Second Coming' and 'The Waste Land': Capstones of the Western Civilization Course" (*CollL* 13:240–53) are predominantly pedagogical: she argues that these two poems are the perfect way to end a Western civilization survey course and then gives the teacher some less interesting pointers on how to teach them. William K. Bottorff thinks he has identified a song Eliot alludes to in "Mrs. Porter's Moon and 'Red Wing' " (*ELN* 22,iv[1985]:58–59). S. A. Cowan finds "Echoes of Donne, Herrick, and Southwell in Eliot's *The Waste Land*" (*YER* 8:96–102). Robert Crawford makes an unconvincing argument in "Rudyard Kipling in *The Waste Land*" (*EIC* 36:32–46) about the influence of Kipling's short stories on the poem. Equally unconvincing but at least less solemn about it is William D. Jenkins's argument, in "On Finding (Fool's?) Gold in 'The Waste Land' " (*BSJ* 36,iii: 99–102), that *The Waste Land* echoes A. Conan Doyle's *The Sign of the Four*. In "T. S. Eliot's *The Waste Land*" (*Expl* 45,i:45–47), P. Marudanayagam argues even less convincingly that the passage in Part V about "the third who walks always beside you" is a reference to a Tamil myth. Finally, Giles Mitchell gives us a dreadful psychoanalytic study in "T. S. Eliot's *The Waste Land*: Death, Fear,

Apathy and Dehumanization" (*AI* 43:23–33) that reproaches Eliot's characters for refusing "to confront death realistically," however one does that.

Richard A. Silvia's "T. S. Eliot's 'Ariel Poems' " (*Expl* 45,i:41–42) finds a correspondence between the "Ariel" sequence and Lancelot Andrewes's 1622 Nativity Sermons. In a less substantive study D. P. Edmunds emphasizes "The Literal in Eliot's 'Journey of the Magi' " (*CRUX* [10/1983]:27–31). Both studies of *Murder in the Cathedral* —the only play receiving separate attention this year—remain on the level of unsatisfactory generalities. Carmen Gago Alvarez gives a Heideggerean summary of the play in "Becket—Being and Its Transcendency" (*Estudos Anglo-Americanos* [São Paulo] 7–8 [1983–84]:74–80). James E. Robinson's central thesis in "*Murder in the Cathedral* as Theatre of the Spirit" (*R&L* 18,ii:31–45) is that the "play is not only Christian drama; it is Theatre of the Spirit." But he never makes it clear what distinction he is trying to draw here, nor why it is a useful one to draw. Of even less note is Jagdish V. Dave's "T. S. Eliot's *Four Quartets* in Relation to the *Bhaghvadgita*" (*LCrit* 20,iii[1985]:26–38), one more rehash of a familiar topic. Two source-hunting essays in the *Yeats Eliot Review* indicate that the whole theory of source studies presently operative in Eliot studies needs to be rethought. Max Keith Sutton's "*John Inglesant* and 'Little Gidding' " (8:119–22) argues that J. H. Shorthouse's historical novel *John Inglesant* is an important source for "Little Gidding." Carol E. Stuart's "*Lilith* and 'Burnt Norton': More Echoes from the Garden" (8:103–08) argues that George MacDonald's "adult fairytale" *Lilith* influenced "Burnt Norton." Stuart reveals the flaws in her methodology: "Although there is no evidence that Eliot knew MacDonald's work, it would be very difficult indeed to prove that he did *not* know it." This is simply not good enough: the critic has to provide some evidence in favor of his or her argument, not rest content with pointing out a lack of counterevidence. Unfortunately, similar principles seem to be at work in many recent essays on *The Waste Land* as well.

It is with relief that I can end this section with the best essay on the later poetry of this year, Martin Warner's "Philosophical Poetry: The Case of *Four Quartets*" (*P&L* 10:222–45), a fine defense of the poem and the genre of philosophical poetry against the charge that it falls between the two stools of philosophy and literature. I do not think Leavis's criticism of the poem on this score needs to be taken as seriously as Leavis himself is for some reason taken in England, but Stead shows that the discussion over the value of *Four Quartets* is still very much a live one, and Warner's essay is a good antidote to Stead.

***e.* The Criticism.** Only three essays on the criticism came to my notice this year. Jacqueline Rose's "Hamlet—the *Mona Lisa* of Literature" (*CritQ* 28,i&ii:35–49) is primarily about *Hamlet*, but her Lacanian reading of psychoanalytic criticism of the play takes its starting point and much of its direction from Eliot's essay on *Hamlet*, even though Eliot comes across as the antifeminist villain of the piece. Michael Ryan's "Eliot's Assumptions" (*Crazyhorse* 26[1984]:67–78) contains a number of interesting observations, though I am not quite sure what makes them hang together. Miroslav Beker's "Eliot, Saussure, and the Russian Formalists" (*Twentieth Century Literatures*, pp. 643–48) offers a fairly interesting if cursory comparison of Eliot's ideas in "Tradition and the Individual Talent" with those of the Russian Formalists. We have come further in recentering Eliot's poetry than we have in recentering his criticism, since uninformed gibes at Eliot and the New Criticism are still a staple of our critical discourse. But the time has come to react against the reaction against Eliot's criticism, to see once again what a good—as well as important—critic he was.

New Mexico State University

9. Faulkner

M. Thomas Inge

There were two major thrusts in Faulkner scholarship this year. A great number of critics addressed the controversial topic of Faulkner's treatment of women in the fiction with impressive results. While the path is thorny and fraught with misunderstanding, several essays brought new light to bear on the subject, though things are still far from resolved. The other major development was in biography, primarily in the interpretation of the factual and fictional records through a variety of critical approaches, psychological and otherwise. The interesting thing is that these 12 books and 100 articles demonstrate that there is no consensus among scholars about critical method; thus every type is to be encountered. This is a sign, I believe, of the richness of the texts and the genuine genius of Faulkner.

i. Bibliography, Editions, and Manuscripts

The bibliographic control of primary and secondary material is conveniently assisted by two dependable projects: William Boozer's quarterly checklists in issues of *The Faulker Newsletter*, which is especially attentive to foreign publications, and the annual "Survey of Research and Criticism" in the Faulkner issue of *MissQ*, rather strict and acerbic in its judgment in that it "ignores articles that are deficient in scholarship or originality." Four critical surveys of mostly 1984 and 1985 books are Panthea Reid Broughton, "Faulkner Biography and Bibliography" (*RALS* 13:41–52); Helen McNeil, "Homage to the Inevitable" (*TLS*, 27 June:704); Michael Grimwood, "The Paradigm Shift in Faulkner Studies" (*SLJ* 19:100–112); and Calvin S. Brown, "These Thirteen Faulkner Books" (*SR* 94:167–80). "Benjy's Sound and Fury: A Critical Study of Four Interpretations" (*REALB* 4:265–90) by Michael Buckwalter evaluates the criticism of Olga W. Vickery, Wolfgang Iser, Donald Kartiganer, and John T. Matthews on *The Sound and the Fury*. The pattern of translations and development of critical opinion on Faulkner in two countries are traced with attentive detail by Catherine Georgoudaki in "The Greek Reception of William Faulkner" (*NMW* 18:1–34) and Jan Nordby Gretlund in "William Faulkner's Strange Career in Danish" (*NMW* 18:35–52).

Noel Polk's "corrected text" edition of *Absalom, Absalom!* from Random House is a faithful reproduction of the original typescript submitted by Faulkner for publication and largely preserves the original inconsistencies and eccentricities. So this is a different text. Whether it is a better text depends on one's belief that what the author submitted is inevitably superior to what was published after the house editing and proofreading were done.

From his seeming inexhaustible supply of unpublished manuscripts, Louis Daniel Brodsky, with the assistance of Robert W. Hamblin, has edited *Country Lawyer and Other Stories for the Screen* (Miss.). Of the three screen treatments, only the title piece demonstrates the marvelous range of Faulkner's narrative ability and is his only effort to adapt Yoknapatawpha material for the movies. "The Life and Death of a Bomber" and "The Damned Don't Cry" are of negligible interest, but I do not see why "Country Lawyer" was not filmed the way he wrote it. It had the makings of a remarkable film. James B. Meriwether has edited one of the several versions of the story generally known as "Spotted Horses" before it came to rest in *The Hamlet*, this one titled interestingly enough "As I Lay Dying" (*MissQ* 39:369–85). Except for an occasional incongruity between language and the point of view of a youthful narrator, the version is quite effective, and we get a closer view of Flem Snopes than usual. A generally neglected but key public statement by Faulkner was his 1952 address to the Delta Council, which is reprinted along with two photographs of the occasion in *The Delta Council: Fifty Years of Service to the Mississippi Delta* (Stoneville: Delta Council) by William M. Cash and R. Daryl Lewis.

Following the footsteps of the textual critics will soon be possible for all of Faulkner's fiction with the *William Faulkner Manuscripts* project approaching completion by Garland Publishing. Edited by Joseph Blotner, Thomas L. McHaney, Michael Millgate, and Noel Polk, with James B. Meriwether serving as senior consulting editor (a veritable who's who of Faulkner scholarship), 36 volumes were published by 1986 with another eight to come. Each volume or set collects and photographically reproduces the manuscripts, typescripts, and selected galleys for each work. What is unexpectedly interesting is the canceled material on the versos of some pages (Faulkner never threw away a scrap)—drafts of letters and essays, shopping lists, fictional genealogies, and so on. The set will be an invaluable storehouse of fascinating material and should generate a good deal of soundly considered textual scholarship.

ii. Biography

Although there are few revelations in Jim Faulkner's *Across the Creek: Faulkner Family Stories* (Miss.), the nine brief sketches have the value of coming from someone who spent a good deal of time with Faulkner as his favorite nephew (Jim is the son of brother John). The informed reader will recognize the sources of many incidents and characters in the fiction, but the stories also have a charm of their own. There are plenty of biographical glimpses of Faulkner from an admiring friend in *Conversations with Malcolm Cowley* (Miss.), ed. Thomas Daniel Young. Dan Brennan briefly recalls "A Visit with Faulkner" (*SatR*, May/June:72) in 1940.

Louis Daniel Brodsky, in "Faulkner's Life Masks" (*SR* 22:738–65), assembles everything Faulkner said about the profession of authorship in his fiction, letters, and interviews and applies the material to a survey of his life in an attempt to understand "Faulkner's dissatisfaction with himself as a physically inactive individual and with his role as a writer." The result is an intriguing piece of biographical scholarship that works without recourse to the clichés and categories of psychological criticism. In a similar biographical exercise, "Faulkner's Self-Portraits" (*FJ* 2,i:2–13), Michael Gresset examines Faulkner's portraits of himself in the fiction and poetry, which Gresset sees as efforts on the author's part to say: "Through my work, I have added myself to actuality, not because I have existed but because I have written." Both essays are of considerable interest.

Carl E. Rollyson's "'Counterpull': Estelle and William Faulkner" (*SAQ* 85:215–27) makes better sense of the author's marriage and his relationships with other women than have most other biographical accounts. Rollyson makes out a strong case for Estelle as Faulkner's "inspiration, his nemesis, and his first love." In "William Faulkner and the Faulkner Family Name" (*Names* 34:255–65), O. B. Emerson and John J. Hermann summarize everything that has been said about the change in spelling of the family name and conclude that it primarily had to do with Faulkner's enabling others to pronounce the name correctly and defining himself within his own community. This should be the last word necessary on the matter. Although the topic needs further exploration, Robert Roper's "Faulkner & West vs. H'wood" (*California* 2,i:144, 153, 161–62) makes a beginning at supporting the seldom-argued point that the lives of writers in Hollywood were of greater creative importance to them than we are encouraged to believe, especially for Faulkner and Nathanael West, who once hunted wild boars together on Santa Cruz Island. Mike Granberry's "Bearing with Carvel Collins" (*Southern Magazine* 1,iv: 28–29) offers some reasons why Collins's long-awaited biography of Faulkner has yet to appear. *The Faulkner Newsletter* continues to publish memoirs, letters, and other items of biographical interest.

Faulkner makes an interesting appearance in a novel this year, Lawrence Wells's *Rommel & The Rebel* (Doubleday). Using the historical fact that several German military officers visited Mississippi in 1937 to study the 1864 battle strategy of Nathan Bedford Forrest, Wells imagines what might have happened had one of the officers been Field Marshal Erwin Rommel under an assumed name and encountered Faulkner in Oxford. The scenes with Faulkner and the Oxford milieu have the ring of authenticity (the author lives there), and an unlikely premise becomes quite credible in Wells's skillful narrative.

iii. Criticism: General

Much like the essay by Brodsky mentioned above, Michael Grimwood's *Heart in Conflict: Faulkner's Struggles with Vocation* (Georgia) is a study of the ways Faulkner viewed his vocation as a writer, but from a distinctly Freudian point of view (modified though by the theories of Erik Erikson). Some of the material has been reviewed here earlier as essays (see *ALS 1984*, p. 173, and *ALS 1985*, p. 167). I remain apprehensive about the reductive nature of such psychological criticism, which often seems to make the creative act into simple therapy for the writer, a way of resolving tensions in the private life. Grimwood focuses on the apprenticeship years and what he sees as a period of decline after *Absalom, Absalom!*, especially the "articulately disordered narratives"—*The Wild Palms, The Hamlet, Knight's Gambit,* and *Go Down, Moses,* works which fail because "Faulkner's literary vocation was fatally rooted in deception and fraudulence." The deception was a result of unresolved tensions between the two sides of his personality as an illiterate bumpkin and a sophisticated aesthete. Grimwood's insights are often compelling and his arguments engaging, so the book requires attention whether or not one agrees with him. He also provides a good deal of useful historical/cultural context as background for his theories.

Also concerned with psychology (as well as anthropology) is Constance Hill Hall's *Incest in Faulkner: A Metaphor for the Fall* (UMI Research Press), except the application is to the work rather than the writer. Hall finds the theme of incest pervasive in Faulkner's fiction. Social scientists have suggested that the purposes of incest taboos have to do with survival—"the propogation of the species, the cohesion of society, and the integration of the individual"—and all of these are illustrated in the novels. For Faulkner, incest was a metaphor for Original Sin, and Hall amply supports her thesis by thorough examinations of *Flags in the Dust*, *The Sound and the Fury*, and *Absalom, Absalom!* Especially striking are the parallels she finds between these novels and Milton's *Paradise Lost* (in fact the study might well have been subtitled a comparative analysis of Faulkner and Milton on the theme of incest), and between *Flags in the Dust* and Thomas Mann's *Death in Venice*. The Miltonic parallels deserve further study.

Although the title does not make this clear, James A. Snead's *Figures of Division: William Faulkner's Major Novels* (Methuen) is about the language and rhetoric of social and racial segregation in human and literary discourse, with Faulkner serving as the example of a writer who weaves the logic of segregation and arbitrary social division into his fiction and then breaks it down conceptually for the reader. The rhetorical strategies of the dominant class are the "figures of division" that Faulkner analyzes and questions through characters who deny or cross social and racial boundaries in the pursuit of a more accurate reality and the reunion of what only seem to be opposites. There are individual chapters on *The Sound and the Fury*, *As I Lay Dying*, *Light in August*, *Absalom, Absalom!*, *The Hamlet*, and *Go Down, Moses*. The close analyses of language and rhetoric require very careful reading, but semioticians and followers of the Yale school of literary criticism should have no problem.

Richard Gray's *Writing the South* is an attempt to answer the question, "Is there such a thing as the South?" by examining the writings of southerners who have created the idea of a South in the process of seeing and describing it. In the chapter on Faulkner (pp. 165–

216) Gray discusses the novelist's assumption that he created a unified fictional world. "The tale of Yopnapatawpha County, the premise is, can somehow be separated from the books in which it is told, and indeed from its teller; it stands apart from them . . . ." For Faulkner, Yoknapatawpha "*became* the South: not just an emblem of the South but his way of understanding it and using it to encode experience." Using principles of linguistic theory and structural anthropology in a balanced and sensible way, Gray discusses such themes as sense of place, the past, evil, sexuality, self-consciousness, and the relationship between reality and language in the fiction, with special attention to *The Sound and the Fury*.

iv. Criticism: Special Studies

The major thematic concern for criticism this year was Faulkner's attitudes toward and uses of women in his fiction, primarily promoted through the publication of the proceedings of the 1985 Faulkner and Yoknapatawpha Conference on "Faulkner and Women" but also by the publication of a portion of one book, two general essays, and several articles focusing on specific works. The intense light shown by such a variety of first-rate critical sensibilities will have a considerable impact on the studies to come on this topic.

Seven of the 15 conference papers in *Faulkner and Women* are general essays. Joseph Blotner's "William Faulkner: Life and Art" (pp. 3–20) categorizes the fictional women and aligns them with real women who might have served as models, and Ilse Dusoir Lind examines "The Mutual Relevance of Faulkner Studies and Women's Studies" (pp. 21–40), especially in the areas of gender definition, ideology, and psychological theory. In "Faulkner's Critics and Women: The Voices of the Community" (pp. 41–57), John N. Duvall reads some of the earlier commentary on the subject and demonstrates how it often elucidates the attitude of the critic rather than Faulkner.

Sergei Chakovsky discusses a number of "Women in Faulkner's Novels" (pp. 58–80) in a broad critical context and finds that Faulkner moves during the development of his career from depicting women as stereotypes to seeing them as individuals, and that androgyny became for him "a romantic symbol of woman's humanity." In "Meditations on the Other: Faulkner's Rendering of Women" (pp. 81–99), Philip M. Weinstein argues that primarily the women are "in the service of the narrative urge, present throughout his career, to probe the deepest recesses of his men." Mimi R. Gladstein's survey of "Mothers and Daughters in Endless Procession: Faulkner's Use of the Demeter/Persephone Myth" (pp. 100–111) notes that Faulkner used the myth optimistically to affirm not only the relevance and continuity of women but the human will to survive.

The essay that explores the most interesting new territory is "Faulkner and Women Writers" (pp. 270–94). Judith Bryant Wittenberg surveys those women writers who may have influenced the fiction. What is especially striking is her discussion of the problems in language, attitude, and assumptions that arise when someone even undertakes to discuss critically the idea of a female writer influencing a male writer. The reader truly learns something new.

The paper by Mimi R. Gladstein mentioned above is excerpted from her chapter on Faulkner in *The Indestructible Woman in Faulkner, Hemingway, and Steinbeck* (UMI Research Press). Here the discussion of the Demeter/Persephone myth is placed in a larger context of Faulkner's conscious and subconscious use of various regional and universal mythologies, but the larger discussion makes clear what the essay does not—that Gladstein believes that Faulkner basically was a misogynyst. Although the current scholarship seriously questions that viewpoint, I suppose one can still adhere to it, but at this stage it is quite surprising to find someone holding, as Gladstein does, to the thesis that Faulkner was a pessimistic Naturalist and prophet of despair, and to see someone quoting with approval Gustaf Hellstrom of the Swedish Academy: "Faulkner has often been described as a determinist. He himself, however, has never claimed to adhere to any special philosophy of life. Briefly, his view of life may perhaps be summed up in his own words: that the whole thing (perhaps?) signifies nothing." We know better than that now, and both Hellstrom and Gladstein should know that those last words are Shakespeare's, not Faulkner's.

Two feminist essays on Faulkner are Anne Goodwyn Jones's "Gender and the Great War: The Case of Faulkner and Porter" (*WS* 13:135–48) and Gail L. Mortimer's "The Smooth, Suave Shape of Desire: Paradox in Faulknerian Imagery of Women" (*WS* 13:149–61), paired in the same journal issue. Jones examines the influence of World War I on gender definitions in the male and female imagination as seen in the fiction of Faulkner and Katherine Anne Porter, and describes how they questioned the traditions of the southern gentleman and lady, respectively. Mortimer contends that usually "Faulkner's protagonists are brooding, troubled men whose encounters with women tend to leave them feeling baffled and helpless," and she examines specific kinds of imagery having to do with water, urns, and vases through which he suggests both positive and horrifying responses to the feminine. Both are balanced, sensible essays.

A long-neglected aspect of Faulkner's work was served well in 1986 through the publication of *Faulkner and Humor*, the proceedings of the 1984 Faulkner and Yoknapatawpha Conference. Seven of the 13 essays address specific novels and will be discussed below under individual works. Thomas L. McHaney recounts "What Faulkner Learned from the Tall Tale" (pp. 110–35) and traces how he worked away from the influence of "the fin de siècle decadents to, or back to, the antebellum Southern humorists" during the course of his career, and greatly benefited thereby in content and style. Hans Bungert's "Faulkner's Humor: A European View" (pp. 136–51) proves that German readers and critics have always been attuned to Faulkner's humor. He also pinpoints important characteristics of that humor in the style, language, and structure of the fiction. My own contribution to the volume, "Faulkner Reads the Funny Papers" (pp. 153–90), is an illustrated survey of the influences specific comic strips may have had on his early cartoons and the later fiction, especially E. C. Segar's *Popeye* on *Sanctuary* and George McManus's *Bringing Up Father* on *Pylon*. Barry Hannah's "Faulkner and the Small Man" (pp. 191–94) is a suggestive sketch that affiliates Faulkner's baggy figure around Oxford with Charlie Chaplin's little tramp.

"Lacan and Faulkner: A Post-Freudian Analysis of Humor in the Fiction" (pp. 195–215) by James M. Mellard is an application of the humor theories of Sigmund Freud as reinterpreted by Jacques Lacan to the comic practice of Faulkner with revealing results. Careful reading is required, but the results are most rewarding. In " 'Fix My Hair, Jack': The Dark Side of Faulkner's Jokes" (pp. 216–31), George Garrett finds that all of Faulkner's fiction, even the most tragic, is interlaced with his humor. It is often sardonic but always affirms a comic vision which he sustained despite the vicissitudes of his literary career and personal life. Garrett's criticism, like his fiction, is always lucid and full of insight.

Faulkner's attitudes toward the culture of place and region, the rituals of urban and rural communities, are thoroughly explored in the chapter "William Faulkner: The Memphis-Oxford Connection," in Ted R. Spivey's *Revival* (pp. 62–84). Spivey finds that Faulkner saw "Memphis as part of the American megalopolitan sprawl engulfing traditional Southern communities and destroying all memory of ordered moral life." Faulkner's connections with a nearby state are explored in several articles in a pamphlet by Frank Burns, *Mr. Faulkner and Tennessee* (Tennessee Homecoming '86), mostly biographical connections and uses of Tennessee territory in the fiction. Also concerned with place is Elizabeth Duvert's "Faulkner's Map of Time" (*FJ* 2,i:14–28), a study of his intentions in creating his own map of Yoknapatawpha County and how it becomes an icon of his "vision of landscape as spatialized time." This is a perceptive study of how time relates to space in Faulkner's imagined world, and its implications are extensive.

Duvert notes the influence of Henri Bergson on Faulkner's conception of time, a connection more fully explored in two chapters of Paul Douglass's *Bergson, Eliot, and American Literature*. "Deciphering Faulkner's Uninterrupted Sentence" (pp. 118–41) reviews critically the previous discussions of Bergson's influence and locates the most important parallel in Faulkner's nonstop sentences meant to embrace the whole of human experience. "Faulkner and the Bergsonian Self" (pp. 142–65) compares their belief that freedom is directly related to self-knowledge and self-acceptance. Douglass successfully asserts the continuing relevance of Bergson to understanding modern American literature, especially Faulkner. Both Joseph M. Flora's "Cabell and Faulkner: Connections, Literary and Otherwise" (*Kalki* 8:271–75) and Carvell Collins's "Likeness Within Difference: Cabell and Faulkner" (*Kalki* 8:276–83) outline parallels rather than demonstrate influence. The biographical connections between Faulkner and Stark Young are summarized in Susan Snell, " 'Aristocrat' and 'Commoner': The Professions and Souths of Stark Young and William Faulkner" (*SoQ* 24,iv:93–100). Doreen Fowler and Carl Herzig identify a woman writer quoted in *The Town* in a note on "The Faulkner-Djuna Barnes Connection" (*FJ* 1,ii:77–78). In "The Town That Was an Open Wound" (*CLS* 23:24–43), Mary E. Davis briefly notes parallels with and uses of Faulkner's fiction in that of Colombian writer Gabriel García Márquez.

v. Individual Works to 1929

Among Faulkner's early novels only *The Sound and the Fury* received individual critical attention this year. If Paul Douglass has revived the Bergsonian theories of time in their applicability to Faulkner, Bernhard Radloff does the same for Martin Heidegger by applying his explanation of human temporality in two essays: "The Unity of Time in *The Sound and the Fury*" (*FJ* 1,ii:56–68) and "Time and Timepieces: A Note on Quentin's Section of *The Sound and the Fury*" (*ELN* 23:51–57). The first proposes a structuralist analysis of Dilsey's experience as one which "expresses the unity of the three dimensions of time" (that is, past, present, and future) and the second explores the structure of the time-field in Quentin's section as expressed through his consciousness. Both arguments are carefully reasoned. Richard Feldstein's "Patterns of Idiot Consciousness" (*L&P* 32:10–19) traces the series of associational sequences used by Faulkner to achieve a psychologically sound pattern of idiot consciousness in Benjy's section of the novel.

While it has been suggested from time to time that Jason Compson should be viewed as a humorist, this idea is given full exploration in two excellent essays in the *Faulkner and Humor* volume, James M. Cox's "Humor as Vision in Faulkner" (pp. 1–20) and William N. Claxon's "Jason Compson: A Demoralized Wit" (pp. 21–33). Cox finds humor to be at the very heart of all Faulkner's fiction, especially *The Sound and the Fury*, where to be aware of Jason's humor is "to be fully in touch with the humanity of the large loss Faulkner is at once envisioning amd enacting." Cox fully supports his thesis and produces one of the best essays ever written on Faulkner's comedy. Claxon finds that Jason practices three forms of wit—self-irony, riddle, and humorous scenic description—which elicit a degree of admiration even as they illustrate his dark and irredeemable malice. Both essays elucidate the thin line between tragedy and comedy and their inextricability. In "Faulkner's Benjy, Hemingway's Jake" (*CollL* 13:300–304), Merritt Moseley briefly compares two literary castratos, and Arline R. Standley compares *The Sound and the Fury* with *Fogo Morto* by Brazilian novelist José Lins do Rego as examples of regionalism in "Here and There: Now and Then" (*LBR* 23:61–75).

vi. Individual Works, 1930–1949

All the novels from the second decade of Faulkner's career received some attention this year, with *As I Lay Dying* and *Absalom, Absalom!* being the front-runners with eight articles each and *Light in August* next with six. Charles Palliser's "Predestination and Freedom in

As I Lay Dying" (*AL* 58:557–73) sensibly expands on the traditional view that the novel stresses the importance of words vs. deeds, the unreality of language vs. the reality of action, and examines the attitudes of Addie and Darl to argue that "Faulkner is establishing a crucial distinction between real and pretended belief in the predestined nature of Providence or the Word of God." In "*As I Lay Dying*: Literary Imagination, the Child's Mind, and Mental Illness" (*SoR* 22:51–68), David Kleinbard provides further support for Faulkner's intuitive grasp of psychological theory through an analysis of Darl, who shows how incipient schizophrenia can both encourage and cripple imagination and insight. Laura Mathews argues, in "Shaping the Life of Man: Darl Bundren as Supplementary Narrator in *As I Lay Dying*" (*JNT* 16:231–45), that in order to resolve the technical difficulties of multiple narrators and authorial control, Faulkner allows Darl to serve as a primary authorial narrator to assist the reader. She contends this to be true in spite of Darl's schizophrenia and ultimate insanity.

Patricia R. Schroeder traces how Faulkner has successfully woven elements of southwestern humor, black humor, and classical comedy into an affirmation of the comic vision in "The Comic World of *As I Lay Dying*" (*Faulkner and Humor*, pp. 34–46). A. M. Potter turns to the Bible, both Old and New Testaments, as a way of explicating "The Role of 'Cash' Within the Religious Structure of 'As I Lay Dying' " (*Theoria* 65[1985]:49–64), but the text of the novel is read too literally in this theological interpretation. Charles Chappell's "The Mathematical Bequest of Addie Bundren" (*FJ* 1,ii:69–74) outlines a clever explanation for the ambiguous reference in Addie's only interior monologue to the three children that belong to Anse, but only a mathematician will fully grasp it. Some interesting parallels between *As I Lay Dying* and Anne Tyler's *Dinner at the Homesick Restaurant* are discussed by Adrienne Bond in "From Addie Bundren to Pearl Tull: The Secularization of the South" (*SoQ* 24,iii:64–73). The novels do elucidate each other and the similarities are striking, but there is no evidence that Tyler was intentionally updating Faulkner's story. Ann Lecercle-Sweet's "The Chip and the Chink: The Dying of the 'I' in *As I Lay Dying*" (*FJ* 2,i:46–61) is a translation of an essay previously published in French and reviewed here (see *ALS 1985*, p. 459).

All three studies of *Sanctuary* focus on Temple Drake and take issue with the traditional negative view of her paradoxical character, the combined innocence with depravity and her seeming roles as nymphomaniac and corrupt whore. Robert B. Moore in "Desire and Despair: Temple Drake's Self-Victimization" (*Faulkner and Women*, pp. 112–27) argues that Temple is a victim of evil and the novel is about the process whereby the victim becomes the victimizer. Moore betrays, however, a distinct masculine perspective: when he says Temple is "fair game for our sexual fantasies," surely he means for men. "Bewildered Witness: Temple Drake in *Sanctuary*" (*FJ* 1,ii: 43–55) by Elisabeth Muhlenfeld contends that our failure to take into account the fact that Temple is an adolescent and not a woman causes us to misunderstand her behavior. Muhlenfeld's reading of the novel with this in mind greatly clarifies many ambiguities, including the perjury at the end. Dianne Luce Cox, "A Measure of Innocence: *Sanctuary*'s Temple Drake" (*MissQ* 39:301–24), reminds us that we need also to take into account that Horace Benbow tells the story and his views are colored by his own sexual obsessions. Cox's reading is compatible with Muhlenfeld's and supplies as well some interesting parallels with Shakespeare's *Measure for Measure*.

"In Praise of Helen" (*Faulkner and Women*, pp. 128–43) by André Bleikasten surveys the use of classical myth and pastoral in *Light in August* and sees Lena (Helen) as Faulkner's tribute to feminine fertility, endurance, and triumph. Doreen Fowler's "Joe Christmas and 'Womanshenegro' " (*Faulkner and Women*, pp. 144–61) addresses the charge of antiwomanism in Faulkner's fiction by examining the context for it in *Light in August* and convincingly argues that through Christmas Faulkner was indicting a sexist and racist society for which he had no admiration. In "Fusion and Confusion in *Light in August*" (*FJ* 1,ii:2–16), Arnold Weinstein finds that the reconciliation of opposites represented by Joe Christmas and Lena Grove is accomplished by the confusion between various characters and names, especially between Joe and Lena's baby at the end. The argument is more complex than this but eminently reasonable.

As the title indicates, " 'Keep Your Muck': A Horneyan Analysis of Joe Christmas and *Light in August*" by Marjorie B. Haselswerdt (*Third Force Psychology*, pp. 206–24) represents an application to Faulkner of the theories of Karen Horney and other "Third Force" psychologists (as distinct from the Freudian and the behaviorist groups). Christmas is found to be a type of aggressive personality called "arrogant-vindictive." While the description fits on the whole,

I am not sure it tells us anything new. This approach also leads to a literal interpretation that distorts the novel and causes the critic to conclude strangely that *Light in August* appeals to "our less wholesome impulses." Doreen Fowler's essay should be read as a corrective to this one. Robert L. Feldman's "In Defense of Reverend Hightower: It Is Never Too Late" (*CLAJ* 29:352–67) makes out a strong case for Hightower as a character who symbolizes the potential for spiritual growth open even at the end of life. In "The Levity of *Light in August*" (*Faulkner and Humor*, pp. 47–56), Virginia Hlavsa sees the parallels between the 21 chapters of the novel and the 21 chapters of the Gospel of St. John as a humorous game plan on Faulkner's part. Maybe so, but as Faulkner once said about parallels between Oedipus and Joe Christmas, "The similarity is there but it was not by deliberate intent. It was by coincidence—not accident but coincidence" (*Faulkner and the University*, 1959, p. 72).

The continuing relevance of biographical criticism is amply and impressively demonstrated in "Money and Matter in *Pylon* and *Wild Palms*" (*FJ* 1,ii:17–29) by Karl F. Zender, a conclusive study of financial transactions and materialistic concerns in the two novels and how they reflect Faulkner's life and artistic attitudes. Gail L. Mortimer provides a thorough reading of *The Wild Palms* as a Freudian rejection of transcendent love as illusion, with special attention to the anal compulsive behavior of the characters, in "The Ironies of Transcendent Love in Faulkner's *The Wild Palms*" (*FJ* 1,ii:30–42). Laurie A. Bernhardt's "'Being Worthy Enough': The Tragedy of Charlotte Rittenmeyer" (*MissQ* 39:351–64) shifts the usual critical focus from Harry Welbourne to Charlotte Rittenmeyer in *The Wild Palms* and finds her more admirable a figure than do most critics, her tragic flaw being "her inability to see love, like art, as a creative, life-giving act."

The eight essays on *Absalom, Absalom!* demonstrate a variety of critical approaches. The most original may be "Opening Pandora's Box: Re-Reading Compson's Letter and Faulkner's *Absalom, Absalom!*" (*CentR* 30:358–82), another in a series of similar studies by David Krause (see also *ALS 1983*, p. 166, and *ALS 1984*, p. 168), this one providing "a close consideration of Faulkner's strategies in presenting Quentin reading his father's letter and manipulating our reading of that reading." It is a little like being lost in the hall of mirrors but fun. In "*Absalom, Absalom!*: An Ontological Approach to Sutpen's 'Design'" (*Mosaic* 19:45–56), Bernhard Radloff develops the idea that since "Sutpen's design arose out of the oral tradition, an analysis of the semantic and temporal structure of this design will lead us back into the heart of the narrative movement of the novel." The argument is effectively articulated.

Deborah L. Clarke asserts with forceful conviction in "Familiar and Fantastic: Women in *Absalom, Absalom!*" (*FJ* 2,i:62–72) that the women in the novel are full of inherent contradictions, real and unreal, ordinary and extraordinary, and therefore are fantastic, and the narrative structure being shaped by them takes on the fantastic attitudes they embody. The importance of Shreve as storyteller and the effect this has on narrative strategy and meaning are accounted for in "Shreve's Bon in *Absalom, Absalom!*" (*MissQ* 39:325–35) by Steve Price, while David Paul Ragan tries to explain why Quentin responds so passionately to meeting Henry Sutpen at the end of the novel when he visits Sutpen's Hundred in " 'The Tragedy Is Second-Hand': Quentin, Henry, and the Ending of *Absalom, Absalom!*" (*MissQ* 39:337–50). Ragan believes it is the shock of recognition in Henry of his own problems (as explored in *The Sound and the Fury*) that disturbs Quentin.

"The Chronology and Genealogy of *Absalom, Absalom!*: The Authority of Fiction and the Fiction of Authority" (*SAF* 14:191–97) by Robert Dale Parker surveys the discrepancies between the novel and the chronology and genealogy added later by Faulkner and concludes that we are totally disallowed from trusting either as final authority and thus left in a suspended state of fictionality. Susan Swartzlander's " 'That Meager and Fragile Thread': The Artist as Historian in *Absalom, Absalom!*" (*SoSt* 25:111–19) takes note of these same discrepancies and suggests that they are purposeful—"to force the reader to surrender misguided perceptions of the past, those that depend on inconsequential details," and "confront the fundamental human features of history." She then provides an intelligent reading of the novel as a commentary on history. However, I am not sure either Parker or Swartzlander provides a satisfactory explanation for the discrepancies. Mary Ann Dazey's "Truth in Fiction and Myth in Political Rhetoric: The Old South's Legacy" (*SoSt* 25:305–10) is a comparison of the public addresses of U.S. Senator John C. Stennis and the fiction of Faulkner (both had similar Mississippi backgrounds) on the causes of the Civil War, with *Absalom, Absalom!* serving as a main source.

In an effort to explicate the vague phrase "no bloody moon" used by the blockade-runner, Jenny Du Pre, and Bayard in *The Unvanquished*, Winifred L. Frazer argues that it means "no bloody woman" in "Faulkner and Womankind: 'No Bloody Moon'" (*Faulkner and Women*, 162–79). The argument is not persuasive, but her general comments on the women in the novel are enlightening. "Reading Faulkner's *The Unvanquished*" (*CollL* 13:217–39) by James Hinkle is a set of glossary notes on words, phrases, and references in the first two sections of chapter one of *The Unvanquished* ("no bloody moon" is not included). This is a preview of a forthcoming "Reading Faulkner" series of books under Hinkle's editorship from the University Press of Mississippi, intended to provide line-by-line commentaries on the major novels and stories. Jane Isbell Haynes supplies one more analogue for the Celia Cook story in *The Unvanquished*, *Intruder in the Dust*, and *Requiem for a Nun*, in "Another Source for Faulkner's Inscribed Window Panes" (*MissQ* 39:365–67).

vii. Individual Works, 1940–1949

Seven of the nine new articles on works from the third decade are devoted to *Go Down, Moses*. "The Speech Community of *The Hamlet*" (*CentR* 30:400–414) by Louise K. Barnett is a sensible appreciation of the part language and speech plays in that novel, and "I'd Rather Be Ratliff: A Maslovian Study of Faulkner's *Snopes* [*sic*]" by Marjorie B. Haselswerdt (*Third Force Psychology*, pp. 225–39) is a reprint of an essay previously reviewed here (see *ALS 1981*, p. 157).

Three of the essays on *Go Down, Moses* consider its uses of humor. Daniel Hoffman, "Faulkner's 'Was' and Uncle Adam's Cow" (*Faulkner and Humor*, pp. 57–78), identifies with authority the folk humor and folklore on which Faulkner probably drew in "Was," and Nancy B. Sederberg, "'A Momentary Anesthetic of the Heart': A Study of the Comic Elements in Faulkner's *Go Down, Moses*" (*Faulkner and Humor*, pp. 79–96), identifies the two types of comedy used (anecdotal comedy and humor of belittlement) and moves through several portions of the book to elucidate them. "Twain and Faulkner: Miscegenation and the Comic Muse" (*Faulkner and Humor*, pp. 97–109) by William Bedford Clark is an informative comparison of *Go Down, Moses* and Twain's *Pudd'nhead Wilson* which effectively demonstrates that Faulkner could do Twain one better in transforming tragic concerns into comedic scrutiny.

"Isaac McCaslin and the Possibilities of Vision" (*SoR* 22:37–50) by Susan V. Donaldson praises Ike as one character who breaks free of repetition and entrapment in Faulkner's fiction to a vision beyond tradition and history. Donaldson meticulously traces Ike's development and notes some revealing biographical parallels as well. John Limon, in "The Integration of Faulkner's *Go Down, Moses*" (*CritI* 12:422–38), enters an exhaustive analysis to make the simple point that the book "has an enigma at the center of its mysteries, around which it cannot cohere," and that the enigma is the character Rider in "Pantaloon in Black" who cannot be understood. But the essay is about many other things—Stanley Fish's concept of interpretative communities, the integrationist politics of Martin Luther King, and the criticism of Edward W. Said—ingeniously handled and not easily summarized. It is an important essay. "McCaslin and Macomber: From *Green Hills* to *Big Woods*" (*FJ* 2,i:29–36) by John M. Howell notes some possible borrowings from Hemingway in Faulkner's "The Bear," especially animal analogues. The evidence is interesting but not compelling. James Harrison's note on "The Old People" (*Expl* 44,ii:41) is an explication of a 220-word sentence from the text in the form of another single sentence of commentary of over 240 words, an effort I suppose at a minor satiric tour de force.

John E. Bassett's "Gradual Progress and *Intruder in the Dust*" (*CollL* 13:207–16) is an intelligent political reading of that novel to clarify Faulkner's attitude on segregation in the 1940s. Bassett's treatment of themes also clarifies the novel's place as a transitional work in Faulkner's career. *The Faulkner Investigation* by Ross Macdonald and Eudora Welty (Cordelia, 1985) is a limited-edition pamphlet reprinting Welty's 1948 review of *Intruder in the Dust* and a brief note by Macdonald on Faulkner's story "The Hound." In an introductory note Ralph B. Sipper connects the three writers biographically. Welty makes some significant comments on Faulkner's humor and style.

viii. Individual Works, 1950–1962

Three novels from the last period of Faulkner's career were the subject of one essay each. "Time and Punishment in Faulkner's *Requiem for a Nun*" (*Renascence* 38:245–55) by Doreen Fowler argues convincingly that the seemingly unconnected and disparate elements of *Requiem* actually "blend and merge to show that no matter how far apart individuals or events may seem to be, they are in reality part of one network—time." Faulkner's views of time are particularly well articulated. Noel Polk's "Woman and the Feminine in *A Fable*" (*Faulkner and Women*, pp. 180–204) selects one seemingly unimportant scene in which an old man, three women, and a child appear and demonstrates that not only is it "an emblem for the entire novel" but for "Faulkner's entire fictional oeuvre." This is accomplished through a sensitive reading of the feminine nuances of the novel, and Polk succeeds in asserting its importance in the Faulkner canon as much more than a "pious aberration." In "*The Reivers*: Revision and Closure in Faulkner's Career" (*SLJ* 18:53–61), John E. Bassett reads the novel in the light of earlier fiction to observe the degree to which it revises that material, introduces new characters, and allows Faulkner to move away from the irony and "dialectic of voices that complicate" the major novels. The narrator, Grandfather Lucius, is Grandfather Faulkner bringing the lifetime's work to a comic resolution. I would like to think that Bassett is right.

ix. The Stories

Of the three general essays on the short stories, two have to do with feminine themes. In "Woman and the Making of the New World: Faulkner's Short Stories" (*Faulkner and Women*, pp. 205–19), Alexandre Vaschenko notes the impressive gallery of women to be found therein but focuses on those in "A Courtship," "Mountain Victory," and "Delta Autumn." Each has a female figure, an Indian, a white, and a black, respectively, whose presence helps define the thematic concerns with crucial points in southern and American history. The insights are sensible and informative. Myriam Díaz-Diocaretz, in "Faulkner's Hen-House: Woman as Bounded Text" (*Faulkner and Women*, pp. 235–69), undertakes to determine Faulkner's artistic design for women in 10 short stories, using the analogy of women as hens confined by the boundaries of henhouses. The essay is clever and has useful insights. In "William Faulkner's Detective Stories" (*Archiv* 222[1985]:136–44), Wolfgang Schlepper finds interesting ways to relate the 10 stories of *Knight's Gambit*, especially through their concern with the themes of truth and justice.

Among the five individual stories treated, "A Rose for Emily" continues to attract the most attention. One would think that little remains to be said about this story, yet James M. Mellard rings some new and interesting changes in "Faulkner's Miss Emily and Blake's

'Sick Rose': 'Invisible Worm,' *Nachträglichkeit*, and Retrospective Gothic" (*FJ* 2,i:37–45). The title nearly says it all, but basically William Blake, the Gothic tradition, and the psychoanalytic concept of "deferred action" are used to elucidate the text, all handled with a nice sense of humor on Mellard's part. Two more explicators have a go at the story: Elizabeth Carney Kurtz (*Expl* 44,ii:40) believes that Emily tucked Homer Barron away in the manner of a southern girl who puts away a rose to dry and be preserved between the pages of a book, and Alice Hall Petry (*Expl* 44,iii:52–54) compliments the precision of language by analyzing one sentence from the story.

The Petry explication is quite useful, as is her essay "Double Murder: The Women of Faulkner's 'Elly'" (*Faulkner and Women*: pp. 220–34), which cleverly interprets "Elly" as an allegory of "the clash between the Old and New South in psychoanalytic terms" and thereby clarifies a much misunderstood story. "Black Culture in William Faulkner's 'That Evening Sun'" (*JAmS* 20:33–50) by Dirk Kuyk, Jr., Betty M. Kuyk, and James A. Miller substantially supports the idea that basically it is Nancy's story and that it moves so deeply into Afro-American culture that the young white narrator and even Faulkner himself could not understand much of what it meant. John K. Crane's "But the Days Grow Short: A Reinterpretation of Faulkner's 'Dry September'" (*TCL* 31[1985]:410–20) explores the title's meaning as applied to Minnie Cooper and Jackson McLendon, who along with Hawkshaw Stribling are equally central to the plot and theme, which has to do with entering a barren middle age. A reading of "Faulkner's 'Golden Land' as Autobiography" (*SSF* 23:275–80) by Michael Grimwood finds that the story not only paints a scathing portrait of Southern California but also reflects on his ambivalence toward his family, his home, and his literary vocation. Grimwood's arguments are plausible, and like so much of the best scholarship published this year his essay demonstrates that the depths of Faulkner's fiction are far from being critically exhausted: it is the critic who will be exhausted first.

Randolph-Macon College

10. Fitzgerald and Hemingway

Gerry Brenner

The ticket stubs continue to show Hemingway outdrawing Fitzgerald by three to one. But while *Tender Is the Night* surprisingly upstaged *The Great Gatsby*, more surprising were curtains rising to a new Hemingway novel and falling to all but one old novel, *The Sun Also Rises*. That the Fitzgerald-Hemingway marquee still attracts patrons is vouched for by the steady flow of former dissertations-become-books from UMI Research Press, which accounted for one-third of the books on both authors.

i. Bibliography, Texts, and Biography

Three bibliographies appeared this year, two of them William White's always thorough, semiannual "Hemingway: A Current Bibliography" (*HemR* 5,ii:57–61; 6,i:118–20). The third was Joseph Wenke's "*Tender Is the Night*: A Cross-Referenced Bibliography of Criticism," in Milton R. Stern, ed., *Critical Essays on F. Scott Fitzgerald's* Tender Is the Night (Hall, 247–69). Giving one section to periodicals and one to books, Wenke chronologically lists over 300 English-language entries in periodicals and 140 in books. But only 18 entries from the 1980s get recognition, blunting an otherwise useful tool.

Another posthumous Hemingway novel, *The Garden of Eden* (Scribner's), promptly became a cause célèbre. With customary Scribnerian disingenuousness, the text's front matter makes no mention of Tom Jenks's editing of this 247-page novella from a considerably larger set of manuscripts with contending and complementary plots, themes, and characters. Despite mixed reviews and divergent responses from scholars, the long-rumored-about novella is a welcome addition to the Hemingway shelf, if only because its first half strikes some quite contemporary chords—androgyny and lesbianism—before it reverts to type and strums a weary doting-woman tune. In a nutshell: into her recent marriage to young novelist David Bourne, the identity-troubled and erotically experimental Catherine brings Marita, whom she promptly beds *à la lesbos*. While Catherine's sadistic, dominating, and destructive ways quickly erode the marriage, Marita's adoration of David salvages from the ménage à trois a blancmange twosome. When Catherine burns a set of David's stories —one woven into the narrative ("An African Betrayal," *Sports Illustrated* 5 May, pp. 58–72)—she also torches the marriage, and Jenks has Hemingway turn out a clichéd text: a coming-of-age hero-artist flanked by a troublesome foreground (Bitch-Goddess vying with Corn-Goddess) and troubled background (Giant-Killing Father).

The posthumous works will continue to appear, according to Gregory Hemingway, who has told me that next is *Jimmy Breen*, an unfinished novel of the 1920s. In the meantime scholars continue to ruminate over the manuscripts in the Kennedy Library and to be beset by permissions and access problems. To minimize such problems, Hemingway Society ex-president James Nagel has issued "Hemingway Guidelines for Permission and Publication: Background and Comment" (*HemR* 5,ii:34–36). But the death of Mary Hemingway has promptly outdated one guideline. The nine other guidelines are so general that scholars wishing to use the Kennedy Library materials need heed but one: "write for permission to use materials" before trekking to Boston; and inquire whether other scholars have recently received permission for quoting from those materials. The guidelines instruct scholars to request permission to quote from *published* material from Scribner's and *unpublished* material from Hemingway Foundation lawyer Alfred Rice. But Nagel might have added that until this year one of Rice's practices was to pass along requests he received to Charles Scribner, Jr., putting permission decisions in the hands of a publisher whose clear conflicts of interest impeded the work of more than one scholar.

That the House of Scribner has been a poor caretaker to its best-known authors is not news. But James Hinkle's "'Dear Mr. Scribner' —About the Published Text of *The Sun Also Rises*" (*HemR* 6,i:43–64) shows that Scribner's has done a shamefully shoddy job in its publications of Hemingway's best novel. Hinkle meticulously tallies some 4,000 (yes, four thousand) differences between Hemingway's finished typescript and the published text of *Sun*; locates different wordings at 125 places in the typescript and the published text, over 70 certainly by Hemingway; fingers 60 demonstrable errors in spellings, accent marks, and foreign words; and notes a mere five corrections to the 1926 text in the 1953 second edition. Hinkle wryly argues the irony of such an error-riddled text in light of the obsessive exactitude that Hemingway makes a part of Jake Barnes's character. And he convincingly proves that "the published text of *SAR* was apparently *never* seriously copyedited in detail by *anyone* on the Scribner *editorial* staff." By right and duty, contends Hinkle, the text ought to be corrected, if only to honor Hemingway's intention "to avoid wrong spellings, wrong names, wrong foreign words in his own work." Hinkle's appendix of the differences between Hemingway's final typescript and the present published text will let scholars emend their foul texts, pending a fair text that Scribner's new parent, Macmillan, should be nudged to publish.

Besides Hinkle's corrigenda, scholars can also number in their copies of *Sun* the 67 writing sessions that it took Hemingway to draft the novel, thanks to William Balassi's "The Writing of the Manuscript of *The Sun Also Rises*, with a Chart of Its Session-by-Session Development" (*HemR* 6,i:65–78). Carefully describing the contents of each of the seven notebooks and the opening 32 sheets on which Hemingway began the novel, Balassi briefly discusses Hemingway's difficulties focusing the early drafting sessions and goes on to note, by the fourth notebook, a transition from the self-explanatory narrative of the novel's first half to the second half's more literary, symbolic, and suggestive technique. His chart records each session's word totals, locates the material of the manuscript in the published text, and remarks omissions, additions, and occasional comments so as to clarify differences between the manuscript draft and the finished text. Balassi's findings are useful: not a single scene added in revision, three manuscript sessions altogether eliminated from the finished text, and surprisingly few major revisions, even though revisions added one-fifth to the text's word totals. But the article's value lies in its descriptive clarity, enabling scholars to determine for themselves the significance of changes and to observe Hemingway's difficulties in writing some segments, as in the sharply decreasing word counts for the sessions that produced the closing scene between Jake and Brett in Madrid. In contrast Frederic Joseph Svoboda's *Hemingway and* The Sun Also Rises (1983) imposed designs and thematic interpretations on the manuscripts, blurring their sequence and making reconstruction difficult.

Add to the list of foul texts "The Short Happy Life of Francis Macomber," for as has long been known the anthologized version differs from that published in September 1936. In "A Lost Passage from Hemingway's 'Macomber'" (*SB* 38:328–30), Leger Brosnahan compares the typescripts that *Cosmopolitan* and Scribner compositors worked from. The *ribbon* typescript Hemingway carefully corrected "in great detail" for *Cosmopolitan* differs from the carbon copy he sent to Scribner's, one he corrected independently of, and "much less carefully" than, the ribbon typescript, for errors corrected in the ribbon went uncorrected in the carbon. Brosnahan also reconstructs what must have caused Scribner copy editors to delete a 100-word passage, one that he believes should be restored to future publications of the story.

Of 13 texts Hemingway wrote during his two-year "Chicago period," five saw print in Peter Griffin's *Along with Youth* last year, and three of those same five, plus three others, have gotten critical comment in Michael Reynolds's *The Young Hemingway* (below). But Griffin, without commentary, simply plugs the stories in where he thinks they chronologically belong, and Reynolds so disperses his discussion that Hemingway's development as a writer of fiction is hard to integrate. Paul Smith integrates that development in "Hemingway's Apprentice Fiction: 1919–1921" (*AL* 58:574–88), surveying and dating the 13 texts, classifying them according to three "styles"—Chicago, Italian, and Michigan—and discussing the characteristics of each style. Smith also corrects some misdating by Griffin, explains why the "maudlin and lofty vacuities" of the letter portion of "Portrait of the Idealist in Love," printed in Griffin, are not Hemingway's work, and discusses two early versions of Hemingway's story *inaccrochable*, "Up in Michigan."

New to the year's bookshelf is Michael Reynolds's fine first biographical installment, *The Young Hemingway* (Blackwell), a volume that secures Reynolds's place as the new dean of Hemingway's historical scholars. He gives the fullest accounting yet of the cultural milieu out of which Hemingway grew, leaving off with Hemingway and Hadley at the railing of the *Leopoldina* in New York harbor, en route to Paris. Reynolds has pored over all sorts of public records in Oak Park, Illinois. The result wobbles between a welter and a wealth of sociohistorical detail that wants to prove that Hemingway was a product of his culture strongly influenced by Teddy Roosevelt's values (the strenuous life, physical fitness, self-reliance) and experiences (military heroics, big-game hunting, and self-publicizing postures). See-sawing against Reynolds's habit of historical pedantry is some belletristic self-indulgence, for he occasionally lapses into writing about Hemingway as though he were Hemingway writing about young Nicholas Adams. But between the pedant and the belletrist is the careful scholar clarifying three images: Self-Inventing Ernest (tracking Hemingway's versions of his war experiences and the problems he created for Hadley during their courtship); Imitative Ernest (knowledgeably discussing and identifying popular authors' themes, plots, characters, and techniques in Hemingway's early fictional experiments); and Diplomatic Hadley (detailing the delicate tact required to win to wedlock a mercurial courter.) Reynolds's most interesting finds are two. One, the importance to Grace Hemingway of Ruth Arnold, a voice student who became a household fixture from 1907 to 1919, when Dr. Hemingway dismissed from the house this confidante, sister spiritualist, and possibly lesbian lover. Two, Dr. Hemingway's long history of "a nervous condition," chronic depression and paranoia, symptoms that not only caused him to prescribe for himself therapeutic vacations to New Orleans in 1904 and 1908, but also swam in the gene pool that flowed into his famous son as well.

Francis Kroll Ring, Fitzgerald's 20-year-old secretary during his final 20 months, returns to that brief stint in her memoir, *Against the Current: As I Remember F. Scott Fitzgerald* (Creative Arts, 1985). But she "remembers" shopworn information—his relationships to Sheilah Graham, Scottie, Raleigh cigarettes, and Gordon's gin; his scriptwriting of "Babylon Revisited." Or she retails trivia—his preference for turtle and black bean soups, for eating Smithfield's deviled ham from the tin. Or she draws upon sources of information other than her own memory—as for Fitzgerald's skirmish with Arnold Gingrich over the Pat Hobby stories. Ring duly applauds herself as funereal functionary: making mortuary arrangements, corresponding with Fitzgerald's executor, inventorying the flotsam and jetsam, and expressing her dismay with Edmund Wilson's summary outline of the ending of *The Last Tycoon.* Padded with photos, notes, letters, and telegrams—occasionally inaccurately transcribed in the text—Ring's slim volume has scholarly value only because her letter to Wilson may reveal some of Fitzgerald's plans for the ending of *Tycoon.*

From biography to memoir to snapshot: collector Matthew J. Bruccoli gathered 40 newspaper and magazine "interviews" for *Conversations with Ernest Hemingway* (Miss.). The earliest pieces include the New York *Sun* feature on "the first wounded American from the Italian front," with one version of his wounding, and the Oak Park High School *Trapeze* account, with the heroic version commonly retailed: the wounded Hemingway carrying a wounded, etc. The later pieces include frequent blurbs by Harvey Breit and George Plimpton's classic interview. Neither new information nor fresh perspectives are here; indeed, the last dozen "conversations," all in Cuba, blur one into another with barefoot Ernest, pert Mary, and the automatic lines: of having four novels "in the bank," of not talking about what he's working on lest it get lost in the telling, of daily work habits.

The corrective to such thin biographical supplements is James D. Brasch's "Hemingway's Doctor: José Luis Herrera Sotolongo Remembers Ernest Hemingway" (*JML* 13:185–210). A corrective as well to errors in Norberto Fuentes's *Hemingway in Cuba* (1984), Brasch works from four interviews—by Canadian (1971), Cuban (1970, 1984), and Russian (1971–74) interviewers—of Hemingway's longtime personal physician and friend. In Herrera's early friendship with Hemingway during the Spanish Civil War and his subsequent intimacy in Cuba between 1941 and the time Hemingway left Cuba in 1959, Brasch finds a paternalism that Hemingway often deferred to. It enabled Herrera to censure Hemingway for excessive drinking in the late 1940s and to write a long letter (transcribed) advising him against an infatuation with Adriana Ivancich that threatened domestic problems. More significant are Herrera's views of Hemingway's sympathy and support for Castro's overthrow of Batista. Brasch includes a transcribed portion of the earliest interview with Herrera. Herrera figures again in N. Ann Doyle and Neal B. Houston's "Ernest Hemingway, Adriana Ivancich and the Nobel Prize" (*NMAL* 9,i [1985]:Item 5). Anticipating the prize as early as 1950 (Faulkner's year) and again in 1953 (Churchill's), Hemingway wrote the Italian contessa in the latter year, saying that were he awarded it, either she or Herrera must accept it for him, making no mention of Miss Mary's candidacy as recipient. But when notified of the award in 1954, Hemingway failed to ask Adriana to be his stand-in, eliciting from her a cool congratulatory letter, quite unlike the condolatory one of the previous year. Perhaps this is matter for gossips, but its value lies in making accessible paraphrased information from two of Adriana's letters to Hemingway and three from him to her, letters not in Baker's *Selected Letters.*

One-upping last year's essay by Scott Donaldson on the same subject is Donald Pizer's discerning and provocative "The Hemingway-Dos Passos Relationship" (*JML* 13:111–28). Intrigued by both writers' recurrent use of the other in autobiographical portraiture and fictional caricature, Pizer contends that their "spasmodic brooding" led each to unconsciously project onto the other "the tormenting anxieties of his own psychic life." Reexamining Katy Smith, Dos Passos's wife and a woman for whom Hemingway had carried the torch before and during his courtship of Hadley, Pizer finds her "intimately connected in Hemingway's feelings with failure," both as a woman he failed to possess except in fantasy and, as the years passed, as a powerful reminder of his failed marriage to Hadley. Rivals in love and politics, the men broke friendship over whether acts by communists during the Spanish Civil War constituted betrayal, and the break yielded Hemingway's portrait of Dos Passos as Richard Gordon in *To Have and Have Not.* In Pizer's view, Gordon's adultery and his wife's vicious accusations reflect Hemingway's self-accusations and anxieties over personal and political betrayals, all of which he projects on Dos Passos, both here and later in his false portrayal of him as the pilot fish of *A Moveable Feast.* In like fashion Dos Passos sought to exorcise his preoccupation with masculine competitiveness through caricatures of Hemingway in *Chosen Country* (1951) and in *Century's Ebb* (1975). Pizer's provocative analysis correctly sees that one writer's portrayal of another can constitute an "inward exploration . . . to find symbolic constructs for the expression of the deepest center of his own being." But it is arguable whether betrayal lurks at the core of Hemingway's being, and whether Dos Passos alone best reflects that concern. After all, *A Moveable Feast* identifies the name of betrayers as Legion.

Two biographical appetizers: David Harrell offers a not-so-final note on Lady Brett's model in "A Final Note on Duff Twysden" (*HemR* 5,ii:45–46). To settle conflicting versions of her death, Harrell dug up the medical and mortuary records to add to Sarason's version (*Hemingway and the Sun Set*) of her death from pulmonary tuberculosis in June 1938 in Santa Fe, New Mexico. He verifies that she was cremated in Albuquerque on 28 June, the day after her death, that her ashes were returned to Santa Fe, and that no funeral service was held. *R.I.P.*? Not quite, for still unresolved, Harrell finds, is the matter of her name. Was it Mary Smurthwaite, as *Burke's Peerage* lists it? Or was it "'Mary Duff Stirling Byron, eldest daughter of B. W. Smurthwaite of Prior House, Richmond, Yorkshire,'" as Carlos

Baker records? And was *that* her father's name or was it "Smurthwaite Sterling," as her death certificate gives it? Surely Jake Barnes, who knows Bocanegra's origins and the brand of cigarette stubs Lady Brett left in a bed table drawer, could have given definitive answers, even though he was but a mere journalist. And it is to a "left-wing British journalist," Claud Cockburn, that Cecil D. Eby turns in "Bothering to Explain Hemingway's 'How Do You Like It Now, Gentlemen?'" (*HemR* 5,ii:47–48). Cockburn's 1956 autobiography, *In Time of Trouble*, records a delightful anecdote in Madrid's Florida Hotel that occasioned Hemingway's refrain.

ii. Influence Studies

Notwithstanding the qualification to loop back to Reynolds and Smith, as well as forward to Wilkinson (see *iii. a.* below), if the quality and quantity of this year's influence studies were any yardstick, then the anxiety of influence in both writers would appear measurable with an inchstick. In "The Mystery of Ungodliness: Renan's *Life of Jesus* as a Subtext for F. Scott Fitzgerald's *Great Gatsby* and 'Absolution'" (*C&L* 36:15–24), Bryce J. Christensen compares Gatsby's romantic idealism and Platonic self-generation with that of Renan's Jesus, who was similarly capable of the "great act of originality" necessary to join the "great family of the true sons of God." Undergirding the comparison is Fitzgerald's letter asking Scottie whether she had recently read a good book, listing, among others, Renan's *Jesus*. The comparisons remark both heroes' attempts at bridging time and eternity, history and myth. Christensen finds Rudolph Miller (aka Blatchford Sarnemington) in "Absolution" similar to the un-Christian, self-creating, son-of-God James Gatz, for like Renan's Jesus, they too act on the belief that "the creations of the imagination are irreconcilable with and superior to the reality they defy, . . . to the mundane world of truth." But is Jesus—Renan's or Matthew's or Luke's—the only instance in history of divine self-promotion? Barry J. Scherr briefly doffs his cap to Keats before contrasting *Tender* to Lawrence's *Women in Love* in "Lawrence, Keats and *Tender Is the Night*: Loss of Self and 'Love-Battle' Motifs" (*RecL* 14:7–17). He highlights the destructive dominance of Gudrun-like Nicole over Dick Diver to show their failure to achieve the "star-polarity" that Rupert Birkin and Ursula Brangwen achieve through their healthy love-battles. And in case you, too, have long wondered about the source for Nick Carraway's irreverent thought of asking Gatsby to show Daisy his rubies after dazzling her with his mounds of shirts, then follow George Monteiro's "Gatsby's Rubies" (*NMAL* 9,ii[1985]:Item 10) back to Marvell's "Coy Mistress" where "Thou by the Indian Ganges' side/ Should'st rubies find."

Michael S. Reynolds's "A Supplement to [His] *Hemingway's Reading*" (*SAF* 14:99–108) lists 93 more books that "passed through Hemingway's hands." Drawn from Baker's *Selected Letters* and the recently accessible correspondence between Hadley Richardson and Hemingway, the titles, when added to the over-9,000 items already identified in Brasch and Sigman's *Hemingway's Library* and Reynolds's *Hemingway's Reading*, warrant Reynolds's puckish conclusion: "For too long scholars have wanted Hemingway to be Huck Finn grown older. They have been looking at the wrong boy. Eventually he will be seen more as Tom Sawyer, the middle-class boy who knew the game rules, for he learned them out of books." And one of those books would include Longfellow's 1850 poem of "divergent friendship," "The Fire of Drift-Wood." Its distinct echoes in the setting and the emotional states of two characters whose conversation "begins nostalgically" and "becomes increasingly emotional and sporadic" in "The End of Something" are well argued by Janet L. Florick and David M. Raabe in "Longfellow and Hemingway: The Start of Something" (*SSF* 23:324–26). Buttressing the indebtedness, Florick and Raabe point to "Hoof prints on another's mug," Hemingway's line from a high school football poem that parodies Longfellow's "Footprints in the sands of time" from "Psalm of Life." Less convincing is George Monteiro's tenuous and coy "This Is My Pal Bugs: Ernest Hemingway's 'The Battler' " (*SSF* 23:179–83). Abstracting the triangle of an affectionate relationship between a black (Bugs) and a white (Ad) as observed by another white (Nick), Monteiro remarks a parallel triangulation in Melville's *Benito Cereno*, for Babo's ministrations to Benito equally mystify naive Captain Amasa Delano. The parallel exists, but not the evidence that from the 9,100 books Hemingway's hands hefted, one contained Melville's great epistemological story. After all, the Melville renaissance was an infant when Hemingway wrote his story. Oddly, the same parallel, but identified only as Lowell's *Benito Cereno*, gets recognized in Joyce Dyer's "Hemingway's Use of the Pejorative Term 'Nigger' in 'The

Battler'" (*NConL* 16,v:5–10); she also finds Bugs "a dangerous, greedy Negro," disingenuously exploitative, "forcing his will on a pathetic (but not lunatic), defeated and frail ex-boxer."

Hemingway's influence on subsequent writers burdens two items. Michael Moorhead sees Francis Macomber in the traits of an Irwin Shaw deputy in "Hemingway's 'The Short Happy Life of Francis Macomber' and Shaw's 'The Deputy Sheriff'" (*Expl* 44,ii:42–43). And Frederick Busch, in "Islands, Icebergs, Ships Beneath the Sea" (in his *When People Publish*, pp. 97–112), discusses "After the Storm" and its narrator's "anticontemplative prose of action"; but this is prolegomenon to a lengthy review of the novels of John Hawkes, tracing in them Hawkes's acknowledged use of the haunting imagery from "After the Storm," "a sunken ship, looming like an underwater city," and a bejeweled, drowned woman with floating hair.

iii. Criticism

***a.* Full-Length Studies.** A pair of books from UMI Research Press gave Fitzgerald some needed play. In the flood tide of the New Criticism Dan Seiters's *Image Patterns in the Novels of F. Scott Fitzgerald* would have been timely. But problems bedevil this decade-old dissertation and its anachronistic net-fishing for schools of imagery. The format sets up five image patterns—transportation, communication, light and dark, dirt-disease-decay, and water—and follows them lockstep through each novel, summarizing in two pages at the end of each chapter what the imagery has shown; the formulaic scheme reads like a transposed card file. Because the imagery applies to *The Sun Also Rises*, *Tess of the d'Urbervilles*, *Our Mutual Friend*, and *Gulliver's Travels*, it reveals less about Fitzgerald's aesthetic preoccupations than about imagery common to hosts of writers. Seiters's classification system could use some help from Linnaeus: my retina registers the genus *water imagery* amid such species as rain, snow, rivers, seas, etc.; but my retina finds no object in trying to register the abstractions of transportation and communication, concepts higher up a classification ladder. The chapter on *Gatsby* shows the datedness of Seiters's study, acknowledging neither recent narratological considerations nor more conventional point-of-view problems that roost with Nick Carraway, a narrator whom Seiters credits with the capacity for clear moral vision and redemption: "If Nick is corrupt—as he may well be before his association with Gatsby humanizes him—

the sole moral center of the novel is the story Nick tells, the story he can tell because now he can peer beneath the surface and find the human being." But whosoever can peer can also skew his report of that at which he peered.

By far the better UMI Research Press book on Fitzgerald is Wheeler Winston Dixon's *The Cinematic Vision of F. Scott Fitzgerald*, a fine study of Fitzgerald's Hollywood connection: his screenplay writing, the adaptations of his fiction on film, his several stints in Hollywood, and the effects of his scriptwriting on his creation of *The Last Tycoon.* Part biographical revisionism, Dixon corrects the conventional view of Fitzgerald's failures by regarding such impediments as changed assignments, censorship problems, and collaborative impasses. Examining Fitzgerald's work on a number of scripts, especially *Infidelity*, he notes his study and grasp of film techniques, particularly the shift from dialogue-burdened scenes to visually complex structures. Fitzgerald's long-standing problems with and exploration of narrative point of view in *Gatsby* and *Tender* prompt Dixon to analyze several of Fitzgerald's scripts for their innovative use of camera angles and devices for rendering ambiguities to film viewers. Although it was perhaps useful to trace back through those same two novels for Fitzgerald's penchant for "filmic" tendencies, the chapters on those novels tend toward the catalog pedantry of Seiters's image-mongering. Nevertheless, Dixon establishes a firm and full context for viewing Fitzgerald's development away from the lush poetic textures of his major novels and toward the verbally spare but visually complex texture of *Tycoon*, a texture compounded of scenic speed and "extensive use of iconographs and gestures to convey meaning."

Three of this year's books on Hemingway are journeyman studies. J. Bakker, *Ernest Hemingway in Holland, 1925–81: A Comparative Analysis of the Contemporary Dutch and American Critical Reception of His Work* (Humanities), chronologically summarizes and comments on all the reviews of Hemingway's works in Dutch periodicals and better-known national newspapers, comparing them with those in Robert O. Stephens's 1977 *Critical Reception*, each of which he also summarizes. He includes synopses of two dozen general articles on Hemingway, translations of two interviews, descriptions of 22 of the periodicals from which the reviews came, documentation on the reviews, and the conclusion that while American reviewers show greater outspokenness in praise and rejection than their Dutch counterparts, there is "remarkable similarity" in the responses of both groups. The first half of Harriet Fellner's refurbished 1977 dissertation, *Hemingway as Playwright*: The Fifth Column (UMI Research Press), is interesting, for she discusses specialized information: the play's critical reception as text and as production by the Theatre Guild; the script alterations by Benjamin "Barney" Glazer; preproduction problems; casting; pre-New York tryouts; and the play's brief life between 6 March and 18 May 1940. Succinctly describing the métier of New York theater in 1940, Fellner also proves that while the play was a financial failure, losing between $28,000 and $91,000, nevertheless it had a "respectable run," its 87 performances comparing well against the year's other drama. The second half of Fellner's book replows Hemingway's political and journalistic work surrounding *Fifth Column*, remarking on his documentaries (*Spain in Flame* as well as *Spanish Earth*), his speech to the Second American Writers' Congress, his articles for NANA and *Ken* (giving synopses of the 28 former and 14 latter), his stories of the Civil War, and his use in *Fifth Column* and *For Whom the Bell Tolls* of material he wrote or experienced as foreign correspondent. In *Hemingway and Turgenev: The Nature of Literary Influence* (UMI Research Press), lured by Hemingway's several references to Turgenev and urged on by the borrowers' cards from Sylvia Beach's Shakespeare and Co. that prove Hemingway's extensive reading of the Russian author's works, Myler Wilkinson circumstantially argues Turgenev's shadow on Hemingway's work. Wilkinson knows Turgenev's literary context, but, notwithstanding invocations of Harold Bloom's influential *Anxiety of Influence*, the idea that Hemingway's stories and *Sun Also Rises* are, respectively, indebted to *Sportsman's Sketches* and *Fathers and Son* does not wash. Indeed, Turgenev's stories keenly register landscapes and the natural world in which peasant life occurs; but Hemingway renders a markedly psychological natural world with an altogether different style and without Turgenev's monochromatically elegiac mood. Even less persuasive is Wilkinson's attempt to make Jake Barnes cousin or brother to Bazarov, latter-day descendant of the Byronic rebel. Loosely equating Jake's bitterness and disillusionment with Bazarov's profound nihilism, Wilkinson shows that he too is a victim of influence: of the critical clichés that overlook Jake's self-pitying and morally censorious unreliability. Jake may be well enlisted as Bazarov's "literary cousin." So too are a platoon of characters, each caught in the "essential discontinuity between generations," each needing only to salute himself as a "latecomer who, finding no legitimate place for his aspirations or ideals within culture, must search within himself for the values and codes which will make existence possible. This yearning for a lost aristocracy of the spirit in a world which no longer provides inherent meaning is the question which haunts the pages of late romantic writers such as Turgenev and Hemingway." And Fitzgerald. And Faulkner. And Bellow. And . . . . Straining to bond his two figures, Wilkinson resorts to tenuous thumbnail discussions that link Hemingway to the Imagists, to other Russion novelists, and even to Isaac Babel.

The fourth of the new Hemingway books is a revised edition of the classic and valuable *Ernest Hemingway* (TUSAS 41) by Earl Rovit and Gerry Brenner. Besides some minor cosmetic editing of the original chapters, the authors include a new chapter, "Of Memory and Melancholy: The Posthumous Works," discussing *A Moveable Feast*, *Islands in the Stream*, *The Dangerous Summer*, and *Sports Illustrated*'s 1971–72 three-part account of Hemingway's 1953–54 African safari, *African Journal.* A new annotated bibliography and a much-amplified notes and reference section "indicate the tip of the titantic iceberg of scholarship and criticism that has been building so vigorously in Hemingway studies" since the 1962 publication of Rovit's original edition. While Rovit's ideas have proven durable, his text has seen such hard service by library users that this revised edition is a welcome replacement for the dog-eared, underscored, and margin-filled old versions that lean on newer neighbors.

***b.* Collections.** In *Critical Essays on F. Scott Fitzgerald*'s Tender Is the Night (Hall), Milton R. Stern gathers in chronological sequence a score of reviews and a dozen standard essays (e.g., Bruccoli, Stanton, Doherty, Trachtenberg) on Fitzgerald's vexingly majestic novel. In addition are three new items and his own introduction, an overview of the novel's reception and criticism on it. While the selected reviews show strong divergences, the reprinted essays tilt toward cultural-historical readings that buttress Stern's conviction that *Tender* is "the great American novel of history in the twentieth century." In his own "*Tender Is the Night*: The Text Itself" (pp. 21–31), Stern picks up the long-standing debate over the original versus the revised endings, joins the scholarly chorus that "Scribners has not proved to be a conscientious custodian," and cogently explains why the facts of composition and revision both challenge the critical preference for the original version and call at least for "a carefully edited fair edition of each version." James W. Tuttleton, in "Vitality and Vampirism in *Tender Is the Night*" (pp. 238–46), links Nicole Diver and Zelda to the vitality-draining and destructive women of Keats's "Lamia," "La Belle Dame sans Merci," and "Endymion," curiously ignoring the castration motifs in the displacement of virility with vitality. For Joseph Wenke's bibliography see section i, above.

c. **General Essays.** While no general essays were dealt to Fitzgerald, the 10 dealt Hemingway were all small cards. Genevieve Hily-Mane's "Point of View in Hemingway's Novels and Short Stories: A Study of the Manuscripts" (*HemR* 5,ii:37–44) observes that Hemingway continually experimented with point-of-view combinations, commenting on nearly 20 works in which manuscript drafts and final versions seesaw between first-person and omniscient narrators. Quoting often from manuscripts without acknowledging permission to do so, Hily-Mane displays superb Gallic disdain for the policies Nagel articulates in his article (see *i*, above), immediately preceding hers. In "Silent Ernest" (*Literature's Silent Language: Nonverbal Communication* [Peter Lang], pp. 89–116), Stephen R. Portch (see *ALS 1983*, p. 171) examines the nonverbal signs and codes that punctuate such dialogue-heavy stories as "Killers" and "Hills Like White Elephants," arguing that in this pair and other stories Hemingway requires readers alert to nonverbal meanings, for in them, in "the total context of the story and the rhythms of the dialogue, we can hear the tones of voice without ever having them described." But hearing nonverbal meanings is slippery business, Portch obtuse to Jig's sarcastic last line in "Hills"; and assigning such meanings, while legitimate with a performed story, is a radically flawed approach to the unperforming text that one silently reads from a page. Nevertheless, Portch clocks the hour and 50 minutes the killers spend in Henry's lunchroom and the 35 minutes Jig and her American man await the train to Madrid, explaining that while the dialogue of these intervals demands interpretation, so do the intervals of silence that take up the larger amounts of time.

In a posthumous essay probably written in the early 1970s, "Ernest Hemingway: The Stylist of Stoicism" (in his *The Critic Agonistes: Psychology, Myth, and the Art of Fiction*, ed. Eric Solomon and Stephen Arkin [Washington, 1985] pp. 133–60), Daniel Weiss crafts an insightful but tenuously organized essay. Calling Hemingway's stoicism psychological rather than philosophical, his protest personal rather than social, his style "neurotic by definition, occlusive rather than illuminating," Weiss discusses a constellation of psychological issues: Hemingway's traumatophilic repetition compulsion, his behavior of shock, the absolute coalescence of his separate identity with that of his father, and his resemblance to his contemporaries, all of whom both worked in a literary epoch that was "an exhibition of imbalances," and walked in "a tilted world." But Weiss concludes that "Hemingway's own lopsidedness, which was a sort of insulation around a core of lacerated nerves, has an honorable quality."

Hemingway and the woman problem shows a faint pulse. In her chapter on Hemingway in *The Indestructible Woman in Faulkner, Hemingway and Steinbeck* (UMI Research Press, pp. 47–73), Mimi Reisel Gladstein attempts to redress the conventional view of Hemingway's exclusively male world in which women are objects playing "the role of functionary in man's fulfillment." Drawing upon both the influence on Hemingway's life of Grace Hemingway, Agnes von Kurowsky, and Hadley Richardson, and the duality of the Jungian archetype of the Great Mother as nourishing and destructive, Gladstein argues the complexity of a quartet of "indestructible" heroines—Lady Brett, Pilar, Maria, and Renata. Enduring women who provide a positive note of optimism in a vision otherwise pessimistic, they are "projections" of Hemingway's responses to the influential trio who "mothered" him because they too mother their men. Interesting though Gladstein's discussion of the Pilar-Maria/Demeter-Persephone parallels is, she fails to explain why Hemingway's mothering heroines represent a role other than "functionary in man's fulfillment." Bickford Sylvester also attempts to redress Hemingway's women in "Winner Take Nothing: Development as Dilemma for the Hemingway Heroine" (*PCP* 21:73–80). Using the analogy of Nick Adams's development and the characteristics of the bildungsroman, Sylvester melts down several heroines into a composite woman, charting her development into the self-realizing, mature, and increasingly independent figures of Marie Morgan, Maria, and Renata. Staunch feminists will likely deride Sylvester's attempt at elevating handmaidens to personhood.

Deserving brief mention are four items. In her *From Fact to Fiction: Journalism and Imaginative Writing in America* (Hopkins [1985], pp. 135–64), Shelley Fisher Fishkin devotes a chapter to the correspondences and differences between Hemingway's careers as journalist and fiction writer, matters more amply dealt with last year in J. F. Kobler's *Ernest Hemingway: Journalist and Artist*. Reworking Hemingway's indebtedness to the rules laid down for writers at the Kansas City *Star*, "one of the most admired and influential newspapers in the country" when young Ernest covered a beat, Fishkin also focuses on the stories and vignettes of *In Our Time* and deals well with the problems of Hemingway's involvement in the *Spanish Earth* documentary—before abruptly ending her chapter, as if Hemingway died with Robert Jordan at that pass in the Guadarrama mountains. Citing passages from *Bell Tolls, Have Not* and *Farewell*, Charles M. Oliver in "Hemingway's Merger of Form and Meaning" (*Lang&S* [1985]18:223–31) notes that "elements of form—repetition of words, the rhythm of a passage, the length of sentences"—merge with meaning to enhance meaning and emotive response. In "The Aesthetics of the Visible and the Invisible: Hemingway and Cézanne" (*HemR* 5,ii:2–11), Erik Nakjavani discusses phenomenological theory and the aesthetic aims of Cézanne to establish similarities in the painter's and the writer's artistic goals: "to save the visible and the seen from our intellectual inclinations," to achieve "an unmediated vision," to evoke the invisible latent in the visible. While Nakjavani identifies the last of these as Cézanne's spatial corollary to Hemingway's iceberg theory, his abstractions take root in no specific works, his discussion invoking the definition of a liberal: someone with both feet planted firmly in the air. In a complementary article, "Moving in the Picture: The Landscape Stylistics of *In Our Time*" (*L&S* [1985] 18:363–76), Paul M. Hedeen discusses a number of Cézanne's techniques and then alleges to find them at work in brief descriptive passages from several stories; but his examinations of the miniscule passages add little to readings of the stories.

d. **Essays on Specific Works: Fitzgerald.** Even without benefit of Stern's collection (above), *Tender Is the Night* would have rivaled *Gatsby* for modest attention this year, each novel receiving a pair of substantial essays. The headier of the two on *Tender* is Richard Godden's "Money Makes Manners Make Man Make Woman: *Tender Is the Night*, a Familiar Romance?" (*L&H* 12:16–37). Godden sketches an economic analysis of the historic shift in capitalism from classical imperialism's "sphere of accumulation" to late capitalism's "sphere of reproduction" in order to claim that "the novel's psychiatric vocabulary operates primarily as a metaphor whose subject is the relocation of accumulations." I can trot along with Godden as he points out the often-recognized landscape of paternal incest. But I stumble at the hurdles of his finish lines, such as that incest, "the key to Fitzgerald's understanding of the relationship between identity and economics," "creates *dis*integral selves through a multiplication of roles which, by analogy," he compares "to a shift in economic emphasis. An intersection between psychological and economic trauma registers precisely how a change in the history of capital changes the history of bourgeois selfhood." Angus P. Collins takes me to a more recognizable intersection in "F. Scott Fitzgerald: Homosexuality and the Genesis of *Tender Is the Night*" (*JML* 13:167–71). Using the early Francis Melarky drafts of the novel, he claims their homosexual material resulted in a "paralyzing sense of vocational emasculation" because of Fitzgerald's inability to resolve matters of his own sexual and professional identity. But Fitzgerald could complete the novel after realizing "that his choice of career [was] far less reprehensible than his failure to practice it," after substituting for the homosexual theme Dick Diver's deeply rooted feelings of moral apostasy.

Far superior to Godden's essay is Geof Cox's equally Marxist "Literary Pragmatics: A New Discipline. The Example of Fitzgerald's *Great Gatsby*" (*L&H* 12:79–96). Finding an intertwining of commercial and aesthetic interests in Fitzgerald's excited response to the dust-jacket illustration that Max Perkins sent him for *Gatsby*, Cox launches a trenchant analysis of the social-class underpinnings and commodity-centered commercialism that so strongly influence highbrow literature, literary critics, and educated readers. At odds with recent reading theories—German Reception, American Reader-Response, and French Semiotic—Cox demands at least equal time for "literary pragmatics," which hunts out the cultural ideologies embedded in literary texts, seeks to unmask the power relations disguised in semantic contexts, and attempts to explode "the twin ideological supports of much current literary criticism: 'the reader' and 'the text,'" replacing them with *classes of readers* and *book-commodities*, terms that insist upon the capitalistic enterprise that undergirds the allegedly "pure" study of literary texts. And so he dances attention on alternate versions of Nick Carraway's beginning sentence, on the old 1970 Scribner Research Anthology on *Gatsby*, on chapter two's paragraphs about the valley of ashes and Doctor Eckleburg's eyes, and on the Fitzgerald revival of the 1940s both to underscore the class bias that infiltrates the production of meanings in the novel and to emphasize "that Literature is a category finally controlled by the publishing industry, and Literary criticism has an ideological role within this control." Offsetting Cox is one of the best essays on *Gatsby* in years, Arnold Weinstein's "Fiction as Greatness: The Case of *Gatsby*" (*Novel* [1985]19:22–38.) Dismayed by moral fervor begat by readings of the novel, Weinstein celebrates the novel's sustained focus on "the notion of making something from nothing," which he identifies, of course, not only as credo for Jay Gatsby and affiliated American Dreamers, but also as "a paradigmatic formula for literature itself." Reading the novel as an "experiment in semiosis," Weinstein applauds Fitzgerald's ludic abilities, his "consummate hero of belief," and—in a brilliantly sustained analysis of the "Blocks' Biloxi" exchange in the New York hotel room—his verbal high jinks, lexical artifice, and modernist, semiotic wizardry. For Weinstein the novel's greatness lies in its commitment to the power of the dream, the power of fiction, in its willingness "to hint, more than once, that fiction just might take you all the way." Although Louis K. Greiff's "Fitzgerald's *The Great Gatsby*" (*Expl* 44,iii:49–51) belongs in another league, it merits inclusion here because his attention to the telephone-call motif in the novel reconsiders interesting questions over the calls that did not reach Gatsby on his last day.

Fitzgerald's stories continue to await the degree of critical inquiry Hemingway's routinely receive, although three of them found responding readers. After differentiating among distinct shifts in narrative voice in "Four Voices in 'Winter Dreams'" (*SSF* 23:315–20), Gerald Pike argues that the story marks a stylistic turning point in Fitzgerald's early career. In "Fitzgerald's 'O Russet Witch!': Dangerous Women, Dangerous Art" (*SSF* 23:443–48), Leland S. Person, Jr., freshly reads Merlin Grainger's strongly ambivalent fascination with Alicia Dare's fabulous alter ego and finds in Fitzgerald's 1921 story oppositions that reveal his "fears about the dangers of male-female relationships and the self-destructive power of his art." The best of this small group is Patrick D. Murphy's "Illumination and Affection in the Parallel Plots of 'The Rich Boy' and 'The Beast in the Jungle'" (*PLL* 22:406–16). The comparisons with James's story are not vital, but they clarify Fitzgerald's accomplishments, particularly his double subversion of the "moment-of-crisis" story, subverting the hero by having Anson Hunter fail to change during the course of the story and subverting the Conradian narrator by having him fail to learn anything from Hunter's failure because of the narrator's "flagrant subjectivity," flawed critical ability, and blindly envious desire to imitate Hunter.

***e.* Essays on Specific Works: Hemingway.** Of 11 essays on *The Sun Also Rises* three are particularly noteworthy. The only original one is John Atherton's "The Itinerary and the Postcard: Minimal Strategies in *The Sun Also Rises*" (*ELH* 53:199–218). A self-confessed "aficionado of Gérard Genette's poetics of narrative," Atherton examines both the linguistic patterns in varied minitexts—postcards, telegrams, letters, messages, and dialogues—and the painstakingly attentive recorder of texts, events, places, and sequences, Hemingway's narrator-guide Jake Barnes. Atherton finds the novel not the narration of "a quest or a voyage of discovery" but of a prearranged trip to places every inch of whose terrain Jake has previously reconnoitered and experienced, "so that the narrating appears as one uninterrupted recognition of sites visited before, places reseen and refitted into some preexisting scheme of things." But this view calls for discussion of thematic or psychological implications in such a narrator; Atherton dismisses the call by quickly classifying Jake-the-narrator an archivist whose narration seeks to shift the responsibility for narrating "elsewhere." E. Miller Budick finds Jake a maturing narrator in her narratological "*The Sun Also Rises*: Hemingway and the Art of Repetition," (*UTQ* 56:313–37). Regarding Jake's self-reflexive text as one that presents himself as a narrator of Cohn's, others', and his own stories, Budick differentiates two Jakes. Jake the Undiscerning can read well Cohn's story and Cohn's reading but is blind to Cohn as a projection of himself, misreads his own story, and inattentively registers but cannot interpret the redundancies, doublings, and duplications in his narrative (" 'I had the feeling of going through something that has all happened before' "). Jake the Discerning is an artist-critic who, Budick unconvincingly insists, acquires "self-referential, self-knowing, and self-controlled experience" in the episodes in San Sebastian and Madrid. In contrast to such readings of Jake in narratological garments, H. R. Stoneback finds him wearing the garb of a pilgrim in "From the rue Saint-Jacques to the Pass of Roland to the 'Unfinished Church on the Edge of the Cliff' " (*HemR* 6,i:2–29). From textual references and allusions to such places as Roncevaux, Bruges, Senlis, Tours, Sainte Odile, St. Etienne du Mont, and Pamplona, Stoneback strums the old song of Hemingway's Catholic sensibility to new choruses, the sustained pilgrimage motif that certifies both Jake's role as a "*jacquet* (the common term for a pilgrim)" and his narration as Hemingway's *Liber Sancti Jacobi.* Discords in Stoneback's erudite account include hieratic dismissal of non-religious readings of the novel, dogmatic insistence that Jake's journey harvests spiritual growth, blindness to Jake's secular activities as pilgrimic impedimenta, and repetition of material Stoneback earlier articulated in Donald R. Noble's 1983 collection of essays, *Hemingway: A Revaluation.*

In "The Festival Gone Wrong: Vanity and Victimization in *The Sun Also Rises*" (*ELWIU* 13:115–33), Robert Casillo weds the terminology of René Girard to the shopworn Hemingway "code" to issue a tortuous reading of scapegoating, rituals, and their relationship to Jake's confused and confusing treatment of Cohn as "the projected and unacknowledged image" of Jake's and the in-group's confusion. As for Jake's pimping, naturally it signifies "the imitative sickness and masochism of mediated desire." Another wedding occurs in Frank Scafella's "*The Sun Also Rises*: Owen Wister's 'Garbage Pail,' Hemingway's Baggage of the 'Human Soul'" (*HemR* 6,i:101–11). Scafella recounts and quotes from the correspondence between Wister and Hemingway, a correspondence Wister initiated in 1928 and continued into 1936, six years after Hemingway quit responding, presumably because of Wister's paternalistic censure of "garbage"—that is, Hemingway's smut and apparently excessive fidelity to actual conversation in his work. Onto the back of this biographical minichapter Scafella yokes a reading of Jake Barnes's magnanimous, reliable, and confessional narrative, a narrative rooted in the archaic function of feasts and fiestas, "attended only by members of a clan, at which those who [had] quarrelled were, in the sacrament of eating and drinking, reconciled."

Hispanophile Allen Josephs reiterates the aesthetic and religious importance of bullfighting to Hemingway and *Sun* in "*Toreo*: The Moral Axis of *The Sun Also Rises*" (*HemR* 6,i:88–99). But he also tracks Hemingway's changes in adopting, modifying, and finally transforming his novel's torero from the actual Cayetano Ordóñez to the legendary "Guerrita" to the mythic Romero, whose bullring behavior Hemingway alters to kill *recibiendo* (receiving the bull) rather than *volapié* (routinely taking the sword to it). The bullfight is also like a medieval tournament, according to Kim Moreland's "Hemingway's Medievalist Impulse: Its Effect on the Presentation of Women and War in *The Sun Also Rises*" (*HemR* 6,i:30–41), which exercises the conventions of courtly love to examine the novel's men as knights-errant who serve well and poorly Lady Brett, a degraded modern woman who, failing to honor the criteria of the courtly order of love, makes ignoble requests of her knights, "spurring them to moral degeneration." Judging Brett by alien categories seems to continue to be her fate, as further evidenced by a pair of essays by Wolfgang E. H. Rudat, "Brett's Problem: Ovidian and Other Allusions in *The Sun Also Rises*" (*Style* [1985]19:317–25), and "Hemingway's Brett: Linguistic Manipulation and the Male Ego in *The Sun Also Rises*" (*JEP* 7:76–82). In the former Rudat frolicks in the literal and figurative translation of Brett's name as board, ski, and boat—which men, of course, nail or ride, and which Hemingway consciously intended so as to obscure his sexist attitudes toward Brett's model, Duff Twysden. The relationship between the wild allusions and a conventionally religious reading of the novel's ending escaped me. Rudat continues to knead Brett's name in the second essay, folding in her real-life model, Lady Duff Twysden, whose unusual name, *duff*, is "a northern English version of *dough*," thereby making Brett a loaf of bread shared by many eaters. John W. Aldridge tries to link "Big Two-Hearted River" to *Sun* in "*The Sun Also Rises*—Sixty Years Later" (*SR* 94:337–45), maintaining that the minimalist prose of both works not only accounts for the unidentified trauma of the story but also the omissions of "some acute unpleasantness" that Jake cannot confront because it threatens his "psychic equilibrium and might cause a dangerous 'flooding' of consciousness." If Aldridge missed the scene of Jake standing naked before a mirror, gazing at his genital disfigurement, and crying, maybe he missed an idiot repeating the scene in *The Sound and the Fury*, a parallel not missed by Merritt Moseley in "Faulkner's Benjy, Hemingway's Jake" (*CollL* 13:300–304).

With one exception, scholar-critics called back some perennial puzzlers among Hemingway's stories. Which whore to put our money on went another round this year. In "Taking on the Champion: Alice as Liar in 'The Light of the World'" (*SAF* 14:225–32), William J. Collins adds more information on the boxer both Alice and Peroxide lay claim to, showing that neither woman tells the truth about her relationship with him. But this is the prelim to Collins's main event, that Alice's lies have a "realistic outlook that force her to accept what she is now in a world she never made"; in contrast, Peroxide's "retreat into a solipsistic fantasy" creates "an oasis of unreality that permits her to deal with her life on false, easy terms." Counterpunching is Howard L. Hannum in "Nick Adams and the Search for Light" (*SSF* 23:9–18). Reviewing the story's criticism, bringing in more boxing history, adding Christian and literary allusions, and throwing some low blows—the punchy dialogue between the iridescent beauties replays the fight between Ketchel (read Peroxide) and Johnson (read Alice)—Hannum argues that Peroxide has some information while Alice, who "shows no verifiable knowledge of Ketchel's life and career," gulls Nick and others merely with her "determined manner." How to read Nick's return to the battlefront is the nub of Kenneth G. Johnston's " 'A Way You'll Never Be': A Mission of Morale" (*SSF* 23:429–35). Rejecting the ostensible reason for his return—at the bidding of his military superiors to boost the Italian troops' morale—Johnston argues that Nick is at the bidding of his medical superiors whose therapeutic motive is to boost Nick's own morale and restore his self-confidence, to "exorcise some of his fear and self-doubt." Neither booster takes.

Two of Hemingway's stories fell into the hands of pedants. The lesser pedant was Susan Beegel, whose "The Death of El Espartero: An Historic Matador Links 'The Undefeated' and *Death in the Afternoon*" (*HemR* 5,ii:12–23) locates a source other than *Afternoon*'s Maera for Manual of "Undefeated." From an eight-page manuscript chapter for *Afternoon*, "a false start on a chapter about bullfighters killed in the ring," Beegel tracks down another Manuel Garcia, a torero known as El Espartero who was gored to death in 1894 and whom she compares with Maera and Manuel to conclude that the story's torero resembles Espartero more than Maera. To such information, however, she adds gobs of taurine research and even an appendix in Spanish. The greater pedant was Oddvar Holmesland, whose "Structuralism and Interpretation: Ernest Hemingway's 'Cat in the Rain' " (*ES* 67:221–33) allegedly brings structuralist principles to disabuse at length a host of critics who have erroneously assigned symbolic meanings to the story's cats. But Holmesland stoops to similar symbolic signification, pulling Hermes and a host of "metaphors of spiritual equivalents" from the window that the American wife looks out. And what construct does such structuralism erect? That "the meaning of the cat cannot be defined more explicitly than as a metaphor for the wife's instinctual desire for a vital openness to life."

The often ignored story freshly considered is "The Sea Change,"

Hemingway's delicately etched, sympathetic portrait of a lesbian. In "Perversion and the Writer in 'The Sea Change'" (*SAF* 14:215–20), Robert E. Fleming examines the story's literary allusions, a manuscript alternate ending, and Hemingway's frequent habit of populating his fiction with writers who embody his own problems. These let Fleming dismiss interpretations that quibble over whether Phil himself becomes homosexual and attend instead to Phil's quasi-allegorical role as a writer who will perversely use others' experiences, however sordid or unpromising, and impose a "sea change" on them; he will, that is, transform them into beautiful and enduring art, as Phil's allusion to "Ariel's Song" from *The Tempest* indicates.

University of Montana

Part II

11. Literature to 1800

William J. Scheick

This year in colonial American studies Benjamin Franklin attracted more attention than did Thomas Jefferson, a perennial favorite of recent studies of the Revolutionary period. Especially noteworthy are J. A. Leo Lemay's expert wrestling with the Franklin literary canon and Christopher Looby's excellent probe into the nature of deferral, displacement, and reconciliation in Franklin's *Autobiography.* The outstanding achievement in the field is Cathy N. Davidson's remarkable study of the rise of the novel in late 18th-century America.

i. Puritan Poetry

Harrison T. Meserole's valuable anthology has been reissued with a few revisions and a new title, *American Poetry of the Seventeenth Century* (Penn. State, 1985). This volume includes all of Michael Wigglesworth's *The Day of Doom,* which figures early in Douglas Robinson's *American Apocalypses: The Image of the End of the World in American Literature* (Hopkins, 1985, pp. 55–62). Robinson concludes that unlike Jonathan Edwards's later frustrated effort to democratize the Last Judgment, Wigglesworth is satisfied with a rigid sense of who is excluded from heaven, a sense that even Christ is not free to alter; for Wigglesworth the elect have undergone a transformation of self, a splitting off of a drosslike evil Other. In contrast to Wigglesworth's anticipation of a dramatic eschatological transformation, Anne Bradstreet desired a sense of permanence in the present. According to Albert J. Von Frank, in *The Sacred Game: Provincialism and Frontier Consciousness in American Literature, 1630–1860* (Cambridge, 1985, pp. 11–26), Bradstreet was uncomfortable with the changes accompanying her emigration to New England and wrote her early verse in order to focus on immutable truths, a focus which protected her imagination from the brute facts of the American wilderness. Bradstreet thought of earthly existence as "lonely . . . with pleasures dignif'd," and this sense of the pleasures of life is found as well in the late poems of another Puritan poet, Richard Steere. The difference between his early and late writings, explains Donald P. Wharton in "The American Poetry of Richard Steere" (*AmerP* 3,iii:2–12), does not signify an abandonment of faith by the poet, whose work tends to emphasize art over description and showing over telling.

The newly discovered first extant publication of a poet who energetically intermingles his faith and his sense of earthly wonder is edited by Thomas M. Davis in "Edward Taylor's Elegy on Deacon David Dewey" (*PAAS* 96:75–84). Not death but life is the concern of "The Christian Hero and the Classical Journey in Edward Taylor's 'Preparatory Meditations. First Series' " (*HLQ* 49:113–32), in which Michael Schuldiner identifies Taylor's meditational pattern with both Calvin's paradigm of the first stage of spiritual growth in assurance and with the classical model of the first stage (departure) of the hero's journey. Taylor's linguistic journey into the ineffable provides the focus of Carter Martin's "A Fantastic Pairing: Edward Taylor and Donald Barthelme" (*The Scope of the Fantastic—Theory, Technique, Major Authors*, ed. Robert A. Collins and Howard D. Pearce [Greenwood 1985], pp. 183–90), which argues that the poet uses (especially in "Meditation 2.48") opacity of statement and metaphor to confound rationality and to cause the reader to derive meaning through hesitation.

Rationality and meaning come together for Taylor in biblical types, the subject of Karen Rowe's repetitive, somewhat tedious *Saint and Singer: Edward Taylor's Typology and the Poetics of Meditation* (Cambridge). Rowe traces Taylor's sources to Thomas Taylor's *Christ Revealed* and Samuel Mather's *Figures or Types of the Old Testament*, and she distinguishes between ceremonial typology and sacramental typology. In the early meditations of the second series (2.2 to 2.15), Taylor is exegetically conservative, avoiding the application of ceremonial types to history or to people and limiting the application of types beyond Christ to *exempla fidei*. A little later in this series (2.16 to 2.25) the poet sometimes eschews typical parallels and prefers provocative conceits as a means of transforming analytic doctrine into fervid desires to perform devout service. In time Taylor comes to prefer sacramental typological themes over those of ceremonial typology, and then (as in 2.102 to 2.111) he seeks out a larger variety of typological signification; now he sometimes transforms conventional antitheses, based in part on typological reasoning, into a transcendent unitary vision. In many of the meditations near the end of his life Taylor moved from typology to allegory, particularly as manifest in Canticles, which informs his sense of identification with Solomon and David; in these late poems he finds a transcendent language suggesting that he has achieved a sense of nearly having arrived at the longed-for destination of marriage to Christ in heaven. Particularly in these poems the poet manages to do what he could previously only achieve now and then: to engraft ingeniously his personal pleas for salvation into the figural (typological) development of his meditations and thereby to redesign and personalize age-old images. Excellent as a resource on the meanings of Taylor's typology, Rowe's analysis unfortunately makes no case for the poetry, a problem she blames on Taylor, who is for Rowe "a poet with limited skill, but glorious ambitions."

ii. Puritan Prose

Congregationalist ministers like Taylor turned to Scripture not only for types but also for clues to the proper time period of the Sabbath, which is the topic of "John Cotton's Treatise on the Duration of the Lord's Day" (*PCSM* 59[1982]:505–22), ed. Winton U. Solberg. Cotton believed that the Sabbath lasted from sunset on Saturday to sunset on Sunday, and he was equally concerned with the function of the sermons he prepared for this occasion. In "John Cotton and the Rhetoric of Grace" (*EAL* 21:49–74) Eugenia DeLamotte suggests that in his sermons Cotton links experiential knowledge to a rhetoric which provides nonintellectual ways for the listener to experience the influx of grace; Cotton juxtaposes figurative language with abstractions in a way which tends to impart doctrine rather than merely to illustrate it, a method which at once endows his metaphors with life without abandoning Scripture. If Cotton's sermonic rhetoric is more subtle than it first appears, so too was his position on baptism and common grace after the controversy surrounding Anne Hutchinson. Norman Pettit ("Cotton's Dilemma: Another Look at the Antinomian Controversy" [*PCSM* 59(1982):393–413]) is certain that Cotton was less repentant than he seemed, that he did not readily discard his low conception of baptism, and that he continued to deny any direct connection between common grace and effectual conversion.

That Cotton is not quite what he appears is also the subject of

The Interpretation of Material Shapes in Puritanism: A Study of Rhetoric, Prejudice, and Violence (Cambridge), a wild book in which Ann Kibbey unconvincingly claims that Cotton's rhetoric manifests a variety of phonic repetitions stressing the primacy of the interrelationship of word sound over meaning, even to the extent of contradicting the meaning of the sermon: to turn away from the world, the very world that is given primacy by the material acoustic shapes of the words. But the verbal effects in Cotton's discourse that Kibbey singles out seem more the accidents of the nature of the English language than the deliberate design of the minister. Cotton, Kibbey explains further, interprets Solomon in Canticles as the prophetic, visionary cleric speaking in sacred tropes, but interprets the bride, "who is a silent audience *despite her literary appearance of speech* in the poetry," as dissociated from the same sacred interpretive signs attributed to Solomon (emphasis added). Kibbey does not argue away the fact that the bride is not in fact silent or that in the traditional exegeses of the Song of Solomon, to which Cotton and other Puritans had access, the bride represents the Church; Kibbey only asserts away the bride's status. And she then rushes into the hasty conclusion that the bride is merely a female (signifying profane imagination), a material object, a nonlinguistic *figura* different from the sanctioned living icon of the Solomon-like authoritative male minister. Because women represented profane imagination, Kibbey recklessly continues, "Puritan women were potentially a threat to the social and natural order simply because they were women," with the consequence that "Puritan women lived under the threat of sanctioned violence from Puritan men," a violence (including murder) sanctioned by such spokesmen as Cotton.

Some of the more than 400 books available to Cotton while he was a fellow at Emmanuel College are listed in "Emmanuel College Library's First Inventory" (*TCBS* 8[1985]:514–56), ed. Sargent Bush, Jr., and Carl J. Rasmussen. The minister who said, "Mr. Cotton repents not, but is hid only," is seen in the context of English Puritanism in *God's Caress: The Psychology of Puritan Religious Experience* (Oxford), in which Charles Lloyd Cohen studies the spiritual relations of Thomas Shepard's converts and concludes that they were personally self-assured moderates rather than neurotic personalities. The English roots of Puritanism as well as the Renaissance uses of Ramean logic, both seminal in Cotton's and Shepard's thought, are usefully discussed again in the late Leon Howard's *Essays in Puritans and Puritanism*, ed. James Barbour and Thomas Quirk (N. Mex.). Respect for Cotton and his peers by the next generation came under attack by Solomon Stoddard, who accused establishment ministers of an excessive veneration of the past, especially ecclesiastical tradition. As Phillip F. Gura remarks in "Solomon Stoddard's Irreverent Way" (*EAL* 21:29–43), Stoddard claimed that such spokesmen as the Mathers used the veneration of their predecessors as a veil to hide the fact that these contemporaries of Stoddard were actually altering tradition.

A more belligerent attack on Increase Mather (and Jonathan Edwards) appears in Jefferson Humphries's "The Sorcery of Rhetoric in French and American Letters" (*MR* 28[1985]:178–97), which argues that Mather quotes aphorisms that run counter to his own citation of them, that Mather (like Edwards) merely represses the paradoxicality of aphorisms by resorting to the idea of the Logos. Clues to Mather's resignation from the presidency of Harvard are provided by Harley P. Holden in "Commentary on Selected Correspondence Between Increase Mather and Sir William Ashurst" (*PCSM* 59[1982]: 211–29).

Some thoughts similar to those of Increase's son, Cotton, concerning courtroom procedures are noted in "The Salem Witchcraft Trials: Samuel Willard's *Some Miscellany Observations*" (*EIHC* 122:207–36), ed. David C. Brown. In "Cotton Mather, Physico-Theologian" (JHI 47:583–94) Jeffrey Jeske focuses on *The Christian Philosopher* to reveal a Matherian persona who respects reason and science, endorses a mechanistic interpretation of the universe, and retreats from the sacerdotal, jeremiadal, and affective preoccupations of his earlier writings. A Puritan persona of sorts interests Lawrence Rosenwald, whose "Sewall's *Diary* and the Margins of Puritan Literature" (*AL* 58:325–41) argues that Sewall feels that his life is so firmly fixed at the center of his attention that he readily diverts his thought to the periphery of that life, a dramatic margin replete with a luring variety countering the monotonous conformity of the censoring public life at its center. A shift of authorial focus occurs as well in Edward Johnson's *Wonder-Working Providence*, in which Andrew Delbanco ("Looking Homeward, Going Home: The Lure of England for the Founders of New England" [*NEQ* 59:358–86]) sees the historian's inability to sustain his initial energy; Johnson's book winds down and falls into disarray as it confronts the defection of colonists returning to England.

iii. The South

In *Writing the South* Richard Gray offers a chapter (pp. 1–30) on the colonial South that traces how the pastoral ideal of the pamphleteers, who imagined an emergent aristocracy, evolved into a sense of loss that nurtured for later colonists a dream of recovering a yeoman republic based on English literary and legal traditions. The colonial southern mind, especially in Virginia, moved from hope to nostalgia, a sense of the future to a sense of the past, from the ideal of the good farmer to the model of the fine gentleman. Settlers' dreams, Gray reasonably contends, collided with the realities of the New World, the people, and their ruthless methods of personal advancement; but these dreams helped them to manage the harshness of the strange place.

That imagination and reality conflict as well in the various treatments of Nathaniel Bacon's attempt to take command of Virginia is the subject of an essay by W. H. Ward in *No Fairer Land*: "The 'True Narrative' of Bacon's Rebellion" (pp. 21–31). In this same volume Charles J. Churchman awkwardly reads Samuel Davies's verse as pre-Romantic (pp. 50–66), and Meta Robinson Braymer limply concludes that in his plays St. George Tucker stumbles, but at least he was trying to walk (pp. 87–100). A picture of colonial plantation life in South Carolina appears in "George Ogilvie's *Carolina; Or, the Planter* (1776)" (*SLJ*, special issue), a long narrative poem edited and annotated by David S. Shields.

As bibliographic aids to the study of colonial southern literature there are Sam G. Riley's *Magazines of the American South* (Greenwood) and his *Index to Southern Periodicals* (Greenwood). Also helpful is *South Carolina Imprints, 1731–1800: A Descriptive Bibliography* (ABC-Clio, 1985), by Christopher Gould, Richard Parker Morgan, and Marcus A. McCorison.

iv. Edwards and the Great Awakening

Harry S. Stout's *The New England Soul: Preaching and Religious Culture in Colonial New England* (Oxford) reminds us of the importance of aurality in the culturally impoverished wilderness of the New World. He reviews the place of the sermon not only as popular culture, but also as a social sacrament which served as a facilitator of grace and a way ritually to transform everyday experience into the divine word. Stout particularly emphasizes the Great Awakening, when debates raged concerning the place of the sermon, which regard was questioned by people like George Whitefield. The nature of the debate between Whitefield and more conservative clergy is considered as well in Dennis Barone's "James Logan and Gilbert Tennent: Enlightened Classicist versus Awakened Evangelist" (*EAL* 21: 103–17), which indicates that whereas Logan believed in an authoritarian system and a hierarchical structure in society, Tennent questioned these patterns and argued that true human worth is not determined by social status. Consequently, Logan used rhetoric as a classicist in order to maintain authority, while Tennent opposed such formal rhetoric.

For a time Jonathan Dickinson shared some of Tennent's views, but that he came to modify his enthusiasm for the religious revival of the Great Awakening is the topic of "A World of Double Visions and Second Thoughts: Jonathan Dickinson's *Display of God's Special Grace*" (*EAL* 21:118–30) by David Harlan. Dickinson's book is a dialogue about religion in which both participants grow in their understanding and finally evince a moderate position, which reflects the author's inward doubts. If Dickinson became a moderate, Andrew Croswell remained a radical. In "'A Second and Glorious Reformation': The New Light Extremism of Andrew Croswell" (*WMQ* 43: 214–44), Leigh Eric Schmidt describes Croswell's belief that only a contentious spirit willing to disrupt established society could reverse New England's religious and social dissolution and resurrect God's order.

Croswell was debated by David Brainerd, whose journals were edited by Jonathan Edwards in an effort to restrain the radical New Lights. In two articles, "The Life of David Brainerd: Comments on the Manuscript and Text" (*YULG* 60:137–44) and "Prelude to Mission: Brainerd's Expulsion from Yale" (*NEQ* 59:28–50), Norman Pettit repeats much of what he already reported in the introduction to his edition of Edwards's work (*ALS 1985*), reminding us that Edwards deleted much which might have put Brainerd in a bad light and thereby presented him as a representative figure rather than as an individual. Another figure in Edwards's life, his father, makes an appearance in "A Great Awakening Conversion: The Relation of Samuel Belcher" (*WMQ* 44:121–26), ed. Kenneth P.

Minkema, who believes that the language of this spiritual relation (c. 1740) by one of Timothy Edwards's parishioners is richer in emotional language than are earlier relations.

The sermonic language of Timothy's son is scrutinized in "Jonathan Edwards on Rhetorical Authority" (*JHI* 47:395–408), in which Stephen R. Yarbrough grounds Edwards's communication theory less on John Locke than on the Ramist thought of Alexander Richardson. With grace, in Edwards's view, one's vision achieves a refined focus and can now see unity in Scripture and nature (God's beautiful communicated art); this communication of grace gives the saint authority to interpret and to teach. A specific application of Edwardsian rhetorical management is detected by Rosemary Hearn, whose "Form as Argument in Edwards' 'Sinners in the Hands of an Angry God'" (*CLAJ* 28[1985]:452–59) suggests that in this sermon an initial use of deductive reasoning gives way eventually to the inductive form in the last part of the work, where the argument is interlaced with powerful imagery; this pattern, Hearn notes without going into detail, makes the reader choose between options and ponder the consequences of what will logically follow.

Edwardsian rhetoric of another kind interests R. C. De Prospo in his overly long *Theism in the Discourse of Jonathan Edwards* (Delaware, 1985), which points to an Edwardsian discursive pattern (termed theism) based on the ultimate dichotomy between creator and creation, an ontological pattern indefinitely generating hierarchical dualities or divisions which human vision cannot be relied upon to discover. Edwards was inspired, De Prospo maintains, by the inexpressiveness of the visible world, a lack of sufficient expression of truth that orients Edwards toward what lies beyond nature, the supernatural. Edwards did use analogies, but an analogy is only a similitude implying a gap between what is compared and so must never be mistaken for an identity. This same sense of gap is underscored by providence, which does not work in nature as it does against it, for providence is superior to time. In these terms, then, De Prospo's Edwards doubts the human ability to know God, even in a personal experience of conversion. All of this is thoughtful and sometimes insightful, though it is given heavy-handed treatment by De Prospo, who rummages among the formulators of deconstructive theory for support. For me the main trouble with this study is the nagging question of whether De Prospo has only said finally that in emphasizing the utter disparity between creator and creature Edwards was a thorough Calvinist. But even a Calvinist believes in the Incarnation, that wondrous event (for a Christian) which closes any gap between deity and humanity. Nor am I convinced of De Prospo's asserted conclusion that the paradigm of utimate duality is distinctively characteristic of American literature and culture.

In complete opposition to De Prospo, and more convincing, is Paula M. Cooey, whose *Jonathan Edwards on Nature and Destiny: A Systematic Analysis* (Mellen, 1985) argues that in Edwards's thought nature—sensible and sentient reality—is subordinate to but not detached from its creator, that the order and interrelationships of nature manifest the deity. Nature is the deity's act of self-communication aimed at fulfilling its divine destiny of self-glorification, a view that Cooey defines as the systematic underlying theme informing Edwards's coherent vision. Cooey's sense of Edwards's understanding of nature seems to me to be accurate, but she fails to realize that she cannot use this concept in a *special* claim for Edwards. The notions she details are precisely those of Edwards's Puritan predecessors; in fact, they constitute a main current of Augustinian influence on Reformation theology. There are other problems too: Cooey ignores completely the place of predestination in her analysis of history as the syntax of the grammar of nature; she does not avail herself of the useful Augustinian distinction between *natura naturans* and *natura naturata*, which distinction would have significantly shortened her study; she asserts, rather than argues, that Edwards reads nature anagogically, not allegorically; she overlooks Edwards's *History of the Work of Redemption*, which describes the end of time (nature) as a universal conversion experience; and she takes the "Personal Narrative" at face value, as if no one had ever suggested that this work might evince rhetorical strategies managed in terms of both a persona and an intended audience. A literal reading of the "Personal Narrative" also appears in "The Mystical Journey of Jonathan Edwards" (*SMy* 8[1985]:20–29), in which J. R. McNerney notes that this Edwardsian document points out important features of its author's mysticism that informed his emotionalism during the Great Awakening.

v. Franklin, Jefferson, and the Revolutionary Period

In *The Canon of Benjamin Franklin, 1722–1776: New Attributions and Reconsiderations* (Delaware), J. A. Leo Lemay provides a most valuable consideration of 96 writings, of which 39 are newly attributed to Franklin. And for still later works there is *Papers of Benjamin Franklin, Volume 25: October 1, 1777, through February 28, 1778* (Yale), ed. William B. Willcox.

David M. Larson's "Benevolent Persuasion: The Art of Benjamin Franklin's Philanthropic Papers" (*PMHB* 110:195–217) concerns Franklin's adoption of a persona, such as that of an experienced old man giving good advice, in order to establish a common ground with his audience by appealing at once to its self-interest and its altruism. Another Franklin persona designed specifically with an audience in mind is the subject of "Benjamin Franklin, the Inveterate (and Crafty) Public Instructor: Instruction on Two Levels in 'The Way to Wealth'" (*EAL* 21:248–53), in which Patrick Sullivan studies how, on the one hand, Franklin uses proverbs to appeal to the passive reader who slavishly follows advice and, on the other hand, uses dramatic context and a rhetorical mutual qualification, stressing life's complexities, to appeal to the sophisticated reader who prefers to judge and evaluate independently.

Not Franklin's sense of two types of audience, but his division between urban and pastoral matters interests James L. Machor, whose "The Urban Idyll of the New Republic: Moral Geography and the Mythic Hero of Franklin's *Autobiography*" (*PMHB* 110:219–36) argues that Franklin reconciled his attraction to pastoral values and his commitment to city life by creating an urban hero making a fresh start in a symbolic landscape, a hero transplanted from an old oppressive city to a new city beyond the horizon. Franklin's awareness of audience and of the need to reconcile conflicting feelings are the subjects of Kenneth Dauber's "Benjamin Franklin and the Idea of Authorship" (*Criticism* 28:255–86) and Christopher Looby's "'The Affairs of the Revolution Occasion'd the Interruption': Writing, Revolution, Deferral and Conciliation in Franklin's *Autobiography*" (*AQ* 38:72–96). Dauber interestingly observes that the language of the *Autobiography* is never inferior or superior to its audience, which fact permits an easy relation between author and reader; this language, moreover, reflects culture interiorly, obliterates beginnings and endings outside this culture, and never permits the reader to inquire into anything beyond the text for explanations about what is narrated. Looby excellently remarks how the conciliatory language of the *Autobiography* is valued by Franklin for its association with his father (an envied model in the skillful use of language) and with

Britain, against whose authority he initially rebelled; this language represents a new form of authority and a return to order, which Franklin thought was threatened by the rhetorical excesses and the activity associated with the Revolutionary War (an event oddly absent from the text). Looby argues that the first part of the *Autobiography* expresses Franklin's wish to defer the Revolution, while the subsequent parts express both misgivings concerning the war and a desire to repress the memory of it in the interest of restoring social and political order.

For Leo Braudy in *The Frenzy of Renown* (pp. 366–71) Franklin's desire in his autobiography to associate what is best for himself with what is best for others is a form of civic narcissism; moreover, Franklin's consideration of his self as fashionable and marketable heightened his sense of personal will, but it risked a psychic alienation and a commoditization of that self in the future. Not alienation but Franklin's and Jefferson's integration of the emerging American culture and its natural environment interests Myra Jehlen, whose *American Incarnation* (Harvard, pp. 59–66) argues that whereas in *Notes on the State of Virginia* Jefferson praises nature in the new republic as an incarnation of national spirit, in a letter (1753) Franklin defends American ideology by pointing to nature. The principal events of Franklin's public self are entertainingly emphasized, with few errors of fact and with a few new interpretations of his political involvements, in Esmond Wright's *Franklin of Philadelphia* (Harvard). In "Milton and Franklin" (*EAL* 21:44–48) Eid A. Dahiyat documents Franklin's high regard for the 17th-century poet, and in "Benjamin Franklin and Cooper's *The Pioneers*" (*ELN* 24:73–78) Michael Clark claims that Judge Temple is fashioned after Franklin.

That Franklin was a master of accommodation is one point made by Robert A. Ferguson in "'We Hold These Truths': Strategies of Control in the Literature of the Founders" (*Reconstructing American Literary History*, pp. 1–28), which suggests that the founders had a faith in words as stabilizers capable of reshaping crude facts and, consequently, used the language of imposition, negation, reduction, and avoidance to create an impression of unifying consensus that in actuality only masked the mix of antithetical tendencies of the uncertain world of the 1770s. A gap between perceived reality and ideal occurred as well in the poetry of this period, explains David S. Shields in "Mental Nocturnes: Night Thoughts on Man and Nature in the Poetry of Eighteenth-Century America" (*PMHB* 110:237–58).

In poetry by James Ralph, Richard Lewis, Philip Freneau, and Thomas Godfrey, Jr., Shields sees a pessimistic view of the relation of humanity to nature, a doubt that nature is designed to be comprehended by reason; this doubt creates a tension with these poets' articulated belief that nature evinces order and will redeem mankind from its own flawed, unstable, and self-deluding human nature.

The man who thought that Franklin should be appointed as the first vice president in George Washington's administration makes an appearance in *Classica Americana: The Greek and Roman Heritage in the United States* (Wayne State, 1984), in which Meyer Reinhold observes the profound influence of the authors of classical antiquity on such leading figures as Thomas Jefferson, among others. That the grounds of Jefferson's theory of property, theory of educational development, and theory of human powers differed from those of John Locke is argued by David M. Post in "Jeffersonian Revisions of Locke: Education, Property Rights, and Liberty" (*JHI* 47:147–57). Jefferson's friend and ally in his fight for religious freedom is the subject of "Safety in Numbers: Madison, Hume, and the Tenth *Federalist*" (*HLQ* 49:95–112), in which Edmund S. Morgan indicates the ways Madison agreed with Hume on the nature of republican government, but daringly differed from him in the reasoning behind the views expressed in the *Federalist*.

Not Locke or Hume, but Voltaire and Rousseau might have had an effect on a compatriot of Jefferson and Madison; the influence of these philosophers on Thomas Paine's radicalism, as well as of his Quaker inheritance, his early exposure to poverty in London, and his experience of corruption in the customs and excise service, is detailed in David Powell's *Tom Paine: The Greatest Exile* (St. Martin's, 1985), which *imagines* Paine's responses to the social, economic, and political conditions of the first 37 years of his life. Paine's use of language drawn from both revolutionary politics and a secularized republican apocalypse emphasizing human perfectability is remarked in "The Revolutionary Millennialism of Thomas Paine" (*SECC* 13[1984]:65–77) by Jack Fruchtman, Jr.; and the traditions behind the eschatological beliefs of colonial figures, including secular versions like Paine's, are detailed in Ruth H. Bloch's *Visionary Republic: Millennial Themes in American Thought, 1756–1800* (Cambridge).

The man about whom Paine wrote a vicious analysis, accusing him of treachery in personal friendships and hypocrisy in public life, interests Barry Schwartz, whose "The Character of Washington: A

Study in Republican Culture" (*AQ* 38:202–22) recovers what Washington meant in the 18th century and concludes that neither classical nor religious ideals molded the image of Washington during the early republic, a power-wary society which did not see him as a charismatic or authoritorian hero. The portrait of Washington and others as presented in verse in English books, pamphlets, journals, and magazines published from 1763 to 1783 is bibliographically noted in Martin Kallich's *British Poetry and the American Revolution* (Whitston).

vi. The Early National Period

In *New England Literary Culture* (pp. 84–102) Lawrence Buell concludes that New England Neoclassicism was not a transient fashion symptomatic of American cultural immaturity, but a posture of moral monitoring and visionary self-consciousness similar to that of the Puritans and of the Romantics to come. New England Federalists made use of such literary strategies as the jeremiad in order to legitimize the new republic and its literature in response to fears that anarchy might prevail. A literary strategy of another kind employed to combat the tyranny of slavery is remarked in "A Slave's Subtle War: Phillis Wheatley's Use of Biblical Myth" (*EAL* 21:144–65), in which Sondra O'Neale studies how Wheatley's management of connotations of blackness, in terms of biblical allusions and types, subverts racial attitudes prevailing during her time. Newly discovered verse written five months before the poet's death is edited by Mukhtar Ali Isani in " 'An Elegy on Leaving ———': A New Poem by Phillis Wheatley" (*AL* 58:609–13).

Not fear of social anarchy or anger over slavery, but early national anxiety over the tension between tired urban sophistication (imitative of English culture) and pastoral backwoods simplicity interests Albert J. Von Frank, whose *The Sacred Game* (pp. 42–60) discusses Royall Tyler's search for an American wholeness that preserved something of Yankee barbarism. The barbarism of slavery is under attack in Tyler's *The Algerine Captive*, which Cathy N. Davidson considers in *Revolution and the Word* (pp. 192–211); Davidson focuses on Tyler's use of modes of apparent irresolution to highlight both the problems of the political and social culture of the new nation and the need for the republican values of individual responsibility, conscience, and action. That Tyler tried to bridge the extreme forces of 18th-Century America is also the subject of Richard S.

Pressman's "Class Positioning and Shays' Rebellion: Resolving the Contradictions of *The Contrast*" (*EAL* 21:87–102), which discloses how Tyler creates an illusion of agrarian culture being subsumed into mercantilist culture, while in fact in his play Tyler uses Federalist values to chasten mercantilists in order to bring them closer to agrarians; Tyler, who is concerned with reconciliation between these two social classes, criticizes the self-aggrandizement of the wealthy (which trait contributed to Shays's Rebellion) and, at the same time, distances himself from a strongly democratic, egalitarian stand.

Another author of comedy appears in "English Satire and Connecticut Wit" (*AQ* 37[1985]:13–29), in which Peter M. Briggs focuses principally on John Trumbull's struggle to domesticate his muse when he tended to laugh at the British with humor borrowed from the English tradition of satire; Trumbull and his fellow wits experienced difficulty in imagining America, for politics can change, but a state of mind in matters of culture is difficult to transcend. Cultural concerns informed, as well, Joel Barlow's political pamphlets, which are scrutinized by Gregg Camfield in "Joel Barlow's Dialectic of Progress" (*EAL* 21:131–43). Camfield emphasizes Barlow's use of paradox as an expression of his sense of a fundamental antithesis in human character between social form and natural morality, which oppositions people try to synthesize. Culture and the question of the originality of early national humor also interest Robert Secor, whose "The Significance of Pennsylvania's Eighteenth-Century Jest Books" (*PMHB* 110:259–87) argues that during this time American humor did not merely imitate English examples and, even when it did, it reveals prevalent American social attitudes. An author whose comic manner discloses a specific problem in early national culture is treated by Mark R. Patterson in "Representation in Brackenridge's *Modern Chivalry*" (*TSLL* 28:121–39), which insightfully explores the problematic nature of representation in the new country. Pitted against each other in Brackenridge's work are the Federalist view (endorsed by the author) of metaphoric or figurative representation (suggesting an autonomous detachment of the elected from the electors) and the anti-Federalist view of metonymic representation (suggesting a functionally associative continuity between the elected and the electors). In revealing the illusion of metonymic representation, which is akin to metonymic narrative sincerity, Brackenridge's book favors metaphor and allegory, which didactically direct its readers to think figuratively rather than literally.

The didactic function of Noah Webster's efforts is suggested in *The Politics of American English*, in which David Simpson remarks Webster's motives in studying American idiom, the influences behind his work, and his belief that the common speech of the new nation would socially bind its people. Simpson makes clear that much-debated linguistic concerns, such as punctuation and phonetic spelling, informed the postrevolutionary self-consciousness of the new nation. In their role as editors Webster and Brackenridge figure also in *American Literary Magazines*, ed. Edward E. Chielens, which describes and analyzes periodicals of the early national period, including the *Monthly Magazine and American Review*, edited by Charles Brockden Brown.

vii. Brown and Contemporaries

Cathy Davidson's excellent, fresh *Revolution and the Word* studies the entire milieu of late 18th-century American practices in printing, publishing, loaning, and inscribing novels. Central to her argument is the conclusion that sentimental fiction sometimes critiques patriarchial authority and frequently goes against the grain of its stated moral purpose (as in William Hill Brown's *The Power of Sympathy*), whereas picaresque books sometimes critique American politics and usually set forth unreconciled contradictions. Davidson's study is important for rich insights into early American writings which have not generally elicited such sophisticated criticism. Even when she turns her attention to a favorite of critics, Charles Brockden Brown (pp. 236–53), she offers new suggestions, such as the possibility that the ending of *Arthur Mervyn* is deliberately left open to two contradictory interpretations: did individuality or egomania triumph? Brown's purpose behind this ambiguity, Davidson argues interestingly, is to force the reader of his romance to take an active part in making judgments and decisions in the uncertain cultural world of the reader and the novel.

Brown's reflection of the confused culture of the new nation interested other critics as well. In "*Wieland*: 'Accounting for Appearances'" (*NEQ* 59:341–57), Beverly R. Voloshin reinforces our current sense that Brown's romance registers doubts concerning the Lockean model of the mind and sensationalist psychology, which fail to come to terms with the ambiguity of appearances and of human motives, especially in postrevolutionary America. The rapidly changing transitional culture of the early national period figures as well in Daniel A. Cohen's "Arthur Mervyn and His Elders: The Ambivalence of Youth in the Early Republic" (*WMQ* 43:362–80), which points out that Arthur's behavior and language are not the product of rigid rectitude, self-serving duplicity, or confusing antagonistic tension between conscious and unconscious motivations; they are determined by conflicting imperatives nurtured by an unstable culture, replete with generational conflict, in which it is not clear to Arthur how a young man should act as he vacillates between childish subordination to his elders and adult independence. Postrevolutionary tension is also discussed in "Picking up the Knife: A Psycho-Historical Reading of *Wieland*" (*AmerS* 27:115–26), Bill Christophersen's attempt to correlate Clara's troubles with the potential dangers facing the young nation; in Clara's experience of a crisis in identity, survival, self-assertion, and self-understanding, the dark underside of Federalist America is depicted.

That America can be understood and rationally analyzed by those who, like Edgar, can read its primitive iconography is the interesting claim of Dennis Berthold in "Desacralizing the American Gothic: An Iconographic Approach to *Edgar Huntly*" (*SAF* 14:127–38). Berthold sees in this romance a mergence of English gothic tradition and early local color, a mixture peculiarly American, wherein Edgar identifies such American icons as a tomahawk and mocassins to diffuse terror, come to terms with his situation, and orient himself both geographically and psychologically. That this early romance is not far removed from Brown's last two novels is argued in Donald A. Ringe's historical essay for the Bicentennial Edition of *Clara Howard* and *Jane Talbot* (Kent State), which also includes a review of their critical reception.

The critical reception and the context of the fiction and plays of another novelist are reviewed in *Susanna Rowson* (TUSAS 498), in which Patricia L. Parker also notes Rowson's unconventional views of marriage, her creation of independent women, and her particularly American attack on wealth and rank. Rowson's *Charlotte Temple* and Hannah Webster Foster's *The Cocquette* have been separately reissued in handsome, handy editions (Oxford) with introductions by Cathy N. Davidson, who emphasizes the ways Rowson's book reflects the insecurities of the early national period and how it was changed to suit its various publishers' sense of its audience; in Foster's work Davidson detects a complexity disguised within stereotypes and an *apparent* conservative moral that actually affirms female independence, questions the problematic nature of marriage for women, and exposes the injustices of patriarchal culture. Davidson also authored "Female Authorship and Authority: The Case of Sukey Vickery" (*EAL* 21:4–28). Vickery had to contend in the early republic with the idea of fiction as a lie capable of corrupting youth; like Rowson's work, Vickery's diary, letters, poems, and single epistolary novel present independent women, the gender expectations of the time, and an anatomy of marriage. Many of these observations about Rowson, Foster, and Vickery, together with some discussion of *The History of Constantius and Pulchera* and of work by Judith Sargent Murray and Tabitha Gilman Tenney, appear in Davidson's *Revolution and the Word.*

viii. Miscellaneous Studies

In "The Idea of Discovery as a Source of Narrative Structure in Samuel Hearne's *Journey to the Northern Ocean*" (*EAL* 21:189–209), Bruce Greenfield scrutinizes Hearne's sense of conflict between European expectations or intentions and the author's actual, local experiences, a tension that distorts the plot of discovery in the book and reveals that plot to be illusory. Literature of discovery appears as well in the three-volume edition of *The Complete Works of Captain John Smith (1580–1631)* (No. Car.), in which editor Philip Barbour praises Smith as a reliable ethnographer, geographer, encyclopedist, and colonization theorist. Barbour's impressive work is graced with a textual apparatus, annotations, a biographical dictionary, and a chronology of events for Virginia (1608–12) and New England (1602–20).

Some descendants of the Native Americans met by Smith appear in A. LaVonne Brown Ruoff's "American Indian Authors, 1744–1899" (*Critical Essays on Native American Literature* [Hall, 1985], ed. Andrew Wiget, pp. 191–202), which mentions a Samson Occom sermon that saw several editions in 1772. That we do not have the facts about Native Americans or their experience with the settlers of colonial America is argued by Jane Tompkins in " 'Indians': Textualism, Morality, and the Problem of History" (*CritI* 13:101–19), which reviews the relativistic perspectives of Perry Miller, Alden T. Vaughan, Francis Jennings, Calvin Martin, James Axtell, and J. Norman Heard.

Perry Miller figures as well in Francis T. Butts's thoughtful "Norman Fiering and the Revision of Perry Miller" (*CRevAS* 17:1–26), which concludes that contemporary interpretations of Miller's work have misattributed to him an overemphasis on intellectual matters, a distorted and monolithic reading of Puritan culture, and especially a misinterpretation of Jonathan Edwards. Butts finds that Fiering's studies supplement Miller's work more than they overthrow it.

Two useful reference tools are provided in *American Newspaper Journalists, 1640–1872* (DLB 43), a biographical dictionary edited by Perry J. Ashley, and *Annals of American Literature, 1602–1983* (Oxford), a chronological list of major American literary works with parallel listings of important historical events edited by Richard M. Ludwig and Clifford A. Nault, Jr.

With the foregoing labor of commentary in mind, let me take my leave with John Smith: "there is a great difference betwixt the directions and judgment of experimental knowledge, and the superficial conjecture of variable relation. . . . These are the inducements that thus drew me to neglect all other employments, and spend my time and best abilities in these adventures, wherein . . . I have had many discouragements."

University of Texas at Austin

12. 19th-Century Literature

James Woodress

There has been no slackening of scholarly interest in the lesser 19th-century authors who fall within the purview of this chapter. For Irving and Cooper it was a big year, no doubt attributable to the continuing appearance of volumes in their respective definitive editions. Irving is represented by 19 items, including two volumes in the Irving edition and a book-length collection of essays. Cooper generated 16 items, including a book and two volumes in the Cooper edition. As for other writers, 11 of the popular women authors received attention, and, surprisingly, there was a book on Longfellow, plus what I thought the most interesting article I read in preparing this chapter, Helen Carr's essay on "The Myth of Hiawatha." Among the post-Civil War writers, Henry Adams and Sarah Orne Jewett were the most discussed in 1986, while Howells and Crane lagged behind. The best book I read this year was Frederick Turner's splendid biography of John Muir, which actually appeared too late in 1985 to be reviewed here last year.

i. General Studies

There was a great deal of variety in the books and essays on general topics this year, but none seemed to me a major contribution to the study of the 19th century. One I found of considerable interest, however, was James Kinney's *Amalgamation: Race, Sex, and Rhetoric in the Nineteenth-Century American Novel* (Greenwood). This is, in the words of the series editor, "the definitive study of miscegenation in American literature." It deals with 63 novels written between *Modern Chivalry* (1792) and Cable's *Gideon's Band* (1914). Some of the novels, like *Modern Chivalry* or *The Last of the Mohicans*, treat the subject very tangentially, and others are totally forgotten works, such as Richard Hildreth's *Archie Moore* (1836), the first anti-slavery novel, but well-known novelists like Simms (*Beauchampe*) and Howells (*An Imperative Duty*) tried their hands at this theme.

As might be expected, this book devotes a chapter to the most famous novel of miscegenation, *Pudd'nhead Wilson* (1894).

A very useful book appeared in Steven E. Kagle's *Early Nineteenth-Century Diary Literature* (TUSAS 495), which surveys 27 works and continues the author's previous study of colonial diaries. The diaries are discussed under the classifications of spiritual diaries, journals of travel and exploration, diaries of situation, life diaries, and Transcendentalist journals. Emerson and Bronson Alcott are treated (Thoreau is omitted), but their journals are too well known to need much discussion. The book's value lies in the attention given to little-known diarists such as Samuel Cole Davis, Zebulon Pike, and Philip Hone. A very different sort of book is David Wyatt's *The Fall into Eden: Landscape and Imagination in California* (Cambridge), a study that focuses on the unfolding of the Edenic myth of California in the imaginative literature of the 19th and 20th centuries. It begins with the California encounters of Dana, Zenas Leonard, and Frémont, follows with the early naturalists, then turns to Muir, Clarence King, and Mary Austin, who "celebrate the liberation conferred by a particular California region" and see landscape as validating human behavior. The second half of the book deals with later writers, Norris, Steinbeck, Chandler, Jeffers, and Snyder. Norris, with Steinbeck and Chandler, maps "the advance of human hopes against the steady encroachments of space."

Other books treating general topics in 1986 were essay collections. Patricia Ann Carlson edited *Literature and Lore of the Sea* (*Costerus* 52), which contains two pertinent essays: Haskell Springer's "Call Them All Ishmael?: Fact and Form in Some Nineteenth-Century Sea Narratives," and Joan Tyler Mead's " 'Spare Me a few minutes i have Something to Say': Poetry in Manuscripts of Sailing Ships." The former essay discusses six sailor narratives, including Dana's *Two Years before the Mast*; the latter gleans verse from the logbooks in New England museums of 19th-century sailing ships. Among the 350 poems scribbled in the margins of logbooks, Mead found no Melvilles. J. Lasley Dameron and James W. Mathews edited *No Fairer Land*, which contains Jan Bakker's "Some Other Versions of Pastoral: The Disturbed Landscape in Tales of the Antebellum South" (pp. 67–86). This volume is dedicated to the memory of Richard Beale Davis, one of the original contributors to *ALS*. Bakker discusses several very minor writers, the most prominent of whom is James Kirk Paulding, and examines pastoral and antipastoral motifs. *No Fairer Land* also includes Jack E. Surrency's "The Kentucky Tragedy and Its Primary Sources" (pp. 110–23).

Taylor Stoehr's *Words and Deeds* contains two essays, "Realism and Verisimilitude" and "Realism and Ethics," that should be of interest to readers of this chapter, but I could not find anything in them that I could use. The final general collection is James Barbour and Thomas Quirk's edition of *Romanticism: Critical Essays in American Literature* (Garland), which contains all reprinted essays by excellent critics, among whom are Kenneth Burke, Joel Porte, Daniel Hoffman, Frederick Crews, and Floyd Stovall. Paul S. Koda's "Chicago Conference on the Nineteenth-Century Book: Books on the American Frontier" (*PBSA* 80:219–41) is a report on a conference at the University of Chicago in 1985 with summaries of papers on such topics as trade sales, book fairs, parcel sales, Mathew Carey and the origins of 19th-century book publishing, subscription publishing, and the dissemination of popular books in the Midwest and Far West.

A final item of general interest is *American Literary Magazines*, ed. Edward E. Chielens, in which Donald Yannella has written brief profiles of three journals: *The Literary World* (1847–53), which under the editorship of Evert A. Duyckinck and later his brother George carried material that was unique in the period for its high quality and broad coverage; *The Lowell Offering* (1827–30), which contained material written solely by women who worked 12 and more hours six days a week in New England textile mills; and *Yankee Doodle* (1846–47), which attempted in its short life to be an American *Punch*.

ii. Irving, Cooper, Simms, Bryant

The two latest volumes in the Irving edition are James Tuttleton, ed., *Voyages and Discoveries of the Companions of Columbus*, and Sue Fields Ross, ed., *Journals and Notebooks* (Twayne). The former, volume 12 of the complete works, contains the writing Irving did in Spain in the 1820s after completing his life of Columbus. It has 172 pages of appendices and over 200 pages of textual apparatus, all prepared according to meticulous CSE standards. The latter volume is a mixed bag of material dating from Irving's return to the United States after 17 years abroad. It begins with the journal of Irving's trip west and ends with passages copied from Elizabethan and Jacobean plays, miscellaneous notes, and account books. Here one can find that on 16 May 1840 Irving paid $.25 for a broom and on 3 June paid $.81 for horseshoeing. Another Irving title appeared when the University of Oklahoma Press reprinted in paper Edgeley Todd's 1961 edition of *The Adventures of Captain Bonneville*. This classic account of the fur trade in the Rockies is well edited and contains handsome illustrations.

Papers presented at a conference at Hofstra University in 1983 have been collected in Stanley Brodwin, ed., *The Old and New World Romanticism of Washington Irving* (Greenwood). Ralph M. Aderman in "Washington Irving as Purveyor of Old and New World Romanticism" argues that Irving wrote in a mode dictated by the nature of the material. "Preconceived theories . . . had little influence" and "as he grew older, romantic attitudes began more and more to dominate his writing," and his literary material was influenced by prevailing literary style in Europe and America. Joy Kasson in "Washington Irving: The Growth of a Romantic Writer" argues that in *The Sketch Book* Irving found his voice and made the transition to a prose style that could be called romantic. He infused earlier forms of the sentimental essay and travel literature with his special brand of melancholy introspection, passionate concern for the human heart, understated humor. The voice also owed a great deal to his own drastic shift in fortune, culminating with the bankruptcy of the family business. Jeffrey Rubin-Dorsky in "Washington Irving as an American Romantic" believes that "in *The Sketch Book* Irving created a kind of autobiographical fiction that is closer in spirit to the literature of the romantic period than to its predecessors in the eighteenth century. It is nothing if not a positive assertion of Irving's own individuality and of his own unique reaction to the phenomenal world." Peter Christensen in "Washington Irving and the Denial of the Fantastic" analyzes *The Alhambra*, which shows that Irving "coped most successfully with his aversion to the fantastic through the marvelous." Judith G. Haig's "Washington Irving and the Romance of Travel: Is There an Itinerary in *Tales of a Traveller*?" answers the subtitle's query with a "no." William Owen's "Reevaluating Scott: Washington Irving's 'Abbortsford' " declares that while Irving had much personal regard for Scott, he "found that his talents, interests, and American origins required him to distance himself from Scott."

Other essays in this collection include Michael R. Katz's "Pushkin's Creative Assimilation of Zhukowsky and Irving"; John Frey's

"Irving, Chateaubriand, and the Historical Romance of Granada" (the writings of both on the same topic allow comparison of Old and New World romanticism); Loretta Sharon Wyatt's "The Charm of a Golden Past: Iberia in the Writings of Washington Irving and Antonio Gonçalves Dias"; Lee Fortanella's "Washington Irving's *Tales of the Alhambra* and Early Photography in Spain"; and John Joseph's "The Romantic Lie: Irving's 'A Tour on the Prairies' and Stendhal's *Promenades dans Rome*." Finally, there are David R. Anderson's "A Quaint, Picturesque Little Pile: Architecture and the Past in Washington Irving" and William L. Hedges's "*The Knickerbocker History* as Knickerbocker's History." The last essay analyzes the historicity (almost nil) and zaniness (abundant) in Irving's first book. "The pity is that this provincial American did not realize the power that he had unlocked with this laudable new world brashness." As his literary career went on, he tensed up with worry about how the Old World was going to read him.

Four additional articles on Irving appeared in various places, two of them by Jeffrey Rubin-Dorsky: "Washington Irving and the Genesis of the Fictional Sketch" (*EAL* 21:226–47) and "Washington Irving: Sketches of Anxiety" (*AL* 58:499–522). The former essay argues that Irving's great achievement was in turning the popular travel sketch into a fictional form that became uniquely his. Later 19th-century writers (Hawthorne, Melville, Howells, Twain) followed Irving's pioneering efforts. Irving accomplished this through his creation of a persona, Geoffrey Crayon, and his ability to draw, which gave a painterly quality to his work and an emotional dimension. The latter essay tries to replace the traditional view of Irving as the genial though diffident tourist indulging his fancy for aristocratic culture amid the finery of the Old World with the image of an author with a very different personality. *The Sketch Book* was a triumph achieved despite Irving's depression over the bankruptcy of his brothers' business, self-doubt, and a crippling cultural insecurity. Brigitte Bailey's "Irving's Italian Landscapes: Skepticism and the Picturesque Aesthetic" (*ESQ* 32:1–22) compares Irving and Allston, whose aesthetics evolved from 18th-century England. Irving's scenes do not go beyond a rational amusement to a higher purpose (as Allston's sometimes did); they are habitually qualified by skepticism. David W. Pancost's "How Washington Irving Published *The Sketch Book*" (*SAF* 14:77–83) explodes as a myth Irving's account of having to publish his book at his own expense because of threats of piracy. Piracy was not a problem, and Irving took his time in getting the book out.

The two new volumes in the SUNY Cooper edition are Kay Seymour House, ed., *The Pilot*, with introduction and explanatory notes also by House, and *Gleanings in Europe: The Rhine*, with introduction by Ernest Redekop and Maurice Geracht and text established by Thomas Philbrick and Geracht. The latter volume reprints Cooper's second travel book, his account of Europe in 1832. Both volumes carry the CSE seal. James D. Wallace's *Early Cooper and His Audience* (Columbia) is a solid, no-nonsense little book that starts from the observation that if Cooper had to invent the American novel, he also had to invent an audience. Wallace proceeds to investigate the American literary scene at the time Cooper began to write to find out how Cooper achieved his success. He includes a chapter on Charles Brockden Brown's failures, then traces the evolution of Cooper's art from *Precaution* to *The Spy* to *The Pioneers*. The conclusions of this study are not very surprising: Cooper hit on American subjects, fulfilling a public demand for a new kind of fiction suited to America. He adapted literary structures from models he knew to be popular, but he also used subliterary narratives such as legends and traditions, and he did a shrewd job of publishing and marketing. One might also conclude that a lot had happened in the United States between Brown's failure in 1800 and Cooper's success a quarter of a century later in terms of a larger reading public and the amount of its disposable income. An article that complements Wallace's book is Renata R. Mautner Wasserman's "The Reception of Cooper's Work and the Image of America" (*ESQ* 32:183–95), which observes that Cooper's relationship with his public was not uniformly good during his career. Wasserman discusses the angry reaction in England to his *Notions of the Americans* because the Old World would not accept America as coming of age and contrasts the contrary acceptance of the Leatherstocking Tales, which presented a mythic, dreamlike world that readers were comfortable with.

Most of the articles on Cooper, as usual, dealt with the Leatherstocking Tales. There were three essays on *The Pioneers*: Michael Clark's "Caves, Houses, and Temples in James Fenimore Cooper's *The Pioneers*" (*MLS* 16:227–36) and "Benjamin Franklin and Cooper's *The Pioneers*" (*ELN* 24:43–78); and Douglas Anderson's "Cooper's Improbable Pictures in *The Pioneers*" (*SAF* 14:35–48). Clark's first essay argues that Cooper used architecture in *The Pioneers* as metaphor and symbol to an extent heretofore unnoticed and that awareness of the novel in the historical context of American architecture helps to a better understanding of the author's intentions. The novel is organized by the numerous architectural references. Clark's other essay suggests that the portrait of Judge Temple owes a debt both to Cooper's father and Franklin, but the argument is pretty tenuous. Anderson's essay holds that Cooper was not interested in "pictorial plausibility" but created visual images designed to be "fuller than simple vision can make it." "Cooper is a master at employing description as a means of capturing fundamental dramatic conflict in a single, condensed image." And he treats more than the visual: "he emphasized the invisible" in his descriptions. Cooper belongs with the great imaginative writers in his ability to "engage the mind's infinite eye."

Other articles in 1986 dealt with *The Pathfinder*, *The Deerslayer*, and the Leatherstocking Tales in general. Steven Blakemore's "Language and World in *The Pathfinder*" (*MLS* 16:237–46) analyzes language in the novel to conclude that Cooper is creating a world in which conflict is essentially linguistic, a world where language itself is the problematic source of friction and fragmentation. April Selly in "I Have Been, and Ever Shall Be, your Friend: *Star Trek*, *The Deerslayer*, and the American Romance" (*JPC* 20:89–104) starts with the concept that the most enduring American classics revolve around the friendship of two males, usually of different races. She draws parallels between the male relationships in *The Deerslayer* and *Star Trek*. General articles were Bryant N. Wyatt's "Cooper's Leatherstocking: Romance and the Limits of Character" (*CLAJ* 29: 295–308) and a chapter in Richard Forrer's *Theodicies in Conflict*. Wyatt characterizes Natty Bumppo as "an embodied oxymoron: a Christian savage, a learned ignoramus, a humble braggart, a girlish *macho*, a sinless killer." Natty dies not quite an ideal hero but an admirable failure. Forrer sees the Leatherstocking Tales as an extended treatment of the problem of theodicy. Cooper was the first person to recognize the moral challenge that the Westward movement posed for both the literary and religious imagination. Central to Cooper's dramatizations of the seemingly irreconcilable conflict between the Indian way of life and civilization is whether the frontier itself can give rise to the kind of religious vision that reconciles their opposing values.

Another chapter in Forrer's book deals with *Wyandotté* and *The Spy.* Forrer sees Cooper in these novels as moving toward "the conclusion that the polarities created by the Revolution can be accommodated only by a dual moral perspective that transcends conventional norms." Donald Ringe in "The Source for an Incident in Cooper's *The Redskins*" (*ELN* 24:66–68) believes that the incident of the canopied church pew comes from James Thacher's *Military Journal During the American Revolution,* a book Cooper mined for *Lionel Lincoln.* In one of the essays in *Literature and Lore of the Sea,* Robert D. Madison ("Cooper's *The Wind-And-Wing* and the Concept of the Byronic Pirate") argues that Cooper's seventh sea novel (1842) creates a pirate of the Byronic type as in *The Corsair* and *Lara,* and that though the novel has been dismissed by most critics it is a product of Cooper's maturity. The penultimate item on Cooper this year is Robert Erwin's "The First of the Mohicans" (*AR* 44:148–60), a witty reflection on the career and significance of "the misadventures of our most passé, antiquated, aboriginal famous writer." Erwin traces sardonically the history of Cooper scholarship and its efforts to keep him in the canon. Finally, there is Ivan Melada's "'Poor Little Talkative Christianity': James Fenimore Cooper and the Dilemma of the Christian on the Frontier" (*SNNTS* 18:225–37), an interesting essay dealing with Cooper's concern for the place of Christian teachings on the frontier. While Natty Bumppo is a bloodthirsty killer in *The Last of the Mohicans* (1826), in *The Deerslayer* (1841) he struggles "to accommodate the teachings of a higher spiritual state to the necessities of survival on the frontier." This last-written of the Leatherstocking Tales is "the most consistently religious by virtue of its preoccupation with Christian ethics."

Other contemporaries of Cooper fared poorly and some not at all. Simms inspired only one article, John McCardell's "Poetry and the Practical: William Gilmore Simms" in *Intellectual Life in Ante-Bellum Charleston.* This is an essay on Simms and Charleston and Simms as a professional man of letters in antebellum Charleston at a time when a literary career there was a novel undertaking. Bryant gets little attention these days, but Steve Olson in "A Perverted Poetics: Bryant's and Emerson's Concern for a Developing American Literature" (*ATQ* 61:15–21) looks at Bryant's "Fourth Lecture on Poetry" as anticipatory of Emerson. Bryant, he argues, was the first person to "formally introduce into American poetical theory the complex relationship among poetry and nature and the influence of the past." Norbert Krapf has put together an anthology of tributes to Bryant in *Under Open Sky: Poets on William Cullen Bryant* (Fordham), an attractive little volume containing both essays and poems. The editor's contributions in prose, "William Cullen Bryant's Roslyn [Long Island] Poems" and "Walking with Walt Whitman and William Cullen Bryant: A Fantasy," have been previously published, as was John Hollander's piece, but there are in addition some engaging little articles: Vince Clemente's "Bryant's 'To a Waterfowl' and the Painter W. S. Mount," Richard Wilbur's "A Word from Cummington," and William Jay Smith's "The Bryant's Cottage in Cummington." In addition, Richard Ellman reminisces about his student days at Stanford and Yvor Winters on "Thanatopsis," and Richard Eberhart recalls memorizing the poem in his youth. Among the poems in the volume is a fine one by William Stafford, "At Bryant's Grave."

iii. Popular Writers (Mostly Women) and Humorists

One of the significant trends in 19th-century American literary scholarship is the rediscovery of the popular women writers. Eleven of the 14 women writers I cover in this chapter are discussed in this section, in the chronological order of their births. Sarah Orne Jewett will be treated with the realists of the post-Civil War period, and Kate Chopin and Grace King will appear among the fin de siècle writers.

Cathy N. Davidson in "Female Authorship and Authority: The Case of Sukey Vickery" (*EAL* 22:4–28) wishes to revive Vickery's forgotten novel *Emily Hamilton* (1803), arguing that it is one of "the most sustained critiques of sexual mores written in America during the early national period." It focuses on women's expected passive domesticity in this era. Vickery published only one novel, then put away her pen and produced nine children. Carolyn L. Karcher's "Censorship, American Style: The Case of Lydia Maria Child" (*SAR* 287–303) is an account of how a popular author was ostracized and hurt economically after she published an antislavery tract in Boston in 1833, and how she made a comeback. Joel Myerson wishes to revive another obscure work in his "Mary Gove Nichols' *Mary Lyndon*: A Forgotten Reform Novel" (*AL* 58:523–39). This is an autobiographical novel (1855) by a very untypical 19th-century woman who was active in movements promoting dietary and health reform. The heroine of the novel leaves her husband after an unhappy marriage and argues that marriage without love is legalized slavery. Contemporary reviewers attacked the novel as subversive of public morals.

Stowe inspired two articles and a chapter in a book this year: Johanne M. Smith's "Feeling Right: Christianity and Women's Influence in *Uncle Tom's Cabin*" (*ESQ* 32:122–34); Amy Schrager Lang's "Slavery and Sentimentalism: The Strange Career of Augustine St. Clare" (*WS* 12:31–54); and Lawrence Buell in *New England Literary Culture*. Smith's article makes the point that although Stowe wrote her novel to do something about ending slavery and reminded her women readers of their Christian responsibilities in the struggle, the novel makes it clear that right thinking could not do the job. The Christian submissiveness of Tom, Mrs. Selby, Eva St. Clare, and St. Clare's mother only strengthens the institution of slavery. In the end it seems that only divine retribution can end slavery. Lang's essay is a discussion of how Stowe put sentimentalism, which traditionally had supported the status quo, to the service of abolition. St. Clare represents Stowe's effort to combine the knowledge and power of men with the goodness of women and "thus to bridge the gap between private feeling and public action." But the dual nature of St. Clare presented Stowe with a structural problem of blurring the gender differences of her character, and thus she had to kill him off. Buell's chapter on Stowe deals with *The Minister's Wooing* and Hawthorne's *The Scarlet Letter*. He sees both writers as the most ambitious and distinguished chroniclers of New England history. Both suffuse their work with ambivalence toward Puritan repressiveness. "The central device in both books is to take an undogmatic, intuitively perceptive, liberal female sensibility and set it against a more traditional, dated, culture-bound male sensibility."

Judith Fetterley in " 'Checkmate': Elizabeth Stuart Phelps's *The Silent Partner*" (*Legacy* 3:17–29) finds in this novel a reversal of the popular notion that women talk and men are silent. It "seeks to articulate the phenomenon of inarticulateness and to give voice to the fact of voicelessness." The novel investigates how those who are denied access to speech express themselves. Joanne Dobson's "The Hidden Hand: Subversion of Cultural Ideology in Three Mid-Nineteenth Century American Women's Novels" (*AQ* 38:223–42) is a feminist reading of Susan Warner's *The Wide, Wide World*, E. D. E. N. Southworth's *The Hidden Hand*, and A. D. T. Whitney's *Hitherto*. Dobson believes these novels subvert the principle of self-sacrifice and domestic submission that dominated the American cultural ethos of ideal femininity in the 19th century. In all three novels the authors struggled with the contradictions of feminine submissiveness and individuality. Rosemary Whitaker's "Helen Hunt Jackson" (*Legacy* 3:56–62) is a profile with special attention to Jackson's relationship with Emily Dickinson.

Louisa May Alcott was the subject of four items in 1986. Lynette Carpenter's "Did They Never See Anyone Angry Before?: The Sexual Politics of Self-Control in Alcott's 'A Whisper in the Dark' " (*Legacy* 3:31–41) is a feminist reading of one of Alcott's thrillers, a lurid Gothic tale in which her pent-up anger is released. But the story ends ambivalently, as the heroine comes to learn the dangers of anger and the wisdom of self-control. Joel Myerson and Daniel Shealy have made two contributions to Alcott's life and canon: "Louisa May Alcott's 'A Wail': An Unrecorded Satire of the Concord Authors" (*PBSA* 80:93–99) and "Three Contemporary Accounts of Louisa May Alcott with Some Glimpses of Other Concord Notables" (*NEQ* 59:109–22). The former reprints the satire, which may have been read at a meeting of the New England Women's Club in 1886. It views Emerson, Hawthorne, Channing, Thoreau, and Bronson Alcott as they struggled against celebrity hunters. The latter reprints two letters and a reminiscence by people who knew Alcott briefly. Shealy alone has reprinted Alcott's report of a lecture by Emerson in 1868 from *The National Anti-Slavery Standard*: "Louisa Alcott's Account of Emerson's 'Poetry and Criticism' " (*Concord Saunterer*, 18 December 1985: 47–48). The final essay in this group is Melody Graulich's "Mary Hallock Foote (1847–1938)" (*Legacy* 3:43–50), a profile of this New York-born writer who wrote and illustrated stories of the West. Illustrative of the revived interest in the popular women writers of the 19th century is the reprinting by Rutgers University Press of three collections: Elizabeth Ammons, ed., Rose Terry Cooke, *How Celia Changed Her Mind and Selected Stories*; Carolyn L. Karcher, ed., Lydia Maria Child, *Hobomok and Other Writings on Indians*; and Joyce W. Warren, ed., Fanny Fern, *Ruth Hall and Other Writings*.

Popular male writers received less attention in 1986 than the women. Edward Wagenknecht wrote another book on Longfellow: *Henry Wadsworth Longfellow: His Poetry and Prose* (Ungar), the first full-length study of this poet since he published *Henry Wadsworth Longfellow: Portrait of an American Humanist* (1966). It seems doubtful if Wagenknecht's graceful little book will revive much interest in this onetime schoolroom poet, but the study is written with the author's usual charm and perception. Longfellow was fading fast when I began teaching in the late '40s, and his reputation has continued to dim; to one who grew up with *Evangeline* and *The Courtship of Miles Standish*, however, the book has the effect of meeting an old friend. The publisher's blurb is accurate: "The best possible introduction to the poet for those who are approaching him for the first time." It was a considerable surprise to read Helen Carr's excellent article, "The Myth of Hiawatha" (*L&H* 12:58–78), an essay that reexamines the emergence of a self-consciously American literature and discusses some of the problems associated with this movement. It focuses on the production and reception of a poem which set out to be the great American epic. "The poem gave to its readers . . . a myth which helped to make possible, for America, the acceptance of the displacement and destruction of the Indian, and for Europe the ravages of imperialism." Longfellow selected, changed, and altered his sources (*Kalevala*, Schoolcraft, and others) to achieve this result. To this end he created the simple, childlike Hiawatha, and the poem anesthetized American anxieties over the Indian. It further reproduced uncritically the prejudices of its contemporary readers. The result was the most popular poem of the 19th century or of any century, if sales figures are the measure.

Wayne R. Kime's *Donald G. Mitchell* (TUSAS 489) adds another forgotten author to the Twayne series. Kime argues that the literary achievement of Mitchell (who wrote under the pen name of Ik Marvel) deserves a thorough contemporary assessment. Although most of Mitchell's work has been happily forgotten, Kime thinks that *My Farm of Edgewood* (1863) is a minor classic. Although most people, if they have even heard of him, know J. G. Holland only as a friend of Dickinson, he was a popular writer and editor of *Scribner's*. Robert J. Scholnick's "J. G. Holland and the 'Religion' of Civilization in Mid-Nineteenth Century America" (*AmerS* 27:55–79) surveys the career of Holland and the impact of his writing and editing on American culture. "Holland's extraordinary popularity attests to the needs of millions of Americans to receive a message that was at once practical, yet spiritual, challenging, yet reassuring, realistic, yet hopeful, traditional in its religious language, yet non-denominational, universal in its rhetoric, yet insistently nationalistic."

Two other humorists, one totally forgotten and the other nearly so, round out this section of my essay. Edward J. Piacentino has edited and introduced Mortimer Neal Thompson's *Doesticks: What He Says* (Scholars' Facsimiles), and John J. Pullen has written an entertaining little article on Artemus Ward: "Who Wrote 'The World's Best Book Review'?" (*NEQ* 59:252–59). Pullen argues convincingly that Ward invented the review: "Those who like this sort of thing will find this the sort of thing they like." This review often has been attributed to Lincoln and claimed by Max Beerbohm.

iv. Southern Writers

Some of the writers corralled here are humorists and could have been discussed in the previous section, but "Southern Writers" is a homogeneous designation for authors below the Mason and Dixon Line and will accommodate the humorists and others nicely. Jane S. Gabin's *A Living Minstrelsy: The Poetry and Music of Sidney Lanier* (Mercer, 1985) is the first book on Lanier since 1972. It focuses completely on the relationship between Lanier's music and his poetry. Gabin does not claim his compositions were significant (he had no formal training in counterpoint or harmony), but he was an accomplished flutist. One insight that seems interesting and important is her argument that Berlioz's *Symphonie Fantastique* gave Lanier the idea for the structure of "The Marches of Glynn." Lanier is our only poet who was a professional musician. A competent study.

Two pertinent essays appeared in *Intellectual Life in Antebellum Charleston.* Michael O'Brien's "Politics, Romanticism, and Hugh Legaré: 'The Fondness of Disappointed Love'" traces the career of Legaré and his relationship to Charleston intellectual life. Steven M. Stowe's "City, Country, and the Feminine Voice" deals with the novels of Carolyn Howard Gilman and Susan Petigru King and the fictional diary of Mary Chesnut as reflections of South Carolina life and the role of women in the antebellum South.

Three relevant essays appeared in *No Fairer Land.* James W. Mathews's "A Yankee Southerner: The Aesthetic Flight of Samuel Gilman" surveys the career of a minor literary man and Unitarian preacher in Charleston. Benjamin McClary's "George Washington Harris's 'Special Vision': His Yarns as Historical Source" traces the vicissitudes and fortunes of *Sut Lovingood* and argues that these yarns "should be a major sourcebook for studying the mid-nineteenth century Appalachian mountain communities of its origin." Joseph H. Harkey's "Some Adventures of Captain Simon Suggs: The Legacy of

Johnson J. Hooper" surveys Hooper's creation of Simon Suggs, but there seems to be nothing new here.

Other essays dealt with Thomas Bangs Thorpe, Charles Henry Smith (Bill Arp), and Joel Chandler Harris. Robert J. Higgs's "The Sublime and the Beautiful: The Meaning of Sport in Collected Sketches of Thomas B. Thorpe" (*SoSt* 25:235–56) argues that Thorpe was a pioneer in writing about sport and tries to extract from his tales what sport means to him. The conclusion: it meant "restraint, skill, courage, humor, compassion." David B. Parker, Jr., in "Bill Arp and the North: The Misreading of a Southern Humorist" (*SoSt* 25:257–73) surveys Arp's career as an unreconstructed southerner, but he thinks that northerners have misread him. Arp "was clearly in favor of reconciliation" with the North after the Civil War, but "he insisted that peace be on his terms." Eric L. Montenyohl's "Joel Chandler Harris' Revision of Uncle Remus: The First Version of 'A Story of the War'" (*ALR* 19:65–71) reprints the original version of "A Story" as it appeared in the Atlanta *Constitution* in 1877.

My final item in this section deals with Constance Fenimore Woolson, who was not a southerner but who spent some of her adult years in the South before becoming an expatriate and writing about the region. Sharon L. Dean's "Constance Fenimore Woolson's Southern Sketches" (*SoSt* 25:274–83) regards Woolson as "one of the more successful Northerners to write about the South during Reconstruction and as a writer with the ability to understand, without sentimentalism, the social conditions of the South." One of the significant aspects of her southern fiction is that she never judged. Joan Myers Weimer in "Women Artists as Exiles in the Fiction of Constance Fenimore Woolson" (*Legacy* 3:3–15) believes that although Woolson was a successful writer, her sense of exile is reflected in her work. She was preoccupied with the problem of the woman as artist, but her voice is assured, ironic, in control. To the women artists in her fiction she assigns debilitated lives. Her characters' situations seem to reflect her deepest feelings about women and art.

v. Howells and the Age of Realism

There were no new books on Howells this year, but there were five good articles, one of which was outstanding. The last was Amy Kaplan's " 'The Knowledge of the Line': Realism and the City of Howells's

A Hazard of New Fortunes" (*PMLA* 101:69–81). The title refers to the "line at which respectability distinguishes itself from shabbiness," which Basil and Isabel March perceive as they house-hunt in New York. Kaplan sees Howells's first novel of the metropolis as his effort to deal with the problem of urban existence at a time when the city was regarded as a serious menace to civilization. She calls it a narrative of settlement that seeks to control a foreign and unreal territory, and she thinks the long house-hunting scene at the start is appropriate.

Sarah B. Dougherty in "Howells, Tolstoy, and the Limits of Realism: The Case of *Annie Kilburn*" (*ALR* 19:21–39) sees a significant influence in Howells's novel from Tolstoy's *Que faire*? (1886) and also sees compatibility between Howells's realism and Tolstoy's Christian socialism. Sam B. Girgus's "The New Age of Narcissism: The Sexual Politics of Howells's *A Modern Instance*" (*Mosaic* 19:33–44) discusses Howells's novel as "an Americanized version of Greek tragedy of incest, passion, and jealousy." He sees the "complex set of relationships in *A Modern Instance* concerning parents, daughter and lover" as constituting "a sexual politics of love and authority that interact with the changing cultural environment." He analyzes Bartley Hubbard's character in terms of Freud's "On Narcissism" and Marcia's relationship with her father in terms of other Freudian essays. The "crime of the characters in the novel is their inability to love outside of themselves."

Fleda Brown Jackson's "A Sermon Without Exegesis: The Achievement of Stasis in *The Rise of Silas Lapham*" (*JNT* 16:131–47) is a closely argued demonstration that "the novel as a whole is a metaphor for a world held in tension between the rise and fall of mythic rhythms." Jackson goes on to say that the world of the novel "is composed of the background music of natural rhythms and the discordant scales of the civilized world played *together*, one on top of the other." She cites many passages in which contradictions balance each other to produce stasis. The novel "reflects a vision of human existence which offers few claims to ultimate moral solutions." The final Howells item is George Arms's "A Sidelight on Howells" (*ALR* 19:73–77), which turns up some interesting annotations by Howells's doctor in copies of Howells's novels.

Three other realists treated in articles this year were Rebecca Harding Davis, J. W. De Forest, and Harold Frederic. Frances M. Malpezzi's "Sisters in Protest: Rebecca Harding Davis and Tillie Olsen" (*ReAL* 12:1–9) is a slight piece noting Olsen's discovery of and the impact of Davis's *Life in the Iron Mills* on her *Yonnondio.* Robert W. Antoni in "*Miss Ravenel's Conversion*: A Neglected American Novel" (*SoQ* 24:58–63) reminds us that despite Howells's high praise this early realistic novel never has attracted the attention it deserves. Fritz Oelhschlaeger in a good article, "Passion, Authority, and Faith in *The Damnation of Theron Ware*" (*AL* 58:238–55), argues that Frederic's novel "presents sexuality, especially female sexuality, as something proscribed by a male authority which fears it." The novel traces consequences of this: the blight in Ware's marriage, the disordered sex of Celia Madden, and the effeminization, regression, and adolescent prurience that emerge in Theron. The novel is a critique of the way corrupt authority poisons sexuality. It also discredits every authority figure in the novel. Another essay on Frederic is W. Jean Marshall Clark's "Harold Frederic's *The Market Place* and Voluntarism" in *Amid Visions and Revisions.* Clark discusses Frederic's use of Schopenhauer and Nietzsche in his last novel. Voluntarism (life force) comes from Schopenhauer modified by Nietzsche as the will to power, and is exemplified in the protagonist of the novel. Two more volumes in the Frederic edition, which has moved to the University of Nebraska Press, came out in 1986: *The Damnation of Theron Ware*, text established by Charlyne Dodge and the history of the text by Stanton Garner, and Larry Bromley, ed., *Gloria Mundi.* Both volumes carry the CSE seal.

Nineteen eighty-six was a bumper year for Sarah Orne Jewett scholarship, chiefly due to a special issue of the *Colby Library Quarterly*, which published a selection of papers from a conference held in Portland in 1985. Elizabeth Ammons in "The Shape of Violence in Jewett's 'A White Heron' " (22:6–16) argues that Sylvia's decision not to let the ornithologist have the heron denotes resistance to the institution of heterosexuality, or it is the rite of passage that the girl refuses to take. Sylvia chooses not to pass over into the world of adult female sexuality, as it is defined by the culture. Josephine Donovan in "Nan Prince and the Golden Apples" (22:17–27) sees the apple tree in *A Country Doctor* as symbolizing the paradisical woman's community envisioned in the literature of the 19th-century local-color school. Nan Prince is an Artemis-Diana figure. The novel expresses directly the central theme of late-19th-century women's literature: whether to leave the mother's garden for the realms of patriarchal knowledge. Marti Hohmann's "Sarah Orne Jewett to Lillian M. Munger: Twenty-three Letters" (22:28–35) prints letters of counsel to a minister's daughter 13 years her junior. Marilyn E. Mobley in "Rituals of Flight and Return: The Ironic Journeys of Sarah Orne Jewett's Female Characters" (22:36–42) notes that Jewett often uses flight imagery to describe the real and imaginary journeys of her female characters. This characteristic belies an ambivalence toward her native region and demonstrates an unflinching admiration for the self-reliant women. Gwen Nagel's " 'This Prim Corner of Land Where She Was Queen': Sarah Orne Jewett's New England Gardens" (22: 43–62) is a discussion of gardens, which figure prominently in Jewett's fiction, usually tidy plots confined by fences, associated with the past, and lovingly cultivated by women. They provide her with a rich matrix of themes: garden lost, garden under siege, garden possessed.

Sarah W. Sherman in "Victorians and the Matriarchal Mythology: A Source for Mrs. Todd" (22: 63–74) believes that Walter Pater's essay on the myth of Demeter and Persephone showed Jewett how to make the connection between rural Maine and the matriarchal goddesses. Carol J. Singley's "Reaching Lonely Heights: Sarah Orne Jewett, Emily Dickinson, and Female Initiation" (22:75–82) is a comparison of the work of the two writers in which Singley sees portrayals of individual female growth that are strikingly similar. The final Jewett essay is also by Josephine Donovan: "Silence or Capitulation: Pre-patriarchal 'Mothers' Gardens' in Jewett and Freeman" (*SSF* 23:43–48). The author discusses "A White Heron," in which she sees Sylvia's decision not to reveal the nest of the bird as a deliberate choice of "feminine nature over patriarchal culture." She sees Freeman's "Eveline's Garden" as illustrative of a woman's rejection of the feminine realm in order to enter the patriarchal realm.

Sylvia Bowman has added *Edward Bellamy* as the 500th volume in the Twayne United States Authors Series, which she edited before her retirement. As perhaps the leading authority on Bellamy (she published her first book on him in 1958), Bowman has made a distinguished addition to the series. It follows the usual procrustean pattern for TUSAS volumes, packing everything into a brief compass, but it makes a good introduction to the author of the influential *Looking Backward*. Also this year there was Nancy Snell Griffith's *Edward Bellamy: A Bibliography* (Scarecrow), pages 3–50 covering primary bibliography and pages 53–161 secondary bibliography. One notes, for instance, 31 editions of *Looking Backward* down to the Penguin edition of 1982.

vi. Nonfiction Writers

There was much interest in Henry Adams in 1986. The Library of America brought out in its usual attractive format Adams's *History of the United States of America during the Administrations of Thomas Jefferson and James Madison*, ed. Earl Harbert, in two volumes. Getting this important work back into print and putting Adams's original nine volumes into two easily portable ones is a real service to scholarship. The texts that Harbert chose to reprint are the last printings containing Adams's revisions. Both volumes contain excellent notes.

Of the seven articles on Adams, Viola Hopkins Winner contributed two: "Henry Adams and Lafayette Square, 1877–1887" (*VQR* 62:478–89) and "Style and Sincerity in the Letters of Henry Adams" in *Essaying Biography*. The former is a charming re-creation of the Washington social life and friendships of Henry and Marian Adams, and the latter is a good analysis of Adams as a letter writer. Winner writes that Adams regarded letter-writing as a form of literary expression and consciously aimed at stylistic perfection. The 4,500 extant letters that Adams wrote between 1858 and 1918 "are in a class of their own in nineteenth-century American literature, comprising a major literary work equal to, if not surpassing, *The Education of Henry Adams* and *Mont-Saint Michel and Chartres*." Raymond Carney in "The Imagination in Ascendancy: Henry Adams' *Mont Saint Michel and Chartres*" (*SoR* 22:506–31) characterizes Adams's book as a meditation journey "across strange seas of thought and feeling. It is the narration of a voyage of the imagination across interior landscapes." Adams is interested (as were Hawthorne, Melville, Thoreau, and Whitman) in "testing the condition in which certain free movements . . . are still possible in . . . the 'prison' of space and time and actual human society." Carney sees Adams as a modernist. Len Gougan in "Adams in the Garden: Sex, Symbol and Myth in *The Education of Henry Adams*" (*JEP* 7:261–69) notes that Adams defines the American experience of the Civil War as a fall from innocence to experience, as Adam and Eve similarly fell. Two articles on Adams appeared in John E. Gedo and George H. Pollock, eds., *Psychoanalysis: The Vital Issues*, Vol. 1, *Psychoanalysis as an Intellectual Discipline* (International, 1984): Mark R. Schwehn, "Reviewing Henry Adams," and George Moraitis, "The Two Readings of *The Education of Henry Adams*." Schwehn's essay, which is chiefly of interest to psychologists, reports on the author's determination, in working with a psychoanalyst, of his own biases in reading Adams's *History*. Moraitis's article, which has a similar appeal, is an account of his reading *The Education* twice three years apart. After the second reading he concluded that *The Education* represents a historian's effort to go beyond the writing of history and to reveal parts of himself in an attempt to make history. It reveals not only his ideas but also the spectacles through which the author perceives the world and develops his ideas. The reader can use the spectacles either to understand the author's personality or to see the world as Henry Adams saw it. A final item on Adams is James M. Mellard's "The Problem of Knowledge and *The Education of Henry Adams*" (*SCR*ev 3:55–68), a dense article that tries to "locate *The Education* in the gap between the contiguous epochal epistemes that, on the one side, formed both history and the novel and, on the other, formed the ideology of modernism in narrative genres that had previously depended upon naive realist epistemologies."

Perhaps the most significant book to fall within my purview this year is Gerald E. Myers's *William James: His Life and Thought* (Yale). I am not competent to give an expert opinion on this work, but it is a careful, detailed (628 pages) intellectual guide to James's thought by a CUNY professor of philosophy. After a chapter on James's life and career, it devotes successive chapters to consciousness, sensation and perception, space, time, memory, attention and will, emotion, thought, knowledge, reality, self, morality, and religion. Myers keeps the focus on James's thought, and his own analysis is not obtrusive.

An interesting and felicitously written article by Monroe Spears is "William James as Culture Hero" (*HudR* 39:15–32), which uses as a springboard recent works on James by Jacques Barzun and Howard Feinstein. Spears examines "the special affection and admiration he [James] evokes from his readers." He compares James to Samuel Johnson as a master of the language, who wrote for a common reader and scorned those who refused to do the same. He finds many other parallels, such as a belief in the "superior validity of actual experience to any kind of theory or abstraction or doctrine." Frank Lentricchia's "On the Idologies of Poetic Modernism, 1890–1913: The Example of William James" (*Reconstructing American Literary History*) sees James as a seminal influence on modernism. He notes that Frost, Robinson, Stein, Eliot, and Stevens all were at Harvard when James taught there. "James' refusal to look back in either anger or delight, his exuberant vision of historical work as *present act* unencumbered by the anxieties of the backward look, is the equivalent in American philosophy of the characteristic modernist literary desire to make it new." The final item in this group is W. S. Di Piero's "William James and Henry James" (*TriQ* 67:93–107), an engaging essay on William as "a renowned European American" and Henry as "the most famous American European of his time." The purpose of the essay is to sketch certain character formations dramatically acted out in their works. William's contribution was to fuse passionate interest in facts with equal devotion to abstract generalization. "William described the thinker's problem. Henry enacted the artist's procedure."

Parkman takes a beating from Kim Townsend in "Francis Parkman and the Male Tradition" (*AQ* 38:97–113), a feminist reading that finds him less than heroic, "perhaps the first of all too many examples of the American male's destructive quest for manhood." *The Oregon Trail* "remains one of the American male's most authoritative texts on going West to prove one's manhood." A reading of Parkman as he represents himself, the essay tries to recognize him for what he was and the damage he has done by perpetuating the "canon's most powerful motifs and myths about the sexes."

The most enjoyable book of the year for me was Frederick Turner's *Rediscovering America: John Muir in His Time and Ours* (Viking, 1985), an excellent biography, felicitously written, based on a thorough familiarity with Muir's writings and his papers at the library of the University of the Pacific. Though Muir's life has been told several times, this perhaps is the most satisfactory biography. Muir's romance with the Sierra Nevada, his love for Jeanne Carr, who was responsible for getting him out of the mountains to make a career writing, his studies of the glaciation of Yosemite Valley, his meeting with Emerson in Yosemite in 1871, his efforts to make Yosemite a national park, his struggle to persuade Congress to preserve the forests, his relationship with Theodore Roosevelt, all are well told. In addition, the book is equipped with an excellent set of notes.

vii. Crane, Norris, and the fin de siècle

A special issue of the *Syracuse University Library Associates Courier* was devoted to Crane, occasioned by the university's acquisition of the Schoberlin Crane Collection, an important addition to the already extensive Crane holdings at Syracuse. James B. Colvert's "Searching for Stephen Crane: The Schoberlin Collection" (21:5–34) describes the new holdings and the collector's career in gathering material for a biography never completed. In doing so Colvert writes a fascinating account of the vagaries of Crane biography. Other items in the collection: Stanley Wertheim and Paul Sorrentino, eds., "New Crane Letters in the Schoberlin Collection"; Thomas A. Gullason, ed. and intro., "The 'Lost' Newspaper Writings of Stephen Crane"; "Schoberlin's Annotated Copy of *War Is Kind*" by Donald P. Vanouse; and the printing of some newly discovered writing by Crane's mother and his sister Agnes, introduced by Paul Sorrentino.

Stanley Wertheim also has written "Cora Crane's Thwarted Romance" (*CLC* 36:26–37), which provides a footnote to Crane biography. The article details Cora Crane's life in the months following her husband's death, a period in which she fell in love with Poultney Bigelow, an American journalist, who occasionally had visited Brede Place. George Monteiro's "Stephen Crane, Dramatist" (*ALR* 19:42–51) traces Crane's "love-hate courtship of the theater" from his college days, when he wrote a sort of scenario for a dramatic interlude, to the end of his career. Crane once made a plan, never carried out, to collaborate on a play with Conrad. He never finished a full-length play, though he tried his hand at plays from time to time.

Michael J. Collins's "Realism and Romance in the Western Stories of Stephen Crane" in Barbara Meldrum, ed., *Under the Sun: Myth and Realism in Western American Literature* (Whitston, 1985), analyzes "The Five White Mice," "The Bride Comes to Yellow Sky," and "The Blue Hotel" to show that Crane applied elements of the Western romance form to realistic content, evident in the focus on internal rather than external experience. Another article in the same collection, Chester L. Walford's "Classic Myth Versus Realism in Crane's 'The Bride Comes to Yellow Sky,'" sees Crane's tale as showing the fall of the old West in a comic manner; he uses a mock-epic rendering of a Western sub-myth, "the showdown."

Prescott S. Nichols in "*The Red Badge of Courage*: What Is Fleming Fleeing?" (*L&H* 12:97–101) argues that Crane was trying to achieve realism and had a social message (that Fleming was fleeing reality in life in the context of both war and peace). The final Crane item is Thomas A. Gullason, ed., "A Cache of Short Stories by Stephen Crane's Family" (*SSF* 23:71–106), which reprints tales by Crane's mother and his sister Agnes. Gullason thinks that these stories probably influenced Crane's own stories.

Frank Norris received an unusual amount of attention in 1986 with a new edition of selected works, an addition to his canon, and three articles. Donald Pizer selected texts and wrote the notes for the Library of America's *Frank Norris: Novels and Essays*. Included in this edition are *Vandover and the Brute*, *McTeague*, *The Octopus*, and over 100 pages of essays. The essays are reprinted from their original sources rather than the 1903 Doubleday posthumously published collection, which has no authorial sanction. The text of *Vandover* is the only possible one, that revised and added to by Charles Norris. The text of *McTeague* is the first printing, which presumably Norris saw through the press, and *The Octopus* is reprinted from the fifth printing, which incorporates substantive changes no doubt made by Norris.

Robert C. Leitz III in "'Christmas in the Transvaal': An Addition to the Norris Canon" (*SAF* 14:221–24) reprints from the San Francisco *Sunday Examiner* of 17 December 1889 an episode foreshadowing the Boer War. Linda A. Dover's "*A Man's Woman*: The Textual Changes" (*RALS* 13:165–83) reports on the many textual changes Norris made between serial and book version, apparently in an effort to improve what he admitted had been "slovenly put together." Another article in *Reconstructing American Literary History* deals with Norris: Walter Benn Michaels, "Corporate Fiction: Norris, Royce, and Arthur Machen." Michaels discusses flaws in *The Octopus* and Royce's only novel, *The Feud at Oakfield Creek*, because they seem to embody the concept of corporate entity, as outlined by Arthur Machen, Jr., in the *Harvard Law Review* (1911). Although the law treats the corporation as a person, the real existence of the corporation does not make it a person. Finally, Barbara Hochman in "Loss, Habit, Obsession: The Governing Dynamic of *McTeague*" (*SAF* 14:179–90) is not satisfied with previous critical views holding that the novel is organized by the tenets of naturalism. She believes that the structure pivots on the problem of personal loss. What animates *McTeague* is not the desperate lust for gain but rather the haunting fear of loss. All the characters may be interpreted from this perspective, and their fear provides tension, as they struggle to contain the chaos beneath the surface of life within a stabilizing medium.

James Lane Allen, Bliss Carmen, Ambrose Bierce, and Kate

Chopin were the subject of one article each this year. Lee Harding in "From Romance to Realism: James Lane Allen's Revisions of *A Kentucky Cardinal*" (*MissQ* 39:41–52) argues that Allen's revisions between the 1894 and 1900 editions of his novel moved in the direction of greater realism. James Doyle's "Canadian Writers and American Little Magazines in the 1890's" (*CanL* 110:177–83) discusses Carmen's editorship of *The Chap Book*, one of the early little magazines, and his introduction to American readers of other Canadian writers. Alice Hall Petry in "E. A. Robinson's Bierce Connection" (*MarkhamR* 15:1–2) argues from internal evidence that "How Annandale Went Out" was influenced by Bierce's story "The Coup de Grace." Not very convincing.

Interest in Kate Chopin may be falling off. After a dozen essays in 1984, there were only three essays plus a Twayne volume in 1985, and this year there were just two items: Barbara C. Ewell's *Kate Chopin* (Ungar) and Carole Stone's article, "The Female Artist in Kate Chopin's *The Awakening*: Birth and Creativity" (*WS* 13:23–32). Stone argues that Edna's memories of childhood and her immersion in the sea are emblems of regression in the service of progression toward an artistic vocation. She goes forward to a new conception of self, herself as an artist. Her romanticism is positive because it catalogues her imaginative power. She sees through the delusion of romantic love after confronting the horror of giving birth. Ewell's 216-page book includes notes, bibliography, and index. It is about 50 percent longer than Peggy Skaggs's TUSAS *Kate Chopin*, reviewed in this chapter last year, and covers about the same ground. Per Seyersted's critical biography is still the essential book on Chopin, and the criticism in this volume does not add anything to Robert Arner's 1975 monograph. Nonetheless, Ewell's book is a competent study and will be useful for beginners.

Another fin de siècle New Orleans writer was the subject of an article by Edward J. Piacentino, "The Enigma of Black Identity in Grace King's 'Joe'" (*SLJ* 19:56–67). Piacentino analyzes a tale that treats the enigmatic identity crisis of a black slave who becomes disoriented after the death of his benevolent master. This is a story of character that deals realistically with race relations in the antebellum South, but King at the end, unwilling to break step with southern racial attitudes, fabricated a safe and sentimental denouement.

University of California, Davis

13. Fiction: 1900 to the 1930s

John J. Murphy
and Stephen L. Tanner

Interest in the writers of this period continues to grow and reflect the redefining of the canon. Cather is by far the major figure, followed closely by Wharton, whose work is enjoying a renaissance, and Dreiser, who maintains a fairly high plateau of interest. Stein constantly grows in stature, while interest in Dos Passos and London flags. Certain writers, like Lewis and Stark Young this year, enjoy flashes occasioned by centennials and special issues, but such interest seldom reestablishes reputations. Since this chapter is jointly authored this year, we think it helpful to indicate that sections i, ii, v, vii are authored by Murphy, iii and iv by Tanner, and vi is a collaboration.

i. Willa Cather

Five books and more than a score of articles testify to the constantly and rapidly growing interest in Cather and her fiction. At the forefront of major contributions this year is Susan J. Rosowski's *The Voyage Perilous: Willa Cather's Romanticism* (Nebraska), which shapes Cather's career into dramas involving imaginative vision and artistic re-creation of the world, into discoveries of archetypal truths and struggles toward selflessness when art is undermined by modern materialism, and into explorations of the chaotic gothic underside of the romantic imagination. Of particular value is the use here of early stories to trace Cather's imaginative creation of Nebraska through symbols and myth and to arrive at that vision of the New World so successfully achieved in *O Pioneers!* and *My Ántonia.* Rosowski's chapters on these prairie novels, *The Song of the Lark,* and *A Lost Lady* are among the best in her book. In *The Song of the Lark* Cather focused on the psychology of the artist-heroine, Thea Kronborg, exploring imaginative growth from negative to positive romantic stances in ways that resemble Wordsworth's awakening sense of artistic power in *The Prelude*. The Wordsworth connection is also evident in *My Ántonia*, which is to American fiction "what Wordsworth had introduced to English poetry a century earlier—the continuously changing work." *A Lost Lady*, like *My Ántonia*, dramatizes tensions between the ideal envisioned by the mind and the reality of the object envisioned (the prairie heroine). Rosowski is perhaps even more original in treating Cather's last and lesser-known novels. These are offered as dramas of the underside of romanticism, "when resolution is thwarted and irreconcilables triumph." To prepare for these, a catalog of the demonic forces in Cather is included, from apprentice stories to major novels. In this vein, *Lucy Gayheart* is discussed as Bram Stoker's *Dracula* retold from the female point of view, and *Sapphira and the Slave Girl* is considered from the perspective of the inevitable threat of the irrational. Less positive aspects of the study include Rosowski's restricting Cather's romanticism to the British version. Because of this narrowing, *O Pioneers!* and *The Professor's House*, for example, are not treated as thoroughly as they might be. Then, too, the romanticism thesis is less adequate for comprehensive treatment of the novels of Cather's middle career. The commentary on *My Mortal Enemy* is excellent in treating Myra Henshawe's turning from outworn sentimentalism but less satisfactory in explaining the religious orthodoxy of Myra's last days. Similar problems are evident in the discussions of *Death Comes for the Archbishop* and *Shadows on the Rock*. There are fine insights into narrative voice, symbolism, doubling episodes and twinning imagery techniques, but these are somewhat marred by encyclopedic understanding of the faith compelling the characters. Overall, however, Rosowski's is definitely a major study, unique in its intensity to grasp and shape the Cather canon.

Judith Fryer's *Felicitous Space: The Imaginative Structures of Edith Wharton and Willa Cather* (No. Car.), due to chaotic organization and lapses in focus, is a decidedly lesser contribution. I will comment on the work in general and review the Cather component at this point and save the Wharton for the next section. The jewels of insight on fiction and the concept of space are found long distances apart here, and these distances are as infuriating as they are intriguing. Fryer's seems to be criticism by association, allowing her interest, say, in Eastlake furniture to occupy a page or more before arriving at the reason why she is including this material in the first place. The first fifty pages concern, among many other things, male and female orientations to space, sexual conditioning, the skyscraper, the White City of the 1893 Columbian Exposition, Virginia Woolf's desire for a writing space, Charlotte Gilman's *Herland*, and so on. The rest of the study is divided equally between Wharton and Cather. The Cather section (pp. 201–342) concentrates on *Alexander's Bridge, O Pioneers!*, *My Ántonia, The Song of the Lark, The Professor's House, Death Comes for the Archbishop*, and *Shadows on the Rock*. Fryer's attempt to show how symbols work from objects in *Alexander's Bridge* is of interest, and the parallels she draws between this first novel and Wharton's *The Age of Innocence* are intriguing. However, while insightfully placing *O Pioneers!* and *My Ántonia* in the French "realist" tradition of Millet and the Barbizon painters, she reduces these important novels to feminist versions of the western experience. Fryer makes much of Cather's interest in primitive storytelling, in *My Ántonia* especially, in uniting teller, tale, and listener. However, the major thesis of space is often obscured by application to desert floor and sky as well as to houses, caves, and towers; in fact, the thesis here is so broad and undefined that the reader becomes confused as to the point being made. Spatial considerations are easier to understand and more appropriate when Fryer applies them to Thea Kronborg's bedroom and cliff-dweller cave in *The Song of the Lark*, Professor St. Peter's garden and study in *The Professor's House*, and Jeanne LeBer's enclosure in *Shadows on the Rock*. Professor St. Peter becomes a pivotal figure, a "Cartesian man . . . dividing mind and body and celebrating in this division the supremacy of the rational," while the more physical Thea and Ántonia consolidate rather than divide. This synthesis is accomplished on a different level by Jean Latour in *Death Comes for the Archbishop*; through his cathedral, the vastness of the southwestern landscape is made intimate and felicitous. Fryer works from space concepts to establish *Shadows on the Rock* as a "woman-centered view of historical experience," and while this may be debatable, the parallels made between recluse LeBer's mystical world and Cecile Auclair's domestic one are contributive. Despite the acceptable insights, however, the study is marred by a glut of details and by textual and factual distortions made to fit the very elusive central thesis: Jeanne LeBer's "tower" is moved mysteriously from Montreal to "[give] focus to the Rock of Quebec in the same way as the tower at Mesa Verde defines the pale little houses built into the side of the cliff." A very rare winter coffee klatch in *O Pioneers!* is passed off as typical of female bonding in

Cather, and Johannes Vermeer, who painted interiors, is made into a landscape painter for purposes of comparison to the window scene in *The Professor's House*. The potentials in *Felicitous Space* cry out for reorganization and reediting; it is surprising that a major university press failed to see to these.

The late L. Brent Bohlke left us an important aid to Cather scholarship in his collection *Willa Cather in Person: Interviews, Speeches and Letters* (Nebraska). Bohlke says Milchael Millgate's collection of Faulkner interviews (*Lion in the Garden*, 1968) gave him the idea for a similar Cather collection. Most of the pieces here are from newspapers and magazines and have never been published in book form, and having them between covers presents the novelist as a woman of the world with opinions about contemporary letters and events. In his brief but informative introduction Bohlke depicts Cather as being torn between enjoying public notice and resenting its intrusions on her time and energies. He also notes that she was not above creating fictions about herself, and includes a 1903 interview which depicts her as experiencing a "ranch period" when she "did not go to school at all." Some of the things to be learned from *Willa Cather in Person* are that Cather did not consider *Alexander's Bridge* an industrial novel, that she did not intend Niel Herbert to be the focus of *A Lost Lady*, that in 1925 she defended *One of Ours* as her best book, and that she considered *Death Comes for the Archbishop* and *Shadows on the Rock* as experimental fiction. Particularly helpful to critics, perhaps as a warning, is Cather's refusal to be held responsible for public utterances because she felt her opinions were constantly changing—a warning to be taken to heart by current critics who use her adolescent journalism to prove their theories about her later novels. Burton Rascoe observed that she was uninhibited and used "good, colloquial, and pungent words," and her reference to a well-known academic as a "mutton head," should underscore this warning. Highlights of the Bohlke collection include a 1922 New York *Herald* interview concerning violinist David Hochstein, the prototype of David Gerhardt in *One of Ours*; a report of the 1925 Bowdoin College lecture on technique in fiction; and a 1933 NBC radio talk on the novel.

Willa Cather (1985), ed. Harold Bloom, becomes yet another addition to the burgeoning Chelsea House series of "Modern Critical Views." Bloom reprints 15 representative essays from 1937–84, although unfortunately six of these have been reprinted in either *Willa*

Cather and Her Critics (1967) or *Critical Essays on Willa Cather* (1984). In his introduction Bloom, perhaps (as he betrays in his comment on the present neglect of Cather) because he comes to Cather less than steeped in the flood of recent criticism, makes some refreshingly perceptive comments about her "difficult art," associates her "systematic resentment of her own era" to the "relation between paranoia and homosexuality," and places her near Faulkner in eminence as a modern American writer. He makes a bit much of her supposed anti-Semitism, however, while minimizing her spiritual journey as characterized by "the archaic and not . . . the supernatural." Among the recent criticism gathered by Bloom is the "Introduction" from a 1983 edition of *A Lost Lady* by John Hollander (Limited Editions Club), which comments perceptively on Niel Herbert's "illusory hope" of his "elusive object," Marian Forrester. Hollander divides the novel into patterns of losses and concludes that it makes us aware of the knowledge that "can only come in response to loss." As the product of unusually meticulous scholarship, Marilyn Arnold's *Willa Cather: A Reference Guide* is a model contribution to the G. K. Hall series of bibliographies and also a badly needed guide to Cather criticism. I say badly needed because increasing numbers of critics demonstrate little or no knowledge of criticism on Cather as they somewhat cavalierly apply contemporary critical theories to her fiction. As a result, many of their attempts falter from insufficient grasp of texts and from useless strategies to prove the already established. Arnold covers secondary sources from 1895 to 1984, arranging these, each with its clear and extensive abstract, according to year and in alphabetical order according to author. She also provides an index of authors and a subject index which includes titles, characters, and topics.

Among the major novels, *The Professor's House* drew most attention. David Laird's "Willa Cather and the Deceptions of Art" (*Interface*, pp. 51–59) contains brilliant insights on this novel and *My Ántonia* as works in which life is sacrificed to artistic patternings of it. While Jim Burden's re-creation of reality in *My Ántonia* might authenticate existence, Godfrey St. Peter's comparable attempt in *The Professor's House* demands the surrender of adult human relationships and would direct him to death but for his chance rescue by Augusta (real life). Thus the end of this novel, concludes Laird, resists conventional closure. In "Pioneer or Gadgeteer: Bergsonian Metaphor in the Work of Willa Cather" (*MQ* 28:130–40), Eileen T.

Bender considers *The Professor's House* with *One of Ours*, "Before Breakfast," and "The Best Years" to establish Cather as an anti-technocrat rather than anti-scientist. Bender disassociates Cather from Professor St. Peter's condemnation of science and suggests that pioneer scientist Tom Outland and violinist David Gerhardt in *One of Ours* are fellow victims of modern exploitation. "The Ambiguities of Escape in Willa Cather's *The Professor's House*" by Thomas F. Strychacz (*SAF* 14:49–61) illuminates the complexity of the novel by showing that many of its supposed "absolute opposites" can be construed as correspondences, and that the urge to possess and exploit is in some measure an attribute of Tom Outland as well as of the materialists in Godfrey St. Peter's life. Strychacz sees the Professor and even Tom as seeking freedom in restriction and confinement: "as Tom's story comments on the corrupt world of Hamilton, one views even the moving account of Tom's summer on the mesa through the eyes of cruel experience." Frank G. Novak, Jr., is on target in "Crisis and Discovery in *The Professor's House*" (*CLQ* 22: 119–32) in stating that the key to the resolution of the Professor's story is in "Tom Outland's Story" and that the Professor's experience deepens him in a religious direction; but Novak is simplistic in seeing Tom and Louie Marsellus as, respectively, the good and bad guys. Unfortunately, Bill Christophersen's "Between Two Houses: Architecture as Metaphor in *The Professor's House*" (*NDQ* 53,i[1985]:89–96) only sketchily relates to the expectations of the title and fails to distinguish clearly among primitive, historical, and modern houses; however, it does contain a few interesting but undeveloped insights concerning Cather's employment of chance in the naturalistic tradition. In "The 'Case' of Willa Cather" (*WAL* 20:275–99) John B. Gleason refutes Leon Edel's argument in his famous psychological case study of *The Professor's House* (in *Stuff of Sleep and Dreams*, 1982) that Cather in writing this novel is somewhat beside herself due to the marriage of her friend Isabelle McClung, and instead sees the novel as a carefully controlled achievement in tragic vision in which America is judged ambivalently. "Memory, Myth, and *The Professor's House*" by John N. Swift (*WAL* 20:301–14) associates Cather's complex trauma with Tom Outland's and Professor St. Peter's stories, which depict somewhat narcissistic religious and psychological pilgrimages toward origins. What is revealed, however, is the "factitiousness of all origin . . . as an attempt to heal a common human state of mutability, failure, and ultimate loss." Leaning heavily on

Freud, Swift makes interesting connections between Louie Marsellus and the tower of Cliff City as paternal symbols.

The annual *Literary Issue* of the *Willa Cather Pioneer Memorial Newsletter* (30:11–38) contains a wealth of commentary on *My Mortal Enemy*, the briefest and perhaps most problematic of Cather's novels. In "The Dantean Journey in Cather's *My Mortal Enemy*" (pp. 11–14) I see religion as a key to the puzzling protagonist, Myra Henshawe, claiming that the novel "can be viewed as an allegory of the apostosy of a soul—its days of sin, its punishment, its journey back to God," which like the journey in Dante's *Divine Comedy* "includes the confessional ritual, the crucifixion image, the ascent to the mountaintop, and the vision of dawn." Merrill Skaggs makes some valuable comments about the narrator of this novel being defective in vision and a reflection and a frame for protagonist Myra Henshawe in "Nellie Birdseye" (pp. 14–16); however, Skaggs exaggerates a bit in making Nellie a significant destructive force and Myra's "mortal enemy." Mildred R. Bennett uses ideas from Eric Fromm's *The Art of Loving* to assess the Henshawes' marriage in "Myra's Marriage" (pp. 16–19), concluding that their love is symbiotic, with Myra dominating and Oswald submitting. Bennett interestingly observes that because Myra has been improperly disposed toward love and failed to find God, when dying she becomes obsessed with the Church. In "Gems and Jewelry: Cather's Imagery in *My Mortal Enemy*" (pp. 19–22) Kathryn T. Stofer explores the ambivalent meanings of Cather's use of amethysts, topazes, opals, and pearls to "underscore the personalities of Myra and Oswald Henshawe and . . . reveal the human frailties in the love story they live." Jean Tsien develops the novel's potential as an indictment of money and its corrupting power in "The Fascinating Complexity of *My Mortal Enemy*" (pp. 22–25), but then suggests connections between spiritual fulfillment and wealth, concluding that Cather's ambivalence about wealth adds to the novel's realism.

Cather's neglected first novel occupied two critics. Elizabeth Ammons in "The Engineer as Cultural Hero and Willa Cather's First Novel, *Alexander's Bridge*" (*AQ* 38:746–60) perspectivizes the novel against the background of literature about engineers and the myth of Progressive Era optimism. Ammons's uncovering of Cather's friend Viola Roseboro's "The Mistaken Man" as a possible source is especially valuable. The essay is somewhat flawed by feminizing, however; Cather is made out to be unsympathetic to the protagonist of her novel, whom Ammons depicts as a weakling, and toward the male world in general and American progress. Has Ammons forgotten Cather's own fondness for trains and that Captain Forrester in *A Lost Lady* is heroic to Cather because he "imagined" the railroads across the country? In "Willa Cather's 'Consequences' and *Alexander's Bridge*: An Approach through R. D. Laing and Ernest Becker" (*MFS* 32:191–202), Fritz Oehlschlaeger uses the works of the two psychiatrists to explain the tension between isolation and engulfment in schizoid temperaments like Keir Cavenaugh's in the 1915 short story and Bartley Alexander's in the earlier novel. Laing's idea on the role of marriage in protecting the self from engulfment through mutuality illuminates the significance of Alexander's death, when his wife "let him go" into nothingness. Cather's other "first novel," *O Pioneers!*, generated four very varied responses. Ann Moseley's "Mythic Reality: Structure and Theme in Cather's *O Pioneers!*" in *Under the Sun: Myth and Realism in Western American Literature*, ed. Barbara Howard Meldrum (Whitston, 1985; pp. 93–105), defines, without making use of the last decade of criticism, Cather's brand of realism as experience structured in mythic patterns and shows how the Greek myth of Demeter and Persephone and the Pawnee myth of the Father Heaven and Mother Earth union parallel Jungian concepts in Alexandra Bergson's dreams and search for equilibrium. Warren Motley's "The Unfinished Self: Willa Cather's *O Pioneers!* and the Psychic Cost of a Woman's Success" (*WS* 12:149–65) is an argument that the novel is the public code of a writer jealously guarding her privacy. Motley sees Alexandra Bergson's being forced to assume male tasks as causing her fear of passion and other abnormalities, and claims that she disguises even from herself her love for Marie (as Cather hid her passion for other women) but felt betrayed when Marie made love to Emil. On safer ground is Cynthia K. Briggs's "The Language of Flowers in *O Pioneers!*" (*WCPMNewsl* 30:29–30), which should be considered by all interpreters of the novel for Cather's figurative use of flowers, trees, vegetation of all kinds (Briggs's title is too narrow), and which uses as a basis of interpretation various Victorian sourcebooks on the significance of flora. A good companion piece is "Flower Imagery in a Willa Cather Novel: *A Lost Lady*" (*PVR* 12 [1984]:66–72) by Edward J. Piacentino, who traces the range of Niel Herbert's reactions to Marian Forrester through various flowers he associates with her, from lilacs and roses through withering gardenias.

There was some interest in several Cather short stories. "Caesar and the Artist in Willa Cather's 'Coming, Aphrodite!'" by Alice Hall Petry (*SSF* 23:307–14) is a bit reductive in making the dog Caesar the symbol of painter Don Hedger's "artistic sensibility" attempting to protect his master from sexual relationships, but suggests a link between Cather's dog and one of the same name in Mary Wilkins Freeman's "A New England Nun," which either Petry or someone else should follow up. In "Aphrodite and the Factory: Commercialism and the Artist in Frost and Cather" (*SoAR* 41:49–63), Donald G. Sheehy speculates that Frost, who praised Cather's "Coming, Aphrodite!" in a 1921 letter, was influenced by the story in writing his play "In an Art Factory." Both works have as their theme the conflict between artistic integrity and popular reputation. The story clearly defines Cather's choice of the former, while the play reflects Frost's conflict between lofty idealism and a desire for fame and fortune. Alice Hall Petry perceptively sees sculptor Harvey Merrick's homosexuality as a key to Sand City's hesitant and fumbling reaction to the return of his body and to his student Steavens, a possible lover, in "Harvey's Case: Notes on Cather's 'The Sculptor's Funeral'" (*SDR* 24,iii:108–16). Petry draws interesting parallels between Merrick and Paul in "Paul's Case" and points out Merrick's family background as a classic case of sexual confusion. Although a bit forced in places, Petry's "Both Sides of the Mirror: Willa Cather's 'A Gold Slipper'" (*MarkhamR* 15:53–56) is a good analysis of how singer Kitty Ayrshire, without realizing its chilling effect on him, forces industrialist Marshall McKann to regret the senseless sacrifice of his aesthetic self.

Miscellaneous items include pieces on two prairie novels and on Cather's letters. In "Willa Cather's *One of Ours*: A Novel of the Great Plains and the Great War" (*Midamerica* 11[1984]:20–33), Raymond J. Wilson III suggests that Claude Wheeler goes to war to conform to and be accepted by his materialistic society rather than to reject or escape it, and that Cather's views on the war are represented in violinist David Gerhardt's cynical realism rather than in Claude's naïveté. Richard C. Harris's note, "Jim Burden, Willa Cather and the Introductions to *My Ántonia*" (*WCPMNewsl* 30:33–34), tries to argue that the 1926 deletions from the 1918 description of Jim Burden in the Introduction reflect Cather's growing pessimism and exhaustion, and perhaps an altered sense of the Jim-Ántonia relationship. In "Cather's Published 'Unpublished' Letters" (*WCPMNewsl* 30:25–29), Marilyn Arnold makes available some previously published letters and letter excerpts. One of these concerns the cornerstone of a

Nebraska hospital and appears in Bohlke's collection. More significant to literary scholars are a letter to Fanny Butcher in which Cather selects *War and Peace* as the novel which she would have most liked to write, excerpts from letters to a Colby College professor concerning her youthful visit to A. E. Housman and her personal collection of Sarah Orne Jewett correspondence, an exchange with Cyril Clemens about the intranslatability of *Huckleberry Finn*, and comments on Steinbeck's language poverty, Columbus's Catholicism, and the effect of World War II on literature in letters to Father Harold C. Gardiner. "An Interesting Willa Cather Letter" by Julian Mason (*AL* 58:109–11) uncovers a letter to Henry W. Boynton which expresses difficulty getting on with the writing of *My Ántonia* due to the marriage of Isabelle McClung and the death of Isabelle's father.

ii. Edith Wharton

Among the writers of this period Wharton runs second to Cather in critical interest. The Wharton section in Judith Fryer's *Felicitous Space* (pp. 53–199) focuses on the influence of Art Nouveau females, Loie Fuller dances, Raphael's Villa Madama, etc., etc., on *The House of Mirth*, *The Custom of the Country*, *The Age of Innocence*, *Ethan Frome*, *Summer*, and Wharton's autobiography, *A Backward Glance*. Fryer says that Wharton makes a case against space without a moral center in *The House of Mirth* and that disorder in spatial arrangements reflects chaotic human intercourse and the absence of private retreats necessary for spiritual re-creation. Lily Bart's tragedy results from rootlessness and lack of private shelter or sense of home. Her desire for space leads to her possession as an object by men, a possession she resists to her death. Fryer uses *The Decoration of Houses* again and again, and appropriately so, to indicate the ideal balance Wharton saw as necessary between the public and private selves. The need for order is also stressed in *The Custom of the Country*. Undine Spragg is a Lily Bart without a moral sense, and she leaves a wreckage of lives behind her as she tries to gratify her inchoate desires. In considering this novel as an "urban pastoral," Fryer discusses Undine's mistaken sense that through change of space she will achieve change of identity, and juxtaposes this to Ralph Marvell's sea-cave retreat (fine old traditions as set against chaotic new power). Fryer notes in *The Age of Innocence* the contrast of Newland Archer to Henry James's Spencer Brydon in "The Jolly Corner," who, unlike

Archer, has the courage to explore the rooms of his locked consciousness, and she focuses on old New York's suitable rooms of female ritual as a refuge for Wharton in a modern, male age of war. Fryer has more positive things to say about May Welland than some other recent critics, or at least she attempts to understand why May, as a member of a women's community in decline, is defensive. Ellen Olenska is seen as existing for Archer in the private refuge of his study. There are perceptive comments about *A Backward Glance* as Wharton's attempt to fix her persona in the Whitman tradition and to lift the veil and expose the secluded, private place of mystery and creativity. *Ethan Frome* is analyzed from the perspectives of the male narrator and the female reader. Ethan's house is seen as the key to situation and character, as the small, imprisoning space within which insignificance gathers significance. Finally, *Summer* is envisioned spatially as the dream between the nightmare of the Mountain and the town of Nettleton. There is much to learn about Wharton from Fryer, especially in what she has to say about the autobiography and *The Decoration of Houses* as integral to Wharton's concept of public and private selves, but there is much that we would rather not know because Fryer fragments and obscures the theme of space.

Harold Bloom has given Chelsea House treatment to Wharton also, representing critics from 1968–85 in 10 solid essays. In his introduction to *Edith Wharton* Bloom tries to launch the novelist into some literary mainstreams by associating her with Edwards, Emerson, Hawthorne, Melville, and Wallace Stevens, with Balzac, Browning, James, and Ursula K. Le Guin, and with Nietzsche, Schopenhauer, and Robert Penn Warren; however, he concludes that her gift for social reductiveness prevented her from being a visionary. A Wharton bonanza of 26 love letters to Morton Fullerton is available in the University of Texas *Library Chronicle* (31[1985]:6–107) with commentaries on them by Alan Gribben (" 'The Heart Is Insatiable' ": A Selection from Edith Wharton's Letters to Morton Fullerton, 1907–1915") and Clare Colquitt ("Unpacking Her Treasures: Edith Wharton's 'Mysterious Correspondence' with Morton Fullerton"). Gribben introduces this selection from the 300 pieces of Wharton correspondence to her lover acquired from a Paris owner in 1980 by the Harry Ransom Humanities Research Center in Austin. These letters, which will be included in *The Letters of Edith Wharton* presently being edited by R. W. B. and Nancy Lewis, reveal Wharton's uneasiness and vulnerability as well as Fullerton's typical pattern of dealing with older women friends—passionate interest, conquest, silence, and neglect. The selection reveals Wharton's concern about divorcing her husband as well as her literary interests and opinions. Colquitt provides an afterword to the letters in noting the "radiant reasonableness" which attracted Wharton to Fullerton as well as the "balance" she sought to control a potentially disorderly situation. Although Colquitt establishes Fullerton's unsavoriness, she reminds us that Wharton valued him as a friend until her death. What is most important is his impact on her art: "The 'experience of loving' not only awoke the writer 'from a long lethargy, a dull acquiescence in conventional restrictions'; it also gave Wharton her first opportunity 'to do justice to the tender sentiment in fiction' by allowing her the chance to locate that 'mystic' space in her letters where she could both contain and express her love."

Among general articles on the fiction is Lawrence Jay Dessner's "Edith Wharton and the Problem of Form" (*BSUF* 24[1983]:54–63), which views Wharton as an experimentalist applying forms to incoherent and fragmentary life situations while obscuring important ironies from the general reader, collapsing structure in *The House of Mirth*, and undercutting her central sensibilities in *The Age of Innocence* and *The Reef*. Dessner sees her as confusing novel and short story techniques and is most positive about the integration of the four novelettes in *Old New York*. In "Edith Wharton's Profession of Authorship" (*ELH* 53:433–57), Amy Kaplan uses *A Backward Glance* to explore the strategy Wharton used to separate herself from the genteel dilettantism of the popular domestic "lady novelist." *The Decoration of Houses* becomes Wharton's attempt to transform woman's sphere by making her the architect of domestic space rather than an inmate in a domestic prison (shades of Fryer!). Such professionalizing of the private self, which has its counterpart in Wharton's development as a novelist, becomes fraught with dangers to the self. Kaplan explores stories like "The Pelican" and "The Expiation" as well as *The Touchstone* and *The House of Mirth* as expressions of Wharton's ongoing struggle to achieve equilibrium between her private and professional lives and to rise above the charge of merely exploring the private realms of the rich. Worthy of note here is the reprinting in the anniversary issue of *Yale Review* (75:229–38) of Wharton's 1927 essay "The Great American Novel," in which she laments the poverty of Main Street mediocrity increasingly associated with America, suggests that people were more interesting subjects when they were isolated, unequal, and had an ornate religion, and invites novelists to explore modern international culture rather than provincial America.

Analyses of individual works included "The Death of the Lady (Novelist): Wharton's *House of Mirth*" (*Representations* 9[1985]: 133–49) by Elaine Showalter, who considers this novel the turning point in Wharton's career from lady to serious modern novelist. Although Lily Bart's death signifies the death of the Perfect Lady, she dies awakened to the "vision of a new world of female solidarity . . . . Lily dies . . . so that working women like Gerty Farish and Nettie Struther may live and grow." Showalter also credits the novelist with depicting changes in men's lives: "Wharton's critique of the marriage system is not limited to the economic dependency of women but also extends to consider the loneliness, dehumanization, and anxiety of men." This is definitely a solid article on a major work. In "Wharton's *House of Mirth*" (*Expl* 44,iii:39–40) Laura Niesen De Abruna uses references to the French moralist La Bruyère's *Les Caracteres* as clues to Lawrence Selden's detachment from frivolous society as well as to his isolation, which contributes to Lily Bart's death. *The Custom of the Country* is the subject of "Edith Wharton and the Fiction of Public Commentary" (*WHR* 40:189–208) by Robert Caserio, who struggles with theories of Fredric Jameson, Hannah Arendt, and Hanna Pitkin in order to distinguish Wharton's school of representative realism as including within it that which it misses. Elmer Moffatt, he says, is Wharton's contribution to a list of characters including Dreiser's Frank Cowperwood and Faulkner's Flem Snopes who challenge through fabrication the shared reality that seems the foundation of the realistic mode: "through Moffatt and his relations with the other characters . . . Wharton confronts all the difficulties fabrication sets for realism, and accordingly she structures her novel as an implicit debate among representational concepts." Slightly less heady is Alexandra Collins's "The Noyade of Marriage in Edith Wharton's *The Custom of the Country*" (*ESC* 9[1983]:197–212), an earnest attempt to apply Friedrich de la Motte Fouque's *Undine* to Ralph Marvell's marriage to Undine Spragg and to explore the conflict between social reality and ideal existence, seeing both partners as using marriage to escape the entrapments of their respective pasts but as incapable of rising beyond them. In retreating from the vulgarities of the business world and shooting himself, Ralph "becomes the undine himself, . . . victimized in the world of human society . . . ."

Wharton's most popular work is R. B. Hovey's subject in "*Ethan Frome*: A Controversy about Modernizing It" (*ALR* 19:4–20), which quite convincingly shoots down recent "narcissistic" readings by Cynthia Wolff and Elizabeth Ammons, faulting Wolff for, among other things, feminizing the text by psychoanalyzing Ethan rather than Zeena after attributing the genesis of the novel to Wharton's dominating mother, and faulting Ammons for emphasizing the difficulty of women's lives while exploring a text devoted to a male character's tragic stature. Hovey asserts that his own realistic and unfashionable approach to this novel, even though it is touched by Freudianism, is at least faithful to the text and, unlike that of the feminist scholars, repairs rather than renovates it. Peter L. Hays sees the red pickle dish in *Ethan Frome* as a possible source for Fitzgerald's story "The Cut-Glass Bowl" in "Edith Wharton and F. Scott Fitzgerald" (*EdWN* 3,i: 2–3). Adeline Tintner turns her attention to a somewhat neglected work in "'False Dawn' and the Irony of Taste in Changes in Art" (*EdWN* 1,ii[1984]:1, 3, 8). Tintner sees sources for Lewis Raycie, his taste in painting, and his gallery in early New England collector James Jackson Jarvis and in Thomas Jefferson Bryan's New York Gallery of Christian Art, and says that Wharton's fickleness-of-taste theme is ironically underscored for current readers because some of the painters considered eclipsed at the novel's writing have since returned to grace. This novelette is paired with its companion in "'Feminized Men' in Wharton's *Old New York*" (*EdWN* 3,ii:2–3, 12). Here Mary Margaret Richards approaches Lewis Raycie and Hayley Delane in *The Spark* as in the same company as the women New York society has destroyed, as men reduced, inarticulate, ineffective, yet superior to their male peers in moral stature. Surprisingly, *The Age of Innocence* is beginning to suffer neglect and is represented here only by John Kekes's somewhat scholastic argument of a few years ago, "The Great Guide of Human Life" (*P&L* 8[1984]: 236–49), that Ellen Olenska's decision not to divorce and Newland Archer's not to marry are instances where social convention and personal fulfillment are not as opposed as modern readers presume. Indeed, "part of the reason Ellen and Archer love each other is that they . . . have . . . been shaped and formed by their society." "To discard its conventions would be to destroy themselves psychologically and morally." Kekes acknowledges D. Z. Phillips's discussion of this novel in *Through a Darkening Glass* (Notre Dame, 1982, pp. 9–29). Jean Gooder's "Unlocking Edith Wharton: An Introduction to

The Reef" (*CQ* 15:33–52) is about the novelist's being underrated because of the society she inherited and because of the cool professionalism with which she approached it. Gooder has interesting things to say about "Souls Belated," "The Other Two," "Autres Temps," "Xingu," and "Roman Fever" before she approaches the novel she is introducing, in which she says that clinical, classical artistry contrasts with the theme of anarchic, sensual awakening, and that behind it lurks the figure of George Sand. The intriguing duality reflects Wharton herself, who hoped, like her heroine Anna Leath, to find a bridge between West Fifty-fifth Street and life. In "Life's Empty Pack: Notes Toward a Literary Daughteronomy" (*CritI* 11[1985]: 355–84), Sandra M. Gilbert questions the effects of two centuries of powerful literary ancestresses on female sexuality paradigms as alternatives to Freud's and Lévi-Strauss's accounts of female maturation, using George Eliot's *Silas Marner* and Wharton's *Summer* as studies of the obstacles and terrors along the "circuitous path" Freud envisioned to trace heterosexual femininity. Gilbert concludes that these texts discover "no viable alternative to filial resignation." *Summer*, from Charity Royall's viewpoint, is "about both renunciation and resignation," and from Lawyer Royall's, it is "about the roles of cultural authority to which men are assigned and about the women who are assigned . . . to them to signify that authority."

Among the miscellaneous are some James-Wharton items. In "Wharton and James: Some Literary Give and Take" (*EdWN* 3,i: 3–5, 8), Adeline Tintner includes in her network of possible influences and borrowings James's "The Birthplace" as in debt to Wharton's "The Angel at the Grave," his "The Tree of Knowledge" as influencing her "The Recovery," her "Copy" in debt to his "Broken Wings," her "The Moving Finger" as a reminder of his "The Special Type" and "The Tone of Time," her *The Touchstone* as in debt to his "The Given Case," and the last page of *The Wings of the Dove* as inspired by *The Touchstone*. Tintner's "Henry James's 'Julia Bride': A Source for Chapter Nine in Edith Wharton's *The Custom of the Country*" (*NMAL* 9:16) establishes Wharton's debt to James through exploration of textual parallels and proposes that Wharton's Undine Spragg fulfills the possibilities and promise of James's title character. In "Henry and Edith: The Velvet Glove as an 'In' Joke" (*HJR* 7:21–25), Jean Frantz Blackall sees the private thrust of the James story as his recognition of his own deficiencies as a man as well as of Wharton's as a writer, but says that James received creative inspiration from

Wharton's "The Fruit of the Tree" in its employment of hands and gesture for metaphor. Linda W. Wagner suggests in "A Note on Wharton's Use of *Faust*" (*EdWN* 3,i:1, 8) that the ironic use of a line from Goethe's poem might be the source of the title of *The Custom of the Country*, and further indicates that *The Age of Innocence* draws from *Faust* in imagery and character relationships. Alfred Bendixen supplements the recent guide to Wharton studies in the *Edith Wharton Newsletter* (2,ii[1985]:1–8) with a valuable commentary on criticism from 1983–85 in "Recent Wharton Studies: A Bibliographic Essay" (*EdWN* 3,ii:5, 8–9), and in the same issue (pp. 6–7) Scott Marshall provides a map for places between Manhattan's Washington Square and Twenty-eighth Street that are important in Wharton's life and fiction.

Wharton scholars should check the *Edith Wharton Newsletter* (in its fourth volume at this writing) for frequent commentaries on criticism. Listed below are several publications listed in the *Newsletter* worthy of mention but previously overlooked in this chapter. Diana Zacharia Worby contends that Wharton equivocates about women's rights in her fiction in "The Ambiguity of Edith Wharton's 'Lurking Feminism'" (*MHLS* 5[1982]:81–90). In "Triangles of Defeat and Liberation: The Quest for Power in Edith Wharton's Fiction" (*PCL* 8[1982]:18–26), Lois A. Cuddy examines tripartite relationships in *The House of Mirth*, *Ethan Frome*, and *The Age of Innocence*. The text of the Wharton-Clyde Fitch collaboration on the dramatization of the first of these novels is provided in Glenn Loney's *The House of Mirth: The Play of the Novel* (Fairleigh Dickinson, 1981), which includes a commentary on the relationship between novel and play. The "creative impulse" of heroines is the concern of Alexandra Collins in "The Art of Self-Perception in Virginia Woolf's *Mrs. Dalloway* and Edith Wharton's *The Reef*" (*Atlantic* 7[1982]:47–58). In "Reality and the Puritan Mind: Jonathan Edwards and Ethan Frome" (*JEP* 4[1983]:238–47), Frederik L. Rusch examines Ethan's decisions in the light of Edwards's belief in human moral responsibility. Leon Edel probes Wharton's life as the source of the horror in "All Souls" in "The Nature of Literary Psychology" (*Jour. of the American Psychoanalytic Association* 29[1981]:447–67). Finally, Suzanne Poirier notes the irony of how the encouragement to write contributed to Wharton's divorce in "The Weir Mitchell Rest Cure: Doctor and Patients" (*WS* 10[1983]:15–40).

iii. Sinclair Lewis

This was a banner year for Sinclair Lewis scholarship due to the 1985 centennial of his birth. A conference was held in February of that year at St. Cloud State University in St. Cloud, Minnesota, near Sauk Centre, Lewis's birthplace, and the papers appeared this year under the title *Sinclair Lewis at 100: Papers Presented at a Centennial Conference*, ed. Michael Connaughton and published by St. Cloud State University (1985). Also intended to correspond with the centennial was *Critical Essays on Sinclair Lewis*, ed. Martin Bucco (Hall). This latter collection contains 41 essays and reviews spanning about 70 years. Bucco's introduction (pp. 1–27) and two of the essays appear for the first time. After beginning with the observation that recent critics have been more understanding and tolerant of Lewis's aesthetic deficiencies than was Mark Schorer, author of the major biography, Bucco surveys Lewis's books and posthumous collections, briefly describing their content and reception. He concludes with a survey of books about Lewis. The 188 notes to his 17-page essay contain a wealth of bibliographical information. One of the essays appearing for the first time in this collection is Robert E. Fleming's "*Kingsblood Royal* and the Black 'Passing Novel'" (pp. 213–21), an influence-and-parallels study linking Lewis's novel with James Weldon Johnson's *The Autobiography of an Ex-Colored Man* (1912) and other novels treating the situation of a black person passing for white. The second essay appearing for the first time is James Lundquist's "The Sauk Centre Sinclair Lewis Didn't Write About" (pp. 221–33). Lundquist suggests that *Main Street* is as disturbing for what it omits about Lewis's hometown as for what it includes. The death of his mother when Lewis was a child and the litany of deaths and accidents in the local newspapers of the period contributed to psychic scars that travel and marriages could not heal.

The papers in *Sinclair Lewis at 100* are diverse in subject and approach and uneven in quality and significance. There are 23 of them, which is less than the number actually presented at the conference; some of the others have been published or are scheduled for publication elsewhere. A few trends or clusters are discernible. Five essays attempt to place Lewis in a midwestern tradition. David Crowe's "Illustrations as Interpretation: Grant Wood's 'New Deal' Reading of Sinclair Lewis's *Main Street*" (pp. 95–111) is an interpretive analysis of Wood's nine illustrations for a 1936 edition of the novel and explores the relations between the work of these two midwestern artists. William T. Morgan's "Sauk Centre as Artifact: The Town as Seen in History, Painting, Architecture, and Literature" (pp. 135–55) is an exposition of the city's history from 1858 to 1903 that provides background for Lewis's midwestern roots. Two essays compare and contrast Gopher Prairie with the more recent fictional Minnesota small town of Lake Wobegone. In "From Gopher Prairie to Lake Wobegone: From Sinclair Lewis to Garrison Keillor" (pp. 113–23), Wayne H. Meyer concludes that the main difference between the towns is that Keillor is a humorist, Lewis a satirist; Keillor's attitude toward his subject is more ambiguous, more sympathetic. F. Garvin Davenport in "Gopher-Prairie-Lake-Wobegone: The Midwest as Mythic Space" also recognizes Keillor's as the more gentle and accepting satire and suggests that both towns can be viewed as "mythic space," by which he means a people's attempt to make sense of their environment. David D. Anderson's "Sinclair Lewis and the Midwest Tradition" (pp. 253–65) is a general assessment of Lewis's career and recognition, concluding that Lewis is important for psychological, sociological, and historical rather than literary reasons. Lewis was not a great writer, but his best works are still relevant for reasons other than aesthetic. This familiar view is also expressed by one of the essays not concerned with the midwestern element in Lewis's artistic vision. According to W. Gordon Milne ("Lewis's Muted Influence as Artist and Social Commentator," pp. 87–93), the force of Lewis's attack on American culture is blunted by a lack of artistic skill. Technical flaws (mostly in the form of overdoing and excess) mar his varied and exhaustive social satire.

As expected in such a conference, several papers attempt to promote neglected or disesteemed works. Clara Lee R. Moodie tries in "The Book that Has Never Been Published" (pp. 201–12) to persuade us that Lewis's 126 stories should be collected into one book. They reveal better than the novels, she argues, the values or norms on which his satire was based. But it will probably take more forceful arguments than she provides to entice a publisher into such an undertaking. The attempt by Elmer F. Suderman in "The God Seeker in Sinclair Lewis's Novels" (pp. 227–34) to stimulate interest in *The God Seeker* by focusing on its religious ideas is even less successful. James T. Jones is more persuasive promoting a neglected novel in "A Middle-Class Utopia: Lewis's *It Can't Happen Here*" (pp. 213–25).

He argues along two lines: first, that the novel is an interesting contribution to the Utopia genre, and, second, that it extends the social critique of Lewis's major novels to a fuller and more honest comment on the middle class. He sees London's *The Iron Heel* and Hawthorne's *The Blithedale Romance* as important influences on Lewis's novel. London's influence is also examined by Robert L. Coard in "Jack London's Influence on Sinclair Lewis" (pp. 157–70). Lewis at one time sold story ideas to London, and Lewis's writing contains a number of references to London and his works. Coard's arguments concerning London's influence are, as he himself admits, largely conjectural. Two other alleged influence studies, one connecting Lewis with the southern writer T. S. Stribling and another linking him to J. F. Powers, are merely exercises in the ingenuity of perceiving parallels.

Two essays focus on the feminine perspective. Lydia Blanchard's " 'Grey Darkness and Shadowy Trees': Carol Kennicott and the Good Fight for Utopia *Now*" (pp. 125–33) persuasively asserts that Lewis's vision of "female empowerment," while growing out of traditional treatment of the theme, was prophetic of future needs and circumstances. He went beyond Cather and Wharton, who viewed empowerment as achievable through nurturing and civilizing, and recognized that these approaches do not work in the twentieth century. Eleanor H. Lincoln, C.S.J., in "Carol Kennicott, Survivor" (pp. 245–52), provides a mostly personal and subjective interpretation of Carol in support of the thesis that she differs from the heroines of *The Awakening* and *The House of Mirth* because she is a reformer and survivor who never loses her freedom to be herself.

Other noteworthy papers from the centennial conference include Martin Bucco's informative examination (pp. 179–89) of Lewis's "Book Week" column in *Newsweek*, which ran from 4 October 1937 to 18 April 1938. As a book reviewer Lewis was witty, impressionistic, partisan, and self-assertive. Roger Forseth explores Lewis's excessive drinking and its effects on his writing in "Sinclair Lewis, Drink, and the Imagination" (pp. 11–26) and concludes that Lewis lived in a state of "unresolved alcoholism" that produced "emotional poverty" in his later fiction. One of the highlights of the collection is Glen A. Love's "Babbitt's Dance: Technology, Power, and Art in the Novels of Sinclair Lewis" (pp. 75–85). This penetrating and authoritative essay describes Lewis's fascination with power and technology and interprets *Babbitt* as a study of power and powerlessness in urban industrial America. The shadow hero is the architect-designer that Lewis never successfully realized in his fiction. At the end of *Sinclair Lewis at 100* is "A Sinclair Lewis Checklist: 1976–1985," a supplement to Robert E. and Esther Fleming's *Sinclair Lewis: A Reference Guide* (Hall, 1980).

The most significant article outside the two collections prompted by the centennial is Joel Fisher's "Sinclair Lewis and the Diagnostic Novel: *Main Street* and *Babbitt*" (*JAmS* 20:421–33). Fisher ingeniously argues that what we have read as limitations in Lewis are actually "part of a comprehensive and radical intellectual exercise." Lapsing at times into obfuscating jargon, he makes some rather abstruse connections between the marriage contracts in Lewis's novels and the contract between the individual and nation in America. Much of the intellectual complexity he discovers in Lewis's diagnosis of American culture is, one suspects, the product of his own fertile ingenuity.

iv. Theodore Dreiser and H. L. Mencken

Richard Lingeman's *Theodore Dreiser: At the Gates of the City, 1871–1907* (Putnam's) is clearly the most significant contribution to Dreiser studies this year. Beginning with Dreiser's childhood poverty, this first volume of a projected two-volume biography tells of his lonely and sexually troubled adolescence, his courtship and marriage, his struggle to succeed in journalism, and his frustrating beginning as a novelist. It builds up to a climax in the story behind *Sister Carrie*, which it tells more fully than has been done before. Lingeman, a social historian, is skilled at capturing the tenor of the period as it impinges on Dreiser's life. Energetically amassing material, including letters and diaries unavailable to earlier biographers, he has constructed a biography rich in information but less successful in imaginatively conveying his subject's bewildering personality. Also, the small amount of literary criticism, while competent, serves essentially biographical purposes and adds little to our understanding of Dreiser's fiction. Lingeman, executive editor of *The Nation*, is keenly interested in the social issues of the period and emphasizes Drieser's social consciousness and politics. The book includes 18 pages of photographs.

Another large addition to Dreiser scholarship are the two volumes of Thomas P. Riggio, ed., *Dreiser-Mencken Letters: The Correspondence of Theodore Dreiser and H. L. Mencken, 1907–1945* (Penn.). The more than 1,200 letters exchanged between these two friends are one of the major correspondences in American literature. Only 238 of the 1,204 letters have been previously published, and only 168 of them are not printed in full; these consist of repetitions or trivial material and are listed and described in an appendix. This collection has been meticulously edited for the benefit of scholars. With few exceptions typographical errors have been retained and notes explain illegible words and the position of marginalia. The letters are arranged in six sections, each with an introduction. These sections mark important biographical or historical divisions or stages in the friendship. Mencken's letters to Helen Dreiser, written after Dreiser's death, appear in an appendix. Another appendix includes 19 reviews and reminiscences useful for understanding the interaction of the two men. Twenty-four photographs of Dreiser, Mencken, and friends are scattered through the two volumes. This collection has the all too rare quality of being at the same time a boon to scholarship and delightful reading for many kinds of readers. Pennsylvania has other Dreiser projects under way, including volumes of Dreiser's journalism, letters, diaries, and related writing.

Bibliographical information appeared this year in the usual updated checklists in *Dreiser Newsletter*, which, incidentally, announced that it would become *Dreiser Studies* with the spring 1987 issue. And a book-length secondary bibliography was published: *Theodore Dreiser and the Critics, 1911–1982: A Bibliography with Selective Annotations* by Jeanetta Boswell (Scarecrow). Such a bibliography was needed—the last one appeared in 1975, and much has been written on Dreiser in the interim. Unfortunately, however, this bibliography is marred by carelessness and inconsistent annotation (see Frederic E. Rusch's review in *DrN* [17,ii:14–16] for specific and telling examples).

Sister Carrie was the only Dreiser novel to receive significant attention. James L. Machor points out in "Carrie's Other Sister" (*SAF* 14:199–204) that "the holograph of the novel reveals that Dreiser originally conceived Minnie as a slightly warmer, more human individual capable of eliciting sympathy and understanding from readers." Slight but significant changes in the final version made her more a part of the unsympathetic environment that threatens to debase

Carrie's spirit. Philip L. Gerber's "The Tangled Web: Offstage Acting in *Sister Carrie*" (*DrN* 17,ii:1–8) argues that Carrie's repeated dissimulation and role-playing before she becomes an actress serve as counterpoint to her rise to prominence on the stage. Joseph Epstein in "The Mystery of Theodore Dreiser" (*NewC* 5,iii:33–43) provides a substantial general essay on Dreiser that revives the perennial paradoxes of the man versus the artist. He suggests that neglect of Dreiser by recent theory-oriented criticism is partly to the good because such neglect leaves his fiction to readers who assume a link between character and destiny—the link which Epstein considers the main tradition of the novel. As for the mysterious relation between Dreiser's personality and his art, Epstein suggests that in some writers imagination is in the service of intelligence—with Dreiser the opposite is true.

In Mencken scholarship this was a memorable year for letters. The two volumes of Dreiser-Mencken correspondence have been described above. Because Mencken was a prolific and entertaining letter writer, the attention given to his correspondence is understandable. *"Ich Kuss de Hand": The Letters of H. L. Mencken to Gretchen Hood*, ed. Peter W. Dowell (Alabama), includes 138 of 248 communications Mencken sent between 1926 and 1930 to a young admirer who became a friend desirous of marrying him. This friendship has received only passing mention by biographers. The letters, which ended abruptly when Mencken married someone else, are of considerable interest because they are a product of the years of his greatest popular acclaim and because Gretchen Hood was a bright, independent, and accomplished woman who stimulated Mencken's epistolary skills. Dowell's introduction describes and explains the relationship, and some of Gretchen Hood's annotations of the letters, made late in her life, are included.

The articles on Mencken this year are devoted nearly exclusively to matters of biography. Robert A. Hohner's " 'The Woes of a Holy Man': Bishop James Cannon, Jr. and H. L. Mencken" (*SAQ* 85:228–38) describes Mencken's relationship with a prominent and respected Methodist clergyman and temperance reformer who became embroiled in scandal in the early 1930s. Hohner's purpose is to show that Cannon was not the narrow and unscrupulous fanatic he is usually considered to have been and that Mencken was surprisingly conservative in some matters. Jason D. Duberman's "H. L. Mencken and the Wowsers" (*ABC* 7,v:3–14) and Kenneth W. Amrhine's "The Day

Mencken Was Arrested" (*Menckeniana* 98:10–12) both treat the "Hatrack" test case in which Mencken sold the banned spring 1926 issue of *American Mercury* on the Boston Common to Reverend J. Frank Chase, secretary of the New England Watch and Ward Society. Duberman's is the more complete and informative account. Jean-Maurice Poitras in "Leonard Keene Hirshberg and Henry Louis Mencken" (*Menckeniana* 97:1–7) describes the bizarre career of a doctor turned con man with whom Mencken once collaborated to produce a book on the surprisingly unlikely subject *What You Ought to Know about Your Baby*. Richard J. Schrader in "'But Gentlemen Marry Brunettes': Anita Loos and H. L. Mencken" (*Menckeniana* 98:1–7) explains that in their 1920s association Loos attempted in vain to impress Mencken with her intelligence. "The Saturday Night Club Diary of Louis Cheslock" (*Menckeniana* 97:8–13) is the fourth and concluding segment of the diary. The entries begin 24 November 1948 with Mencken's stroke and end with his death seven years later. They provide intimate details by a close friend on Mencken's illness and death. (Also, in the friendship area, Stephen Young's "The Mencken-Lewis Connection" reviewed in *ALS 1985* as in *Menckeniana* 95:10–16 should be corrected to 94:10–16.)

In September the board of directors of the Enoch Pratt Free Library in Baltimore announced that the library will publish (through Knopf) Mencken's own diary. The five volumes (2,100 pages of double-spaced typing) cover the years 1930 to 1948. Sealed for 25 years after his death, the diary was opened in January 1981 and made available to selected scholars, who were forbidden to quote or paraphrase it. This new material is discussed by Carl Bode in a new foreword to the 1986 paperback reissue of his *Mencken* (Hopkins).

The diversity of Mencken's enduring appeal is revealed in three articles from markedly different political perspectives that all focus on the need of current American society for a critical voice like Mencken's. Scott Lahti in "The Fourteenth Colony" (*National Review* 31[Dec.]:52–55), Alfred Kazin in "H. L. Mencken and the Great American Boob" (*Menckeniana* 99:1–7), and James Seaton in "The Truth-Value of Bourgeois Hedonism" (*JAC* 8,iii[1985]:53–57), representing respectively the conservative, liberal, and Marxist points of view, all find Mencken's style and method a congenial model and lament the lack of such a vibrant personality and entertainingly destructive style to support their own quarrels with contemporary American society.

v. Gertrude Stein

Two collections of critical essays and a two-volume edition of correspondence highlight the year's work on Stein. Editor Michael J. Hoffman in his introduction to *Critical Essays on Gertrude Stein* (Hall) makes clear and interesting what is sometimes unclear but interesting—Stein's purposes and the fever chart of her reception by reviewers and critics. Hoffman evaluates the important criticism, pieces he has included as well as those omitted: pioneer estimates by Mabel Dodge, Carl Van Vechten, Sherwood Anderson, and Edmund Wilson; in-depth analyses by Kenneth Burke, B. F. Skinner, and others; negative estimates by Wyndham Lewis and Michael Gold; academic touchstones by Donald Sutherland, Allegra Stewart, John Ashbery, and Richard Bridgman. The collection contains four substantial, previously unpublished essays. Poet Laura Riding Jackson in "The Word-Play of Gertrude Stein" (pp. 240–60) places Stein within the modernist linguistic revolution and measures her against T. S. Eliot and other contemporaries. Jackson finds Stein personable, honest, and healthy in daring "to equate modernity with a real barbarism, as compared with the equivocal disposition of the critical definers of a new era of literature and art disembarrassed of the old standard objectives of progress. These raided the past as a mortuary repository for ghostly substance for the supposedly purged present." Elyse Blankley also sees "Stein's disdain of tradition as [separating] her from the male giants of modernist literature," but her essay, "Beyond the 'Talent of Knowing': Gertrude Stein and the New Woman" (pp. 196–209), is devoted to Stein's rejection of the university route to sexual equality as within the patriarchal tradition. Focusing on the early novella *Fernhurst*, *The Making of Americans*, and *Tender Buttons*, Blakely outlines Stein's strategy toward originality by revolutionizing the English language. In "A Rosy Charm: Gertrude Stein and the Repressed Feminine" (pp. 225–40), Lisa Ruddick uses *Tender Buttons*, *A Long Gay Book*, and *G.M.P.* to show that "Stein moved from a [William] Jamesian notion of selective attention to a psychoanalytic one" that the "interesting fact of mental life . . . was no longer that we suppress . . . in the interest of survival . . . but that we *repress* aspects of experience in the interest of instituting culture. What we repress is . . . important . . . . the mother and the female body; . . . Stein uncivilizes us by bringing these back into view." Jane Bowers's "The Writer in the Theatre: Gertrude Stein's *Four Saints in Three Acts*" (pp. 210–25) explores the famous libretto as a geography of Stein's mind, as a landscape where writing and performance, or writing and speech, are reconciled through a structure preplanned to make the audience feel that the plan is being created during performance. Harold Bloom gives Stein the benefit of his editorial skills in *Gertrude Stein* (Chelsea House). Unfortunately five of the 15 essays reprinted here are duplicated in *Critical Essays* (these two series should cooperate to avoid such duplication). Bloom includes some of the same early portraits, uses Sutherland's work as the beginning of academic assessment, and includes later criticism by Bridgman, William H. Gass, Marianne DeKoven, and Jayne Walker. In his introduction Bloom calls Stein "the greatest master of dissociative rhetoric in modern writing" but says that the only religion she espoused was American self-reliance. He admires *The Geographical History of America* for its theory of abstraction and places Stein in the tradition of Whitman and Emerson for the freedom and wildness she associated with the human mind. *The Letters of Gertrude Stein and Carl Van Vechten, 1913–1946*, ed. Edward Burns (Columbia, 2 vols.), offers in hundreds of pieces of correspondence the "daily everyday living" aspect of Stein's life missing from major biographical studies. As Burns indicates in his concise introduction, what these letters lack in rich self-scrutiny, intellectual excitement, and literary cajoling they make up for in sincere, mutual devotion, revealing Stein's need for love and approval and Van Vechten's need to serve and support. Although he served as literary agent of sorts for Stein, Van Vechten's letters to her fail to reveal an understanding of her writing, and hers to him lack the profundity of her letters to Thornton Wilder or Wendell Wilcox. Instead, they reveal a family in which Stein played "Baby Woojuns" to Van Vechten's "Papa" and Toklas's "Mama Woojuns." Burns concludes that this collection brings to light "the nearby objects and people and places that were grist for Stein's writing . . . ." Carefully edited with copious notes, a "Coda" of Van Vechten's correspondence to Toklas after Stein's death, appendices devoted to the first meeting between Stein and Van Vechten, Stein's unfinished portrait of Van Vechten, as well as bibliographies on both correspondents, these volumes are a milestone in Stein scholarship.

Criticism on Stein outside these collections was substantial and intelligent. Catharine R. Stimpson provides a fascinating consideration of the physical Stein as depicted by her supporters and detractors and as utilized by herself in transforming "the monstrous into pleasure and into art" in "The Somagrams of Gertrude Stein" (*PoT* 6 [1985]:67–80). Despite her radicalism Stein was sexually discreet and believed that passion was but part of a whole: "Indeed, in Stein's more abstract writing, the body disappears into language utterly, or becomes an example of a linguistic category." Charles Caramello's "Reading Gertrude Stein Reading Henry James, Eros Is Eros Is Eros Is Eros" (*HJR* 6[1985]:182–203) is devoted to Stein's aspirations to be James's successor and, in her treatment of James in *Four in America*, combines, as he did, portraiture and narrative. Caramello sees Stein as differing from her fellow moderns and, like James, as "a figure enduring popular indifference or derision while . . . pressing the boundaries of psychological realism." "Gertrude Stein: From Outlaw to Classic" by Cyrena N. Pondrom (*ConL* 27:98–114) concludes favorable reviews of three recent Stein studies (Marianne DeKoven's *A Different Language* [1983], Randa Dubnick's "The Structure of Obscurity" [1984], and Jayne L. Walker's *The Making of the Modernist* [1984]) with a call for a redefinition of modernism to accommodate writers like Stein, H.D., Edith Sitwell, and Virginia Woolf as well as Eliot, Pound, and Yeats. "Some [modernists,] like Eliot at one extreme, never lost their longing for unitary order . . . . others, like Stein . . . at the other extreme, celebrated semantic anarchy . . . ." In "Gertrude Stein: The Pattern Moves, The Woman Behind Shakes It" (*WS* 13:33–46), Linda Mizejewski argues that approaching *Tender Buttons* through A. N. Whitehead's theories of ongoing self-creation clarifies Stein's attempts to blur distinctions between self-delineation and flux, and provides a way of understanding the tension between "self" and interrelatedness in the fictions of Virginia Woolf, Charlotte Gilman, Katherine Mansfield, and Kate Chopin. "Gertrude Stein's Mediating Stanzas" by Elizabeth Winston (*Biography* 9:229–46) analyzes the 1932 poem *Stanzas in Meditation* as the underside of Stein's using the Toklas persona and clear voice in writing the popular *The Autobiography of Alice B. Toklas*. The 164 stanzas reveal the vulnerable and complex personality behind Stein's struggle with the self-effacement she found necessary in order to celebrate her own genius, and also reveal a more independent Alice Toklas than in the *Autobiography*. *Stanzas in Meditation* also explains the solicitous Stein of *Everybody's Autobiography*.

vi. Sherwood Anderson, Jack London, and John Dos Passos

Anderson criticism these days is hardly a rich, exciting area, but there were a few highlights. In " 'The Young Thing Within': Divided Narrative and Sherwood Anderson's *Winesburg, Ohio*" (*MQ* 27:422–37), A. Carl Bredahl considers Anderson's masterpiece in the tradition of *Main-Travelled Roads* and *Go Down, Moses* as a narrative straining toward new forms and values after the collapse of the old order. The struggle toward narrative wholeness in Anderson's work is reflected in urges of art and sexuality to connect isolated characters and bridge the divisions between their stories. Clare Colquitt's "The Reader as Voyeur: Complicitous Transformations in 'Death in the Woods' " (*MFS* 32:175–90) examines the web woven by the narrator to implicate the reader in the "masculinist convention" of "dehistoriz[ing] woman by objectifying her into art." The undaunted David D. Anderson puts Sherwood in company with Dreiser and Bellow by focusing on the city experiences of the protagonist in the first novel of each writer (*Windy McPherson's Son, Sister Carrie,* and *Dangling Man*) in "Chicago Cityscapes by Theodore Dreiser, Sherwood Anderson, and Saul Bellow" (*MMisc* 13[1985]:43–49). For each the city marks an ending and a beginning; for each the city is subjective—what he chooses to see—and a way toward elusive fulfillment. In "Sherwood Anderson, Chicago, and the Midwestern Myth" (*Midamerica* 11[1984]:56–58), critic Anderson continues with the Chicago theme, seeing *Winesburg, Ohio, Windy McPherson's Son, Mid-American Chants, Poor White Marching Men, Horses and Men,* and *Dark Laughter* as expressions of Anderson's being both sold and disillusioned by what that city came to represent—the collapse of Jefferson's idea of a free and orderly society into one of material gain and spiritual emptiness. Charles E. Modlin prefaces a printing of the Newberry Library typescript of Anderson's comments during a 1931 debate in "Sherwood Anderson's Debate with Bertrand Russell" (*WE* 12,i:4–11). Obviously relishing his role as countrywise philosopher to Russell's straight man, Anderson ironically (having abandoned his first wife and children) defends and calls for the preservation of the family and motherhood, opposes state child rearing, and blames a faulty economic system for failures and distortions in rearing children. Hilbert H. Campbell, in a final tidbit, " 'The hills lovely': Lyricism in Sherwood Anderson's Diaries" (*WE* 12,i: 12), uses excerpts from the diary jottings during the Virginia years to take us through the seasons with Anderson and demonstrate that his poetic gifts lie here rather than in his two volumes of verse.

Near the end of his life Jack London was powerfully affected by the writings of Carl Jung and employed Jungian ideas in the tales of the South Seas he wrote during his last year. Jeanne Campbell Reesman suggests in "Jack London—Kama'aina" (*JLN* 18[1985]: 71–76) that these tales deserve more attention for the way the Jungian archetypes informing them lend coherence and power. She does little more than summarize the tales, however, noting the Jungian themes. A more penetrating examination of them is provided by David A. Morland in "The Quest that Failed: Jack London's Last Tales of the South Seas" (*Pacific Studies* 8[1984]:48–70). Frustrated, isolated, and physically ailing in his final year, London grasped Jungian psychology in hope of finding scientific support for free will. The stories in *On the Makaloa Mat* (1919) and *The Red One* (1918) reflect his conflicts and questionings as he tested his philosophical positions against Jungian ideas. Ultimately he found the insights from Jung inadequate for replacing his skeptical materialism.

In "Jack London in the Tradition of American Sea Fiction" (*American Neptune* 46:188–99), Bert Bender, who is working on a history of American sea fiction since *Moby-Dick*, asserts that the American tradition of sea fiction begun by Cooper and reaching its zenith in *Moby-Dick* continued to develop into the twentieth century, with London being the first full-fledged heir after the golden age of 1840–51. To make his case, he focuses on *The Sea Wolf*, *The Mutiny of the Elsinore*, *Michael*, *Brother of Jerry*, and "The Water Baby." A significant new approach to London and to naturalism in general is displayed in Lee Clark Mitchell's "'Keeping His Head': Repetition and Responsibility in London's 'To Build a Fire'" (*JML* 13:76–96). This subtle and brilliant stylistic analysis uses London's story to demonstrate that the often deprecated style of naturalism is not inept, but actually expresses the determinism underlying naturalism and is radically different from the style of realism. The maladroitness of the style reflects a metaphysic; it unsettles our conception of agency by distorting customary linguistic usage. Mitchell subjects London's style to a more detailed and sophisticated scrutiny than it has hitherto received.

Dos Passos is represented this year in veteran critic Donald Pizer's "The Hemingway–Dos Passos Relationship" (*JML* 13:111–28). Pizer explores the way the two writers brooded on each other in the form of autobiographical portraiture and fictional caricature. Dos Passos married Katy Smith, whom Hemingway had previously known and written about. This caused tension in the two men's relationship, as did Hemingway's aggressive athleticism, their respective roles in the radicalization of American writing during the '30s, and their disagreement during the Spanish Civil War. Pizer argues that in their writings about each other Hemingway used Dos Passos as a scapegoat on which to project his own guilt and fears about himself, and Dos Passos used Hemingway as a means of diminishing the value of personal qualities Dos Passos lacked but for a while desired. "Each one had a powerful ghost in his own psychic closet to exorcise—the one of guilt at the betrayal of a loved one, the other of a desired but later rejected code of masculinity."

vii. Southern and Western Writers

The southerner receiving most attention this year, due in part to a delayed reaction to his centenary in 1981, is Mississippian Stark Young, to whom the *Southern Quarterly* has devoted a special issue (24,iv). Robert C. Peterson introduces the seven essays by noting Young's failure to rise above his emotional attachment to Mississippi to attain moral vision and by calling for a systematic exploration of Young's aesthetic and its relevance to his achievement as a fiction writer. In "Stark Young: The Southern Roots" (pp. 17–40) John Pilkington highlights the formative influences of Young's great uncle Hugh McGehee, who provided the writer with a sense of family affections, speculates that the early death of Young's idolized mother "had a bearing on his homosexuality," and suggests that his stepmother's mother, Grandmother Lewis, made the southern past live for him. Kathryn Lee Seidel in "Seeing the South: Ideology, Vision, and Visual Arts in Stark Young's *So Red the Rose*" (pp. 80–92) sees uniqueness in Young's use of art objects, portraits, and photographs in his most popular work to communicate the values, aspirations, and self images his planter class held dear. She gives her thesis complexity in noting that Young's admiration for such self-esteem does not prevent his readers from drawing their own conclusions about the inequity and oppression that sustained it. Veronica A. Makowsky whets our appetites to read Young's stories in her "Mothers and Invention in *The Street of the Islands*" (pp. 68–79) as she argues that the concern with abstractions that ruins Young's novels for many readers works in this 1930 collection of six stories and five vignettes, which establishes patterns of masculinity and femininity and traces the power and decline of maternal love as well as the gestures used to sustain it. G. Frank Burns's "Art and Society: Stark Young's Theory of Literary Form" (pp. 55–67) is essentially a discussion of novels *The Torches Flare* and *River House*, a fictional rendering of Anton Chekhov's *The Cherry Orchard*, as reflecting Young's theory of art, one emphasizing the wholeness of organic (agrarian) society rather than the disorderliness of modern industrial society and "thoroughly consistent with the principles stated over and over again in his career as a drama reviewer." V. F. Gutendorf's "Stark Young: A Critic for All Seasons" (pp. 41–54) makes a strong claim for Young as the finest American theater critic of the first half of this century, at the forefront of a group of men who established serious native theater (George Jean Nathan, Joseph Wood Krutch, John Mason Brown, and Brooks Atkinson). Gutendorf says that Young was distinguished even among these for his experience in production, direction, and design, and as a translator. Young's theories emphasized art over message; in his reviews the legendary performances of Eugene O'Neill, Thornton Wilder, and Tennessee Williams plays live on. Adeline R. Tintner continues her literary archaeology in "James's Legendary Letter to Stark Young Surfaces" (pp. 8–16), quoting from the recently uncovered original of Henry James's letter to "the young man from Texas." Tintner reviews the circumstances occasioning the writing of the letter and speculates that Young, who shared James's love of theater, may not have been as indifferent to the Master's fiction as he sometimes boasted. In "'Aristocrat' and 'Commoner': The Professions and Souths of Stark Young and William Faulkner" (pp. 93–100), Susan Snell speculates on why Young was not as helpful as he might have been in launching Faulkner into print, concluding that differences in class, age, and address—Young was at home in New York and Faulkner in Oxford—were contributing factors.

A new issue of *Kalki* (8,iv[32]) kept alive the reputation of James Branch Cabell through comparisons to Faulkner. In "Cabell and Faulkner: Connections, Literary and Otherwise" (pp. 271–75), Joseph M. Flora reads Faulkner's reference to *Jurgen* in his Appendix to *The Sound and the Fury* as an acknowledgment of his debt to a fellow southerner who preceded him in working out the tensions of his heritage by creating a mythical country. Carvel Collins compares Cabell's and Faulkner's uses of myth in "Likeness Within Difference:

Cabell and Faulkner" (pp. 276–83). While Cabell put the mythical on the surface and rejected surface realism, Faulkner, benefiting from James Joyce's experiments, preserved the realistic surface but placed beneath it a mythical substructure. The saga of the imaginary country was not of prime concern to either; each planned the arrangement of his collected works unchronologically to clarify themes. "Manuel as Savior of Poictesme" by Harlan L. Umansky (pp. 284–90) sees the contribution to Cabell's mythical kingdom of the elusive subject of the Biography of Manuel as defined by his followers' need to live by dreams rather than reality. In "Cabell's Journey to Antan" (pp. 301–04) Desmond Tarrant discusses the real theme, missed by "hundreds" of reviewers, of *Something About Eve* as man's attempt, despite his nature, at spiritual fulfillment. "*The Duchess of Malfi* and *Jurgen*: The Shadow as Conscience" by W. L. Godshalk sees the Webster play as one of the immediate sources for the detachable shadow in *Jurgen*. Allen R. Swope's "The Cabell-Bailey Correspondence: 1945–1949" (pp. 293–300) introduces the printing of five Cabell letters to naturalist Harold H. Bailey and Bailey's wife, Laura, concerning the restoring of a deteriorating vacation spot once dear to the novelist. Cabell's letters over a four-year period record his own decline and the passing of his literary reputation.

After experiencing the energy devoted to Young's and Cabell's work, one wonders why a novelist of quality like Ellen Glasgow (and I might add Elizabeth Madox Roberts) receives so little attention. The single contribution on Glasgow is a biographical one by David L. Ribblett, "From Cross Creek to Richmond: Marjorie Kinnan Rawlings Researches Ellen Glasgow" (*VC* 36:4–15), which tells of the frustrations encountered in the last year of her life by the author of *The Yearling* in interviewing Glasgow's ex-fiancé, Henry Anderson, and maid, Anne Bennett, for a proposed biography of the Virginia novelist, and of her encouragement in the project by Cabell.

Among westerners Wister and Rölvaag receive ongoing if scanty attention. "Musical and Literary Influences on Owen Wister's *The Virginian*" by Gerald Thompson (*SAQ* 85:40–55) emphasizes, among other "influences," Richard Wagner's Ring of the Nibelungs and the Bible, paralleling Lohengrin and Wister's hero, the Grail scenes in *Parsifal* and scenes on the Virginian's honeymoon island, and Mosaic law and the code of the West. While these are significant comparisons, others are forced; equating "martyred" cattle rustler Steve with St. Stephen and the Virginian with St. Paul, for example, diminishes

Thompson's more valid insights. Forrest G. Robinson's "The Virginian and Molly in Paradise: How Sweet Is It?" (*WAL* 31:27–38) is a fine analysis of the implications of a paragraph near the end of Wister's popular novel in which the hero betrays the "three competing dimensions" to his interior life: the pull toward a free but cruel natural code, the pull toward the constraints and order of civilization, and the pull toward the oblivion of innocence and death. Robinson suggests also that our view of Molly Stark is colored by a narrator in love with the hero and jealous of her. The most comprehensive of the Rölvaag pieces, "The Great Plain: Rölvaag's 'New World Sea'" by Emilie De Grazia (*Literature and Lore of the Sea*, pp. 244–55), considers *The Third Life of Per Smevik*, *The Boat of Longing*, *Pure Gold*, and the trilogy (*Giants in the Earth*, *Peder Victorious*, and *Their Father's God*) as studies of alienation from the sea, the consequences of which in Beret lead to denial of sexual passion and in Per Hansa, his son, and other heroes to a search for substitutes in a landlocked environment "that, however faintly reminiscent of the motions of the sea, has hardened and trivialized original natural longings." "Rölvaag's Beret as Spiritual Descendant of Ibsen's Brand" by Priscilla Homola (*SDR* 24,ii:63–70) places Per Hansa's wife in *Giants in the Earth* with the tragic hero of *Brand* as stern pietists who victimize worldier loved ones—Beret, her husband, and Brand, his mother; then contrasts the spiritually isolated Beret with Brand's wife, Agnes, who shares her husband's ideals, and concludes by noting that, unlike the Ibsen characters, neither Beret nor Per Hansa experiences tragic vision. Einar Haugen in "'Dear Sara Alelia': An Episode in Rölvaag's Life" (*NAS* 31:269–82) records the tracking down of a mysterious, "restricted" Rölvaag letter, which is included at the end of her article, to a female admirer in Norway. Through correspondence between 1924 and 1931 Mimmi Swensen (Sara Alelia of the letter) provided response from Norway to Rölvaag's output as he tried to sweeten her chronic bitterness and share with her his views on writing and his philosophy of realism. Finally, Jennifer Bradley's "Woman at the Golden Gate: The Last Works of Gertrude Atherton" (*WS* 12:17–30) summarizes the California novelist's use of San Francisco, especially in the books after her return to the city in 1931 (*The House of Lee*, *The Horn of Life*, and *Golden Gate Country*), as typical of the United States and as an appropriate setting for exploring the efforts of women to succeed in professional employment. Although Atherton minimized the difficulties faced by women in attaining success, some of her work is less optimistic and describes the dangers women encounter: "Its final message is that even with talent, luck, and help from friends, the woman who lacks self-criticism and a specific, self-directed program for achievement, dooms herself to disappointment."

Brigham Young University

14. Fiction: The 1930s to the 1960s

Virginia Spencer Carr

i. "Art for Humanity's Sake"—Proletarians

***a.* Richard Wright, Edmund Wilson, and Others.** Joyce Ann Joyce's compact book, *Richard Wright's Art of Tragedy* (Iowa), studies Wright's ingenious use of language in *Native Son* to illuminate the dichotomies in the life of Bigger Thomas and the process by which Wright "synthesizes these dichotomies." Joyce's fresh look at the structure, setting, characterization, point of view, and technique of *Native Son* supports her argument that Bigger Thomas is not merely a victim of his environment and caught condition as a black; he is a tragic hero. She also presents an enlightening discussion of Wright's *The Long Dream* as a bildungsroman.

Wright was the subject of several notable essays in 1986, including Louis Tremaine's "The Dissociated Sensibility of Bigger Thomas in Wright's *Native Son* (*SSF* 14,i:63–76), which argues that by "looking at, rather than away from, Wright's handling of character, plot, and narration, one discovers that these elements point directly to a dissociated sensibility lying at the heart of Bigger Thomas," whose essential dilemma is his continuing inability "to express his emotional experience in ways that make its meaning accessible both to his own consciousness and to the consciousness of those around him." It is this conflict between experience and expression, his "dissociated sensibility," that makes of Bigger Thomas a "mass of unsatisfied urges" that define his existence. A recurring motif in the novel is that Bigger's need is to communicate, yet his instinct is to dissemble. Tremaine suggests that the lawyer Max should not be taken as a mouthpiece for the Communist party, but for Bigger himself as a "fantasy come true." Also of note is Robert James Butler's "The Function of Violence in Richard Wright's *Native Son*" (*BALF* 20:9–26). Butler examines the body of criticism pertaining to Wright's preoccupation with violence—Cowley, Baldwin, Nathan Scott, Cecil Brown, Addison Gayle, and others have considered Wright's use of violence "compulsive"—then argues that Wright was "always in full artistic control." Butler sees Bigger as a "richly imagined character" with a "soft and humane" side to his temperament that "naturally responds to what he perceives as the opportunities of America"; yet he is caught up in a world that forces upon him the dehumanizing options of "numbing apathy and destructive violence." Butler rejects views critical of Wright for Bigger's murder of Mary (some call it fortuitous) and sees Bigger's act as essential to the revelation of his divided self. Wright reveals a world that "encourages and even necessitates fear and hatred but violently blocks love and understanding at every stage." Certainly worth reading, also, is Tony Magistrale's comprehensive "From St. Petersburg to Chicago: Wright's *Crime and Punishment*" (*CLS* 23:59–70), which addresses important similarities between *Crime and Punishment* and *Native Son* and Wright's admitted debt to Dostoevski, who "heightened Wright's awareness of the psychological dimensions of physical space" and gave him a model of the criminal mind. Another interesting essay is John E. Loftis's "Domestic Prey: Richard Wright's Parody of the Hunt Tradition in 'The Man Who Was Almost a Man,'" (*SSF* 14: 437–42), which likens the story to such other initiation tales as Faulkner's contemporaneous "The Old People," yet with certain "parodic implications" that reveal the dramatic "disparity between black and white possibilities of growth and development in American society." Loftis concludes that Wright succeeds in a "sophisticated manipulation" of a complex literary tradition, the hunt, to embody his vision, and that he is by no means the crude, careless, or "technically unpolished writer" that some critics have labeled him. "*Black Boy* and the Trauma of Autobiographical Rebirth" by Donald Gibson (*Callaloo* 9:492–98) provokes interest in Wright's autobiographical writing by considering the ways that the imagination alters one's self-perceptions in writing that is thinly disguised as fiction, both in organization of materials and emphasis. Gibson compares Wright's rendering of his own self-portrait in *Black Boy* with the treatment of the same material by a literary biographer. An excellent piece of scholarship is Yoshinabu Hakutani and Toru Kivchi's "The Critical Reception of Richard Wright in Japan: An Annotated Bibliography" (*BALF* 20:27–61), listing 134 items published through 1984.

The Fifties: The Diaries of Edmund Wilson, ed. Leon Edel (Farrar, Straus & Giroux), depicts a more staid Wilson than do the journals of the '20s, '30s, and '40s. Wilson kept his later diaries and journals with greater regularity than those which recorded his earlier years, and it is obvious that he intended them to be published. *The Fifties* is largely a retrospective journal of the man, the critic, and the artist. The entries are more formal and stylistic, recording a happening, encounter, or observation of a recent time rather than summarizing the date of entry.

T. Dan Young's *Conversations with Malcolm Cowley*, another splendid book in the Literary Conversations Series of the University Press of Mississippi, handily supplements Cowley's own *And I Worked at the Writer's Trade* (Viking, 1978). Lay readers, scholars, and writers alike will be interested in Cowley's observations of other writers of his generation whom he knew firsthand, and of the effects of their successful careers and fame upon their relationships with each other. Cowley ranked Faulkner (whom he edited), Hemingway, Dos Passos, Fitzgerald, and "possibly Wilder and Wolfe" as the most important American writers of his time, then added: "Wolfe I have very mixed feelings about." Of Hemingway he ventured: "As a man in relation to other writers—Dos Passos, for instance—his ethics were lower than a snake's belly." Of the many splendid interviews and conversations in the collection, several stand out, including "Thirty Years Later: Memories of the First American Writers' Congress" (by Daniel Aaron, Malcolm Cowley, Kenneth Burke, Granville Hicks, and William Philly) and Joseph Haas's brief interview/essay of 1971, "Malcolm Cowley: Literature Was a Substitute for Religion in the Twenties." Donald Faulkner's "A Conversation with Malcolm Cowley" and John King's "Cowley: He Found the Lost Generation" are fine concluding essays.

Glenda Weathers's "The Territorial Imperative in *Studs Lonigan*" (*SAQ* 51:101–13) examines the manner in which James T. Farrell develops his naturalistic trilogy by documenting Lonigan's ritualistic and sexually motivated actions according to Darwinian theory. Weathers concludes that Farrell portrays Lonigan—and Irish-Catholics in general—as victims of territorial forces.

Robert L. Heath's *Realism and Relativism: A Perspective on Kenneth Burke* (Mercer) is a cogent and illuminating study of Burke's search for a vital aesthetics (in which there is a "dramatatistic connection between idea, action, and artist appeal") and his evolution of a rhetoric of careful consideration of the sociology of shared perspectives. Burke's perspectives and his vital concern for the state of the country are set against the politics of the times, most notably the

'20s and '30s. His early goal, posits Heath, was a search to understand how language could be used to achieve artistic appeal, and, later, how writers and words may serve society. His literary experiments and his lapse from the conviction that certain truths guide social order and human relations left him an avowed relativist. By advocating a view of language that stresses action rather than literal naming, Burke demonstrates how symbols are more than names for things, hence his commitment to linguistic realism. Despite the careful references to Burke's work and to that of other critics, Heath's study would be more useful to scholars if he had included a selected bibliography of primary and secondary sources. Essays of note on Burke are Clayton W. Lewis's "Identifications and Divisions: Kenneth Burke and Yale Critics" (*SoR*, 22:93–102) and David K. Rod's "Kenneth Burke and Susanne K. Langer on Drama and Its Audience" (*QJS* 72:306–17). Lewis uses the deconstructionist concepts of "presence/absence" and "text division" to explore the "points of identity and division" between Burke—whose last major work appeared in 1966—and the Yale critics "who swept through literary studies in 1977." Lewis identifies Burke's texts as "social acts which intend to make a difference in the way men and women live," whereas the Yale critics "write texts within the very much reduced boundaries of philosophical and literary discourse." Rod's essay concludes that "neither theorist sees any general need for dramatic performances to be adaptive" and that the dramatic works contain resources "within the formal expressiveness of the work" to elicit the "desired responses from particular audiences." For both Burke and Langer, concern for individual audiences is subordinate "to an emphasis on the expressiveness of the dramatic work itself."

James Thurber's "The Secret Life of Walter Mitty" is convincingly examined by Terry Thompson in "Look Out for that Buick! Mitty vs. Machine" (*NConL* 16,ii:11–12) as man's struggle to cope with the growing mechanization of his simple world and his subsequent victory through fantasy. In "Coitus Interruptis: Sexual Symbolism in 'The Secret Life of Walter Mitty'" (*SSF* 23:110–13), Hal Blythe and Charles Sweet discuss the phallic symbolism in Mitty's daydreams from which the story's unity is derived. Mitty places himself in daydreams of heroic postures in which he can assume control and compensate for his inadequacies in real life. Mrs. Mitty physically interferes with Walter's fantasies, dominating his life and robbing him of sexual control.

Naomi Diamant's "Linguistic Universes in Henry Roth's *Call It Sleep*" (*ConL* 27:336–55) treats the novel as a truncated bildungsroman and demonstrates how it employs Yiddish as the normative language to establish boundaries. The exterior landscape of Roth's novel is "represented by a series of concentric circles, determined by linguistic criteria."

***b.* John Steinbeck, John Dos Passos, and Others.** John H. Timmerman's *John Steinbeck's Fiction: The Aesthetics of the Road Taken* (Oklahoma) makes excellent use of other Steinbeck scholarship and many of Steinbeck's previously unpublished letters. Timmerman carefully traces the evolving artistic beliefs and techniques at the center of everything Steinbeck wrote and appraises his work in juxtaposition with his declared aesthetic standards for excellence and his "strong, true purpose." Timmerman notes Steinbeck's use of biblical allusion and animal imagery, his genius for characterization, and his teleological and nonteleological thinking, and he sees Steinbeck both as realist and daring symbolist whose fiction is best read for its revelation of human nature through character and for his genius with language. Important shorter works on Steinbeck include Ray Lewis White's "*The Grapes of Wrath* and the Critics of 1939" (*RALS* 13[1983]: 134–64) and Kiyoski Nakayama's annotations of "Steinbeck Criticism in Japan: 1981–1983" (*StQ* 19:12–19). White confirms that contemporary reviewers of *The Grapes of Wrath* (the essay annotates 110 of them) wrote of the "same cruxes" that scholars have addressed repeatedly in subsequent decades, such as the author's maturity since his previous work, the "effectiveness of the intercalary chapters," the coarse language, the "individuation or compositeness" of characters, the "political implications of individual social responsibility," the combining of art and propaganda, and the consideration of *The Grapes of Wrath* as "The Great American Novel." White notes, too, the comparisons made of *The Grapes of Wrath* with social novels by Hugo, Dickens, Tolstoy, Stowe, Zola, Sinclair, and Lewis. In its "breadth and scope" reviewers were reminded of the poetry of Whitman and the novels of Wolfe, Dos Passos, and Margaret Mitchell. They also drew parallels with the poetry of MacLeish and the films of the '30s.

Overlooked last year was Donald Pizer's excellent essay, "The 'only words against POWER SUPERPOWER' Passage in John Dos Passos' *The Big Money*" (*PBSA* 79:427–34), which examines Dos

Passos's method of composition revealed in an early draft and in the setting copy. Central to recent approaches to *U.S.A.*, says Pizer, is the realization that Dos Passos "attributes the failure of American life principally to our failure to maintain the strength and integrity of American ideals as they are expressed in the 'old words' of the American Dream." Pizer points out that in *U.S.A.*, Dos Passos demonstrates how the resultant "corrupt warping of language and thus of all feeling and expression affects every range of experience." Words may be "all we have against the power of the Harlan County sheriff." Although the Camera Eye persona in Dos Passos's text accepts that America is "two nations," Dos Passos realizes that the "informed understanding can, through art, reveal the injustice of this condition and thereby seek to regenerate and make operative the ideals of America enshrined in the old words." A 1986 essay by Pizer, "The Hemingway-Dos Passos Relationship" (*JML* 13:111–28), is a superb tracing of the long and complex relationship of Hemingway and Dos Passos, their break after a long friendship, and their subsequent brooding in the form of autobiographical portraiture and fictional caricature, which Pizer sees as a "largely unconscious attempt by each writer to project into the other some of the tormenting anxieties of his own psychic life and thus of his work as a whole." A book-length study by Pizer of Dos Passos's writings through *U.S.A.* is forthcoming.

Kay Boyle: Artist and Activist (So. Ill.) by Sandra Whipple Spanier is the first book-length study devoted solely to the work of Boyle and is long overdue. Researched with Boyle's cooperation and laced with letters from Boyle correcting, emending, or supporting Spanier's readings, the book is both a well-written critical biography, and, to a degree, autobiography. It traces Boyle's development as an artist and assesses the author's remarkable achievement from the '20s, when in France her "life and art became permanently entwined," to the '80s, including Boyle's recent fiction and essays on political and social issues. Spanier's study should provoke new acclaim and critical interest in Boyle, who is one of the finest stylists of the 20th century and a writer of great social conscience.

Two essays of note on Harriette Simpson Arnow are William J. Schafer's "Carving Out a Life: *The Dollmaker* Revisited" (*AppalJ* 14:46–50) and Nancy Carol Joyner's interview "Harriette Simpson Arnow" (*AppalJ* 14:52–55). Schafer admits that the book's "over-fussy phonetic spelling" is sometimes "so peculiar as to defeat its own purpose of making the talk audible," that the novel sprawls with "too many Dickensian waifs and eccentrics shuttling in and out of its pages," and that the ending may be "too reminiscent of Tom Joad's vision at the end of *The Grapes of Wrath.*" But he also calls *The Dollmaker* a "masterly achievement" and a "noble effort of the imagination" that is "too big and too serious to ignore." Joyner catches well the spirit of Arnow and her region through her questions about Arnow's Kentucky rearing and early interest in storytelling, her attitude toward being labeled an "Appalachian writer," her writing apprenticeship, and her opinion of other writers.

An entertaining biography with a breezy style and diction that is often outrageous, yet quite fitting for its subject, is Leslie Frewin's undocumented *The Late Mrs. Dorothy Parker* (Macmillan). Dorothy Parker fans may want to take a look at a previously unpublished short story, "Spain, For Heaven's Sake!" (*Mother Jones* 11, February–March:40–42), which reportedly evolved from an admirer's response upon reading Parker's 1939 article in *The New Masses* complaining that she could not get "serious pieces about the issues of the day accepted" because she was known strictly as a humorist. The woman urged Parker to keep doing what she did "so well" and to leave the "so-called serious writing to others," which is precisely what Parker did. Parker as poet is the subject of a brief piece by Ruthmarie H. Mitsch, "Parker's 'Iseult of Brittany'" (*Expl* 44,2:37–40), which reviews the Tristan and Iseult legend, then examines how Parker seizes its essence in two stanzas by shifting the point of view to a minor character in the legend, thus revealing in characteristic fashion her "pessimism with bite just beneath the polite surface."

ii. Southerners

***a.* General.** Only two books of general interest seem worthy of mention this year, last year's *Images of the Southern Writer* (Georgia, 1985) by Mark Morrow and Richard Gray's *Writing the South.* Morrow's book is notable for its 48 splendid photographs of the South's leading contemporary poets and fictionists taken from 1979 to 1983 and for the sensitive yet revealing biographical commentary accompanying each picture. The introduction is by Erskine Caldwell, who probably surprised no one by his comment that he never reads other writers.

***b.* Robert Penn Warren, the Agrarians, and Others.** Mark Lucas's tidy volume, *The Southern Vision of Andrew Lytle* (LSU), examines carefully Lytle's *Bedford Forrest and His Critter Company* as his "accession to a tradition" and a southern identity, surveys his involvement in the Agrarian literary movement, and notes the continuity of Lytle's agrarianism from *I'll Take My Stand* to his book of family memoirs, *A Wake for the Living* (1975), which, says Lucas, makes readers "intensely aware of the currents of time and change" in Lytle's culture. An especially insightful chapter concerns Lytle's "career shift from polemical to fictional expression and the dense social texture of Lytle's fictional world." Lucas also directs the reader's attention to the intricate layering of Lytle's most important work, *The Velvet Horn*, which is also the subject of Thomas M. Carlson's essay, "A Reading of Andrew Lytle's *The Velvet Horn*" (*SoR* 22: 15–36). Carlson concentrates on the importance of Jack Cropleigh's use of language and his progression from a confusion of words to an informed and informing rhetoric, then carefully explicates Lytle's work, chapter-by-chapter, and points to the mystery of Joe Cree's death and Lucius's parentage as unifying elements in the novel. Carlson's treatment of symbol is excellent, and he employs Lytle's commentary to illuminate and support his own interpretation. The essay gives careful attention to all of the novel's major characters, but Carlson's understanding of Jack's personality, actions, and central importance seems especially complete. This article is a significant contribution to study of *The Velvet Horn*.

William Bedford Clark's "Robert Penn Warren's Love Affair with America" (*SoR* 22:667–79) is a superb discussion of Warren's interest in and concern with the American past, present, and future. Clark begins with a brief examination of Warren's poem "Bicentennial," which indicates not only the poet's concern for the state of the nation at that time, but his belief in its potential. The critical perspective that coexists in Warren's writing with faith in America's creed is central to his often ambivalent feelings about the country. Clark uses interviews with Warren and his speeches to create a coherent picture of Warren's ideology. Important to Clark's study, also, is Warren's role as a "social historian" and his belief in the artist's social function. For Warren, the strength of the society depends upon its individuals and their sense of "selfhood," and literature is a means of getting in touch with the self. His admiration for Jeffersonian vision is combined with a profound awareness of its deficiencies. Warren is convinced of the importance of studying history and is concerned about the tendency of Americans to ignore their past with a self-satisfied and mistaken sense of invincibility. Clark observes that Warren's faith in the nation is tempered "by an acknowledgement that, being merely human, we often promise ourselves more than we can deliver—or have bargained for." The essay is a lucid study that expands critical understanding of Warren and his work.

A fascinating interview that brings out the poet's characteristic wit and careful consideration is Tom Vitale's "A Conversation with Robert Penn Warren" (*OntarioR* 25:5–13). The Warren of the interview is an active poet who has great admiration for other writers and a strong sense of his own history and artistic formation. His account of the genesis of *All the King's Men* is particularly interesting, as is his recollection from youth of a mandatory training in the memorization and recitation of poetry. Warren sees himself as a poet and stresses the danger of "self-imitation." In response to Vitale's question about the evaluation of a poetic line, Warren replied, "You have to have more of a context. But the line itself must fully be what it means." Then he demonstrated his idea with a well-chosen line from *Antony and Cleopatra.* Vitale's questions are well directed and designed to elicit such engaging responses as Warren's remark that "any poet's work is a long attempt to define himself."

Warren is included in the series "The State of Letters: The Critics Who Made Us" (*SR* 94:99–111), in which Monroe K. Spears presents a refreshing study of Warren as critic. Spears discusses Warren's major critical works, including the textbooks *Understanding Poetry* and *Understanding Fiction* (coedited with Cleanth Brooks), *Selected Essays* (1958), and *Democracy and Poetry* (1975). Despite Warren's unwillingness to present himself as a critic, observes Spears, his literary analyses and theories have been widely influential. In *Understanding Poetry* Warren and Brooks espoused a method of literary analysis based on close attention to the text and an awareness that poetry belongs to "the everyday world of experience and change, which it interprets and which it can affect." As a critic, Warren is detached from any particular critical theory and works from a moral and democratic stance, often tending toward historical or biographical interpretations. He is also a devoted advocate of the authors in whom he recognizes genius and can often be seen writing about himself as he comments on their works. Spears's article is interesting, and he achieves his goal of presenting Warren's strength as a critic.

Jan Nordby Gretlund's "The Last Agrarian: Madison Jones's Achievement" (*SoR* 22:478–88) is a solid biographical and critical study. After a brief background sketch of Jones's life, Gretlund summarizes each of the author's novels, from his first effort, *The Innocent* (1957), to his recent work, *Season of the Strangler* (1982). Gretlund places Jones at the end of the agrarian tradition, pointing to his concerns about disappearing southern traditions and the problems of the modern South. Although Jones's view is essentially a pessimistic one, his novels always contain characters who maintain their integrity in the face of upheaval. According to Gretlund, Jones illustrates the individual's dependence on society, while suggesting "that every individual is ultimately responsible for his own actions." Gretlund's discussions of all of Jones's novels are useful and sound, but the attention directed toward the popularly unsuccessful novels such as *Forest of the Night* (1960) and *Passage Through Gehenna* (1978) and the unpublished collection, *Tales of Dixie*, is particularly timely and fills a need in Southern literary studies.

c. Flannery O'Connor, Eudora Welty, and Carson McCullers. One of the best studies of writers of the modern South is Louise Westling's *Sacred Groves and Ravaged Gardens: The Fiction of Eudora Welty, Carson McCullers, and Flannery O'Connor* (Georgia), which thoughtfully examines the interrelations of a coherent, distinctively feminine literary tradition. As Westling points out, much of what is unique and most powerful in the writings of Welty, McCullers, and O'Connor stems from their experience as women in a society that "officially worshipped womanhood but in its imaginative life betrayed troubled, contradictory undercurrents." Unless they are seen "fully in this light," explains Westling, their work will be judged by ill-fitting standards. Westling posits that nowhere else in American literature "is there a group of accomplished women writers so closely bound together by regional qualities of setting, character, and time," and that the writings of Welty, McCullers, and O'Connor are richly illuminated by mutual comparison. By concentrating on their treatment of the problems of identity, on the role of the mother and on attitudes and relationships of characters with their mothers, on the ways in which men are perceived, and on the "distinctively female uses of place and symbol" in their writings, Westling defines superbly the differences of these writers as well as their similarities and concerns as women.

Outstanding book-length studies devoted wholly to O'Connor are Frederick Asals's *Flannery O'Connor: The Imagination of Extremity* (Georgia), Harold Fickett and Douglas Gilbert's *Flannery O'Connor: Images of Grace* (Eerdmans), Edward Kessler's *Flannery O'Connor and the Language of the Apocalypse* (Princeton), Marshall Gentry's *Flannery O'Connor's Religion of the Grotesque* (Miss.), and *The Correspondence of Flannery O'Connor and the Brainard Cheneys*, ed. Charles Ralph Stephens (Miss.). Kessler's splendid volume in the Princeton Essays in Literature series places O'Connor in the company of such apocalyptic poets as Blake and Eliot, and contends that only through poetic metaphor could O'Connor "shatter the mirror held up to external nature and declare that fiction is neither true nor false—but fiction." By using lively metaphors and "exposing counterfeit speech," O'Connor was able to transform and transfigure the "phenomenon of straightforward, referential prose," and, through such verbal strategies, to engage the unknown for what Eliot spoke of as "raids of the inarticulate." Gentry's study examines astutely the paths toward redemption taken by the author's major characters, who unconsciously use the grotesque to redeem themselves despite narratorial bias. Of Gentry's five groups of characters who achieve redemption, only one, the innocents, redeem themselves without using the grotesque. Yet redemption remains for O'Connor an abstract, idealized moment, the specifics never quite clear, insists Gentry. Stephens superbly edits the lively and informative exchange of letters between O'Connor and the Brainard Cheneys, and his work nicely complements Sally Fitzgerald's hefty volume of O'Connor correspondence.

Significant short studies of O'Connor's work include Nancy Ann Gidden's "Classical Agents of Christian Grace in Flannery O'Connor's 'Greenleaf'" (*SSF* 23:201–02), which argues that O'Connor's common theme of Christian grace is combined subtly with classical myth (sun/Apollo, bull/Dionysus) "in the service of Christian conversion." John Ower's "The Penny and the Nickel in 'Everything that Rises Must Converge'" (*SSF* 23:107–10) demonstrates that the physical features of the coins and their associations illuminate the attitudes of the characters and the major themes through a web of associations. The Jefferson nickel, for example, is seen both as suggestive of the aristocratic heritage from which Julian's mother draws her values and of the rituals of human equality toward which Jefferson worked. A. R. Coulthard's " 'Keela, The Outcast Indian Maiden': A Dissenting View" (*SSF* 23:35–41) is a refreshing and well-documented interpretation that runs contrary to critical consensus. Instead of viewing the tale as a parable of racial oppression and guilt, Coulthard sees it as a comic account of a pathetic loser who casts himself as a remorseful villain in an attempt to be "somebody." Shirley Foster's "Flannery O'Connor's Short Stories: The Assault on the Reader" (*JAmS* 22: 259–72) is a fine discussion of O'Connor's comic and ironic use of calculated undermining of the reader's expectations and of her ability to shock and puzzle. Still another essay of note is William E. Meyer's "Flannery O'Connor's 'Two Sets of Eyes' " (*SoSt* 3:284–94). Meyer focuses on the conflict of O'Connor's "two sets of eyes" (the Catholic church and the eyes of her own locally rooted observations) and categorizes O'Connor's characters into visionaries, children with a propensity for blind faith, "judgmental female observers," and "intellectual eyeballs."

Louise Westling's "Flannery O'Connor's Revelations to 'A' " (*SHR* 20:15–22) is an engaging study of the correspondence between O'Connor and the as yet unidentified "A" and of the effect of A's probing comments on O'Connor's writing. According to Westling, this correspondence, which began in 1955 and ended in 1964, clearly shows how "A" forced O'Connor to face the sexual "ambivalence" in her writing and her reluctance to accept femininity. Through intelligent and insistent questions concerning the nature of violence and sexuality in O'Connor's work, "A" not only revealed things to O'Connor about her writing that she had not recognized, but actually influenced O'Connor's later writing. Westling draws on the letters to examine O'Connor's use of female characters who are or will be defeated by a male force of some kind. Westling's account of the correspondence is engaging, and she applies what the letters reveal about O'Connor to the stories themselves. Another study of O'Connor's correspondence is Ashley Brown's "An Unwritten Drama: Susan Jenkins Brown and Flannery O'Connor" (*SoR* 22:727–37). Interesting both from a literary and historical perspective, Brown's article presents letters of O'Connor, Susan Jenkins Brown, and Caroline Gordon concerning the possible dramatization of O'Connor's work. Ashley Brown points out that this exchange of letters is typical of the period, for many southern writers sought advice concerning the theatrical potential of their work. William Rodney Allen's complex and convincing article, "The Cage of Matter: The World as Zoo in Flannery O'Connor's *Wise Blood*" (*AL* 58:256–70), provides an exploration of O'Connor's use of the zoo as a symbol of the human condition. Agreeing with recent critical consensus that defends *Wise Blood's* structure and unity, Allen examines O'Connor's blending of images of animals and confinement to create the zoo metaphor. Two short works worthy of attention are D. G. Kehl's intriguing study, "Flannery O'Connor's Catholicon: The Source and Significance of the Name 'Tarwater' " (*NConL* 15,ii:2–3), and Terry Thompson's "The Killers in O'Connor's 'A Good Man Is Hard To Find' " (*NConL* 16,iv:4), a thoughtful examination of O'Connor's use of ironical names. Important always is the annual *Flannery O'Connor Bulletin*, which this year includes eight very different essays: Ted R. Spivey's revealing "Flannery O'Connor's Quest for a Critic" (pp. 29–33); John R. May's excellent "The Methodological Limits of Flannery O'Connor's Critics" (pp. 16–28); Kenneth Scouten's " 'The Partridge Festival': Manuscript Revisions," recounting some of the frustrations of working with O'Connor's manuscript (pp. 35–41); Bill Oliver's convincing "Flannery O'Connor's Compassion" (pp. 1–15); Mary Whitt's "Flannery O'Connor's Ladies" (pp. 42–50); Michael Heher's "Grotesque Grace in the Factious Commonwealth" (pp. 69–81), Gary M. Ciuba's "The Fierce Nun of *The Last Gentleman*: Percy's Vision of Flannery O'Connor" (pp. 57–66); and Victoria Duckworth's "The Redemptive Impulse: *Wise Blood* and *The Color Purple*" (pp. 51–56). All are worthy of detailed comment, but space does not permit.

Floyd C. Watkins's "Eudora Welty's Natchez Trace in the New World" (*SoR* 22:708–26) takes its text from "First Love," "A Still Moment," and *Robber Bridegroom*, Welty's three fictional works that present the spirit and history of early America and the "double vision" therein. According to Watkins, this double vision grows out of coexisting opposite tendencies in frontier life, violence and tragedy vs. humor and joyfulness. Watkins also writes of the coexistence of the real and the imaginary or fantastical, a coexistence that blurs the limits of fact and makes history seem like fiction and vice versa. The supernatural settings of these stories are unique in Welty's fiction, points out Watkins, who sees these tales of early America as "apt versions of America's real and fairy tale beginnings." Carey Wall's "Eudora Welty's *Delta Wedding* and Victor Turner's 'Liminality' "

(*SoSt* 25:220–34) is a substantial examination of the theme of change in Welty's novel as seen in terms of the theories of Victor Turner, a renowned anthropologist. After aligning himself with those critics who view change in the novel as a positive force, Wall attempts through an application of Turner's theories to disprove John Edward Hardy's contention that the novel lacks a unified action. Wall sees the Fairchilds existing in a period of "liminality," which Turner defines as "the process by which people produce changes in the structures by which they live." Wall applies the tenets of Turner's theory to *Delta Wedding* in exacting detail by drawing connections between the theory and its actualization by the novel's characters. His ultimate aim is to show that change is a positive force and that the collective actions of the Fairchilds create the "concerted action" which the novel has been accused of lacking. Wall's article is probing and clear, considering the complexity inherent in his thesis. An excellent and comprehensive essay is Suzanne Marrs's "The Metaphor of Race in Eudora Welty's Fiction" (*SoR* 22:697–707), which examines the roles of black characters in *Delta Wedding* and *The Golden Apples*. Although Welty's focus in most of her fiction is upon the white population, her fictional depiction of black life is rich and complex. According to Marrs, the black characters in these two works both actually and symbolically represent Welty's themes of human separateness, the simultaneous freedom of blacks from white society and their oppression under it, and superstition and the acceptance of mystery. Marrs posits that Welty "uses these aspects of black life to develop her major themes, themes which extend to all life."

A nearly exhaustive effort, executed in the manner of the French *explication de texte*, is Charles Clerc's "Anatomy of Welty's 'Where Is the Voice Coming From?'" (*SSF* 23:389–400). Clerc provides excellent discussions of Welty's use of interior and dramatic monologue, the story's background in fact, and the history of its creation. In his study of the narrative persona, Clerc draws an interesting correlation between modern psychological theories of the assassin personality and Welty's fictional assassin. This article provides a wealth of information and should be of value to readers of Welty's story. Essential to Welty scholars is Pearl Amelia McHaney's expansive "Eudora Welty Checklist: 1973–1986" (*MissQ* 39:651–98).

Alice Hall Petry's "Baby Wilson Redux: McCullers's *The Heart Is a Lonely Hunter*" (*SoSt* 25:196–203) is a convincing refutation of Oliver Evans's contention that the Baby Wilson shooting incident has little connection to the main narrative. Petry views the incident as central to the novel and argues that it exemplifies an important theme for McCullers concerning the nonrealistic roles that people impose upon others, which lead, in turn, to their own abject disappointments and downfalls.

Three important books have emerged on Lillian Hellman since her death in 1985: William Wright's *Lillian Hellman: A Life* and *Lillian Hellman: The Image, The Woman* (both Simon & Schuster), and *Conversations with Lillian Hellman*, ed. Jackson Bryer (Miss.). Wright's in-depth biography reveals a formidable personality whose "combative reflexes" put off most people with whom she came in contact. It was also Hellman's "refusal to go the way of a good second-rate playwright" that irked her critics more than anything else, insists Wright. The book is notable, too, for its debunking of the image presented in Hellman's several books of memoirs, for its candid portrait of Hellman's propensity for untruths and her ability to "manipulate truth," for its treatment of what lay behind Hellman's controversial defamation suit against Mary McCarthy (an action that evoked extraordinary agreement and support for McCarthy, whose televised accusations of Hellman's habitual lying had prompted the suit), and for its revelation that Hellman's "Julia"—reportedly her friend—was someone Hellman never knew. Wright presents the actual Julia (Muriel Gardiner Buttinger), whose life closely parallels the woman in the book. An excellent companion study for Hellman scholars and lay readers alike is Jackson Bryer's *Conversations with Lillian Hellman*, in the Literary Conversations series of the University Press of Mississippi. Arranged chronologically, the items span Hellman's long and colorful career as playwright, film writer, and memoirist. In light of Wright's revealing biography, the most interesting interviews are those in which Hellman ventures her opinion of other playwrights and her own plays and movie scripts, and discusses her Hollywood blacklisting and feelings about Hollywood and the film industry in the '30s and '40s, the ramifications of her statement before the House Committee on Un-American Activities, and her involvement with Dashiell Hammett and his effect upon her work.

Lillian Smith, A Southerner Confronting the South (LSU) by Anne C. Loveland is an informative and useful first major book on Smith which retrieves the author from much of the obscurity she feared and resented at the hands of reviewers, editors, and such organizations as the National Institute of Arts and Letters, which in

1965 awarded her $500 from the Artists and Writers Revolving Fund "as a gesture of appreciation" for her accomplishments. Smith returned the check, declaring that to accept it would be "humiliating," since the organization had not seen fit to grant her an award for any of her books or to offer her membership. Loveland's scholarly narrative reveals meticulous research executed with the cooperation of Smith's family and of her close friend and professional associate, Paula Snelling. But the book seems less an engaging biography than a compendium of reportage concerning the life and controversial career of a woman who was far ahead in her time in Georgia in her social consciousness and civil rights activism. The reader is told a great deal about the author of *Strange Fruit*, *Killers of the Dream*, *The Journey*, *One Hour*, *Now is the Time*, *Our Faces, Our Words*, and *Memory of a Large Christmas*, but misses the sense of immediacy in Loveland's tale-telling that makes a biography especially engaging. Scholars would appreciate, also, a bibliography of Smith's work and a chronology. This book confirms that Smith will be remembered chiefly not for her novels—or even for one novel, *Strange Fruit*—but for her relentless fight for integration and human rights in the South.

The work of Katherine Anne Porter attracted little attention in 1986. "Porter's 'The Jilting of Granny Weatherall'" (*Expl* 44,ii:37) by Robert Meyers contributes to the group of theories concerning the identity of the mysterious individual who had supported Ellen Weatherall when she almost fainted with embarrassment upon the realization of her jilting. Meyers argues convincingly that in her confused memory Ellen is thinking of her father, who is the only likely candidate for the enraged outburst.

An important addition to Wolfe studies is Jimmie Carol Still Durr's essay, "*Look Homeward Angel*, Thomas Wolfe's *Ulysses*" (*SoSt* 24:54–68). Durr examines Wolfe's extensive indebtedness to Joyce, often underestimated by other critics yet evident in numerous comparisons between *Ulysses* and *Look Homeward, Angel*. Both Joyce and Wolfe were concerned with autobiography, and both employed stream-of-consciousness techniques. Durr also mentions the two writers' love of language and their attempts to expand the limits of expressiveness. In addition to sharing a belief in the dignity of the commonplace, both employed the themes of human isolation and the search for a father. Durr is careful to point out that Wolfe's debt to Joyce does not diminish his own standing as an artist. This well-written and thought-provoking essay is thoroughly evidenced.

iii. Expatriates and Émigrés—Miller, Nabokov, and Rand

Although J. D. Brown's *Henry Miller* (Ungar) is a tidy and well-written introductory study of Miller's life and work, the most eminently readable and informative book on Henry Miller in 1986 is Leon Lewis's *Henry Miller: The Major Writings* (Schocken). Lewis's survey of Miller's "acolytes and adversaries" is a useful overview of Miller scholarship, and his illuminating discussion of Miller's life and works confirms the reasons for Miller's extraordinary and enduring appeal. Lewis considers the development of Miller's narrative consciousness parallel to Camus's conception of rebellion (as set forth in *The Rebel*) in that Miller "decided to stop trying to adjust to a world which was rejecting all of his best efforts to get along" and chose instead to "construct his life and his art in terms of a personal rebellion that finds meaning in *anything* that the self does." Lewis, who likens the boldness and arrogance of Miller's proclamations in *Tropic of Cancer* to Whitman's barbaric yawp, posits that Miller was almost never in "the right place at the right time," having arrived in Paris after the original "lost generation" had returned to America, and later having settled in Big Sur when he was "too old to be anything other than an example to the Beat writers in California." Lewis sees much in Miller that forecasts the direction of post-World War II literature in America, yet believes that he was "too much the humanist and Yankee individualist to really become *un homme revolte*." Miller is "built out of F. R. Leavis's 'Great Tradition' more than one would suspect," continues Lewis, and he cannot go "far enough back into primitive America or far enough forward into unknown country to stake out his own ground."

Of interest, too, is *Dear, Dear Brenda: The Love Letters of Henry Miller to Brenda Venus* (Morrow), written when Miller was in his mid-eighties, divorced from his fifth wife, largely bedridden, and reportedly "mad with love." Of limited appeal is Kathryn Winslow's *Henry Miller: Full of Life* (Los Angeles: J. P. Tarcher), a chatty, informal memoir by a friend who met Miller in 1944 soon after his move to Big Sur and opened "M" in Chicago's Jackson Park art colony, a gallery and bookshop to help relieve Miller's financial distress by selling his work and giving him most of the proceeds. For ten years "M" was a gathering place for readers who admired Miller's work, says Winslow, as well as for avant-garde painters, writers, poets, and sculptors who sought there an oasis in "the desert of Chicago."

Essential to Nabokov scholars is Michael Juliar's *Vladimir Nabokov: A Descriptive Bibliography* (Garland), which is thoroughly indexed, including first lines. Also important is Andrew Field's exhaustive and revealing *V.N.: The Life and Art of Vladimir Nabokov* (Crown), which has been described as a "brilliant piece of detective work and analysis," especially given the fact that Nabokov "designated in his will that his personal papers could not be made public until seventy-five years after the deaths of his wife and son." A fascinating and revealing interview is Emory George's "Remembering Nabokov: An Interview with Victor Lange" (MQR, 25:479–92). The informed and well-directed questions to Lange, a colleague of Nabokov's at Cornell for 10 years, provoke insightful recollections regarding Nabokov's unorthodox but effective teaching style, his eccentricities and character traits, his "aristocratic perspective" on the world, his theories concerning the translating process, and his keen sense of worth as a writer. Other excellent Nabokov scholarship includes D. Barton Johnson's "The Labyrinth of Incest in Nabokov's *Ada*" (*CL* 38:224–55), David Galef's "The Self-Annihilating Artists of *Pale Fire*" (*TCL* 31[1985]:421–37), Marianna Torgovnick's "Nabokov and His Successors: *Pale Fire* as a Fable for Critics in the Seventies and Eighties" (*Style* 20,i:22–41), J. H. Garrett-Goodyear's " 'The Rapture of Endless Approximation': The Role of the Narrator in *Pnin*" (*JNT*: 192–203), and Lance Olsen's "A Janus-Text: Realism, Fantasy, and Nabokov's *Lolita*" (*MFS* 32:115–26).

Although Barbara Branden refers to her book on Ayn Rand as a biography, Branden lacks the biographer's essential objectivity because of her own personal relationship with Rand. *The Passion of Ayn Rand* (Doubleday) is an intimate memoir that covers Rand's early years with a wide-angle lens, then moves in for close-ups in which Branden herself is seldom beyond camera range. Branden and her husband Nathaniel had a tightly bonded, 19-year friendship with Rand and her husband, Frank O'Connor. The Brandens were first devoted pupils of Rand's, then disciples and teachers of her controversial philosophy. All seemed harmonious until Nathaniel Branden (Rand's "intellectual heir") and Rand became lovers, with the consent of their spouses. That Branden could write about it at all with some measure of objectivity is extraordinary in itself, for the lives of all four were shattered, and only she survived to tell the tale. Although the book contains almost no documentation, its substance having been derived chiefly from dozens of interviews before their breach and from the intimacies of their shared lives, Branden's story rings true. It will shatter many illusions about the philosopher/author whose cultist teachings (and her two best-sellers, *The Fountainhead* and *Atlas Shrugged*) won for her as many disciples as outraged critics.

iv. Easterners and Westerners

Wallace Stegner is the subject of an outstanding interview by Suzanne Ferguson entitled "History, Fiction, and Propaganda: The Man of Letters and the American West: An Interview with Wallace Stegner" (*Literature and the Visual Arts*, pp. 3–22). The interview was intended to concentrate on Stegner's environmentalism and its relation to his fiction, but it became a wide-ranging discussion of the themes recurrent in both his fiction and nonfiction. Ferguson identifies those themes as "the visionary courage of those who explored the West and wrote its story in the nineteenth and early twentieth centuries, the nature and value of various kinds of writing and the role of the writer in dealing with real and invented materials, the difficulty of matching a commitment to life, the present destruction of natural resources, and the American ideal of public service." Stegner is convinced that art and propaganda are separate; yet throughout his career he has also "courted the danger of the 'contamination' of his art by his convictions about the world." He speaks of the "new nonfiction fiction"—whose genesis is often attributed to Capote—as something he himself had done many years earlier in his "Joe Hill book," *The Preacher and the Slave*, and proposes that the genre goes back at least to *An American Tragedy*.

Cheryl J. Plumb's *Fancy's Craft: Art and Identity in the Early Works of Djuna Barnes* (Susquehanna) is a slim volume that views Barnes's work against a background of symbolist assumptions and methods and notes how consistently Barnes's writings focus on moral integrity and on the superior sensibility, represented in her work by artist figures. Whereas most critics have emphasized Barnes's dark vision and privateness at the "expense of the embattled vitality at the center of her work," Plumb examines Barnes's techniques of style and literary experimentation and the moral awareness of her characters that alternately repel and attract her readers. Plumb attributes Barnes's being on the outside of the American literary mainstream to the difficulty of her prose and its demands upon readers of "discerning engagement," to her frank treatment of women's sexuality (which provoked only temporary interest), and to her emergence into an American literary tradition dominated by the realism and naturalism of Crane, Dreiser, Norris, Lewis, and Anderson, who were less daring in subject matter and verbal experiment. Plumb agrees with criticism that Barnes's characters are often types, but also argues that the author is successful in combining abstract suggestion with psychological intensity.

A well-informed essay on Bernard Malamud is Joel Salzberg's "Irremediable Suffering: A Reading of Malamud's 'Take Pity' (*SSF* 23:19–24). According to Salzberg, critics have overlooked important aspects of Malamud's story by focusing too much attention on the thematic center. Salzberg gives a thorough reading of "Take Pity," pointing out the way in which the Holocaust and the poverty of the Depression bring dual meaning to the comedic narrative. Salzberg's excellent comparison of Malamud's Eva with Melville's Bartleby exemplifies his adept positioning of "Take Pity" in a literary and critical context. Charles E. May's "Something Fishy in 'The Magic Barrel' " (*SAF* 14:93–98) is a readable article which sets out the critical controversy concerning Malamud's narrative technique. May asks whether the reader is to read the story as realistic fiction or fairy tale, since the story opens in a fairy-tale manner and quickly moves to realism. In addition to being sound Malamud criticism, May's article contains good ideas for reading any work of fiction, suggesting that the reader allow the world of reality and imagination to mesh with his own imagination. A brief piece worthy of mention is Arthur Coleman's "*The Iron Mistress* and *The Natural*: Analogue or Influence?" (*NConL* 16:11–12). Coleman analyzes the "close allegorical and thematic resemblance" between Paul I. Wellman's *The Iron Mistress* and Malamud's *The Natural*, both of which concern legendary heroes (Jim Bowie and a baseball player) who share similar upbringings and are portrayed as invincible.

v. Iconoclasts and Innovators

Warren French's *Jack Kerouac* (TUSAS 507) is one of the best of the recent volumes in the series. Especially useful to Kerouac scholars is the chapter entitled "The Town and the City," a study of his last major work, *Vanity of Duluoz*, which he wrote to replace *The Town and the City* and the much earlier *Maggie Cassidy.* Taken together, these early and late books present a consistent picture, concludes French, who is not as fond of the novel *Desolation Angels* as he is of the others. Contrary to the opinion of many critics, French does not think Kerouac succeeded in the total canon in creating a legend; rather, he provided his countless readers over the years with a "remarkable case study of Kerouacism."

Sanford Pinsker's "*The Catcher in the Rye* and All: Is the Age of Formative Books Over?" (*GaR* 40:953–67) argues the importance of Salinger's novel as the formative book of the decade for him and for most other readers who grew up in the '50s.

In "A Novel of Despair: A Note on Nathanael West's *Miss Lonelyhearts*" (*Neophil* 703:475–78), Helge Normann Nilsen agrees with other critics who view Miss Lonelyhearts's quest for order as religious in its intensity, but argues cogently that the novel conveys complete metaphysical disillusionment without any hope for redemption. Dieter Schulz's "Nathanael West's *A Cool Million* and the Myth of Success" (*Studien zur englischen und amerikanischen Prosa*, pp. 164–75) argues that the key to the merits of *A Cool Million*, aesthetic and otherwise, lies in West's parody of the Horatio Alger success novels. Schulz in this splendid essay points out that West refused to commit himself to any of the current ideologies; yet, "paradoxically, the West of *A Cool Million* came as close as anyone to an aesthetic realization of an insight that is essential to Marxism." He also came to terms with the American Dream and bourgeois ideology.

One of the most important books of the year is Jeffrey Miller's carefully prepared and invaluable *Paul Bowles: A Descriptive Bibliography* (Black Sparrow), which reveals the full range of Bowles's versatility as poet, novelist, short fictionist, translator, set designer, and composer. The book is well indexed and should be a boon to collectors of Bowles's books, music, and memorabilia. *Out in the World: Selected Letters of Jane Bowles, 1935–1970*, edited by her biographer, Millicent Dillon (Black Sparrow), has been long awaited by readers who have appreciated the scant writings of Jane Bowles (most notably her play, *The Summer House*, and her novel, *Two Serious Ladies*) and know something of her physical illnesses and gradual decline into madness. Most of the letters in this collection were written to Bowles's husband, Paul, and are filled with references to such people as Tennessee Williams (who considered her the "most underrated writer in American literature"), Truman Capote, Oliver Smith, Cecil Beaton, Gore Vidal, Audrey Wood, and countless other well-known persons whose lives touched hers and her husband's over the years. The letters are candid and revealing, but the collection as a whole would have been better served had the editor provided a fuller introduction and more context.

H. P. Lovecraft provoked no new books or major articles in 1986, but last year's *Lovecraft Studies* (spring and fall) brought forth some good essays by Barry Bender, Donald Burleson, S. T. Joshi, Steven Mariconda, Will Murray, and Robert Price.

Daniel Dickinson's "What Is One to Make of Robert Heinlein?" (*MFS* 32:127–31) is a comment on the social messages in the novels *Stranger in a Strange Land* and *The Moon is a Harsh Mistress.* Dickinson points out the contradiction in Heinlein's personal philosophy between his claim to write only for the money and his messages to the reader to the contrary. He divides Heinlein's writing into three periods and notes the changes in Heinlein's new fiction, particularly the 1982 novel *Friday.*

A fine first biography of S. J. Perelman is Dorothy Hermann's *S. J. Perelman: A Life* (Putnam's). Hermann comments that it was work on her first book, *Malice Toward All* (a study of prominent Americans of the 20th century who were both "blessed and cursed with the gift of social wit"), that led her inevitably to the writing of Perelman's intimate biography. Hermann was intrigued by Perelman, who seldom had "a good word to say about anyone, but always had a witty one." Perelman, like John Dos Passos, compartmentalized his friends. He knew a great many people, but few knew anything about the existence of his other friends or the nature of their relationship. For example, Max Wilk, who also published a book on Perelman in 1986 (a memoir that records a friendship begun in 1969 when they met in London while Wilk was writing for British television and film), is not even mentioned in Hermann's book. Readers would be interested in juxtaposing Hermann's life of Perelman with Wright's biography of Hellman or with Bryer's collection of interviews with Hellman, since Perelman and Hellman were in New York and Hollywood during the same periods and knew many of the same people. Wilk's book, *And Did You Once See Sidney Plain?* (Norton), subtitled *A Random Memoir*, is a slight and not very witty one. Although the drawings by Al Herschfeld are splendid and Wilk's sense of timing in his lightly dropped anecdotes is rather nice, the name-dropping and self-indulgence that characterize the minichapters will probably put off most readers.

vi. Detectives

A fine collection of essays for enthusiasts of police and detective fiction is *Cops and Constables: American and British Fictional Policemen*, ed. Earl F. Bargainnier and George N. Dove (Bowling Green). An especially notable essay is Barrie Hayne's historical overview, "Anthony Abbot's Thatcher Colt" (pp. 10–32), which places Colt in the tradition of the omnipotent detective and second only to Ellery Queen as the heir to Van Dine. An informative introduction by the editors (pp. 1–8) defines and contrasts the British detective and policeman with his American counterpart. Whereas the figure of the police detective who teams up with an intelligent amateur is fairly common in British fiction, it is virtually nonexistent in American tales. According to Bargainnier and Dove, the British policeman tends to perceive patterns by backing away from the situation and taking "the broad view" (and tends to verbalize what he is thinking); the American policeman "throws himself into the middle of it" and talks "only about the necessity for getting on with the job." Dove, who edited the seven "cops" essays, supplies a splendid one himself—"John Ball's Virgil Tibbs and Jack Tallon" (pp. 43–54). Mary Jean DeMarr's sensitive "Dell Shannon's Luis Mendoza" (pp. 69–85), reveals the bleak texture of Mendoza's world of criminality and brutality, a world relieved only by his few brief hours of hearth and home. Bargainnier's six "constables" essays are notable, also.

Chandler's work is the subject of two recent book-length studies: Peter Wolfe's *Something More Than Night: The Case of Raymond Chandler* (Bowling Green, 1985), published too late for last year's *ALS* essay, and William Marling's *Raymond Chandler* (TUSAS 508). Wolfe devotes considerable attention to a psychological dissection of Chandler's character. Especially interesting is his examination of the prominence of sadism and homoeroticism in Chandler's work, supporting the popular view that Chandler's detective hero, Philip Marlowe, is a repressed homosexual. Whereas critics have condemned Chandler for his vicious stereotyping of minorities, Wolfe offers excerpts that present minorities more favorably. Marling provides an excellent biographical introduction to Chandler and acknowledges his debt to Frank MacShane's *The Life of Raymond*

Chandler (1976), calling it "meticulously researched" and "carefully and fairly written." Marling surveys the Chandler criticism and deems Chandler a superior writer to Hammett, with whom he is most often compared. He also argues that Chandler has transcended the bounds of crime fiction in which earlier critics confined him, but that he has not received his due as a serious writer.

Georgia State University

15. Fiction: The 1960s to the Present

Jerome Klinkowitz

If literary criticism were as systematic as art history, we would have no lack of labels for the ongoing styles of fiction and critical response. Literary epochs, however, roll by more slowly than the frantic gallery-directed parade of Abstract Expressionist, Pop, Op, Hard Edge, Minimal, Superreal, and New Symbolist approaches; and so when a genuinely new style of writing is named, the occasion is noteworthy. No matter that the term, "Minimalism," is borrowed from art and that its characteristics remind one of the superrealistic or photorealistic paintings of Richard Estes and Ralph Goings. In 1986 critics and scholars directed considerable energy, with occasional intelligence and insight, into trumpeting this new theme, the first identifiable movement in contemporary American fiction since the great wave of innovation in the 1960s.

i. General Studies

First noticed in *ALS 1985* (p. 288) with guest editor Kim Herzinger's special issue of *Mississippi Review* (nos. 40–41), Minimalism has spread across the spectrum to be the most frequently studied topic this year. Alan Wilde's "Shooting for Smallness: Limits and Values in Some Recent American Fiction" (*Boundary* 13:343–69) reconsiders Donald Barthelme's fear that a "stubbornly persisting humanist heritage" would not release its grip on fiction evolving from an ahumanist, postmodern age. New realists such as Joan Didion, Ann Beattie, and Raymond Carver "grudgingly take for granted" the controllable world made in man's image that distinguishes humanist values. Yet these contemporaries hardly see such stability as a value; it is, instead, a "leaden, enthralling certainty that everything wearies, stales, and disappoints," which brings these writers into conformity with the postmodern critiques of Heidegger, Foucault, Barthes, and Derrida. Picking up a theory from Herzinger's special issue, Sven Birkerts speculates in "The School of Lish" (*New Republic* 13 October:28, 30–33) that Gordon Lish, former editor of *Esquire* now at Knopf and a fixture at writers' conferences and MFA programs, has fostered a style of realism identifiable as "the natural effluence of an electronically connected, stimulus-saturated culture." Birkerts attacks this style as "an abrogation of literary responsibility" which fails to venture anything more than "a passive recollection of fragmentation and unease," the same charges neoconservative critics made against innovative writers who had deserted realism two decades before. That surface predominates over depth is clear from *Esquire*'s annual August fiction issue, which E. L. Doctorow introduces as an example of the storyteller's authority to "make and remake the world," but which in its presentation implies that the camera has both the first and last word: each story is prefaced by a lavish full-page color portrait of the author on location, posed "in character" (Thomas McGuane on a Key West dock imagined from *Ninety-Two in the Shade*, Louise Erdrich as the barefoot Indian maiden, fair of face), the collection ending with Harold Brodkey, Derek Walcott, Barry Hannah, Jim Carroll, Anderson Ferrell, and—heading the parade as "Captain Fiction"—Gordon Lish himself, all of them modeling clothes by Henry Grethel and Sero. As with rock music videos, a phenomenon contemporaneous with Minimal fiction, more care has been taken with the visual presentation than with the product itself; the photos cost more than the stories, and may well have dictated the fiction's selection. In "A Few Words About Minimalism" (*NYTBR* 28 December:1–2, 25), John Barth traces the evolution of this form from ancient sources and ascribes its current eminence to "our national hangover from the Vietnam war," the energy-crisis reaction against excess and wastefulness, declines in writing and reading skills, loss of attention spans, and a reaction against the irony and dense intellectualism of the previous decade's innovations. In general, our culture has tired of an advertising-induced verbal overkill, and hence younger writers are literally driven to understatement in order to be noticed.

Positive or negative, the culture is presently awash in consideration of this Minimalist trend, with anthologies and special issues devoted to both fictional examples and critical debates. The best of the former is editors Robert Shapard and James Thomas's *Sudden Fictions* (Peregrine Smith Books), which complements 70 stories with an extensive group of comments from authors, editors, and critics on the phenomenon devoted to "seeing the structure of the work in its entirety." A more ponderously moral tone bogs down the discussion in "The Writer in Our World," a special symposium issue of *TriQ* (65), in which Terrence Des Pres, Carolyn Forché, Mary Lee Settle, and several other writers and critics talk in elegant circles around Benjamin DeMott's complaint that fiction no longer contains "a full responsiveness to life." This familiar despair with the present can be traced to a deliberate short-sightedness. DeMott declines to recognize any criticism more avant-garde than his own (and that having been formulated over two decades ago), and editor Reginald Gibbons has shown his own bias elsewhere in *TriQ*, taking the vast majority of stories in the journal's quarter-century anthology from his own recent tenure and disregarding the quite different style of work published by founder Charles Newman and his successor Elliott Anderson. A more balanced and much more extensive range of consideration is offered in *Critical Angles* (So. Ill.), where editor Marc Chénetier assembles 13 younger scholars from England and Western Europe for fresh looks at authors as diverse as Walker Percy and Gilbert Sorrentino. Rather than decry losses, Chénetier's critics examine what is actually present in these texts, and find that by broadening their view beyond "the endless series of humanistically inclined commentaries" one can see how referentiality itself can become a stylization (Alide Cagidemetrio), that author-reader relationships are as complex as any human ones (Heide Ziegler), that any narration is a form of exile from the real (Claude Richard on Percy's *The Moviegoer*), and that "the energy of an absence" can generate a workable intimation of perfection (Johan Thielemans on William Gaddis and Gilbert Sorrentino). New light is shed on the polar extremes of innovative and Minimal fiction in Régis Durand's and Marc Chénetier's complementary essays on these movements' two leading figures, "On the Pertinaciousness of the Father, the Son, and the Subject: The Case of Donald Barthelme" (pp. 153–63) and "Living On/Off the 'Reserve': Performance, Interrogation, and Negativity in the Works of Raymond Carver" (pp. 164–90). Rather than unveil and decipher (a modernist practice), Barthelme adopts a Lacanian dramaturgy of performance, an effect in which the subject "pulsates" its active presence. Carver, the supposed realist, uses ambiguity and suspension to destabilize his own subject and clarify its existence as a product of competing visions, fusing his stories "so that they detonate a few minutes after one has read them."

Among more particularized interpretations of the contemporary are two fine collections published by Greenwood Press, editor Stanley Trachtenberg's *The Postmodern Moment* and editor Larry McCaffery's massive (and nearly exhaustive) *Postmodern Fiction*. Trachtenberg joins the sentiment expressed by contributor Philip Stevick ("Literature," pp. 135–56) that against modernism's rage for "summary insight" the postmodern fictionist "repeats, parodies, slows things down" by emphasizing the "performative rather than revelatory, superficial rather than immanent, aleatory rather than systematic, dispersed rather than focused." McCaffery's 600-page volume shows how in three decades the experiments of postmodern fiction have moved in directions toward science fiction (Welch D. Everman), parafictional journalism (John Hellmann), metafiction (Sarah E. Lauzen), feminism (Bonnie Zimmerman), the poetic (Ron Silliman, Fred Moramarco), and textual bases for realism (R. Radhakrishnan). Tom LeClair's "Postmodern Mastery" (pp. 117–28) praises the control of vast extremes evident in the meganovels of Barth, Coover, Heller, McElroy, Pynchon, and DeLillo, which are "texts of bliss" as much as any of the reductive works favored by Roland Barthes. LeClair feels there is a latent "literary authority" within postmodern uncertainty which justifies these expansive views; in "Experimental Realism" (pp. 63–78) I disagree, finding that close attention to surface action yields the same priority of performance over product that characterizes the most abstract innovative fiction.

Both Trachtenberg's and McCaffery's volumes speak of the necessary reformation of the canon so that postmodern achievements can be counted for something else besides the obvious lack of modernist and humanist qualities that DeMott and the *TriQ* panelists regret. Sacvan Bercovitch's *Reconstructing American Literary History* would seem to present just such an occasion, but its only contemporary fiction analysis is Wendy Steiner's thoroughly conventional "Collage or Miracle: Historicism in a Deconstructed World" (pp. 323–51), in which one novel solidly within the canon—Pynchon's *The Crying of Lot 49*—is read in the context of Eliot's *The Waste Land*, which indicates certain obvious differences between modern and postmodern values but which does little to answer questions argued by the *TriQ* and Greenwood Press contributors. More pertinent is Richard

Kostelanetz's *The Grants Fix* (RK Editions), which demonstrates how the vested interests and self-serving practices of public grants organizations use a humanistic, antiexperimentalist bias to encourage work on outmoded, academically "safe" subjects, while branding anything that challenges the status quo as "incompetent." A companion to Kostelanetz's *The End of Intelligent Writing* (1974) which showed how fiction was shaped by commercial pressures, *The Grants Fix* helps explain the overtly conservative and self-rewarding nature of the National Endowment for the Humanities, whose history reveals a funding of redundant scholarship while consistently ignoring innovative work (which hindsight now demonstrates to have become the new mainstream, albeit without the help of public funding).

Other extraliterary influences on the form of fiction are explored in "Penned In" (*CritI* 13:1–32) by Richard Stern, who finds that the International PEN Congress contradicts the writer's essential solipsism—enforced collegiality throws this natural talent off balance. In "Poets Who Write Fiction: 'What's Your Primary Form?'" (*Coda* 13,v:1, 14–19), Susan Mernit learns that Marge Piercy, Erica Jong, Rita Dove, May Sarton, W. S. Merwin, Mark Strand, George Garrett, and John Balaban feel compelled to write both fiction and poetry because to stick to just one form would show they are "outdated" and leave too much writing time unused.

Literary theory continues to enhance readings of fiction, most rewardingly in Marcel Cornis-Pop's "Inside a Stratified Whale: Melville's Textual Semiotics and the Postmodern Novel" from editor John Deely's *Semiotics 1985* (Univ. Press, pp. 286–301), which takes the layering of texts in *Moby-Dick* as a device for understanding the rhetoric of narrative structuring and destructuring central to the work of Kurt Vonnegut, Steve Katz, and Richard Brautigan. Game theory informs John Kuehl's "The Ludic Impulse in Recent American Fiction" (*JNT* 16:167–78), from the typography of Raymond Federman's *Double or Nothing* through the alphabetical play of Gilbert Sorrentino's *Splendide-Hôtel* and Walter Abish's *Alphabetical Africa* to the interplay of multiple texts in Sorrentino's *Mulligan Stew*. William C. Dowling's "The Death of the Game in Contemporary Baseball Fiction" (*MQ* 27:344–60) takes Jim Bouton's *Ball Four* as an example of how conventions of an athletic contest can be "exploded" to provide a new narrative structure; while Johan Huizinga's *Homo Ludens* encourages an idyllic view of baseball as a lazy stream through summer as celebrated by Roger Angell and John Updike, Bouton redirects this focus from the larger community back to the actual conduct of the game and season. The postmodern visions of Ihab Hassan, Roland Barthes, and William H. Gass (as a critic) inform Christopher Butler's excellent "Skepticism and Experimental Fiction" (*EIC* 36:47–67), where Abish's *How German Is It?* and Barthelme's *Great Days* respond to recent skeptical readings of illusionary realism in both philosophy and literary theory, replacing the transparent with the opaque.

Two book-length surveys—the fewest by far in recent times—and two volumes of commentary by fictionists themselves round out the year's general critiques. In *Passionate Doubts: Designs of Interpretation in Contemporary American Fiction* (Iowa), Patrick O'Donnell suggests that the very process of interpreting the author's supposed lack of voice creates a presence beyond the intertext. Those limits which postmodern fiction strives to exceed—origin, frame, and temporality—keep reappearing, if only as shadows or secrets, in the work of Hawkes (a linguistic self paradoxically suppressed in *Travesty*), Barth (whose *Letters* consumes itself in reduplicated narrative orders), Pynchon (*Gravity's Rainbow* as a book of traces), and Elkin (whose *The Franchiser* celebrates the plurality of worlds and interpretations). My own *The New American Novel of Manners* (Georgia) finds Richard Yates, Dan Wakefield, and Thomas McGuane employing the semiosis of Roland Barthes to both generate and express their own narrative actions of signs at work in a culture, bringing the novel of manners back into postmodern currency. A bracing lyrical spirit informs fictionists Michael Stephens's *The Dramaturgy of Style* (So. Ill.) and Paul Metcalf's *Where Do You Put the Horse?* (Dalkey Archive). Stephens explores the fiction of Hubert Selby, Gilbert Sorrentino, Teresa Cha, and Stephen Dixon to show how the genre's "imaginary landscape is evoked by virtue of a voice that sees," a process analagous to the dramatist's and actor's art of evoking the sense of something "happening for the first time" by virtue of pacing, rhythm, and tone. Metcalf ranges more widely and more critically, faulting John Gardner for limiting himself to "the decadence of the conventional novel form" when the materials of *The Sunlight Dialogues* demanded so much more, and praising Guy Davenport for mining the more nativistically American resources of particulars which refuse to congeal as conventions say they should.

ii. Isaac Bashevis Singer, Norman Mailer, Philip Roth, and Chaim Potok

Jewish-American writers have joined their colleagues from the American South in abandoning their previous "separatist core" and assimilating more general traditions, Jules Chametzky suggests in *Our Decentralized Literature* (Mass.). Singer avoids the paralysis of history and filial pieties by becoming the epic chronicler and celebrant of well-lived lives; Roth expands his region of interest beyond Bellow's by counseling that "the *neighborhood* is *over*"; coincidentally, William Styron shifts the action of *Sophie's Choice* into this newly integrated neighborhood as a way of moving beyond the categories previously defining his writing. Roth's allegiance to the mannerist tradition is reaffirmed in Adeline R. Tintner's "*The Prague Orgy*: Roth Still Bound to Henry James" (*Midstream* 31,x[1985]: 49–51), in which Henry James's *The Middle Years* links the Zuckerman trilogy with this newly written epilogue. Ranging even more widely through the culture is the Norman Mailer characterized by Laurence Goldstein in *The Flying Machine* as a reconciler of two worldviews whose self-conscious struggle with words reflects the transformation of will reported in *Of a Fire on the Moon*. *Why Are We in Vietnam?* also shows cultures in conflict, from machine power versus the wilderness to the overkill of bombers and helicopters as opposed to the ritual of a bear hunt. The only writer discussed within the Jewish-American tradition this year is Chaim Potok, whose interview with Elaine M. Kauvar (*ConL* 27:291–317) centers on the conflicts and rewards inherent in religious belief (with asides on Picasso and Freud as influences on his isolation of characters and interpretation of history); *Davita's Harp* is discussed with the focus on its heroine, the first woman in Potok's work as a central character.

iii. William Styron, Walker Percy, and Anne Tyler

Scholars and critics feel that writers of the American South, unlike contemporary Jewish-Americans, are maintaining a special status for their fiction. Even though the decades since World War II have effaced differences and cost the South its "unique subject to teach," these writers' "systems of perception have survived material change," says Richard Gray in *Writing the South.* Styron's *Sophie's Choice* perfects this "amphibious" capability by being part old and part new, discussing its own making as a disengagement from the South while the terms of those discussions keep it emphatically southern in perception. Walker Percy and John Barth try to reject the South, but the most successful in forging a new style is Barry Hannah, whose new voice couched in a jazz-rock rhythm is defiantly postmodern. Yet the deepest thinker remains Percy, who wonders why mankind is so sad in this century of pleasure and plenty, and finds an answer by "demoting" the South's models of belief to acknowledge a world now amorally avoiding the responsibility of sin.

Styron shows his mastery of parody by playing with texts inside his narrative, according to Lucille M. Schultz in "*Lie Down in Darkness*: A Story of Two Processions" (*SLJ* 18,ii:62–75); Styron's reversals establish the real as fraudulent and vice versa. Taking on a more controversial subject in "A Psychological Redefinition of William Styron's *Confessions of Nat Turner*" (*Third Force Psychology*, pp. 240–61), James R. Huffman claims that earlier critics' inability to explain behavior does not mean these scenes and characters are inexplicable or false. Nat himself is not dehumanized (the Elkins thesis) nor simply neurotic (Freud), but is more responsive to conditions of childhood and dream (Horney's understanding of anxiety).

Walker Percy continues to inspire the best criticism. William Rodney Allen's *Walker Percy: A Southern Wayfarer* (Miss.), while tempted to present a hagiography of the author and an exhaustive exegisis of his critics (all couched with a plot summary of the holy text), combines a good understanding of the generating principle of the novels (protagonists with weak fathers) with Percy's own thematic intent (rejecting a stoic, skeptical heritage). Allen seeks insight among such influences as Mark Twain, Robert Penn Warren, and Ernest Hemingway; in *The Politics of Reflexivity* (Hopkins) Robert Siegle takes a more rewarding postmodern approach to *Lancelot* by plumbing its reflexive commentary as a recurrent pattern of Kierkegaardian existentialism, "a blankness at the heart of the watching and waiting."

A thematic study which would have profited from attention to technique is offered by Anne G. Jones in "Home at Last, and the Homesick Again: The Ten Novels of Anne Tyler" (*HC* 23,ii:1–13), in which "self" seeks a way out of the conflict between the desire for perfect, blissful union and the reality of separation. Homesickness is the result of such an unattainable quest, and Tyler uses this sense to inform tone. Personal psychic growth, family as community, and meditations on mutability are indeed issues of human personality; but as with too much criticism of southern authors, less thought is given to writing technique than to the compelling themes of region and soul.

iv. John Updike and John Cheever

Updike's rich resources allow critics to extend their own theses, James M. Mellard's *Doing Tropology* finding that lyrical expressiveness in *The Centaur* signals a metaphorical return to resonance (in which only our language can capture the already existing "grand images of the world"), Robert Siegle's *The Politics of Reflexivity* reading *Rabbit, Run* as a debunker of boyhood mystiques, revealing the emptiness at the heart of selfhood and the way meshed social relations ensnare the ideal—for Rabbit, inside and out resolve themselves in a final emptiness expressed reflexively in the hero's running (which gets him nowhere). More than once Updike has written novels whose themes (space exploration, African dictatorship) depart from his familiar domestic interests, and in "Updike and Contemporary Witchcraft" (*SAQ* 85:1–9) Charles Berryman considers how *The Witches of Eastwick* presents metaphors for the way artistic practice flirts with its dark roots in deviltry, in the process avoiding the more conventional uses of realism (as in Malamud's *Dubin's Lives* and Bellow's *Humboldt's Gift*) and confession (Roth's Zuckerman triology) to explore this theme.

That mannerists may be Romantics at heart is suggested by Martin Bidney's " 'The Common Day' and the Immortality Ode: Cheever's Wordsworthian Craft" (*SSF* 23:139–51); motifs of sun, prison, heart, and nature link poems and story, with the day's changing modes of sunlight serving Cheever as a prose poem. This process throws words such as "common" and "day" into high relief, enhancing our metaphoric understanding of light. An insightful look at the writer's own behavior is provided by Dana Gioia in "Meeting Mr. Cheever" (*HudR* 39:419–34), where the author spends a week visiting Stanford with his son for freshman orientation and muses about his religious beliefs, view of the writer's role in ordinary life, and stylistic practice.

v. Realists Old and New

The newer issues of realism, from the moral impatience with abstract innovation to the emerging style of Minimalism discussed in *i.*, have eclipsed the attention formerly shared by more established practitioners. John Malcolm Brinnin's *Truman Capote: Dear Heart, Old Buddy* (Delacorte) continues the trend toward viewing Capote as a historical figure most interesting for his impact on one's own life, here an expansion of Brinnin's autobiographical piece in *Sextet.* Establishing the Gardner canon is Jeff Henderson's goal in "John Gardner's *Jason and Medeia*: The Resurrection of a Genre" (*PLL* 22:76–95); challenged with evoking the *epos* of an age long past, Gardner expands his scale and enhances the "moment of significance" so our more skeptical age can understand and sympathize, reflecting his characteristic belief in "the fecundity of time's possibilities and the potential for alternative or even multiple futures." More critical of this self-professed moralist's achievement is Richard Gilman, whose "Novelist in a Mirror" (*NYTBR* 20 July: 11–12) finds his work "tone-deaf and blind to nuance" and pathetic in its clumsy lunging after the "secrets" of existence. "The sad truth is that he was an inconsolable aspirant after literary size and significance, a writer with a hundred maimed styles and so, finally, with none."

How jazz rhythms structure narrative is detailed by Timothy Dow Adams in "A Momentary Stay Against Confusion: Frank Conroy's *Stop-Time*" (*Crit* 27:153–66), while a neoclassical style of intelligence does the job elsewhere, according to Steven Moore in "Alexander Theroux's *Darconville's Cat* and the Tradition of Learned Wit" (*ConL* 27:233–45). George Plimpton's interview, "The Art of Fiction: E. L. Doctorow" (*ParisR* 101:22–47), reveals an author concerned with voice, from how Hemingway's *The Garden of Eden* shows how a familiar style can become an exhaustive trap to Doctorow's own fascination with the techniques of oral history. Different ideas of structure can radically influence characterization, says Steve Yarbrough in "Andre Dubus: From Detached Incident to Compressed Novel" (*Crit* 27:19–27). Contrasting views of myth and time achieve a similar result as described by Peter Clark in "Classical Myth in William Kennedy's *Ironweed*" (*Crit* 27:167–76) and by David Black in "The Fusion of Past and Present in William Kennedy's *Ironweed*" (*Crit* 27:177–83). Thomas McGuane's first collection of stories, *To Skin a Cat*, prompts interviews with Liz Lear in *Shenandoah* (36,ii:

12–21) and Kay Bonetti in *MissR* (9,i:73–99). McGuane tells Lear about his homes and literary influences, and responds to insightful questions about man and nature. Bonetti draws him out on the bad aspects of academic influence and the evolving rise of emotional content in his work which has redirected his intent to be a comic novelist.

Minimalism marks its acceptance into the critical canon with Christina Murphy's *Ann Beattie* (TUSAS 510), in which the writer's craft is praised as "post-postmodern." Beattie uses small spaces as integers, articulating her message with what is *not* said. While critics fault her absence of resolved conflicts, she is in fact a nonmimetic writer striving for indeterminacy and relativism. "Ann Beattie's Children as Redeemers" (*Crit* 27:197–212) by Jane Bowers Hill makes the same argument referentially, that such redemptive figures show "that life may be fragmented and uncertain without becoming meaningless." A similar but far less successful attempt to recast Raymond Carver as a humanist mars Mark A. R. Facknitz's " 'The Calm,' 'A Small, Good Thing,' and 'Cathedral': Raymond Carver and the Rediscovery of Human Worth" (*SSF* 23:287–96), which reads these stories as moral preachment about real people rather than as artistic constructions on the page. Carver has indeed become the fulcrum for critical interpretations of this new, "minimal" style of fiction. He is the first major writer since Hemingway to have a life story as agonizingly dramatic as his fiction, and so the temptation is great to approach his characters in the same spirit with which we respect the struggles of his life. The reverse approach, which critics of the Minimal use just as easily, is to summarize a Carver or Beattie story and lament its lack of "human" dimension and depth, code words which really mean the critic cannot imagine a role in it for Joan Collins. As with any style of fiction, attention must be directed to technique before filling up pages with sermons to the choir about the need for human verities and the "better things" we expect from literature.

More intelligent uses of mimesis—as technique—are made in readings of Bobbie Ann Mason, Jay McInerney, Breece Pancake, and Harry Crews. In "Making Over Or Making Off: The Problem of Identity in Bobbie Ann Mason's Short Fiction" (*SLJ* 18,ii:76–82), Albert E. Wilhelm finds that a thematic contrast between identity formed by tradition and identity demanded by the present lets Mason draw her characters as either doers or seekers ("making over or making off"). Sanford Pinsker's "Soft Lights, Academic Talk: A Conversation with Jay McInerney" (*LitR* 30:107–14) reveals an understanding of *Bright Lights, Big City* as pattern and structure rather than mere topicality. Wilhelm returns with "Poverty of Spirit in Breece Pancake's Short Fiction" (*Crit* 27:39–44), an argument which complements Geoffrey Galt Harpham's contention in "Short Stack: The Stories of Breece D'J Pancake" (*SSF* 23:265–73) that "nondevelopmental revelation of character" remains possible even in Aristotelian terms. Harry Crews, however, continues to be read in terms of his mixture of comedy and violence, a valid but predictable approach used by David K. Jeffrey in "Murder and Mayhem in Crews's *A Feast of Snakes*" (*Crit* 27:45–54).

vi. Joseph Heller, Ken Kesey, Kurt Vonnegut, and Richard Brautigan

Heller's first two novels continue to interest critics, in both cases quite productively. *Catch-22*'s structural complexity draws on dramatically timed flashbacks and reinterpretations of repeated scenes, according to Robert Merrill in "The Structure and Meaning of *Catch-22*" (*SAF* 14:139–52); its three sections provide a perspective for Yossarian's "effective moral response" in which conventional liberalism ascends to fable. *Something Happened* supports James M. Mellard's thesis in *Doing Tropology* that a Lacanian displacement of desire can be expressed in the search for a signifier/phallus; the desire for completeness creates a narrative structure in the end acquiescing to an Oedipal reliance on the imaginary as a substitute for the indeterminacy of symbol. For *Hayden's Ferry Review* (1:99–108) Jay Boyer conducts "A Conversation with Joseph Heller" centering on the novelist's use of Malamud's language in *Good as Gold* and the publishing history of *Catch-22*. "Shifting Roles in the Symbolic Scenario of the 1960s: *Hero* and *Narrator* in Ken Kesey's Fiction" (*Anglo-American Studies* 5:129–44) presents Marcel Cornis-Pop's case for Kesey's fiction reflecting "a type of cultural *intertextuality* characteristic of postmodern fiction," with the interplay of the hero's and narrator's voices speaking for the turmoil of the 1960s. Fred Madden agrees with the counterpoint of these two roles; his "Sanity and Responsibility: Big Chief as Narrator and Executioner" (*MFS* 32:

203–17) presents McMurphy as the individual whose supposedly despicable behavior preserves sanity as opposed to group conformity, while the Chief's narrative distortions express the author's view of the group's dehumanizing practices.

Although resisting the label, Kurt Vonnegut continues to interest critics as a science fiction writer. Joseph Sigman praises his thoughtful and thematically persuasive use of physics, especially as interrelated with theology, in "Science and Parody in Kurt Vonnegut's *The Sirens of Titan*" (*Mosaic* 19,i:15–32). *Cat's Cradle* is a straighter style of SF, Daniel L. Zins suggests in "Rescuing Science from Technocracy: *Cat's Cradle* and the Play of Apocalypse" (*SFS* 13:170–81), which instead of parodying the subgenre's clichés actually uses its techniques to help readers face problems they might otherwise ignore, notably the apocalyptic consequences of failing to rescue science from technocracy. The necessary commitment to historical actuality present in even *Slaughterhouse-Five*'s most fantastic scenes makes Vonnegut just as much a realist as James T. Farrell, Barbara Foley insists in *Telling the Truth: The Theory and Practice of Documentary Fiction* (Cornell); while her range of examples is admirable, her tendency to reduce all innovation, especially the stridently anti-Aristotelian variety, to a replay of simple mimesis oversimplifies the arguments of Robert Scholes, Raymond Federman, Mas'ud Zavarzadeh, and Ronald Sukenick, all of which are dismissed in a two-page cavalcade, the hysteria of which has not been seen since John Gardner's *On Moral Fiction.* Final words on the late Richard Brautigan grace two helpful essays in *Exquisite Corpse* (14:i–ii), Keith Abbott's "Brautigan in Bolinas" (pp. 12–13), which complements last year's regretful accounts of the writer's childhood poverty and adult lack of self-control, and Ed Dorn's "Richard Brautigan: Free Market Euthansia" (p. 13), which recasts him as a humorist, at ease with memories of his childhood and drawing strength from his environment rather than being destroyed by it.

vii. Thomas Pynchon, John Hawkes, Donald Barthelme, and Robert Coover

No major work on John Barth makes 1986 an odd year, but a shift in attention to Robert Coover is a welcome innovation in criticism.

Thomas Pynchon, however, remains an inexhaustible resource, mined with most success by Robert D. Newman. His *Understanding Thomas Pynchon* (So. Car.) sees this author's obsession with naming and identity as an expression of our age's problem with realism; Pynchon appreciates the "fixed identity" of Calvinism's predestination as an escape, but finally rejects it as an abstract distinction which cannot share the middle ground of vitality his fiction celebrates. A fancier of underground movements, Pynchon is a Luddite, his spirited writing style objecting to the "intellectual parochialism that regulates the cultural machinery." In *The Flying Machine* Laurence Goldstein sees *Gravity's Rainbow* as an event in itself, with the rocket as an erotic fantasy in which body aspires to spirit; apocalypse is seen in Puritan terms as a victimization of the world. Campbell Tatham finds a metaphor for textual rearrangement in "Tarot and *Gravity's Rainbow*" (*MFS* 32:581–90), while Lance Olsen's "Deconstructing the Enemy of Color: The Fantastic in *Gravity's Rainbow*" (*SNNTS* 18:74–86) uses fantasy to question structures of both story and culture, including aesthetic and moral tastes, all as a way of crossing over into an area the culture has suppressed. "For Once, Then, Pynchon" (*TSLL* 28:182–208) by Michael Kowalewski finds Pynchon's personal elusiveness consonant with his fictive practice in which "the culturally encyclopedic impulses . . . render him invisible behind all they encompass"; this "incorporative impulse" is explored for its "narrative energy and exuberance," which in turn generates the fiction. *Pynchon Notes* remains indispensable as the major repository of Pynchon scholarship; with such a small canon, the full breadth can be covered in each issue, with the most ground broken by Adrian Emily Richwell in "*The Crying of Lot 49*: A Source Study" (17:78–80), detailing structural similarities with *Oedipus at Colonus*.

In "A Newly Envisioned World: Fictional Landscapes of John Hawkes" (*ConL* 27:318–35), Carol A. MacCurdy studies the unforgettable and provocative verbal pictures which ground Hawkes's imagination; this "dream-energy" releases his fancy from representative constraints, providing "not only his writing process but also his artistic raison d'être" in which imaginative depth balances the conscious level of life. Donald Barthelme's success with a lack of teleological commitment is explored by Thomas M. Leitch in *What Stories Are: Narrative Theory and Interpretation* (Penn. State); his "Daumier" projects surrogates which imply no particular line of development and therefore contradict the idea of an ending even as they end the story itself (a practice Leitch prefers to Vonnegut's arranging teleological opportunities but then not using them). Walter Evans compares a story's structure with that of conventional Westerns in "Comanches and Civilization in Donald Barthelme's 'The Indian Uprising'" (*ArQ* 42:45–52), noting that the reader's knowledge of townspeople-Indian relations is assumed as a convention.

Robert Coover's Fictions (Hopkins) offers Jackson I. Cope's cogent readings of this author's experiments with genre, especially as he expands it to include Mikhail Bakhtin's preference for dialogically multiple relations within the text over the monological sense of authorial control. The carnivalistic allows Coover to use different voices not as competing points of view, in which one or another stands the chance of proving itself correct, but as a vast interplay of textural textuality based on coexistence and interaction. L. L. Lee considers the thematic implication of both Coover's form and content, finding that they are played off "received attitudes" toward the artist (who disappears) and toward formal content (here reshaped as fable), an approach which makes "Robert Coover's Moral Vision: *Pricksongs & Descants*" (*SSF* 23:63–69) an important piece of scholarship. Less helpful because of its unwillingness to see the formal implications of content (here studied for its sexual implications) is Ann R. Morris's "'Death-Cunt-and-Prick Songs,' Robert Coover, Prop." in Jan Hokenson and Howard Pearce, eds., *Forms of the Fantastic* (Greenwood, pp. 209–15).

The best overall study of innovative fiction's central core comes from Janusz Semrau, whose *American Self-Conscious Fiction of the 1960s and 1970s: Donald Barthelme, Robert Coover, Ronald Sukenick* (Posnan, Poland: Adam Mickiewicz University Press) shows how self-consciousness more than compensates for the loss of belief in external reality. For Barthelme the world is fragmentary, for Coover ephemeral, and for Sukenick paradoxical. Yet all three refuse to despair and turn to a reexamination of narrative art, finding that its initial promises of cohesion, presence, and authority were based on axioms no longer workable for their world. Barthelme learns how to employ signs as signs (especially when some of them are lies), while Sukenick transcends Coover's impatience with language to show that it is all that certainly exists. The new fiction they have invented is hence a positive rather than nihilistic event.

viii. Ronald Sukenick, Raymond Federman, and Steve Katz

Janusz Semrau's countryman Jerzy Kutnik provides another example of how Eastern Europeans and especially Poles have been most responsive to the American innovations too often dismissed by stateside critics as being insufficiently moral to merit serious attention. Kutnik's *The Novel of Performance: The Fiction of Ronald Sukenick and Raymond Federman* (So. Ill.) devises a performance theory from the art criticism of Harold Rosenberg, the theater of Allan Kaprow, the music of John Cage, the poetic theory of Charles Olson and practice of Frank O'Hara, the dramatic experiments of Richard Schechner, and the "counter-poetics" of Jerome Rothenberg by which he explicates Sukenick's and Federman's full canon, including their own criticism and theory (each has published major scholarship as well as fiction). Kutnik's advantage is to see that certain problems with realism cannot be resolved with simple readjustments but require "a whole new vision of literature" which these writers provide. Whereas other critics have turned to philosophy and psychology, Kutnik works with these fictions within the context of artistic (and not merely intellectual) debate.

Julian Cowley of King's College, London, also demonstrates a grasp of innovations which too often elude American critics, and in two pieces for *Critique*, "Ronald Sukenick's New Departures from the Terminal of Language" (27:87–99) and "A Disintegrating Song: The Fiction of Steve Katz" (27:131–43), he shows how Sukenick articulates experience beyond language and Katz "disintegrates" presumptive views of reality with improvisational style as song. There are tragic actualities which defy verbal formulations, and both writers have devised techniques for expressing them, often relying on words as printed phenomena rather than as semantic units. Robert Siegle's *The Politics of Reflexivity* (Hopkins) focuses this argument on the relationship between language and fiction in Katz's *Moving Parts* (where truth is generated by the art of telling); Sukenick's *98.6* experiences the limits of language and its attendant systems as a way of going beyond language itself. A helpful discussion among Sukenick, Coover, Hawkes, Barth, and Jonathan Baumbach concludes the symposium edited by Lois Oppenheim, *Three Decades of the French New Novel* (Illinois, pp. 195–209). Barth speaks for the variousness of our "Anglo-Saxon literature," a notion Sukenick at once corrects; more pertinent is Baumbach's teacherly list of 12 points of commonality, from a rebelliousness against received notions to an openness to cinematic technique.

ix. John Irving, Gilbert Sorrentino, Stephen Dixon, and Guy Davenport

After several years of growing critical attention, 1986 finds John Irving having to speak for himself, although his interview with Ron Hansen (*ParisR* 100:74–103) is rich in both anecdote (J. P. Donleavy's cruelty to John Cheever at Iowa) and insight (the passion of Dickens, Vonnegut, and Grass as an influence). Stephen Dixon fascinates Richard Martin in "The Critic as Entertainer: Ten Digressions and a Diversion on Stereotypes and Innovation" (*Amst* 30:425–27) as an author who does not merely parody stereotypes but employs them as a narrational mode. Michael Stephens's chapter on Dixon in *The Dramaturgy of Style* (So. Ill.) praises his control of the New York native's breathless, nervous voice, a cadence which creates and not merely expresses his fiction (pp. 211–30); another New Yorker, Gilbert Sorrentino (pp. 85–101), generates narratives from a condition of grousing irritability, "a wrathful judging of others" which as a tragic flaw both creates and limits his style. Guy Davenport receives long-overdue attention from Alain Arias-Misson ("Erotic Ear, Amoral Eye," *ChiR* 35,iii:66–71), who faults *Apples and Pears* for its moral vagueness and ascribes the flaw to Davenport's veneration of objecthood (an emphasis of the noun over verb) which keeps the author from considering consequence.

x. Literature of the Vietnam War

Because the great disruption of the Vietnam War coincided with the remarkable wave of innovative fiction, critics are challenged to explain both radically new social and artistic dimensions when it comes to the war literature, and invited to draw causal connections. John Hellmann's *American Myth and the Legacy of Vietnam* (Columbia) is strongest on the social and cultural aspects, tracing a post-World War II vision of Puritan redemption through the obstacles erected by postmodern times—most notably the new mythos that while Americans still share a feeling of national uniqueness and special mission, they must now "shed the notion of a virgin national birth excepting their nation from the universal fallibility of human character and history." More formal critiques distinguish Timothy J. Lomperis's *'Reading the Wind': The Literature of the Vietnam War* (Duke), which in its synthesis of a wide-ranging conference on the subject incorporates the war writer's struggle to express the previously unknown with the more general postmodern notion that older conventions no longer suffice; while reserving judgment, John Clark Pratt offers a lengthy bibliographic commentary which reveals how immense and wide-ranging this literature is, surely a large and important part of the American literary experience.

Pointed critical judgments on this war literature seem reserved, at present, for essays rather than books. In "Narrating the Facts of War: New Journalism in Herr's *Dispatches* and Documentary Realism in First World War Novels" (*JNT* 16:97–116), Evelyn Cobley shows how Herr does not confuse "realism" with the "real," yet stops short of postmodern indeterminacy by allowing factual assertions to "authorize clearly delineated messages," even though those assertions are not grounded in documentary truth. Ward Just sorts through these arguments on a personal level in "Vietnam—Fiction and Fact" (*TriQ* 65:215–20), admitting that the real challenge is facing what one thinks rather than what one is supposed to think. My own "Writing Under Fire: Postmodern Fiction and the Vietnam War" in Larry McCaffery's *Postmodern Fiction* (Greenwood, pp. 79–92) considers how the fictive search for meaning in these novels parallels the innovationists' struggle to devise non-Aristotelian forms, the unreal nature of the war complementing the eclipse of realistic conventions. Yet some writers used the war as a provocation for conventional, issue-oriented response, a style which stays with them through later nonwar fictions—so Daniel L. Zins suggests in "Imagining the Real: The Fiction of Tim O'Brien" (*HC* 23,iii:1–12). Implications of conscience framed as hypothetical fictions, answering the question "What if . . . ?," are the generating principle of O'Brien's work as described by Marie Nelson in "Two Consciences: A Reading of Tim O'Brien's Vietnam Trilogy" (*Third Force Psychology*, pp. 262–79).

xi. Women

That feminism is larger than narrowly political issues is clarified by Judi M. Roller in *The Politics of the Feminist Novel* (Greenwood). When relationships between men and women become power-structured, patriarchy usually rules, making women a minority in economic, political, and social terms. Such characters' split lives are drawn by Ann Roiphe, while Erica Jong thrives on heroines who mount a victory over the part of their lives indoctrinated by society. For Marge Piercy, victory is a matter of definite action, while Judith Rossner's characters who cannot find themselves are in fact missing out on the community of women. False unities do have their enticements, as in Marilyn French's *The Women's Room*, but Helen Yglesias's *How She Died* shows how positive steps are always possible. A less successful study is Thelma J. Shinn's *Radiant Daughters: Fictional American Women* (Greenwood). Her realistic characters are "purposely chosen" for their "frames of reference," a tactic which obscures the authors' art and thematic intent; as a result, Updike's women are easily attacked as functions rather than people, Susan Sontag's creations are admired as models from the author's own life (which Shinn appreciates more acutely than the fiction), while Grace Paley's complex fictions are reduced to plot summaries relating to a "matrilineal subculture." A far more sensitive reading of referential concerns is provided by Paula Bennett in *My Life a Loaded Gun* (Beacon); here Sylvia Plath's need for her mother's approval is translated into the fictive notion of a successful marriage providing a successful identity, with *The Bell Jar* feeding on this duplicity in the author's relation to the world, at once relying on social restrictions while making autonomy a necessity for survival.

Mary Doll's "Joan Didion" (DLB *Yearbook 1986*, pp. 247–52) finds the author of *Democracy* facing a narrative tradition which dictates a solution to problems in a way that contradicts life, and so Didion places herself against this tradition while remaining within it, reporting the action while rejecting its assumptions about history. Rosellen Brown talks at length about *Civil Wars* in the interview conducted by Melissa Walker for *ConL* (27:145–59), including how this novel blends her political activism with her personal life and how a style evolves to express this combination.

xii. Science Fiction, Horror, and the American West

Subgenres breed their own subculture of criticism, producing much for the specialist but little for the generalist (and even less that has impact on the direction of literary studies). A prominent exception is editors George E. Slusser and Eric D. Rabkin's *Hard Science Fiction* (So. Ill.), the best essays of which interrelate questions about "the possible counterhumanism and fabulatively exhaustive nature of SF based on rigorous postulation and the working out of concrete physical problems," a subject which transcends the Trekkiness of too much science fiction criticism. A validly idea-oriented critique is offered by Peter Ruppert in *Reader in a Strange Land* (Georgia), which studies Ursula K. Le Guin's *The Dispossessed* as an examination of tensions between utopian and antiutopian possibilities without relying on a utopian solution and Marge Piercy's *Woman on the Edge of Time* as a naturally relentless investigation of social systems dominated by racial and sexual prejudice, both of which offer the reader "a precariously open vision" which inhibits simple answers. An ethnographics of the SF subculture is provided by William Sims Bainbridge in *Dimensions of Science Fiction* (Harvard), together with a helpful ranging of the genre from hard SF (rationality and control) through new wave (inner space and aesthetic truth) to fantasy (free artistic imagination).

The finest insights into horror fiction are found in Gregory A. Waller's *The Living and the Undead: From Stoker's* Dracula *to Romero's* Dawn of the Dead (Illinois). Stephen King, Waller's favorite contemporary, plays received notions against each other to provide an added tension; he is less optimistic than his predecessors, enlarging the possibilities for evil by virtue of its "multiple threat" of inhabiting the many and not just the one.

The American West, whether concerned with the cowboy novel, Chicano, or Native American writing, is a field which sets itself reductive limits: surveying fiction to see how it fits the form occupies most critics, whose works are best described (and evaluated by) their titles in bibliographical lists. A refreshing change, of interest to generalists for what it adds to our understanding of American narrative in general, is James Ruppert's "Mediation and Multiple Narrative in Contemporary Native American Fiction" (*TSLL* 28:209–25). The mediators use epistemological frameworks of various cultures to pattern and illuminate each other, creating a true artistic dynamic; such fiction writers are far more than anthropological curiosities, for instead of fitting one cultural stereotype they use their position to generate structures and actions, which may indeed be the proper anthropological understanding of all fiction.

University of Northern Iowa

16. Poetry: 1900 to the 1940s

Linda Wagner-Martin

Frank Lentricchia's "On the Ideologies of Poetic Modernism, 1890–1913: The Example of William James" (*Reconstructing American Literary History*, pp. 220–49) describes the complex philosophical milieu at the turn of the century. Because James was one of the seminal Harvard philosophers, along with Royce and Santayana, assessing his influence separately is difficult, but the freedom to find a personal aesthetic stemmed in part from this nexus of idea. Harvard students Stevens, Robinson, Eliot, Frost, Stein, Dos Passos, and Cummings, among others, surely benefited from association with these men—and through them, with Emerson's concepts. One point of Lentricchia's study is simple chronology: that this most energetic period of philosophical modernism—1890–1913—occurred in the "big blank" of American poetry, because the deaths of Longfellow, Whittier, Bryant, and Lowell had occurred from 1878 to 1894.

The sense of the artistic experimentation that dominated poetry during these years and later is caught in Peter Quartermain's two-volume *American Poets, 1880–1945* (DLB 45, 48). Essays written by individual critics chart the lives and describe the work of poets ranging from Bob Brown and Genevieve Taggard to Ezra Pound. Each volume includes more than 40 essays, most carefully presented. Susan Stanford Friedman on H.D., Carol Shloss on Louise Bogan, Karen F. Stein on Elinor Wylie, and many other critics deserve commendation for their work.

An important corrective to conventional interpretations of American Modernism appeared this year: Shari Benstock's far-reaching study, *Women of the Left Bank, Paris, 1900–1940* (Texas). Drawing on the lives and work of more than two dozen women writers, Benstock critiques standard Modernism as being elitist, narrow, and generally remote from central cultural interest (a view shared by O. B. Hardison, Jr., in "Great Walls and Running Fences," *SR* 94:384–417). Benstock treats the work of H.D., Stein, Djuna Barnes, Margaret

Anderson, Mina Loy, and many other writers whose salons and residences in Paris protected and furthered their feminist art and lifestyles. As she unearthed the rich history of these writers, women "whose lives and works have been considered marginal," Benstock found that "our working definitions of Modernism—its aesthetics, politics, critical principles, and poetic practices—and the prevailing interpretations of the Modernist experience had excluded women from its concerns." She was forced to recognize "the misogyny, homophobia, and anti-Semitism that indelibly mark Modernism."

A more predictable study of Modernism is Margaret Dickie's *On the Modernist Long Poem.* Considering the major long poems of Eliot, Crane, Pound, and Williams, Dickie insists that the length and fragmentary nature of each poem was a valid artistic principle. Each "started with a beginning that could not begin and a sense of structuring that had immediately to be dismantled or overcome." Although she recognizes that the process was different for each poet, Dickie also finds each poet frustrated because the idea of content embodied in the long poem never generated structure. She sees much of the poets' frustration stemming from the fact that these contemporary poems needed to use public language, yet their source of imagery as well as language remained, in keeping with the Modernist principle of selection, private. The obscurity of Crane's *The Bridge* and Williams's *Paterson* accrued less from their choices of images than from the apparently simple language, language which was intrinsically private and therefore not what it appeared.

With the somewhat even distribution of dissertations in American poetry this year (three each on Stevens and Williams, two on Robinson Jeffers and Frost, one on H.D. and Louise Bogan, and four each on Hart Crane and Marianne Moore), it appears that critical trends are creating change in the established subjects for graduate investigation. Some Modernist work has only begun to be fully and accurately read, as Hardison and James Applewhite point out in the *Sewanee Review* Modernist issue (384–439), calling for more attention to Hart Crane, Gertrude Stein, Williams, and Stevens.

i. Wallace Stevens

Interest in Stevens as person continues with Joan Richardson's *Wallace Stevens, A Biography: The Early Years, 1879–1923* (Morrow). From a childhood of pleasant times in bucolic Reading, Pennsylvania, to an adolescence already reflecting the changing times of the new century, Stevens was a quiet and curious young man. Richardson notes that Stevens's life parallels Einstein's.

A special student at Harvard—his father had three boys in college, a condition that qualified Stevens for a shorter course—Stevens admired William James, Charles Eliot Norton, and George Santayana, and maintained a friendship with the latter for many years. His first profession was journalism, and he reported for the New York *Tribune*, all the while writing poetry. When Stevens was 24, he met Elsie Kachel Moll, then 18. He evidently idealized the young woman—who had little education and little interest in his poems—and they were married after a five-year courtship. Richardson had access to the courtship letters; what emerges, and occupies a large part of the book, is a portrait of an indecisive Stevens. Unable to decide whether to stay in New York, whether to marry, whether to practice law, Stevens finally did marry. When Elsie discovered that many of her courtship poems were also published, she felt betrayed and began expressing anger over Stevens's publications and honors. Although she provided stability for Stevens, and assumed the mother role (one important section describes the aftermath of the death of Stevens's mother), it becomes clear that Elsie also drove her husband further and further into the world of poetry.

The sense of Stevens as indecisive and somewhat remote accrues in *Secretaries of the Moon: The Letters of Wallace Stevens & José Rodríguez Feo*, ed. Beverly Coyle and Alan Filreis (Duke). This 10-year correspondence between the established poet and the young Cuban Harvard student, written between 1944 and 1954, provides interesting literary history. It also gives a view of Stevens that is sometimes uncomplimentary, as when he seems bent on avoiding Rodríguez when he visits New York or Boston.

The only critical study of Stevens published in 1986 is Jacqueline Vaught Brogan's *Stevens and Simile: A Theory of Language* (Princeton), which makes accessible several technical patterns in the poetry. In several essays ("The 'Form/and Frame' of 'As If' in Wallace Stevens" [*AmerP* 3:34–50] and "Wallace Stevens: 'The Sound of Right Joining'" [*TSLL* 28:107–20]), Brogan anticipated her text by dealing with separable elements of the larger picture. Language *is* meaning. Stevens's phrasing is much more a part of his oeuvre than most critics recognize. His use of similes containing the word *like* suggests that language is in itself less than representational, or perhaps that presentation of "the thing" is itself problematic. Brogan sees Stevens's insistence on using similes as at odds with Imagist, and much Modernist, poetry (there the palm was given to compression). From the start of his career, Stevens was striking out on his own, caring little for the fashionable. But his language tendencies grew to become his way of not only writing about his world, but of looking at that world as well. Stevens's mode was always self-reflective; he consistently put his poetry to use as an instrument observing his aesthetic position. As if he were writing in a private code, Stevens gave priority to constructions in his art in much the same way that other artists might have privileged themes. Without what Brogan feels is the essential key to understanding Stevens's work, a description of his language phrasing, other avenues of criticism are handicapped.

The number of essays on Stevens's work has remained constant over the past few years. Because many of them are comparative, they are published in a variety of places. Michael Wood compares Stevens with Paz ("The Poet as Critic, Wallace Stevens and Octavio Paz," *Reinventing the Americas*, pp. 325–32) in that both believe in history, both define reality in similar terms. So far as their individual roles in art go, however, Paz lives in a "haunting unreality" while Stevens can hardly avoid true reality—accounting partly for the polemic tone of some of his work. Frank J. Warnke chooses Stevens's "Credences of Summer" to illustrate that Stevens is like the meditative poets of the Baroque, delighting in ambiguity ("Rilke, Valéry, Stevens: The Meditative Imagination and the Lyric" in *Explorations: Essays in Comparative Literature*, ed. Matoto Ueda, Univ. Press). Unlike Rilke and Valéry, Stevens is not a mythic poet, and he strips his lyric of any trappings of myth.

Frank Kermode uses Stevens's poem to establish an important theme, reflective of interests in modern philosophy—that there is as much fascination with the movement of the mind that accompanies meditation as there is in the meditation itself ("The Plain Sense of Things," *Midrash and Literature*, ed. Geoffrey H. Hartman and Sanford Budick [Yale]). He chooses Stevens's "The Snow Man" to describe his ideas about the process of language. One of the avenues of accessibility for Stevens's work is this comparative entry. Kathleen L. Komar uses a variant of this approach in "The Issue of Transcendence in Rilke's *Duineser Elegien* and Stevens's *Notes Toward a Supreme Fiction*" (*Neophil* 70:429–41). Her comparison is that both Rilke and Stevens share a belief in the power of language to rejuvenate existence. The poet, accordingly, in the activity of using language to name, creates permanence for the ephemeral and provides an answer for the ontological status of limited, physical, human existence.

Ihab Hassan stresses the importance of Stevens's belief system in "Imagination and Belief: Wallace Stevens and William James in Our Culture" (*WSJour* 10:3–8). He finds that the two shared an "agreement in reality" but that, within that agreement, Stevens leaned toward a "fastidious disbelief." James, in contrast to Stevens, rarely evoked the imagination. Jonathan B. Imber's "The Vocation of Reason: Wallace Stevens and Edmund Husserl" (*HumanS* 9:3–19) stresses the modern faith in the power of mind to come to terms with, and to create terms for, the world and life in the world. Again in phenomenological terms, these writers both dealt with problems of clarifying experience—and routes to do that through language. Alex Argyros in "The Residual Difference: Wallace Stevens and American Deconstruction" (*NOR* 13:20–31) places Stevens's work within the atmosphere of the New Critics, Phenomenologists, Heideggerians, and Derridian Deconstructionists. Stevens's poems are suitably "protean." Argyros outlines what he calls the misappropriation of J. Hillis Miller and Joseph Riddel of Derrida in order to confute the New Critics. Rather, says this author, Stevens's writing is "simply a particularly felicitous example of a certain kind of reflexivity indigenous to literature in general." The contradictions in Stevens's work—he who sees reality as "wholly other" and he who sees it as the final fiction—can be resolved by the critic who can "think textuality and reality together without ablating either one into the other." He discusses "An Ordinary Evening in New Haven" and decides that "reality can be both fiction and fact, both text and extra-text."

Similarly, Melita Schaum explains the interest in the later Stevens poems as a reflection of newer critical approaches ("'Preferring Text to Gloss': From Decreation to Deconstruction in Wallace Stevens Criticism," (*WSJour* 10:84–99). She begins with the work of Riddel and Roy Harvey Pearce, continues to that of Miller, and concludes with the later Riddel and Helen Vendler. For all these approaches, Schaum sees the reductionary element at work, claiming that Stevens's poems defy most critical paradigms. In "Wallace Stevens' Reader Poems and the Effacement of Metaphor" (*WSJour* 10: 67–75), Alan D. Perlis suggests that some of Stevens's poems would benefit from the approach of Paul de Man, that of positing a reader reading text in his own text. Perlis begins with "The Reader" and uses that as gloss for "Phosphor Reading by His Own Light" and other Stevens poems. The apparent interest, even self-consciousness, makes each text a likely source of what Perlis calls "the phenomenology of perception. While the poet's images serve to evade the reality of the world external to mind, they say a great deal about the 'imagined land': the world of the mind itself."

Several essays this year describe personal bonds. B. J. Leggett's "Wallace Stevens and Marianne Moore: Two Essays and a Private Review" (*WSJour* 10:76–83) is a good summary of Stevens's gratitude for Moore's championing of his poetry (Moore calls him "America's chief conjurer—as bold a virtuoso and one with as cunning a rhetoric as we have produced"). Although Stevens and Moore did not meet until 1943, he admired her work much earlier; and after they had met, his praise was most often for her personal integrity, not for her poetry. The most interesting part of the essay is Stevens's describing Moore as creating a "new romantic" in her work. Dana Wilde sees Stevens himself as exploring the problems of the romantic ("Romantic and Symbolist Contexts in the Poetry of Wallace Stevens," *WSJour* 10:42–57) but always intrigued as well with "the crystalline suggestiveness characteristic of symbolism." The process of search dominated Stevens's poems; he rested not in romantic transcendence but rather "on the periphery of Nietzsche with a sense that the imagination alone could order the world for any individual." Wilde contends that Stevens had a vital sense of place, which contributed to his vision of man essentially in context, in a world, as in "The Comedian as the Letter C." In "Strategies of Smallness: Wallace Stevens and Dickinson," Fred Miller Robinson discusses poems from "Inchling" to "Bantams in Pine-Woods" (*WSJour* 10:27–35). He finds the two alike in their privileging of smallness, reflecting perhaps their Emersonian traditions. Robinson suggests, in fact, that the similarities are so great that Stevens might have been thinking of Emily Dickinson when he wrote "Woman Looking at a Vase of Flowers" or "Conversation with 3 Women of New England."

One of the central essays on Stevens's work this year is Mark Halliday's "Stevens and Heterosexual Love" (*ELWIU* 13:135–55). Like Wordsworth, Stevens placed great importance on "mental states achieved in solitude, states of calmness and non-desirous joy." Stevens seemed to be a poet disinterested in romantic love, and when he refers to love it is almost always a metaphor for the imagination. Stevens knows he avoids this problematic area of experience, Halliday thinks, and is troubled by his own omission of the topic. He becomes, then, a man intolerably disturbed by love and its demands. Because his treatment of romance is so ethereal, Stevens never pays any woman the compliment of presenting her fully (see "Arrival at the Waldorf" and "Red Loves Kit"). Mary Arensberg emphasizes the link in Stevens's poetics between the "fantasy of desire or lovers' discourse" and the invention of a poem ("'Golden Vacancies': Wallace Stevens' Problematics of Place and Presence," (*WSJour* 10:36–41). She traces the development of this theme in Stevens's use of "the first idea" (his phrase), his doomed search for transcendence, and his evocation of primal scenes. Through his choice of Key West at one extreme and New Haven at the other, Stevens builds a continuum from the unreal to the real, locations for his constant search.

Another relatively personal slant appears in Jay Dougherty's "Stevens' Mother and 'Sunday Morning'" (*WSJour* 10,ii:100–06). Self-descriptive, the essay traces Stevens's firm Christian upbringing—and the role his mother played in it—and proceeds to read the poem biographically, with much attention to Stevens's mother and her last days. Other 1986 essays focus on such poems as "Wallace Stevens' 'Vacancy in the Park' and the Concept of Similitude" (Jacqueline V. Brogan, *WSJour* 10:9–17), "Stevens' 'Peter Quince at the Clavier' and Pericles" by R. W. Desai (*ELN* 23:57–60), "The Argument of 'Sunday Morning'" by Lyle H. Smith, Jr. (*CollL* 13:254–65), "Stevens' 'The Death of a Soldier': War or Peace?" by Charles D. Hanson (*Expl* 44:33–34), and David Galef's "Resemblance and Change in Wallace Stevens' *Three Academic Pieces*" (*AL* 58:589–608). The last essay posits that Stevens sees the combination of essay and poems ("The Realm of Resemblance" followed by "Someone Puts a Pineapple Together" and "Of Ideal Time and Choice") as marking a change in his manifesto, coming five years after his *Notes Toward a Supreme Fiction.* In this late middle phase Stevens seemed willing to accomplish more with less, more willing to see the realities of life for what they are.

ii. William Carlos Williams

The most important publication in 1986 for assessment of Williams was *The Collected Poems of William Carlos Williams*, Vol. 1, 1909–

1939, ed. A. Walton Litz and Christopher MacGowan (New Directions). Finally ordered and complete, this fertile, almost unclassifiable bounty of poems has for years resisted an academic hand. The editors have maintained chronology—as much as is known—and have published the previously uncollected poems between the volumes reprinted within this edition. It is a useful and even critical work. Yet even in the midst of congratulating the editors on their achievement, one notes that Dennis M. Read found and published three lost Williams poems (sent to *The Little Review* and never returned) in *AL* (58:422–26). "To the Shade of Po Chü-i," "The Cats' Month," and "Daybreak," submitted in 1920, are as careful and as characteristic as any poems we have previously recovered.

Very little new critical work appeared this year. The one book is Harold Bloom's collection, *William Carlos Williams* (Chelsea House), all reprinted essays with a short, summary introduction (Bloom published similar collections this year on Hart Crane and Robert Frost). An important essay is "Mrs. Williams's William Carlos" by Julio Marzan (*Reinventing the Americas*, pp. 106–21). In it Marzan points out how uneasy Williams was with his mother's Puerto Rican origin. Although Spanish was the language spoken in the Williams home when the boys were small, Williams pretended it was French, and he often attributed much of his rearing to his English grandmother. His avoidance of his mother's nationality and language was more than ambivalence. Marzan asserts that "Williams gives signs of being psychologically blocked from writing about Elena's life in a manner that does not hint of either the historical persona's shame or the poet's condescension." Williams's privileging of the Anglo-American over the Spanish could not disguise his interest in Latin American writers, in his Spanish past, and in his language affinity. But his writing about his mother, sentimental and given to self-deception, showed the conflicts he felt about having to claim that culture. Marzan's study is long overdue.

In contrast to this essay, Donald D. Kummings's "Williams' *Paterson*: The Vernacular Hero in the Twentieth Century" (*AmerP* 4: 2–21) covers mostly old ground, though his comparison with Whitman has some interest. Brian A. Bremen's " 'The Radiant Gist': 'The Poetry Hidden in the Prose' of Williams' *Paterson*" (*TCL* 32:221–41) adds the dimension of Byron Vazakas's *Transfigured Night* to the origin of Williams's epic. Victor P. H. Li's "The Vanity of Length: The Long Poem as Problem in Pound's *Cantos* and Williams' *Pater-*

son" (*Genre* 19:3–20) makes the point that the long poem is intentionally inclusive, an apparent stay against oversimplification or reductionism. Even though the modern long poem tries to deny genre, it creates a new kind of form, one expressive of the poet's anxiety. It shows the poet's despair with conventional lyric. Bernhard Radloff discusses the way Williams attempts to shape his experience in "Name and Site: A Heideggerian Approach to the Local in the Poetry of William Carlos Williams" (*TSLL* 28:140–63). Radloff traces the impetus for Williams's fascination with structure that could reflect temporality to Heidegger, particularly his use of design or "Auf-riss." He selects four poems to illustrate what he finds as the progression in the poet's use of language to open the reader's consciousness: "The Yachts," "The Red Wheelbarrow," "The Locust Tree in Flower," and "Asphodel, That Greeny Flower."

Interesting essays in the *William Carlos Williams Review* (12,i) include Bruce Clarke's "The Fall of Montezuma: Poetry and History in William Carlos Williams and D. H. Lawrence" (pp. 1–12); Anne Waldron Neumann's linguistic study, "Diagramming the Forces in a 'Machine Made of Words': Williams' 'Red Wheelbarrow' as Picture Poem," (pp. 13–20); and shorter pieces by George Monteiro and Peter Schmidt. Barbara Herb Wright and Dan Piper contribute unpublished Williams letters to the same issue.

iii. H.D. (Hilda Doolittle)

H.D., born in 1886, received a quantity of attention in this her centenary year. Special issues of *The Iowa Review* (16,iii), ed. Adalaide Morris, and *Contemporary Literature* (27,iv), ed. Susan Stanford Friedman and Rachel Blau DuPlessis, appeared, as did the National Poetry Foundation volume, *H.D.: Woman and Poet*, ed. Michael King. Some of H.D.'s previously unpublished work was also brought to print this year: *Ion*, her ostensible translation of a play by Euripides, was published by Black Swan Press with an afterword by John Walsh which quotes from H.D.'s criticism, and several pages by H.D. on Euripides. H.D. called her approach in rendering the Greek in vers libre "transformation"; her edition of *Hippolytus Temporizes* makes no claim to being any kind of translation. It is a montage of H.D.'s characteristic themes, partly inspired by the play by Euripides for which it is titled. This too has an afterword by Walsh and is published by Black Swan. From New Directions appeared H.D.'s

Nights, probably written in the early 1930s and credited to "John Helforth," the narrator of the frame tale within. A study of a bisexual woman who commits suicide, the novella self-reflexively describes her love affair with the young houseguest, David. That becomes the second part of the novella. It follows the first half, "Prologue," ostensibly told by the narrator as her suicide is described, its reasons conjectured. With a preface by Perdita Schaffner, H.D.'s daughter, the text is intriguing in its multilayered irony.

Rachel Blau DuPlessis's book, *H.D.: The Career of That Struggle* (Indiana) follows her important 1985 *Writing Beyond the Ending: Narrative Strategies of Twentieth-Century Women Writers* (Indiana) which has much material about H.D. In her recent study of H.D., DuPlessis tries to deal with four kinds of authority: cultural authority, authority of otherness or marginality, gender authority, and sexual or erotic authority. Intertwined, they occur throughout H.D.'s writing, though in somewhat different patterns. DuPlessis uses such a description to explain why H.D.'s writing is often difficult. She describes the early poetry and the pull of classical art and thought, and then the overwhelming production of H.D.'s prose (during two sets of years, 1920–25 and 1933–34). H.D. wrote three groups of novels in those years, a *Magna Graeca* set that includes *Hedylus* and *Palimpsest*; the "Madrigal cycle" (*Paint It To-day, Asphodel, HERmione*, and the later *Bid Me to Live* (*A Madrigal*); and a Borderline group. According to DuPlessis, one cannot read H.D.'s important late poems without seeing how she constructed these fictions in order to unify her female experiences such as sexuality and motherhood with creativity. DuPlessis's comments about rescripting and her study of "romance" are both helpful.

The *Contemporary Literature* special H.D. issue includes Pound's tribute to H.D. (1961); four chapters from H.D.'s extant first novel, *Paint It To-Day* (1921), as *kunstlerroman*; and a number of fine essays. Alicia Ostriker's "What Do Women (Poets) Want? H.D. and Marianne Moore as Poetic Ancestresses" (pp. 475–92) stresses these poets' strengths, viewing H.D.'s *Helen in Egypt* as her "Cantos" and the work of both women as heroic, emphasizing continuities over dualities and centralizing material which is usually repressed. Ostriker sees both Moore and H.D. as creating for themselves the roles of mothers.

Adalaide Morris's "A Relay of Power and of Peace: H.D. and the Spirit of the Gift" (pp. 493–524) explains that H.D. did not live her life according to a Western ethic. Her treatment of money, of motherhood, and of writing identity (her ever-changing signature as author) puzzles observers; clearly, H.D. was not an acquisitive Western woman. Morris's theory is that H.D. operated under principles which Marcel Mauss has termed "the gift economy," and a reading of her fiction and poetry using that ideology proves satisfying. Eileen Gregory describes the similarities between Sappho and H.D. (and all women lyricists) in "Rose Cut in Rock: Sappho and H.D.'s *Sea Garden*" (pp. 525–52). Her reading of many of the early lyrics is masterful. "Fishing the Murex Up: Sense and Resonance in H.D.'s *Palimpsest*" (pp. 553–73) by Deborah Kelly Kloepfer suggests the wit with which critics of H.D. delve into her craft as process of self-knowledge: "Text becomes, then, both what is sought and the means of seeking it(self)." A good, economical reading of H.D.'s prose, as is Joseph Milicia's "H.D.'s 'Athenians': Son and Mother in *Hedylus*" (pp. 574–94).

The Iowa Review compilation is equally strong. It also includes essays by Alicia Ostriker and Rachel Blau DuPlessis, as well as Diana Collecott, whose 1985 *Critical Quarterly* essay, "Remembering Oneself: The Reputation and Later Poetry of H.D." also deserves notice (27:7–22); "Running," a memoir by Perdita Schaffner; "Fortune Teller," the missing second chapter of H.D.'s *The Gift*; and H.D.'s own reflection on herself entitled "H.D. by Delia Alton." The centerpiece of the issue is Susan Stanford Friedman's "Emergences and Convergences" (pp. 42–56), a moving account of her own re-vision of H.D.'s work, and H.D.'s importance to readers through time.

Other important essays collected in *The Iowa Review* are Barbara Guest's meditation on biography; Paul Smith's "H.D.'s Flaws," which places her work in the larger context of questioning the politics of modernism (pp. 77–86); and H.D.'s friend, Silvia Dobson, recalling World War II in England ("'Shock Knit Within Terror': Living Through World War II"). Both this essay and that of Donna Krolik Hollenberg ("Art and Ardor in World War One: Selected Letters from H.D. to John Cournos") draw heavily on H.D.'s correspondence.

H.D.: Woman and Poet includes another two dozen expert essays, as well as a good bibliography compiled and annotated by Mary S. Mathis and the editor. Generally more substantial essays, these cover the range of subject matter from biography (Adalaide Morris, Janice S. Robinson, Barbara Guest) to reminiscence (Dobson, Sarton, Walsh, Schaffner) to close critical readings of the prose (L. S. Dembo,

Jeanne Kerblat-Houghton, Joseph Milicia) and poetry (Albert Gelpi, Kloepfer, Dale Davis, Mary K. DeShazer, Ostriker, and DuPlessis). A fascinating section deals with H.D.'s career as actress and film critic: Anne Friedberg's "Approaching *Borderline*"; Diane Collecott's "Images at the Crossroads: The 'H.D. Scrapbook' "; and Charlotte Mandel's "Magical Lenses: Poet's Vision Beyond the Naked Eye." This assemblage of more than 500 pages is rich and informative.

Other essays on H.D. are Elizabeth A. Hirsh's " 'New Eyes': H.D., Modernism, and the Psychoanalysis of Seeing" (*L&P* 32:1–10), a study of the author's use of tableau-like scenes of dramatic revelation which hold the center of the thematic import; Margaret M. Dunn's "H.D.'s *Trilogy*: A Portrait of the Artist in Full Bloom" (*CEA* 48: 29–37), high and reasoned praise for H.D.'s World War II poem collections; and Susan Stanford Friedman's "Gender and Genre Anxiety: Elizabeth Barrett Browning and H.D. as Epic Poets" (*TSWL* 5:203–28), which analyzes the women's reformulation of epic conventions to fit their own stories, as well as their female voices. Both experienced genre anxiety, both feminized epic convention, and both achieved striking narrative intertextualities (in *Aurora Leigh* and *Helen in Egypt*). Friedman's work is a touchstone not only for H.D. criticism, but for women's literature in general. Two essays by Melody Zajdel are also helpful: " 'I See Her Differently': H.D.'s *Trilogy* as Feminist Response to Masculine Modernism" (*Sagetrieb* 5[Spring]: 7–15), in which the clear sense of community within H.D.'s last three poem collections counters the pervasive modernist alienation; and "Portrait of an Artist as a Woman: H.D.'s Raymonde Ransom" (*WS* 13:127–34), a study of a central H.D. protagonist who appears in both *Palimpsest* (1926) and "Narthex" (1928).

iv. Marianne Moore, Gertrude Stein, Louise Bogan, Sara Teasdale, Edna St. Vincent Millay, Harriet Monroe, and Elinor Wylie

Taffy Martin's *Marianne Moore: Subversive Modernist* (Texas) brings to the reading of Moore's poems a different sense of context. Rather than discuss separate works, Martin sets out from the start her belief that Moore "responded to the twentieth century with humorous irony and aggressive optimism. Her blend of ideas was unique in its time. She was both at the center of twentieth century modernism and at its outer limits." Martin finds the years Moore edited *The Dial* highly influential. Not that she was ever removed from theory, or from friendships with other writers and artists, but during those years she was particularly voicing exciting ideas. Martin's use of indeterminacy and radical ambiguity to read Moore is apt; she admonishes the reader to think of Moore's sly smile as one reads the epigrammatic endings that solve nothing, and the quotations that disfigure rather than enhance.

In contrast to this study, Grace Schulman's *Marianne Moore, The Poetry of Engagement* (Illinois) seems tepid. The book includes good readings, but predictable ones. Schulman points to some general truths about structure and aligns Moore with Stevens in their search for a poetic way to describe the workings of the mind. That Moore is a serious reflective poet has long since been proved.

New sensitivity to Gertrude Stein's *Tender Buttons* as poetry, not just experimental writing, prompts essays by Linda Mizejewski, Lisa Ruddick, Catharine R. Stimpson, and—briefly—Elyse Blankley. The last credits Stein's writing *Tender Buttons* with revolutionizing her native tongue ("Beyond the 'Talent of Knowing': Gertrude Stein and the New Woman," *Critical Essays on Gertrude Stein*, ed. Michael J. Hoffman [Hall], pp. 196–209). Lisa Ruddick, in "A Rosy Charm: Gertrude Stein and the Repressed Feminine" in the same collection (pp. 225–40), explicates Stein's extensive private language code, necessary to refer not only to her lesbianism but also as "the vehicle for a sophisticated set of insights about gender and culture" which anticipate current psychoanalytic and feminist theory. She accordingly reads *Tender Buttons* as a meditation on the female body and "its relation to a symbolic order that suppresses the female." Ruddick attends to the objects of Stein's poetry (stains, secretions, body parts, clothing) and relates them to the conventional family romance. Defying the authority of the father, Stein writes *Tender Buttons* as "a prolonged enactment of the return to the mother."

Linda Mizejewski ("Gertrude Stein: The pattern moves, the woman behind shakes it," *WS* 13:33–47) draws usefully on Hélèn Cixous and Alfred North Whitehead, as she also connects Stein with Charlotte Perkins Gilman, Kate Chopin, and other turn-of-the-century women writers. While Stein was writing out of the same frustrations and using much of the same imagery (rooms, furnishings, enclosures), she drew on a much more defiant presentation of a woman's possible life. Mizejewski thinks Stein achieves some larger sense of defiance in *Tender Buttons* because her concern is with changing the language she feels trapped in, rather than reacting thematically to her frustrations. Stein's flight for freedom takes the form of "a consciousness that is deliberately breaking down categories of perception, time, space, and language." Catharine R. Stimpson's "Gertrude Stein and the Transposition of Gender" (*The Poetics of Gender*, pp. 1–18) places Stein's poetry in the context of her generally subversive stance toward modernism. Her direct confrontation with gender issues, her humor, her willingness to be the outsider, all suggest a steady awareness far beyond the usual sense that Stein as writer stumbled from one avant-garde position to another. Stimpson sees Stein's turn to poetry in 1910 as the most calculated of her literary moves, because poetry at that time was so exclusively the province of the male elite. In what she achieved in *Tender Buttons*, Stein made readers reconstitute patriarchal ideas about both poetry and gender.

John Muller's "Light and the Wisdom of the Dark, Aging and the Language of Desire in the Texts of Louise Bogan" (in *Memory and Desire: Aging—Literature—Psychoanalysis*, ed. Kathleen Woodward and Murry M. Schwartz [Indiana], pp. 76–96) is equally important. He contends that from the first Bogan knew the fascination with the Other, the process of riskily identifying with passion and self-fulfillment. Her own fearful and precarious relationship with her mother, who led an illicit sexual life in addition to her existence as wife and mother, forced Bogan to question many of the psychological assumptions about living, as well as about poetry. In Bogan's work, light is never simply redemptive. It is rather a metonymy of the other (Other), an ironic reminder of the attraction of the repressed and consciously unknown. Muller finds that this pattern of imagery of light has at least double significance throughout Bogan's work—and her life.

Sara Teasdale by Carol B. Schoen (TUSAS 509) is a good study of the conflicts of the Victorian woman becoming an artist. There is much information given concisely about the women poets and artists who supported Teasdale as she grew into her art in St. Louis, New York, and Chicago, woven as it should be with the events of her fragile personal life—marred as it was with ill health, depression, and an increasing inability to cope with life. After her divorce from Ernst Filsinger and Vachel Lindsay's suicide (when she had married Filsinger, she had rejected Lindsay), Teasdale saw little reason to fight the depression that had become customary for her, and she died a suicide. Schoen provides a good assessment of Teasdale's importance to modern poetry, both in her art and in her friendships, both of which have been undervalued.

Edna St. Vincent Millay has received similarly good readings in two essays, Debra Fried's "Andromeda Unbound: Gender and Genre in Millay's Sonnets" (*TCL* 32:1–22), a comparative study in which Millay's work is compared with writing by Wordsworth, particularly in sonnets that have gender as subject; and Suzanne Clark's "Jouissance and the Sentimental Daughter" (*NDQ* 54:85–108). The latter takes the tactic of seeming to agree with objections about Millay's work (as sentimental, adolescent, romantic), and then reverses the reader's expectations. She claims that Millay also does some reversal, because just when we expect the good mother to become a martyr, she does not. Millay's poetry seems to do much of what Edith Wharton's fiction was attempting, to stay within a readership that expected certain themes, and yet to end up in an ambiguity that in effect denied those thematic implications. Clark calls this "a slippage about the position of the subject." She concludes, "Millay's poetry becomes a gesture of definition enacted at the margins of identity and the self she does not define is the character of the Woman as Poet." She reminds the present-day reader that Kristeva might be of more use in reading Millay than would Edmund Wilson. A special issue of *Tamarack* (3,i[Fall 1985–86]) includes John J. Patton's "The Variety of Language in Millay's Verse Plays" (pp. 8–16); Norma Millay's reminiscence, "The Saga of *Conversation at Midnight* in the Living Theatre" (pp. 36–58); and shorter essays by Frank Caldiero and James A. Brophy, Jr.

Ann Massa's essay on Harriet Monroe's place in late nineteenth-century Chicago helps one appreciate Monroe's skill in editing *Poetry*—and keeping it running ("'The Columbian Ode' and *Poetry, A Magazine of Verse*: Harriet Monroe's Entrepreneurial Triumphs," *JAmS* 20:51–69). Monroe was paid $1,000 for her 2,200-line ode for the dedication ceremonies for the Chicago World's Fair in 1892. Then it was canceled, but she got parts of it back in (and other sections set to music and played). Massa's skillful telling of this story and of Monroe's later rounding up of support for *Poetry* lends credence to her calling Monroe "a poetic businesswoman."

One short item on Elinor Wylie deserves mention: Terence A. Hoagwood writes on "Wylie's 'The Crooked Stick'" and the poet's expert use of antithesis (*Expl* 44:54–57).

v. Hart Crane and Robinson Jeffers

An important book on Crane's work appeared, presaging more accurate readings to come. (Crane's is a poetry that will yield to many of the approaches now in use, and the recently completed dissertations suggest his appeal.) Paul Giles's *Hart Crane: The Contexts of "The Bridge"* (Cambridge) is a useful and interesting study. Recognizing that Crane's "bridge" reflected both his wide cultural insight and his skepticism about the "progress" of his culture, Giles's approach is to locate Crane's work in relation to Joyce's *Ulysses* and *Finnegans Wake*, and to see it as a tour de force of language play—specifically of the pun. The title itself puns in various ways, and from that opening readers will miss Crane's satire and humor if they read too literally. Giles organizes into such emphases as "business world," "burlesque," "Ouspensky and Whitehead," "Dada," "Freud," and other chapters as provoking for what they say about the culture of the early 20th century as what they say about Crane.

Crane's "Cape Hatteras" is discussed by Laurence Goldstein in *The Flying Machine* in connection with Lindbergh's flight, Kitty Hawk, the spirit of the mythic in man's conquering space. Goldstein spends time on the influence of Harry Crosby, with whom Crane lived for a time. He also ties Crane with Muriel Rukeyser's "Theory of Flight," the title poem from her Yale Younger Poets collection in 1935, which played off Crane's *Bridge* concept. Goldstein also mentions Robinson Jeffers, Archibald MacLeish, Allen Tate, and Robert Frost.

Relationships between Crane and other writers are the topics of "Un encuentro de Lorca y Hart Crane en Nueva York" (*Insula* 41: 1–12) by B. Russell Thomson and J. K. Walsh, and Celeste M. Schenck's "When the Moderns Write Elegy: Crane, Kinsella, Nemerov" (*CML* 6:97–108). Discussing pastoral elegy, Schenck explicates Crane's "Voyages," Kinsella's *A Country Walk*, and Nemerov's *Elegy for a Nature Poet*.

Jeanetta Boswell's *Robinson Jeffers and the Critics, 1912–1983: A Bibliography of Secondary Sources with Selective Annotations* (Scarecrow) lists a surprising number of essays and reviews, arranged alphabetically by critic instead of by year of publication. This guide foreshadows the work being done by Timothy Hunt (a complete edition in several volumes of Jeffers's poetry); it complements the essays appearing in *The Robinson Jeffers Newsletter*, ed. Robert J. Brophy.

vi. Robert Frost

Only one monograph appeared dealing with Frost's work, and that in part, but it was a good year for critical essays. Several relate to the still-fascinating topic of Frost as contradictory person. Donald G. Sheehy takes on the Lawrance Thompson controversy by discussing Thompson's journals, in which it becomes clear that once Thompson had read Karen Horney's *Neuroses and Human Growth* he saw everything in Frost's behavior as neurotic. Frost's vacillation between antipathy and intimacy was an even greater problem to his biographer than it was to most of his friends (Thompson's journal attests to that as well). This scholarly approach to the problem of why Thompson's biography seemed so critical is useful and interesting ("The Poet as Neurotic: The Official Biography of Robert Frost," *AL* 58:393–410).

Philip L. Gerber interviewed William Jewell, the son of classmates of Frost, in "Remembering Robert Frost" (*NEQ* 59:1–27). While Jewell's father had a fondness for Frost, his mother distrusted him, called him a "scalawag," and lamented that her husband loaned Frost over $600 (which was never returned). This interview records what Jewell calls Frost's "extraordinary dependence" on his wife, though he also acknowledges that the poet frustrated Elinor's considerable talents completely. Frost's granddaughter, Lesley Lee Francis, contributes "A Decade of 'Stirring Times': Robert Frost and Amy Lowell" (NEQ 59:508–22), a memoir that sheds more light on Lowell than on Frost. The two poets were friends and debated often the use of dialogue, form, regional themes (Lowell insisted Frost was a regional poet, though he never claimed to be). Lowell did much to enhance Frost's reputation; she felt that she had helped to discover him, though Francis feels that she never understood his humor and read his work too literally.

Robert Crawford's "Robert Frosts" speaks of the wide range of possible occupations Frost saw before him, and the many layers of irony inherent in his work; he wanted multiple lives, multiple roles, multiple masks (*JAmS* 20:207–32). From 1885 to 1892 he held a variety of jobs, and his eclectic vision allowed him to stay up in many areas of knowledge. As subversive a portrait as the mask of a New England farmer was, it allowed him to be many other things. Rather than being the rational intellectual (another role he played), he was descended from the Scottish visionary line and loved Scotch poems, folktales, "voices." He was probably named for Burns. "Mending

Wall," written in 1913, was written about his experience visiting in Scotland, yet it appears to be a perfect reflection of the New England experience. In this context, Crawford finds Frost's "The Road Not Taken" completely ironic: he was always faced with many more than two choices, and the oversimplified course of action expressed here would have never satisfied Frost the person.

Some insight into the formation of the Frost persona occurs in Ronald Bieganowski's "Sense of Time in Robert Frost's Poetics: A Particular Influence of Henri Bergson" (*RALS* 13[1983]:184–93). By studying the marginalia by Frost in his copy of the 1911 edition of Bergson's *Creative Evolution*, Bieganowski formulates several theories of poetry for Frost. One of the most important is the persistence of the past into the present, as "West-Running Brook" illustrates. Because Frost quoted Bergson for at least 35 years, there is little question that he found the philosopher's ideas compatible. W. David Shaw's "The Poetics of Pragmatism: Robert Frost and William James" (*NEQ* 59:159–88) also draws parallels between the modernist philosophy and the poet's aesthetic. Frost said repeatedly that he had been influenced by James, though he had never taken a course from him at Harvard. Pragmatism permeated his theories about language, people, and religious belief. Shaw points out that Frost was consistently interested in "keeping open other frameworks," a condition of mind that owed much to William James.

Scott Donaldson studies Frost's characteristic use of oblique or evasive statement in "Frost, Dickinson, and the Strategy of Evasion" (*CP* 19:107–16). He notes that Frost often made references to both Dickinson and her poems in his public performances and readings, and that his methods of concealing his personal feelings are akin to hers. Both view the poem as a means of play, or game; both link metaphor and parable.

A fresh approach to Frost's poetic structure is the thesis of Robert T. McPhillips ("Diverging and Converging Paths: Horizontal and Vertical Movement in Robert Frost's *Mountain Interval*," *AL* 58:82–98). This close reading of the 1916 collection of poems provides good information about Frost's care to create a powerful experience for the reader. McPhillips begins his discussion with the opening poem, "The Road Not Taken," agreeing with Crawford's view that the poem is highly ironic. In this case Frost was able to keep traveling both roads: the choice is feigned; the poet is not limited in ways other people are. In another sense, one of the two roads is horizontal, referring to time and history; another is vertical, keeping in touch with space, the imagination, and timelessness (and placing this poem in the tradition of the American visionaries). Using Gaston Bachelard's work on phenomenological space, McPhillips stresses the contradiction between the houses Frost's characters inhabit and the lives they lead away from those houses, in nature. Within the home, most of Frost's personae lead bleak, stoic lives; what happiness does exist occurs outside. As the closing poem, "The Sound of Trees," suggests, the best choice for the poet may be the "reckless" one described in that poem. Taken as a composite and closely structured whole, *Mountain Interval* is a very different "statement" than it is sometimes read as being.

Fritz Oehlschlaeger considers the uses of metaphor in "West toward Heaven: The Adventure of Metaphor in Robert Frost's 'West-Running Brook'" (*CLQ* 22:238–41). George F. Bagby, Jr., focuses on "Frost's Synecdochism," particularly in his poems about nature (*AL* 58:379–92). Bagby's point is that Frost often moves in his poems from a description of a scene or an image to some comment about its significance ("from sight to insight"). Using this technique, which is found as well in the work of Emerson and Thoreau, Frost also draws on 17th-century British poetry. There is nothing symbolic or realistic about his use of synecdoche. As a style, it has the consequences of leading to punning, double meanings, a predictable structure, and a seemingly slight subject matter.

Another essay on Frost as nature/pastoral poet is Barbara Currier Bell's "Frost on Humanity in Nature" (*ArQ* 42:223–38), in which she defines six roles Frost plays in the natural world, ranging from Sufferer to Seer. Related to this nexus is Walter Stiller's "The Dominion of Violence in the Poetry of Robert Frost" (*MHLS* 9:65–73). D. Bradley Sullivan tackles those enigmatic late writings in " 'Education by Poetry' in Robert Frost's Masques" (*PLL* 22:312–21). Placing the masques in relation to the poet's belief that metaphor could order the world, Sullivan finds them critical of that notion: they "explore the failure of cherished metaphors and the human reaction to such failures." They question what happens when the world takes its metaphors too seriously? And they warn of the difficulty of letting well-established metaphors go. Robert F. Fleissner ties Frost's *A Masque of Reason* to Shakespeare's *Hamlet* and Goethe's *Faust* in *The Prince and the Professor: The Wittenberg Connection in Marlowe, Shakespeare, Goethe, and Frost, a Mahlet/Faust(us) Analogy*

(Carl Winter). The last section of the monograph deals with Frost, as he was influenced by these earlier writers, especially with the entire Faust legend. Unless I missed some important connections, the chief tie seems to be in Fleissner's critical imagination.

vii. Other Poets

Archibald MacLeish: Reflections, ed. Bernard A. Drabeck and Helen E. Ellis, is a fascinating informal "autobiography" (Mass.). In interviews conducted from 1976 through 1981, MacLeish gave the editors what he called "the autobiography of my professional life." The text, culled from that material, is arranged into chapters by chronology. Most interesting are the sections on MacLeish living in Paris (at odds with the reminiscences of Malcolm Cowley), his friendships, and his wife Ada's singing career.

Martin Bidney stresses the importance of Mephistopheles and the Eternal Feminine in the writing of Edgar Lee Masters, in "Beethoven, the Devil, and the Eternal Feminine: Masters's Goethean Typology of Redemption" (*PLL* 22:187–205). Masters especially admired Goethe's "philosophic wit and metamorphic vision."

A philosophical question of a more intense but also less attached kind is the concern of James Mack. In "John Crowe Ransom's Moments: A Reconstruction in the Post-Scientific Mode" (*REALB* 4: 233–64), he offers a speculative reconstruction of the ideas—not the exact verbal contents—of an early manuscript, later destroyed, dealing with "moments of experience," and applies the exercise to "a reconstructed understanding of Ransom's significance as a man of letters." This Ransom is both a post-Romantic and a postscientific poet, one whose "attachment to the romantic values implicit in the idea of moments, coexisting uneasily alongside systematic, modern aspects of his mind, makes him more difficult and interesting than we have imagined."

Shyamal Bagchee's "The Western-ness of Yvor Winters's Poetry" (*SDR* 24:148–65) seems to reduce Winters's large concerns with art to those of a local colorist, whereas Lewis P. Simpson ("The Critics Who Made Us—Allen Tate," *SR* 94:471–85) makes the work of Allen Tate seem central to Modernist poetics. Simpson's point about *The Man of Letters in the Modern World* is that Tate's life and aesthetic are perfectly displayed in this seemingly random collection. Simpson sees the work driven by the force of Tate's "critical will."

Thomas Daniel Young acts as editor in *Mississippi Quarterly* (39: 53–78) for "Quo Vadimus? Or the Books Still Unwritten, Part II," a 1964 symposium held at Kenyon College in honor of John Crowe Ransom, moderated by Robie Macauley. The discussion by Robert Lowell, Ransom, Stephen Spender, Robert Penn Warren, and Allen Tate centers on the work of Stevens, Pound, Eliot (and the impact of *The Waste Land*), Dos Passos, and Plath, a transcription that shows the reason these poets were such important figures to modern and contemporary literary opinion.

Michigan State University

17. Poetry: The 1940s to the Present

Richard J. Calhoun

i. Overviews

In taking over the section on our most contemporary poetry from Lee Bartlett, who has carried out this assignment with great critical aplomb and with careful organization for six years, I believe I should state the premises on which I am operating. There is a difference in selection of items this year from past years. The MLA Bibliography is now available in advance through the computer sources of Knowledge Index. Any item listed there I made every effort to include, and I added to this a search through all periodicals which had proved rich sources for Lee Bartlett during the preceding six years. I want to be as inclusive as possible. As editor of a small literary magazine, I know the feeling of disappointment and resentment when a worthy item is left out. I have learned what I suspected before. Many of the most interesting articles on contemporary literature appear in little magazines that are not always the most readily available. I have had to write and follow up with telephone calls to get many items I needed, and not always with success. The author of this section, more perhaps than for any other section, needs help in the way of offprints and suggestions of items that might be overlooked. I do promise that significant items that did not make my review this time will next time.

I have tried to give a concise account of each item with some indication of what I found its value to be. I have probably erred on the side of too much summary and too little judgment. I have also combined and simplified the subheadings that Professor Bartlett used in order to make it possible to get more items into the space I have been allowed. My own tastes are fairly broad and, in my own self-assessment, without too much bias. I like to think that I tilt in the favor of experiential poetry and open forms, though I have a formalist bias that has to come from being of that graduate school generation that had a full dose of the New Criticism.

More than anything else I had hoped to begin with the discovery of a major book on contemporary poetry. Unfortunately, this is not the year for one. Last year was the year of Robert von Hallberg's *American Poetry and Culture, 1945–1980*. This year could have been the year of Harold Bloom's *Contemporary Poets* (Chelsea House), except that his book is a collection mostly of reprints of significant essays on contemporary poets, with only two new essays; even the introduction was written in 1974. It is, nevertheless, a useful and interesting collection of the best on contemporary poetry from the perspective of the establishment (and specifically Yale) view of modern poetry. In his "Editor's Notes," Bloom admits that the perspective is narrow, since 11 of the 28 essays are by Richard Howard, John Hollander, and himself. He comments that three poets "lost to us, but still included among the living," Elizabeth Bishop, Robert Fitzgerald, and James Wright, are "still very much part of the poetry of the contemporary scene, as Robert Lowell, John Berryman, Randall Jarrell perhaps no longer are." Bloom refreshingly shares none of that current view that evaluation has no place in scientific criticism. He knows the best: Ashbery, Ammons, and Merrill are of "the eminence of Warren and Bishop," and Robert Penn Warren is "our greatest living poet." Gwendolyn Brooks is "the foremost black woman poet." If his judgments are not explicit by statement, they are implicit by selection. For example, his own essay on James Dickey considers only that poet's "early motion," through *Helmets*; Allen Ginsberg is still a bard to some, but to Bloom resembles James Macpherson's "Ossian"; he is "not moved" by the work of Amiri Baraka, or the recent poetry of Adrienne Rich; May Swenson and John Hollander rank among the "unduly neglected." It will be interesting to keep his judgments in mind as we look at the scholarship on contemporary poets for 1986 to determine which poets, living and dead, are regarded as part of the contemporary scene.

John Hollander's new essay on Robert Penn Warren, "Modes and Ranges of a Long Dawn" (pp. 9–17), is an attempt to begin this collection of essays with a late assessment of Warren as "our wisest man of letters," who is "not only part of the literary landscape, but, more significantly, part of the way in which we view the landscape." He is a poet of personal and public history, from which the moments he creates have since *Promises* (1957) "grown more passionate and complex." It is this increasing intensity and complexity that Hollander has chosen to trace in an essay in which he has come to praise our first poet laureate and senior poet, not to criticize him. This is first-rate praise. The only other new essay pertinent to my chapter is Bloom's own, "The Poetry of Robert Fitzgerald" (pp. 19–25), in which he sees Fitzgerald occupying the same place among moderns that Walter Savage Landor held among Romantics, as an elegiac poet and lyric master who could invest classical form with personal passion. The remaining essays, though not new, are recent, informative, and still of critical interest. In spite of the fact that so much is covered by so few, this is one of the best collections of essays on contemporary American poetry, and one of the most comprehensive, from Warren to Daryl Hine. Brief biographical and bibliographical notes on each living poet are included.

The book next in interest is Andrew Ross's *The Failure of Modernism*, primarily for its attempt to discern the failures in modernism that led to postmodernism. To Ross modernism was a series of attempts to eliminate subjectivity from poetic form and language in order to establish a discourse more authentic or "true" to our experience of the natural world. Modernism failed because it confused philosophical assumptions with applicability to literary texts. He focuses on three writers who were poets and something else—Eliot, poet and philosopher; Olson, poet and historian; Ashbery, poet and art critic—all with a view of language as a medium in which a poet could solve theoretical problems. Olson proposed objectivist alternatives—"a nonlinear approach to history and a new spatial realism incorporating phenomenological models into poetic discourse." Ross analyzes the difficulties of converting this theory to practice in the *Maximus poems*. John Ashbery has attempted to internalize the temporal problems that bothered him by displacing the problem of subjectivity onto the reader and through adoption of the Renaissance tradition of a painting perspective. This is interesting reading in the persistence of problems that bothered modernist poets into postmodernism, but it is heavy going. The most interesting chapter is on Ashbery.

For an overall view of recent poetry Jonathan Holden's *Style and Authenticity in Postmodern Poetry* (Missouri) is about the best we have from 1986, at least in the early chapters. Unfortunately, his focus is lost in the last half of the book. Borrowing from Northrop Frye, Holden classifies postmodernism as a low mimetic mode of poetry, a "vernacular poetry of personal ethos," with its origins in a tradition stretching through Frost and Hardy back to Wordsworth. Modernist writers sought to formalize poetry and organize it into structures recognizable as art. They sought literary analogues. Postmodernist writers deviate from fixed-form conventions and traditional prosody and seek nonliterary "communal" analogues, such as confession and conversation, over the impersonal literary analogues. The great modernist poems tend to be about poetry itself. The postmodernist poet turns his attention away from his poem, toward his experience. Holden also wishes to show that the "fully achieved poetic form" must locate in a sense of the general while presenting an experience which is also typical. This is simply the old particular versus general argument, one of the oldest in the history of literary criticism applied to postmodernism. He describes the poet's real task today as personal mythmaking, explaining his sorrow by use of some mythology or other, finding "some little, summarizing song." In the change from modernism to postmodernism the authority of the lyric voice is replaced by the authenticity of the confessional or conversational voice. Written otherwise, postmodernist poems face the danger of undermining distinctions between fiction and history and run the risk of "losing poetry." He gives us two examples, one running the risk of failure, John Ashbery's "The Man on the Dump," and an example of "success," Richard Hugo's "Degrees of Gray in Philipsburg." I agree with much of Holden's theory as perfectly true and obvious. More examples would be helpful, but the last chapters seem to wander from the thesis as if already published essays had to be fitted in. The first part is interesting though hardly new except for the attention devoted to postmodernist nonliterary analogues.

Sherman Paul's *In Search of the Primitive* (LSU) explores very narrowly an important subject in recent poetry, primitivism, by selecting three poets (David Antin, Jerome Rothenberg, and Gary Snyder) he values for their radically innovative work and their desire to restore the role of poetry as oral art. Of greatest value is the chapter on Gary Snyder. The potential value of the book for some may be diminished by the free-association style and daybook organization. Paul's style mirrors the irritation arising from his belief that these three poets have been excluded by the establishment because they have been doing something valuable, "talking at the boundaries." The form is dialectic, featuring a series of running responses to the poets he is concerned with, and, in the chapter on David Antin, even a minute disagreement with Marjorie Perloff. My main regret with a subject as important as the primitive is that he could not include other poets, e.g., Dickey, Kinnell, Stafford.

Another important subject in contemporary poetry, autobiography, is broached in Paul Christensen's "Postmodern Bildungsromans: The Drama of Recent Autobiography" (*Sagetrieb* 5,i:29–40). Unfortunately, the surface is only scratched. Christensen identifies two dialectically opposed conceptions of the self which developed after 1945. One saw the self as separate and unrelated to nature except in acts of contemplation; the second viewed it as the "blighted figment of a blind, amoral determinism." Christensen is concerned with the attempt to remake the self by turning to ancient civilizations, to primitive and non-Western sources of belief, for a new conception of human nature. For this new stage in the formulation of the self, writers like Olson, Snyder, Ginsberg went to other cultures—Mayans and Aztecs in the case of Olson, Japanese and Buddhism for Snyder, India and Hinduism for Ginsberg. All this is true but hardly news. What I would have liked was a clearer delineation of the relationship between sources and that self as it appears in later autobiographical poetry.

The contributions to the *New York Quarterly* on the "Present State of American Poetry" are of occasional interest. In a spirit of good humor Robert Peters (30:115–20) finds the dominant poem today to be an "experiential" first-person poem derived from the trivia of one's life. A variant is the "wistful poem of dead forebears and children." A more literary version is represented by "Fulbright poems," those with "foreign, mostly European settings." The serious rival for the experiential first-person poem is the "bucolic poem," somewhat in the mode of Robert Frost and best represented recently by some of the poetry of William Stafford and James Wright. The classification may be a bit frivolous, but it does remind me of poems I have read, sometimes to my regret. As to what is wrong today, Peters simply blames the established writing programs and establishment magazines for "sanitizing poetry and stifling imagination." He singles out for condemnation institutions that used to be supporters of the new (Iowa Writing Program) and a periodical that believes it still is (*American Poetry Review*) and urges support for enlightened small publishers and journals who publish unknown and lesser known writers.

Richard Kostelanetz (*New York Quarterly* 31:115–19) laments that poets can no longer gain the prominence with the lay public that a Lowell, a Ginsberg, or a Plath had in the 1950s or 1960s. Even publication by a large commercial firm cannot guarantee this kind of attention. The good news is that it is a good time for fair remuneration for poets. The bad news is that the system of awards supports work that tends toward the more conventional than the innovative. Rewards for experimental poetry are nonexistent. Kostelanetz is not alone in this view, but the fault seems not to be that of little magazines.

A few other items are minutely relevant. The debate goes on about strict form and open forms. Wayne Dodd in an editorial essay, "The Art of Poetry and the Temper of the Times" (*OhR* 37:6–14), makes a case that the poem of the open form has been the main direction of American poetry ever since the publication of James Wright's "The Branch will not Break." Philip Levine, Louis Simpson, and Robert Bly are presented as examples of the current viability of open poetry. The alternative conservative judgment is given (*NER* 8:217–41) by Fred Muratori, who believes that modern poetry is suffering from a technical incompetence because poets no longer have "paid their dues" in the traditional forms. He is encouraged, however, by a group of young poets new to these pages who are undertaking the discipline of working with sonnet forms—Richard Kenney, Molly Peacock, Jilia Alvarez, and Gregory Djanikian. Muratori's thesis is a bit contrary to the more generally held belief that one sure thing contemporary poets have going for them is their technical competence.

Sherod Santos in "Notes Toward a Defense of Contemporary Poetry" (*NER* 8:284–96) enumerates the usual complaints about contemporary poetry and attempts a reply: there are no great poets; there is a sameness to all our poets; our poets are not sufficiently engaged in issues of immediate political or social concern. He confronts these criticisms with the "inclusiveness" of James Merrill's poetry, "the poetic craft" of Elizabeth Bishop, and "the variety of political subjects" pursued by Adrienne Rich. Andrew Hudgins explores the element of "risk" in "Risk in Contemporary Poetry" (*NER* 8:526–53). For one interested in what in modernism may have caused postmodernism the special issue of the *Sewanee Review*, Art Modern and Modernism (94,iii), may be worth examining, especially the article by contemporary poet James Applewhite, "Modernism and the Imagination of Ugliness" (pp. 418–39).

A European perspective emerges in Marc Chénetier's *Critical*

Angles. This collection of essays is intended to demonstrate European critical awareness of contemporary American literature. What it reveals is an almost exclusive preoccupation with American fiction. Only Ellman Crasnow's "Figure and Ground in Modern American Poetry" (pp. 60–76) turns to recent poetry. The approach, borrowing from Auerbach, Heidegger, and Derrida in an attempt to discover the strategic figures and settings used for confronting the modern abyss, is especially informative on the use of landscape by Ammons and Ashbery. The approach reminds one of the 1960s, when there was a serious concern with Heidegger and existentialism in American criticism.

There is a lament for the loss of the poet as critic in Robert von Hallberg's "American Poet-Critics since 1945" (*Reconstructing American Literary History*, pp. 280–99), to which I am responsive because I once wrote a review of James Dickey as critic with the plaintive title, "Whatever Happened to the Poet-Critic?" Von Hallberg evokes a poetic world when a young Robert Lowell could learn from the criticism of Tate, Eliot, Blackmur, Winters (and, I would add, from his teacher Ransom) what modernism had meant. He reminds us that the poet-critic was interested in problems of craft and in readings of poems. The history of literary criticism in English has been a history of poet-critics. In contrast, he finds a good deal of what has been written as criticism by poet-critics (e.g., by Robert Bly) in their concern with political writing embarrassing. He does mention exceptions in the work of Donald Hall, John Hollander, and Robert Pinsky; he fails to mention James Dickey who in his critical writings undoubtedly had some influence on postmodernism.

The last item for this section is the most entertaining, Laurence Goldstein's *The Flying Machine*, an attempt to survey the mythos created by the modern literary imagination about technology in its least earthbound manifestation, "the flying machine." Goldstein believes this symbol of man's extraterrestrial yearnings is used most powerfully when there is a dialectic tension between godlike pilot figures and the mass of earthbound humanity. Modern writers surveyed include H. G. Wells, Yeats, Hart Crane, Frost, Muriel Rukeyser, and James Dickey. Surprisingly, there is only brief mention of Randall Jarrell, who has clearly written the most famous aviator poem since World War II. His "Death of the Ball Turret Gunner" deserves its status "as the classic epitaph of the blasted gunner," but it does not fit Goldstein's thesis. Jarrell is not capable of the ambivalence described by James Dickey in his poem "The Firebombing," as he recalls the aesthetic detachment he felt in his plane far above the city he was firebombing below. Goldstein devotes a chapter to Rukeyser's long early poem, "Theory of Flight," as her challenge to Hart Crane's "Cape Hatteras." I am more impressed with his explication of Dickey's poem.

ii. The Middle Generation: Roethke, Lowell, Jarrell, Shapiro, Schwartz, and Nemerov

If a group portrait in retrospect was ever needed, it is of what was known appropriately in the 1950s and 1960s as "the middle generation." It is these poets who meant contemporary poetry in the 1950s and whose reputations have suffered in the 1980s when there seems to be more interest in their lives than in their works. In *The Middle Generation: The Lives and Poetry of Delmore Schwartz, Randall Jarrell, Robert Lowell, and John Berryman* (Archon), Bruce Bawer has attempted this portrait. Because he attempts to give us the lives as well as the works, his effort becomes just a bit too ambitious, too quick to see each individual poet in terms of group characteristics. On the other hand, he does establish that these poets had a sense of group awareness. Bawer shows in detail how they began under the common influence of Eliot and other modernists and then left Eliot behind as all found new subjects and forms from themselves and from one another. What is new in this study is the emphasis on "from one another." Bawer is convincing in his stress on the common traumas of turbulent childhoods, absent or dead fathers, overbearing mothers, which led to defenses in the form of compulsive personal habits and to an obsessive devotion to poetry which tragically crippled them as men but also provided their poetry with its greatest beauty and strength. Unfortunately, the biographical sketches overstress the eccentricities and compulsions, as if these were the only stuff of their daily lives, and he makes dubious claims for all, especially that there was a strong repressed homosexuality in all except possibly Jarrell. I agree that these troubled poets sought to vanquish their sense of alienation through their poetry. But Bawer overdramatizes when he makes the claim that their hunger for knowledge was "nothing more or less than a wish to find God." They wanted God to stand up and say "Here I am." Finally, it is a pity that the poet who is usually associated with this group and whose reputation has remained the highest, Theodore Roethke, is excluded from this group because of individual differences in his attitude toward poetry. It makes one feel that something must be wrong with the thesis.

Roethke does receive attention in a survey of criticism in Randall Stiffler's *Theodore Roethke: The Poet and His Critics* (American Library Association). As part of a series, the book has a prescribed form, a review of all the important reviews of each book, followed by an overview in the context of overall themes. In the overviews Stiffler does a good job of tracing how criticism has revealed the developing mysticism of Roethke in the greenhouse poems and in the Lost Son narratives. Stiffler is also effective in chronicling the literary influence of Roethke on students like Carolyn Kizer, James Wright, David Wagoner, Richard Hugo, but also beyond these to an impact on major poets like Ammons, Ashbery, Kinnell, Levertov, Merwin, and Snyder.

Though this is not a banner year for Roethke criticism, there is yet another explication of his most explicated poem, "My Papa's Waltz" (Ronald R. Jansen, *Expl* 44,ii:51–54), which I liked. Jansen brings out all the contrasts, the formality of the waltz and the informality of Papa, the grim vision of helpless boy (a bit overstated) and the rather hilarious image of the drunken father trying to step formally through the paces of the waltz, perhaps to imaginary music. Jansen sees in the drunken sway a parody of the formal dance. Balancing off this humor of incongruous contrasts are family portraits of drunken father (again a bit overstated), angry mother, desperate child (definitely overstated). The final contrast is between the explicit waltz and an implicit dance of death. The whole here is definitely more than the sum of the parts, and we have what is rare, a good old-fashioned explication. Another explication requires only to be recorded: Nancy Ann Smith reads "Where Knock Is Open Wide" (*Expl* 44,iii:69–80) in the context of what she regards as the key passage, "a real hurt is soft."

Harold Bloom's doubts about the continuing significance of Robert Lowell would seem to be allayed by the appearance in 1986 of an important collection of essays on Lowell, *Robert Lowell: Essays on the Poetry*, ed. Steven Gould Axelrod and Helen Deese (Cambridge), featuring an unusually high number—nine—of new essays. This is an important collection intended to reassess Lowell's poetry and to restimulate critical thinking by turning attention from the private life of an imperfect human being to a still important poet. We are reminded by Axelrod in his introduction and by Marjorie Perloff in her essay that Lowell has been savaged by biographers far more than Robert Frost. Axelrod, "Lowell's Living Name: An Introduction" (pp. 1–25), provides the context for the reexaminations and the best explication thus far of the poem "George III." Jay Martin's reprinted "Grief and Nothingness: Loss and Mourning in Lowell's Poetry" (pp. 26–50) directs attention to the sense of loss and mourning in Lowell's personal life and shows how he copes with this in his poetry. Albert Gelpi, "The Reign of the Kingfisher: Robert Lowell's Prophetic Poetry" (pp. 51–69), reevaluates *Lord Weary's Castle*, reconfirming to some extent Jarrell's judgment of "masterpiece." Sandra Gilbert (another reprint) rereads "Skunk Hour." Lawrence Kramer (the third reprint) looks again at the "Life Studies" sequence. Perloff's article, "*Poètes Maudits* of the Genteel Tradition: Lowell and Berryman" (pp. 99–116), is a review of recent biographical revelations and a new look at how Lowell transcends the personal in poems in *Life Studies* and *For the Union Dead.* Alex Calder, "*Notebook 1967–68*: Writing the Process Poem" (pp. 117–38), chooses the sonnet sequences in *Notebook* for his reevaluation. Calvin Bedient in "Illegible Lowell (The Late Volumes)" (pp. 139–55) contends that in his late volumes Lowell often found the full development of his art. Alan Holder, "Going Back, Going Down, Breaking: *Day by Day*" (pp. 156–79), and A. Kingsley Weatherhead, "*Day by Day*: His End Game" (pp. 217–30), examine *Day by Day.* Helen Deese directs attention to "Lowell and the Visual Arts" (pp. 180–216). George McFadden, "'Prose or This': What Lowell Made of a Diminished Thing" (pp. 231–55), returns to the last work, *Day by Day*, seeing it as a fitting coda in itself to Lowell's poetic achievement. This is a timely tribute to a poet whose reputation needs critical rescue, and one of the most uniformly impressive collections of essays I have encountered recently.

Also worthy of comment is Katharine Wallingford's "Robert Lowell and Free Association" (*Mosaic* 19,iv:121–33). This article begins with mention of a letter Lowell wrote in 1949 to George Santayana, which seems to follow the psychoanalytic technique of free association. From this letter, Wallingford argues that Lowell made poetry out of the free associational process because it was natural for him to think this way. He was usually able to transmute associational material into successful poetry, thereby gaining both a sense of spontaneity and a means of alternating between detachment and involvement. The point is worth making, but more could be said about how Lowell, always the careful craftsman, controls the free association. William Doreski (*CEA* 48,iii:38–49) makes a minor point, suggesting the influence of Baudelaire and Rimbaud on the change of Lowell's persona in *History* from the customary humble voice to an impassioned witness to societal corruption. Baudelaire may have taught him to subdue fears in the very design of poetry, and Rimbaud asserted the superiority of the poet to a corrupt and disintegrating society. All this is made to seem very plausible. Ronald K. Giles explores a major poem in "For the Union Dead" (*CollL* 13: 266–71), and another one of Lowell's best receives consideration by Alice Hall Petry, "That 'Tudor Ford' Reconsidered: Robert Lowell's 'Skunk Hour'" (*PLL* 22:70–75).

Randall Jarrell's reputation as a poet may have received a boost from the great interest in Mary Jarrell's edition of the letters, and from the announcement of the new authorized biography to be written by William Pritchard. Stuart Wright has produced *Randall Jarrell: A Descriptive Bibliography 1929–1983* (Virginia), a handsome bibliography of all his primary works. Volume 35 of *Field* offers "Randall Jarrell: A Symposium," which turns from two decades of emphasis on Jarrell's criticism back to the poetry. There are 10 essays, the majority by young poets, which, though very brief, make a rather impressive case for the poetry. One of the charges made against Jarrell as a poet in the 1960s, the plainness of his language, is made a virtue. He is compared to the great American poets of the plain style—Whitman, Frost, Williams—as well as praised for his ability to convey a sense of childhood wonder. Laura Jensen in "Potential for Whole Totem" (pp. 10–13) contrasts the serious worldview of Jarrell with the playful side that emerges in the letters. She finds the explanation for his serious side suggested in the early poem, "The Bad Music," written perhaps out of a disappointment in love. She conjectures that Jarrell's fate was formed by women, to whom as a poet he has always been sensitive, something that women writers today should appreciate. Bruce Weigel in "An Autobiography of Nightmare" (pp. 15–18) revisits Jarrell's most explicated poem, "The Death of the Ball Turret Gunner," to speak for the literalness as well as the figurative structure, the stark effectiveness of the unadorned presentation of death underlying an attitude of "the indignation of acceptance." C. D. Wright, in "Mission of the Surviving Gunner" (pp. 19–20), makes the minor point that only the state and not the actual enemy is blamed in this and other Jarrell war poems. Fred

Chappell in "The Longing to Belong" (pp. 23–29) shows how Jarrell uses the child as outsider not only to express a longing to belong to some humane order of existence but also to admit movingly that this sort of order cannot exist in the world we know. There is, consequently, not a single poem depicting a genuinely happy child in all of Jarrell. David St. John (pp. 33–36) regards "Seele im Raum" as a "stunning dramatic monologue" that embodies many of Jarrell's lifelong concerns and influences, such as love of fable and folktale, close reading of Freud, devotion to Rilke and things German, and empathy for the isolated sensibility, especially that of women. Ralph Burns, "The Plain Truth in 'The Truth'" (pp. 39–42), defends the poem against James Dickey's charge that it lacks the power to rise above the sentimental to a meaningful level. The simple persona and plain language are suitable for a poem spoken by a child after an air raid, and save the poem from sentimentality. David Young in "Day for Night" (pp. 46–49) resurrects one of my favorite Jarrell poems, "Nestus Gurley," about "a man's mythologizing of his paperboy." Nancy Willard in "Radiant Facts" (pp. 51–54) chooses the children's poem "Bats," reminding us that Jarrell turned to poems for children when he could not write other poems, and contending that this poem, and perhaps others of this ilk, should be as well regarded as his more serious work. Marianne Bourch, "Rhetoric and Mastery" (pp. 57–61), looks at "Field and Forest" as a poem willfully and profoundly "plain." She tries to tie together the two parts, the view from an airplane above and the commentary on the farmer below, with what she regards as the functional symbolism of the fox and the cave. Finally, David Walker, in "The Shape on the Bed" (pp. 64–67), surveys Jarrell's poems on childhood to identify what Robert Lowell meant when he called Jarrell our most "heartbreaking poet." I have summarized each of these essays because, taken together, they make a good case for Jarrell as poet. It will be interesting to see how far this new interest in Jarrell goes toward reevaluating his reputation and his place among this former "middle generation."

Patricia Rodger Black in "The Atom Bomb: Jarrell's Dream Work and *The Lost World*" (*MissQ* 39:31–40) reconsiders Jarrell's last work, which was not generally well received at the time of its publication but which is now finding its admirers. She begins with Jarrell's puzzling statement that he was writing a book of poems about the atom bomb. Her explanation draws on Jarrell's admiration for the dream work of Freud and his acceptance of the belief that the unconscious helps the poet write a good poem. *The Lost World* originated in threats of atomic destruction current then, removed to the setting of the world of American fantasies, Hollywood, and drawing on memories of the set of an old dinosaur movie. This is an interesting idea, but the article does not quite make a case. I mention J. A. Bryant, Jr.'s *Understanding Randall Jarrell*, part of the series of paperbacks on contemporary writers begun in 1985 by the University of South Carolina Press, last because, although it may be of some value to students as an introduction, it contributes little new to a reevaluation of Jarrell. Bryant makes the unremarkable claim that Jarrell was a modernist with romantic tendencies in spite of himself, and that he wrote best on subjects that were personal and required sympathy. He lists the useful influences, adding one sometimes forgotten—that of Ernie Pyle on the war poetry. He is disappointing on Jarrell as a critic and does not provide a clear portrait of Jarrell, as he impressed most of his contemporaries, as an intellectual. The best of the several explications are those on "Nestus Gurley" and on "Woman," two very fine poems.

Hayden Carruth, in "A Salute in Time" (*CEA* 48,iii:21–24), part of a tribute to Karl Shapiro, recalls Shapiro's *Person, Place, and Thing* (1942) as the first book by a contemporary poet he encountered and the war poems as the first to make an impression, even before Jarrell's, and states that he still regards Shapiro's "An Essay on Rime" as the only contemporary essay in verse worth reading. Robert Phillips, "Karl Shapiro and His Latest Poems" (*CEA* 48,iii:24–28), begins with the observation that reputations can change and lists poets whose reputations are nearly forgotten and poets we have lost; but Shapiro, he continues, still writes poems like the "The Sawdust Boys" and "The Cathedral Bells," which have not received the attention they deserve because his most recent volume of poems, *Love and War, Art and God*, was published by a small press (Stuart Wright) in the South.

There is still no great interest in Delmore Schwartz, only a lone item, Jo Brans's "The Mission for Plato in Delmore Schwartz" (*CentR* 30:507–28). It begins with Schwartz's statement in the preface to *Summer Knowledge* that "every point of view, every kind of knowledge and every kind of experience is limited and ignorant" to stress that, notwithstanding, Platonism serves as the basis for his best poetry. This is hardly news about the poet whose reputation has suffered more than that of any other of the middle generation. Robert Phillips contributes an edition with introduction of Schwartz's "bagatelles," 19 short essays, most never before published (*The Ego Is Always at the Wheel* [New Directions]).

Howard Nemerov was born within a decade of the Middle Generation poets, but was even more than Shapiro apart from the group. John F. Skinner contributes "Semantic Play in the Poetry of Howard Nemerov" to *Literature in Performance* (6,ii:44–59), indicative of the interesting dimensions that can come from such an approach. Skinner contends that Nemerov's poems "abound with play" and discusses games, puzzles, jokes, play motifs, wordplay, and what he calls "semantic tensiveness," the contradiction between what words say and "feel" in poetry, as functional in several poems.

iii. The Poetry of Women—Bishop, Rich, Levertov, Plath, Forché, and Sexton

It was a strong year for scholarship and criticism on women's poetry, a year in which it was made clear that the poets in the forefront of women's studies are those who are politically engaged for feminism and/or against war. There were at least two important books. The first of these is Alice Suskin Ostriker's *Stealing the Language: The Emergence of Women's Poetry in America* (Beacon). The subject is both the triumph of woman's poetry, beginning in the early 1960s, and the choice made then to explore "experiences central to their sex and to find forms and styles appropriate to this exploration." Women poets began confronting the view that asserting true poetry is genderless is a "disguised form of believing that poetry is masculine." This is an important book for focusing very convincingly on the years 1960 to 1965, even though some might not agree that women poets have "stolen the language" from male poets or that prior to this time women poets had a sense of being imprisoned in an "oppressor's language." Ostriker does make a case for inequities and for women poets being at their best when they express anger in social or political terms. Rich and Levertov score very well by this criterion; others like Plath are regarded as vacillating between past roles and present, and as writing poetry that reflects this tension. *Stealing the Language* is most effective at discussing the strategies women have devised to subvert and overcome what has been denied to them as women poets—authoritative expression. Ostriker contends that as a result of this struggle strong personae have emerged; when a woman poet today says "I" she is likely to mean herself. The mask "has grown into flesh." The book will help students of contemporary poetry realize that the late '50s and early '60s are noted for other things than the rise of Beat and confessional poetry.

Equally important to women's studies, but more limited in its coverage, is Paula Bennett's *My Life a Loaded Gun.* The thesis here is that the female poet has lacked the male poet's long-established tradition of "self-exploration and self-validation." She has been torn between "restrictive definitions" of what a woman is and her own fears of seeming unwomanly. Consequently, the speaking voice in the poetry has lacked the power of experience. The three poets considered here, Emily Dickinson, Sylvia Plath, Adrienne Rich, have had to dissociate their creative power from their woman selves only to discover that to function at their best they have had to heal the internal divisions and accept the actual self as "the base on which a woman poet must work." The thesis suits the development of Adrienne Rich best, but it is also used to explain the power of Sylvia Plath's best poems as coming from her sense of betrayal by her husband. For some tastes too much credence may again be given to the importance of a "rage for order" theory, suggesting Medusa as the effective symbol for the woman poet's liberated self and as the explanation for the best of woman's poetry. Bennett demonstrates convincingly the importance of the bond established among women poets in the '60s.

The best book on an individual woman poet of this period is Claire Keyes's *The Aesthetics of Power: The Poetry of Adrienne Rich* (Georgia). Keyes traces Rich's rejection of her earlier masculine persona, which had brought her early notice, leading her to rebel against a male-dominated world and to discover new experiential and poetic possibilities for women. Keyes does admit the danger that Rich's commitment to feminine ideals may be regarded as a limitation to her universality, but concludes that Rich is without doubt a major poet.

Further support for Paula Bennett's view of the power of the Plath poems written between 26 September 1962 and 5 February 1963 comes from Marjorie Perloff, "The Two Ariels: The (Re)Making of the Sylvia Plath Canon," pp. 308–34 in *Poems in Their Place: The Intertextuality and Order of Poetic Collections* (No. Car.). Perloff contrasts Plath's intentions for *Ariel* with the book actually edited and published by her husband, Ted Hughes. She contends that Hughes left out poems and added others that make Plath's suicide look like the inevitable climax of her disease, in order to direct attention from the impact on Plath of her sense of betrayal from her husband's affair with the wife of a mutual friend. Perloff not only asserts the power of the omitted poems but also contends that those published, such as "Daddy," would gain even more power and greater lucidity by restoration of the context Plath intended for them. Perloff's essay offers reasonable conjecture and even fascinating literary detective work based on a knowledge of manuscripts and the journals. It would get my award as one of the most interesting essays of the year.

This was a decent year for Elizabeth Bishop scholarship, and a very good one for consideration of the political poetry of Denise Levertov and Carolyn Forché. Carolyn Handa's "Vision and Change: The Poetry of Elizabeth Bishop" (*AmerP* 3,ii:18–34) is a nicely structured explication of an anecdotal remark which leads her to an analysis of the importance of "slightly self-mocking" grim humor in Bishop's poetry. The remark, made to Elizabeth Stevenson, was: "It would add interest, certainly, to your book if you could have a footnote saying I'd been shot in the Brazilian Revolution of April Fools' Day, 1964, but I wasn't." Handa not only finds this characteristic of Bishop's tone but of her syntactical arrangement, a long hypothethical clause, followed by a shorter, rapid statement of the actual situation. The tone and syntax both are expressive of the tension in the poetry between withdrawal from the world and resignation to life. This is the kind of article that attracts an editor's attention to a manuscript readily; it begins interestingly and then makes something of the beginning. Alfred Corn's "Elizabeth Bishop's Nativities" (*Shenandoah* 36,iii:21–45) lengthily discusses religious allusions in Bishop's "Nativities" and tries to show that Bishop is responding to and defining herself against Robert Lowell's *History*. Finally, there is a source study that also adds to the story of the mutual admiration of the two poets for their respective work, Martha Carson Bradley's "Lowell's 'My Last Afternoon with Uncle Devereux Winslow': The Model for Bishop's 'First Death in Nova Scotia'" (*CP* 19:117–31).

No woman poet receives more attention than Denise Levertov. Jane Hallisey, "Denise Levertov . . . Forever a Stranger and Pilgrim" (*CentR* 30:281–91), connects Levertov's poetry to her religious and familial heritage. This perspective, as well as her personal view, helps fuse the real world of social and political concern with the spiritual world. Of more significance is Richard Jackson's "A Common Time: The Poetry of Denise Levertov" (*Sagetrieb* 5,ii:5–46).

This rather difficult article attempts to tie Jean Paul Sartre's description of time in *Being and Nothingness* as a "shimmer of Nothingness on the surface of a strictly atemporal being" with Levertov's concern with time and the question of how one writes poems to give a fullness and being to nothingness. Jackson contends that in Levertov there is always something that transcends the particular, even though she had to come to understand in her later poetry that her own language and her own time sense "may also deteriorate." This is suggested as a reason for the avoidance of the "I" and subjective modes in much of her later poetry.

Two items deal with Levertov's turn to political poetry. Nancy Sisko's "*To Stay Alive*: Levertov's Search for a Revolutionary Poetry" (*Sagetrieb* 5,ii:47–60) focuses on *To Stay Alive* as a record of Levertov's inner and outer experience, with her younger sister Olga as the first standard for self-judgment of her effort to "save the world," then moving on to a hagiography in which she catalogues her personal saints of war resistance as a new standard. Levertov finds she cannot accept physical discomfort, and she is unable "to bend her poetry absolutely to her will." This article is valuable for outlining a dramatic structure and specifying a major conflict in the book. Lorrie Smith, "Song of Experience: Denise Levertov's Political Poetry" (*ConL* 27:213–32), attempts far too much for an essay, a discussion of seven volumes of political poetry. She does make a good case that with Levertov we have an example of "a deeply ethical imagination grappling with difficult political issues over the last twenty years." Smith also attempts to see her conflict as the dilemma of poets of this generation with growing political consciousness, a personal poetry that explores political implications of the poet's own life and environment, and the use for the most part of traditional forms and idioms. Smith believes that current postmodernist romanticism, influenced by Williams, has gradually learned to accommodate a disjunction between personal and political anguish. This is an interesting theory which requires more evidence.

Joan Dargan's "Poetic and Political Consciousness in Denise Levertov and Carolyn Forché" (*CEA* 48,iii:58–67) provides a transition from Levertov to the other woman poet whose political poetry is still attracting critical attention. Both poets have constructed the effective persona of a witness or observer reporting "the domestication of horror" in a matter-of-fact style that increases the effect. Levertov affirms life in all its forms and in its dignity. Forché stresses learning from her fellow artists and her own experience that a commitment to social justice must transcend natural boundaries. Not much is new here, but it is good to have the comparison and contrast. John Mann, "Carolyn Forché: Poetry and Survival" (*AmerP* 3,iii:51–69), believes that recent poets have turned from the question of whether poetry can be political to whether poetry can be adequate to a century that has witnessed the Holocaust and other crimes against humanity. The latter is answered successfully in Forché's poetry because despair is somewhat moderated by the act of the poet speaking, and she commands an effective tension between silence and the scream. As part of a symposium on "The Writer and Our World," Forché gives in "Lesson in Commitment" (*TriQ* 65:30–38) her own account of her experiences in El Salvador as observer and as poet. This most detailed account begins with her going to Spain to translate a Salvadorian poet living there, her work for Amnesty International, her experiences and private emotional release in writing the poems, and her problems in publishing them.

In the criticism of 1986, confessional poetry is out and political poetry is in, just as the political film seems to be. Political poetry has its problems, as Nan Nowik demonstrates in the work of three writers in "Mixing Art and Politics: The Writings of Adrienne Rich, Marge Piercy, and Alice Walker" (*CentR* 30:208–18). The personal and confessional rather than the political poetry of Anne Sexton invites only one item, but an interesting one dealing with an important relationship in the poetry: Diana Hume George, "How We Danced: Anne Sexton on Fathers and Daughters" (*WS* 12:167–78).

iv. The Rest: Major and Minor Poets

***a.* Olson, Snyder, Berry, Ginsberg.** A grouping here is not intended to imply that these poets are of less importance or are of one poetic faith and practice. The influence of Charles Olson is still being explored; Stanley Kunitz was honored for a distinguished career; James Dickey is getting attention for his poetry once more, mostly in a newsletter devoted to his work; W. S. Merwin always attracts notice; Ammons and Kinnell are poets of power to their admirers; Merrill and Ashbery are considered major poets; then there is perhaps the major poet, Robert Penn Warren. The problem is that I have space for only a cook's tour of who is and will be of greatest critical interest and as to whether poetry is still "cooked" and "raw," experiential or formalist.

Michael F. Harper contrasts Olson with his mentor, Ezra Pound, and finds a different concept of history from Pound's in "The Sins of the Father and Ezra Pound" (*AmerP* 4,i:30–54), an attempt to disagree with Paul Bove and find development in Olson. The importance of Olson to postmodernist poetry is now a matter of historical record in William McPheron's *Charles Olson: A Bibliographic Guide to the Critical Reception, 1941–1983* (Garland), which documents a long and a distinguished career from Olson's first published essay on Melville through the definitive edition of *The Maximus Poems*. McPheron seems to cover everything published by Olson and all the critical reaction in English and the foreign language reception, offering critical testimony to his strong influence on contemporary poetry.

Woon-Ping Chin Holaday, in "Formlessness and Form in Gary Snyder's *Mountains and Rivers without End*" (*Sagetrieb* 5,i:41–52), begins by quoting Snyder's "I am a striver not a finisher" and relating him to "anti-closure" conceptions of poetry. Holaday goes on to argue for the influence of Mahayana Buddhist philosophy on Snyder's theory that there is no distinction between "formlessness" and "form." Patrick D. Murphy, "Penance or Perception: Spirituality and Land in the Poetry of Gary Snyder and Wendell Berry" (*Sagetrieb* 5,ii: 61–72), compares the two poets in their use of archetypes of "The Promised Land" and "The Garden" in landscape and nature poetry. Berry stays primarily in the Judeo-Christian tradition, with appropriate emphasis on creation, the garden or earth in its natural state, especially stressing the importance of agrarian stewardship of the land. Snyder goes beyond this tradition, drawing from shamanism, Hindu-Buddhist beliefs, and even North American primitivism; he does not believe in the Fall and he is more interested in nature as a frame for "a poetic vision quest." Murphy tells me more about Berry than about Snyder. One other item, Donald Jacob Leed's "Gary Snyder: An Unpublished Preface" (*JML* 13,i:177–80), documents an early influence by publishing the preface prepared for Snyder's translation of Han Shan's *Cold Mountain Poems*. Allen Ginsberg is represented by two testimonies on influence. His own essay, "Pound's Influence" (*APR* 15,iv:7–8), is a listing of the teachings of Pound, stressing especially the matter of "attention to the tone or pitch of syllables tending toward music in our poetry." Jennie Skerl provides an account of "Ginsberg on Burroughs" (*MLS* 16:271–78).

***b.* Bly, Stafford, Wright.** Robert Bly scholarship benefits from William H. Roberson's *Robert Bly: A Primary and Secondary Bibliography* (Scarecrow). Roberson also includes Bly's essay, "In Search of an American Muse," commenting that "the American poet has much to do alone," without traditions. And he contributes an essay of his own, "Some Thoughts on Robert Bly," stressing Bly's belief that poets operate under a moral imperative to involve themselves in political and social studies and commenting on the variety of Bly's poetry—nature poems, satirical, surrealistic, and political poems—a point not made by many recent critics. Richard Sugg's Twayne volume, *Robert Bly* (TUSAS 513) also appeared this year, providing the usual competent introduction to poetry and prose with a very sparsely annotated bibliography. In this case a Twayne volume was strangely long overdue. Sugg surveys the poet and explicates the poems adequately. He makes a strong (to some, an overstated) case for Bly as a man of letters, showing the full variety of his career. He concludes sensibly that Bly's reputation will rest on his poetry, where his main achievement has been "his exploration and a re-creation in poetry of an imaginative geography of the human psychic landscape."

William Stafford is the subject of a pamphlet by David A. Carpenter, *William Stafford* (WWS 72). Carpenter stresses Stafford's belief that an individual's psychological and spiritual health depends upon an almost "religious identification with the relatively wild, non-human world." In his later poetry Stafford appreciates the wilderness less for itself than for its value as a contrast to the human world. Two of the strengths of his poetry are his uncertainties and frustrations and his contrasting determination to continue to make discoveries about himself and the world through his writing, no matter how disheartening those discoveries may be. This is a well-written, coherent introduction that may oversimplify a bit but in general rings true. J. Gill Holland is enlightening in a reading of Stafford's fine poem, "Traveling Through the Dark" (*Expl* 45,i:55–58).

James Wright is represented by "The Music of Poetry" (*APR* 5,ii: 43–47), a talk he gave as part of the "Poetry in the Schools" program. Published here for the first time, it makes the point that to talk about poetry is to talk about the structure of poetry and the sound of poetry; to talk about the music of poetry is to talk about particular poems. Wright is also the subject of an interesting article by Jim Elledge," The Land Deep in Sound: Insects in the Poetry of James Wright" (*AmerP* 4,i:72–77). Elledge demonstrates that there is a heavy reliance on nature in Wright's imagery, an important aspect of which is his use of insects which take on a significance beyond their roles in nature: in many poems a person's lack of individuality and his helpless struggle against various societal, economic, and psychological forces are indicated by the use of insect metaphors.

***c.* Kinnell and Dickey.** Galway Kinnell and James Dickey are not neglected. Joyce Dyer, "The Music of Galway Kinnell's *Mortal Acts, Mortal Words*" (*NConL* 16,iii:5–8) makes a point that had not gone unnoticed, that music is important in all volumes of Kinnell's poetry. But Dyer develops this point to show how different types of notes in his poetry, "chords of beauty," "grace-notes of hope," and "courage songs," urge us to accept our mortal state. In *Mortal Acts*, as in later poetry, mortality is what Kinnell struggles to accept and celebrate through song. To Kinnell there cannot be the terrible silence of a nihilistic universe so long as there is sound. David Kleinbard, in "Galway Kinnell's Poetry of Transformation" (*CentR* 30:41–56), stresses Kinnell's romantic faith in the imagination as having "taken the place" of the Divine Savior. Stones in his poetry are not markers of death but symbols of "miraculous new life." James Dickey benefits from having a newsletter devoted to his poetry and prose. Dickey has always placed his poetry first, but most of his critics choose to write on his prose, finding new and not so new things to say about his first novel, *Deliverance*, certainly Dickey's great success of the 1970s. The Fall 1986 *James Dickey Newsletter* (3,i) reprints very brief testimony by younger poets on the impact of his poetry on them, offered at a conference at DeKalb College. Betty Adcock ("James Dickey: Man Made of Poems," pp. 2–5) praises both the natural world described and the man-made artifacts of the poems themselves, the subject matter and the craft. David Bottoms ("Witnessing for the Worldly Mystic," pp. 6–9) stresses the influence of *Buckdancer's Choice* on poets of his generation and then the impact of Dickey's personality, with all its own wonderful personae. T. R. Hummer (" 'The Thousand Variations of One Song': James Dickey and the Impetus of Influence," pp. 9–12) remembers the "energy of his poetry," and singles out "The Firebombing" as a great political poem of the 1960s, a sentiment I would second. David Smith ("A Kinsman's Signature," pp. 13–19) praises Dickey as an experiential poet of the New South." He singles out "May Day Sermon" as something new as well as a fusion of ecclesiastical vision. One novelist contributes.

Philip Lee Williams chooses "The Heaven of Animals" and "The Lifeguard" and reveals that the title of his own novel came from his being haunted by the line "At the heart of a distant forest" ("In the Beginning: '*At The Heart of a Distant Forest*'," pp. 26–28). These testimonies remind us of just how important a poet Dickey was in the 1960s. Nothing is said about the later poetry. Eugene McNamara ("James Dickey's 'The Eye-Beaters': Poetry of The Burning Bush," pp. 20–24) does direct attention to one of the poems that seemed to mark new directions in Dickey's work. "The Eye-Beaters" explores through a dual track, poem and gloss, "a man's thought process as he encounters senseless and randomly inflicted pain." Reason is useless. The visitor must cope with his imagination alone, accept the primacy of the savage self, and write the poetry of "The Burning Bush." The participatory aspect of the poem is stressed; the reader is invited to go into his own deep self. I find nothing new here, but I am glad to see attention redirected to one of Dickey's most powerful poems, overlooked because of the slight regard given his poems of the '70s.

***d.* The Grand Old Men: Warren and Kunitz.** This is the place for brief mention of tribute paid to Robert Penn Warren and Stanley Kunitz. The tribute to Warren is a collection of essays, *Time's Glory: Original Essays on Robert Penn Warren*, ed. James A. Grimshaw, Jr. (Central Arkansas). The glory in this uneven volume consists of two essays by the authors of the best books on Warren, a new essay on the nonfiction by James Justus ("Warren and the Narrator as Historical Self," pp. 109–18) and on the poetry by Victor Strandberg ("Poet of Youth: Robert Penn Warren at Eighty," pp. 91–106). Stanley Kunitz was always a poet who sought his own way into the poetry of his age, and, for that reason, may not have always received his proper critical recognition. *A Celebration for Stanley Kunitz: On His Eightieth Birthday* (Sheep Meadow Press) pays tribute through poems by fellow poets, but it also includes a few essays. These are mostly reminiscences which have the value of suggesting the impact of Kunitz as a sophisticated and an intellectual poet conversing with his fellow poets, with artists who met at his home, and in his garden with friends and his plants. Kunitz is a poet who achieved success early, and befriended other poets who needed his encouragement, like Theodore Roethke. What is remembered here is the staying power of the conversationalist.

v. Poet as Craftsman: Ashbery, Merwin, Merrill, Rexroth

John Ashbery is, not surprisingly, of great interest to critics. There are more articles than can receive the comment they deserve. John Rawson in "A Poet in the Post-modern Playground" (*TLS* 4 July:723–24) judges Ashbery as the most highly regarded living poet in America and compares him extensively to Wallace Stevens. Lee Edelman, "The Pose of Imposture: Ashbery's 'Self-Portrait in a Convex Mirror'" (*TLC* 32:95–114) gives us a reading of a complex and important poem in terms of the title, which specifies that the poem is an attempt to redirect attention from the portrait of the self to the distinctive angle of the portraiture. Edelman sees the self-portrait as an entrance into Joyce's "a mirror within a mirror"; the self-portrait mirrors not the self but the process of mirroring the self. This is a sophisticated analysis of the poem as "deconstructive self-poetry," drawing on structuralism and especially on deconstructionism. The same poem is viewed from another angle by Thomas Getz, "John Ashbery's 'Self-Portrait in a Convex Mirror' and Henry James's 'The Liar'" (*SHR* 13:42–51), who argues that it is intended "as convex mirror" of James's story. Thomas Gardner, "Reading Ashbery" (*CEA* 48,iii:50–57), makes the same point developed in more detail by Lee Edelman. Ashbery's work grows out of a tension, the desire to capture immediate experience and the accompanying awareness that what is isolated is not the moment itself but always and only form. The most informative piece of criticism on Ashbery is David Bromwich's "The Self Against Its Images" (*Raritan* 5,iv:36–58). Bromwich makes it clear that he is dealing with a poet who writes about life "with the guarded pleasures of one who cannot possess it." He refers to the picture of the artist in "Syringa" as a person so receptive to the stimulus of present things as to be unconscious of his role in creating them. Bromwich goes to the right poems for suggesting consistent views of poet and poetry.

Mark Christhilf in *W. S. Merwin The Mythmaker* (Missouri) classifies Merwin as both modernist and postmodernist. He believes that with *The Moving Target* Merwin transformed his poetic style, contributing significantly to the emerging postmodernist aesthetic, but that there are not "two poets named Merwin." Both modernist and postmodernist share "a vitalizing concern with the relationship of poetry and mythology." In the volumes immediately following *The Moving Target* Merwin assumed the role of mythmaker, giving imaginative order to world, to history, to individual existence. In the '80s, however, he became more ambivalent towards this role. Christhilf is interesting in that he relates Merwin's view of poet as mythmaker to the context of poetry in the last four decades. I value most highly his comments on the autobiographical memories of Merwin's boyhood in *Unframed Originals* (1982), conflicting with Merwin's growing uncertainty about the place of personal experience in his poetry, a concern shared with contemporaries like Bly and Wright.

The best I can say of Judith Moffett's *James Merrill: An Introduction to the Poetry* (Columbia) is that it is an adequate introduction for undergraduates to the major works and themes of a very important poet whose work deserves a much more definitive analysis. It does not demonstrate the importance of Merrill to postmodernist poetry or show why he may be the most imaginative of living poets with a remarkable talent for short lyrics and, more rare, for the long poem. D. L. McDonald's "Merrill and Freud: The Psychopathology of Eternal Life" (*Mosaic* 19,iv:159–72) focuses on a singular aspect of Merrill's poetry, his imitation of Ouija board experiences. Freud is brought into the picture because the Ouija board is a means of producing verbal material without conscious control, a variant of the free association on which psychoanalysis relies. The specific influence argued for here is Freud's case history of Daniel Paul Schreber, and the point is made that Merrill's occult journey begins in conflicts comparable to Schreber's.

vi. A Miscellany

***a.* Booth, Ignatow, Levine.** Who else received attention? Philip Booth, whose interview with Stephen Dunn was published (*NER* 8: 134–58). Of interest here are the comments on the influence of Thoreau because of living at Lincoln, Massachusetts, near Walden, and on the more contemporary influence of Richard Wilbur. Teaching Wallace Stevens brought Booth to a realization of the importance of being more abstract, of "trying to get at ideas." If I offered one, this would receive my award as the most interesting interview of the year. David Ignatow receives "Three Appreciations" (*AmerP* 3,ii:32–52) from Dianne Wakoski, Linda Wagner, and Milton Hindus. Wakoski finds him to be "the most American" among our first-rate poets, Apollonian in his longing for perfection and Dionysian in his knowledge of human failures. Wagner praises the "spirit of openness" in his poems, an acceptance of both the anger and joy of living in which he tries to include the reader. Hindus finds in the "active element of sympathy" in his poetry something which isolates Ignatow from poets now much as Whitman and Williams were isolated from their contemporaries. Appreciations seem much in vogue with the graying of our poets. This is one of the better contributions. Jerome Mazzaro's "David Ignatow's Post-Vietnam War Poetry" (*CentR* 30:219–27) compares Ignatow to Whitman in an ability "to touch on many subjects and many people," and shows that his Vietnam-era experiences have led him in his poetry to seek to remind America that "variety," "compassion," and "individualism" are still alive and well.

Robert Hedin's "In Search of a New World: The Anarchist Dream in the Poetry of Philip Levine" (*AmerP* 4,i:64–71) makes another contribution to analysis of political poetry by showing how the moral courage of "the Spanish anarchists," particularly Buenaventura Durruti, is a model of social behavior for Levine. Donald Gutierrez, in "Musing with Sappho: Kenneth Rexroth's Love Poem 'When We with Sappho' as Reverie" (*AmerP* 4,i:54–63), is a defense of reverie not as "escapist activity," but a form of transcendence, "a valuable removal from the world of time." Reverie is placed in the context of Gaston Bachelard's concept of "significant day-dreaming." This is a detailed and informative reading of the poem.

***b.* Bowles, Dorn, Oppenheimer, Wagoner.** In a special issue of *Twentieth Century Literature* on the expatriate writer Paul Bowles edited by Edward Butscher and Irving Malin, Butscher offers "Paul Bowles as Poet: Excursions of a Minimal Anti-self" (350–72), a discussion of *Next to Nothing: Collected Poems*, all the poems Bowles wanted to preserve. Bowles, as poet and fiction writer, is placed in the tradition of "Poe, Faulkner and other Gothic Writers." Tandy Sturgeon offers "An Interview with Edward Dorn" (*ConL* 27:1–16), a poet with Black Mountain and Charles Olson connections who has never sought wide commercial circulation, publishing with "people not houses." Dorn comments on his relationship with Olson, and on the excitement of teaching and writing poetry. Joel Oppenheimer is not as well remembered as Black Mountain poet or as a contributor to the *Black Mountain Review*. He is the subject of a study by David Thibodaux, *Joel Oppenheimer: An Introduction* (Camden House).

Thibodaux discusses changes in Oppenheimer's poetry from the '50s to the '80s, and makes a comparison between the use of phenomenology in his poetry and that of Roethke and Lowell.

Gail Miller offers "Interview with David Wagoner" (*JNT* 7:45–49). The most interesting moments are Wagoner's views on performing poetry and on the relationship of rhyme to dance in his poetry and in that of others. A step beyond the interview is the mass interview. In *Conversations with South Carolina Poets* (Winston-Salem, N.C.: John F. Blair), Gayle Swanson and William B. Thesing have printed an account of conversations with several poets, including Bennie Lee Sinclair, Gilbert Allen, Ennis Rees, Susan Ludvigson, and Alice Cabaniss, on whether the poet is losing his appeal to the American audience and on the responsibility of the poet to himself, to his art, and to society. In the era of postmodernist return of the poet in the poem, the emphasis on interviewing or on conversations with poets is still much in vogue. Unfortunately in this book the greatest interviewee of all, James Dickey, is included only as author of the foreword.

Similarly, after a decade or more of interest in autobiography, not surprisingly the informal conversation of poets is being heard in heavily autobiographical criticism. The best of the lot this year are Anthony Hecht's *Obbligati: Essays in Criticism* (Atheneum), criticism on contemporary poetry, including comments on Wilbur and Lowell, and William Stafford's wise and interesting *You Must Revise Your Life* (Michigan). Lewis Turco takes on academic critics and their underestimation of the professionalism of poets in *Visions and Revisions: Of American Poetry* (Arkansas). Paul Metcalf in *Where Do You Put the Horses?: Essays by Paul Metcalf* (Dalkey Archive) speaks for an American tradition of personal experience and physical immediacy in contemporary poetry.

I must take notice of collections of other minority poetry, Cardelia Candelaria's *Chicano Poetry: A Critical Introduction* (Greenwood) and Barbara R. Gitenstein's *Apocalyptic Messianism and Contemporary Jewish American Poetry* (SUNY), the latter including sections on significant poets such as John Hollander, Anthony Hecht, Howard Nemerov, and Jerome Rothenberger.

For next to last I have saved perhaps the most current movement, described in Lee Bartlett's "What Is Language Poetry?" (*CritI* 12: 741–52), a concept a mere decade old. Bartlett traces it back to Ron Silliman's *Alcheringa* (1975) and Stephen Fredman's *Poet's Prose:*

The Crisis in American Verse (Cambridge, 1983), and uses the term to describe the most recent "group" of American poets, including Michael Palmer, Ron Silliman, Michael Davidson, Ljn Hejinian, and Barrett Watten, for whom the critical act of deconstruction is a means of poetic creation. Bartlett sees this movement as a reaction against "a prevailing aesthetic" and a critique of the "workshop poem," combining Sapir and followers with Karl Marx.

I shall conclude with what might be the answer of the '80s to Donald Allen's *The New American Poets 1945–1960*, which documented the ascendancy of open forms. This is *Strong Measures: Contemporary American Poetry in Traditional Forms*, ed. Philip Dacey and David Jauss (Harper). The open forms were for the '60s; traditional forms, as evidenced here by Ashbery, Kinnell, Merwin, and many others, are for now.

Clemson University

18. Drama

Walter J. Meserve

If the distinction between drama and theater remains vague for some scholars, it is not a concern of most people involved in practical theater. For them, everything is theater; the material they provide their actors is a script for the stage rather than the reader; they are far more interested in the rehearsal notes of Hal Prince than the footnotes of Ruby Cohn, and they have never heard of *American Literary Scholarship*. Clearly, a disparity between approaches to the study of theater art prevails. Although conversations among actors, theater managers, and literary people at the first meeting of the American Dramatic Fund Association in 1849 led some observers to hope for a united effort between playwrights and theater practitioners, effective cooperation has been long in coming. And more years evidently must pass before scholars of performance and those of dramatic literature accept any theoretical common ground and take advantage of each other's expertise.

Presumably, this space is reserved for scholarly commentary on American drama—those literary works written to be produced in the theater which may also be enjoyed by the casual reader. The medium for which the literature was created being a performing art, however, it is sometimes difficult for the scholar to limit observations to the effect of the dramatist's pen when the play was written for the sound of the actor's voice and for a response from a live theater audience. The art to be judged in its final form is obviously a cooperative art; yet it is an art which may be assessed from various points of view. Consequently, studies of both dramatic literature and of performance must be considered. Few scholars, indeed, draw a clear distinction between the theater and the drama; the prejudices of those who do are as obvious as ever.

i. Literary and Theater Histories

Publication dates of American dramas are carefully noted in Richard M. Ludwig and Clifford A. Nault, Jr.'s *Annals of American Literature*,

1602–1983 (Oxford). This admirable calendar, organized to provide basic information on the main literary output in fiction, nonfiction, drama, and verse for any given year, includes a comparison listing of historical events and features a substantial index for more effective usage. The reader of Marcus Cunliffe's *American Literature to 1900* (New York: Peter Bedrick), however, would have no idea that any plays were written in America before 1900. *The Flower and the Leaf: A Contemporary Record of American Writing Since 1941* (Viking, 1985) collects many perceptive essays by Malcolm Cowley, who, unfortunately, has had little to say about the drama. America has not enjoyed a critic of Cowley's stature who has been concerned, not with productions in the theater, but with American dramatic literature. It is a sign of enlightenment, however, when Ben Forkner and Patrick Samway, Jr., editors of *A Modern Southern Reader* (Atlanta: Peachtree Publishers), include a section on the drama (pp. 349–455), with commentary on the contributions of Tennessee Williams, Lillian Hellman, Paul Green, and others, along with the texts of *The Glass Menagerie* and *The Member of The Wedding*.

In *Heralds of Promise: The Drama of the American People During the Age of Jackson, 1829–1849* (Greenwood), I have described the conditions endured by American playwrights and evaluated their contributions to American literature during a particularly promising period in the history of American drama. Dividing my attention between the popular work of the journeymen and the efforts of the literary playwrights, I present a core of American playwrights who certainly had a potential for success, only to be thwarted by the idiosyncrasies of Jacksonian culture. Basically, I am interested in drama as literature which may achieve its ultimate expression on stage with the artistry of sensitive theater productions. Therese Fischer-Seidel limits this interest to a single approach in *Mythenparodie in Modernen Englischen und Amerikanischen Drama*; for a review, see Rolf Meyn's essay on German contributions in chapter 20, Foreign Scholarship. Much less concerned with terminology, Zoltán Szilassy writes about *American Theater of the 1960s* (So. Ill.), a decade which he finds particularly striking for its "theatrical equilibrium." In clear and forceful prose, stressing an interdisciplinary approach, Szilassy treats both American drama and theater in America. In Part I, Rebellious Drama, he discusses all of Albee's plays as fusions of tradition and innovation, an Americanization of our European heritage. Also in the work of Arthur Kopit and Albee, whom he terms models of the '60s, as well as that of Jack Richardson and Jack Gelber, he finds a continuing debt to European theater. Logically enough, Szilassy highlights "humanistic alternatives" in the plays of Barrie Stavis, an American dramatist who is highly respected in many parts of the world and yet seriously neglected by American critics. In Part II Szilassy comments perceptively on the confusing kaleidoscope of happenings, performance theories, avant-garde theater, and, finally, regional theater, where he predicts a positive future for American drama. As a European critic, fascinated with American experiments, yet aware of America's continuity with the past, Szilassy gives American playwrights, theater artists, scholars, and critics a thoughtful view of their drama and their theater.

Mary C. Henderson's *Theater in America* (Abrams) is clearly the work of an historian of the theater. Concerned with the "Americanization of drama and theater" and the "fun and fury" of the collaborative effort, this book is carefully written to inform and to bring pleasure. Henderson discusses producers, playwrights, directors and choreographers, actors, designers of scenery, costume, and lighting, as well as theater architecture and theater "Beyond Broadway." The section on playwrights (pp. 42–87) begins with O'Neill but reverts to the earlier periods with excellent if brief commentary on American dramatists before 1915, whose work she considers largely from the point of view of an actor or producer. Emphasizing the work of O'Neill, she sadly neglects the 1920–40 period, while providing slight commentary on Tennessee Williams, Arthur Miller, and contemporary dramatists. Nevertheless, this lavishly illustrated history is an excellent addition to one's library and is particularly good on theater architecture. Another clearly written and beautifully illustrated volume, *Stage for a Nation: The National Theatre, 150 Years* (Univ. Press, 1985), by Douglass Bennett Lee, Roger L. Meersman, and Donn B. Murphy, traces the history of this Washington, D.C., theater from its beginnings through its golden years in the mid-19th century to its embarrassing closing in 1948, due to the racial prejudice of its managers, and its eventual reopening in 1952. A final work, David Savran's *The Wooster Group, 1975–1985* (UMI Research Press), is unmistakably theater history. Confessing to be utterly captivated by "madness and chaos," Savran relishes the experimental and occasionally vulgar actions of this offbeat group and provides a detailed commentary on what he terms their "politicized deconstruction." In describing the group's achievements, such as the high point of *Hula* (1981) when all the actors urinate upon the stage, Savran reemphasizes his thesis that the group members enjoy what they do.

ii. Reference Works

Each year a number of reference volumes are published for the general use of the student of drama and theater. Some are parts of a series, such as *The Encyclopedia of the New York Stage, 1920–1930* (2 vols., Greenwood), ed. Samuel L. Lister and Holly Hill, which will eventually provide the titles, staging details, descriptions, and critical response for every legitimate professional production in New York, on or off Broadway. The present volumes have 2,500 entries plus 10 appendixes listing such information as awards, long runs, theaters, foreign companies, and selected bibliographies. *The Federal Theatre Project: A Catalog—Calendar of Productions* (Greenwood), compiled by the staff of the Fenwick Library, George Mason University, provides information on 2,745 productions of the FTP. *Contemporary Theatre, Film and Television*, vol. 3 (Gale), continues a biographical guide to critics, playwrights, and theater artists in the United States and Great Britain. This volume adds the personal data, photographs, and "sidelight comments" of 700 such individuals, including James Baldwin, Christopher Durang, Frank Gilroy, Jonathan Levy, David Rabe, Larry Shue, Jean-Claude Van Itallie, and Richard Wilbur. Gordon Samples's *The Drama Scholars' Index to Plays and Filmscripts*, vol. 3 (Scarecrow), is a guide to plays and filmscripts in selected anthologies, series, and periodicals. By design, the volumes index plays from the beginning of recorded dramatic literature to 1983. Each of the 146 world dramatists listed in Walton Beacham's *Research Guide to Biography and Criticism* (Research Publishing) is represented by a chronology and bibliography, an evaluation of biographies, autobiographies, and critical works as well as entries in dictionaries and encyclopedias. American dramatists included are Lorraine Hansberry, Lillian Hellman, Arthur Miller, Eugene O'Neill, Clifford Odets, Royall Tyler, Thornton Wilder, and Tennessee Williams.

For American theater historians Weldon B. Durham's *American Theatre Companies, 1749–1887* (Greenwood) is the first of a three-volume set. Each of the 81 entries in this volume includes an essay describing the policies and practices of the theater company as well as artistic and commercial achievements. Company personnel and yearly repertories are included, along with a bibliography and a valuable cross-reference. The concept of this project is excellent, but the entries are seriously uneven: listings of repertories range from none to 11 pages of small print; basic resources are sometimes not used; writing styles vary in effectiveness. In *The Great Stage Lives* (New York: Facts on File) Sheridan Mosley has selected 200 "distinguished theatrical careers of the past and present" for a simple narrative presentation of information, nothing critical. Joe Jefferson and William Gillette are there, along with James Earl Jones; Edwin Forrest is missing, but William McCready is included. For actors, particularly young actors, *Early Stages: The Professional Theater and the Young Actor* (New York: Walker Publishing Co.) by Walter Williamson gives advice, somewhat romanticized and in the form of illustrative stories, on entering the profession. Appendixes give information on theaters, casting notices, and theater terms. For playwrights the *Dramatists Sourcebook* (TCG), ed. M. Elizabeth Osborn, provides an annual guide to professional opportunities among its constituent theaters, plus general information for playwrights. Mollie Ann Meserve's *Playwright's Companion* (Bloomington, Ind.: Feedback Theatrebooks) is an annual submission guide to playwriting contests and to a broad range of American theaters that accept new plays.

Two brief monographs by the same person, Paula De Caro, substantiate old opinions: *A Study of the Problems of the American Theatre* and *A Study of the Problems of the European Theatre* (Holt, Minn.: Beech Tree Press). Based on interviews with 96 actors, directors, playwrights, etc. (all listed in an appendix), the first book treats financial problems, actor training, the competition of television, and funding suggestions. The author concludes that current conditions stimulate less adventuresome and less rewarding theater. In the words of David Mamet, "The American theater is up the creek." With the second booklet De Caro observes that the American theater is not alone with its problems.

iii. Bibliography and Criticism

Two bibliographical essays this year deserve particular attention. Jüngen Wolter's "Recent Books on American Drama and Theater: A Bibliographical Survey, 1980–1985" (*Amst* 31:261–81) provides a succinct and acute evaluation of books, which Wolter divides into four major categories. More importantly, Wolter declares that after long neglect the American drama is now an appropriate topic for serious criticism. Joyce Flynn employs a cultural perspective in "Melting Plots: Patterns of Racial and Ethnic Amalgamation in American Drama Before Eugene O'Neill" (*AQ* 38:417–38). Explaining that "no ethnic group was left unaffected in natural life on the stage," she suggests the importance of American drama for historians of culture and provides an extremely well-footnoted argument in the process. In addition to these two essays, Charles A. Carpenter's "Modern Drama Studies: An Annual Bibliography" (*MD* 29:241–353) lists 203 entries for 61 dramatists from Albee to Willson. Suzanne Wise's *Sports Fiction for Adults: An Annotated Bibliography of Novels, Plays, Short Stories and Poetry with Sports Settings* (Garland) lists only seven plays and is of little value.

The high point of the year for the promotion of scholarship in American drama was the advent of a new journal, *Studies in American Drama, 1945–Present*, ed. Philip C. Kolin and Colby Kullman. It promises much as a new outlet for scholars. *Anthony Slide's Selected Theatre Criticism*, vol. 3:1931–50 (Scarecrow), provides selected reviews and basic production information for 115 plays, most of them American. The only critic to publish a book of essays this year was Benedict Nightingale, who spent the 1984–85 theater season in New York and wrote his views in what he finally admitted was "becoming a somewhat querulous journal," *Fifth Row Center: A Critic's Year On and Off Broadway* (Times Books). In his casual and sometimes gossipy style, Nightingale discusses the work of several American playwrights, singling out Mamet and Shepard as the only "really interesting American dramatists currently producing work" and the musical as "the broadest form in which Americans excel." Although he bemoans the "wretched fiscal predicament" of the theater, his most British comment is perhaps his most painful: "New York may be able to manage without British actors, but where would it be without British plays?"

iv. Anthologies

Unfortunately, there is still no adequate anthology for the teacher who wishes to acquaint students with the entire range of American drama from its beginning to the present—or even to World War II. There are, however, an increasing number of collections of American plays which, although they do not solve many problems for teachers, have the admirable objective of making people aware of American drama. One publisher, the Theatre Communications Group, has stated that it wants to support and encourage the publication of American plays of the past. *Strictly Dishonorable and Other Lost American Plays*, ed. Richard Nelson, is the latest volume, printing Preston Sturges's *Strictly Dishonorable*, Bartlett Cormack's *The Racket*, Damon Runyon and Howard Lindsay's *A Slight Case of Murder*, and Sidney Howard's *The Ghost of Yankee Doodle*. Lowell Swortzell's *Six Plays for Young People from the Federal Theatre Project (1930–1939)* (Greenwood) reviews the FTP interest in children's theater, provides notes for the six plays, illustrations, a list of children's theater units in the FTP, a good bibliography, and a half-dozen interviews with people who knew the project's work. Celebrating the ninth year of the Women's Project, Julia Miles has edited *Women Heroes: Six Short Plays from the Women's Project* (New York: Applause Theatre Book Publishers). *Plays from the New York Shakespeare Festival* (New York: Broadway Play Publishing) is introduced by Joe Papp and includes Marvin Cohen's *Necessary Ends*, Jack Gilhooley's *The Time Trial*, Miguel Pinero's *Short Eyes*, David Rabe's *Streamers*, Dennis J. Reardon's *The Leaf People*, and Ntozake Shange's *For Colored Girls. . . .*

v. 18th- and 19th-Century Plays

Some years ago Richard Moody argued that the early Indian treaties in America were examples of America's first drama. I have never found his argument particularly convincing, and I have supported the inclusion of various 18th-century dialogues as part of the beginnings of American drama. I have also contended that some of the great preachers, particularly Cotton Mather, came close to dramatic composition. Now David E. Williams suggests another possibility: "Behold a Tragic Scene Strangely Changed into a Theater of Mercy: The Structure and Significance of Criminal Conversion Narratives in Early New England" (*AQ* 38:827–47). Exploring some 28 narratives or execution sermons in which criminals elucidated their progress from sinner to saint, Williams suggests something equivalent to the modern one-person show where a complete reversal of character is acted out. In another fine essay on early American drama, Richard S. Pressman—"Class Positioning and Shays's Rebellion: Resolving the

Contradictions of *The Contrast*" (*EAL* 21:87–102)—relates the play to the social-political activities of March and April 1787 and explains the moral lesson it provided the Federalists.

Among several essays dealing with drama and theater in the 19th century, Lewis Leary's concern for the "1776–1815" period (pp. 68–70) in Louis D. Rubin, Jr.'s *The History of Southern Literature* (LSU, 1985) includes basic information on Robert Mumford and William Wirt and, with new research among the papers at Williamsburg, is particularly good on the dramatic efforts of St. George Tucker. Although Billy J. Harbin's "Letters from John Parke Custis to George and Martha Washington, 1778–1781" (*WMQ* 43:67–93) reveals nothing about the plays of George Washington Parke Custis, the essay presents a clear picture of the relationship of the playwright's father to his stepfather and something of the playwright's family background. Arthur W. Bloom corrects, supports, and expands existing information on "The Jefferson Company, 1830–1845" (*ThS* 27:89–153) in an extremely detailed investigation (303 footnotes) which surely takes advantage of every scrap of information available. In "Cheers! Tears! and Laughter: Popular Drama in 1883" (*JPC* 19:85–93), William Goldhurst takes a single month in 1883, December, and tells about the melodramas that one might have seen on New York stages. Although the author draws some conclusions about marriage, willful women, and the function of the theater at the time, the essay is most valuable for its particular information about William Young's *The Rajah*, Judge G. C. Barrett's *An American Wife*, and Augustin Daly's *728; or, Casting the Boomerang*. Goldhurst's criticism of Steele Mackay's *Hazel Kirke* as an adaptation of Shakespeare, however, seems farfetched.

Dion Boucicault will never be renowned for his literary style, but he knew how to provide an evening's entertainment for his generation. *George Spelvin's Theatre Book* (7:1986) reprints *London Assurance*, *Old Heads and Young Hearts*, and *Used Up*, ed. Sven Eric Molin and Robin Goodfellowe with a brief introduction by Richard Fawkes. Mark Twain, on the other hand, had an exceptional way with words but could not write good plays; he did, however, love minstrel shows. Anthony J. Berret, S.J., "Huckleberry Finn and the Minstrel Show" (*AmerS* 27:37–49), suggests the influence of the minstrels which Clemens so enjoyed on the structure, dialogue, songs, and themes in *Huckleberry Finn*, particularly chapters 1 through 19. S. Ramaswamy tries to evaluate the success of *The Belle of Amherst* as a means of revealing the poetic consciousness of Emily Dickinson. His essay, "*The Belle of Amherst* As a One-person Play," appears in *IJAS* 15 (1985):81–84. David Leon Higdon argues that Henry James's *The American* "seems to have directly reshaped Lillian Hellman's memories and intentions" as they are revealed in *The Little Foxes*. In "Henry James and Lillian Hellman: An Unnoted Source" (*HJR* 6[1985]:134–45), Higdon mentions in particular Regina's refusal to get medicine for Horace and a murder in which medicine is withheld as described in chapter 22 of *The American*.

vi. Entering the 20th Century

Scholarly interest in 20th-century dramatists remains reasonably predictable. Eugene O'Neill always attracts attention, and with his centennial celebration in 1988 there will certainly be increased activity among the O'Neill enthusiasts. As Arthur Miller tries, thus far in vain but with hope, to create as he did 30-odd years ago, his name fades from the contents pages of scholarly journals. Tennessee Williams's current popularity among critics is inevitable—deservedly so, of course, but not without that irony which must accompany the ending of a career. There is less to explain Edward Albee's sudden appeal, but the rush of articles and books is nonetheless real. Recent exuberant interest in the work of Sam Shepard continues, joined by critics who find hope for American drama and theater in the plays of David Mamet and David Rabe. Although still a constant part of contemporary drama scholarship, criticism of black drama is settling into a more substantial mode, as it should if black drama is to be established, not as an esoteric theater, but as part of the American drama.

***a.* Eugene O'Neill.** *"Love and Admiration and Respect" The O'Neill-Commins Correspondence* (Duke), ed. Dorothy Commins, presents some 242 letters—82 written by O'Neill—all carefully footnoted and interspersed with excerpts from Saxe Commins's "memoirs" and a good selection of pictures. Commins was senior editor at Random House and close friend of O'Neill, whom he first met at the Provincetown Players, and his letters and O'Neill's responses provide fresh insight into the dramatist's work. Travis Bogard's foreword (pp. xi–xxi) is an enlightening and necessary introduction to these letters, which are astutely divided into four periods of O'Neill's life—1920–29, 1930–32, 1933–39, and 1940–53. Perhaps one learns more about O'Neill's character than his work from these letters, especially the relationship between Gene and Carlotta, while the excerpts from Commins's "memoirs" include such excellent commentary as the nice reference to Edward Sheldon. And there is O'Neill's memorable reference to *The Great God Brown* (24 May 1942): "I still think this play one of the most interesting and moving I have written" (p. 205).

A number of essays were written this year showing a relationship between O'Neill and a contemporary, either in general or with a particular issue in mind. James Fisher, for example, describes the relationship between "Eugene O'Neill and Edward Gordon Craig" (*EON* 10,i:27–30). Linda Ben-Zvi considers "Susan Glaspell and Eugene O'Neill: The Imagery of Gender" (*EON* 10,i:22–27) with special attention to Glaspell's *The Verge*. Stephen Watt's "O'Neill and Otto Rank: Doubles, 'Death Instincts,' and the Trauma of Birth" (*CompD* 20:211–30) accomplishes the major objective of good criticism: it helps illuminate the work of art. In this clear and interesting discussion of doubling, Watt examines Rank's *The Double* and *The Trauma of Birth* as a "means" to explore O'Neill's split or identical characters. His psychoanalytic readings of *More Stately Mansions* and *Long Day's Journey into Night* are particularly effective. Illustrating his argument with references to *Strange Interlude*, Peter Egri distinguishes between retrogressive motifs and retarding motifs to show how the action of the latter creates an epic division of the dramatic plot, thus fusing the epic and the dramatic. His essay is entitled "The Fusion of the Epic and Dramatic: Hemingway, Strindberg and O'Neill" (*EON* 10,i:16–22). Martha Bower suggests that the way in which O'Neill presents women as succeeding in a normally male business world appears to coincide with his relationship with Carlotta beginning in 1927. Showing fine research based on Carlotta's diaries at Yale University, Bower traces her concept through Sara Melody in *Touch of the Poet* and *More Stately Mansions*, Leda Cade in *The Calms of Capricorn*, and the heroine of *The Career of Bessie Bowlan*. The title of this interesting essay is "The Cycle Women and Carlotta Monterey O'Neill" (*EON* 10,ii:29–33).

Among essayists concerned with particular plays, Stephen A. Black shows a sensitive appreciation of O'Neill's artistry and attitude toward life in "Let the Dead Be Dead: A Reinterpretation of *A Moon for the Misbegotten*" (*MD* 29:544–55). In "The Tragic Cosmology of Eugene O'Neill: *Desire Under the Elms*" (*EON* 10,ii:25–29), Preston Fambrough concentrates upon mystery, emphasizing the "thin' " which haunts Eben and Abbie, underlies the "desire" of the title, and as a demonic element distinguishes the tragic cosmology of O'Neill's play. Michael Mikoś and David Malroy argue unconvincingly for "Reymont's *The Peasants*: A Probable Influence on *Desire Under the Elms*" (*EON* 10,i:4–15). John Alvis states his thesis clearly in "On the American Line: O'Neill's *Mourning Becomes Electra* and the Principles of the Founding" (*SoR* 22:69–85): "The character of American life and of America's self-understanding changes according to changes in the dominant conception of equality and liberty." Unfortunately, Alvis's poorly argued and wandering commentary reveals little and has slight value for O'Neill scholars. The usually astute Peter Egri also appears to have little to say concerning a tenuous thesis in "High Culture and Popular Culture in Eugene O'Neill (*Strange Interlude*)," pp. 55–76, in Charlotte Kretzoi, ed., *High and Low in American Culture* (Budapest: L. Eötvös University). Basically, Egri sees the play as an experimental attempt to fuse high culture and popular culture while employing psychological realism in an attempt at epic drama. The discussion is not effective. In one final item Marcelline Krafchick compares " 'Hughie' and *The Zoo Story* (*EON* 10,i:15–16) to support her thesis concerning the transformation of "a listener into a participant."

***b.* Arthur Miller.** Basing his discussion on five elements which he considers constant in tragedy—conflict, suffering, tragic irony, awakening, and a metaphysical dimension—Santosh K. Bhatia writes about *Arthur Miller: Social Drama as Tragedy* (Heinemann, 1985). With close attention to six of Miller's plays—the best discussion deals with *The Crucible*—Bhatia argues that all are tragedies, plays set in a tragic framework in which the social theme does not diminish the tragic intensity. In "The Monomyth and Arthur Miller's *After the Fall*" (*Studies in American Drama, 1945–Present* I:49–60), Steven R. Centola discusses the play in terms of the monomyth as presented in Joseph Campbell's *The Hero with a Thousand Faces.* Arguing that the play meets his criteria by "transmuting the personal drama into a symbolic drama of universal significance," Centola describes a hero who ventures forth, encounters, wins victory, and returns with a certain power. Quentin, he concludes, is such a hero. Emphasizing the theater conventions and playwriting techniques that distinguish *Hamlet* and *Death of a Salesman,* M. C. Anderson accepts the fact that 20th-century man lacks the freedom of his Greek and Elizabethan peers to challenge fate and achieve nobility ("*Death of a Salesman*: A Consideration of Willy Loman's Role in Twentieth-Century Tragedy" (*CRUX* 22,ii:25–29).

Although a concept of tragedy stimulated these literary scholars to express themselves, a historian provides one of the most interesting essays on Miller—Edmund S. Morgan, "Arthur Miller's *The Crucible* and the Salem Witch Trials: A Historian's View" (pp. 171–86) in *The Golden & Brazen World: Papers in Literature and History 1650–1800* (Calif., 1985), ed. John M. Wallace. Acknowledging the problems of both artists and historians in separating the unreal from the unique, the timeless from the temporal, Morgan questions Miller's treatment of his subject matter. He feels that Miller knew his characters as human beings but not as Puritans, that the action in Salem, Puritanism being what it was, was not as strange and awful as Miller suggests. Interpreting Proctor's decision as a triumph of man over man rather than man over Puritanism (which he assumes is Miller's view), Morgan contends that audiences watching *The Crucible* are allowed to "escape" the full impact of Proctor's act because the play is set in a past era.

c. Tennessee Williams. Evaluating Tennessee Williams's contribution to American drama—that is a major and tantalizing task for literary and theater scholars. In the meantime, however, a great many people will have something to say, and on the basis of their observations and a lot of careful research and study an acceptable assessment will eventually be made. Interviews can be a good source of information from which careful conclusions can be drawn. *Conversations With Tennessee Williams* (Miss.), ed. Albert J. Devlin, includes some 35 interviews with such people as George Freedley, William Inge, Mike Wallace, and Arthur Gelb spread over the years from 1940 to 1981. Dotson Rader's *Tennessee: Cry of the Heart* (Doubleday, 1985) records a lot of observations, some distasteful, few that are verifiable, most of them self-conscious and of no value to scholars.

Tennessee Williams's attachment to and preoccupation with the South, particularly New Orleans, has been the basis for several essays. According to Pnina Rafailovich, "Tennessee Williams's South" (*SoSt* 23[1984]:191–97) was the South of the present viewed through myths, the Old South as a "lost garden" where Williams became absorbed with the dispossessed white aristocrat and the oppressed black. Milly D. Barranger, "New Orleans as Theatrical Image in

Plays by Tennessee Williams" (*SoQ* 23,ii[1985]:38–54), traces a changing image of the city as it is revealed in *A Streetcar Named Desire, Suddenly Last Summer*, and *Vieux Carré*. Within the French Quarter and the Garden District Barranger discovers a microcosm of Williams's parade of lost and maimed humanity. Ted R. Spivey's "Tennessee Williams: Desire and Impotence in New Orleans" (*Revival*, pp. 122–38) is a loosely structured assessment of Williams's achievement, in which New Orleans, peopled with impotent, narcissistic, and destructive personalities, rises as a major symbol. *The Glass Menagerie* and *A Streetcar Named Desire* are major illustrations. W. Kenneth Holditch's "The Last Frontier of Bohemia: Tennessee Williams in New Orleans, 1938–1983" (*SoQ* 23,ii[1985]:1–37) examines "the biographical details of his association with New Orleans." This is an excellent essay, carefully descriptive of the places Williams lived in New Orleans and filled with references to his plays. It is also well illustrated and, as the author hopes, truly helps one understand "the nature and extent" of New Orleans' influence upon the dramatist.

Numerous essays treat individual plays. Lindy Melman, for example, explains that Blanche is trapped by southern tradition and condemned by that world of illusion as well as the conflict it generates—"A Captive Maid: Blanche Dubois in *A Streetcar Named Desire*" (*DQR* 15:125–44). In "Williams' *A Streetcar Named Desire*" (*Expl* 43,ii[1985]:44–45), Bert Cardullo argues that the newsboy scene evokes Blanche's own lost innocence. Jere Huzzard, "Williams' *Cat on a Hot Tin Roof*" (*Expl* 43,ii[1985]: 46–47), explains that this play is about the sexual ambivalence of males toward females. June Schlueter compares the Treat Williams/Ann-Margret version of *Streetcar* with the Marlon Brando/Vivien Leigh movie—"Imitating an Icon: John Erman's Remake of *A Streetcar Named Desire*" (*MD* 28[1985]:139–47). Francis Gillen studies the play-within-a-play creative process in "Horror Shows, Inside and Outside My Skull: Theater and Life in Tennessee Williams's *Two-Character Play*" (pp. 227–31), in Jan Hokenson and Howard Pearce, eds. *Forms of the Fantastic: Selected Essays from the Third International Conference on the Fantastic in Literature and Film* (Greenwood). Helen E. Moritz, "Apparent Sophoclean Echoes in Tennessee Williams' *Night of the Iguana*" (*CML* 5[1985]:305–14), buttresses her idea that Williams dealt with great and enduring themes by comparing Nonno and Hannah to Oedipus and Antigone, Shannon with Oedipus, and the Iguana with the Furies. Another essay in *Classical and Modern Literature* (6:

287–303), "Classical Motivations in Tennessee Williams," attempts to show that Williams was widely read. The author, John Douglass Minyard, appears to be interested primarily in refuting a comment by Gore Vidal and finally admits that much of his evidence is a "reflection of the general intellectual climate of [Williams's] age."

The most important of any of the essays on individual Williams plays is Gilbert Debusscher's "And the Sailor Turned into a Princess: New Light on the Genesis of *Sweet Bird of Youth*" (*Studies in American Drama, 1945–Present* I:25–37). From an eight-page fragment discovered in the Texas archives, Debusscher learns of a sailor named Casky who obviously became the Princess Kosmonopolis and draws some conclusions about Williams's writing process. A final essay establishes Williams's importance to the theater of Norway since World War II—Hans H. Skei, "The Reception and Reputation of Tennessee Williams in Norway" (*NMW* 17,ii[1985]:63–81). Statistics abound in this essay, in which Skel concludes that Williams's plays, with O'Neill's, represent American drama in Norway, although they are not often read in universities.

***d.* Edward Albee.** A surge of interest in Albee just as this playwright appears ready to disappear into the academic world shows a gathering of forces among those who value his efforts in propelling American drama into the post-World War II world theater. Certainly Albee was among the first to support Laurence Kitchen's mid-century view of America as a "Potent intruder." Preparation for Albee's assessment is obviously under way. Richard Tyce's *Edward Albee: A Bibliography* (Scarecrow) is a good indication, with more than 2,700 citations. *Critical Essays on Edward Albee* (Hall), expertly edited by Philip C. Kolin and J. Madison Davis, supports this view. Their introduction (pp. 1–40) is a model bibliographical essay, insightful and well organized with well-documented commentary on each play. Reviews include two on *The Zoo Story* and *The Death of Bessie Smith* translated from the German for the first time. With a few exceptions, the essays are reprints. One striking addition is Lea Carol Owen's "An Annotated Bibliography of Albee Interviews, with an Index to Names, Concepts and Places" (pp. 200–218), a listing of 75 interviews from 1960 to 1986.

Anne Paolucci has written a number of critical works on Edward Albee. "Albee and the Restructuring of the Modern Stage" (*Studies in American Drama, 1945–Present* 1:3–23) further explains her approach in *From Tension to Tonic* as she commands a new set of critical guidelines in assessing Albee's contribution to the theater of the absurd. In "The Illusion and Reality of Happiness in Edward Albee's *The American Dream*" (*KAL* 26[1985]:57–64), Arun Pant explores once again the vacuity of the social life represented as the reality which lies beneath the illusions of commercialism, but brings nothing new to our attention. Philip C. Kolin's "Of Jets, Milk Trains and Edward Albee's *Seascape*" (*NMAL* 9:Item 9) associates fear, loss, and death with the recurring jet "booms" which are termed unpleasant reminders of inescapable death. Two new essays in the Kolin-Davis selection of *Critical Essays on Edward Albee* are by Matthew C. Roudane. "A Monologue of Cruelty: Edward Albee's *The Man Who Had Three Arms* (pp. 187–92) assesses the playwright's latest experimental techniques as a means of lecturing his audiences on the way in which Americans create monsters. Roudane's second contribution to the volume, "A Playwright Speaks: An Interview with Edward Albee" (pp. 193–99), is less successful. Conducted on 12 February 1985, this is Roudane's third interview with Albee, but aside from Albee's usual observations that "drama is an attempt to make things better," that "the function of a good play is to communicate," Roudane's questions do not generate good conversation or stimulating comment. In "God and Albee's *Tiny Alice*" (*Studies in American Drama, 1945–Present* 1:61–71), Dennis Grunes tries, as have others in the past, to explain the "wonder" and "mystery" of the play as a revelation of Christian attitudes, but has difficulty in revealing more than the mystical appreciation of the staunch Albee enthusiasts.

***e.* Sam Shepard, David Mamet, and David Rabe.** For some critics the worldwide reputation of post-Vietnam theater in America must be measured by the work of these three dramatists. Although Shepard has appeared to excite critics unduly over the past few years and his popularity continues, scholarly interest is not completely responsible. As a movie actor and extravagant personality in general as well as a skillful playwright, Shepard attracts audiences. The latest book, *Sam Shepard: The Life and Work of An American Dreamer* (St. Martin's) by Ellen Oumono, illustrates popular curiosity rather than artistic achievement. Oumono's subject is a hero, her concerns his private life, writings, and general activities. Her writing style is chatty and based on stories taken from interviews with people who know Shepard. Such an approach has its place in bookstores, but scholars need to have sources identified and quotations footnoted. None of that information is presented in Oumono's book. Arthur Ganz's approach to Shepard's work is, on the other hand, scholarly and insightful, typical of Ganz's good criticism. "Sam Shepard: Iconographer of the Depths" appears in *The Play & Its Critics* (pp. 211–38). Writing about a playwright whose attraction is largely his "pictorial drama of extraordinary theatrical and verbal force," his visual imagery, his repetitious and obvious themes in plays less thought than wrought, Ganz compares Shepard with Pinter and Williams and calls him a "genuinely poetic writer" with more sympathy and affection for the past than the present.

Christopher Bigsby provides a particularly clear, sensible, and perceptive overview of Shepard in "Sam Shepard, Word and Image" (*Critical Angles*, pp. 208–19). Emphasizing Shepard as a product of off off Broadway theater and the growth of regional theater whose plays deal with people who do not understand the forces operating on them, Bigsby sees a romantic fatalism in Shepard's plays, their mythic background, and their sensitivity to people who have a special fascination with life's mysteries. Bert Cardullo explains "Sam Shepard's Use of the Monologue in *Curse of the Starving Class*" (*NMAL* 9:Item 11) and warns readers against the pleasures of its excessive use. In another slight essay, Dennis Carroll overextends his argument concerning theme-centered and character-centered cuts in "The Filmic Cut and 'Switchback' in the Plays of Sam Shepard" (*MD* 28 [1985]:125–38). There were fewer articles in 1986 than in past years, but the observations of Ganz and Bigsby are well worth reading.

One sure sign of a playwright's growing reputation among scholars is a bibliography. Listing plays, nonfiction, interviews, criticism, reviews, and biographical material, J. Madison Davis and John Coleman provide "David Mamet: A Classified Bibliography" (*Studies in American Drama, 1945–Present* 1:83–101). Matthew C. Roudane's "An Interview with David Mamet" (pp. 73–82) in the same issue of this fine new journal was conducted on 4 December 1984. Mamet thinks of himself as a teller of stories in which he has a point to make, ideas to communicate in language as poetic as he can create. Guido Almansi's admiration for David Mamet centers on the playwright as "poet and critic, chronicler and parodist of the stag party and of all social occasions and situations precluding women." In "David Mamet, A Virtuoso of Invective" (*Critical Angles*, pp. 191–207), Almansi points out the male prejudices, the degrading language, the violence, and the lying, swearing, gesticulating characters with plotless lives, but argues for comic interpretations of "our consumer's society" which he feels Mamet portrays. It is not for the brutality of the text that one may dislike Mamet's plays, he contends, but for the society presented. In "Revealing Illusions in David Mamet's *The Shawl*" (*NConL* 16:9–10), Philip C. Kolin refers to Mamet's use of particular verbs and metaphors as well as theatrical devices "to exorcise his audience's need for magic (or illusion) while paradoxically demonstrating their dependency on it."

Kolin has also contributed an essay on David Rabe—"Staging *Hurlyburly*: David Rabe's Parable for the 1980s" (*TA* 41:63–78). Concerned that this emphasis upon the drug generation of the 1980s is really the "horror play for our age," Kolin analyzes the characters, plot, language, gesture, costume, movement, and stage devices to conclude that *Hurlyburly* extinguishes the sense of humanity in man. It is "better to be a thing than a human being." Pamela Cooper makes a popular-culture comparison in "David Rabe's *Sticks and Bones*: The Adventures of Ozzie and Harriet" (*MD* 29:613–25). Contending that Ozzie's family is a microcosm of the American capitalistic culture that "bred the media, the journalists, the war itself," she understands the play as one attack upon the "instant culture" produced by the media and a critique of the society they also transformed.

***f.* Black Drama and Theater.** Billy Jo Turner's essay on "The Harlem Renaissance and the Social Commitment Theater: Parallel Lines Which Met" (*JASAT* 17:3–9) suggests a new critical approach in establishing black drama as an appropriate element in the development of American drama. Arguing that "a humanitarian as well as an aesthetic *ficelle*" brought together those two social movements, Turner shows how black plays of the 1920s found outlets in the social commitment theater of the 1930s. It is an important point, well argued, carefully written. In "Mother, Sister, Wife: A Dramatic Perspective" (*SoR* 21[1985]:770–89), Anthony Barthelemy attempts to identify Lorraine Hansberry's *A Raisin in the Sun* as part of a literary debate in which the playwright set out to answer a negative image of woman created in Theodore Ward's 1938 play, *Big White Fog*. Barthelemy feels that this hostility shown to women was part of a misogyny pervading Western culture and that Hansberry capped the debate appropriately in her play. Quoting Ed Bullins's view that the goal of black theater may be achieved through a "creative struggle" toward a collective form, Nicholas Canaday traces Bullins's own progress toward that form which "necessitates a feeling of community." The essay is entitled "Toward Creation of a Collective Form: the Plays of Ed Bullins" (*Studies in American Drama, 1945–Present* 1:33–47).

Edward J. Mullen, ed., *Critical Essays on Langston Hughes* (Hall), considers Hughes's plays in his introduction (pp. 22–27), concluding that they added little to his reputation and merely represented Hughes's personal growth and the growth of the civil rights movement in America. He would have improved his volume had he paid closer attention to Hughes's real achievements in the theater. Even Richard K. Barksdale's "Miscegenation on Broadway: Hughes's *Mulatto* and Edward Sheldon's *The Nigger*" (pp. 191–99), written especially for the same collection, does not attempt to do Hughes justice in American drama; the essay is good as far as it goes, arguing that Hughes's play is far more penetrating psychologically than Sheldon's early work. But it is unfortunate that more would not be written in this collection on the author of nine full-length plays. William Torbert Leonard's *Masquerade in Black* (Scarecrow) treats the history of whites in blackface. There is a pertinent irony in my listing it at this point after the celebration of a writer who could not get a haircut in his hometown of Lawrence, Kansas. Leonard's work is immensely detailed as he considers the "Genesis" of blackface in America through Jim Crow, the minstrels, and the Tom shows. He stretches his thesis by mentioning later plays of miscegenation—*Madame Butterfly*, *The Nigger*, *The Octoroon*, *Brass Ankle*—but his concept is good. Lists of actors performing Othello and other white actors who worked in blackface in films plus a respectable bibliography are interesting, but the book is a great disappointment for scholars, light, chatty, and directed to popular reading. Nowhere can you trace quotations, nor are there any notes to identify information and resources!

vii. And in conclusion . . . .

Musical drama has generally been considered one of the premiere achievements of American theater, although the quality in very recent years has not been outstanding. Meanwhile, the British have suddenly mastered the art once considered foreign to their talents. Alan Jay Lerner's *The Musical Theatre: A Celebration* (McGraw-Hill) is of value mainly because it was written by the author of *My Fair Lady*, whose personal and amusing anecdotes are interesting to read. His memory, however, is faulty, while his opinions are somewhat casually supplied, and the book, filled with factual inaccuracies, is of little value to students. Ken Bloom's *American Song: The Complete Musical Theatre Companion* (Facts on File, 1985) includes 42,000 songs from 3,300 shows with the informational listings in volume 1 and a plethora of indexes and cross-references in volume 2. It repeats and supplements information found in David Hummel's *The Collector's Guide to the American Musical Theatre* (new ed. in 1984). Susan L. Porter discusses "English-American Interaction in American Musical Theater of the Turn of the Century" (*American Music* 4:6–19). With attention to American texts as well as American adaptations of English musicals, Porter explains the popularity of these early musicals and stresses their dependence upon the English theater.

For the record I must mention here briefly two essays on the work of Elmer Rice, the only successful American dramatist whose plays were produced in New York before World War I and after World War II. The first is a reprint of "Elmer Rice, Liberation and the Great Ethnic Question" by Jules Chametzky, who includes it in a volume he edits, *Our Decentralized Literature: Cultural Mediations in Selected Jewish and Southern Writers* (Mass.). In "Names and Numbers in *The Adding Machine*" (*Names* 34:266–74), Russell F. Brown considers a theory of numbers in naming.

Skipping through the decades of modern American drama, one should welcome *The Journals of Thornton Wilder, 1919–1961* (Yale, 1985) ed. Donald Gallup. Some 772 entries explain a great deal about Wilder—how he worked, thought, and functioned in society as a writer. His habit, begun in 1938, was to "go and tell it to the journal," and there we find comments on other writers—Gide, Whitman, Joyce, Poe, Emerson, Melville—on his theories, and on his plays, particularly *The Emporium*, an uncompleted play of which Gallup publishes two scenes. Gallup also footnotes all entries superbly, and the "Foreword: Born to Read and Write" (pp. vii–xxiv) by Isabel Wilder shows her memories of special events and her pride in her brother's accomplishments. Jackson R. Bryer has edited *Conversations with Lillian Hellman* (Miss.), some 27 interviews with Hellman from 1936 to 1981. Offering insights into her playwriting career and into particular plays as well as her views on people, politics, and the women's movement, the volume is obviously of great value to anyone interested in Hellman.

In "Humor, Dreams and the Human Conditions in Preston Jones's 'A Texas Trilogy'" (*SoQ* 24,iii:14–24), R. C. Reynolds attempts to answer the question: what is the value of the real Texan in expressing the human condition? The essay is entertaining because there are many quotations from Jones's humorous dialogue, but the question is never answered. "Seeing with Clarity: The Visions of Maria Irene Fornes" (*Theater* 17:51–56) is an interview conducted by Scott Cummings. The usual information on Fornes's playwriting career and her work with the Actors' Studio is climaxed with her comments on her workshop, which she describes as "a discipline for writing." Involved in a larger thesis, Susan Harris Smith shows the interest of American playwrights in classical mythology—from Achilles through Narcissus and Orpheus to Prometheus and, especially, Venus: "Twentieth-Century Plays Using Classical Mythic Themes: A Checklist" (*MD* 29:110–39). With reference to theater through these decades I will mention William Torbert Leonard's *Once Was Enough* (Scarecrow), a popular rehearsal of 104 Broadway productions for which there were no second nights.

"Ethics and Responsibilities" (*DGQ* 23,ii:15–23) records the response of Christopher Durang, Donald Margulies, Jeffrey Sweet, and Wendy Wasserstein to the question of ethical responsibilities of a playwright. Although as usual in these panel discussions participants wander from the issue, they all agreed that telling the truth is always basic. Their conclusion obviously holds for critics and scholars, too. One writes what one believes is true. Such a critic is Eric Bentley, called the first critic of modern theater by Michael Bertin, ed., *The Play & Its Critics*, whose introduction (pp. xii–xxvii) assesses Bentley's contributions but makes only a parenthetical observation that he was also a playwright. Distinctive among contemporary scholar-critics, Gerald Weales writes "American Theater Watch, 1985–1986" (*GaR* 40:520–31), which is easy to read, witty, urbane, obviously well informed, and clearly informative. Touring regional theaters this past season, Weales was impressed with a production of Sam Shepard's *A Lie of the Mind*, which he regards as a visual-verbal event dramatizing Shepard's concern for the decay of the American family. He enjoyed the ghost story quality of David Mamet's *Prairie du Chien* and *The Shawl* and was fascinated by Wallace Shaun's *Aunt Dan and Lemon* in spite of the ugly thoughts dramatized. Lee Brewer's *The Gospel at Colonus* and Bob Telson's views of *Oedipus at Colonnus* were among his more pleasant experiences in the theater which, as usual across regional America, can and does produce a lot of good, bad, and indifferent new plays each year. In truth, the same might be said of scholars and critics.

City University of New York

19. Themes, Topics, Criticism

Michael J. Hoffman

I believe that in 1986 I read more books relevant to this chapter than during any previous year. While there seems to be no end to our capacity to generalize and theorize, what I find most striking is how theories that seemed innovative or even shocking a few years ago have now simply been absorbed into the discourse of books on "non-theoretical" topics. Most discussions of literature are simply different from what they would have been before.

In order to keep this chapter down to something like a manageable size, I have summarized more than in the past. I have reserved the most extended analyses for works about American literature, and, in order to cover as many books as possible, I have tried to capture the essence of works in other categories in about a paragraph. Even so, I have had to leave out many books that were sent to me. The five categories this year are American Literature, Gender Studies, Modernism, Theory of Narrative, and Literary Theory. In each section I have, for the most part, discussed the books in alphabetical order.

i. American Literature

I am pleased to begin with two collections of essays, edited by Sacvan Bercovitch, which articulate the debate within American literary studies over the "new historicism." The first, which Bercovitch prepared with Myra Jehlen, is *Ideology and Classic American Literature*, a collection that views literary history as the continuous manifestation of ideologies, defined less as doctrines than as unconsciously held social and cultural assumptions. The other book, *Reconstructing American Literary History*, collects essays by contributors to the new Cambridge History of American Literature, which is scheduled for publication in the early 1990s. The Cambridge History (also edited by Bercovitch) and the Columbia History of American Literature (edited by Emory Elliott, himself also a contributor to the Cambridge

History) provide a larger focus for the reinterpretation mentioned above.

Of the two books I find *Ideology and Classic American Literature* to be the more problematic. (What follows borrows freely from the review I wrote of this work for *American Literary Realism, 1870–1910*). In her introduction Myra Jehlen discovers the new emphasis on ideology in two sources: first, "the increasing recognition that the political categories of race, gender, and class enter into the formal making of American literature such that they underlie not only its themes, not only its characters and events, but its very language." Ideology then becomes all-pervasive, and not merely doctrinal. The second source is "the education of American critics in European theories of culture including a complex tradition of ideological theory" (p. 1). Jehlen adds to these the increasing self-consciousness of American critics, by which she means our understanding that "subjectivity now constitutes an inextricable part of our understanding of reality" (p. 6), and the resultant need for critics to explore their assumptions before making statements. Most writers in this collection expose not only the ideological assumptions of the "classic" authors; they deliberately expose their own as well.

Ideology and Classic American Literature is organized into four categories: "Reassessments," containing essays by Henry Nash Smith, Leo Marx, Richard Slotkin, and Gerald Graff that look at earlier attempts at literary history before the current ideological self-consciousness; "Perspectives," which turns to Myra Jehlen, Houston A. Baker, Jr., Alan Trachtenberg, and Carolyn Porter—at least three of them associated with the "new" literary history—to deal with larger ideological issues (e.g., the novel and the middle class, reification) that follow more traditional ideological concerns; "Texts," in which Robert H. Byer, Jonathan Arac, Jane Tompkins, and Michael T. Gilmore read classic American texts according to the "new" ideological method; and, finally, essays by the "new" literary historians Paul Royster, Emory Elliott, James H. Kavanagh, and Donald E. Pease examining Melville as a case study. Bercovitch sums up the book in an afterword.

I am troubled to discover that seven of the 16 essays (other than the introduction and afterword) have been published before, one piece as early as 1977 and five as chapters in full-length books. In addition, this book seems to vacillate by its very structure between the old and new understandings of ideology. Its attempt at balancing the two only succeeds in confusing us.

Some of the best essays have appeared as chapters in Slotkin's *The Fatal Environment*, Porter's *Seeing and Being*, Tompkins's *Sensational Designs*, and Gilmore's *American Romanticism and the Marketplace.* The other essays which I think have most to teach us about ideology are by Robert H. Byer on Poe's "The Man of the Crowd"; Jonathan Arac on *The Scarlet Letter*; James H. Kavanagh on "Benito Cereno"; and Donald E. Pease on "Melville and Cultural Persuasion," which attempts to show how F. O. Matthiessen's consciousness of Hitler when he wrote *American Renaissance* caused him to see Captain Ahab as a proto-fascist. Interestingly enough, the best definitions of the "new" ideology come in essays on specific literary texts rather than in general essays that attempt to define the concept.

Because *Reconstructing American Literary History* (Harvard English Studies 13) is dominated by contributors to the Cambridge History, it presents a more coherent position. The authors share a common stance, what Bercovitch calls the "self-reflexiveness that characterizes this period of critical interregnum" (p. viii). It is worth quoting the editor's stated principles at length, not only because they assert the current book's assumptions but because they reflect a set of principles guiding both the major literary histories. These essays, says Bercovitch,

> share similar convictions about the *problematics* of literary history: for example, that race, class and gender are formal principles of art and therefore integral to textual analysis; that language has the capacity to break free of social restrictions and through its own dynamics to undermine the power structures it seems to reflect; that political norms are inscribed in aesthetic judgment and therefore inherent in the process of interpretation; that aesthetic structures shape the way we understand history, so that tropes and narrative devices may be said to use historians to enforce certain views of the past; that the task of literary historians is not just to show how art transcends culture, but also to identify and explore the ideological limits of their time, and then to bring these to bear upon literary analysis in such a way as to make use of the categories of culture, rather than being used by them. (p. viii)

A good example of the use of these principles occurs in the opening essay, " 'We Hold These Truths': Strategies of Control in the Literature of the Founders," in which Robert A. Ferguson explains the conflicting cultural factors that determined the textual context of such documents as the Declaration of Independence. This "consensual" literature contains "a genuine mix of antithetical tendencies":

> The thought of the Enlightenment, by definition, dwells upon the human context. Psychologically, it presumes an understanding of the world through apparent faculties. Politically, it expresses itself in the rule of law. American religious thought, in contrast, turns upon revelation and divine sanction. Psychologically, it waits upon a supernatural grace that transforms. Politically, it takes the millennial aspects of Puritanism to project a special American destiny upon the history of the world. (p. 20)

In another stimulating essay Walter Benn Michaels relates naturalistic fiction to corporate culture: "In naturalism, no persons are natural. In naturalism, personality is always corporate and all fictions, like souls metaphorized in bodies, are corporate fictions" (p. 219).

This volume contains many excellent essays; aside from those already mentioned, I can especially recommend Barbara Packer, "Origin and Authority: Emerson and the Higher Criticism"; Sandra M. Gilbert, "The American Sexual Poetics of Walt Whitman and Emily Dickinson"; Philip Fisher, "Appearing and Disappearing in Public: Social Space in Late-Nineteenth-Century Literature and Culture"; and Wendy Steiner, "College or Miracle: Historicism in a Deconstructed World."

History and not theory is the subject of Alexander Bloom's compendious *Prodigal Sons: The New York Intellectuals & Their World* (Oxford), a study of half a century of New York Jewish secular intellectual life. Bloom studies typical backgrounds among the major figures in both their immigrant group and home life, along with education at the City College of New York or Columbia, and the role of certain institutions of culture, such as, for instance, the *Partisan Review*, *Commentary*, *Dissent*, *The Public Interest*, and the *New York Review of Books*. I found it fascinating to read about the internecine battles, the egoes, and the passion with which intellectual matters occupied combative minds. The book includes biographical sketches of a number of prominent writers, among them Alfred Kazin,

Saul Bellow, Norman Podhoretz, Irving Howe, Harold Rosenberg, and Clement Greenberg. Bloom follows many of them from the fringes of American society through 1930s radicalism, then through the postwar period as they confronted the destruction of European Jewry, and on to more recent times when many of the same figures became leaders of the neoconservative movement. Bloom writes well, has a feel for major ideas and intellectual and aesthetic disputes, and gives the reader a sense of the historical drama involved.

A companion volume is *The Rise of the New York Intellectuals:* Partisan Review *and Its Circle, 1934–1945* (Wisconsin), by another historian, Terry A. Cooney. Focusing on one of the cultural instruments discussed in Bloom's book, Cooney follows the *Partisan Review* from its founding in 1934 as a Communist publication to the development of its anti-Stalinist position within a few years and to its anti-Soviet, democratic liberalism by the end of World War II. Many of the same actors are on stage here, particularly Philip Rahv and William Phillips, leading figures in establishing the journal's editorial policy. The Stalinist/Trotskyite dispute plays a major role, as does the effort of these (mostly) Jewish urban intellectuals to delineate an American intellectual and cultural tradition that was peer to Europe's. More a book for specialists than Bloom's, *The Rise of the New York Intellectuals* should interest anyone concerned with the recent modern period.

A book that studies how gender and ethnicity interrelate is Mary V. Dearborn's *Pocahontas's Daughters: Gender & Ethnicity in American Culture* (Oxford). The subjects studied are all women who come from one of the hyphenated American ethnic groups. Dearborn believes that "strong similarities, in fact, exist between the male and female ethnic literary traditions; no feature of the ethnic female tradition is exclusively female" (p. 189); the difference lies more in emphasis than theme. Because "the ethnic woman's novel is more heavily weighted toward the family," Dearborn has considered each "in its domestic sense" (p. 191). Chapter titles give a good sense of the subject matter: "A Case Study of American Indian Female Authorship"; "Strategies of Authorship in American Ethnic Women's Fiction: Midwiving and Mediation"; "Black Women Authors and the Harlem Renaissance"; "Fathers and Founding Fathers: The Making of Little American Women"; " 'America is a lover's land': The Pocahontas Marriage, Part I"; and "Miscegenation and the Mulatto, Inheritance and Incest: The Pocahontas Marriage, Part II." The final chapter, excepting the afterword, is "Gertrude Stein's *The Making of Americans* as an Ethnic Text." A student of Werner Sollors, Dearborn finds among her chief influences Oscar Handlin on ethnicity and Simone de Beauvoir on feminism.

Carol Fairbanks writes about frontier women novelists in *Prairie Women: Images in American and Canadian Fiction* (Yale). She synthesizes a broad array of reading (over 100 works, she claims) into a series of historically based general topics, such as "Women and the Prairie Landscape," "First Wave Women," "White Women and Indians," and "Second Wave Women." The thematic approach works well here, and from it we learn much about the nature of women's lives on the prairie and the roles, attitudes, and perceptions they shared. Fairbanks is often in dialogue with Annette Kolodny, who has probably written the most important theoretical work about frontier women writers. The book contains interesting graphics and photographs.

Students of southern American literature will be happy to discover another book by Richard Gray, author of *The Literature of Memory: Modern Writers of the American South.* The current book, *Writing the South*, concentrates on the development of a southern regional consciousness and on the South as both an idea and part of a continuing cultural dialectic. While not exactly claiming that the South is an invention, Gray shows how that region's writers have tried to "invent" their particular place in it at the time they are writing. The book uses works of specific crucial times in southern history, such as the colonial period, the period before the Civil War, and the latter part of the 19th century during and after Reconstruction, and it then deals with important 20th-century writers who have tried to come to terms with their southern heritage. Both major and minor figures are subjects of Gray's scrutiny, and each of his discussions connects the writers closely with their historical moment. I liked all of this book, but I found especially useful the chapters on the manifesto *I'll Take My Stand* and on William Faulkner's career as a southern writer.

Irving Howe's *The American Newness*, originally given as the William E. Massey, Sr., Lectures in the History of American Civilization, is an effective essay on the pervasiveness of Emerson in 19th-century American literature. "I venture," says Howe, "cameo descriptions of three segments of American writing in the nineteenth century: the literature of work; the literature of anarchic bliss; and the literature of loss, announcing and mourning the end of 'the newness.'" The first is Emersonian; the second "assumes the Emersonian vision, or any other republican idea, will be thwarted"; and the third, the post-Civil War segment, "can be understood as a bitter reaction to the hopes of 'the newness'" (p. 65). Howe's cameo descriptions are elegant and personal, often impassioned to the point that he realizes he is being unfair. But Howe is a literary figure in his own right and arrogates to himself a privilege that scholars usually eschew. This stimulating little book is full of good ideas that are often insufficiently worked up.

One could not have the same criticism of Myra Jehlen, *American Incarnation*, a carefully developed theoretical and scholarly argument which posits that American individualism emanates from a direct relationship with the physical fact of this land and this country. While most of its chapters will probably be discussed elsewhere in *ALS 1986*, I should like to comment a bit on what I consider to be one of this year's important books in American literature. For Jehlen "the decisive factor shaping the founding conceptions of 'America' and of 'the American' was material rather than conceptual; rather than a set of abstract ideas, the physical fact of the continent" (p. 3). When settling this "virgin land, the modern spirit completed its genesis by becoming flesh in the body of the American continent." Her central concern becomes, then, "the ideology of this incarnation as it fulfilled Europe's ideal liberalism, and as it is represented, appropriately incarnate, in the form and matter of American writing" (p. 4).

This strong book clearly asserts a thesis about the development of American letters and culture. Jehlen concentrates on how the imperatives of narrative strategy and ideology interact to create the formal dimension of such writers as Jefferson, Emerson, Hawthorne, and Melville; and her readings of these writers are fresh. I am not as taken with her epilogue, "After the Culmination," in which she attempts to make the vision relevant for today without the detail necessary to make the argument convincing. Nonetheless, this is a book that should go on the shelf with other successful overviews of the classic period in our literature.

Brief mention goes to John J. McDermott, *Streams of Experience: Reflections on the History and Philosophy of American Culture* (Mass.). This collection of essays and lectures by a student of American philosophy is loosely tied together by an emphasis on the empirical and pragmatic strain of thought in American philosophers and thinkers. The names of Emerson, William James, and John Dewey continually crop up as either subject matter or reference points for McDermott's reflections on major experiential questions. The writing is clear and the materials familiar; the book is primarily a set of cultural reflections rather than an important contribution to American literature or American studies.

In his brief book, *The Crowd in American Literature* (LSU), Nicolaus Mills has written an essay on the portrayal of crowds in American writing, tracing perspectives on that topic from Adams and Jefferson to narratives by Poe, Melville, Hawthorne, Twain, Howells, Dreiser, Steinbeck, and Ellison. Mills also includes an interesting appendix (with reproductions) on the crowd in American painting. He deals "in chronological order with three major crowds: the revolutionary crowd of John Adams and Thomas Jefferson, the majority crowd of the classic American novel, and the working-class crowd of America's social realists. In the last chapter [Mills discusses] the rise of the modern media crowd in terms of Ralph Ellison's *Invisible Man*" (p. 8). He avoids deprecating words such as "rabble," "mob," and "riot" to speak simply of "a gathering defined by its collective identity of purpose" (p. 9).

I am convinced by Mills's assertion that in the era of the Revolution the idea of the crowd was much more positive than it was for the classic American novelists, whose work "reflects an abiding fear that in America democratic men are the enemy of democratic man." On the other hand, in realists like Howells, Dreiser, and Steinbeck, the portrayal of working-class crowds suggests that these gatherings challenge not the freedoms of individuals, "but the social and economic structure of the country" that denies them "money," "power," and "recognition of [their] needs" (p. 12). Mills's ultimate aim is "to show what happens when the crowds of American literature with their multiple associations challenge the hegemony of the pastoral and timeless images traditionally used to define the meaning of America" (p. 13). These writers raise basic questions about the locus of power in a young democracy, and Mills gets to the heart of the issue with each of his subjects, whether they are political philosophers or novelists. Like most good essays, this little book opens up a lot of questions it does not have time to explore.

As we have already seen, the study of American literature has entered a more self-conscious phase, with a number of works that focus on how scholarship is conducted in that field. Among the interesting books in this vein is Russell Reising's *The Unusable Past: Theory & the Study of American Literature* (Methuen), which analyzes several major theories of American literature, including those of F. O. Matthiessen, Henry Nash Smith, Leo Marx, Leslie Fiedler, Richard Poirier, R. W. B. Lewis, Richard Chase, Sacvan Bercovitch, Charles Feidelson, Jr., D. H. Lawrence, Yvor Winters, and Perry Miller. (Major omissions include Marcus Cunliffe, Leon Howard, and Robert Spiller.) Readers familiar with Howard Mumford Jones's *Theory of American Literature* (1948) will recognize that Reising takes a different tack, not focusing on how the "theory of American literature" developed historically, but looking at the problem topically and reading the texts of American literary theorists from the perspective of the "new Historicism" and poststructuralist analysis.

Reising is highly critical of the systematic thought of almost all his theorists. What he sees as a major "problem for theorists of American literature is to elucidate *how* American texts refer to American social forms, and *what* that mode of reference means. What theorists have done in the past is to skirt the issue by declaring social and historical questions ancillary to their projects" (pp. 34–35). Reising believes that critics who have attempted "to clear a space for American literature as a reformist or revolutionary voice against American society . . . have failed to purge their theories of crucial aesthetic and political assumptions which stifle their objections" (p. 47). An important task of the new literary history will be to expand the canon of works studied. This expansion "should be carried out on two fronts: by abandoning the 'major author' bias and by broadening the conceptual focus of literary study to include the social significance of American texts" (p. 222). Reising finds in Mikhail Bakhtin a possible rationale for formulating "a new appreciation of the heterogeneity of American literature, a heterogeneity often blurred or denied by the polarization of canonical/noncanonical, major/minor, aesthetic/social," even though Bakhtin's "intra-textual bias . . . fails to extend his awareness of dialogism beyond any specific novel into the 'novelization' of literary traditions or critical paradigms" (p. 234). In the foregoing summary I have stressed Reising's own point of view, but readers will also find interesting his critiques of other theorists written from that perspective.

A well-written contribution to American literary regionalism is contained in Anne E. Rowe's *The Idea of Florida in the American Literary Imagination* (LSU). Neither a literary history of Florida nor a source study, this book examines the use of Florida as subject and theme in American literary works, including that state's influence on such writers as Emerson, Hemingway, Irving, Henry James, Marjorie Kinnan Rawlings, and Wallace Stevens. The book is organized thematically, with such chapter titles as "Vestiges of a Romantic Past," "The Garden Spot of God's Green Footstool," "The Last Wild Country," and "The Single Artificer of the World." It contains some excellent photographs and has useful bibliographical apparatus for those who wish to pursue the subject further.

An important book, and one that is bound to provoke a lot of controversy, is Werner Sollors's *Beyond Ethnicity: Consent and Descent in American Culture* (Oxford). For Sollors the history of ethnicity in our literature and culture is defined by a dialectic between the principles of "consent" and "descent." "Descent relations are those defined by anthropologists as relations of 'substance' (by blood or nature); consent relations describe those of 'law' or 'marriage.' Descent language emphasizes our positions as heirs, our hereditary qualities, liabilities, and entitlements; consent language stresses our abilities as mature free agents and 'architects of our fates' to choose our spouses, our destinies, and our political systems" (p. 6). Sollors provides an excellent summary of the book's intentions and contents, which I quote in full:

> This book investigates the origins and ambiguities of the term "ethnicity" and illustrates some of the newer theories (Chapter 1); describes the importance of New England's typological vision for the emergence of different peoplehoods in America (Chapter 2); discusses the melting pot in some unusual contexts (Chapter 3); surveys the strange rhetorical conjunction of melancholy Indian and family drama in American popular culture (Chapter 4) and pursues developmental lines from Indian to urban motifs (Interlude); looks at and interprets some tales of consent and descent (Chapter 5); develops some mental maps of the idealism of group-affiliation thinking (Chapter 6); attempts to get closer to the mysteries of generational counting and ancestor constructing in America (Chapter 7); and, finally, considers some formal implications of writing on themes of ethnicity (Chapter 8). (p. 18)

Because the subject of ethnicity is often fraught with emotion and rhetorical posturing, it may be that Sollors's dispassionate centrism will bring forth the wrath of those committed to one side or another of the consent/descent debate. Nonetheless, scholars should be grateful for the care with which Sollors tries to establish definitions and reasonable intellectual boundaries, as well as for the extraordinary range of his reference—from Puritan typology to modernist fiction. Here, for instance, is Sollors's definition of ethnic literature: "works written by, about, or for persons who perceived themselves, or were perceived by others, as members of ethnic groups, including even nationally and internationally popular writings by 'major' authors and formally intricate and modernist texts" (p. 243). And here is the author's wry yoking of ethnic regionalism with rubrics taken from Puritan imagery: "America seems to be filled not just with Celadon's valleys but also with harmoniously coexisting and overlapping ethnic groups on errands into the wilderness, and regions on the hill—here to save us from the surrounding evils. This may be one reason for the aestheticization of regional and ethnic life, the pervasiveness of moralism in ethnic and regional studies, and the individualization of region and ethnic groups. But how can individuality be constructed as a representation and metaphor of group identity?" (p. 194) Of course, it is also the case "that in America *all* writers can view themselves romantically as members of some out-group so that combining the strategy of outsiderism and self-exoticization can be quite contagious" (p. 31). In its range, clarity of thought, and judicious judgment, *Beyond Ethnicity* establishes itself as a major study of American literary ethnicity.

One of the longest books sent to me for review is *American Literature and the Academy: The Roots, Growth, and Maturity of a Profession* (Penn.), by Kermit Vanderbilt, an excellent history of the academic study of American literature in this country. Although the book goes back as far as Moses Coit Tyler, it really concentrates on two events: the *Cambridge History of American Literature* (1917–21) and the *Literary History of the United States* (1948). In analyzing and describing the process by which each enterprise came to press, Vanderbilt examines the politics and history of the profession, including sketches of most of its important scholars and a lively reconstruction of the debates that shaped our perceptions of American literature throughout the first half of this century and beyond. The book has benefited from full archival research, along with interviews of some of the survivors, and it reprints a number of interesting photographs. The publication of this volume is particularly welcome because of the impending publication of the Cambridge and Columbia histories of American literature, which will eventually, no doubt, inspire their own histories.

Brief mention goes to an excellent regional study by David Wyatt, *The Fall into Eden: Landscape and Imagination in California* (Cambridge). This book suggests that in California setting assumes a kind of mythological status originally created when the first settlers encountered the landscape. Wyatt begins with early writers like Richard Henry Dana and John C. Frémont, moves into the later 19th century with such writers as John Muir and Mary Austin, and then concentrates on such 20th-century figures as Frank Norris and John Steinbeck, concluding with a chapter on Robinson Jeffers and Gary Snyder. This well-written, thoughtful book provides close readings of the various authors along with an informed reflection on the nature of regionalism and how the California variety differs from what one finds elsewhere. It also contains excellent illustrations.

ii. Gender Studies

I have retitled this section because the concerns originally associated with Women's Studies have expanded to include a more general concern with gender as a determining factor in literary and cultural studies. The first book in this section illustrates that concern: Dennis Baron, *Grammar and Gender* (Yale). Baron—whose *Grammar and Good Taste* I reviewed earlier—is concerned with the ways men and women influence the language and the ways the language influences them. Baron's approach emerges from linguistic and philological scholarship, and his tone ranges from sober to ironic. His intention is to "examine how attitudes toward men and women have become attitudes toward language, attempting to place in historical perspective the current debate over sex and language; and we will show not simply how gender-related reforms of language have failed in the past but how views of grammar and gender have been distorted in the past" (p. 10). Baron discusses the subject categorically, looking at such matters as gender-related pronouns, words with feminine endings, and the ways men and women supposedly use language differently. The attempt to create sex-neutral nouns is centuries old, and of the attempt to create such words as salesperson Baron says that "their success as words is secondary to the success of their social design" (p. 189). While he stays out of gender politics, he does point out the historical roots of some current attempts to avoid gender-specific language, without the emotional tone in which such topics are often discussed.

A more ideologically committed book is *The Newly Born Woman*, by Hélène Cixous and Catherine Clement (Minnesota), trans. Betsy Wing. First published in France in 1975, this work has become a classic feminist text. For Cixous and Clement the difference between male and female lies in the concept of "feminine *jouissance*" (p. 82) and in the way it writes itself—e.g., with the "white ink" (p. 94) of mother's milk. The idea that the feminine expresses itself through writing with the body and through sexual play arises because there is no way to understand the feminine "without being trapped within an ideological theater where the proliferation of representations, images, reflections, myths, identifications, transform, deform, constantly change everyone's Imaginary and invalidate in advance any conceptualization" (p. 83). Because we are trapping within logocentric thinking, feminine writing (*écriture feminine*) must break through the relationship of signified and signifier to indulge in the free play of the latter. But this writing can only be posited, never described, and it can be written by men as well as women. Heavily influenced by Lacan's belief that the unconscious is like a linguistic system, the authors exhort: "Woman must write her body, must make up the unimpeded tongue that bursts partitions, classes, and rhetorics, orders and codes, must inundate, run through, go beyond the discourse with its last reserves, including the one of laughing off the word 'silence' that has to be said, the one that, aiming for the impossible, stops dead before the word 'impossible' and writes it as 'end'" (p. 95). A knowledge of this difficult, compelling book is essential to any understanding of radical French feminist theory. I found Sandra Gilbert's introduction very helpful.

For those who wish to know more about the historical and literary dimensions of French feminism, I recommend a brief survey by Claire Duchen called *Feminism in France: From May '68 to Mitterrand* (Routledge). This book places the growth of French feminism within the context of the 1968 "revolution" and its aftermath. Duchen explains difficult concepts well, and her tracing of origins includes not only the political events but the intellectual influences of Foucault and Lacan, and the central roles played by Hélène Cixous and Luce Irigaray. This is a good book to read before tackling *The Newly Born Woman*.

Brief mention goes to Mary Eagleton, ed., *Feminist Literary Theory: A Reader* (Blackwell). This short book is divided into "Finding a Female Tradition," "Women and Literary Production," "Gender and Genre," "Towards Definitions of Feminist Writing," and "Do Women Write Differently?" Unfortunately, the brief selections are no more than snippets, and so the book is useful only as an introduction to titles and authors, though these are extensive and quite appropriate. Even though the author's comments at the head of each section are interesting, I doubt that the book would be a useful teaching aid in spite of its comprehensiveness. One- and two-page selections are simply not long enough.

Gender and Reading, ed. Elizabeth A. Flynn and Patrocinio P. Schweikart, collects essays on the impact of gender as a meaning-giving process for the reader. Divided into "Research and Theory," "Texts," and "Readers," the book covers a variety of topics, most of them literary, and, given its nature, it seems fairly coherent. I found the most interesting materials in the first and third sections, particularly in "The Reader's Construction of Meaning: Cognitive Research on Gender and Comprehension," by Mary Crawford and Roger Chaffin; "Gender Interests in Reading and Language," by David Bleich; and "Gender and Reading," by Elizabeth A. Flynn. There is a good selected bibliography.

The essays in Alette Olin Hill's *Mother Tongue, Father Time* (Indiana) review the rise in consciousness during the last decade of a feminist theory of language. Concerned mainly with the differences between "woman's language" (the ways women speak) and "sexist language" (the ways in which men, and frequently women, speak about women), the book reviews the research done since 1975 in a lively, moderately polemical style, looking at such issues as whether there are genetic differences that affect how men and women speak, the matter of pronouns, the patronizing "terms of endearment" with which men often address women, and what these mean in terms of the full discourse. This is a good-humored book, because the author has an excellent ear for our linguistic absurdities. For those interested in the subject, it might be well to read it in conjunction with Baron's more sober, scholarly work.

Brief mention goes to Mary Jacobus, *Reading Women: Essays in Feminist Criticism* (Columbia), an excellent volume in the Gender and Culture series, but one that contains few essays on American topics. Jacobus, an important feminist critic, writes heavily Freudian readings that make use of Lacan and his followers among French feminists—Luce Irigaray, Julia Kristeva, and Sarah Kofman. Readers interested in theory will find those essays quite useful, particularly "Judith, Holofernes, and the Phallic Woman," "*Dora* and the Pregnant Madonna," and "An Unnecessary Maze of Sign-Reading."

Elizabeth A. Meese's *Crossing the Double-Cross: The Practice of Feminist Criticism* (No. Car.) mixes the practical and theoretical, emphasizing the political and heuristic aspects of theory more than the abstract. She plays a great deal with the punning possibilities in the words "cross," "crossing," and "double-cross," emphasizing not only the concept of betrayal but also crossing boundaries and cross-fertilization. Some of the latter occurs between American authors, and some between American and British authors, as in the relationship between the writings of Virginia Woolf and Tillie Olsen. Meese's topics include the stories of Mary Wilkins Freeman, Zora Neale Hurston's *Their Eyes Were Watching God*, and Marilynne Robinson's *Housekeeping*. I found the theoretical chapters very useful: "Crossing the Double-Cross: The Concept of 'Difference' and Feminist Literary Criticism" and "In/Conclusion: The Problem of Theory and the Practice of Feminist Literary Criticism."

In *The Poetics of Gender*, also part of the Columbia series on Gender and Culture, Nancy K. Miller has edited the proceedings of a colloquium on that topic held in 1985 at Columbia. The assembled participants included many of the best-known feminist critics, and, although the sense of unity in the collection is not strong, the quality of individual essays is high. Many critical issues in the study of gender are discussed, and I can particularly recommend the papers by Mary Ann Caws, Alice Jardine, Susan Rubin Suleiman, Domna C. Stanton, Elaine Showalter, and Nancy K. Miller.

An even more important collection of essays is *The Female Body in Western Culture: Contemporary Perspectives* (Harvard), ed. Susan Rubin Suleiman, most of the essays having been published in an oversized issue of *Poetics Today* (1985). This well-organized and integrated collection takes as its topic one of the central items of contemporary theory, the relation of the body and sexuality to consciousness and language. The editor's opening essay, "(Re)writing the Body: The Politics and Poetics of Female Eroticism," establishes some terms of the argument, which is concerned with the conventional labels of man and woman and assumes that biological determination is insufficient. Much of this argument derives from radical

French feminist thought, particularly the work of Monique Wittig. The contents of this collection are divided into the following provocative categories: Eros, Death, Mothers, Illness, Images, Difference. Contributors include Catharine R. Stimpson, Thomas G. Pavel, Alice Jardine, Julia Kristeva, Mary Ann Caws, Mieke Bal, and Naomi Schor. A key question raised by the discussion: If gender differences are primarily conventional, what is the future of difference?

Eros and Power: The Promise of Feminist Theory (Penn.), by Haunani-Kay Trask, ranges over many disciplines to articulate a theory of how woman's erotic powers can be grounded in a utopian vision of the good society. Trask believes that our concepts of sexuality and gender have been conventionalized by patriarchal societies whose interests have been served by perpetuating male domination. The book is divided into two sections. The first analyzes "Male Power" in a wide-ranging historical, sociological, and philosophical synthesis to show how male dominance has been established and perpetuated. The second presents the book's radical utopian vision, in which the "Feminist Eros" provides the basis for a new society at whose center lies the mother as life-giver and protector. This is the kind of book with which one loves to argue and from which one emerges with a sense that old materials have been freshly presented.

iii. Modernism

This brief section opens with a collection originally published in *boundary 2: Postmodernism and Politics* (Minnesota), ed. by Jonathan Arac, volume 28 in the series Theory and History of Literature. The various essays explore the question of whether in fact there is a phenomenon called postmodernism, and if so, what its characteristics are. Although Arac's introduction tries valiantly to create a coherent book, this set of essays seems rather disparate in approach and subject matter, ranging from studies of Ezra Pound and reader-response criticism to essays on such critical figures as Theodor Adorno, Raymond Williams, and Fredric Jameson. Questions about postmodernism merge with those about poststructuralism, and it is fascinating to watch content and technique merge throughout the debate. The book explores the issues fairly well, but it does not come close to resolving the problem.

Shari Benstock's *Women of the Left Bank: Paris, 1900–1940* (Texas) is a major contribution to the study of modernism. This lengthy, well-stocked book has something significant to say about most of the women writers who lived in Paris during the time of high modernism, and more than any book I know it develops a sense of a strong community in which women writers worked and were nourished. Benstock, while informed by the scholarship of others, seems to have something fresh to say about most of her authors, including Djuna Barnes, Adrienne Monnier, Sylvia Beach, Janet Flanner, Gertrude Stein and Alice Toklas, Jean Rhys, and Edith Wharton. While not a major contribution to our theoretical understanding of modernism, the book adds much to the historical record; more important, it allows us to see the impact of the women's community in Paris, and it breaks down the notion that the only important American modernists in that city were Hemingway, Fitzgerald, Stein, and, later, Henry Miller. It offers a wealth of good photographs.

A large collection of essays on modernism has been edited by Monique Chefdor, Ricardo Quinones, and Albert Wachtel, *Modernism: Challenges and Perspectives* (Illinois), the product of a conference at the Claremont Colleges. The 21 distinguished contributors write on topics that are historical, artistic, and literary. The three sections contain historical overviews, practical readings of modernist artists and schools, and discussions of postmodernism. Although no single essay transforms our understanding of modernism, I found many of them quite instructive: e.g., Robert P. Morgan, "Secret Languages: The Roots of Musical Modernism"; Robert Wohl, "The Generation of 1914 and Modernism"; Harvey Gross, "Parody, Reminiscence, Critique: Aspects of Modernist Style"; JoAnna Isaak, "The Revolution of a Poetics"; Renee Riese Hubert, "Paul Klee: Modernism in Art and Literature"; and Ihab Hassan, "The Culture of Postmodernism."

Another perspective on modernism comes in Stephen W. Melville, *Philosophy Beside Itself: On Deconstruction and Modernism* (Minnesota), volume 27 in the Theory and History of Literature series. Instead of exploring modernist roots in stylistic or structural phenomena, Melville locates them in patterns of thought, showing how modernist consciousness ultimately gives rise to the patterns of a poststructuralist consciousness of language. The first chapter, "On Modernism," is an interesting discussion of backgrounds, and the titles of following chapters give some sense of how the book's argument progresses: "A Context for Derrida," "Psychoanalysis and Deconstruction," "Paul de Man: The Time of Criticism," and "Psychoanalysis, Criticism, Self-Criticism." The book is pervaded more by the presence of de Man than Derrida, and Melville's deconstructive reading of classic psychoanalytic texts is sensitive and ingenious.

iv. Theory of Narrative

I have changed the title of this section from the theory of "fiction" in order to turn the topic to the study of narrativity and away from the study of, say, the novel or some vague concept of "fictionality." The first title deals with those books that straddle the border between works of fiction and works of fact—Barbara Foley, *Telling the Truth: The Theory and Practice of Documentary Fiction* (Cornell). This study claims that Marxism does not have adequate theories of mimesis or genre. Foley's grounding in Marxist theory is strong. She traces the ways in which ideological changes that followed the development of a capitalist economy led to a concern for "authentic" documentation in novels and others works of narrative, and she follows this changing ideology from Defoe to more recent practitioners of the documentary narrative, such as John Dos Passos and Ernest Gaines. In her theoretical section Foley talks about the problems of "borders," "assertion," "the referent," and "the subject." Her chapters of practical criticism are "The Pseudofactual Novel," "The Historical Novel," "The Modernist Documentary Novel," and "The Afro-American Documentary Novel." Marxist scholars and students of narratology will enjoy this well-written, committed book.

Thomas M. Leitch's *What Stories Are: Narrative Theory and Interpretation* (Penn. State) takes a position contrary to the structuralist one (à la Gerard Genette) which opposes "story" (the events) and "discourse" (the medium through which the events are narrated). The author describes his book as a "tendentious study of narrative in rhetorical or transactional terms . . . a study of the conditions under which a given discourse might be displayed as a story and of the relations stories established with their audiences that permitted them to operate as stories" (p. x). The book deals most heavily with the ways a storyteller or narrator interacts with the reader or audience and how those sets of expectations control the ways in which the narratives develop. Leitch is a professor of film as well as English, and his understanding of narrative is informed by that medium as well as by the living theater. The book develops its theory as much out of fictional texts as out of contact with "theorists," and its common-sense approach is welcome.

Wallace Martin's *Recent Theories of Narrative* (Cornell) is a useful summary of the theories of narrative that have emerged since 1945 and have influenced the ways we think and write about not only novels and stories but history and biography. Martin is conversant with French, Russian, American, German, and British theorists, and I found his summaries to be clear and accurate. He is also aware of the ways stories can outstrip theories, and so he is not inclined to overvalue the latter. The book is helpful not only for its summation of theories but for the sense of historical development it conveys about how the theory of narrative has emerged as a scholarly field.

In *Fictional Worlds* (Harvard) Thomas G. Pavel combines philosophical sophistication about fictionality with a knowledge of literary theory. This impressive book discusses the relationship between statements about the "real" world and those about fictional worlds and analyzes the differences and similarities between the two kinds of statements. "By proposing a survey of the semantics of fiction, I am attempting to pave the way for a theory sensitive to the nature and function of imaginary worlds, the representational force of fiction, and the links between literature and other cultural systems" (p. vii). Pavel feels that it is time for such a study after the long hiatus caused by a dominant theory which said we could talk only about what was "in the text." "The moratorium on referential issues," he says, "has by now become obsolete. Freed from the constraints of the textualist approach, theory of fiction can respond again to the world-creating powers of imagination and account for the properties of fictional existence and worlds, their complexity, incompleteness, remoteness, and integration within the general economy of culture" (p. 10). Pavel, himself a novelist, deals well with the "reality" of fictional worlds, organizing his argument into "Beyond Structuralism," "Fictional Beings," "Salient Worlds," "Border, Distance, Size, Incompleteness," "Conventions," and "The Economy of the Imaginary." The book is well-written, well-informed, and imaginative.

Robert Siegle's *The Politics of Reflexivity: Narrative and the Constitutive Poetics of Culture* (Hopkins) explores the constant reflexive interplay of the elements of narrative with both the structures of the narrative itself and with the elements of "real world" culture that control the shape of that narrative structure as well as the "subject" of the novel. This is a useful concept, though difficult to explain, and the author has not fully managed to convey his topic's complexity clearly. Nonetheless, this book does manage to bring many post-structuralist insights into a discussion of the theory of narrative. Siegle focuses his study on readings of four novels: Thackeray's *Vanity Fair*, Conrad's *Chance*, Robert Penn Warren's *World Enough and Time*, and John Fowles's *The French Lieutenant's Woman*. In each case he shows how the novel comments self-reflexively on its own structure.

v. Literary Theory

In this section I shall include those works that are more generally theoretical and seem to me to have the best chance of being read in the future. I shall begin by discussing three collections of theory. The first, ed. Hazard Adams and Leroy Searle, *Critical Theory Since 1965* (Florida State), is a large, compendious collection not organized by topics. It is simply a set of the most interesting theoretical essays "arranged chronologically by year of publication, writing, or first presentation as a lecture, rather than by some imposed rubric" (p. ix). The editors reject organization by rubric because they "have not seen an anthology of the history of criticism arranged by rubric that has not been disconcerting to work with" (p. x). An appendix reprints 16 essays published before 1965 which could have, but did not, appear in the earlier Adams anthology, *Critical Theory Since Plato* (1971). It is difficult to fault the selections in this book because they are from most of the prominent theorists of our time. There are, however, no essays by Georges Poulet or Roland Barthes, and there is too little representation of the structuralist movement. The collection's size might also be a bit intimidating, and the double-column format is made more forbidding by type that is too small.

A collection that *is* organized by rubric has been put together by Robert Con Davis, *Contemporary Literary Criticism* (Longman). The eight categories, each containing about four essays, are "Modernism: The Call for Form," "Formalism," "The Historical Dialectic," "The Sexual Dialectic," "Depth Psychology and 'The Scene of Writing': Jung and Freud," "The Structuralist Controversy," "The Affective Response," and "The Poststructuralist 'Texte.'" The essays range from T. E. Hulme, T. S. Eliot, and Ortega y Gasset in the early part of the century to the best-known critics active within the last 20 years. (Both Poulet and Barthes are here, by the way.) While this book also has the hateful double-column format, the large type is in fact quite readable. I should also add that Davis's introductory materials are very successful in preparing the reader for the various sections and individual essays. In this book the rubrics do work, and it is the one I would assign for a course in 20th-century literary theory.

The third collection is much more specialized, *Deconstruction in Context: Literature and Philosophy* (Chicago), ed. Mark C. Taylor. These essays have been selected in order to set deconstruction into a historical context that is both literary and philosophical. Taylor traces a philosophical tradition that proceeds from Immanuel Kant and G. W. F. Hegel through such 19th-century figures as Søren Kierkegaard and Friedrich Nietzsche (half the book contains essays from the 19th century) and into the 20th century, with Ludwig Wittgenstein, Jean-Paul Sartre, Maurice Merleau-Ponty, Maurice Blanchot, and Jacques Derrida. Taylor's introduction does a masterful job of explaining the problems faced by this philosophical tradition and its various authors. Reading through these selections will explain a great deal to students and skeptical readers about the nature of deconstruction and where it fits into modern intellectual life.

The translations of Mikhail Bakhtin continue in *Speech Genres & Other Late Essays* (Texas), trans. Vern W. McGee. The collection was edited by Caryl Emerson and Michael Holquist, both names familiar to readers of Bakhtin, and there is an excellent introduction by the latter. We are probably reaching the end of the line with Bakhtin manuscripts unless some unknown items show up. These essays are mostly from the end of that distinguished career, some of them full length and some fragments. The most important are "The *Bildungsroman* and Its Significance in the History of Realism (Toward a Historical Typology of the Novel)" and "The Problem of Speech Genres." Most concerns here are familiar, but the latter essay does enrich Bakhtin's theory of discourse.

The study of Freud's writings as texts for literary analysis is exemplified in a densely argued little book by Leo Bersani, *The Freudian Body: Psychoanalysis and Art* (Columbia). The book contains deconstructive readings of certain Freudian texts, principally *Civilization and Its Discontents*, *Beyond the Pleasure Principle*, and *Three Essays on the Theory of Sexuality*. Bersani argues that "the psychoanalytical authenticity of Freud's work *depends on* [his italics] a process of theoretical collapse," which is a "function of its own development." In addition, "the particular type of textual density" that concerns Bersani can "be defined as a tension between certain radical speculative movements and the wish to practice and even to institutionalize the speculative process itself" (p. 3). The author sees Freud's work as part of a continuum that includes the Marquis de Sade, Stéphane Mallarmé, Henry James, Samuel Beckett, and Pier Paolo Pasolini, the Italian filmmaker. His readings are clever, unforced, and nonformulaic; the rhetorical technique opens up the texts rather than closing them. A very stimulating book.

There has been a stirring of interest once again in the writings of R. P. Blackmur, whose work has been somewhat neglected recently. Dennis Donoghue has edited his *Selected Essays* (Ecco), adding to them a good introduction that contains an appreciation of that subtle critic. Donoghue favors Blackmur the close reader of texts; he includes only one essay on a general topic, "A Critic's Job of Work," along with Blackmur's classic readings of Henry James, Henry Adams, Fyodor Dostoevski, W. B. Yeats, and Wallace Stevens. I would have liked to see a few more of Blackmur's theoretical texts such as "The Lion and the Honeycomb" and "A Burden of Critics." In tandem with this book is the first full-length discussion of Blackmur as a theorist, *Wayward Skeptic: The Theories of R. P. Blackmur* (Illinois), by James T. Jones. This is a good overview of its subject, although Jones himself derives theory from Blackmur as much as he explains Blackmur's theories. He discusses Blackmur's language and theory of language, his theories of poetry and overall critical theories, the influences on his work, his readings of other writers, and Blackmur's own poetry. I am pleased to see this revival of interest in a critic whose concern with how language and rhetoric work are close to the interests of contemporary critical theory.

Paul A. Bové's *Intellectuals in Power: A Genealogy of Critical Humanism* (Columbia) is less a history of modern criticism than a study of the ways intellectuals are shaped by modern political and historical phenomena and of the ways they have expressed the dominant historical forces of their time. Clearly a student of Nietzsche and Foucault, Bové claims that there is "no way to understand the past and present social and cultural role of advanced literary education and criticism except by trying to see it as situated within an entire range of discourses and institutions whose own metier is power and interest" (p. ix). The task of Bové's genealogist is to discover the bases of power within a critical and cultural situation and to show

how leading thinkers operate to overcome the power inherent in a tradition that attempts to coerce thought and action. The paradox is that there is no escape. "This representation of the genealogist is, then, thoroughly inscribed within the tradition it hopes to refute; it cannot be otherwise" (p. 11). How to set oneself free from a coercive tradition and to discover texts within a canonical tradition that subvert that tradition are tasks that add to the paradox. Subjects of Bové's analysis include Nietzsche, Michel Foucault, Edward Said, I. A. Richards, and Erich Auerbach. His final chapter, "Critical Negation: The Function of Criticism at the Present Time," with its allusion to Matthew Arnold, is an astute analysis of contemporary theory. Although wordy, the book is one of the better recent overviews of recent modern theory.

Another posthumous collection by Paul de Man is contained in *The Resistance to Theory* (Minnesota), volume 33 in the Theory and History of Literature series. Most of these pieces were written in de Man's last years, the most important ones being the title essay and "Reading and History," which concerns the University of Konstanz school of criticism. It is difficult to overestimate the importance of de Man to contemporary theory, a fact that is reinforced by a special issue of *Yale French Studies* (no. 69), entitled *The Lesson of Paul de Man.* The issue contains a series of eulogies delivered at a memorial service, a last lecture by de Man entitled " 'Conclusions' (on Walter Benjamin's 'The Task of the Translator')," also reprinted in *The Resistance to Theory*, a section of essays called "Reading de Man," another section entitled "Reading with de Man," and a "Bibliography of Texts by Paul de Man." The high quality of most of this collection testifies to the power of de Man's teaching and his influence. Among the contributors are Shoshana Felman, Barbara Johnson, Jonathan Culler, Michael Riffaterre, Geoffrey H. Hartman, J. Hillis Miller, and Howard Felperin.

There is also a book by Jacques Derrida, *Memoires for Paul de Man* (Columbia), trans. Cecile Lindsay et al., which was originally presented as The Wellek Library Lectures at the University of California, Irvine, in 1984, shortly after de Man's death. Not merely a tribute to de Man, who Derrida believes is the most important figure among American deconstructionists, these are moving remarks by someone whose writings have always seemed so emotionally forbidding. It is a difficult book but one which provides the reader with a good account of deconstruction and de Man's role in formulating it.

Derrida points out, as did his colleague, that the deconstructive process is always at work within the text itself; it is not imposed from without by a critic. "Deconstruction," he says, "is not an operation that supervenes *afterwards*, from the outside, one fine day; it is always already at work in the work; one must just know how to identify the right or wrong element, the right or wrong stone . . . the disruptive force of deconstruction is always already contained within the architecture of the work . . ." (p. 73). The informality of the lecture format makes this book perhaps the most accessible entrée I know into Derrida's work.

Two books on Derrida deserve mention, for they contain some of the best exegeses of his methods we have yet had. In *The Tain of the Mirror: Derrida and the Philosophy of Reflection* (Harvard), Rodolphe Gasché writes about Derrida's work from within the criticism of reflexivity and reflection. Beginning with Hegel's criticism of Kant, Gasché follows the tradition through Edmund Husserl, Martin Heidegger, Hans-Georg Gadamer, and Derrida. To read the book one should have a grounding in these philosophical texts as well as in those by Derrida. Although conceptually difficult, the book is written with clarity, and it places Derrida within a philosophical context and tradition better than any book I have read. Also effective in some of the same ways is *Derrida and the Economy of Difference* (Indiana), by Irene E. Harvey. The author, a professor of philosophy, goes against received opinion among her colleagues to say that Derrida is indeed a philosopher, and in some ways the most important one we have had since Heidegger. She too locates Derrida within a long tradition of European philosophy, and she claims that deconstruction is not simply a tool for textual analysis but also an approach to metaphysics. Harvey's interest lies in her using Derrida to develop a philosophy of textuality.

I should like to mention briefly the translation of two of the late Michel Foucault's books. The first, *The Care of the Self* (Pantheon), trans. Robert Hurley, is the third and "possibly final" volume of *The History of Sexuality*. It traces that history during the early Christian centuries in Rome. Foucault analyzes the writings of Roman thinkers as well as early Christians, and in them he finds the beginnings of modern attitudes toward sexuality, including its relation to the family and the inclusion of love, intimacy, and sexuality in the relations of husband and wife. One looks in vain for many statements of the methods behind Foucault's "archaeological" research. It is rather by implication that we see how Foucault amasses evidence and draws conclusions. One should not, by the way, underestimate the amount of basic library research this so-called theorist did. The book is well-written and well-researched, and the examples are continuously fascinating. The other book is *Death and the Labyrinth: The World of Raymond Roussel* (Doubleday), trans. Charles Ruas, the only book of literary criticism Foucault wrote. Roussel was a turn-of-the-century French writer seen as an eccentric by his contemporaries because he dealt with "found" objects and language, but who has lately come to seem like a precursor of the major modernists. An introduction by the poet John Ashbery is helpful in introducing us to this writer before we experience him through Foucault's mixture of biography, descriptive analysis, and criticism. Foucault's method seems quite original, but since I have not read Roussel, I cannot comment on the substance of his remarks.

John Frow's *Marxism and Literary Form* (Harvard) develops a systematic Marxist theory of literary history from within the context of poststructuralism. Frow sees "literary criticism as an institution and a set of institutionally regulated practices. To see the activity of literary criticism in this way is to reverse the traditional patterns of methodological reflection, which have been concerned with the epistemological protocols governing reading, and to tie the practice of reading instead to the procedures of an apparatus of disciplinary training" (p. 2). Influenced by Louis Althusser, Fredric Jameson, and Mikhail Bakhtin, this well-written and well-informed book is one of the best systematic presentations of Marxist literary theory around. Frow has a rich grounding in major Marxist as well as contemporary non-Marxist texts on theory.

Any book by René Girard is an event, and this year's event is *The Scapegoat* (Hopkins), trans. Yvonne Freccero. This volume studies "texts of persecution," by which the author refers to writings that describe mass phenomena of violent persecution written from the persecutor's point of view. Girard describes the stereotypes that exist in such documents: (1) "description of a cultural crisis, that is, a generalized loss of difference"; (2) "crimes that 'eliminate differences' "; (3) "whether the identified authors of these crimes possess the marks that suggest a victim" to the writer and the intended audience; (4) "violence itself" (p. 24). It is the juxtaposition in the document of two or three of these stereotypes that "indicated persecution." "Their existence convinces us that (1) the acts of violence are real; (2) the crisis is real; (3) the victims are chosen not for the crimes they are accused of but for the victim's signs that they bear . . . ; (4) the import of the operation is to lay the responsibility for the crisis on the victims . . . ," to destroy them or at least banish "them from the community they 'pollute'" (p. 24). Girard focuses on a number of historical documents, such as Guillaume de Machaut's *Judgment of the King of Navarre*, that demonstrate the validity of his thesis, and he looks for an overall pattern that might explain such events. He finds it in the Christian Passion which expounds on the same pattern of violence and mass victimization, except that it is told from the point of view of an innocent victim. The events Girard describes are, thus, reversals of the Passion. A mere summary cannot do justice to the richness of this brief and beautifully written book.

Two books about Jacques Lacan make important contributions to our understanding of his work. Ellie Ragland-Sullivan's *Jacques Lacan and the Philosophy of Psychoanalysis* (Illinois) is the best analytic summary of Lacan's work that I have read. It is a straightforward presentation of the major tenets of Lacan's system of thought, including his "theory of the human subject," his notion of the "four fundamental concepts of Psychoanalysis," his "theory of cognition," his theory of the relationship of "signifier, signified, and sign," and the "question of gender identity." Ragland-Sullivan believes that Lacan "may well be the most important thinker in France since René Descartes and the most innovative and far-ranging thinker in Europe since Friedrich Nietzsche and Sigmund Freud" (p. ix), and it is from that perspective that she has written a dense, richly argued book. One should certainly have absorbed a bit of Lacan before reading it, however. A more "literary" approach is contained in *Figuring Lacan: Criticism and the Cultural Unconscious* (Nebraska), by Juliet Flower MacCannell, which studies the role of figurative language in Lacan and its meaning in his theories. MacCannell is interested in Lacan's tropes and in how his ideas mirror the culture. Not as straightforward as Ragland-Sullivan's exegesis, this book is more digressive and playful, occasionally lapsing into opacity, but mostly an interesting meditation that uses Lacan as its base.

I end this section with René Wellek's two volumes on criticism during the first half of this century, which are also volumes 5 and 6 of *A History of Modern Criticism, 1750–1950* (Yale). *English Criticism, 1900–1950* and *American Criticism, 1900–1950* are both fairly straightforward summaries, scrupulously fair-minded and compendious. Their tone is relatively old-fashioned, but Wellek is always linguistically sophisticated. There are excellent chapters in the former book on the Bloomsbury Group and on T. S. Eliot, I. A. Richards, and F. R. Leavis, as well as many good summaries of such lesser lights as Arthur Symons and T. E. Hulme. The American volume goes through the New Criticism and discusses Edmund Wilson, R. P. Blackmur, Kenneth Burke, Yvor Winters, and the Chicago School, as well as many others. The scholarship in both volumes remains astonishingly comprehensive, and Wellek has also informed himself about contemporary critical theory (although he is unhappy with much of poststructuralism). These are not books one would normally read through as narratives; they are most useful as reference works, and the summaries of individual authors are unsurpassed. One volume remains to be published, *Criticism on the Continent of Europe, 1900–1950*, an area that in fact represents Wellek's greatest expertise.

vi. Conclusion

This was a year of competence but not great excellence in the field of theory. I do not think I have read any work that will change the ways we read literature in general (except perhaps René Girard's) and American literature in particular (except perhaps Werner Sollors's), although some metatheoretical works in the American section make one look forward to the major literary histories currently in preparation. We are now in something of a critical interregnum, with the decline of deconstruction announced everywhere and the "new literary history" ready to take its place and waiting to find a major theorist to articulate its principles.

University of California, Davis

20. Foreign Scholarship

i. East European Contributions

F. Lyra

The absence of any books on American literature from the Soviet Union for 1986 provides an opportunity for a closer look at two substantial studies published in 1985 but only now available. One is by Tamara Naumovna Denisova, *Ekzistentsializm i sovremennyi amerikanskii roman* [*Existentialism and the Contemporary American Novel*] (Kiev [1985]: Naukova Dumka), the other by Georgii Pavlovich Zlobin, *Po tu storonu mechty. Stranitsy amerikanskoi literatury XX veka* [*On This Side of the Dream: Pages of Twentieth-Century American Literature*] (Moscow [1985]: Khudozhestvennaya Literatura).

Denisova's is the first Soviet study of the influence of existentialism on American literature. On the chance that it might be thought dated, she insists that "existentialism has become instilled in the flesh and blood of Western civilization." She rests the justification of her book on two premises: the inadequacy of earlier studies by Sidney Finkelstein, Richard Cohan, Charles Glicksberg, and others, though she acknowledges respect for their work and is partly indebted to them; and the conviction that existentialism is organic to American literature, contrary to the opinion of some Soviet scholars, notably A. M. Zverev, who considers existentialism an extrinsic phenomenon. Denisova makes a strong case for the importance of the movement. In a long introductory chapter, "Ways and Fortunes of Existentialism: In Place of an Introduction," she provides a balanced overview, including a brief discussion of Christian existential thought, her shrilly Marxist protestations notwithstanding. In analyzing American fiction she moves within a contradictory framework: having stressed the importance of existentialism in American literary culture, she refutes its manifestations in the work of major writers. The second chapter of her book, "The Problem of the Self in the Contemporary American Realistic Novel," reveals a missionary spirit intended to save Dos Passos, Wolfe, Fitzgerald, Faulkner, and Hemingway for realism. Her reading is necessarily selective, of course, but her omissions seem telling. For instance, in discussing Faulkner she passes over such works as *Pylon*, *The Wild Palms*, and *A Fable*. In a subchapter, "The Self and Morality in the Postwar Novel," she deals with John Updike, Joyce Carol Oates, John Gardner, and Robert Penn Warren as illustrations of an assumption with a foregone conclusion: American writers have basically remained realistic; their preoccupation with the self in general, which began with Charles Brockden Brown, manifests a certain existential predisposition, but American culture could never have produced a system like existentialism, and she says why. To be sure, authors such as Jack Kerouac, Norman Mailer, Saul Bellow, Richard Wright and James Baldwin, William Styron, and Thornton Wilder, who are discussed in the third chapter, "In the Circle of Existentialism and Beyond Its Boundaries," had in various degrees bouts with existentialism, but "none of them can be called an existentialist." Wilder, in her opinion, comes closest, but a work like *The Ides of March* "reaches significantly beyond the frame of existentialist philosophy." Denisova strains to absolve these authors of their susceptibility to existentialism, except for Bellow. She reluctantly approves of some Soviet critics of his work, especially those discussing his earlier fiction. She is particularly critical of his "conformism," "which contrasts with the stoic humanism of the progressive writers and thinkers openly professing existentialism." As to Wright and Baldwin, they are existentialist in method only. The baggy character of the chapter allows her to include authors of such diverse qualities as Kerouac and Styron; the former manifests traits which bring him close to existentialism, but the latter is basically a realist. The last chapter, "After Existentialism," presents a rambling survey of "counterculture" and "the absurd" and their offshoots, which Denisova connects with existentialist philosophy. There are brief discussions of the "neo-avant-garde which has produced nothing worthy of attention," New Journalism, the aesthetics of Susan Sontag and Ronald Sukenik, black humor—a characteristically American product with roots in American folklore—and brief profiles of William Burroughs and John Barth. Thomas Pynchon receives favorable attention on account of his flashes of realistic writing, but is criticized for his "neglect of economic laws of social development." Denisova recognizes the social criticism contained in "particular fragments of the work of black humorists," and contrary to an earlier assertion she admits that "black humor as art can be connected with existentialism, only now it is called postexistentialism." At the end she announces the demise of the school and its offshoots. But the "exhaustion" of black humor does not yet mean the death of modernism. The study closes with the ritualistic equation of modernism and bourgeois culture and with the announcement that the American realistic novel has reached a new stage in the form of "romantic realism," which today characterizes not only Gardner's work but also "progressive American realistic literature." Despite the all too familiar jargon that Denisova applies occasionally and the dichotomization of literature into realist and modernist "schools," *Ekzistentsializm* gives fair treatment to contemporary (and not so contemporary) novelists. An American writer's anti-Marxist worldview does not automatically invite condemning criticism any more, as was so often the case in past Soviet writing about American literature.

Zlobin's *On This Side of the Dream* is by his own admission less a scholarly than a critical work. Relieved of academic restraints, he has made full use of the freedom to produce a protean book in which the absence of structural unity, complemented by literary sophistication, graceful style, and suitable criticism of Soviet academic writing on American literature, makes pleasurable reading. Zlobin writes about the "living existence" of literature and not about "process"—a perennial theme in Soviet academic literary scholarship. Naturally, realism, historicism, and moral seriousness remain for him the highest standards by which to judge a writer's accomplishments. Among contemporary American novelists who, he thinks, have come closest to his ideal, at least in their work of the '70s, are Heller, Gardner, James Jones, Baldwin, and Styron. He is not enthusiastic about such modernists as Barth and Pynchon, who are dealt with in a few paragraphs, yet he remains open to their art. But the "commercial-conformists"—for instance, James Michener and Arthur Hailey—are treated with profound disparagement. Zlobin deplores the inadequate attention given by Soviet scholars and critics to American minority literatures. To make up partly for the deficiency, he looks at the work of a host of black writers (Toni Morrison, who is commended for her "magic realism" in *Song of Solomon*, Alice Walker, Baldwin, and Alex Haley) and a few American Jewish authors (Bellow, Singer, and Malamud), and provides a few paragraphs on the American Irish novel. In a separate chapter Zlobin discusses the war novel and John Hersey's writings, especially *The Call* which he considers in some respects better than Mailer's and Jones's classics.

The lack of thematic unity in Zlobin's book is compounded by the incongruous treatment of particular writers and topics. Analytical chapters on some writers' single works, for example, Faulkner's *The Sound and the Fury*, Steinbeck's *The Grapes of Wrath*, Hemingway's *For Whom the Bell Tolls*, and Styron's *Sophie's Choice*, alternate with chapters characterizing an author's general output, as is the case with Barrie Stavis, John O'Hara, Thornton Wilder, and Edward Albee. There is also a section entitled "American Tragedies in Midcentury" in which Zlobin analyzes single plays by Eugene O'Neill, Arthur Miller, Lillian Hellman, Tennessee Williams, and Stavis. Specialists will not find any new exegetical themes in his texts, but within the general context of the Soviet reception of American literature some of his opinions provide refreshing insights into the works of several writers. For example, he presents a critical review of the Soviet reception of Faulkner, pointing out the paradoxical nature of his work. Some of Zlobin's statements are hard to accept, though, as when he interprets the structure of *The Sound and the Fury* as a "movement" toward realism and takes it as a general characteristic of Faulkner's entire opus. Open-minded Soviet readers have certainly welcomed Zlobin's chapter on *For Whom the Bell Tolls*, until recently Hemingway's most neglected work in the Soviet Union. Zlobin suggests why: Robert Jordan was thought to have embraced the Republican cause out of disappointment with life; his love affair, says Zlobin, is not a manifestation of the "carpe diem spirit" of a man at the edge of the grave. Zlobin points out the complexity of the novel, revealing Hemingway's desire to present the Spanish Civil War truthfully.

Some of the authors discussed in Denisova's and Zlobin's books were subjects of short publications in various periodicals and collections of articles published in 1986 which were not available for review. *Stilicheskoye issledovaniya khudozhestvennogo teksta* [*Stylistic Studies of Artistic Texts*] (Yakutsk) contains two contributions on O'Neill and Hemingway, respectively: L. P. Tchakhoyan, O. B. Reva, "Nestandardnye sintaksicheskie konstruktsii kak kharakternaya tcherta stilya p'es Yu. O'Nila" [Nonstandard Stylistic Constructions as a Characteristic Feature of O'Neill's Style] (pp. 69–79); S. M. Petrova, "Khudozhestvennoye masterstvo E. Khemingueya (*Povest' Starik i more*)" [Hemingway's Artistic Mastery (*The Old Man and the Sea*)] (pp. 106–15). *Realizm v zarubezhnykh literaturakh XIX–XX vekov: K problemakh istorizma* [*Realism in Foreign Literatures of the 19th and 20th Centuries: Toward the Problems of Historicism*] (Saratoga) carries I. V. Razvinova's "Vechnoe i sotsialno-istoricheskoye v novelle U. Folknera 'Bylye Lyudi'" [The Eternal and the Social-Historical in W. Faulkner's story "The Old People"] (pp. 136–46); O. N. Golubkova's "Osobennosti istorizma povesti G. Melvilla Benito Cereno" [Characteristics of Historicism of H. Melville's "Benito Cereno"] (pp. 152–61); and E. V. Staroverova's "Geroi amerikanskoi literaturnoi skazki: Genezis i razvitie" [The Hero of the American Literary Fairy Tale: Origin and Development] (pp. 146–52). In another collection, *Formy raskrytiya avtorskogo coznaniya* [*Forms of Disclosure of Authorial Consciousness*] (Voronezh), E. A. Nikolaeva writes about "Pozitsiya avtora v povesti D. Steinbeka *Nebeskye pastbishcha.* K. voprosu ob ideino-khudozhestvennoi evolutsii pisatelya" [The Position of the Author in Steinbeck's *The Pastures of Heaven*: Toward the Question of the Ideological and Artistic Evolution of the Author] (pp. 121–29); and A. L. Savchenko discusses "Chelovek i mir v svete avtorskoi kontseptsii deistvitel'nosti (R. P. Uarren *Potop*)" [Man and the World in the Light of the Author's Conception of Reality: R. P. Warren's *Flood*] (pp. 107–14).

Whether the relatively large number of short studies of individual works produced at various academic centers signals a new stage in American literary scholarship in the Soviet Union remains to be seen. Most of the studies digest familiar substance, producing little that might be of relevance to the user of *ALS*. But I consider it a duty to list them at least: T. Aunan, "Vliyanie transtsendentalisttskikh kontseptsii na roman N. Gortona *Septimius Felton*" [The Influence of Transcendental Concepts on N. Hawthorne's Romance *Septimius Felton*] (*Uchen. Zap. Tart. Universiteta* 727:5–13); the same issue carries T. Suganova's "Karabl' durakov plyvet po Missisipi: G. Melvill i ego poslednii roman" [A Ship of Fools Sails on the Mississippi: H. Melville and His Last Novel] (*Lit. Ucheba* 3:183–90); L. Rongonen, "Romanticheskie elementy v epose Longfello 'Pesnya o Gaiavate' i tradytsii indeskogo fol'klora" [Romantic Elements in Longfellow's Epic "The Song of Hiawatha" and the Tradition of Indian Folklore] (pp. 49–60); I. V. Golovacheva, "Avtorskii zamysel povesti Genri Dzheimsa *Povorot vinta*" [The Authorial Intention of Henry James's *The Turn of the Screw*] (*Vestnik Leningradskogo Universiteta*, Ser. 2 Istoria, Yazykoznanie, Literaturovedenie 4:46–50); O. Ya. Marchenko, "Kompozitsionno-stilicheskie osobenosti esse G. Dzheimsa" [Compositional-Stylistic Peculiarities of H. James's

Essays] (*Uzb. ANTSSR*, Ser. Obshestv. Nauk 1:77–81); K. P. Krivenko, "Liriko-filosofkii roman N. Uesta *Podruga skorbyashchikh*" [N. West's Lyrical-Philosophical Novel *Miss Lonelyhearts*] (Vestnik Kievskogo Universiteta. *Romano-Germanskaya Filologiya* 20:100–02); A. A. Petrosyan, "Memuary Vil'yma Saroyana" [William Saroyan's *Obituaries*] (Vestnik Erev. Universiteta. *Obshchestv. Nauki* 3:29–35); S. Zhorunuya, "*Kentavr*: Mif, netafora, real'nost'" [*The Centaur*: Myth, Metaphor, Reality] (*Lit. Gruziya* 8:192–95).

N. A. Abineva's "Nachalo znakomstva s Uoltom Uitmanom v Rosii" [The Beginning of Walt Whitman's Reception in Russia] (*Rus. Lit.* 4:185–95) also was unavailable. If the title corresponds to the contents, the Whitman article does not invalidate the observation that among the short monograph studies there was only one on American poetry in this year's crop of publications in the Soviet Union, as far as I was able to ascertain, and it was on a poet whose work has little chance of becoming popular there. He is Robert Lowell, subject of M. P. Kizima's "K voprosu o tvorcheskom metode rannei poezii Roberta Louella" [On the Question of the Creative Method of Robert Lowell's Early Poetry] (*Vestnik Moskovskogo Universiteta*, Ser. 9, 1:84–90), which basically deals with ideological matters rather than poetic questions. To the extent that American critics may have misunderstood Lowell's ideological motives for his break with the New England background, Kizima's article provides a welcome correction, although its thick Marxist coating generates a distortion in the opposite direction. Some of his statements resound with trivial rhetoric: "Lowell's poetry embodies the most common contradictions of the contemporary process in the West—the antagonism between realism and modernism." Kizima strips Lowell's conversion to Catholicism of any spiritual significance, seeing it as yet only another protest against the American establishment, "official bourgeois America." By becoming a Catholic, Lowell "entered the camp of secondary citizens." His search for God manifested a modernist worldview; on a deeper level, however, his Catholicism was antimodernist, an expression of the democratic spirit. Lowell's "religious clothing" had a paralyzing effect: it "prevented him from understanding the great historical meaning of events of those years," i.e., World War II, "in which the United States pursued both liberating and imperialist goals." Kizima's thesis: Lowell's early poetry, steeped in modernism, Catholicism, the Fugitive movement—all negative forces in Soviet opinion—obscured his view of both historical and contemporary reality. Actually, Kizima analyzes only one poem, "Children of Light." By characterizing the poem's irony as formal, the scholar fails to elucidate the inherent contradictions of Puritanism described in it.

There were a number of synthetic studies, a few of which deserve passing notice at least, if only to appreciate the thematic range of this year's Soviet American literary scholarship. In "Amerikanskaya romanticheskaya povest'" [The American Romantic Novella] (*Vestnik Moskovskogo Universiteta*, Ser. 9 Filologiya 5:17–25), E. I. Kumskova proves that *Typee*, *Israel Potter*, and *The Scarlet Letter* have all the distinctive features of the novella. The application of those features to the analysis of American romantic fiction "discloses the capability of romanticism to re-create artistically the external world as productively as it did in the lyrical subjective genres with their fixed attention to the enrichment of the characters' internal world." To pinpoint the difference between the romantic novella and the romantic novel, she provides a brief comparison of *Typee* and *Hyperion*.

The remaining contributions deal with 20th-century literature. Most can do without comment; some were not available. This is the case with O. Alyarkinskii's "Tri versii protesta: Amerikanskie poety 'bitniki' sevodnya" [Three Versions of Protest: American Beatnik Poets] (*Literaturnaya Ucheba* 6:174–83); T. D. Venediktova's "Intellektual'nyi geroi v sovremennoi amerikanskoi proze" [The Intellectual Hero in Contemporary American Prose] (*Problemy Amerikanistiki* 4:261–75); T. E. Nekryach's "O stsenicheskom i dramaticheskom elemente politicheskogo romana SSHA" [On the Stage and Dramatic Element of the American Political Novel] (Vestnik Kievskogo Universiteta. *Romano-Germanskaya Filologiya* 20:100–02).

Much Soviet scholarship on American literature continues to display a divided perspective. Whereas past works, periods, and movements are approached congenially, Marxist presumptions notwithstanding, the contemporary American literary scene tends to be viewed as an ideological and moral battleground. Through numerous publications A. S. Mulyarchik has emerged as the leading exponent of this orientation. In "Poiskakh al'ternativy (O novykh tchertakh sovremennoi literatury SSHA)" [In Search of the Alternative (New Characteristics of Contemporary American literature)] (*Inostrannaya Literatura* 12:212–21), representatives of the antipodean camps include Michener, Hailey, Helen Santmyer, and Ann Beattie on the conservative side, Robert Stone, Joan Didion, Joyce Carol Oates (only as author of *Angel of Light*) in the anticonservative camp. Similar ideological premises delineate the other two of his contributions this year: "Khydozhestvennaya literatura SSHA segodnya: cbet i ten" [American Literature Today: Light and Shadow] (*SSHA* 5:87–96) and "Realizm sub' 'ektivnoy proze' v poslevoennoi literature SSHA (konets 40-kh–nachalo 60-kh godov)" [The Realism of "Subjective Prose" in Postwar American Literature (From the End of the Forties to the Beginning of the Sixties)] (*Problemy Amerikanistiki* 3:90–96). Implicitly, the anticonservative authors are also the most morally sound ones. To M. A. Petrukhina, "Problema nravstvennosti v literature SSHA 70-kh godov" [The Problem of Morality in American Literature of the Seventies] (*Filologicheskie Nauki* 3:44–49), they are Gardner, Styron, and Doctorow. Her praise for their work, however, is qualified by their eclecticism and "occasional lapses in objectivity." L. M. Zemlyanova in "Problema 'Pisatel' i obshchestvo' v usloviyakh sovremennoi kompiuterizatsii literaturnogo dela v SSHA" [The Problem of "Writer and Society" and the Computerization of the Literary Work in the USA] (*Filologicheskie Nauki* 2:15–19) expresses profound concern over the "dehumanization" of literature by the American computer industry designing programs, for instance, of "interaction fiction," an activity which in her opinion fosters American "information imperialism . . . cultural colonization of the world . . . hate toward socialist society and culture." Interaction fiction presents "an image of life which carries the imprint of the spiritual crisis that begot the nihilistic attitude toward the traditions of world literature. The computer industry mocks verbal art through its visual ploys." In another protest article, "Razmyshlaya o nemislimom. Atomnii kontekst amerikanskoi fantastiki" [Thinking About the Unthinkable: The Atomic Context of American Fantastic Literature] (*Inostrannaya Literatura* 11:206–13), Vl. Kakov understandably remonstrates against the "survivalist novel" and science fiction about the atomic era.

Several Hungarian scholars' contributions appeared in the United States and the German Democratic Republic; consequently they do not qualify for commentary in the present section.* Two of these scholars, Charlotte Kretzoi and Péter Egri, also published studies in

* Grateful acknowledgment is due to Zoltán Abády-Nagy, who unfailingly continues to provide the Hungarian material for the annual report. He has also prepared the review of Péter Egri's *Chekhov and O'Neill*, below.

Hungary, though the former's carries the publishing date of 1985. By coincidence the essays happen to be related thematically. In "Clyde Griffiths on Trial: Interpreting *An American Tragedy*" (*Annales Universitatis Scientiarum Budapestinensis.* Sectio Philologica Moderna 16[1985]:41–53), Kretzoi deals with the perennial question in Dreiser criticism, "Whether to consider Clyde Griffiths guilty of murder, or rather, how far is he and/or society responsible for the death of Roberta Alden." Kretzoi desists from rehearsing the various opinions on the matter; instead, she looks at the adaptations of the novel for the stage—Patrick Kearney's and Erwin Piscator's—and for the screen—Samuel Hoffenstein's and George Stevens's—paying special attention to Eisenstein, who pronounced Clyde Griffiths not personally responsible for Roberta's death.

Egri continues to explore O'Neill's work. In a splendidly documented but intricate article, "The Social and Spiritual History of the American Dream: Eugene O'Neill, *A Tale of Possessors Self-Dispossessed*" (*Acta Litteraria Academiae Scientiarum Hungaricae* 1–2:65–89)—its length befitting the subject matter—he tells the story of O'Neill's tormenting and ultimately abortive attempts at realizing his desire of creating a great cycle of 11 plays which would have given dramatic shape to his complex vision of America. In the general opinion of scholars, with only J. Scothia and Egri dissenting, O'Neill was prevented from carrying out his project because of his nervous infirmity and Parkinson's disease. Egri convincingly proves the untenability of that view. He finds "the clue to the secret . . . in a rebellious gesture; to use generic terms: in the revolt of the novel form against the dramatic mould." Though in plays written before the cycle O'Neill succeeded in achieving a synthesis of the epic and the dramatic, "in the Harford saga the novelistic aspect of the dramatic project shattered the framework of the drama sequence." But the failed endeavors proved rewarding: they "dissuaded the dramatist from attempting to write scenic novels and turned his attention to a dramatic pattern from which his greatest tragedies and tragicomedies emerged."

With *Chekhov and O'Neill: The Uses of the Short Story in Chekhov's and O'Neill's Plays* (Budapest: Akadémiai Kiadó) Egri makes an important contribution to international scholarship; he is the first to study the parallels between the works of Chekhov and O'Neill. He ranges far beyond the theme announced in the title. He begins his investigations with a theoretical delineation of the short story and drama and defines three kinds of connections in the protean multiplicity of their varied genetic and generic relationships. In the first type the short story sweeps forward in the direction of drama (Boccaccio, Bandello, and Shakespeare); in the second type drama recedes toward the short story (Hauptmann, Hofmannsthal, and Maeterlinck); and in the third, the short story and drama become integrated. Egri analyzes the ways in which the dramatic principle plays a leading role in the concentric crystallization and coral-like increase of the play under scrutiny, and also considers the model-like treatment of the short-story strategy as a structural and generic pattern in plays which do not possess a direct short-story antecedent. This pattern is shown as a determining factor in the typological parallels between Chekhov and O'Neill as well as the dramatic excellence of Russia's representative dramatist and America's foremost playwright.

Ewa Aumer's "The Social World of Post World War II American Drama" (*Acta Universitatis Wratislaviensis.* Anglica Wratislaviensis 10[1985]:87–93) provides an appropriate transition to a survey of Polish contributions which, with a few exceptions, are rather slender. Aumer drops a great number of names and titles but offers neither much description nor analysis. Her sketchy outline of the American drama after World War II "reveals a clear-cut parallel between the main directions in the social-cultural history of the United States since 1945 and the main trends in recent American drama."

American drama is also the subject of this year's only Polish book-length publication: Teresa Pyzik, *Postac w dramacie. Obraz czlowieka w dramaturgii amerykanskiej* [*Character in Drama: The Image of Man in American Dramaturgy*] (Katowice: Uniwersytet Slaski). Except for the first chapter, "Character in Drama," which presents a comprehensive account of various theories of character construction in plays, the book reads in extensive parts like a historical encyclopedia of American drama, and in some sections of the fourth chapter, "The Image of Man in the Work of the Most Prominent Twentieth-Century American Playwrights," it coagulates into a who's who and what's what in the field. In the second chapter Pyzik describes the chief traditional character types—Patriot, Yankee, Indian, Backwoodsman, Negro, Foreigner; and in the third she surveys the melodramatic versions of man and life in 19th-century American plays. Copiously footnoted, the book is useful mostly for students and general readers.

Scholarship on American poetry was limited to four articles devoted to as many poets. Ludmila Gruszewska-Wojtas examined the structure of artistic space in T. S. Eliot's poetry following the model-building of the "Tartus school." In her "Funkcjonowanie struktur przestrzennych w 'Piesni milosnej J. Alfreda Prufrocka' T. S. Eliota" [The Function of Structural Spaces in T. S. Eliot's "The Love Song of J. Alfred Prufrock"] (*Kwartalnik Neofilologiczny* 2:227–39), she analyzes Prufrock's status in three spaces: the drawing room, the street, and the sea. This structural model, says the author, is also to be found in the other poems of *Prufrock and Other Observations*.

Agata Preis-Smith's "Randall Jarrell—Modern Romantic" (*Kwartalnik Neofilologiczny* 2:155–64) gives the impression of being a fragment from a dissertation adapted for publication. Preis-Smith has found in Jarrell's poetry motifs and themes which constitute its romantic character. They "may be reduced to a few key words that recur throughout Jarrell's entire output and can be found in almost any of his poems. These are words like child, frost, house, ghost, dream, and hunter; also groves, hospitals, concentration camps, patients," and others. "Of all his characteristic motifs, the most conspicuous seems to be that of the child, which, combined with the theme of innocence and experience, gives rise to distinct Romantic echoes."

John Ashbery and Frank O'Hara have been well served by the seventh number of *Literatura na Swiecie*. Apart from numerous translations of their poetry, the issue contains an extensive interview by Piotr Sommer with Ashbery (pp. 241–86), which the Polish translator and critic conducted during the poet's visit to Poland several years ago but was permitted to publish only now. (In the meantime the interview has appeared in *Code of Signals: Recent Writings in Poetics*, ed. Michael Palmer [see *ALS* 1983, p. 354].)

There were only four publications on fiction. Izydor Mielnik, "The Use of Images of Change in Irving's 'Rip van Winkle'" (*Zeszyty Naukowe Wyzszej Szkoly Pedagogicznej w Opolu*. Filologia Angielska 1:107–13), discerns three groups of change images: "those connected with natural phenomena; the ones related to human beings as individuals; and those pertaining to the community of man." Flux unifies the tale as it penetrates all layers of the fictional world. Ryszard P. Jasinski's *Science Fiction: Szkic z dziejow literatury popularnej w Stanach Zjednoczonych i Wielkiej Brytanii* [*Science Fiction: An Essay on Popular Literature in the United States and Great Britain*] (Wrocław: Ossolineum) is less an essay than a rambling survey in the form of short biographies of leading SF writers in both countries. In a somewhat convoluted manner Marek Wilczynski valiantly explores Robert Coover's poetics of fiction and then proceeds to illustrate it with an exegesis of "Seven Exemplary Fictions" in "The Game of Response in Robert Coover's Fictions" (*Kwartalnik Neofilologiczny* 4:513–23). The last and by far the best study of American literature to appear in Poland this year is Richard Martin's "Ishmael Reed: Re-writing America" (*Kwartalnik Neofilologiczny* 4:499–511), a lucid discussion of the five novels preceding Reed's *The Terrible Twos*. Martin manages to integrate his emphasis (perhaps a little too strong with regard to the first three novels) on Reed's historical revisionism with his own iconoclastic ideology and unwonted aesthetics of Hoodooism. Reed appears to be rewriting not only U.S. history but also American literature.

University of Warsaw

ii. French Contributions

Marc Chénetier

There was a rather large production in American literary studies in France this year, and as little space to deal with it as last year. And even less time as I have just come back from a semester's teaching at Princeton, away from the piles of French publications accumulated on my desk, and the deadline draws near. So let me plunge in right away. . . .

***a.* Bibliography.** Useful bibliographies have appeared, tacked on to various publications whose content is further analyzed below. Two deal with particular authors and are appended to issues of *DeltaES*, one on John Hawkes (no. 22, pp. 189–92), the other on William Styron (no. 23, pp. 175–86). Michel Fabre's *AFRAM Newsletters* (nos. 22 and 23) also contain numerous bibliographical items in the field of Afro-American studies. Finally, the issue of *RFEA* given to the study of "Women Writers in the United States" (no. 30) contains a general bibliography by Geneviève Fabre (pp. 501–02) as well as a precious list of "American Periodicals dealing with Feminine Literary Studies" by Françoise Giltard (pp. 503–04).

***b.* Critical Theory and Texts of General Interest.** Also dealing with women's writing but of strictly theoretical import are three essays in

RFEA 30. Paris-based British-born author Christine Brooke-Rose gives her own assessment of the theoretical grounds of feminist criticism in "Problématique de la réception" (pp. 393–98). Ginette Castro's "La critique littéraire féministe: une nouvelle lecture du roman féminin" (pp. 399–413) consists of an evaluation of feminist literary criticism with special emphasis on "gynocritics" focused on the woman writer. Her essay examines major critical trends committed to elucidating the "difference" of female writing. Castro sees "gynocritics" as a subversive enterprise intended to rediscover, revise, and rehabilitate female literary works. In my own "A la recherche de l'Arlésienne: l'écriture féminine dans la fiction américaine contemporaine" (pp. 415–36), I do not oppose this view but choose to examine a precise corpus in order to track down what stylistic specificities could possibly be attributed to an elusive "female writing." My title ("Stalking Nessie," roughly) indicates that I cannot, in situ, find evidence to support the received idea. Possible exceptions I dwell upon are Ursule Molinaro's *Encores for a Dilettante* and Georgiana Peacher's *Mary Stuart's Ravishment Descending Time*. In another issue of *RFEA* (no. 29, "Pensée et ecriture engagées aux Etats-Unis") I confront another general question from a theoretical point of view: the very possibility of "committed writing." My "Ecriture engagée: pléonasme ou oxymore?" (pp. 213–28) wonders whether there is any theoretical basis for such a semantic coupling, whether the very expression is not either pleonastic or oxymoronic.

"What's cooking" in a totally different field is Marie-Claire Pasquier's theme when she examines the impact of "cooking" as theme and metaphor in American letters in "La cuisine et les mots: morceaux choisis" (*RFEA* nos. 27–28:37–50).

Finally, two articles of general import deal with narratology and will be of use both because of their theoretical acumen and their mostly American literary illustrations. They are Maurice Couturier's "Yours Faithfully, the Author" (in *Critical Angles*, pp. 29–44) and Gérard Cordesse's "Note sur l'énonciation narrative" (*Poétique* 65: 43–46).

c. **Poetry.** Following a chronological sequence, to be mentioned here first is Roger Asselineau's "Du côté de chez Whitman" (*Europe* 685:93–95), which deals more specifically with the influence exerted on Jorge Guillen's work by Walt Whitman's poetry. Gilles Farcet's "L'individualisme cosmique d'Emily Dickinson" (*Liberté* 164:68–

75) ties in with this critic's preoccupations with holistic handling of literary texts and his interest in 19th-century texts, as illustrated by his book on Thoreau mentioned below. Michel Duclos's "L'image de Londres dans la poésie de T. S. Eliot et David Gascoyne" (*Annales du GERB* 3:n.p.) is also a thematic piece that draws interesting parallels between both poets' views of London. Jeanne Kerblat-Houghton, in a continuation of her steady analyses of Hilda Doolittle's oeuvre, has this year contributed "But Am I Wrong?: A Study of Interrogation in *End to Torment*" to *H.D.: Woman and Poet*, ed. Michael King (Natl. Poetry Found., pp. 259–77). Pierre Lagayette's single-minded dedication to the work of Robinson Jeffers has produced two studies of detail this year: "L'engagement solitaire de Robinson Jeffers" (*RFEA* 29:251–62) and " 'The Guardian of his gifts': Una and Robinson Jeffers" (*Civilisations* [Paris IV] 12:75–92).

Two articles on living poets remain to be mentioned: Catherine Augustin and Marie-Christine Cunci's collaboration delivered a close analysis of a poem by Adrienne Rich ("Point et contrepoint. autour d'un poème d'Adrienne Rich: 'Sisters.' De l'exploration syntaxique à l'approche de la totalité," *Fabula* 8:35–56), while Rolande Diot contributed "Allen Ginsberg: Humor, Sex, the Bomb and Other Laughing Matters" to *Plutonian Ode*, ed. L. Mintz (University of Maryland, Oct. 85).

Finally, one special piece of work must be mentioned here, a sort of event really: after four years' gestation, Emmanuel Hocquard and Claude Royer-Journoud's bilingual anthology of "L=A=N=-G=U=A=G=E Poets" has come out in two volumes: one consists of the original texts selected from the work of 22 poets (one, Tom Raworth, is British, but publishes in the United States), the other of the translations and adaptations of these texts by myself, Philippe Jaworski, and Claude Richard. Since the rather smaller selections included in the New Directions anthology announced for 1987 and the odd "dossiers" published here and there cannot give an idea of the scope of these works, *21 + 1: American Poets Today* (Montpellier: Delta-BP 5043, 34032 Montpellier Cedex) appears to be a welcome contribution to the sheer knowledge and diffusion of contemporary American poetry.

***d.* Theater.** There is only one major item to be noted in this field this year: a special issue, or "album" as it is called, of *Masques* (Paris), dedicated to the work of Tennessee Williams. Contributions by French scholars include Liliane Kerjan's "La postérité de Tennessee Williams" (pp. 83–89) and three pieces by Georges-Michel Sarrotte: "Tennessee Williams ou l'intelligence du coeur" (pp. 5–7), "La carrière de Tennessee Williams" (pp. 9–17), and "L'homosexualité dans l'oeuvre de Tennessee Williams" (pp. 130–39).

e. Colonial America. An oddity, to begin with: a very little known text of William Penn's, in French, has been published by the Ebor Press (William Sessions, York, England). Entitled *Essai d'un projet pour rendre la paix de l'Europe solide & durable,"* it is a facsimile edition of the only original, so far buried in the Bibliothèque de l'Institut Nobel Norvégien in Oslo, and has been edited by Peter van den Dungen. Although this is not properly French "American Literary Scholarship," this piece of information might be useful to a number of researchers in the field. Also, even though there are very few purely literary matters in this volume, it is worth mentioning that *Autre temps, autre espace: etudes sur l'Amérique pré-industrielle* (sous la direction de Elise Marienstras et Barbara Karsky, Presses Universitaires de Nancy) contains a lot of interesting background material for study of the period. Of direct interest to literary scholars might be the whole first part (pp. 19–90), which deals with religious and political writings of the period, with articles on Thomas Paine by Bernard Vincent ("La stratégie du temps dans *Common Sense*," pp. 77–90) and Pierre-Yves Pétillon ("La plantation dans le *wilderness*": notes sur le cas de la Nouvelle-Angleterre au XVIIé siècle," pp. 35–52), as well as an article by Nelcya Delanoë ("John Tanner Captif entre deux mondes, ou le refus de l'enfermement," pp. 241–54).

This year's contribution to the *Annales du CRAA* by Jean Béranger is his puzzling over the identity of Gilbert Imlay in "Emigration et communauté Utopique dans *The Emigrants* de Gilbert Imlay (?) 1793" (pp. 21–36). Elsewhere (*Civilisations* [Paris iv] 13:11–30) is an article on St. John de Crèvecoeur by Colette Gerbaud: "Terre et culture: un pionnier, Sainte-Jean de Crèvecoeur et divers aspects du phénomène culturel."

f. 19th Century. Of general interest in this area of scholarship is Viola Sachs's "The Language of the Wilderness: The Savage and the Identity of the New World in the American Renaissance," published in Italy in *Letterature d'America*, Anno IV, pp. 19–20. This collection actually bears the date "automno 1983" but was published in the spring of 1986. The other general article to appear on the period is Colette Gerbaud's "Notes sur le mode transcendantaliste," published in *Mode(s)*, a volume of essays put out on the theme of modes/fashions by the Presses Universitaires de Reims and collectively edited by the Société des Anglicistes de l'Enseignement Supérieur (pp. 243–59).

Concerning individual authors, the harvest is rather large. The earliest part of the century is the focus of Noëlle Batt's article, "Washington Irving à la naissance des lettres américaines: un conflit de représentations" (*L'Amérique et l'Europe*, pp. 89–102). Beyond her interest in Irving himself, Batt extends her remarks to the general state of American letters before the advent of the American Renaissance. Edgar Allan Poe is still very much in the French critical eye. Several publications by Claude Richard on the subject are pending; still, this year Roger Asselineau edited another lot of tales (with an introduction, a bibliography, a chronology, and notes) under the title *Poe—Histoires grotesques et sérieuses* (Paris: Garnier-Flammarion), while Gilles Farcet published a "Portrait of the Artist as a Raven" ("Edgar Poe: portrait de l'artiste en corbeau," *Spirale* [Montreal] 55[1985]:11).

Research on the American Renaissance properly said is represented this year by two books. Gilles Farcet's *Henry Thoreau: l'eveillé du nouveau-monde* (Paris: Sang de la Terre) proposes a reading of Thoreau's work under the seldom-used light of Oriental thought. It privileges the spiritual dimension of Thoreau's enterprise of self-discovery and highlights the numerous and intimate connections Thoreau entertains with Eastern philosophies and spiritual classics. Hailed as a "sannyasin" (one that has been "awakened," whence the title of Farcet's book) by the Hindus, Thoreau is here presented as a New England yogi, an approach seldom used by American criticism. This book should be very useful indeed for this reason and for the fact that it veers away very calmly and very consciously from the tonalities generally resorted to by strictly academic criticism. Even though the volume has received most laudatory academic commendations through the foreword given by Arnaud Desjardins and the preface written by internationally renowned Emerson specialist Maurice Gonnaud, it courageously goes against the grain of received ideas and internationalizes Thoreau in a most interesting fashion. The book itself is followed by a conversation on Thoreau with Scotch/French poet Kenneth White, whose interest in things Oriental makes him a natural for this exchange of opinions in the framework defined by Farcet.

Philippe Jaworski's *Melville: le désert et l'empire* (Off-Shore/ Presses de l'Ecole Normale Supérieure) runs parallel to Farcet's book if one considers how profoundly *personal* both books are; it is otherwise light-years away from it methodologically, structurally, philosophically, and stylistically. Entirely devoid of footnotes and of the paraphernalia of academic criticism, Jaworski's book is the result of 15 years' daily reading of and intimacy with Melville's work. It is simultaneously a profoundly passionate book and an intellectually cautious, prudent endeavor. It is an account, in Barthesian words, of the "adventure of a writing," rather than that of the "writing of an adventure." Unmistakably underpinning Jaworski's reading are the works of such Queequeg-like bedfellows as Kafka, Blanchot, Bakhtin, Derrida, Deleuze, and others with whom Jaworski's mind operates in such total symbiosis that footnotes would seem laughably redundant. Does one footnote a conversation? In strange ways Jaworski's book prolongs apropos a single author a thesis developed with great talent by Pierre-Yves Pétillon's *La grand-route* (Le Seuil, 1979), with its catching exploration of the spatial dialectics in American literature. Here, Jaworski opposes "the Empire," that imperial gridding of space by a sovereign ego, to the wanderings, spiritual as well as physical, of the nomad, stalking an eternally recessive threshold. Jaworski traces these two extreme states of consciousness and "meaning" operating in dialogical fashion throughout Melville's works. The accent, emphatically, falls on the act, risks, limits, and stakes involved in writing, and Jaworski adopts a form for his own endeavor which allows one to breathe haltingly along with the meanderings of a meditation that more often than not turns poetical itself, uncompromising in its intellectual rigor as it is humble and unassuming in its rhetoric and claims. The successive chapters deal with *Mardi*, *Redburn*, *White-Jacket*, *Moby-Dick*, *The Piazza Tales*, and *Pierre*.

Concerning the later part of the 19th century are a few isolated pieces, even though Roger Asselineau's article on Twain ("A Transcendentalist Poet Named Huckleberry Finn," *SAF* 13:217–26) endeavors to tie him in with transcendental thought. French influence on the life and works of Kate Chopin is the subject of Jean Bardot's "L'influence française dans la vie et l'oeuvre de Kate Chopin" (*Civili-*

sations 13:31–46). A companion piece in the same volume (Peggy Castex, "Is There a Reader in the House? The Dilemma of Cajun Literature," *Civilisations* 13:47–76) provides interesting background cum reflection on the general scene of Cajun literature.

Five pieces on Henry James bring up the rear of that section. Four of them have self-explanatory thematic preoccupations: P. Hubner's "Henry James et *La Scène Américaine* (1907): le drame transatlantique des cultures" (*Civilisations* 13:79–96), Hubert Teyssandier's "Florence dans *The Portrait of a Lady*" (*Modes* [Paris: Didier Erudition], pp. 154–72), Roger Asselineau's "Innocence et Expérience dans l'oeuvre de Henry James" (*Civilisations* 12:65–74), and Jean-Claude Barat's "Une image du Londres victorien: Henry James témoin du peuple dans *La Princesse Cassamassima*" (*Annales du GERB* 3:n.p.). The fifth, Catherine Vieilledent's "L'intertexte, la pastorale et le lecteur idéal dans *The Aspern Papers*" (*Fabula* 8: 21–34) argues that whereas *The Aspern Papers* is "traditionally viewed as a parable of the 'biographic fallacy,' an intertextual reading based on the 'unconscious' quotation planted at the heart of the text submits this interpretation to a new turn of the screw. The narrator's passion, his abusive cult of the letter and nostalgia of a Golden Age embodied by late Aspern, the aboriginal American artist, are not the ultimate object of the ironic perspective opened by the pastoral emblem. 'The green shade' is also the ambiguous emblem of an irrecuperable beginning, of America as the symbol of modernity, conscious that it cannot escape repetition and metaphoricity."

g. Modernism. The most general article here is André Muraire's "Sur l'écriture 'radicale' aux Etats-Unis dans les années trente" (*RFEA* 29:229–42), which endeavors to single out characteristics of the writings considered "radical" during the period at hand, recalling the impact of that movement. Muraire argues that this sort of writing goes beyond realism "because of its militant spirit which endows it with specific forms and contents. Of particular interest," Muraire finds, "are the centripetal quality of the structure and the hypertrophy of the referent." In the same context—and the same publication (pp. 263–75)—Robert Sayre writes on "Anglo-American Writers, the Communist Movement and the Spanish Civil War: The Case of Dos Passos."

Both Marie-Odile Salati ("Le paradoxe du langage chez Hemingway: le triomphe du non-dit dans la nouvelle 'Hills Like White Elephants,' " *Annales de l'Université de Savoie* 8:51–66) and John Murphy ("Les profondeurs du non-dit dans *The Old Man and the Sea*," *Annales de l'Université de Savoie* 8:67–76) have contributed new analyses of Hemingway; John Atherton's "The Itinerary and the Postcard: Minimal Strategies in *The Sun Also Rises*" (*ELH* 53:199–218) is the English version of the piece published last year in *GRAAT*.

There were rather fewer Faulknerian contributions in 1986 than during the overrich past few years. André Bleikasten, still at work on the second volume of Faulkner's novels for "La Pléiade" (Gallimard), and whose latest book in French on the subject (*Parcours de Faulkner*) will be translated for Indiana University Press next year, contributed "Temps, mythe et histoire chez Faulkner" to *Age d'or et apocalypse, études réunies par Robert Ellrodt et Bernard Brugière* (Publications de la Sorbonne, pp. 173–93) and analyzed Faulkner's modes and powers of description in "Faulkner descripteur" (*RANAM* 19:147–64). As for Giliane Morell, her work on " 'The Wishing Tree,' d'un désir à l'oeuvre" appears in *Civilisations* (12:31–38). *Mode(s)* also contains a piece by Béatrice Rossi-Bouchrara: "La 'Foiesis' ou le mode poétique dans les romans de Faulkner" (pp. 269–77). Faulkner specialist Jean Rouberol turns his attention to another southern writer this year with "Aspects du mythe dans 'The Wide Net' de Eudora Welty" (*Civilisations* 12:51–57), while Caldwell fan Michel Bandry turns his to Thomas Wolfe in "Thomas-George Wolfe-Webber et l'Europe" (*L'Amérique et l'Europe*, pp. 117–30). Wrapping up this series of studies on southern literature, Peggy Castex's "Demonic Grotesque in Flannery O'Connor's 'The Displaced Person': An Exercise in Subversive Ambiguity" (*Civilisations* 12:7–20) is finally to be mentioned.

In France as well as in the United States there seems to be quite a Willa Cather revival under way. The integral works of Willa Cather, never translated before, except for a version of *My Ántonia* published several decades ago amid total indifference, are gradually being published by Editions Ramsay (Paris) in my own translations. So far only two novels have come out: *La Mort et l'Archevêque* (*Death Comes for the Archbishop*) and *Mon Ennemi Mortel* (*My Mortal Enemy*). Lined up for publication are *Pionniers* (*O Pioneers*) and *Une Dame Perdue* (*A Lost Lady*). The rest will follow as the work gets done. In strictly critical terms, to be noted in this connection is "Le regard de Willa Cather sur l'immigration dans *O Pioneers*, *The*

Song of the Lark et *My Ántonia*" (*Annales du CRAA*, pp. 55–66) by Elizabeth Béranger, also the author of an excellent piece on Djuna Barnes ("*Nightwood* ou du sexe d'une belle indifférente," *RFEA* 30: 437–48).

Even though detective novels are not much discussed on the whole, I seize this opportunity to invite reading of a theoretically sophisticated piece of narratological analysis by Yves Le Pellec on Chandler: "Marlowe narrateur, Chandler complice," published in an issue of *Caliban* (23:95–110) entirely given to this particular genre.

***h.* Contemporary Fiction.** This seems decidedly to be the second most explored section in 1986. Elizabeth Boulot has gone back to one of the founding voices of contemporary literary expression and suggested equivalences between experience and writing in two of Kerouac's novels ("Une jeunesse en quête de nouveaux modes d'existence, un écrivain en quête de nouveaux modes d'expression: *On the Road* et *Visions of Cody* de Jack Kerouac," *Mode(s)* pp. 278–87). Barbara Smith Lemeunier has authored a more strictly thematic piece for *L'Amérique et l'Europe* (pp. 131–45): "Henry Through the Looking-Glass: Eastern Europe and America in John Updike's *Bech: A Book.*" Two very sophisticated analyses of Walker Percy's *The Moviegoer* have been added to the stock of stimulating readings offered to Agrégation students in 1986 when Percy's book was on the syllabus. One is by Simone Vauthier ("*The Moviegoer*: proposition de lecture(s)") and came out in *Fabula* (8:99–121). The other, an extremely long piece by Claude Richard, was included in *Critical Angles*, a volume of essays by European critics that I edited. Entitled "The Exile of Binx Bolling" (pp. 77–104), it speculates on parental influence, chance, and simulacra.

Maurice Couturier is recognized as the best French specialist on Nabokov. Even though his interests also take him toward theoretical problems of communication, as the above-mentioned article and a book soon to be published show, his passion for the Master seems to go on unabated. Witness his "Death and Symbolic Exchange in Nabokov's *Ada*" (*CASS* 19[1985]:295–305) and two briefer but pithy articles: "L'effet Lolita," written for a special issue of the *Magazine Littéraire* (233) given entirely to Nabokov, and "Nabokov, professeur" (*Encyclopaedia Universalis*). His efforts on behalf of this essential novelist were relayed this year by the article of another old aficionado, Pierre Gault, who, in *Critical Angles*, wrote a very suggestive formal parallel between the practitioners of two distinct art forms, Nabokov and Balthus ("Between Latency and Knowledge: Figures of Preinitiation in Nabokov and Balthus," pp. 125–44) and by a thematic piece of Simone Lavabre ("Vladimir Nabokov: richesse et problèmes du biculturalisme," *Civilisations* 13:99–106). In another book of essays on the contemporary American novel published in Europe this year (*Essays on the Contemporary American Novel*, ed. Hedwig Bock and Albert Wertheim, Munich: Max Hüber Verlag), Roger Asselineau studied "Norman Mailer's Quest Among the Naked and the Dead and Beyond" (pp. 149–64).

Even though one cannot insist enough on the overall *European* nature of this collection, other texts by French scholars included in *Critical Angles* deal with Guy Davenport (Nancy Blake: " 'An exact precession': Leonardo, Gertrude and Guy Davenport's *Da Vinci's Bicycle*," pp. 145–52), Donald Barthelme (Régis Durand: "On the Pertinaciousness of the Father, the Son and the Subject: The Case of Donald Barthelme," pp. 153–63), and Raymond Carver (my " 'Living On/Off the Reserve': Performance, Interrogation and Negativity in the Works of Raymond Carver," pp. 164–90). Continental theory underpins these pieces, even though they are not in any way direct "applications" of critical methods now so fashionably and transiently prevalent in the United States, where sheer pragmatism plays havoc with theories not conceived to be used in such utilitarian ways. My introduction to the volume attempts to define differences in practical critical methodology from this standpoint among others.

The two annual volumes of essays on American authors published by *DeltaES* this year bore on John Hawkes and William Styron. Both collections include a variety of essays that in turn commend and are critical of the works of these novelists. *DeltaES* 22 (Feb. 86) is the John Hawkes issue. Edited by Pierre Gault, it includes my long general piece on the stylistic evolution of Hawkes's writing ("John Hawkes contre John Hawkes: splendeurs et misères d'une écriture," pp. 13–48), and a series of analyses of particular novels: Georgiana M. Colvile on *Second Skin* ("Paternités dans *Second Skin*," pp. 69–86); Michel Turpin on "*The Blood Oranges* ou l'obscure clarté du texte" (pp. 87–108); Christine Laniel ("La rhétorique de l'excès dans *Travesty*," pp. 129–48) and Jean-Louis Brunel ("Reading *Travesty*," pp. 149–58) on *Travesty*; Pierre Gault himself on *The Passion Artist* ("Le lyrisme de l'homme ordinaire," pp. 159–76).

The William Styron issue (*DeltaES* 23), ed. André Bleikasten, includes a series of very favorable articles (Jacques Pothier's "'You can't go home again'—or can you? Le dépaysement, la honte, le choix" (pp. 35–60); Rachel Price-Kreitz's "William Styron, Nat Turner et les faits historiques" (pp. 77–90), and Marion Brugière's "L'imagination en pélerinage ou la migration du récit dans *Sophie's Choice*" (pp. 137–50), and two very critical ones: Georgiana M. Colvile's "Killing the Dead Mother: Women in *Sophie's Choice*" (pp. 111–36), and above all André Bleikasten's own brilliant and scathing overview of Styron's work: "Un Romancier à façon" (pp. 151–74), which systematically deflates Styron's pretensions and describes him as ever ready to jump on the next media bandwagon that passes.

Thomas Pynchon was on the syllabus of Agrégation two years ago and gave birth to a flurry of critical articles, some of which appeared in 1986. Among them are Maurice Couturier's "Do I Know You? Author-Reader Relationship in *The Crying of Lot 49*" (*CYCNOS* [Nice] 2:n.p.) and Daniel Baylon's "*The Crying of Lot 49*: vrai roman et faux policier?" (*Caliban* 23:111–26). In that same issue of *Caliban* given to the detective novel is Isabelle Grimaud's interesting "'Stranger than Paradise': *Dreaming of Babylon: A Private Eye Novel, 1942*, de Richard Brautigan" (pp. 127–36).

Two isolated (and very contrasting!) articles must conclude this section on contemporary American fiction at the hands of French critics this year. They are Gilles Farcet's "John Gardner: divertissement philosophique" (*Spirale* [Montréal] 57:8–9) and Rolande Diot's "Sexus, Nexus and Taboos versus Female Humor: The Case of Erica Jong" (*RFEA* 30:491–500). Let it also be known that Stanley Elkin was kind enough to give *RFEA* a piece not published elsewhere: "The Contemporary Literature Speech in France" (27–28:157–62). It is the text of the paper Elkin was kept by illness from giving in Paris during the "Day of Contemporary American Literature" in 1985.

***i.* Ethnic Literature.** In terms of attraction, ethnic literature has obviously replaced "redskin" production in the eyes of French researchers. Every year the harvest grows dramatically, and 1986 is no exception.

For practical purposes Michèle Wolf's article must be mentioned first here, as it deals with general problems posed, particularly abroad, by the study of minority writers. It is entitled "Culture Gaps: Difficulties in Comprehending Minority Writers" (*Civilisations* 12:

113–21). Then comes a series of articles published in Jean Béranger's annual Bordeaux publication, *Le Facteur Religieux en Amérique du Nord.* This year's volume (no. 7) includes pieces that deal with often little-discussed minorities: Italian in Jean Béranger's own "De la mort du Père au Dieu retrouvé: mentalités italiennes et crise religieuse dans les romans autobiographiques de Pietro di Donato" (pp. 43–58), Irish in Jean Cazemajou's "Images du catholicisme irlandais dans l'Amérique contemporaine à travers *The Cardinal Sins* et *Thy Brother's Wife* d'Andrew Greeley" (pp. 59–81), Greek in Nicole Ollier's "Nostalgie du père et de la terre orthodoxe dans *Reflections* de Henry Mark Petrakis" (pp. 115–32), and Native American in Bernadette Rigal-Cellard's "Aliénation et initiation mystique dans *Winter in the Blood* de James Welch" (pp. 133–60). Michaël Novak is the theme of Robert Rougé's article in the same ensemble ("Le nouveau pluralisme de Michaël Novak," pp. 207–20).

Other isolated studies of minority literature include Yves Lemeunier's "Amérique et Russie dans *The Rise of David Levinsky,* d'Abraham Cahan" (*L'Amérique et l'Europe*, pp. 7–22) and Jean-Marc Riaume's "Les Sino-Américains dans *The Immigrants* (1978) et *Second Generation* (1979) de Howard Fast" (*Annales du CRAA*, pp. 105–16).

More easily gathered are several sheaves of articles on Chicano, black, and Jewish literature. Marcienne Rocard is our best specialist of the first group. Her "La lutte du chicano sur le plan de l'écriture (ou la face littéraire du mouvement chicano)" (*LanM* 3:45–53) is a central interrogation on the questions posed by writing in the overall struggle of Chicanos. But several good articles on individual Chicano authors also came out in Béranger's publication: Elyette Andouard-Labarthe's "Rudolfo A. Anaya: les racines indigènes et le conflit des religions dans *Bless Me, Ultima,*" (*Le Facteur Religieux* 7:275–306); Ginette Castro's "Mémoire ethnique et religion dans *Rain of Scorpions*" (pp. 307–24), and Serge Ricard's "Un art de la survie: chicanismo et religion dans l'oeuvre de Rolando Hinojosa" (pp. 325–42).

A rather burning question—that of interracial marriage in black fiction—is posed by Claude Julien's " 'Et si l'on restait chacun chez soi' ou les liaisons inter-raciales dans le roman afro-américain" (*RFEA* 29:327–43). Julien writes exclusively on black American fiction and culture and has gone back to one of the classics of this literature in "The eye that cannot/will not see: Location and Intertextuality in Jean Toomer's 'Becky' " (*Les Cahiers de la Nouvelle* 5:23–31). Toomer is also studied in Alain Solard's "Myth and Narrative Fiction in *Cane*: 'Blood-Burning Moon'" (*Callaloo* 8:551–62).

Michel Fabre's work on Richard Wright is very well known in the United States and in France. It is interesting to see that this year he has come out with a piece that may interest both publics for entirely different reasons: "Frantz Fanon and Richard Wright" (in *L'actualité de Frantz Fanon*, ed. Elo Dacy, Karthala). His other contribution to Afro-American studies this year is a study of Ralph Ellison: "The Narrator/Narratee Relationship in *Invisible Man*" (*Callaloo* 7:535–43). Black women writers are the subject of two articles: Elizabeth Béranger's "Le passé composé d'Alice Walker" (*Le Facteur Religieux en Amérique du Nord* 7:23–42) and Geneviève Fabre's "Genealogical Archeology: Black Women Writers in the 1980's and the Search for Legacy" (*RFEA* 30:461–68).

Finally, there was quite a bit of work done on Jewish, and particularly Yiddish-speaking, writers this year. Isaac Bashevis Singer is the "émigré de nulle part" in the article Marc Saporta published in *Civilisations* (13:119–28). For Emmanuelle Farhi, Singer's use of Yiddish is a moral gesture ("Le Yiddish, reflet de la conscience morale," *Civilisations* 13:129–42), and for Mady Atlan "Manhattan" is the "nouveau Yiddishland d'Isaac Bashevis Singer" (*Civilisations* 13:143–56).

There were also three articles on Jewish literateurs included in *Le Facteur Religieux* no. 7: Christian Lerat's "Michael Gold, *Jews Without Money*: ni Dieu ni Mammon" (pp. 189–206), François Brousse's "'Sois Juif dans ta demeure, Sois homme hors de chez toi': *The Rabbi on Forty-Seventh Street* d'Ann Birnstein" (pp. 241–58), and Suzanne Durruty's "Cynthia Ozick et la crise de l'identité juive" (pp. 259–74).

***j.* Science Fiction and the Fantastic.** The second colloquium on science fiction held in Nice at the Centre d'Etudes de la Métaphore saw its proceedings published this year ("Actes du deuxième Colloque International de Science-Fiction de Nice," *Métaphores* 12–13). Contributions by French scholars include Gérard Cordesse's "La terre après la bombe, la complexification de stéréotypes chez Brian Aldiss (*Barefoot in the Head*) et John Crowley (*Engine Summer*)" (pp. 83–94), Denise Terrel's "Is Brian Aldiss's Heliconia a Metaphorical Earth?" (pp. 217–26), and Bernard Sigaud's "L'architecture selon

J. G. Ballard: le creux et le relief: le labyrinthe et la ziggourat, la matrice et le tombeau, casemates et chambres noires" (pp. 291–314).

I do apologize that this year's report should be so sketchy: as production increases and reviewing space remains the same, and as I endeavor to remain within the bounds prescribed by *ALS*, it becomes increasingly difficult to report with any sort of precision on the contents of each article. Comments of any length must be exclusively reserved for full-size books. I hope what boils down progressively to a mere bibliographical report can remain useful to researchers in the field. It is nonetheless cordially submitted despite its programmed shortcomings.

Université d'Orléans

iii. German Contributions

Rolf Meyn

The 1986 harvest is almost impossible to do justice to, given the space available to me, especially because five festschriften appeared this year. They are Winfried Herget and Karl Ortseifen, eds., *The Transit of Civilization from Europe to America: Essays in Honor of Hans Galinsky* (Tübingen: Gunter Narr); Winfried Herget et al., eds., *Theorie und Praxis im Erzählen des 19. und 20. Jahrhunderts: Studien zur englischen und amerikanischen Literatur zu Ehren von Willi Erzgräber* (Tübingen: Gunter Narr); Karl Josef Höltgen et al., eds., *Tradition und Innovation in der englischen und amerikanischen Lyrik des 20. Jahrhunderts: Arno Esch zum 75. Geburtstag* (Tübingen: Max Niemeyer); Maria Diedrich and Christoph Schöneich, eds., *Studien zur englischen und amerikanischen Prosa nach dem Ersten Weltkrieg: Festschrift für Kurt Otten zum 60. Geburtstag* (Darmstadt: Wissenschaftliche Buchgesellschaft); and, finally, Raimund Borgmeier, ed., *Gattungsprobleme in der anglo-amerikanischen Literatur: Beiträge für Ulrich Suerbaum zu seinem 60. Geburtstag* (Tübingen: Max Niemeyer). In addition to these books, several other joint undertakings will be discussed, as well as the usual amount of *habilitationsschriften*, monographs, dissertations, and articles.

***a.* Literary Criticism and Theory: Comparative Studies.** The discussion of postmodern literature, which in many cases amounts to the extrapolation of a theory of what "metafiction" (or its analogous terms) means, has reached an extent in German scholarship that is comparable to Ahab's wresting with the White Whale. A case in point is Rüdiger Imhof's *habilitationsschrift*, *Contemporary Metafiction: A Poetological Study of Metafiction in English Since 1939* (Heidelberg: Carl Winter). A roll call of the writers most drawn upon may illustrate the scope of this study: John Barth, Donald Barthelme, Samuel Beckett, Miguel de Saavedra Cervantes, Robert Coover, Raymond Federman, John Fowles, William H. Gass, Brian Stanley Johnson, James Joyce, Vladimir Nabokov, Flann O'Brien, Gilbert Sorrentino, Muriel Spark, Laurence Sterne, and Ronald Sukenick. Equally impressive is the range of theoreticians incorporated; Imhof cites Heinrich Heine as well as Victor Shklovsky, Siegfried J. Schmidt as well as Robert Alter. Although it is impossible to summarize this 300-page book in a few sentences, some of its results can be pointed out briefly. Imhof is opposed to accusing metafictionists of solipsism. For him the retreat of the postmodernist artist into himself is a legitimate act of self-defense. This retreat is necessary because the brutalization and devaluation of the word, as George Steiner has observed, in combination with a vision of reality that is fragmentary and without a totalizing perspective make traditional fiction obsolete. At the same time Imhof is well aware that self-reflexiveness and self-reflection, the chief characteristics of metafiction, are not confined to postmodernism only. Imhof sees metafiction as part of a tradition which goes back as far as Cervantes, Rabelais, and Sterne. Indeed, "Learned Wits" and "Sternest Jokes," as the author calls two of his most important chapters, have been familiar devices throughout more than three centuries. In other words, metafiction is only partly a contemporary phenomenon.

Not quite as ambitious in scope is another *habilitationsschrift* that I had not had time to look into before. Dietmar Claas's *Entgrenztes Spiel: Leserhandlung in der postmodernen amerikanischen Erzählkunst* (Wiesbaden: Steiner, 1984) tackles a theme which in Imhof's book plays only a marginal role, namely, metafiction as "game" fiction. Claas bases his concept of the "playfulness" of fiction on theories developed by Johan Huizinga, Robert Detweiler, Jacques Derrida, and Jacques Ehrmann. He shows clearly that the three writers under discussion in his study—John Barth, Thomas Pynchon, and Donald Barthelme—play with the artistic principles of classical modernism, including its actualization of mythological substrata, in spite of the apocalyptic trends in much of modern and postmodern American fiction. Claas's concise study ought to be indispensable for all scholars probing the playfulness of postmodern literature.

The use of myth is the sole focus of Therese Fischer-Seidel's comparative study, *Mythenparodie im modernen englischen und amerikanischen Drama: Tradition und Kommunikation bei Tennessee Williams, Edward Albee, Samuel Beckett und Harold Pinter* (Carl Winter). The author starts from a thorough definition of the terms "parody" and "mythos" and their significance for modern drama. She prefers the term "mythos" in favor of "myth," following Northrop Frye, for whom "mythos" also denotes a formalistic term which describes the function of mythological material in literature. According to Fischer-Seidel, Williams, Albee, Beckett, and Pinter had a common foe—19th-century drama and its theater of illusion. They parodied its conventions and used its popularity, which extended far into the 20th century, as a folio on which to create their own concept. At the same time they were still deeply indebted to it, as the plasticity of modern drama amply testifies. In this respect they were in a line with modern media, such as film, in which the influence of 19th-century popular melodrama has remained strong. There are of course differences between British and American drama. The first, Fischer-Seidel holds, puts more emphasis on structure and form, whereas the latter is more concerned with a teleological-progressive view of history. Thus it comes as no surprise that Albee's and Williams's plays are interpreted in this study as dealing with problems of national history. In contrast, the plays of Beckett and Pinter are mainly seen as self-reflexive explorations of the dramatic genre, although Fischer-Seidel cannot refrain from extracting from Pinter's plays mythological structures. Her comparative study is certainly not free from some oversimplifications, especially as she points only to Sir Philip Sidney's *The Defence of Poesy* (1595) and John Dryden's *Essay of Dramatick Poesie* (1668) in order to illustrate the preponderance of form and structure in English dramatic theory. Yet on the whole her book is a refreshing comparative study which contains many astute observations.

"Landeskunde," roughly the equivalent of cultural studies and, when concerned with the United States, of American studies, was the theme of a symposium at the Austrian university of Klagenfurt in 1983. The papers delivered there are published in Franz Kuna and Heinz Tschachler, eds., *Dialog der Texte. Literatur und Landeskunde*

(Tübingen: Gunter Narr). The collection contains not only instructive discussions of the methodology and objectives of this field, but also approaches to the literatures of Great Britain, Canada, and Australia. Most of the contributions, however, are devoted to American literature. Arno Heller's "Literarische Landes- und Kulturkunde als kommunikativer Prozess—ein amerikanisches Beispiel" (pp. 209–29) is a summary of recent priorities in American studies in the United States and short excursions into themes like "Frontier Values and Violence," "Changing Concepts of Nature," and "The Role of Women" and their representation in literary works. Walter Hölbling's "Fiktionale Texte in der Landes- und Kulturkunde: Pragmatische Überlegungen am Beispiel amerikanischer Romane zum Vietnamkonflikt" (pp. 231–58) scrutinizes four novels—Robin Moore's *The Green Berets* (1965), Norman Mailer's *Why Are We in Vietnam?* (1967), Tim O'Brien's *Going After Cacciato* (1978), and John Del Vecchio's *The Thirteenth Valley* (1982)—as four different literary reactions to the Vietnam War. In "Die Metapher als Kulturfigur: Ein literarästhetischer Beitrag zur Landes- und Kulturkunde" (pp. 259–92), Jürgen Peper centers on Donald Barthelme's novel *Snow White* (1967) and its use of metaphors as satirical expressions of contemporary sociological problems. Walter Grünzweig turns to the Austrian-American writer Charles Sealsfield in "Überlegungen zum Verhältnis von Literaturstudien und Landeskunde am Beispiel der Romane von Charles Sealsfield" (pp. 315–37) and points out that it was Sealsfield's aim to convey to his German readers a praiseworthy Jacksonian America, an America that in his opinion could rouse Germans to change their deplorable political situation. Perhaps the most original essay in the collection is Hans-Joachim Lang's "Lobbyismus im amerikanischen Roman des 'Gilded Age'" (pp. 339–59). Lang chooses three novels from the period—Mark Twain and Charles Dudley Warner's *The Gilded Age* (1873), John DeForest's *Playing the Mischief* (1875), and Frances Hodgson Burnett's *Through One Administration* (1883)—to succinctly demonstrate that the portrait of the female lobbyist in all three novels provides us with an uneven picture of the role of women in politics and a disillusioning insight into that ideology which tried to tie women to the home, the hearth, and the crib. Peter Funke concludes the section on America with his essay "Amerikastudien zwischen Forschung und Lehre: Die Zwanziger Jahre im Spiegel von Texten" (pp. 367–96), without doubt the contribution most concerned about methods and didactic means.

***b.* Literary History.** The majority of the German contributions to literary history were directed to the late 19th century. In her fine essay, "The Motif of the Pastor as an Unsuitable Suitor: The Religious Crisis in American Novels of the 19th Century" (*Amst* 31:61–70), Ursula Brumm examines the reflection of a religious crisis, the conflict between an orthodox and a more liberal form of belief, in the second half of the 19th century. She singles out Harriet Beecher Stowe's *The Minister's Wooing* (1859), Henry Adams's *Esther* (1884), Margaret Deland's *John Ward, Preacher* (1888), and Harold Frederic's *The Damnation of Theron Ware* (1896) as novels in which the theme of religious doubt comes out in a love plot, involving a pastor and a female parishioner. In the course of the action a conflict ensues in which the pastor turns out to be unable to fill his role as lover. Brumm does not overlook the fact that all four authors use motifs which had been introduced by Nathaniel Hawthorne's *The Scarlet Letter*. Hester and Dimmesdale serve as models, and Hester even anticipates the later heroines' rejection of a church in which the male element dominates. In the later novels, however, the emphasis is more on the failure of a diluted Protestantism unable to respond to the doubts and needs of men torn between religion and science, individualism and the deficiences of a materialistic society. Also concerned with identifying a motif is Horst Kruse's essay, "The Museum Motif in English and American Fiction in the Nineteenth Century" (*Amst* 31:71–79). Charles Kingsley's *Alton Locke* (1850), Charlotte Brontë's *Villette* (1853), and George Eliot's *Middlemarch* (1871) are compared with Nathaniel Hawthorne's *The Marble Faun* (1860), Mark Twain's *The Innocents Abroad* (1869), and Henry James's *The American* (1877). In all six novels the museum motif occupies a central position. Kruse shows, however, that in the three British novels it is part of a typical bildungsroman, whereas the American authors make the museum a symbol of Europe and a past that holds no promise for them. More devoted to theory but covering the same period (1865–1900) is Winfried Fluck's "Fiction and Fictionality in American Realism" (*Amst* 31:101–12). The author does not see this time span, which for him encompasses "classic American realism," as a dramatic break with an earlier tradition. Rather, he claims, the beginnings of realism must be seen as "interventions into the literary world of romance." Literature was hoped to become a moral and intellectual institution which could open its readers' eyes to the hitherto neglected potential of a democratic American civilization. Thus the emphasis was on communication; in other words, the art-as-model paradigm was replaced by the fiction-as-communication model.

The same literary period is also treated in Hans-Wolfgang Schaller's *habilitationsschrift*, *William Dean Howells und seine Schule: Strukturzüge im amerikanischen Realismus und Naturalismus* (Frankfurt: Lang, 1984), which I had no chance to read earlier. Schaller focuses on Howells, Garland, Norris, and Crane and the processes of adoption and assimilation of European literary theories and techniques of presentation in their works. The impact of national political ideas is by no means neglected. Schaller discusses the achievements of the most important scholars in this field with breadth and fairness. His own findings may not always be too original, but his lucid description of structural developments in realism and naturalism make his study a significant contribution to this period. Schaller holds that Howells clung to the philosophical and moral fundamentals of the Founding Fathers, though the form of his art was shaped by Turgenev and later by Tolstoy, whose panoramic point of view he adopted, and so was able to present a more differentiated picture of society. His typical way of analyzing characters, however, remained. Schaller's thesis is that Howells established the episodic structure in the American novel. Hamlin Garland lacked Howells's cosmopolitanism, hence his works were more autobiographical and contained more social criticism. Schaller thinks that it was owing to Taine's thesis of "race, moment, milieu" that Garland abandoned the concept of regionalism in favor of a national literature. Henry George's *Progress and Poverty* provided him with a synthesis of Jeffersonian egalitarian ideals and Spencerian evolutionary ideas. His younger contemporary Frank Norris was even more strongly influenced by evolutionary ideas, especially those formulated by Joseph LeConte and John Fiske. Love of detail went hand in hand with a very subjective perspective. This subjectivity also characterizes Stephen Crane's work. His handling of reality, however, is different insofar as it is marked by probings into the plausibility of human existence.

Covering American literary history from the beginnings to the present, Klaus Poenicke in "Body, Violence, Text: Probings Toward an 'Ecological Reading' of American Prose" (*Amst* 31:173–86) ponders the implications of an "ecological" hermeneutic which is based on a "cost-efficiency" understanding of culture. Taking examples of American prose from the Puritans and Benjamin Franklin to Thomas

Pynchon, Robert Coover, and Ernest Callenbach, Poenicke illustrates the growing tendencies toward self-destruction which he sees expressed in "certain strategies of evasion and territorialization, especially with regard to nature and the body." This development is, of course, a result of ever-growing urbanization and industrialization, but these factors themselves were hastened by dominant modes of order originating as far back as the 18th century. Urbanization is also the theme of Friedrich Knilli and Michael Nerlich, eds., *Medium Metropole: Berlin, Paris, New York* (Carl Winter). Although the collection of essays dealing with the three cities aims at a comparative view (with the 750th anniversary of Berlin as background), the two papers on New York belong to literary history. Heinz Ickstadt in "New York und der Stadtroman der amerikanischen Moderne" (pp. 111–24) begins with Howells's *A Hazard of New Fortunes* (1889), which he calls a novel against the city, because it depicts disrooted protagonists and an urban environment that is still in the making. In Theodore Dreiser's *Sister Carrie* (1900) a further stage is worked out: the city is both chaos and order, yet none of Howells's moral standards are applied. Carrie is rootless, devoid of morals and of reason, and hence open to the lure of the city. Yet Dreiser was not interested in the manipulation to which the city subjects its inhabitants. Ickstadt understands him as a cultural iconoclast who used the anarchic potential of the city as dynamite against a dominant culture still entangled in moral provincialism. This view, ending in something like the myth of the city, is completely destroyed in John Dos Passos's *Manhattan Transfer* (1925) and F. Scott Fitzgerald's *The Great Gatsby* (1925). New York turns into an artificial world, breathtaking and dynamic, but it becomes also a stifling social, economic, and technological network. The picture of the city is ambivalent; the glamour of the metropolis is undermined by a nostalgic pastoralism and attempts to escape from the city. For a moment the experimentalism of American modernism thrived on its uneasiness about urban culture. Eberhard Kreutzer's "New York in der Gegenwartsliteratur: Bilder der entwirklichten Vertikalen" (pp. 125–42) addresses the theme of metropolis after 1945. He finds the "Manhattan-centricity" of the mental city map repeated in the literary image of New York. In William Gaddis's *The Recognitions* (1955) and Donald Barthelme's *Unspeakable Practices, Unnatural Acts* (1968) and *City Life* (1970), the urban environment appears as a labyrinth of hallucinations and delusions in which objects are misread, situations misinterpreted, communications confused, and persons exchanged by mistake. Kreutzer discerns in this "Unreal City," in which a meaningful reality is not available any more, the perspective of an "unreal vertical." The underground with its subways and subterranean apartments symbolizes atavistic subconsciousness, while the skyscrapers stand for the refinements of civilization. The protagonists, however, are not only members of David Riesman's "lonely crowd" but also very often artists exploring the possibilities of art in modern urban society.

Two other papers dealing with a period in literary history are Franz H. Link's "Jiddische und jüdisch-amerikanische Erzählkunst" (*The Transit of Civilization from Europe to America*, pp. 249–61) and Utz Riese, "Umbrüche in den amerikanischen Literaturideologien zwischen Realismus und Postmodernismus" (*ArAA* 11:3–18). Link's essay is a brief but substantial endeavor to illuminate the transformation from Yiddish to Jewish-American literature, with a special emphasis on Isaac Bashevis Singer. Link thinks that both literatures reached their climax when common human problems became the center of creation. The East German scholar Utz Riese approaches the problem of locating the origins of postmodernism from a strictly socio-historical position. His investigations are based on Peter Bürger's theory of art as an autonomous sphere in bourgeois society. Yet Riese also emphasizes that beginning in the 1890s literature became a consumer good, a development which made it more vulnerable to historical crises; socialist realism became a victim of the cold war because it had not been able to win a broader institutional basis. Yet realism by no means collapsed; it was only turned inside out by writers like Bellow and Malamud.

c. Colonial Literature. All the 1986 essays on colonial literature are to be found in the Galinsky festschrift, *The Transit of Civilization from Europe to America*. As the title suggests, European-American relationships dominate. In her fine essay, "Transfer and Arrival in the Narratives of the First Immigrants to New England" (pp. 29–36), Ursula Brumm examines the recorded reactions of some of the early Puritan immigrants, such as John Winthrop, William Bradford, Richard Mather, and others, to the unknown continent. She cogently shows that the ocean passage mostly appears as a "rite of passage," with stages of separation, transition, and incorporation. The immigrant was prepared to face any danger, toil, and hardship the New

World had in store for him. Gustav H. Blanke, in his "Remarks on the Transit of Ideas: 'America Is West'" (pp. 59–73), makes European writers responsible for the belief that America is west in the sense of geographical location and in the sense of freedom from the restrictions of a hierarchical civilization. American writers turned this idea into a myth of their nation as a paradise of natural goodness and simplicity, predestined to lead mankind into a happier future. Henning Thies also addresses a cultural heritage in his "How to Write Letters: Benjamin Franklin and the European Tradition of School Rhetoric" (pp. 99–117). Franklin was hostile to the study of Latin and Greek, Thies holds, because he thought it too much a matter of social prestige and because it did not correspond with his central value of utility. Nevertheless, Franklin's theories of an English school curriculum, radical as they were, relied heavily on Erasmian ideas and the Latin grammar school with its ideals of public speaking and writing. That these ideals were hard for a later generation to live by is proven in Hans-Joachim Lang's essay, "The Rising Glory of America and the Falling Price of Intellect: The Careers of Brackenridge and Freneau" (pp. 131–43). Lang points to John Witherspoon, first president of the College of New Jersey, as a witness who attributed his success in America to his status as a European intellectual. American intellectuals, unless they belonged to the power elite, had a much harder time on their way to public success, as is demonstrated by the careers of Brackenridge and Freneau. The first resorted to humor as an outlet, the latter to bitterness, but both had to learn that after the American Revolution and the formation of a new ruling class there was no "Rising Glory" for radical intellectuals; they had to adjust themselves to the new situation or die in the gutter. An interesting contribution to the times of Franklin and Freneau, a theme hitherto rarely viewed, is Peter Wagner's "Eros Goes West: European and Homespun Erotica in Eighteenth-Century America" (pp. 145–64). Wagner corrects the view of an 18th-century America as relatively free from erotic literature. Although homespun pornography was not published, bawdy and erotic works were written. In addition, all sorts of erotica from Europe, especially from France, sold very well in colonial America, reaching a climax at the time of the French Revolution. John Cleland's pornographic novel *Fanny Hill* was very popular in Virginia, and in the field of "serious" erotic literature Sterne's *Tristram Shandy* and Boccaccio's *Decameron* led the list. The latter work was also owned by Thomas Jefferson, who was by no means ashamed of his collection of erotica. "Seen from 'below' and from the fields of erotica," Wagner concludes, "the age of Rousseau and Voltaire, even in America, was a macho century adhering to accepted taboos and conservative ways of behaviour."

***d.* 19th-Century Literature.** Our overview will begin with two binational publications. In " 'The Thorn in the Heart'—The Experience of Exile and Assimilation in Emigrant Autobiographies of the Forty-Eighters" (*The Transit of Civilization from Europe to America*, pp. 217–29), Hartmut Grandel discusses the autobiographies of the German immigrants Julius Fröbel, Hermann Körner, and Heinrich Börner, all of them political refugees. Each held a different position toward America, as emigrant, immigrant, or exile. Consequently, their attitudes toward the United States also varied—from a country that was in urgent need of cultural refinement to a newly adopted fatherland which had given the immigrant every chance to start a new life. The binational perspective is also the basis of Jerry Schuchalter's study, *Frontier and Utopia in the Fiction of Charles Sealsfield: A Study of the Lebensbilder aus der Westlichen Hemisphäre* (Frankfurt: Lang). Schuchalter approaches Sealsfield's work both from the angle of the writer's experience in America and from his change of identity from Karl Anton Postl, the Moravian monk, to Charles Sealsfield, the American author. He uses the well-defined concepts of frontier and utopia to illustrate how strongly Sealsfield was influenced by the antebellum tradition in America and how he was able to incorporate the dominant political myths and symbols of his time. For Schuchalter, there is no doubt that Sealsfield's work is one of the most important literary statements on ideology and power in the era of Andrew Jackson.

Book-length studies dealing with 19th-century literature have increased considerably over the last three years. A book that I regretfully failed to comment on earlier is Ludwig Deringer's exhaustive *Die Rhetorik in der Sonettkunst von Jones Very* (Frankfurt: Lang, 1983). The book clearly surpasses all studies of this New England transcendentalist poet that have appeared so far, both in Europe and in the United States, because Deringer provides the reader not only with an excellent insight into Very's sonnet rhetoric, but also into his poetic work as a whole, including the forces that shaped it and its reception. The center of Deringer's book is taken by painstaking analyses of representative and nonrepresentative sonnets on three major themes—religion, nature, and history and politics. Deringer recognizes that Very's rhetoric bears the mark of the classicist tradition, but holds that it was mainly the Puritan tradition which influenced it. Although Very, like his contemporary transcendentalists, believed in nature as a reflection of God's creation, his sonnetry pointed backward. The image clusters of religious typology and borrowings from Puritan sermons, meditations, and jeremiads link him more to Jonathan Edwards than to his contemporary Emily Dickinson.

Very's older contemporary Nathaniel Hawthorne became the subject of a book which will surely arouse some controversy. The thesis of Klaus P. Hansen's *Die empfindsame Theologie Nathaniel Hawthornes* (Rheinbach-Merzbach: Clasen) is that Hawthorne created a personal theology which rests on the concept of a double form of guilt stemming from a sin of passion and a sin of intellect. This idea, of course, has been treated by many critics. Yet Hansen goes on to claim that Hawthorne's "notion of God corresponds to mankind's liability to wickedness" which will be vindicated by God on Judgment Day. This position is far from the Puritan concept of natural depravity. Instead, Hawthorne conceived an "ethic of brotherliness," a community of mortals constantly in danger of lapsing into sin and guilt. But if man sinned, he did so by accident, not because of a natural depravity. This sympathy for the sinner, Hansen claims, links Hawthorne to 18th-century sentimentalism, to David Hume and to Adam Smith's *Theory of Moral Sentiments.* Adopting the method Perry Miller employed in his book on Jonathan Edwards, that is, an approach which combines the history of ideas with intrinsic interpretations, Hansen aims at an "internal biography," a kind of reconstruction of Hawthorne's mind, thereby using the writer's works "not chronologically but systematically, treating it as a quarry." Whether the author is always successful I must leave to the experts, but I am certain that this is a stimulating book which should be translated into English as soon as possible.

Sin, in a national sense, is also behind Maria Diedrich's exhaustive *habilitationsschrift*, *Ausbruch aus der Knechtschaft: Das amerikanische "slave narrative" zwischen Unabhängigkeitserklärung und Bürgerkrieg* (Wiesbaden: Steiner). Diedrich's goal is, as she puts it, "a re-evaluation of the slave narrative as art form in the context of American literary history." Both aesthetic and socio-historical factors are considered. Diedrich not only discusses the historical and political situation of Afro-Americans between 1776 and 1865 in impressive breadth; she also discovers a "divided teleology" in the slave narratives—the goal of Individual freedom, partly realized, and that of freedom for all Afro-Americans. Both remain firmly attached to Jeffersonian ideals, the back-to-Africa syndrome being only a very marginal phenomenon. The main part of the book is devoted to a diligent analysis of textual strategies. Diedrich clearly demonstrates that the principles of equality and resistance, the core of most of the slave narratives, can be traced to the political writings of the American Revolution and the abolitionists. Interestingly enough, however, social inequality is almost never criticized—the "pursuit of happiness" is interpreted as in white society. *Ausbruch aus der Knechtschaft* is undoubtedly the most extensive attempt to cope with the slave narrative that has been published. I sincerely hope that it soon will be accessible to American readers.

Also important is Klaus Martens's *habilitationsschrift*, *Die antinomische Imagination: Studien zu einer amerikanischen literarischen Tradition (Charles Brockden Brown, Edgar Allan Poe, Herman Melville)* (Frankfurt: Lang). Martens neither denies the deep impact of the gothic tradition on these writers nor is he opposed to Leslie Fiedler's and Richard Chase's insistence that 19th-century American writers prefered the romance to the novel. Yet he posits that these novelists were also "antinomic," that is, they played with formal norms and often made their roles as authors writing against their readers the secret themes of their novels. This theory rests on the findings of Fiedler, Bell, Poirier, and many others. Martens supports it by drawing parallels to European contemporaries, e.g., Jean Paul and the brothers Schlegel, and by aligning Brown with Poe, Melville, and postmodern writers. Of the three writers, Martens's treatment of Brown is the most extensive and profound. His thesis is that Brown broke earlier and more thoroughly with the gothic tradition than Melville and Poe and, as far as composition and technique are concerned, dodged it more radically. *Die antinomische Imagination* is a genuine and stimulating contribution to the search for the forerunners of the postmodern self-reflexive mode of writing. Apart from Martens's book, Poe is also assessed in Horst Breuer's "E. A. Poe und Victor Hugo: Zur Quellenlage von Poes Erzählung 'Hop Frog'" (*Theorie und Praxis im Erzählen des 19. und 20. Jahrhunderts*, pp. 219–32). According to Breuer, the story owes its origin not only to the chronicles of Jean Froissart but also to Victor Hugo's verse drama *Le Roi s'amuse* (1832). There are also two essays on Hawthorne in this festschrift. Helmbrecht Breinig's "Crushed Butterflies and Broken Fountains: Hawthorne between Christian Idealism, Romanticism, and Modernism" (pp. 233–48) focuses on "The Artist of the Beautiful" and "Rappaccini's Daughter," two tales published in 1844 when Hawthorne had found emotional stability through his recent marriage. For Breinig there is no doubt that Hawthorne was familiar with Schelling's philosophy of identity, which was transmitted through Coleridge into American transcendentalism. But he remained skeptical, since he was more inclined toward the Christian position "that the world of the spirit was the superior kind of reality." Hence, it is not surprising that Owen Warland's supreme achievement lies in his gaining an idea of the beautiful in its absolute sense. In "Rappaccini's Daughter" we also have the destruction of a work of art, but the shattered fountain reflects poisonous flowers, which suggests that man, nature, and art are hopelessly contaminated. To Breinig, Hawthorne is "something of a premodernist raising such issues," though in the end he was able to take only a halfhearted position. Also concerned with Hawthorne's modernity is Armin Paul Frank in "Making a Romance Work: The Parts Miles Coverdale Plays in Nathaniel Hawthorne's *The Blithedale Romance*" (pp. 249–64). Frank calls the book "the most forward-looking" of the novels, since Hawthorne employed an advanced strategy: Coverdale, the narrator, appears in the guise of a romancer whose cold sympathy for others is far from being altruistic. The real nature of the scrutinizing writer-character can come out only if the reader is able to use similar faculties—mainly those of discovery, speculation, and revision.

Hawthorne's contemporary James Fenimore Cooper is addressed in Heinz Ickstadt's "Instructing the American Democrat: Cooper and the Concept of Popular Fiction in Jacksonian America" (*Amst* 31:17–30). In contrast to the foregoing scholars, Ickstadt does not speculate about tradition and influence but interprets Cooper within the context of the Jacksonian era. He assumes that in the American literature of that time there existed "a partially submerged tradition of bourgeois fiction which is linked, in theory and in practice, to an idea of democracy, an idea of the People." Cooper subscribed to it, like Howells half a century later. To Cooper, America's political institutions were the embodiment of reason, ensuring the precarious balance between individual freedom and collective interest. Literature was nothing short of a public institution which served a didactic purpose, namely, to instruct the American democrat in the history of his nation and its future course. Even in *The American Democrat* Cooper did not resign his faith in the people, though he attacked as "mob" those who did not recognize a social hierarchy based on talent and private property. As late as *Oak Openings* (1848), the last of his Indian romances, written at the time of the Mexican War, Cooper celebrated the myth of the republic in new and sweeping terms. By the time of Cooper's death, the concept of a democratic novel had failed to develop into a "public institution," but the dynamics of Jacksonianism were still at work, as the rhetoric in Melville's *Moby-Dick* proves.

A group of essays is devoted to literature at the turn of the century. Hans-Joachim Lang's "Der Prophet und seine Heldin: Hamlin Garland's *Rose of Dutcher's Coolly*" (*Theorie und Praxis im Erzählen des 19. und 20. Jahrhunderts*, pp. 265–81) scrutinizes both Garland's *Crumbling Idols* (1894) and *Rose of Dutcher's Coolly* (1899) and comes to the conclusion that Garland's "theory of theory-lessness" resulted in a novel which contradicted not only his program but also his own experiences. Franz K. Stanzel concludes the 19th-century overview with an analysis of one of Henry James's lesser known stories in "Wandlung und Verwandlung eines Lügners: 'The Liar' von Henry James" (pp. 283–93). After comparing the two versions of the story, Stanzel is certain that in the "Ur-Liar" James had planned for Colonel Capadose's wife to be the central intelligence, a function given in the final version to the newly invented painter Oliver Lyons. He, not the colonel, turns out to be the real liar and intruder in the end.

***e*. 20th-Century Literature.** Essays on American literature from 1900 to 1945 were definitely in the minority compared with those dealing with the period after World War II. In "The Reverend Duncan McMillan und die Letzten Kapitel in Theodore Dreisers Roman *An American Tragedy*" (*Theorie und Praxis im Erzählen des 19. und 20. Jahrhunderts*, pp. 295–310), Hans Itschert examines a minor character who fascinates most Dreiser critics. Itschert finds it significant that Dreiser called McMillan "A present hour St. Bernard, Savonarola, St. Simeon, Peter the Hermit," all of them dissenters and representatives of an ascetic moralism. McMillan, however, is narrow-hearted and shortsighted, an ironic contrast. Ultimately, Itschert holds, the reverend is a tragic figure whose moral and religious rigor is deeply shaken at Clyde's execution.

Ernest Hemingway keeps German scholars under his spell. Horst

Breuer in "Ernest Hemingway und Otto Weininger: Zur ideengeschichtlichen Kontextualisierung von *The Sun Also Rises*" (*Studien zur englischen und amerikanischen Prosa nach dem Ersten Weltkrieg*, pp. 127–39) claims that the figure of Robert Cohen reflects an anti-Semitism which in the 1920s had reached a climax both in the United States and in Europe. Cohen as a character corresponds to the cliché of the bounder Jew who also appeared in the writings of Cather, Wharton, Eliot, and Fitzgerald. Hemingway could have been influenced by Otto Weininger's *Sex and Character* (1906), a book which Gertrude Stein, T. S. Eliot, and Ezra Pound knew quite well, and which contains a typology of an effeminate Jewish character opposed to a heroic and Germanic one. In his "Hemingway and Goya: Beobachtungen und Bemerkungen" in the same collection (pp. 140–51), Rudolf Haas reminds us that Hemingway knew the work of the Spanish artist Goya quite well, especially his illustrations of the Peninsular War, the collection *Desastres de la guerra*. Both men had witnessed wars, historical crises, and political upheavals. Haas speaks of an "elective affinity" between the two and strongly believes that Goya's influence can be clearly detected in Hemingway's work.

Poetry of the 1920s is dealt with in the Esch festschrift, *Tradition und Innovation in der englischen und amerikanischen Lyrik des 20. Jahrhundert*. Erwin Wolf in "Prufrock, Hamlet und die Tradition" (pp. 18–31) reevaluates Eliot's concept of tradition and is convinced that the poet wanted to free the word "traditional" from its pejorative connotation. Wolf holds that Eliot found in the Shakespeare who created Hamlet a congenial artist who was able to catch a similarly critical moment of social and intellectual history. Thus, J. Alfred Prufrock becomes a modern Hamlet, though not in the psychological sense. He is an impotent man, prematurely aged, a dweller in a city which is the symbol of a lost center. This, according to Wolf, illustrates Eliot's position: whenever tradition (the figure of Hamlet), though transformed, becomes part of the modern consciousness, it ought to be preserved. A similar theme is taken up in Rudolf Sühnel's "Ezra Pound's 'Hugh Selwyn Mauberley' und die Krise der europäischen Kultur" (pp. 56–79). This essay is above all a passionate tribute to Pound, who in spite of his regrettable collaboration with Italian Fascism is celebrated as the cosmopolitan poet who gave alarm when the lights went out in Europe and a cultural vacuum threatened. In Sühnel's opinion, "Hugh Selwyn Mauberley" is not only a renunciation of an exhausted thinking in national categories, but a mobilization of the recollection of the high cultures and their achievements and an overture to the *Cantos.* Lothar Hönnighausen stresses at the beginning of his "William Carlos Williams und die Erneuerung der Lyrik aus der Malerei" (pp. 81–94), that Eliot's and Pound's predominance has been somewhat broken by Williams. Hönnighausen attributes this to the fact that a later generation found easier access to Williams's sensual and direct poetry which received its inspiration from painting, notably from dadaism, surrealism, and cubism. Kurt Gamerschlag's "Robert Lowells 'The Quaker Graveyard in Nantucket': Genetische Notizen zum Melville-Gedicht" (pp. 125–40) turns to a poet who ranks almost as high as Williams. Gamerschlag's essay contains not only an excellent description of the genesis of the poem, but an equally impressive interpretation and a thorough analysis of poetic techniques.

As usual, the 1930s have their proponents too. In his "Nathanael West's *A Cool Million* and the Myth of Success" (*Studien zur englischen und amerikanischen Prosa nach dem Ersten Weltkrieg*, pp. 164–75), Dieter Schulz points to the Horatio Alger connection which "provides the key to whatever merits, artistic or otherwise, the book has." This, of course, has been seen by other West critics. Schulz, however, argues that *A Cool Million* in its diagnosis of contemporary society moves beyond the fascist movements of the time to an exposure of the mechanism of capitalist society. West refused to commit himself to any of the current ideologies, but he was able to aesthetically express the totalitarian grasp of that system. Faulkner's *Absalom, Absalom!* remains the most fascinating novel for German scholars. Lothar Hönnighausen in "The Novel as a Poem: The Place of Faulkner's *Absalom, Absalom!* in the History of Reading" (*Amst* 31:127–40) is dissatisfied with the recent research which overlooks too many of the novel's lyrical qualities. The fragmentation of reality, which in Faulkner's prose turns the flow of time into "moment's monuments," fuses narrative and lyrical elements into a unique style that brings the novelist closer to the lyric poet. This was not a coincidence, Hönnighausen makes clear, because Faulkner assimilated much of his admiration for modern poetry. Black literature of the late '30s is explored in Maria Diedrich's " 'Power to Command God': Zora Neale Hurston's *Moses, Man of the Mountain* and Black Folk Religion" (*Studien zur englischen und amerikanischen Prosa nach dem Ersten Weltkrieg*, pp. 176–85). According to Diedrich, Hurston overcame the fractional aspect of the folk view by transforming the most popular biblical story in black folk religion into a powerful novel, thereby disclosing the totality and richness of this black metaphor.

Articles on American literature after 1945 are abundant in the 1986 harvest. This is not only due to the five festschriften, but also to a fine collection, Hedwig Bock and Albert Wertheim, eds., *Essays on the Contemporary American Novel* (Munich: Hueber). Though most of the contributors are Americans, several German scholars are represented too, and their work is by no means inferior. I can safely say that this collection, with essays on Robert Penn Warren, Saul Bellow, Bernard Malamud, Philip Roth, William Styron, John Updike, Joyce Carol Oates, John Hawkes, Norman Mailer, John Barth, Thomas Pynchon, Robert Coover, Kurt Vonnegut, Jerzy Kosinski, E. L. Doctorow, Toni Morrison, Ishmael Reed, nonfiction writers, and Chicano and Puerto Rican fiction, is a stimulating literary history on modern and postmodern American fiction.

Chronologically, I shall start with another writer, however. Herwig Friedl is one of the very few German scholars who have dealt with Malcolm Lowry. In "Malcolm Lowry and the American Imagination" (*Studien zur englischen und amerikanischen Prosa nach dem Ersten Weltkrieg*, pp. 186–99), Friedl concentrates on Lowry's *Under the Volcano* (1947) and sees in this novel a symbolic interpretation of human existence in the tradition of Melville's *Moby-Dick*. To Friedl, Lowry's novel is a deliberate continuation of the myths the writers of the American Renaissance exploited, the last great fictional renderings of the endeavors of a solitary voyager. Rudolf Haas in his "Form und Sinn bei Vonnegut: Vignetten zu *Cat's Cradle*" (*Gattungsprobleme in der anglo-amerikanischen Literatur*, pp. 230–38) believes *Cat's Cradle* to be in the tradition of Swift, Twain, and Orwell. A more encompassing view of Vonnegut's work is Peter Freese's "Kurt Vonnegut, Jr., or 'Man Got to Tell Himself He Understand'" (*Essays on the Contemporary American Novel*, pp. 225–42), which also contains a fair evaluation of the writer's achievement. Freese sees Vonnegut's merits in the recognition of science fiction as a serious form of literature, in his witty but moral statements on man's predicament, in his contribution to the postmodern tradition of fabulation and fictional strategies, and last but not least in writing *Slaughterhouse-Five*, "one of the undoubtedly great books of post-war literature."

Nonfiction, in some ways the opposite of Vonnegut's way of writing, keeps attracting scholars in Germany. David Galloway dissects Truman Capote's nonfictional technique in "Real Toads in Real Gardens: Reflections on the Art of Nonfiction Fiction and the Legacy of Truman Capote" (*Gattungsprobleme in der anglo-amerikanischen Literatur*, pp. 217–29). The main emphasis is on Capote's *In Cold Blood*, which impresses Galloway as a departure from the linear mode of documentary reporting, since the author rearranged chronology and introduced flashbacks in order to heighten the narrative drama. Peter Bruck in "Facts and Events as Fabulated Realities: The Epistemological Basis of Literary Nonfiction" (*Essays on the Contemporary American Novel*, pp. 335–53) also draws on Capote, but is more interested in theories underlying the nonfiction novel.

It comes as no surprise, though, that the bulk of essays on post-World War II fiction was again devoted to the postmoderns. Bernhard Reitz's "Aspekte postmoderner Geschichtsdarstellung in E. L. Doctorow's *The Book of Daniel*" (*Theorie und Praxis im Erzählen des 19. und 20. Jahrhunderts*, pp. 373–88), an examination of the role history plays in this novel (which has always been a bit neglected in favor of *Ragtime*) is one of the most sensitive I have come across. He holds, and this is by no means farfetched in the light of his convincing arguments, that Doctorow's model of history is largely shaped by the conspiracy theory on which Thomas Pynchon based his novel *V*. In contrast to Herbert Stencil, however, the protagonist Daniel recognizes the fallibility of man. Thus history wins back its humane dimension, and Daniel is able to accept history, his own as well as that of his parents. In his "History, Fictions and Designs of Robert Coover" (*Essays on the Contemporary American Novel*, pp. 205–24), Heinz Ickstadt takes a similar approach, but differentiates between Coover's longer narratives with their interrelation of fiction, history, and myth, and his short stories, which are more or less exercises in narrative design. On the whole, Iskstadt thinks, Coover's fiction is marked by a Jamesian split between an aesthetic world of regenerative ritual and the empty language gestures of public life.

Donald Barthelme is without doubt the most fascinating postmodern writer for German scholars. In his "Barthelme's *Snow White*: Ein Moment in der Geschichte kultureller Dekonzeptualisierung" (*Amst* 31:155–71), Jürgen Peper tries to prove that, though cultural concepts like beauty, love, and education have lost their meaning, Barthelme is still up to preserving a traditional function of the novel, that is, to render an analytic view of a given culture through the medium of a novel. The various intellectual discourses in *Snow White*, in conflict with a very naive form of argumentation, account for its comic tone. But its structureless texture, a result of the collage technique, is a negative commentary on contemporary culture. Paul Goetsch's "Donald Barthelme's *The Dead Father*" (*Studien zur englischen und amerikanischen Prosa nach dem Ersten Weltkrieg*, pp. 200–14) aims in the same direction, though the focus is more on the novel as a rejection of the patriarchal discourse and similar manifestations in modern literature. Harold Bloom, Edward Said, and Roland Barthes almost simultaneously commented on "Text-fathers," and Barthelme, like T. S. Eliot, James Joyce, Samuel Beckett, and Eugène Ionesco, knew that the traditional patriarchal discourse had played out. Postmodern dabbling with history is also explored in Klaus P. Jankofsky's "Sir Gawaine at Liberty Castle: Thomas Berger's Comic Didacticism in *Arthur Rex: A Legendary Novel*" (*Theorie und Praxis im Erzählen des 19. und 20. Jahrhunderts*, pp. 389–404). Jankofsky concedes that Berger's didacticism is couched in multiple irony and humor, but takes it seriously because, he claims, it results from a deep insight into human nature and from a wealth of literary culture.

Besides the postmodern writers, some German scholars tackled recent fiction that does not quite belong there. Evelyne Keitel scrutinizes the two discourses she believes to be at work in Vladimir Nabokov's *Ada* (1969). According to her essay, "Desire in the Text, Desire in Reading: Nabokov's *Ada* and the Intricacies of Literary Response" (*Amst* 31:141–53), there exists a discourse which calls for a reading in the form of an intellectual enterprise and another that comprises an unconscious text, which kindles an erotic tension in the reader by heightening the passion described in the novel. Not so much concerned with textual strategies but with imagination is Franz H. Link's "Auschwitz und die Grenzen der Imagination: Erzähltheoretische Überlegungen zu William Styrons *Sophie's Choice*" (*Theorie und Praxis im Erzählen des 19. und 20. Jahrhunderts*, pp. 311–21). Link interprets the narrator Stingo as a spiritual successor to Melville's Ishmael who tries to find an explanation for evil and sufferings in our world. He is drawn into the vortex of evil, but, like Ishmael, is resurrected. Yet compared with the latter, he is a different kind of narrator, because he is also identical with the author. Styron follows the Defoe tradition of the realistic novel and deliberately blurs the distinction between fiction and history in order to come to an understanding of the Holocaust. But here, Link holds, Styron fails. In the end, the sexual fulfillment Stingo experiences becomes "imaginary love" parallel to the "imaginary evil" the author-narrator indulged in. Thus, the nightmare of the Holocaust is cheapened and drained of its substance. Winfried Herget in "Joyce Carol Oates' Re-imaginationen" in the same volume (pp. 359–71) also theorizes on the imagination, albeit in regard to a border case, a group of short stories by Oates bearing the titles of works of world literature. Herget analyzes only one of the stories by which Oates wanted to express her affection for Joyce, Thoreau, Kafka, Chekhov, and Henry James, proving how deeply Oates's art of short-story writing is shaped by the Chekhov-Kafka-Joyce model. Quite another theme is assessed in an essay on Bernard Malamud's novel *God's Grace* (1982). Horst Meller in "Der Shlemiel fällt unter Raubaffen: Zum Motivhintergrund von Bernard Malamuds *God's Grace*" (*Studien zur englischen und amerikanischen Prosa nach dem Ersten Weltkrieg*, pp. 227–41) puts Malamud's novel in an impressive context. From Mary Shelley's *Frankenstein* to William Golding's *The Lord of the Flies*, almost every possible parallel is mentioned. *God's Grace*, Meller concludes, is an eschatological burlesque in a Tarzan milieu, a moralistic fable of surviving with an inbuilt theodicy turned upside down.

The ethnic component which Meller sees embodied in the schlemiel-like protagonist Calvin Cohn is the main focus of other essays. Günter H. Lenz is one of the few scholars who dealt with black literature in 1986. In his "'Making Our Own Future Text': Neo-Hoodooism, Postmodernism, and the Novels of Ishmael Reed" (*Theorie und Praxis im Erzählen des 19. und 20. Jahrhunderts*, pp. 323–44), he focuses on Reed's novels both from the point of view of postmodernism and from that of black aesthetics. His thesis that Reed's work is an exposure and rewriting of myths (as "ideologies" and "stories") of Western as well as Afro-American history is correct. Whether the novels are as self-reflexive as Lenz sees them is open to discussion. From Afro-American to Amerindian experience: Konrad Gross in his contribution examines fragmentation and discontinuities which for some critics have marred N. Scott Momaday's *House Made of Dawn*. His essay "Erzählen als Ritual: Die Funktion indianischer Tradition in N. Scott Momadays *House Made of Dawn*" (pp. 345–57) is a successful attempt to vindicate this seeming shortcoming. According to Gross, Momaday wanted to argue that because of the fragmentation of Indian traditions, a reconstruction of the old is not possible, that new stories have to be created out of the Indian way of thinking to help master the present. Dieter Herms, one of our few experts on Chicano and Puerto Rican fiction, concludes the survey of ethnic literature with his "Native American, Chicano, and Puerto Rican Fiction: A Survey" (*Essays on the Contemporary American Novel*, pp. 355–74). Herms views the three groups as "oppressed nations within U.S. imperialism" and sees this status prevalent in their ideological expression as well as in their cultural productions. He makes out two phases in its development, the first consisting of protest novels, followed by works of a more complex literary quality. Indian fiction, Herms surmises, is not a part of the Native American social movement, expressing instead a distinct multi-faceted worldview. In contrast, most of the Chicano fiction is rooted in the social movement of "Chicanismo," the identity question is posed more radically, and it is more political—either socialist or anti-imperialist. This also holds for the Puerto Rican novels, which usually center on the themes of identity, cultural clash, and social criticism.

Poetry after 1945 was by no means neglected, thanks to the festschrift *Tradition und Innovation in der englischen und amerikanischen Lyrik des 20. Jahrhunderts* and a few articles scattered elsewhere. Günther Ahrends in his "Die Suche nach dem fernen Feld: Theodore Roethke und die romantische Dichtungstradition" (pp. 150–62) diligently lays bare the romantic tradition which shaped Roethke. The symbolic tendency in his poetry, he claims, can be traced back to Emerson and Whitman, but also to Blake, Wordsworth, and Yeats. Ahrends singles out "The Cycle" as an example of how strongly Roethke's poetry was dominated by Emerson and Whitman's "organic metaphor" in which the lyrical I and the cosmos melted into each other. Wolfgang Karrer follows with "Sein und Schein in John Ashberys 'Leaving the Atocha Station': Die Verdinglichung des modernistischen Paradigmas" (pp. 163–75). Karrer's excellent interpretation starts from the assumption that this poem seems to be a deconstructional text with floating signifiers. Prepositions, conjunctions, and pronouns fail to create a context. Yet, as Karrer lucidly shows, the paradigms clearly delineate the poem as an expression of its creator's dissatisfaction with the notions of time, progress, and mobility, values which Ashbery's once-revered Whitman cherished. My 1986 survey closes with Astrid Schmitt-von Mühlenfels's "Die zeitlose Märchenwelt und ihre zeitgenössische Spiegelung: Zu Anne Sextons 'Transformationen' Grimmscher Märchen" (*The Transit of Civilization from Europe to America*, pp. 263–69), a comparison between the fairy tales of the Brothers Grimm and Anne Sexton's re-imaginations of them, the *Transformations*. Schmitt-von

Mühlenfels demonstrates that Sexton intensified the comic, the grotesque, and even the gruesome, and tried to interpret her own life within the pattern of a fairy tale.

Universität Hamburg

iv. Italian Contributions—1985

Laura Coltelli

The output of Italian scholarly works on American Literature for 1985 was smaller than in the previous year. However, two major publications appeared, both originating from very important conferences: the 1985 issue of *Rivista di Studi Angloamericani* (the annual of the Italian Association for North American Studies) and *Ezra Pound a Venezia*, ed. Rosella Mamoli Zorzi (Florence: Leo S. Olschki Editore).

RSA contains the proceedings of the seventh conference of AISNA, held in 1983 in Catania, devoted to "Italy and Italians in America." Adopting an interdisciplinary approach, the conference analyzed the cultural, literary, and historical aspects of the theme. The literary aspects are discussed in two major papers and in three workshops. Daniel Aaron, in his "The Hyphenate American Writer" (pp. 11–28), first approaches the subject with a general overview: his ideas on the topic, expressed in a 1964 study, must be revised, he maintains, since the process he traced by which the minority writer passed from "hyphenation" to "dehyphenation" is perhaps "overly schematic." In rethinking and completing his original model after the last two decades of resurgence of ethnic pride, Aaron clearly analyzes all "American social and cultural values that thickened and hardened the hyphen for the literary descendants of the New Immigration." By comparing and contrasting Jewish and Italian writers, Aaron further evidences how the dehyphenation process, the passage from "the-old-world-within America" to "the other larger America," has taken a different course for the Italian-American writers, who, unlike the Jewish writers, "seem to have sloughed off the hyphen and disappeared into the American community without extracting all they might have from their inheritance." Aaron rounds off his illuminating evaluation of the ethnic literary achievements by concluding that the new stage is very different from what went before, above all in its synthetic aspect, the "Americanness" of its motivation and strategy.

If "once the hyphen was a pejorative designation," now it is "a plus sign," a means to be distinguished from the mass, so that now the real America is no longer a melting pot but an ethnic patchwork quilt.

In "My Experience as an Italian American Writer," (pp. 67–86), Jerre Mangione speaks of his childhood, of his having a mixed identity in an Italian-American community. Like many other Italian-American writers, writing a book out of his own ethnic background, he confesses, "provides a method of making order out of a sense of having lived in disorder." The world is portrayed at one and the same time with the objectivity of an outsider and the understanding of an insider.

The first workshop, "Italy and Italians in American Literature," includes a careful analysis by Algerina Neri of Cooper's *Gleanings in Europe: Italy*, seen as a valuable piece of travel literature which offers an unusually realistic image of Italy and what Neri considers the most outstanding feature of the book, Cooper's "ability to re-create the feeling of a particular place" ("James Fenimore Cooper's Gleanings of Italy," pp. 103–13). Liana Borghi, in "Anne Whitney: Letters Home" (pp. 115–21), gives a lively description of the Italian experience of the most accomplished woman sculptor of the last century. Through a close reading of Whitney's letters, Borghi re-creates the artistic colony in Rome and above all that of the women artists, "united by a common background and by the search for professional status as women" but also "divided by different artistic aims, competition and the ethics of the marketplace." Both Andrea Mariani's "William Wetmore Story's *Roba di Roma*: The Sculptor's Prose as Painting" (pp. 123–31) and Alberta Fabris Grube's "Edith Wharton's *Italian Background*" (pp. 133–44) are marked by penetrating insights into these particular two books, while Marina Gradoli and Gaetano Prampolini's papers, focusing on Hemingway and Cheever, deal with the recurrence of the Italian setting in the whole body of their work. In her "Italy in Ernest Hemingway's Fiction," (pp. 145–49), Gradoli highlights Hemingway's accomplishments as a writer by investigating his relationship with Italy, a "movement from indifference to involvement." "Italy in John Cheever's Fiction" (pp. 153–69) is a knowledgeable, richly detailed demonstration of how the impact of Italy is reflected in Cheever's work, which does confirm, Prampolini maintains, "the dark vision he had been inspired with by the American scene." "The Sacco-Vanzetti Case and John Dos Passos" (pp. 181–94) is an interesting and well-documented piece by

Gabriella Ferruggia, who examines the treatment of the case in *Big Money* and *The Chosen Country*. The other paper worth mentioning from this workshop is a closely argued study on "Italian-Americans and Jews in Bernard Malamud's Fiction" (pp. 195–211) by Elèna Mortara di Veroli, who explores the effect of the "hyphen," entangled between fragmentation and fusion, "that both separates and joins."

In a study prepared for the second workshop, on "Italian American Writers," Maria Vittoria D'Amico offers a fine analysis of Gilbert Sorrentino's work, noteworthy for the treatment she gives of the language and techniques. In Sorrentino's fiction, D'Amico argues, "total invention and plagiarism are fatally joined . . . in his . . . constant search for a creative prose which could make readers more and more aware of the nude beauty of words, stripped of all metaphorical impediments" ("Paradox Beyond Convention: Gilbert Sorrentino's Fiction," pp. 269–80). In "An Archetypal World: Images of Italy in the Poetry of John Ciardi" (pp. 305–13), Fedora Giordano persuasively sees that Italy seems to appeal most to the poet as "the land of the Great Mediterranean Mother." The closing workshop, "Describing Italian American Experience," includes "Describing the Italian American Self" by William Boelhower (pp. 533–44), "Rosa, the Life of an Italian Immigrant" by Winifred Farrant Bevilacqua (pp. 545–56), and "The Sad Nymph of Margaret Fuller" by Francesca Bisutti (pp. 557–64).

The proceedings of the conference on Pound in Venice include 22 essays. They provide thoughtful insights into Pound's Italian experience, so crucial for understanding his poetry. But approaching and analyzing it, as Mamoli Zorzi points out in her foreword (pp. 5–6), means also taking into account the most important poetic and cultural trends of our time, the influences on Pound and those exerted by his work, and the relationships of the European, American, and Eastern traditions. Thus this rich and stimulating volume is on the whole one of the most important recent publications of Pound scholarship. It gathers the contributions of outstanding Americanists, providing exhaustive studies of broad perspectives, such as Sergio Perosa's "Ezra Pound: per una visione d'assieme (maschere, epica della storia e dell'io" (pp. 7–29); Wolfgang Kaempfer's "L'onnipresenza del tempo nei *Cantos* di Ezra Pound" (pp. 135–45); Alfredo Rizzardi's "Osservazioni sulla tipologia delle immagini nei *Pisan Cantos*" (pp. 147–56); and Marcello Pagnini's "Ezra Pound: episteme del Novecento e acculturazione selvaggia" (pp. 251–62). Pound's relationship with other writers is the focus of "Dante: un modello impossibile" (pp. 79–101) by Nemi D'Agostino and "Ezra Pound e A. E. Housman" (pp. 241–49) by Bianca Tarozzi, while Lionello Lanciotti in his "L'utopia cinese di Ezra Pound" (pp. 207–13) offers a careful account of Pound's Chinese sources and his interpretation of Chinese culture. Of the five essays devoted to Pound and Venice, A. Walton Litz traces a map of the 1913 visit, investigating how the experience of those two weeks reappears in the *Pisan Cantos* ("Pound in Venice, 1913," pp. 31–44). Mary de Rachewiltz, Pound's daughter, in "I livelli di Venezia" (pp. 45–48) presents an unpublished manuscript on Venice by her father: suggestive, intense notes ("La pietra stessa vuol vivere una vita umana. . . . Per portoni di Palazzi: Venezia eterna, acqua e pietra che sembra galleggiare ed essere semplicemente una parte dell'acqua stessa"), written perhaps as a short comment for a movie on Venice. "Pound e le arti visive a Venezia" (pp. 157–70) is a thorough study of the relationship between the poet and the visual arts: Rosella Mamoli Zorzi investigates the analogy between the manner of representation of the two media—poetry and painting—furnishing interesting examples of how some of the Venetian masterpieces of art can be verbally reproduced in Pound's *Cantos*. "Images of Venice in the Poetry of Ezra Pound" (pp. 171–79) by Michael Alexander deals with the Venetian scenes and references to Venice in the *Pisan Cantos*, either topographical, personal, or mythological, concluding that Venice in Pound's work is not "a negative image of decadence and artifice . . . but a human shrine." In "Liguria contro Venezia: due modelli nella poesia di Pound" (pp. 181–202), Massimo Bacigalupo skillfully elucidates the interrelation in the *Cantos* between Venice and Liguria. The *Cantos* are to be seen as a traveler's journal, a "periplus," an Odyssey whose privileged coordinates are Torcello and Tigullio, linked together by that "gold thread in the pattern (Torcello)/al vicolo d'oro (Tigullio)," seeking at the same time elements of similarity in their inner difference and trying to read their ancient message. Pound as translator is the subject of two essays: "Ezra Pound and Creative Translation" (pp. 203–05) by Desmond O'Grady and "Pound alla ricerca di una lingua per Cavalcanti" (pp. 215–34) by David Anderson. In the former, Pound is seen as "the most influential *translator* of poetry of our century," whose pioneering example set up an entirely new approach to verse translation, inventing a new art we may call "creative translation." The latter deals with Pound's version of the *Cavalcanti Poems* and the astonishing differences in the mode of translation.

In another four essays the focus is on particular aspects of specific Cantos, such as Marilla Battilana's well-reasoned essay on the first Cantos and on *Drafts and Fragments* ("Primi Canti e Frammenti finali: il cerchio che non chiude," pp. 117–34). "Per una lettura dei Cantos LXXII, LXXIII" (pp. 49–57) contains an interesting analysis by Maria Luisa Ardizzone, while Guido Carboni in his "I Canti dell'usura e la V Decade: ipotesi sulla forma dei *Cantos*" (pp. 103–15) investigates thematic and structural problems posed by Pound's work, starting from three different yet interrelated points: Canto 45 seen as central to the whole scheme of the *Cantos*; the structure of the *Cantos* as a codification of Pound's aesthetics; and how all this leads to the comprehension and definition of modernism. "In the Station of the Metro" receives attention in Giuliano Gramigna's "Questi volti tra la folla: la doppia iscrizione di Pound" (pp. 59–65), an essay which helps explain, in terms of Freudian *niederschrift*, the process of composition of the couplet. The volume also includes three brief reminiscences by Giorgio Manera, Vanni Scheiwiller, and Giuseppe Santomaso, who had known the poet or worked with him.

The closing essay, by Agostino Lombardo, "Pound e il sogno dell'artista americano" (pp. 263–80), is a limpid, outstanding assessment of Pound's American roots. His profound Americanness, Lombardo maintains, is recognizable above all in his conception of the artist, indeed in what may be defined as the American dream of the American artist. Rejected by Puritans, the artist has accepted his role as an outcast, and in so doing he denounces and destroys the American Dream. But at the same time he creates his own dream, with a tension and clarity of commitment which is peculiarly American. Such an image of the artist who turns himself into a protagonist, a hero, is a constant presence in Pound throughout his early works. Furthermore, the later poet of the *Cantos* can be clearly understood only if we are mindful that along with the creation of his own dream, the American artist also creates the stage on which to act out his role. This is indeed the poetic conquest of the country (starting from Whitman through the Beats), Lombardo goes on, an artistic frontier which is the homologous and the opposite of the historical one, a tendency which is again peculiarly American, for its range and continuous presence both in poetry and in prose. So Pound in the *Cantos* develops an even more far-reaching utopia, the whole world being the stage of his journey.

Somewhat complementary to this conference is the exhibition "Ezra Pound: Un poeta a Rapallo" (1 June–15 July 1985) commemorating the centennial of his birth and illustrating the context in which he lived for so many years, the places that inspired his poetry as well as his activity as promoter of literary and musical events. The exhibition catalog (Genoa: Edizioni San Marco dei Giustiniani) ed. Massimo Bacigalupo, is an invaluable source of unpublished documents, letters, reminiscences, photographs, and local newspapers containing Pound's articles. Bacigalupo, author of studies on the poet reviewed here in the past few years, offers in his introductory essay (pp. 3–7) insightful observations on Pound's stay in Rapallo. His poetry, he maintains, is deeply marked by the places in which it was molded. The *Cantos* are for the Tigullio what Montale's *Ossi di Seppia* are for the Cinque Terre, a sensitive reading of those places, almost a vademecum for visitors. In the microcosm of Rapallo Pound re-created the map of his many interests: musical, educational (the Ezruniversità), literary, making that little town "an international cultural center" as he officially proposed in 1936. In the paper read for the opening of the exhibition and included in the catalog (pp. 92–95), Donald Davie states that Pound made Rapallo his home "more than any city in his native America, more than London where he lived for a dozen years in his youth, more than Paris where he stayed for a shorter time, more than Venice where he lived out his declining years."

To complete this rich harvest on Pound, it is worth mentioning the publication, in a bilingual edition, of *I Cantos* (Milan: Mondadori) ed. Mary de Rachewilts. Considering the many difficulties of her task, it is, on the whole, a fine translation, although some of the subtleties, nuances, and evasive syntax of the original are lost in the passage from one language to the other. In such cases the result is often the evocation of a more definite image in Italian than in the English text.

Other works on American poetry this year include two book-length studies and several essays, three of them introductions to the Italian versions of poem collections by Creeley, Plath, and Rich. A careful analysis of T. S. Eliot's work and the interplay between poetry and critical theories is presented by G. Singh in his *Thomas Stearns Eliot: Poeta, drammaturgo, critico* (Ravenna: Longo). Singh places special emphasis on Eliot's relationship with his contemporaries or precursors and his indebtedness to them. Set within a well-documented cultural and historical context, Singh's analytical reading of Eliot's poetry, criticism, and drama offers an accurate survey aimed at presenting Eliot as the greatest poet-philosopher after Wordsworth and as the greatest religious poet after Milton. Francesco Gozzi's *Letture eliotiane* (Pisa: ETS) is a fine critical reading of "Prufrock" and *The Waste Land* in which a vast array of information about the two works has been gathered, synthesized, and worked into a coherent and persuasive view. This concise and at the same time wide-ranging study demonstrates a variety of sound approaches and is a model, in its format, of critical and scholarly responsibility. This year's interest in poetry has also produced a valuable contribution on Hart Crane. In "F. & H. Il fascino di una sigla" (*Ling&L* 5: 55–80), Pietro Spinucci provides a perceptive study of "For the Marriage of Faustus and Helen," by which Crane takes Eliot (quoting Crane himself) "as a point of departure toward an almost complete reverse of direction," invoking "the poetry of negation" as counterpoise to a poetry with "a more positive content," the "funeral dirge" in opposition to a possible catharsis which Crane linked with the maieutic and visionary quality of poetry. Thus "F. & H.," Spinucci maintains throughout this essay, rich with interesting annotations on Crane's cultural milieu, is a real turning point, embodying "a resurrection of some kind" as Crane wrote, after "the absolute *impasse*" depicted by Eliot in *The Waste Land.*

An extensive and finely translated selection of Sylvia Plath's poems (*Le Muse inquietanti*, Milan: Mondadori) is presented in a bilingual edition by Gabriella Morisco and the Italian poet Amelia Rosselli. In Morisco's introductory essay the many aspects of Plath's poetry are intelligently studied, including the mother and father figures, the recurring theme of the double, the different voices of her female identity, her innovative connections with the grotesque traditions of the female gothic, and the poet's lifelong courtship with death. Adrienne Rich is the subject of two publications. *Come la tela del ragno* (Rome: Editrice La Goliardica) ed. Marina Camboni, contains some poems in bilingual presentation, the Italian version of two essays by Rich, "Power and Danger: Works of a Common Woman" (written as an introduction to *The Work of a Common Woman: The Collected Poetry of Judy Graham*) and "Disloyal to Civilization:

Feminism, Racism, Gynephobia." The closing section includes in translation Alicia Ostriker's essay, "The Nerves of a Midwife: Contemporary American Women's Poetry," and two essays by the editor. In "Come la tela del ragno: la construzione della identità nella poesia di Adrienne Rich" (pp. 146–78), Camboni sees the poetical development closely connected to and coinciding with a self-willed construction of identity, while in "Le parole di Filomela" (pp. 179–214) she offers an extended analysis of the poet's technique, stressing the highly dynamic quality of her poetry. The very structure of the book —poetical and prose texts by Rich together with critical appraisal of her work—provides a general overview while offering at the same time a particularly insightful study of Rich's poetic language. Further on the subject of Rich is an elegant volume, *Lo Spacco alla radice* (Florence: estro editrice), forming the very first publication of a new feminist press, which contains an autobiographical piece "Split at the Root," and the bilingual presentation of *Sources*, edited and beautifully translated by Liana Borghi. Her afterword, "Adrienne Rich e la diaspora dell'identità" (pp. 85–113), is a keen appraisal of the dynamic relationships between personal history, political commitment, and poetry. In this thoroughly researched look at Rich's involvement in lesbian-feminist groups, Borghi traces an accurate map of the American feminist movement in the '80s as well as the genesis and development of the poet's art—her struggle to dig out her roots as she strove to shape a new identity as a lesbian and as a Jew.

Interest in contemporary poetry is also reflected in another bilingual publication of Robert Creeley's *Later* (*Poi*, Venice: Edizioni del Leone), ed. Attilia Lavagno, who provides a short and not always very clear account of Creeley's achievements.

Fiction studies focus on many subjects, starting with one of the first novelists in American literature, Charles Brockden Brown, whose *Alcuin* (Naples: Guida Editore) is insightfully discussed by Rosella Mamoli Zorzi. Her introduction (pp. 5–23) to the Italian version of the novel is a detailed, probing study of the distinctive qualities of *Alcuin* as the first example of feminist utopian fiction. A clear and competent overview of the historical novel and of Cooper's Leatherstocking Tales is offered by Alide Cagidemetrio. Her "La frontiera del tempo nei *Leatherstocking Novels* di James F. Cooper" (pp. 65–94) is included in an interesting volume devoted to the historical novel as a genre, *Storie su storie. Indagine sui romanzi storici (1814–*

1840) (Venice: Neri Pozza Editore). Following an interesting, if faint, track, Giovanni Nicosia in his "Parkman and Manzoni" (*Nuovi Annali della Facoltà di Magistero dell'Università di Messina* 3:695–99) argues that Parkman was somewhat influenced by Manzoni's *Promessi Sposi* in a few passages of his work. Of the three essays on Poe, one treats the detective stories. In "Dupin e i giochi" (*Il lettore di provincia* 16:19–27), Augusto Ponzio offers a fresh insight (though at times overingenious) of "The Purloined Letter" conceived in its structure, he maintains, as a whist game. Another is an accurate and well-constructed introduction by Sergio Perosa to a new paperback edition, in three volumes, of Poe's works (*Racconti del terrore, Racconti del grottesco, Racconti di enigmi* [Milan: Mondadori]). The third, "Edgar Allan Poe e la prima traduzione americana dei *Promessi Sposi*" (*Nuovi Annali della Facoltà di Magistero dell'Università di Messina* 3:451–504), is a well-argued essay, convincing in the main, in which Giuseppe Lombardo demonstrates that Poe was the author of an anonymous review devoted to the English version of Manzoni's *Promessi Sposi* that appeared in the *Southern Literary Messenger.*

The unflagging interest in Henry James once more is strongly borne out in three splendid items, two of them by Sergio Perosa. As one of the most distinguished Jamesian critics, in his introduction to a collection of James's short fiction (*Romanzi brevi,* Milan: Mondadori) he subtly illuminates the writer's artistic phases and his concept of art as a heuristic and resolutive element of life—the organizing principle of what otherwise is fragmentary and evasive. In the course of his analysis of the eight pieces, Perosa offers a discerning commentary and an evaluation of the techniques used by James in his "nouvelles," providing on the whole a very skillful synthesis which should be taken as a model of the introductory essay. The same critical ability is to be seen in a short essay by the same author, "Henry James's Literary Criticism" (*Annali della Facoltà di Lingue e Letterature Straniere di Cà Foscari* 23,ii:213–18) where he stresses that the *Prefaces* "can be read as a manifesto of early modernism just as they prefigure crucial features and concerns of the latest narratology" and that "there is more of James in Genette than meets the eye." Indeed, it is Henry James that provides the starting point for a discussion of the point of view technique in a book-length study by Paola Pugliatti (*Lo sguardo nel racconto: Teorie e prassi del punto di vista,* Bologna: Zanichelli). She offers an exhaustive synthesis of the subject, illustrating and discussing the theories of European, American, and Russian critics, and providing exemplary analyses of some passages by American authors.

Though the flow of scholarly works may have dropped in 1985, Faulkner and Hemingway received their usual share of attention in two original studies, while Fitzgerald is the subject of a short introduction by Roberto Cagliero to a beautiful Italian version of *The Cruise of the Rolling Junk* (*La crociera del rottame vagante* [Palermo: Sellerio]). Rosella Mamoli Zorzi with her customary clarity of exposition and sound scholarship investigates a rather new aspect of Faulkner's early writings, making some fresh observations about his use of fairy-tale materials. Her "L'uso della fiaba in due opere del primo Faulkner" (*Annali della Facoltà di Lingue e Letterature Straniere di Cà Foscari* 22,ii:141–51) is a thoughtful and close reading of *The Wishing Tree* and *Mayday*. The former, she maintains, is perfectly structured according to the theories elaborated by Propp and Greimas, in the best Brothers Grimm tradition, a perfect example of *Kunstmärchen*, mingling elements which belong to the fairy tales with those typical of Faulkner's world. *Mayday*, although bearing an identical structure, is an unsuccessful attempt as a fairy tale owing to the totally different treatment and meaning of the Saint Francis figure and the continuous demythicization of the fairy-tale material achieved by the intermittent use of language with an evident parodistic intent.

One major biographical work appeared in 1985: *Hemingway* by Fernanda Pivano, whose professional and friendly association with the writer covered a span of 30 years. Relying mainly on personal conversations (some of them already published in her *Mostri degli anni Venti*) as well as on earlier biographies, Pivano has created a valuable resource. She includes material of considerable importance, such as unpublished letters by Hemingway which deal with personal and professional matters. Written by means of associations instead of chronological order, some parts may sound episodic and disjointed, but on the whole the book makes pleasant reading for the scholar and general reader alike.

Several articles have been written on other 20th-century authors. In his introduction to the Italian version of a collection of short stories by James M. Cain (*Il bambino nella ghiacciaia*, Palermo: Sellerio), Roberto Birindelli offers a useful investigation of Cain's fiction seen as a skillful mixture of popular and cultural elements appealing to a variegated audience. "La Torre Abolita: una lettura di *Invisible Man* di Ralph Ellison" by Galilea Maioli (*Il lettore di provincia* 16:60–66) is a brief and rather schematic essay dealing with Northrop Frye's theories on romance applied to Ellison's novel. Anna Maria Palombi Cataldi's "Defoe, Golding, Malamud: esiste ancora una speranza?" (*Critica letteraria,* 13,iv:715–25) is an attempt to forge a link between *Robinson Crusoe, Lord of the Flies,* and *God's Grace,* but the result is that the author gives a more descriptive than critical appraisal of the three novels. James Purdy, Ishmael Reed, and Richard Brautigan are the subject of three short essays. "Il primo Purdy: note su *Malcolm*" (*Annali della Facoltà di Lettere e Filosofia dell'Università di Bari* 27–28:315–35) by Stefano Bronzini is an interesting although erratic investigation of Purdy's first novel. "*The Free-Lance Pallbearers* di Ishmael Reed ovvero non più arco di proscenio" (*Il lettore di provincia* 16:41–49) by Franco La Polla provides stimulating evidence about Reed's radical revision of fiction as a genre. "Altre seduzioni: *Trout Fishing in America* di Richard Brautigan" (*Il lettore di provincia* 16:50–59) by Marina Busani offers a few intelligent glimpses into Brautigan's novel seen as a perfectly structured architecture, although it seems to lack narrative strategy.

Surely the most significant work on contemporary fiction this year is a collection of essays on Henry Roth's *Call It Sleep*. *Rothiana, Henry Roth nella critica italiana* (Florence: Giuntina), ed. Mario Materassi, contains articles written over the past 20 years and two unpublished pages from Roth's 1967 diary and Materassi's vivid reminiscences of two of his encounters with Roth. A very useful bibliography—the most current yet published—of primary and secondary sources complements this important contribution. As several of the authors point out, the title, which echoes the closing phrases of the book, remains enigmatic but invites reflection on Roth's sleep or silence as a writer, and the role of sleep in his novel. Little David's sleep is read against a Freudian backcloth by Guido Fink in his essay "Lo schermo del sonno" (pp. 143–54) as he brilliantly weaves in and out of other textual references commenting on the association of reverie and dream with peace but also with death, and the significance of awakening as transition to reality. Freud's theories again establish critical guidelines in Alessandra Contenti's "Identità culturale, infanzia e nostalgia in *Call It Sleep*" (pp. 105–17), a very interesting autobiographical interpretation of the novel where the—partly imaginary—sadness of an unhappy childhood reflects the adult immigrant's sense of loss. According to Elèna Mortara di Veroli's beautiful essay, "Scrivere con il carbone d'angelo, l'arte di Henry Roth" (pp. 45–75), it is the harmony between the child's subjective perception in his desperate search for light and purity to counteract his growing awareness of sin, and the objective, richly documented description of reality achieved partly by the variety of stylistic registers, that constitutes the book's enduring fascination. It furthermore reflects Jewish aspirations to a unitary vision of life. The Jewish theme returns in Guido Fink's bravura piece, "Il viaggio: E così questa è la terra promessa" (pp. 77–85). Fink's allusive reading of the prologue to *Call It Sleep* tells of great expectations giving way to the estranged identity of the immigrant, played out by Roth within the two poles of seeing and being seen. Gordon Poole, in his "David in America: dall'etnicità ebraica all'americanismo cristiano" (pp. 119–42), sees affinity with the American "romance" in the symbolic network and indeed mythical dimensions through which Roth filters social realism, whereby the terrifying father figure is akin to the wrathful God of the Old Testament while David in the electrocution scene is a figure of Christ. The issue of Roth's modernist technique, compared and contrasted by Poole with that of Dos Passos and Eliot, is also examined in "Il caso Henry Roth" by Giordano De Biasio (pp. 93–104), who argues convincingly that caught as Roth was between ideological adherence to Marxism and artistic loyalty to Eliot and Joyce, his use of multiple interlayered stylistic registers, including political parody in the electrocution scene, irrevocably separates this novel from documentary proletarian work. Roth's technique is again the central theme in Mario Materassi's two essays, "Il grande romanzo di Henry Roth (pp. 27–44) and "Sul modulo dell'insieme semantico in *Call It Sleep*" (pp. 155–67). In the former, Materassi dwells revealingly upon the interplay of opposites such as the condensing and stretching of time (likened to James), light and dark, and David's quest for God and his awareness of sin, which are highlighted by perception through the mind of a child in this novel of initiation. In the latter, Materassi gives a very elegant demonstration that Roth used a system of buried analogies to merge the syntagmatic and paradigmatic levels in a manner strikingly different from Joyce.

The only two studies dealing this year with Americans in Europe are Alessandro Gebbia's *La città teatrale* (Rome: Officina Edizioni) and Giuseppe Gadda Conti's "Dos Passos sul fronte francese" (*Nuova Antologia*, 2155:153–75). The first is about American travelers in Rome between 1760 and 1870, such as Story, Hawthorne, Longfellow, Irving, Cooper, and James, and in particular what they wrote on the "theatrical exhibitions" in a country where, in Story's words, "all the world is a stage, but every stage is a world" and in a city where "for high and low, rich and poor, prince and peasant, there is a theatre." Divided into three parts—a general introduction on American travelers in Rome, their ideal itinerary among the picturesque Roman streets or the pompous Catholic ceremonies, and finally their comments on the many performances in Roman theaters—this research is another interesting contribution to the already very rich study of American travelers in Italy. The focus of the second essay is on *One Man's Initiation: 1917*, which Giuseppe Gadda Conti does not consider a "war novel." Although Dos Passos served as an ambulance driver during World War I, he was not involved in frontline battles. He lived, Gadda Conti convincingly maintains, his war experience as an outsider, a spectator, or, better, as an observer, which makes this work a war novel sui generis, dealing only with the adventures of "voluntary gentlemen."

The year 1985 was not particularly rich in the field of theater studies, although a major contribution, *1930s. La frontiera nell'America del New Deal* (Venice: Marsilio Editori), ed. Franco Minganti, is a lively and thoroughly researched book focusing on the "urban frontier" in the '30s. Its first part is a detailed examination of the "social entertainment," while the second is a carefully selected anthology. Together, they offer the reader a critical overview of the period, providing sound analysis and documentation, including Guido Fink's brilliant essay ("Scene di strada nel teatro degli anni trenta," pp. 45–64) on the political drama of the '30s, a drama in many ways a "double" of the urban street. "*Trifles*: lo spazio conquistato" (*Quaderni di Teatro* [August:165–71]) by Alessandra Calanchi is a feminist critical approach to the play by Susan Glaspell, while the introductory essay by Roberto Bertinetti to the Italian translation of three plays by Sam Shepard (*Scene americane*, Genoa: Costa & Nolan) is a well-grounded assessment of the American playwright's literary career, which also clarifies our reading of *Rock Star*, *Buried Child*, and *True West* included in this collection.

University of Pisa

v. Italian Contributions—1986

Massimo Bacigalupo

Few book-length studies were published in 1986, but there were a number of useful editions and translations of texts, four special issues of magazines (*RSA*, *LAmer*, *Verri*, *Galleria*) devoted to one topic, and one festschrift, besides the usual crop of articles. The festschrift, *Letture anglo-americane in memoria di Rolando Anzilotti* (Pisa: Nistri–Lischi), collects five papers given in Pisa, Anzilotti's university, on 2–3 April 1984, and 12 further contributions, followed by a bibliography of his writings. (A more detailed annotated bibliography appeared in *Studi canadesi* 7:41–60.) The festschrift opens with a brief memoir of Anzilotti by his colleague Felice Del Beccaro, which recalls their first 1934 meeting in the Lucca lycée where Del Beccaro was already teaching and Anzilotti came as a student, their common hikes and search for information about Carlo Lorenzini, the creator of Pinocchio, whose pseudonym Collodi comes from a suburb of Pescia near Lucca. Anzilotti had been born in Pescia in 1919 and later, as mayor of the township, saw to the erection of a monument to Pinocchio, which Del Beccaro's article makes one curious to visit. Another important date is 27 March 1951, as it marks a reading in Lucca by Robert Lowell of "The Quaker Graveyard in Nantucket," and by Anzilotti of his loving Italian translation of the poem. It is from this very poem that Agostino Lombardo takes his cue for his discussion of Anzilotti's translations (*Letture anglo-americane*, pp. 21–33), which points out how translation can be both humble and creative, and also a work of criticism, especially when dealing with a difficult original, with the help of the author. Thus Anzilotti's editions of Lowell can be of value not only to readers at large but also to future commentators, who will often find in them authoritative interpretations. (The same is the case with some Italian translations of Ezra Pound.) On the whole, I was struck by the tact with which many contributors to the Anzilotti panel were able to pay homage to their colleague and friend while getting on with their scholarly work. Their contributions will be discussed in the appropriate sections below.

***a.* Critical Theory.** In *Il testo e la sua "performance"* (Rome: Editori Riuniti), Agostino Lombardo addresses in turn theater, poetry, and narrative, giving a few pages to Melville and Hawthorne and claiming that the American romance is paradoxically more "truthful" and advanced than the novel with its illusionary representation. Lombardo closes with a defense of what he calls "imperfect criticism," of the critic's negative capability, as against a too "strong" or too technical approach. (Not surprisingly, the booklet opens with references to Samuel Johnson.)

Franco Moretti's *Il romanzo di formazione* (Milan: Garzanti) is an important study of the bildungsroman, announcing in its first footnote why American literature will *not* be discussed: because of its religious dimension (which it has in common with Russian literature, also omitted from Moretti's survey) and because of the essential confrontation with nature and "the alien (Indian, Black, or savage)." These themes, according to Moretti, are wholly at odds with the secular world of the English and Western European bildungsroman (from Austen and Goethe to Balzac and George Eliot). I hope he will give us a further study on American *and* Russian literature.

Another provocative book of theory, more iconographic than literary, is Ruggero Pierantoni's *Forma fluens: il movimento e la sua rappresentazione nella scienza, nell'arte e nella tecnica* (Turin: Boringhieri), which covers the span from rock drawings to Jackson Pollock and the changing ideas of the physical world as represented in art, philosophy, and literature. *Forma fluens* is an Italian relative of *Steps to an Ecology of Mind* and *Gödel Escher Bach* and is therefore also interesting as a cultural document.

***b.* General Works.** Sergio Perosa's *Teorie americane del romanzo 1800–1900* (Milan: Bompiani) is a translation of *American Theories of the Novel* (see *ALS 1983*). It includes an excellent introductory survey of 19th-century ideas of the novel and their background and 60 excerpts of varying lengths, from Brackenridge to Norris. The book will be indispensable for reference, though it is difficult to read consecutively.

Bianca Tarozzi has written a penetrating account of "Virgilio nella cultura americana," published in *La fortuna di Virgilio: atti del convegno internazionale* (Naples: Giannini), pp. 477–505, which follows Virgil's fine thread from Cotton Mather to Robert Lowell in brief compass. Some observations on Pound and Eliot's responses to Milton compared to Wordsworth and Keats's may be found in my

"Versioni di Milton," printed in *La performance del testo*, ed. Franco Marucci and Adriano Bruttini (Siena: Ticci), pp. 393–405.

c. 17th and 18th Centuries. Tommaso Pisanti has edited an elegant pocket anthology of *Poesia dell'America puritana* (Pordenone: Studio Tesi), with an informative introduction and bibliography and a few notes. Seventeen poets are represented (the original English being printed opposite careful Italian translations), from Bradstreet to Cotton Mather. Marilla Battilana has happily brought together in one volume *Tre donne del New England* (Urbino: Quattro Venti) smooth translations of the *Narrative of Mary Rowlandson*, the *Journal of Madam Knight*, and the *Diary of Anna Green Winslow*, with an afterword that shows much genuine sympathy for and knowledge of the world in which the three women lived. The text is diligently annotated and will be well received by students and readers (it also sports a nice dust jacket). Franca Rossi's *L'idea dell'America nella cultura inglese (1500–1625): vol. 1: diaristica e storiografia* (Bari: Adriatica), looks at America from the point of view of early English accounts, its 364 pages comprising much material in which one may want to dip now and again.

d. 19th Century. Guido Fink continues his brilliant investigation of 19th-century narrative techniques (see *ALS 1978*, p. 468) in his paper, "A Strange Couple: Hawthorne and His 'Gentle Reader' " (*Letture anglo-americane*, pp. 127–45), possibly the first to provide a close reading of Hawthorne's "Little Annie's Ramble," which turns out to have some surprising analogies with *Lolita*. He also edits and introduces *La figlia di Rappaccini* (Bologna: Il cavaliere azzurro). Edgar Allan Poe is allowed to rest, except for a new selection of his poems, *Il corvo e altre poesie*, ed. Silvana Colonna and Maurizio Cucchi (Milan: Mondadori). Melville is well served by Ruggero Bianchi, who has edited the first volume of a projected complete Italian edition, *Typee, Omoo* (Milan: Mursia), adding a thorough biographical and bibliographical apparatus and a 40-page introductory essay, "Sognando Rousseau," on the parallelism and divergence of the two books and their long foreground in cultural history. As for the plan of his edition, Bianchi says he will follow Weaver's 16-volume Standard Edition while taking into account later textual work; the translations are to be all new or newly revised. In the first volume *Typee* is offered in Luigi Berti's 1951 version, fully corrected (Ezra Pound wrote Berti in dismay on 10 December 1942: "But you don't *understand* English!"), *Omoo* in a new and fine translation by Alessandro Monti. Another curious result of Melville worship is the first Italian translation of *Fragments from a Writing-Desk*, published as *Profili di donne* (Maser: Amadeus), ed. Alberto Lehmann and Giulia Bruna Bogliolo, two nonacademics who prove their passion and mettle, though I do not know where they got their information about "the famous Melville *Diary*, not to be published, by the author's wishes, until a century after his death" (p. 23). The book has an interesting introduction, which makes rather high claims for the *Fragments*: "Every work on Melville is truly an 'ewige Arbeit' . . . every work of this author is as important as the others, but the *Fragments* are even more so, as indication and confirmation of a circle, closed but continuous, perhaps inexhaustible in its circularity, also from the point of view of understanding and study" (p. 23). The translation, thoroughly annotated, is followed by a poorly written "Critical Note" and by a biography and a bibliography which includes some items missed even by Bianchi.

Biancamaria Tedeschini Lalli, a contributor to the Anzilotti panel, chooses as a suitable theme "Il superamento dell'alterità della morte in 'Song of Myself'" (*Letture anglo-americane*, pp. 79–93) and gives a close stylistic reading of some of Whitman's meditations on death, ending on the lines: "Prepare the later afternoon of me myself, prepare the lengthening shadows,/Prepare my starry nights." In the same volume Elizabeth Philpott investigates Whitman's Bible connections ("The Song of Songs That Is Whitman's," pp. 267–85), providing some very detailed phonetic evidence. Giuseppe Lombardo, in "Doctor Holmes, Rip Van Winkle e i 'territori dell'Arcadia'" (*Nuovi Annali della Facoltà di Magistero dell'Università di Messina* 4:435–58), gives an interesting portrait of the Autocrat and a careful reading of his occasional poem, "Rip Van Winkle, M.D.," showing how a powerful myth was pared down to an after-dinner joke and how this illuminates Holmes's milieu.

AISNA, the Italian Society for American Studies, organized a centenary Dickinson colloquium in Pisa, 3–4 November 1986, but this year's scholarly yield was not large. Nadia Fusini writes suggestively, in her rather oneiric style, about "Dickinson and ellipsis" in her notable book on women writers, *Nomi* (Milan: Feltrinelli), pp. 43–73. Many of her remarks are rewarding, but hers is criticism-as-meditation and creation, so much so that Dickinson's lines are quoted in Italian, made part of a new work. Barbara Lanati edited what must be the twentieth volume of selected Dickinson poems to appear in Italy (and her second—see *ALS 1976*, p. 451), with a brief introduction. The book has an appealing title, *Silenzi* (Milan: Feltrinelli) and offers 221 poems for the poetry lover's admiration. However, as Lanati notes, the largest Italian selection is still Guido Errante's old two-volume edition of over 300 poems, last reprinted in paperback in 1978 (Milan: Bompiani), which has a good 100-page essay and perceptive annotations.

***e.* 20th-Century Prose.** Henry James got as usual the greatest amount of attention. Agostino Lombardo revises his 1956 edition of *Le prefazioni* (Rome: Editori Riuniti): comparison of the old introduction to the new one (pp. 9–47) shows how carefully he has made changes in almost every sentence, adding or omitting paragraphs and quotations, and writing a provocative new conclusion in which he claims that the Prefaces to the New York Edition are one of the Master's major novels, "the novel of James's narrative process." Lombardo's scholarly care and attention, as well as his instinct for the essential, are as always admirable, and this painstaking revision is (as he confesses) a thoroughly Jamesian matter. To the large stock of Italian translations of James the *Notebooks* were added this year, in a verbatim rendering of the Matthiessen and Murdock edition: *I taccuini*, tr. Ottavio Fatica (Rome: Theoria). Leon Edel's new edition of the *Notebooks* was instead the source of Francesca Durenti's fine translation, with an afterword, of the uncompleted "Hugh Merrow" (*Paragone* 440:20–35). Giovanna Mochi, one of our more astute readers of James, makes some good points about the Master's apparent withdrawal into objectivity by way of the circumscribed viewpoint in "Henry James: le figure dell'autore nelle 'fables for critics'" (*RLMC* 39:309–25). No less than three essays were devoted to *The Turn of the Screw*, besides Pietro Citati's lay observations in *Il sogno della camera rossa* (Milan: Rizzoli), pp. 148–65, which also has chapters on *Italian Hours* and *The Sense of the Past*. Rosamaria Loretelli briefly connects the story with the mechanism of suspension (*La performance del testo*, pp. 163–73). Elsa Linguanti gives an excellent in-depth narratological reading in "Mistificazioni" (*Letture anglo-americane*, pp. 199–227). Luisa Villa contributes a most useful contextual consideration, "Henry James e la ghost story: i fantasmi del positivismo" (*Inventario* 23,xv[1985]:49–68), touching upon Henry and William's interest in the Society for Psychical Research, and thus making a good case for a deliberately planned uncertainty about the apparitions, in conformity with "psychic" studies current at the time. Another good contribution on the ghostly James comes from Remo Ceserani, in "La maschera della Medusa" (*Belfagor* 41:605–20), a sympathetic study of "The Friends of the Friends."

"Gertrude Stein, l'indifferenza" is the title of the Stein chapter of Nadia Fusini's *Nomi* (pp. 115–42), as attractive a piece of writing as her "Emily Dickinson, l'ellissi," mentioned above. "Gertrude Stein is not at all the abstract, intellectual writer that people talk about. To the contrary, she is always concerned with the most prosaic and empirical problems of writing"—and she is, for Fusini, indifferent to pain. Marina Camboni's "Il gioco della mente: linguaggio e metalinguaggio in Gertrude Stein" (*LAmer* 22[1984]:5–34) attempts a stylistic investigation, concluding that "the sense that Stein's phrases and texts show is the circularity of the finite, enclosed and surpassed by the series of possibilities and the non-finite (Bergson's Real)."

Mario Materassi, who published a translation of *Soldier's Pay* (Milan: Mondadori) with a short introduction, is also interested in ellipsis as it figures in Faulkner's works, where the central fact about a story can be perversely withheld, in his reading of " 'That Evening Sun' e il modello della ellissi climactica" (*Letture anglo-americane*, pp. 229–41). The same festschrift includes a well-informed essay by Giulia Pissarello on "Il paradigma dell'inversione in *Nightwood* di Djuna Barnes" (pp. 287–96), and, while I am touching upon expatriatism, Scott Donaldson's helpful "Americans in Italy: The Clash of Cultures in John Cheever's Studies" (pp. 113–26), which refutes the charges of snobbery and condescension leveled at Cheever's Italian sketches.

The Jewish-American event of the year was the publication to great acclaim of Mario Materassi's translation of Henry Roth's *Call It Sleep* (Milan: Garzanti). Guido Fink's review appeared with a 1985 Materassi-Roth interview in *L'Indice* (3,vii:14–15). (Roth's masterpiece was fittingly preceded in Italian bookstores by Abraham Cahan's *Yekl: A Tale of the New York Ghetto*, translated as *Perduti in America* [Milan: SugarCo, 1985] by Mario Maffi, who also provided an introductory note.) Gigliola Sacerdoti Mariani's "Jewish-American Writers of the Fifties: Saul Bellow and Bernard Malamud"

(*RSA* 6:249–62) offers some interesting notes on Hasidic elements in *The Assistant*.

This essay appears in a 326-page issue of *RSA* entirely devoted to "The Tranquillized Fifties" (Robert Lowell's phrase), being the proceedings of the 1985 AISNA conference. The first three sections of the issue are for once interdisciplinary, addressing "The Rise of Globalism," "The Arts" (Guido Fink and Angela Vistarchi on the cinema, Gillo Dorfles and Andrea Mariani on painting), and "The Role of Congress and the Supreme Court." Section four, "The Reduction to Globalism," turns out to be about literature and includes notes on "The Novel of the Fifties" by Barbara Lanati, Blanche Gelfant's interesting rejoinder "An 'Untranquil' Novel of the Fifties: Jack Kerouac's *On the Road*" (on Kerouac's conservatism), two well-argued papers on the critical scene, John Paul Russo's "The New Criticism in Trouble" (pp. 229–47) and Mario Corona's militant and sly "Getting Ready for the Fifties: Or, Criticism Anaesthetized" (pp. 283–93), which debunks some New Critical myths and explications. There is also a survey of "The American College Novel" by Francesca Orestano Vanni, including some comments on *A New Life* made by Bernard Malamud while visiting Sicily in 1985.

Two volumes of American plays were added to the list of Costa & Nolan, a specialized publisher in Genoa: David Mamet's *Teatro* (*The Woods, A Life in the Theatre, Glengarry Glen Ross*) with an introductory note on "Il turpiloquio di Mamet" by Guido Almansi, and Sam Shepard's *Pazzo d'amore* (i.e., *Fool for Love*) with a well-informed preface by Guido Fink.

f. 20th-Century Poetry. Ezra Pound is still the most studied author in the wake of the centenary. Two journals have devoted special issues to him that nicely complement each other. The two fascicles of *Il Verri*, numbered 11 and 12, and edited by me, are in part an update for the Italian reader on Poundian criticism abroad and on Pound's singing school. So No. 11 has poems by Basil Bunting, Donald Davie, Denise Levertov, a story by Guy Davenport, and the first Italian translation of "Three Cantos I," followed by my note "*Urcantos, Propertius, Cantos*: Pound dal ritardo al sorpasso" (pp. 18–22), which sees "Three Cantos" as an appealing but dated attempt, and *Propertius*, paradoxically, as a critique of the *Cantos* (the mythology that Pound's Propertius makes fun of being very prominent in the contemporary early Cantos, including nos. 4–7). *Il Verri* 12 includes, among essays by Donald Davie, Marjorie Perloff, and Michael Alexander, a longish paper of mine, " 'Per parte nostra sappiamo cancellare': al lavoro su due poemetti di Pound" (pp. 64–76), on the travails and revelations of translating and editing Pound's *Mauberley* and *Propertius*. Concerning the latter, Giannina Solimano's review (*Maia* 38,iii:263–65) of my Italian edition of the poem (see *ALS 1985*, pp. 552–53) is worth mentioning as one of not many contributions on the subject from a professional Latinist. For further light on Mary de Rachewiltz's important translation of *The Cantos*, the reader may go to my detailed review, "Una cattedra perpetua" (*L'Indice* 3,iii: 13–14).

In contrast to *Il Verri's* emphasis on foreign scholarship, the special Pound issue of *Galleria* (35,iii–vi), ed. Mary de Rachewiltz and Maria Luisa Ardizzone, gathers articles and notes by Italian writers and scholars. Ardizzone discusses at length Pound's worrying of Aristotle in "La sapienza del sensibile: Pound (Cavalcanti) Aristotele: Prolegomena" (pp. 155–82)—no easy going, as one gathers from the title. The use of the word "wisdom" in connection with Pound may raise a few eyebrows, and altogether Ardizzone takes her subject too solemnly, for Pound's incursions into Aristotle are no more serious than his parody of Propertius. Other original contributions are from Vittore Branca, Anna Caffini (on Carlo Linati), Arturo Cattaneo (on Claudius Rutilius Namatianus), Boris de Rachewiltz (on Peter Goullart and Joseph F. Rock), Vanni Scheiwiller, Aldo Tagliaferri, Rosita Tordi (on Giuseppe Ungaretti). Of special interest is Maria Corti's "Quattro poeti leggono Dante" (pp. 223–43), which compares the approaches to Dante of Osip Mandelstam, Rudolf Borchardt, Olof Lagercrantz, and Pound. A specialist in Dante and Guido Cavalcanti, among others, Corti shows great discretion in appreciating the poet's way of reading and "making new" such great masters. Three of Italy's most prominent poets also have contributions in the *Galleria* gathering: Giovanni Giudici writes of his translation of *Mauberley*; Giovanni Raboni discusses the essential anticapitalism of Pound's economics and *The Cantos* as "the century's greatest monument and richest trove of poetic possibilities"; and Edoardo Sanguineti, most humorously, contributes an "Omaggio a Catullo," seven slangy imitations of the Latin poet bearing the dedication "per E.P., neglected by the young" (pp. 277–80).

Since Sanguineti is a socially engaged and highly intelligent poet and critic, he may mean that it is E.P.'s antagonistic stance that is being ignored by the more conventional young men of letters. For scholars by no means neglect him, though they may not understand him. Caterina Ricciardi contributes "Cantabile/cantobile: traduzione e poetica del suono in Ezra Pound" (*LAmer* 22[1984]:161–84) on the element of sound in Pound's poems and translations, especially those from Arnaut Daniel. Riccardo M. degli Uberti, not a scholar, tries his hand at a translation of *Guide to Kulchur* (*Guida alla cultura* [Florence: Sansoni]), but his work is marred by too many misunderstandings of the original to be of much use. Piero Sanavio's *La gabbia di Ezra Pound* (Milan: Scheiwiller) is a memoir that moves somewhat erratically back and forth in Pound's and Sanavio's lives (the two met in Washington, D.C., and later in Paris), telling once again the story of Pound's incarceration with little new insight and much special pleading (Sanavio is almost unique in attempting a defense of Pound on Jews). One item may be of interest to students of *Mauberley*, namely a comment from Pound in a letter of 1 August 1955, which Sanavio quotes in Italian: "[John] Espey on *Mauberley* corrects a few of the more stupid errors. . . . Espey makes some mistakes of his own, especially on acorns" (p. 158).

In contrast with the usually busy Pound industry, the Eliot front remained quiet but for the publication of a 1,200-page volume of selected poetry, plays, and criticism, *Opere*, ed. Roberto Sanesi (Milan: Bompiani), which has at the end useful excerpts of Italian criticism. The ample bibliography notes another Eliot volume for this year, *Saggi su Dante*, ed. Giovanni Vidali (Cernusco sul Naviglio: Severgnini). This must be the silence before the storm, given the approaching centenary.

Interest in Wallace Stevens is on the rise. *Il mondo come meditazione: ultime poesie 1950–1955* (Palermo: Acquario-Guanda), a volume which I edited, collects for the first time anywhere all the poems from Stevens's last phase, that is, the "Rock" sections of *Collected Poems* and the poems from 1950 onward of *Opus Posthumous*. I give the English text, numbering the lines, with facing Italian translation, and extensive annotations (pp. 199–235), attempting a full account, structural and thematic, of these 57 deceptive and moving poems. Needless to say, the work of Stevens's last years benefits from being seen as a whole, and the accomplishment of some of the later little-regarded sequences, such as "Solitaire Under the Oaks," "Local Objects," and the two poems that follow in *Opus Posthumous*, stands out more clearly. This is the second book of Stevens's poetry to appear in Italy (the first, the small but exquisite selection by Renato Poggioli, came out in 1954, in time for Stevens to be proud of it). That more is soon to come is apparent from Francesco Rognoni's fine translation of, and note on, "The Auroras of Autumn" (*Paragone* 442: 30–46).

If much of Stevens remains untranslated in the language of Petrarch (a poet with whom he may have as much in common as with John Milton), the *Spoon River Anthology* was translated for the third time, mostly accurately, by Alberto Rossatti, who also provided footnotes, while Viola Papetti contributed a sparkling introduction and critical excerpts: *Antologia di Spoon River* (Milan: Rizzoli). Masters's book has been an important one for Italian writers such as Cesare Pavese from the '30s onward, and it remains, as Papetti wittily notes, "an object of love, if not of affection" (p. 23). In the aftermath of the war came the discovery of such experimentors as E. E. Cummings, as Marcello Pagnini recalls in "Il caso Cummings" (*Letture anglo-americane*, pp. 35–57; an English version appeared in *Poetics Today* 6[1985]:357–73). Reading Cummings in *This Is My Best*, writes Pagnini, he and Anzilotti were surprised by the apparent echoes of the manifestos of Marinetti and his fellow Futurists. Pagnini's paper now helpfully places Cummings in that context—cubism, futurism, imagism, vorticism—and provides an exemplary reading of "what a proud dreamhorse." Cummings's admirer Louis Zukofsky is the subject of Cristina Giorcelli's "Parole in musica, musica di parole" (*LAmer* 22[1984]:67–93), a reading of this forbidding poet's so-called *Autobiography*, surely relatively virgin territory. Giorcelli takes a very laudatory view of Zukofsky's experiments, so it is amusing to find Pound writing his disciple on 22 March 1940 that one of these, Zukofsky's rewriting of Cavalcanti's canzone of love, "seems to me harmless undergrad/ exercise" (*Pound/Zukofsky*, ed. Barry Ahearn [New York: New Directions, 1987], p. 200). Giorcelli provides a shrewd account of a later, equally sophisticated Jewish poet, John Hollander, in her reading of *Powers of Thirteen* (*Letture anglo-americane*, pp. 147–64), accompanied by Italian translations of some poems in Hollander's sequence.

Two useful studies of Hart Crane appeared in 1984: Barbara Nugnes's *La conversione al mondo* (Abano Terme: Piovan) and Rita Di Giuseppe's *The Terrible Puppet* (Verona: Libreria Editrice Universitaria). Di Giuseppe's "The Burden of Achievement: Hart Crane's

Last Poem" (*Quaderni di Lingue et Letterature* [Verona] 11:75–89) was originally intended, she writes, as the last chapter of her book but was omitted because "The Broken Tower," though "a beautifully wrought last will and testament," considered "in an afterword to a full-length study would have undermined and cast an anti-climactic shadow over what preceded it." Di Giuseppe's reading leans heavily on Harold Bloom's categories and is not wholly persuasive in its claim that Eliot was the "strong" poet to whom Crane finally succumbed, yet it is thoughtful and well-informed.

The later Robert Lowell is the subject of no less than four contributions: Bianca Tarozzi's translations (with introductory note) of 15 sonnets from *History* (*Almanacco dello Specchio* 12:139–61); Alfredo Rizzardi's sensitive reading of *The Dolphin* (*Letture anglo-americane*, pp. 59–77), Barbara Nugnes's perceptive account of *Day By Day* as Lowell's final poetic crisis, a reduction to tabula rasa ("'Goodbye Nothing': l'ultimo libro di Robert Lowell," *Letture anglo-americane*, pp. 243–65), and my own survey of the last three books in connection with Ian Hamilton's biography ("Un nome vivo: poesia e biografia nell' ultimo Lowell," *Nuova Corrente* 95[1985]: 203–26). Gabriella Morisco introduces May Swenson to Italian readers in her selection of poems, *Una cosa che ha luogo* (Urbino: Quattro Venti), with a careful introduction. Fedora Giordano provides a guide to Nathaniel Tarn's long poem in the Pound-Olson tradition, *Lyrics for the Bride of God*, in "Il mito come metalinguaggio nella poesia di Nathaniel Tarn" (*LAmer* 22[1984]:95–126).

The contemporary American poetry scene is the subject of my survey, "Parole mutate per una realtà mutata: la poesia americana oggi" (*Almanacco dello Specchio* 12:261–88)—the title being a translation of W. H. Auden's "an altering speech for altering things." After sampling several anthologies for an indication of current reputations and noting the present dearth of major figures, I give some attention to such magazines as *Poetry*, *American Poetry Review*, and *The New Yorker*, and the kind of writers they print, from Richard Wilbur to Stephen Dobyns, from John Ashbery to Charles Wright and Dave Smith. The article's final section, "Alone with America," provides thumbnail sketches of the work of John Hollander, Anthony Hecht, James Merrill, and Amy Clampitt, whose poem "The August Darks" comes in for explication. Merrill's trilogy, *The Changing Light at Sandover*, and its Dante connections are also discussed perceptively by Andrea Mariani in "Dal polilinguismo al metalinguismo: il linguaggio dantesco nella trilogia di James Merrill" (*LAmer* 22[1984]: 127–60).

After so much talk of poetry and the fortunes of American verse in Dickinson's "blue peninsula" (Poem 405), I would like to close with some significant lines by the poet Attilio Bertolucci, "America" (*Paragone* 432:3), written, he notes, "on the day of J. F. Kennedy's death." Bertolucci traces within a small compass the story of the rejection of America by many European intellectuals during the cold war, and the rediscovery of that culture in the '60s. "We couldn't any longer," he writes, "chant Poe Hawthorne Melville Dickinson Whitman/gods and demigods who planted gigantic/steps into the earth and vanished/without heirs, not Stephen Crane whose stature was more human/and nearer to us Ernest and Scott/who gave us in prose a music whose *dulcedo*/was as good as verse.//But today we can do this again, thanks to you. So be it."

Università di Udine

vi. Japanese Contributions

Hiroko Sato

In 1986 Japanese interest in American literature was as diverse as ever, with books and articles covering a wide range of writers, from William Bradford to John Irving. This avidity is also shown in Japanese scholars' attraction to the critical theories of reader-oriented criticism, deconstruction, and psychoanalytic criticism. Terms such as "signifier," "signified," "reader/writer," "text," and "displacement" appear with almost sickening frequency in more than half the books and articles reviewed here; these terms, however fresh and bright they were a few years ago, have already deteriorated to the level of clichés. Anyone who is clever enough to handle these critical tools can produce an academic paper of a certain standard, yet its concluding words are almost always predictable. The blind dependence on these borrowed tools, without any of the author's own personal interpretation of literary works, often fails to reveal the individual truth of the works under discussion.

If asked to point out some specific features of the year's achievements, I would like to name two things. One is the fact that much attention was paid to the literature of minority groups—blacks, Jews,

Catholics, and Indians. The other is that some of the most stimulating achievements of the year were done by American scholars teaching in Japan on a permanent basis. As their works were either published by Japanese publishers or came out in our major academic periodicals, I have decided to include a discussion of their works in this survey.

The articles examined here will be restricted to our major periodicals, *EigoS*, *SALit*, *SELit*, and the *American Review*. Unless otherwise indicated, all books mentioned were published in Tokyo.

***a.* 19th-Century Fiction.** Nobody would deny that James Fenimore Cooper is one of the major American writers. However, no serious critical study or research on him had been done by a Japanese until Daisuke Suzuki's *Sakka toshite Cooper wa Ikani Kodoshitaka* [*How Cooper Acted as a Writer*] (Eichosha-shinsha), the first book on the novelist by a Japanese scholar. As the subtitle of the book—"An Observation of the Writer's Life through His Letters"—suggests, this book is not so much a critical study of Cooper's work as an examination of Cooper's relationship with his own time. His social and political credo, his deep concern with the social trends of the time, and his endeavor in publishing more than 40 bulky books—when the American novel was still in its infancy and the publication of novels was not an easy thing—all are indicated through a close examination of his letters. This book is significant as a pioneering work which will serve as the starting point of the study of this great but so far neglected novelist.

Toshio Yagi's *Hakugei Kaitai* [*The Deconstruction of* Moby-Dick] (Kenkyu-sha) is an ambitious book. On the basis of his article "Moby-Dick Mosaic," published in 1983 (see *ALS 1983*, p. 487), Yagi expands his analysis of the novel's textual structure. Following the analytical method employed by Evert Duyckinck, Yagi thinks that this novel consists structurally of four strands—"Story," "Cetology," "Drama," and "Gam." Through unraveling the texture of these four elements, Yagi tries to show the mysteries of the universe created by Melville. Though Yagi's attempt is not wholly successful, the book is delightful to read; charm derives from the fact that the examiner and the examined share the same mentality—a deep interest in, and the strength to face, the chaos of the universe.

As I mentioned, young scholars' interest in deconstruction theories, psychoanalytic criticism, and semiotics is rampant. Nobuko Matsuda's "Dynamics of the Rational and Irrational in Thoreau's *Walden*"

(*SALit* 23:1–15) is one example. Using the theory of "festa" and the pathological psychology of Ludwig Binswanger, Matsuda contends that the irrational psychological elation Thoreau sometimes experienced in his merging with nature "keeps him going in his quest for a higher order of beings." Though presenting a new approach to Thoreau's world, Matsuda's analysis remains superficial, for her understanding of such key words as "rational" and "irrational" seems vague.

Three attempts along this line were made to study Henry James. One is "Theatrical Space as Metaphor—Representative Function in *The Ambassadors*" by Kuniko Izumi (*SALit* 23:35–54). Influenced by Barbara Johnson's "The Frame of Reference" and by the prevalent reader/writer theory, Izumi tries to define the role of Strether in the novel. He is given a place only as a "reader"; hence, he is compelled to play the role of an ambassador who is unable to convey the truth. Hiromi Kawashima's "A New Light on 'The Figure in the Carpet' " (*SALit* 23:56–69) deals with the critics' favorite story once again. Kawashima's point is to show, through an analysis of the characters of the narrator and Corvick and of their attitudes toward literature, that "those who have a passion for the literary secret succeed in leading a passionate life." Kawashima concludes that this is the story of a narrator who has missed a chance to live. More successful than these two is Yasuki Saeki's discussion of *The Ambassadors*: "Theater, City, Painting—A Perspective View of *The Ambassadors*" (*EigoS* 132:54–58). Saeki concentrates on the third, unexpected encounter between Chad and Strether and points out that it is different from the previous two meetings. This time it is Chad who is surprised from behind. This incident is a kind of "discovery scene" and the turning point in Strether's recognition of reality. Here, the significance of theater, painting, and city are merged in Strether's mind, giving him a new insight into reality. Saeki indicates that Strether's "reading" of reality is deepened after this incident.

Margaret Mitsutani's "Kate Chopin's *The Awakening*: The Narcissism of Edna Pontellier" (*SELit* English No.:3–15) is a clever analysis of the novel, presented in a neat and logical form. Mitsutani probes the parallel between Edna Pontellier, the heroine of the novel, and the mythological figure Narcissus and so tries to explain the novel's "somewhat too abrupt ending." Mitsutani rejects Elaine Showalter's interpretation of the ending, which explains Edna's suicidal death as an escape from the harshness of reality. On the other hand,

Mitsutani favors Linda Huf's idea of Edna as a kind of artist. Edna prizes her own self above anything and goes beyond "the role of mother-woman." Through this act, Mitsutani contends, she has "forfeited her place in human society." Hence, Edna realizes that her self is "sacred" and "not to be sacrificed." Mitsutani's article gives a convincing answer to the novel's most controversial issue.

***b.* 19th-Century Poetry.** This year marked, of course, the centennial of Emily Dickinson's death. The July issue of *EigoS* ran a special feature on the poetess, "Emily Dickinson: One Hundred Years after. . . ." Some of the articles are reports on the centennial conferences held in the United States in the spring. One article, though, is Hisashi Noda's informative "The Legacy of a Private Poet" (*EigoS* 132:176–78), an historical survey of the editing of the manuscripts. The most suggestive among the articles gathered for this feature is Shunichi Niikura's "The Poetics of Emily Dickinson—From Metaphorical to Metonymical" (*EigoS* 132:166–68). Niikura characterizes the poet as "a great revisionist" like William Blake, one who did not follow blindly the religious views of New England, but who deconstructed the orthodox typology and created her own poetics. Dickinson herself noticed the ambiguous relationship between "signifier" and "signified," and this led to her metonymical expressions. Her slanted attitude toward the world—a step down from reality—sometimes transformed her expressions from metaphorical to metonymical—an example that words had become "pure inferences."

Yasuaki Suzuki, the president of the Walt Whitman Society of Japan, published a book on his favorite poem, *Whitman "Yurikago no Uta" Kenkyu: Sono Seiritsu to Tenkai* [*A Study of Whitman's "Out of the Cradle Endlessly Rocking"—Its Formation and Development*] (Gendai-sha). Most of Whitman studies in Japan have been done from the standpoint of comparative literature. Taking a new approach, Suzuki closely traces the growth of the poem through an analysis of two earlier poems, "A Child's Reminiscence" and "A Word Out of the Sea." Then Suzuki tells us of the motivation behind the writing of the poem and discusses the expressions, rhythms, imagery, and musical quality of the poem. Based on a genuine personal affinity for the poet and long and assiduous research, this book is quite a valuable work for scholarship. Its publication should mark a new beginning for Whitman studies here.

c. 20th-Century Fiction. This year, unlike recent years, very few studies were done on major writers of the 20th century. The only one in book form is Sanae Tokizane's *Faulkner and/or Writing: On "Absalom, Absalom!"* (Riberu-shuppan, available in English). This book exemplifies what I said about the danger of blindly using borrowed critical tools. Writing under the strong influence of Barthes, Deconstructionists such as Barbara Johnson, and reader/writer criticism, Tokizane analyzes the novel using such terms as "signifier" and "signified," "unlanguage," "reading" and "writing." Unfortunately, her attempt cannot be regarded as successful as a whole, though at some points, such as the discussion of the significance of letters in the novel, Tokizane shows brilliance. But Faulkner's novel is submerged under a deluge of critical terms.

Two articles should be mentioned briefly. Takashi Tasaka's article on F. Scott Fitzgerald's style, "A White Darkness: The World of Oxymoron" (*EigoS* 132:158–66), is an interesting study of Fitzgerald's vision of the world through an examination of his use of oxymorons. Takako Tanaka's "Some Aspects of Silence in *Light in August*: The Importance of Lena Grove" (*SALit* 23:71–86) is a straightforward study which goes back to the first stage of criticism of the novel, Alfred Kazin's "The Stillness of *Light in August*"; it emphasizes the significance of the Lena Grove episode, told by the unnamed furniture dealer to his wife at the end of the novel. Certainly the discrepancy between the words and deeds which is prevalent in the novel remains, but Tanaka concentrates on the fact it is treated as comical here. Tanaka thinks that this brighter view of the power of words gave Faulkner the confidence to create the verbally complex book *Absalom, Absalom!*

As I indicated, several books were published on the literature of minority groups: David R. Mayer's *The American Neighborhood Novel* (Nagoya: The University of Nagoya Press), Atsuko Furomoto's *America Kokujin Bungaku to Folklore* [*American Black Literature and Folklore*] (Kyoto: Yamaguchi-shoten), and Tsuneaki Kato's *America Kokujin Josei Sakka no Sekai* [*The World of American Black Women Writers*] (Osaka: Sogen-sha).

Mayer defines the word "neighborhood" as an urban environment where the people of minority groups gather according to their races and religions. Mayer's book covers Jewish, Catholic, and black writers, such as Ellison, Baldwin, Gaines, Bellow, Malamud, Potok, and O'Connor. Mayer's attempt to distinguish the "neighborhood novel" from the "city novel" and the "immigrant novel" is quite interesting, and through the distinction the characteristics of the writers mentioned above become clearer. However, the most important merit of the book lies in the fact that it provides accurate information about the social, historical, and religious backgrounds of these ethnological and religious groups, information which is indispensable for an understanding of the literature of these writers and yet which is hard to come by for us Japanese. Mayer also wrote "The Neighborhood Novel Defined and Contrasted" (*SALit* 23:101–13), which can be read as a companion piece to the book and in certain ways supplements its discussion.

Furomoto's book is a collection of 11 essays written over the past 15 years. They are divided into two groups: the first part includes studies of Negro spirituals, black folklore, a musical play by Zora Neale Hurston, earlier jazz, and Ellison—that is, black culture before the civil rights movements, while the second part deals mostly with such contemporary women writers as Alice Walker, Toni Morrison, and Paule Marshall. Though it has the appearance of a "crazy quilt," as Furomoto herself admits, the book yet has a unity as a whole—the author's sympathy for, and deep concern with, the issues of black people. In a way it is good to read something which shows a genuine personal involvement with literary works, not spoiled by the indiscriminate borrowing of current critical jargon. However, this kind of book often cannot escape giving the impression of lacking an objective perspective. Here, for example, Furomoto passes severe judgment on traditional writers like Paul Laurence Dunbar and Margaret Walker and on the problems of "passing." Also, as often happens in subjective studies of black literature, Furomoto's view curiously misses the point that the black writers she discusses are Americans and not Africans. After all, the black cultural heritage has been formed under the various and inevitable influences of the white American society. This is why so many contemporary black writers have been concerned with the search for their cultural "roots": they know that, without finding such roots, it is not possible to have something which they can really call their own.

Kato's book deals with three contemporary black women writers: Alice Walker, Toni Morrison, and Paule Marshall. Kato believes that these black women writers are mirrors reflecting the reality of the contemporary world, though why these particular writers were chosen is not clearly stated. Not a book of significant criticism of these writers, Kato's faithful reading of the text and his research in the social and historical background of black people in America will nevertheless be a helpful guide to the world of black women writers for Japanese students.

Other studies of ethnic literature include Konomi Ara's "*Ceremony* as Conducted by a Laguna Woman, L. M. Silko" (*American Review* 20:86–98), Kenji Kobayashi's "Beyond Post-Modernism—Thomas Pynchon and Toni Morrison" (*EigoS* 132:418–22), and "*Native Son*: Bigger Thomas as a New Hero," by Hiroyuki Koguchi (*SALit* 23:87–100, available in English). Ara's article is perhaps the first ever published in Japan on Indian women writers. Silko is regarded as a medicine woman, officiating over a healing ceremony by writing the novel; through reading it, readers also become insiders, participating in the ceremony of regaining humanity.

In his philosophical article, influenced by Hegel, Brecht, and Benjamin, Kobayashi insists that what the contemporary novel must achieve is to stop the stream of time and to emphasize the importance of a specific moment in the even flow of history. Kobayashi thinks that Toni Morrison is a writer who has achieved this difficult task in her novel *The Song of Solomon*.

EigoS ran a feature in its April issue titled "American Culture in the 1960s." Most of the articles, written by Shunsuke Kamei, Masako Notoji, and others, are valuable for their abundant information on the society and the culture of that turbulent decade. However, only one article is on the literature of the time. Junji Kunishige's survey, "Caught in the Meshes of the Absurd" (*EigoS* 132:20–22), is an excellent estimation of the literature of Barthelme, Gass, Barth, Pynchon, Kesey, and others. Kunishige asserts that, though these writers are now condemned for writing not for the general public but for the textual critics, their tours de force in expressing their views of the world were a necessity for the rejuvenation of American literature; without knowing their work, we cannot talk about the literature of the 1970s and after. Kunishige's argument is quite convincing.

On the entertainment side, John Irving has become the most favored among contemporary American writers, with the release of the movie version of *The World According to Garp*. A book titled *The World According to John Irving* (Sanrio) was accepted with great enthusiasm by Japanese youth. This is a kind of potpourri of Irving's own stories and essays, summaries of his major novels, and some critical essays. Almost everyone who writes here seems to be merely enjoying himself in expressing his devotion to his favorite writer, but such articles as Konomi Ara's "The Curious Irving Myth" cannot be ignored. Ara calls Irving "cute" (a Hemingway term) and, keenly seeing through Irving's superficial social concern, doubts his sincerity as a writer.

In closing, I have to mention the progress of a very ambitious work by Toshio Yagi, the serialization of an enormous study project in *EigoS* titled "The Lineage of American Gothic." This is not only a study of American gothic writers; it also traces the gothic mentality in the American mind and starts with William Bradford. This study will be more fully discussed when it comes to its end.

Tokyo Woman's Christian University

21. General Reference Works

David J. Nordloh

If the '60s and '70s were the age, however brief, of the scholarly edition, the '80s are the age of the reference book. The editions, despite NEH support and moderate academic approval, have not been that popular with the publishers, whose impressive expenses are met with mediocre sales—after all, most of the texts being edited are widely available in other forms. Reference books, on the other hand, cost less to produce but sell for more, and to an eternally captive audience of librarians: it does not seem to matter that the contents are obvious repackagings of biographical or bibliographical information available with a bit of effort elsewhere.

Some of the items covered in this chapter this year are of this sadly dispensable, inevitable kind: useful perhaps in the absolute information-collecting scheme of things, but also gratuitous or trivial or badly conceived. And yet there are also some effective single volumes and some excellent series. (In addition to the discussion here, readers interested in reference material should see the "Literary and Theater Histories" section of chapter 18, above.)

Among the notable publications of the current year are *The Concise Oxford Companion to American Literature* (Oxford), James D. Hart's abridgement of the 1983 5th edition of the full-blown *OCAL*, and its new Cambridge University Press competitor, *Cambridge Handbook of American Literature*, ed. Jack Salzman. It is clear from a cursory comparison of the two that the *CHAL* is badly outmatched and may need the equivalent of four or five editions and who knows how many years to match even the *Concise OCAL*. The Cambridge text contains approximately 750 entries to the 2,700 in the *Concise OCAL*. Of the various people named "Adams," for example, *CHAL* identifies only Andy, Brooks, and Henry; *Concise OCAL* identifies those three and Abigail, Alice, Charles Francis, Franklin, and Hannah. Both volumes offer a chronology of American literature and history: *CHAL* mentions two important publications and the Wright

Brothers' flight under 1903; *Concise OCAL* mentions those two publications plus nine more, six additional historical events, and the births of five authors. The only unique feature of *CHAL*—and it is a useful one—is a selected bibliography, by period, of "the most important critical and historical studies of American literature of the last 50 years," with an end date of December 1983.

Annals of American Literature, 1602–1983 (Oxford), ed. Richard M. Ludwig and Clifford A. Nault, Jr., is a comprehensive compendium of historically focused information. Obviously the organization is chronological. Each page is headed by the year date, accompanied by the names of reigning monarch and sitting president, as well as the most recent 10-year U.S. census figures. The major listing which follows is an alphabetical list, by authors, of significant publications of that date. Also on the page are lists of key American political and literary events as well as international ones, including the publication of significant works of world literature and birth/death dates of major world authors. That thoughtfully conceived organization is matched by an elaborate index, cross-referenced to appropriate sections of the book and offering full bibliographical information concerning titles in American literature and birth and death dates. Thus the index becomes in itself a brief primary bibliography. *Annals* is a reference work worth referring to, and for more than one kind of information.

Historical information is also the basic orientation of the 5th edition of *Dickinson's American Historical Fiction* (Scarecrow), ed. Virginia Brokaw Gerhardstein, now ballooned to some 3,048 novels "casting light on some aspect of American history." The titles and synopses are grouped into standard historical divisions like "The American Revolution" and "The Nineteen-Twenties." There must be someone prowling the reference shelves for such silly, insensitive commentary as item 1241: "Crane, Stephen. *The Red Badge of Courage*. Appleton, 1895. Psychological study of a young Union soldier in his first action at the Battle of Chancellorsville in 1863." Or someone who wonders why De Forest's *Miss Ravenel's Conversion* is not here at all. A similar connection of literature and history informs Albert J. Menendez's *Civil War Novels: An Annotated Bibliography* (Garland), intended to supplant—or so the author says—Robert A. Lively's *Fiction Fights the Civil War* (1957). The entries are arranged by author and title, with an index cross-listing them by subject (fantasy, Florida, and Fredericksburg, for example). Menendez's introduction is terribly disconnected, but the entries (see item 235, *The*

Red Badge of Courage, and compare it to that in Dickinson) are at least more sensible and sensitive.

If history dictates the content of these volumes, region shapes two others. Patricia Sweeney has compiled *Women in Southern Literature: An Index* (Greenwood), technically part of a series—"Bibliographies and Indexes in American Literature"—but essentially independent. The text "identifies some 1000 female characters who appear in Southern literature in the United States," in novels, short stories, and drama, but not autobiographical works or memoirs. The vagueness of this primary criterion—is "Southern literature" literature written by southerners or is it literature about the South?—also infuses the introduction and is matched by Sweeney's inclination to interpret rather than to simply identify. And of course there is the terrible limitation built into trying to tell the story: "Grierson, Emily, a lonely and frustrated spinster whose father had run off all her suitors when she was young. She becomes the mistress of a Yankee, then kills him when he tries to desert her. ('A Rose for Miss [*sic*] Emily,' William Faulkner)." On the other hand, *Western Series and Sequels: A Reference Guide* (Garland), ed. Bernard Drew et al., is clearer in its definition of coverage, less presumptuous, and so more useful as a source of information.

Edward E. Chielens has edited *American Literary Magazines: The Eighteenth and Nineteenth Centuries* (Greenwood), part of the series of "Historical Guides to the World's Periodicals and Newspapers" and the first half of a set which will add the 20th century later. The major section of the book, "Profiles of American Literary Magazines, 1774–1900," surveys, in alphabetical order, 92 of the "principal periodicals of the period." Appendixes include a batch of briefer identifications of minor literary magazines and nonliterary magazines with literary contents, and an *OCAL*-style parallel-list "Chronology of Social and Literary Events and American Literary Magazines, 1774–1900." Chielens's volume is something of an alternate version of Frank Luther Mott's work, but with a more strictly encyclopedic orientation. For each major entry there is a historical essay with notes, bibliography of information sources (including reprint editions and locations of major holdings), and a brief publication history (including variant titles and a list of editors). The relegation of such journals as *The Southern Literary Gazette* to the secondary section raises questions about the basis for the distinction between major and minor—which may after all have been dictated by the availability of contributors.

The oddest limitation of *American Literary Magazines*, however, is the absence of a prefatory or index list of the magazines themselves; a user has to hunt the pages to learn what is covered and where.

Douglas Tallack's very long "American Short Fiction: A Bibliographical Essay" (*ASInt* 23,ii[1985]:3–59) supplies an essay surveying major critical discussions of the genre and a separate bibliography, both divided by period and author and the latter section also encompassing reference works and general studies. I strongly recommend it as a starting point for work on Poe, Hawthorne, Melville, Henry James, Stephen Crane, Sherwood Anderson, Katherine Anne Porter, Hemingway, Fitzgerald, or Faulkner. Stan A. Vrana's *Interviews and Conversations with 20th-Century Authors Writing in English: An Index*, Series 2 (Scarecrow) is a starting point of a different and in ways annoyingly wasteful kind. Covering the same period (1900–1980) as Series 1, this volume lists 4,400 items on some 1,100 authors; many of these were among the 3,500 items in volume 1, but not all—and Vrana does not specify which ones. We can wait breathlessly for Series 3, which should be easy enough to produce in the inelegant typescript-facsimile format of this one. And yet the material is valuable collected in this way, and more immediately accessible than it is through citations in *Bio-Base* or the endlessly updating volumes of *Contemporary Authors*. John E. Kramer, Jr.'s "The Actual Setting of American 'College Novels' and 'College Mysteries'" (*LRN* 10,iii:5–35) is a modest and less expensive kind of update, supplementing Kramer's 1981 and 1983 Garland reference books on the topic with coverage of 352 works, arranged under an alphabetical list of the real institutions.

Several publishers added to their ongoing programs of publication concentrating on individual authors. The University Press of Virginia has issued Stuart T. Wright's *Randall Jarrell: A Descriptive Bibliography, 1929–1983* and Wright and James L. W. West III's *Reynolds Price: A Bibliography, 1949–1984*. Garland has issued *Joyce Carol Oates: An Annotated Bibliography* by Francine Lercangee, *Charles Olson: The Critical Reception, 1941–1983: A Bibliographic Guide* by William McPheron, and *A Concordance to the Collected Poems of Sylvia Plath* by Richard M. Matovich. And Scarecrow Press offers *Theodore Dreiser and the Critics, 1911–1982: A Bibliography with Selective Annotations* by Jeanetta Boswell, *Ezra Pound: A Bibliography of Secondary Works* by Beatrice Ricks, and *Robert Bly: A Primary and Secondary Bibliography* by William H. Roberson.

Finally, before I descend to the 1986 additions to the major ongoing reference series, I want to mention three books mostly peripheral to the concerns of *ALS* but nonetheless valuable. René Wellek's *American Criticism, 1900–1950* (Yale), the sixth of seven planned volumes in the author's *A History of Modern Criticism: 1750–1950,* is a masterful, humane, deeply felt statement of a major critic's perspective on American letters. It includes discussions of Mencken, Van Wyck Brooks, Babbitt, Paul Elmer More, Santayana, Spingarn, Edmund Wilson, Trilling, Ransom, Tate, Cleanth Brooks, Robert Penn Warren, Winters, and Wimsatt, as well as chapters on Marxist criticism and the New Criticism. It is not quite fair to set anything next to such an ambitious intellectual enterprise, since the comparison is bound to be odious. Nonetheless, *American Studies: An Annotated Bibliography,* 3 volumes (Cambridge), ed. Jack Salzman, is its own kind of useful contribution to the organization of the raw material in its field, which is often in desperate need of organization. Peter L. Shillingsburg's *Scholarly Editing in the Computer Age: Theory and Practice* (Georgia) does not clear the increasingly dense fog of theoretical discussion of textual scholarship, though it makes an interesting attempt. The book is a statement of personal position rather than a guide (and so very different from Robert L. Oakman's *Computer Methods for Literary Research,* 1980). Still, even readers unfamiliar or uneasy with theory may find some value in Shillingsburg's description of his computer-collation program, CASE (Computer Assisted Scholarly Editing).

Of the too many ongoing reference series, the Dictionary of Literary Biography (Gale) most consistently and productively justifies its existence, by the quality of the essays, a lavish and judicious selection of illustrations (a classroom teacher's delight!), and the coherence of its divisions into genre and period. In their various ways the eight relevant additions to the numbered series issued in 1986 and the unnumbered *Yearbook: 1985* enhance those strengths. *American Screenwriters: Second Series* (DLB 44), ed. Randall Clark, a companion volume to DLB 26, adds biographical essays with filmography of 64 additional screenwriters, including S. N. Behrman and William Faulkner. *American Poets, 1880–1945: First Series* (DLB 45), *Second Series* (DLB 48), and *Third Series* (DLB 54), the last of these divided into two volumes and all edited by Peter Quartermain, cover a total of 136 authors, ranging from Robert Penn Warren and Harte Crane to Sara Teasdale and Thomas Merton to Kenneth Burke and

Van Wyck Brooks. The second volume of DLB 54 also includes a very useful survey of poetry anthologies, with introductions and tables of contents from the most important of these. The contributors to *American Poets* have more firmly established credentials than those who supply the essays for another DLB series within the series, *American Literary Publishing Houses, 1900–1980: Trade and Paperback* (DLB 46) and *American Literary Publishing Houses, 1638–1899* (DLB 49), both ed. Peter Dzwonkoski. The reproductions of bindings, title pages, and publishers' imprints are particularly useful. A third volume on small presses, university presses, and literary reference publishers in the 20th century is also planned. Clyde N. Wilson has edited the third volume in yet another series, this one *American Historians, 1866–1912* (DLB 47), which joins earlier volumes on the 20th century (DLB 17) and on the period 1607–1865 (DLB 30). Henry Adams, John Hay, and W. E. B. DuBois are here, as are appendixes on official government records of the Civil War and excerpts from the influential *Battles and Leaders of the Civil War* (1888)—though I wonder at the emphasis on only this one of several 19th-century comprehensive histories of the event. *Afro-American Writers Before the Harlem Renaissance* (DLB 50), ed. Trudier Harris, is the first of three planned volumes which will treat Afro-American writers up to 1955. It takes the 1920s as its end date and includes Phillis Wheatley, Frederick Douglass, Charles W. Chesnutt, Paul Laurence Dunbar, and lesser figures. The DLB *Yearbook: 1985*, ed. Jean W. Ross, is a permanent record of gossip, "events," and crises. There are essays on the year in literary biography, drama, poetry, and fiction, on the centennials of Ring Lardner, Sinclair Lewis, and *Huckleberry Finn*, and on occasions and conferences, besides updated entries on various authors (this last feature threatening to make the *Yearbook* a mini-*Contemporary Authors* within the DLB program, and thus in library terms indispensable though inconsequential).

Literature Criticism from 1400–1800, vol. 3 (Gale), ed. James E. Person, Jr., includes Phillis Wheatley among the authors given full treatment—bio-critical introduction, list of works, annotated secondary bibliography, and a mass of critical excerpts—and volume 4 in the same series adds Anne Bradstreet. In the same pattern the three 1986 volumes of *Nineteenth-Century Literature Criticism* (Gale), ed. Laurie Lanzen Harris and Cherie D. Abbey, cover 26 authors, five of whom are American: volume 11, Thomas Jefferson; volume 12,

Herman Melville and Francis Parkman; volume 13, Timothy Dwight and Mercy Otis Warren. That pattern also informs the three volumes of *Twentieth-Century Literary Criticism*, ed. Dennis Poupard, with their entries on both authors and works: volume 19, Rachel Crothers, O. Henry, James Weldon Johnson, James Agee, and *Adventures of Huckleberry Finn*; volume 20, Lincoln Steffens; volume 21, Julia Ward Howe, Gene Stratton Porter, and Owen Wister. Volumes 36 through 38 and 40 of *Contemporary Literary Criticism* (Gale), ed. Daniel G. Marowski, cover almost 200 authors, from Allen Ginsberg and Robert Creeley to Garrison Keillor and Mario Puzo. (Other people's tastes may dictate a different set of "froms" and "tos.") Volume 39 of *Contemporary Literary Criticism*, ed. Sharon K. Hall, is something like the DLB *Yearbook* in its essays on the year's events, though obviously with an international ken.

And then there is the granddaddy of the reference enterprise, *Contemporary Authors* (Gale), ed. Hal May. The three 1986 additions bring the series to volume 118. Somewhere in the welter one will find Philip Lamantia and Mary Robison among others. Because of the chaotic lack of chronological or alphabetical order from one number to another, this and the other Gale series provide comprehensive indexes, in every volume or—as in *Contemporary Authors*—every other volume. That service is useful but expensive: in volume 116, for example, the index consumes 315 of the 825 pages.

Finally, there are the additions to the spin-offs from *Contemporary Authors*. The most patently opportunistic is *Contemporary Authors, New Revision Series* (Gale), ed. Linda Metzger and Deborah A. Straub, which has revised its format: the revision volumes no longer replace the original *CA* volumes, they supplement them, and so the reference shelves must groan with the whole lot. The 1986 additions, volumes 17 through 19, update entries on such notables as Alison Lurie, James Thurber, Truman Capote, Paddy Chayefsky, Maya Angelou, and Larry McMurtry. Volumes 3 and 4 of *Contemporary Authors Autobiography Series* (Gale), ed. Adele Sarkissian, include autobiographical essays by Irving Stone and David Wagoner among others. I still feel uneasy about the notion of autobiography created in response to a demand for reference material. I am more comfortable with *American Novelists*, ed. James J. Martine, and *American Poets*, ed. Ronald Baughman: these first two volumes in the newest *CA* concept, *Contemporary Authors Bibliographical Series* (Gale), get closest to being essential. The entries provide both analytical bibliographical essays and primary and secondary bibliographies (including a section on interviews). Every one of the 21 authors treated in the signed essays in the two volumes is clearly "major," and this series promises to be one of the few genuinely crucial resources for coherent information about contemporary authors.

Indiana University

Author Index

Subject Index

GOSHEN COLLEGE - GOOD LIBRARY
3 9310 01086869 1